JORDYNN JACK AND
KATIE ROSE GUEST PRYAL

How Writing Works

A GUIDE TO COMPOSING GENRES WITH READINGS

NEW YORK   OXFORD
OXFORD UNIVERSITY PRESS

Oxford University Press is a department of the University of Oxford.
It furthers the University's objective of excellence in research,
scholarship, and education by publishing worldwide.

Oxford New York
Auckland   Cape Town   Dar es Salaam   Hong Kong   Karachi
Kuala Lumpur   Madrid   Melbourne   Mexico City   Nairobi
New Delhi   Shanghai   Taipei   Toronto

With offices in
Argentina   Austria   Brazil   Chile   Czech Republic   France   Greece
Guatemala   Hungary   Italy   Japan   Poland   Portugal   Singapore
South Korea   Switzerland   Thailand   Turkey   Ukraine   Vietnam

For titles covered by Section 112 of the US Higher Education
Opportunity Act, please visit www.oup.com/us/he for the
latest information about pricing and alternate formats.

Published in the United States of America by
Oxford University Press
198 Madison Avenue, New York, NY 10016
http://www.oup.com

Oxford is a registered trade mark of Oxford University Press.

Library of Congress Cataloging-in-Publication Data

Jack, Jordynn, 1977–
    Writing works with readings / Jordynn Jack and Katie Rose Guest Pryal.
    pages cm
    ISBN 978-0-19-985984-9
    1. English language—Rhetoric—Study and teaching. 2. Report writing—Study and
teaching (Higher) 3. Reading (Higher education) I. Pryal, Katie Rose Guest. II. Title.
    PE1404.J33 2016
    808'.0420711—dc23
                                                        2014009706

Printed in the United States of America
on acid-free paper

BRIEF CONTENTS

PART 5 Presentation   623

Style and Usage Guide   667

Readings   695

CONTENTS

PART 2 Projects   73

PART 3   Writing Process   397

PART 4 Research 487

PART 5 Presentation *623*

Style and Usage Guide   667

Readings 695

Preface: How Writing Works

There are hundreds of genres in the world today—and the list is growing. No single writing course, and no single instructor, can prepare students for every genre, situation, and challenge they will face as writers.

And yet, as the range of genres students are expected to write multiplies (from traditional print essays to multimedia genres to workplace writing), we have found that most textbooks have responded by providing lists of more and more genres to cover in class.

Simply adding to the list of genres does not prepare students for the moment when they must write a genre that they have never encountered before. Nor does the "more genres" approach help students to recognize the differences between genres when they are written for different disciplines or different audiences. Yet every year there are new editions and new textbooks that continue to expand upon what's expected from students—and from our teaching.

The world doesn't need another writing guide; it needs a better writing guide.

While most textbooks teach students *how to write*, our book teaches students *how writing works* by taking a problem-solving approach to writing. Most college writing guides on the market today are primarily *descriptive*—listing the qualities of "universally good" writing—or *prescriptive*—telling students how to write particular genres. *How Writing Works* takes a new approach to genre pedagogy. In the pages of this book, we help students figure out a new genre for themselves, by asking students to figure out how the genre works:

- *"What is it?"*
- *"Who reads it?"*
- *"What's it for?"*

By helping students discover how writing works, our book teaches students how to engage effectively with any writing situation they may encounter at school, at home, or at work.

The main purpose of *How Writing Works* is to prepare students to tackle these challenges by helping them develop a set of transferable skills and intellectual habits that can be applied to any new writing situation. Our innovative Genre Toolkit, discussed in Part 1, provides students with a strategy to use in any writing situation:

First, determine how the genre works, through careful study and analysis; and
Second, make that genre *work for you* in any specific rhetorical situation.

This problem-solving paradigm has many benefits for both teachers and students.

First, in teaching problem-solving to students, this book is much more student-centered than other textbooks. Students are taught to discover, on their own, how to identify, understand, and write unfamiliar genres. This approach makes the book immediately relevant to students' work in future courses and keeps students engaged.

Second, this unique problem-solving approach teaches three habits of mind that are essential for success beyond the composition classroom: (1) self-reliance (by teaching students how to solve writing challenges); (2) self-efficacy (by showing students their own successes with their writing); and (3) self-confidence (by helping students build trust in their own judgment of a rhetorical situation).

Third, this problem-solving paradigm helps instructors achieve the ultimate goal of transfer—that is, helping students take what they've learned in composition and use it in other courses in college. The skills we teach aren't limited at all to any discipline or field. Instead, we offer skills that students can use to understand how writing works when students enter a new discipline: students learn to discover what genres are used in the new discipline and how readers and writers use those genres to generate new information and share ideas.

Depending on the situation, there are thousands of different ways to write effectively. Teachers don't—and can't—teach students all of these different ways. We don't have the time, and in the end, it wouldn't serve our students well. There are as many ways to write as there are writers. There are thousands of different genres and writing situations. But it is our hope that students will only need this one writing guide.

Part 1, The Genre Toolkit: The Process of Discovery

How Writing Works begins with the Genre Toolkit, a flexible set of strategies that students can apply to any writing situation. Instead of a descriptive ("good writing looks like this") or prescriptive ("use these generic conventions") approach, we use a discovery approach. The toolkit helps students identify a genre's structure, purpose, content, style, and audience.

By using the toolkit, students will develop problem-solving habits of mind for future writing situations—identifying what genre to use, how that genre works, and how to use that genre to meet their rhetorical goals.

At the core of the toolkit are three simple questions:

- **"What is it?"**
- **"Who reads it?"**
- **"What's it for?"**

These three questions guide students through the project chapters that follow.

Part 2, The Projects: Writing from Classrooms to Careers and Communities

The second part of *How Writing Works*, the projects chapters, include traditional academic genres that students are likely to encounter in college, such as analyses, essays, and research papers. However, these chapters also include genres drawn from different professions and community situations, such as factsheets, program profiles, and business letters. From these projects, writing instructors can select the genres that will best fit their classrooms and students.

Each project chapter focuses on a genre "family," such as analyses, reports, or reviews. For example, the "analysis" genre chapter includes rhetorical analysis, literary analysis, scene analysis (for a film), and so on. Grouping these analysis genres together shows students how the individual genres share a fundamental purpose—analyses break down something complex into its parts or functions—even as the individual genres may differ in content, form, and audience. In doing so, this genre family approach provides students with techniques they may use to examine other kinds of analyses in the future.

At the start of each chapter, we explain where students are likely to encounter these genres, both in college and in future professions. For example, at the beginning of the reviews chapter, we note that a student might write a film review for a film course in college, or a performance review as a manager for a company. After this brief introduction, each project chapter offers several examples of genres within that family, leading students through a series of examples.

Student and Professional Examples

To make the connections between college writing and workplace or community writing even clearer, we have included examples in every project chapter drawn from students and from professional writers, placing the examples side by side for comparison. For example, in the chapter on argument genres, students will read platform speeches given by a candidate for President of the United States of America alongside a speech by a candidate for college student body president.

Individual, Team, and Multimedia Projects

In college, students write assignments in a variety of ways—as individuals and in teams, in traditional print format, and in many multimedia formats. By writing in these different settings, students learn how to problem-solve at different levels—how to manage a large project in a group, how to tackle a writing project independently or collaboratively, and how to address rhetorical challenges of visual, aural, and oral communication. Therefore, in the project chapters, we have provided projects to suit all of these writing situations. We designed some projects for the individual writer, some for groups, some for traditional writing formats, and some for multimedia formats. This variety of assignments will suit a variety of learning styles and a variety of teaching styles.

Part 3, Processes: Projects Modeled from Start to Finish

Rather than teaching a single, monolithic writing process, *How Writing Works* helps students develop writing processes that work for them. Throughout the book, we include case studies of writing processes used by different students. We also use extended student examples in Part 3 and Part 4 to show how two students worked on major writing projects from start to finish. Students can follow each project and see how elements of a writing process can work for different students in different situations.

In Part 3, we examine elements of writing processes that students can use flexibly, providing *options* rather than *prescriptions*. To show how different students use different writing processes, we model one student's rhetorical analysis assignment alongside another student's research article that he published in an undergraduate journal. From developing a topic to prewriting, to organization and style, Part 3 guides student writers through the myriad ways that a new writer develops a writing process.

Part 4, Research: Connecting Research to Genre

Part 4 pays special attention to research. In particular, Part 4 connects research to genres, noting that the kind of research you do for a project depends in part on the genre you are writing. Connecting genre to research serves two main purposes: (1) we help students consider how genres provide resources for writers to *join a conversation* about a topic, and (2) we stress the importance of using *research as invention*, not just as confirmation of already-held opinions.

To illustrate the elements of a research process, from exploring existing research to integrating and citing sources, we show how one student composed a rhetorical analysis assignment that involved close analysis of texts and research in articles, books, and online sources.

Part 5, Getting It Out There: Presentation, Publication, and Design

Finally, with the rise of digital publishing, service learning, e-portfolios, and similar initiatives, student writing is increasingly expected to do something in the world, not just end up in a pile on a desk. Therefore, with Part 5, we demonstrate how students can get their work "out there"—how they can publish and present their work. Students who work through the process of publishing their work will be better poised for the assignments they will face in college classes and for the realities of the "knowledge economy," which values communication and presentation skills.

Part 5 demonstrates how one student revised his research article into a visual document to illustrate the different rhetorical choices involved in visual composing, and we emphasize how students can proactively get their work out into the world via conferences, traditional academic publications, and online tools.

Teaching Support

We designed *How Writing Works* to support how teachers work. We've taught at a variety of institutions ourselves, so we know how important it is for a textbook to be flexible enough to suit different courses, programs, and institutional settings.

You can choose assignments that reflect the goals, interests, and needs of your students. The problem-solving approach in *How Writing Works* applies equally well to workplace writing, academic essays, or research genres. While we offer plenty of examples in the textbook and the optional reader, you can also select examples from those genres to reflect your students' interests, current issues in your community, and trends in academic research.

Multiple Teaching Approaches

Composition instructors and programs differ widely in approach. Some prefer a process approach, where the emphasis is on developing skills in pre-writing, drafting, revising, and editing. Others prefer a genre-based approach, where students focus on examining and writing a range of documents. Still others might focus on academic writing, on research, or on rhetorical modes. The flexible organization of *How Writing Works* means that this book can be adapted to any of these approaches. In the **Instructor's Manual**, you will find sample syllabi and course schedules for a variety of teaching approaches, including those listed here. And with the **Annotated Instructor's Edition**, newer faculty can immediately teach and easily prepare various lessons directly from the book itself. Additional instructor resources and online materials for student assessment and self-study are also available through our **Companion Website** (http://www.oup.com/us/jack).

Integrated Assignments

It can be difficult for students to compose a major writing project if we don't offer them milestones along the way. In each project chapter, you will find several assignments that belong to a genre "family." Each assignment in a chapter builds on the previous one, so that you can construct a series of small assignments that build to a major chapter project.

The next-to-last section of each project chapter models how one student approached the final chapter project, a tool that you can use to demonstrate to your students the processes and strategies that they can use to complete a major writing project.

Integration with WPA Outcomes

How Writing Works reflects the Council of Writing Program Administrators' (WPA) Outcomes Statement for First-Year Composition.

Outcome	*How Writing Works*	Examples
Rhetorical Knowledge	*How Writing Works* builds rhetorical knowledge by helping students to develop transferable skills and habits. Through practice, we stress the consideration of audience, purpose, rhetorical situation, and style. We believe genre offers a powerful tool with which to develop rhetorical knowledge, because genres epitomize rhetorical situations. By studying a genre, you study its purpose, its audience, the role it creates for the author, and the way that it leads to certain kinds of arguments and appeals.	Chapters 1–3 develop awareness of purpose, audience, and rhetorical situation. Chapters 5–14 demonstrate how specific genres shape reading and writing and help students learn to compose different genres. Chapter 21 devotes attention to style, including voice, tone, and level of formality.
Critical Thinking, Reading, and Composing	Critical thinking, reading, and composing form the bedrock of *How Writing Works*. Our approach guides students through analysis and inquiry into written genres, encouraging students through a process of critical discovery of a genre's conventions. Students then implement what they have discovered when they, in turn, compose the genre themselves.	Chapters 7, 8, and 30 emphasize the use of reading and writing for inquiry, learning, and communicating. Chapters 23–30 teach students to locate, evaluate, analyze, and synthesize research material. Chapters 17, 24, 29, and 30 address the use of digital technologies for research, writing, and presenting information, including the use of scholarly databases and electronic tools for drafting, reviewing, revising, editing, and sharing texts.

Processes	*How Writing Works* not only demonstrates the variety of actions that go into producing a document, but it also models those processes using student examples. Students can see firsthand how other students have tackled complex writing projects by drawing on the actions and techniques given in the text.	Chapters 4, 15–22, and 30 emphasize elements of writing as a process, including generating ideas, revising, editing, proofreading, and collaboration. Multimedia exercises throughout Chapters 5–14 and Chapter 30 emphasize adapting composing processes for different technologies and modalities.
Knowledge of Conventions	Throughout *How Writing Works*, you will find not only examples of written genres in different disciplines, but also examples of how writing processes and strategies can differ across fields. We draw on our own experience as faculty who teach writing in the sciences and writing in law, as well as our research into the wide range of genres assigned in colleges and written across different professions.	Chapters 1–4 and 5–14 stress developing critical skills in identifying common formats and conventions for genres. Chapters 27–28 address appropriate documentation in MLA and APA formats.

Integration with the WPA Framework for Success in Postsecondary Writing

How Writing Works supports development of "Habits of Mind," which were collaboratively developed by the National Council of Teachers of English (NCTE), The National Writing Project (NWP), and the Council of Writing Program Administrators (CWPA). As the CWPA explains on their website, "**Habits of mind** refers to ways of approaching learning that are both intellectual and practical and that will support students' success in a variety of fields and disciplines. The Framework identifies eight habits of mind essential for success in college writing" (http://wpacouncil.org/framework).

Here is a list of the eight habits of mind alongside an explanation of how *How Writing Works* specifically encourages these habits.

"Habit of Mind"	*How Writing Works*	Examples
Curiosity—the desire to know more about the world	By using a problem-solving approach, we encourage students (1) to discover new genres and learn how they work; (2) to discover how disciplines form; and (3) to learn how genres and disciplines work together to create knowledge in the world.	Chapters 1–4 outline a Genre Toolkit that develops curiosity. Rather than presenting guidelines first, *How Writing Works* presents problems or questions, encouraging students to develop their own strategies for understanding genres and rhetorical situations.
Openness—the willingness to consider new ways of being and thinking in the world	Our research chapters stress the importance of identifying a conversation and researching an issue before staking a claim. By staying open to what others are saying about a topic, students can develop stronger arguments and exercise critical thinking about their existing opinions. *How Writing Works* also stresses the value of collaboration in all stages of the writing process, including listening to the advice and opinions of others.	Part 3 models one student's writing process, including multiple writing strategies and attempts at solving problems. Part 4 models how one student worked through a research project, trying out multiple research strategies and weighing different expert opinions before making his own claims.
Engagement—a sense of investment and involvement in learning	*How Writing Works* shows students how written genres are used in different disciplines to make connections and build new knowledge. The research chapters, especially, show students how to extend existing research, rather than simply summarizing it.	Part 3 shows how one student joined a scholarly conversation by researching and writing an article for a scholarly journal in law. Part 4 shows how one student wrote a rhetorical analysis for a class in rhetoric and writing studies by extending claims made in a journal article he found in an undergraduate research journal.
Creativity—the ability to use novel approaches for generating, investigating, and representing ideas	*How Writing Works* introduces students to a variety of research and composing methods, from interviews and field work to traditional library research. It also offers students multiple ways of presenting their ideas, orally and visually, as well as in traditional print form.	Part 5 shows how one student reworked his research paper into a factsheet, drawing on strategies of layout, design, and visual rhetoric.

Persistence—the ability to sustain interest in and attention to short- and long-term projects	By modeling student writing projects from start to finish, each project chapter in *How Writing Works* demonstrates how persistence with a topic, genre, and task pays off.	In Chapters 4–15, students see how individual students worked through each writing project. Parts 3 and 4 model two student writing projects in greater detail, showing how two students worked through a complex writing task, taking advantage of peer and in-structor responses, multiple writing techniques, and library resources.
Responsibility—the ability to take ownership of one's actions and understand the consequences of those actions for oneself and others	*How Writing Works* encourages responsibility by positioning students as active learners of new genres, equipping them with the skills they need to solve problems on their own and with the help of others. Furthermore, the teamwork assignments encourage responsibility for others.	Each project chapter (Chapters 5–14) models how one student used problem-solving skills to tackle an assignment. Each project chapter also includes at least one team-based assignment. Part 3 of *How Writing Works* emphasizes research as a matter of joining a community, which includes crediting others with appropriate attribution.
Flexibility—the ability to adapt to situations, expectations, or demands	*How Writing Works* provides a set of tools or skills that can be applied to different genres, disciplines, and writing situations, helping students to recognize how conventions differ based on the context.	Part 1 offers a flexible Toolkit for understanding any genre and any writing situation, and for identifying the differences between them. Parts 2, 3, and 4 model multiple writing processes for different assignments and situations.
Metacognition—the ability to reflect on one's own thinking as well as on the individual and cultural processes used to structure knowledge	*How Writing Works* builds metacognition skills by encouraging students to think about writing at an abstract level, and then to apply abstract concepts to their own writing experiences and to new written genres. Students learn awareness of genre, discourse communities, and rhetorical situations that they can use to reflect on past writing experiences and apply to new situations.	Part 1 develops a set of metacognitive skills in the form of the Genre Toolkit. Parts 2, 3, 4, and 5 extend that toolkit, offering extended examples and additional tools students can use to understand genres, discourse communities, and rhetorical situations, and to learn how writing produces knowledge in those contexts.

Acknowledgments

How Writing Works began back in early 2011, when we first met the Oxford editor who recruited us for this project, Frederick Speers, for lunch in Chapel Hill, North Carolina. From the very beginning, Fred, along with Carrie Brandon, Executive Editor at OUP, believed in us and in our project, and their belief has sustained us throughout the years. Put simply, this book would not be here if it were not for Fred and Carrie.

Since lunch that day, Jordynn and Katie have had, between them, one wedding, one son, and one daughter. Now, four years later, we have another new arrival: the first edition of *How Writing Works*.

Many other members of the Oxford University Press team, in addition to Fred and Carrie, have helped bring this book to fruition: Meg Botteon, Senior Development Editor, who guided our writing process from day one, and who answered all of our silly questions; Patrick Lynch, Editorial Director; Lisa Black, Permissions Editor; David Bradley, Senior Production Editor; Talia Benamy, Kristina Nocerino, and Garon Scott, Editorial Assistants; and Roger Pellegrini, Editorial Intern. We would also like to thank the OUP art and design team: Michele Laseau, Art Director; Bonni Leon-Berman, Senior Designer; and Todd Williams, Designer. Kelly Morris, University of North Carolina Law Class of 2014, provided valuable research assistance.

Both of us benefited from the support of our friends and colleagues at the University of North Carolina at Chapel Hill. We wish to thank our colleagues in the Department of English and Comparative Literature, especially Erika Lindemann, Jane Danielewicz, Todd Taylor, Dan Anderson, and Susan Irons; and wonderful graduate students Ashley Elizabeth Hall, Chelsea Redeker Milbourne, Risa Applegarth, Sarah Hallenbeck, Heather Branstetter, Oren Abeles, Phil Sandick, Sarah Singer, Emi Bunner, and Erich Werner. Moreover, we benefited from the brilliance of the entire UNC Writing Program faculty and staff, especially the teachers of English 105i, Writing in the Disciplines, with whom we have had the opportunity to share ideas. Professors Alexa Chew and Kaci Bishop of the University of North Carolina School of Law's legal writing program embraced a genre approach to teaching legal writing, helping test ideas and refine them. This book would not have emerged without this network of scholar-teachers who understand genres and why they matter.

Within our professional network, we would like to thank our mentors and colleagues. Jack Selzer, Cheryl Glenn, Stuart Selber, Keith Gilyard, Hepsie Roskelly, Elizabeth Chiseri-Strater, and Nancy Myers provided valuable advice from the perspective of experienced textbook writers. Jessica Enoch, Scott Wible, Janice Fernheimer, Jim Ridolfo, David Gold, Risa Applegarth, and Sarah Hallenbeck joined in our regular dinner at CCCCs and patiently listened as we refined our ideas for *How Writing Works*. Participants and fellow presenters at two genre workshops at CCCCs enriched our thinking, including Charles Bazerman, Anis Bawarshi, Amy Devitt, Rebecca Nowacek, Janet Giltrow, Carolyn R. Miller, Catherine Schryer, Mary Jo Reiff, Jason Swarts, and Elizabeth Wardle.

We also benefitted from the support of other colleagues and friends: Alan Benson, Kevin Browne, Aria Chernik, Aaron Chandler, Rosalyn Eves, Brandy Grabow, Sara Littlejohn, Jodie Nicotra, Ersula Ore, Mary Beth Pennington, Melissa Richard,

Tonya Ritola, Marika Seigel, Stacey Sheriff, Elizabeth Vogel, David Rogers, and many others in the rhetoric and composition community.

The town of West Jefferson, North Carolina, deserves special thanks as host for Jordynn and Katie's annual writing retreats, where the writers could always find a perfect cabin with a view. The folks at West Jefferson Coffee House and Bohemia kept the coffee flowing as Jordynn and Katie wrote, revised, and wrestled with permissions.

Jordynn would like to thank her family for their support. Her husband, Ryon, provided comic relief, cleaned out the litter box, and held down the fort during writing binges. Daughter Penelope came along just in time to urge Jordynn through the book's final stages. Cooper the poodle and cats Ricky and Leo were the most untiring companions, providing unhelpful research assistance such as "typing" on the keyboard, keeping books warm, and providing ambient noise.

Katie would like to thank her husband and her children for their forbearance while she wrote *How Writing Works*. She is not sure that her husband, Michael, had a clear picture of what he was getting into when she signed her publishing contract back in 2011, but he hung in there. She would like to particularly thank her two sons, Adrian and Edward, who have also had great patience, sitting on her lap while she composed, building Lego rockets at her feet while she revised, kicking soccer balls in the yard while she sat on the patio and copyedited.

Last—yet very far from least—we wish to extend a heart-felt ***thank you*** to the many, many reviewers and class-testers who helped to shape this first edition:

Nancy Alexander
Methodist University

Jessie Allen
McCook Community College

Andy Anderson
Johnson County Community College

Diana Badur
Black Hawk College

Ryan Baechle
University of Toledo

Mark Baggett
Samford University

Rebecca Barclay
Christopher Newport University

Mat Bartkowiak
University of Wisconsin–Marshfield

Jill Belli
New York City College of Technology

Kirsten Benson
University of Tennessee

Lisa Bickmore
Salt Lake Community College

Samantha Blackmon
Purdue University

Ryan Bloom
University of Maryland Baltimore County

Allen Brizee
Loyola University

Ron Brooks
Oklahoma State University

Peggy Brown
Collin College

Siobhan Brownson
Winthrop University

Michael Callaway
Mesa Community College

Jennifer Camden
University of Indianapolis

Jackie Cason
University of Alaska

Tom Cerasulo
Elms College

Jimmy Chesire
Wright State University

J. Elizabeth Clark
LaGuardia Community College

Jennifer Consilio
Lewis University

Gail Corso
Neumann University

Kristi Costello
Binghamton University

Douglas Crawford-Parker
University of Kansas

Cheri Crenshaw
Dixie State College

Meg Cronin
St. Anselm College

Brandy DePriest
Trine University

Rebecca Dingo
University of Missouri

Kerry Dirk
Virginia Polytechnic Institute and State University

William Donovan
Idaho State University

Laura Dubek
Tennessee Technological University

Gareth Euridge
Tallahassee Community College

Marie Fitzwilliam
University of Charleston

Kit Frankenfield
Johnson County Community College

Robert B. Galin
University of New Mexico–Gallup

LeAnne Garner
Middle Tennessee State University

Phillip Gregory Gibson
Henderson State University

Cathy Gillis
Napa Valley College

Brandy Grabow
North Carolina State University

Anissa Graham
University of Northern Alabama

Sinceree Gunn
University of Alabama–Huntsville

Kim Gunter
Appalachian State University

Gary Hafer
Lycoming College

Gregory Hagan
Madisonville Community College

Charles Hamilton
Northeast Texas Community College

Debra Hawhee
Pennsylvania State University

Kerry Lynn Henderson
Northwestern State University

Jennifer Hewerdine
Southern Illinois University–Carbondale

Ashley Horak
Kankakee Community College

Patricia Houston
University of Cincinnati

Laurie Hughes
Richland Community College

Robert Imbur
University of Toledo

Michael Johnson
Muskegon Community College

Peggy Jolly
University of Alabama–Birmingham

Nina Keery
Massachusetts Bay Community College

Ashley Kelly
North Carolina State University

Elizabeth Kessler
University of Houston

Koren Kessler
North Carolina State University

Krista Kettler
Washington Bible College

Jennifer Pecora Kettley
Kankakee Community College

Kim Lacey
Saginaw Valley State University

Cheri Lemieux-Spiegel
Northern Virginia Community College

Kristin Le Veness
SUNY–Nassau Community College

Lindsay Lewan
Arapahoe Community College

Darby Lewes
Lycoming College

Karen Linam
University of California, Merced

Glenda Lowery
Rappahannock Community College

Scott Lunsford
James Madison University

Ginny Machann
Blinn Junior College

Lisa Mallory
Atlanta Metropolitan State College

Stephen Mathewson
Central New Mexico College

Carola Mattord
Kennesaw State University

Michael McCamley
University of Delaware

Victoria McClure
South Plains College

Thomas McConnell
University of South Carolina Upstate

David Miller
Mississippi College–Clinton

Susan Miller-Cochran
North Carolina State University

Mary Ellen Muesing
University of North Carolina–Charlotte

David Mulry
College of Coastal Georgia

Elizabeth Nelson
Norfolk State University

Rebecca Nowacek
Marquette University

Mary Jane Onnen
Glendale Community College

Osayimwense Osa
Virginia State University

Jessica Parker
Metropolitan State University–Denver

Karen Patterson
Ohio University

Paul Patterson
St. Joseph's University

Heather Pavletic
Auburn University–Montgomery

Colleen Pawling
University of Memphis

Jenny Pecora
Kankakee Community College

Janina Perez
Long Island University–Brooklyn

Christopher Perkins
College of Southern Nevada

Octavio Pimentel
Texas State University–San Marcos

Kristin Prins
University of Wisconsin–Milwaukee

Amy Propen
University of California–Santa Barbara

Bonnie Proudfoot
Hocking College

Jeff Pruchic
Wayne State University

Jennifer Radke
Long Island University

Alison Reynolds
University of Florida

Thomas Reynolds
Northwestern University

Ana Milena Ribero
University of Arizona

Shawn Rice
Queens College

Johannah Rodgers
New York City College of Technology

Iris Ruiz
University of California—Merced

Robert Saba
Florida International State University

Mark Sanders
Stephen F. Austin University

Deborah Scaggs
Texas A&M University

Jessica Schreyer
University of Dubuque

Precie Schroyer
Northampton Community College

Jessica Serviss
Auburn University

Micah Sivaglio
Borough of Manhattan Community College

Rachelle Smith
Emporia State University

Suzanne Smith
University of Toledo

Ellen Sorg
Owens Community College

Maria Soriano
John Carroll University

David Stacey
Humboldt State University

Lucy Steele
University of North Carolina-Charlotte

Hilary Stillwell
Tallahassee Community College

Christopher Syrnyk
Oregon Institute of Technology

Danielle Tarner
Kansas State University

Mary Ann Tobin
Triton College

Jessica Tomsen
University of Nebraska-Omaha

Heather Urbanski
Central Connecticut State University

Ross Wagner
Greenville Technical College

Julie Watts
University of Wisconsin-Stout

Jennifer Weaver
Wayne State University

Eleanor Welsh
Chesapeake College

Steve Werkmeister
Johnson County CC

Maggie Werner
Hobart and William Smith Colleges

Brett Wiley
Mount Vernon Nazarene University

Amy Williams
Mesa Community College

Rita Wisdom
Tarrant County College-Northwest

Paul Wise
University of Toledo

Sue Yamin
Pellissippi State Community College

Jun Zhao
Marshall University

Jason Ziebart
Central Carolina Community College

PART 1

The Genre Toolkit

1

Asking Questions

The word *genre* refers to a group of documents that all share similar features. As a college student, you will be expected to write a number of different genres—essays, reviews, letters, presentations, and so on. As an employee of a business, you might encounter a different set of genres, such as proposals, profiles, reports, and more. We can't fit all of these different genres into one book, but we can give you tools: tools to help you learn about genres and tools to help you write them.

This chapter will teach you to identify a genre by asking questions.

A. What Is a Genre?

Read the passage below, published in 1855; it is an excerpt from an autobiographical narrative written by Frederick Douglass, an American author, orator, abolitionist, and escaped slave.

EXAMPLE 1: Frederick Douglass, "My Bondage and My Freedom" (excerpt)

Once in Baltimore, with hard brick pavements under my feet, which almost raised blisters, by their very heat, for it was in the height of summer; walled in on all sides by towering brick buildings; with troops of hostile boys ready to pounce upon me at every street corner; with new and strange objects glaring upon me at every step, and with startling sounds reaching my ears from all directions, I for a time thought that, after all, the home plantation was a more desirable place of residence than my home on Alliciana street, in Baltimore. My country eyes and ears were confused and bewildered here; but the boys were my chief trouble. They chased me, and called me *"Eastern Shore man,"* till really I almost wished myself back on the Eastern Shore. I had to undergo a sort of moral acclimation, and when that was over, I did much better.

My new mistress happily proved to be all she *seemed* to be, when, with her husband, she met me at the door, with a most beaming, benignant countenance. She was, naturally, of an excellent disposition, kind, gentle and cheerful. . . . I hardly knew how to behave toward "Miss Sopha," as I used to call Mrs. Hugh Auld. I had been treated as a *pig* on the plantation; I was treated as a *child* now. I could not even approach her as I had formerly approached Mrs. Thomas Auld. How could I hang down my head, and speak with bated breath, when there was no pride to scorn me, no coldness to repel me, and no hatred to inspire me with fear? I therefore soon learned to regard her as something more akin to a mother, than a slaveholding mistress. . . .

Mrs. Auld was not only a kind-hearted woman, but she was remarkably pious; frequent in her attendance of public worship, much given to reading the bible, and to chanting hymns of praise, when alone. . . . The frequent hearing of my mistress reading the bible for she often read aloud when her husband was absent soon awakened my curiosity in respect to this *mystery* of reading, and roused in me the desire to learn. Having no fear of my kind mistress before my eyes (she had then given me no reason to fear), I frankly asked her to teach me to read; and, without hesitation, the dear woman began the task, and very soon, by her assistance, I was master of the alphabet, and could spell words of three or four letters. My mistress seemed almost as proud of my progress, as if I had been her own child; and, supposing that her husband would be as well pleased, she made no secret of what she was doing for me. Indeed, she exultingly told him of the aptness of her pupil, of her intention to persevere in teaching me, and of the duty which she felt it to teach me, at least to read *the bible*. Here arose the first cloud over my Baltimore prospects, the precursor of drenching rains and chilling blasts.

Master Hugh was amazed at the simplicity of his spouse, and, probably for the first time, he unfolded to her the true philosophy of slavery, and the peculiar rules necessary to be observed by masters and mistresses, in the management of their human chattels. Mr. Auld promptly forbade continuance of her instruction; telling her, in the first place, that the thing itself was unlawful; that it was also unsafe, and could only lead to mischief. To use his own words, further, he said, "if you give a nigger an inch, he will take an ell;" "he should know nothing but the will of his master, and learn to obey it;" "if you teach that nigger—speaking of myself—how to read the bible, there will be no keeping him;" "it would forever unfit him for the duties of a slave;" and "as to himself, learning would do him no good, but probably, a great deal of harm—making him disconsolate and unhappy." "If you learn him now to read, he'll want to know how to write; and, this accomplished, he'll be running away with himself." Such was the tenor of Master Hugh's oracular exposition of the true philosophy of training a human chattel; and it must be confessed that he very clearly comprehended the nature and the requirements of the relation of master and slave. His discourse was the first decidedly anti-slavery lecture to which it had been my lot to listen. Mrs. Auld evidently felt the force of his remarks; and, like an obedient wife, began to shape her course in the direction indicated by her husband.

The effect of his words, *on me*, was neither slight nor transitory. His iron sentences— 5 cold and harsh—sunk deep into my heart, and stirred up not only my feelings into a sort of rebellion, but awakened within me a slumbering train of vital thought. It was a new and special revelation, dispelling a painful mystery, against which my youthful understanding had struggled, and struggled in vain, to wit: the *white* man's power to perpetuate the enslavement of the *black* man. "Very well," thought I; "knowledge unfits a child to be a slave." I instinctively assented to the proposition; and from that moment I understood the direct pathway from slavery to freedom. This was just what I needed; and I got it at a time, and from a source, whence I least expected it. I was saddened at the thought of losing the assistance of my kind mistress; but the information, so instantly derived, to some extent compensated me for the loss I had sustained in this direction. Wise as Mr. Auld was, he evidently underrated my comprehension, and had little idea of the use to which I was capable of putting the impressive lesson he was giving to his wife. *He* wanted me to be *a slave;* I had already voted against that on the home plantation of Col. Lloyd. That which he most loved I most hated; and the very determination which he expressed to keep me in ignorance, only rendered me the more resolute in seeking intelligence. In learning to read, therefore, I am not sure that I do not owe quite as much to the opposition of my master, as to the kindly assistance of my amiable mistress. I acknowledge the benefit rendered me by the one, and by the other; believing, that but for my mistress, I might have grown up in ignorance.

• •

Now that you have read this passage, ask yourself the following questions:

- What is it?
- Who reads it?
- What's it for?

Let's try to answer these questions by examining the text more closely.

USE THE TOOLKIT

What Is It?

Looking at Douglass's story, we see that it is an excerpt of an autobiography. We know this because the introduction to the text tells us so, and because the story uses a key feature of the genre of autobiography: it is written in the first person (using "I"). This excerpt focuses on the subject of learning to read and write: Douglass became a "master of the alphabet" and he learned "to read *the bible.*" The excerpt thus tells the story of how Douglass became literate.

Douglass's story of achieving literacy also highlights the connection between literacy and power. Douglass points out the ways that his white slave-owner used "ignorance" to keep Douglass in slavery: "[T]he very determination which he expressed to keep me in ignorance, only rendered me the more resolute in seeking intelligence."

Given these observations, we can say that the genre of this excerpt is a *literacy narrative*, which is a first-person story about learning to read or write that often highlights the power the narrator gains from literacy.

Who Reads It?

Frederick Douglass's autobiographies—he wrote more than one—are widely read. *My Bondage and My Freedom* is often read today in high schools and colleges in the United States, usually to teach students about the history of slavery.

This specific excerpt, however, is also widely taught as a classic example of the genre of the literacy narrative. Literacy narratives are used by students of education, English, language acquisition, and other academic disciplines to explore the powerful impact that learning to read and write can have on individuals as well as on groups.

At the time Douglass wrote his autobiographies, however, the books were important political documents. Douglass and other abolitionists used an autobiography to educate readers about slaves' experiences. Often, these readers would never have known an enslaved person, so Douglass's book would be their only insight into the mind of a former slave. Today, literacy narratives continue to serve a political purpose: for example, to help argue for improved access to educational resources in underserved communities.

What's It For?

At the time he published this autobiography, Douglass would have had multiple purposes for the book. He would have wanted to educate northern, white readers about slavery. He would have wanted to persuade these readers to support abolition of slavery. Many of these readers would have been unfamiliar with the practice of slavery in the American South.

This excerpt, in particular, persuaded readers about the importance of education in the abolition of slavery. As a literacy narrative, the excerpt highlights how slave-holders deliberately withheld education from enslaved people in order to keep them enslaved. When Douglass wrote that "[education] would forever unfit [a slave] for the duties of a slave," he suggested that educating slaves would be a powerful form of rebellion. In this way, Douglass's book also served as a guidebook for escaping slavery.

Congratulations: You Have Just Discovered a Genre

These three questions—*What is it? Who reads it? What's it for?*—will guide you whenever you encounter a new kind of document, or genre.

This book introduces you to the notion of genre as a way to advance your writing skills. In simple terms, a genre is a group of documents that share similarities (called *conventions*).

By studying a genre, you can learn about the goals of writers, the needs of readers, and the kinds of information to include. You can learn about how best to organize a document, how to format it, and what kind of words to use. You can also learn about *why* people write a genre in a particular way.

The conventions of a genre arise in response to situations in which a certain kind of author needs to communicate a certain kind of a message to a certain kind of audience. When situations recur over and over again, they often give rise to genres. The literacy narrative has become a genre in response to situations in which people are excluded or oppressed on the basis of their ability to read and write.

Situations create a need to communicate, and genres arise to fill this need. We call these situations *rhetorical situations* because they present a particular need or opportunity for communication. By *rhetoric*, we mean any attempt to communicate something to an audience—to inform, persuade, challenge, or argue (Chapter 2).

Here are two more literacy narratives to consider. As you read them, think about the genre toolkit questions. What is it? Who reads it? What's it for?

EXAMPLE 2: Abida Sultaan, "Memoirs of a Rebel Princess" (excerpt)

This excerpt is from the autobiography *Memoirs of a Rebel Princess* by Abida Sultaan (1913–2002), an Indian royal and statesperson whose diaries of the twentieth century histories of India and Pakistan present a unique portrait of a vibrant, active life: she was a hunter, a pilot, a sportswoman, a leader, a mother, and a scholar. The following excerpt relates the story of Sultaan's coming to literacy, when she first learned to read the Koran, and how her family celebrated her feat. As you read, think about any preconceptions you might have about gender, Islam, and politics.

Among Muslims, a child's formal education used to start with the Holy Quran when the child reached the age of 4 years, 4 months, and 4 days; the ceremony being called the Bismillah. Born on 28 August 1913 the fateful beginning of my formal education began on New Year's Day 1918. I was at an age when I had begun to appreciate the significance of dates and looked forward to birthdays, Eids, Christmas or New Year, which brought presents, toys and Christmas trees for us children. For the New Year, I had been promised the "greatest gift" of my life—the Bismillah—and I had been looking forward to it as another joyful celebration. Little did I realize what the event held in store for me. Whatever blessings this auspicious New Year may have spelt for Sarkar Amman [Sultaan's grandmother, and the ruler of Bhopal], the drudgery, torture and misery that I suffered from that day onwards was a long nightmare that had a defining influence on my personality and my attitude to life.

Ever since my birth, I had shared Sarkar Amman's apartments and had been put to sleep in a cot placed next to her bed. Now, with the Bismillah, she started waking me up before dawn to perform the *namaz-i-fajr* [early morning prayers]. I was supposed to do the *wuzoo* [ablutions] in ice-cold water and after prayers, report to her for the Quran.

Still half asleep and with eyes closed, I would stagger into the bathroom and promptly put myself to sleep in the empty bathtub until some anxious attendant pulled me out and splashed water on my face, and hurried me off to an impatient Sarkar Amman.

"Have you said your prayers?" she would sternly demand.

5   "Yes." I would lie!

"Then get your Quran." She would growl.

There never seemed to be an end to my Quran. Either I had to recite my lesson to Sarkar Amman's complete satisfaction, or be kept sitting in front of her, chanting and swaying in typical *mullah* style. As we had no electricity, I would read my lesson under a kerosene lamp until daybreak while Sarkar Amman would remain on her *janamaz* [prayer mat] telling her beads or performing additional prayers until 9 a.m. The slightest mistake would draw an angry response, or a slap, from Sarkar Amman. Further mistakes would lead to pinching, tweaking my nose, ear bashing or even knocking my head against the wall.

Then she would transfer me, my Quran and herself, to her little white mattress spread on the floor in the main courtyard. Surrounded by visitors, petitioners, secretaries, Dr. Johory (her personal physician) and several black boxes containing state papers, she would attend to all of us at the same time. The slightest mistake did not escape her notice and no matter how intensely she was occupied, she would react to any mistake with another sharp slap across my face in full public view.

When I started crying, I would be unable to stop and the more I cried, the more I was slapped. Almost tearing off my ears, she would swing my head from side to side and knock it against the wall. To introduce more variety to her punishments, she would pull at my eyelids, pinch my cheeks, or twist my nose, leaving dark bruises and hard lumps all over my face, my nose, behind my ears and on my eyelids. . . .

On the other hand, there were days when I rebelled after the first slap or two and stopped reading. Then no matter how I was tormented, slapped or pinched, I would not utter a single word even though it meant missing my lunch or dinner. It became a test of wills between grandmother and granddaughter. I would go on strike by standing silently without uttering a sound while Sarkar tried to pinch, slap or shake me into submission. Even as a child the rebel in me could not be suppressed and the standoff usually ended with Sarkar Amman giving up—and starting my lessons later. At 9 p.m. sharp, I had to be in bed, next to Sarkar Amman's, where she would be sitting with several of her ladies, cutting *chhalia* [betel nut] until she was ready for her *tahajjud* prayers. No one spoke unless spoken to by Sarkar Amman. So my early childhood was filled with memories of drudgery and interminable torment at the hands of my grandmother.

However, by the tender age of six I had earned the distinction of being the first and only member of Sarkar Amman's family to have completed the Arabic version of the Quran. Bursting with pride and affection, Sarkar Amman generously distributed sweets and rewarded me with a one-day holiday and a kiss! No one had ever kissed me before! Briefly, a light had appeared at the end of a dark, grim tunnel.

By 1921, I had earned my second distinction. I had memorized the *lafzi tarjuma* [the word for word translation of the Quran] before my eighth birthday. As the Quran is in Arabic, which was not taught as a language, the completion of the *lafzi tarjuma* amounted to a remarkable feat of memory achieved by me between the age of six and eight.

Now Sarkar Amman really did explode with pride, "My Abida is incomparable and will be rewarded with a *Nashra* [a ceremony held on completing the first reading of the Quran] ceremony that will put all royal weddings to shame," she announced. I was given a whole week off. It was my first long holiday since the Bismillah four years earlier! After four dark years it seemed that I had stepped out into the sunlight.

··

EXAMPLE 3: Amy Tan, "Mother Tongue"

The literacy narrative excerpted here, titled "Mother Tongue," is written by novelist Amy Tan, daughter of Chinese immigrants. Tan's novels, including *The Joy Luck Club*, have won numerous awards. "Mother Tongue" was originally published in *The Threepenny Review*, a literary journal, in 1990.

Recently, I was made keenly aware of the different Englishes I do use. I was giving a talk to a large group of people, the same talk I had already given to half a dozen other groups. The nature of the talk was about my writing, my life, and my book, *The Joy Luck Club*. The talk was going along well enough, until I remembered one major difference that made the whole talk sound wrong. My mother was in the room. And it was perhaps the first time she had heard me give a lengthy speech, using the kind of English I have never used with her. I was saying things like, "The intersection of memory upon imagination" and "There is an aspect of my fiction that relates to thus-and-thus"—a speech filled with carefully wrought grammatical phrases, burdened, it suddenly seemed to me, with nominalized forms, past perfect tenses, conditional phrases, all the forms of standard English that I had learned in school and through books, the forms of English I did not use at home with my mother.

Just last week, I was walking down the street with my mother, and I again found myself conscious of the English I was using, the English I do use with her. We were talking about the price of new and used furniture and I heard myself saying this: "Not waste money that way." My husband was with us as well, and he didn't notice any switch in my English. And then I realized why. It's because over the twenty years we've been together I've often used that same kind of English with him, and sometimes he even uses it with me. It has become our language of intimacy, a different sort of English that relates to family talk, the language I grew up with.

So you'll have some idea of what this family talk I heard sounds like, I'll quote what my mother said during a recent conversation which I videotaped and then transcribed. During this conversation, my mother was talking about a political gangster in Shanghai who had the same last name as her family's, Du, and how the gangster in his early years wanted to be adopted by her family, which was rich by comparison. Later, the gangster became more powerful, far richer than my mother's family, and one day showed up at my mother's wedding to pay his respects. Here's what she said in part: "Du Yusong having business like fruit stand. Like off the street kind. He is Du like Du Zong—but not Tsung-ming Island people. The local people call putong, the river east side, he belong to that side local people. That man want to ask Du Zong father take him in like become own family. Du Zong father wasn't look down on him, but didn't take seriously, until that man big like become a mafia. Now important person, very hard to inviting him. Chinese way, came only to show respect, don't stay for dinner. Respect for making big celebration, he shows up. Mean gives lots of respect. Chinese custom. Chinese social life that way. If too important won't have to stay too long. He come to my wedding. I didn't see, I heard it. I gone to boy's side, they have YMCA dinner. Chinese age I was nineteen."

You should know that my mother's expressive command of English belies how much she actually understands. She reads the *Forbes* report, listens to *Wall Street Week*, converses daily with her stockbroker, reads all of Shirley MacLaine's books with ease—all kinds of things I can't begin to understand. Yet some of my friends tell me they understand 50 percent of what my mother says. Some say they understand 80 to 90 percent. Some say they understand none of it, as if she were speaking pure Chinese. But to me, my mother's English is perfectly clear, perfectly natural. It's my mother tongue. Her language, as I hear it, is vivid, direct, full of observation and imagery. That was the language that helped shape the way I saw things, expressed things, made sense of the world.

Lately, I've been giving more thought to the kind of English my mother speaks. [5] Like others, I have described it to people as "broken" or "fractured" English. But I wince when I say that. It has always bothered me that I can think of no way to describe it other than "broken," as if it were damaged and needed to be fixed, as if it lacked a certain wholeness and soundness. I've heard other terms used, "limited English," for example. But they seem just as bad, as if everything is limited, including people's perceptions of the limited English speaker.

I know this for a fact, because when I was growing up, my mother's "limited" English limited my perception of her. I was ashamed of her English. I believed that her English reflected the quality of what she had to say, that is, because she expressed them imperfectly her thoughts were imperfect. And I had plenty of empirical evidence to support me: the fact that people in department stores, at banks, and at restaurants did not take her seriously, did not give her good service, pretended not to understand her, or even acted as if they did not hear her.

My mother has long realized the limitations of her English as well. When I was fifteen, she used to have me call people on the phone to pretend I was she. In this guise, I was forced to ask for information or even to complain and yell at people who had been rude to her. One time it was a call to her stockbroker in New York. She had cashed out her small portfolio and it just so happened we were going to go to New York the next week, our very first trip outside California. I had to get on the phone and say in an adolescent voice that was not very convincing, "This is Mrs. Tan."

And my mother was standing in the back whispering loudly, "Why he don't send me check, already two weeks late. So mad he lie to me, losing me money."

And then I said in perfect English, "Yes, I'm getting rather concerned. You had agreed to send the check two weeks ago, but it hasn't arrived."

Then she began to talk more loudly. "What he want, I come to New York tell him [10] front of his boss, you cheating me?" And I was trying to calm her down, make her be quiet, while telling the stockbroker, "I can't tolerate any more excuses. If I don't receive the check immediately, I am going to have to speak to your manager when I'm in New York next week." And sure enough, the following week there we were in front of this astonished stockbroker, and I was sitting there red-faced and quiet, and my mother, the real Mrs. Tan, was shouting at his boss in her impeccable broken English.

We used a similar routine just five days ago, for a situation that was far less humorous. My mother had gone to the hospital for an appointment, to find out about a benign brain tumor a CAT scan had revealed a month ago. She said she had spoken very good English, her best English, no mistakes. Still, she said, the hospital did not apologize when they said they had lost the CAT scan and she had come for nothing. She said they did not seem to have any sympathy when she told them she was anxious to know the exact diagnosis, since her husband and son had both died of brain tumors. She said they would not give her any more information until the next time and she would have to make another appointment for that. So she said she would not leave until the doctor called her daughter. She wouldn't budge. And when the doctor finally called her daughter, me, who spoke in perfect English—lo and behold—we had assurances the CAT scan would be found, promises that a conference call on Monday would be held, and apologies for any suffering my mother had gone through for a most regrettable mistake.

I think my mother's English almost had an effect on limiting my possibilities in life as well. Sociologists and linguists probably will tell you that a person's developing language skills are more influenced by peers. But I do think that the language spoken in the family, especially in immigrant families which are more insular, plays a large role in shaping the language of the child. And I believe that it affected my results on achievement tests, I.Q. tests, and the SAT. While my English skills were never judged as poor, compared to math, English could not be considered my strong suit. In grade school I did moderately well, getting perhaps B's, sometimes B-pluses, in English and scoring perhaps in the sixtieth or seventieth percentile on achievement tests. But those scores were not good enough to override the opinion that my true abilities lay in math and science, because in those areas I achieved A's and scored in the ninetieth percentile or higher.

This was understandable. Math is precise; there is only one correct answer. Whereas, for me at least, the answers on English tests were always a judgment call, a matter of opinion and personal experience. Those tests were constructed around items like fill-in-the-blank sentence completion, such as, "Even though Tom was ____, Mary thought he was ____." And the correct answer always seemed to be the most bland combinations of thoughts, for example, "Even though Tom was shy, Mary thought he was charming" with the grammatical structure "even though" limiting the correct answer to some sort of semantic opposites, so you wouldn't get answers like, "Even though Tom was foolish, Mary thought he was ridiculous." Well, according to my mother, there were very few limitations as to what Tom could have been and what Mary might have thought of him. So I never did well on tests like that.

The same was true with word analogies, pairs of words in which you were supposed to find some sort of logical, semantic relationship—for example, "Sunset is to nightfall as ____ is to ____." And here you would be presented with a list of four possible pairs, one of which showed the same kind of relationship: red is to stoplight, bus is to arrival, chills is to fever, yawn is to boring: Well, I could never think that way. I knew what the tests were asking, but I could not block out of my mind the images already created by the first pair, "sunset is to nightfall"—and I would see a burst of colors against a darkening sky, the moon rising, the lowering of a curtain of stars. And all the other pairs of words—red, bus, stoplight, boring—just threw up a mass of confusing images, making it impossible for me to sort out something as logical as saying: "A sunset precedes nightfall" is the same as "a chill precedes a fever." The only way I would have gotten that answer right would have been to imagine an associative situation, for example, my being disobedient and staying out past sunset, catching a chill at night, which turns into feverish pneumonia as punishment, which indeed did happen to me.

I have been thinking about all this lately, about my mother's English, about achievement tests. Because lately I've been asked, as a writer, why there are not more Asian Americans represented in American literature. Why are there few Asian Americans enrolled in creative writing programs? Why do so many Chinese students go into engineering? Well, these are broad sociological questions I can't begin to answer. But I have noticed in surveys—in fact, just last week—that Asian students, as a whole, always do significantly better on math achievement tests than in English. And this makes me think that there are other Asian-American students whose English spoken in the home might also be described as "broken" or "limited." And perhaps they also have teachers who are steering them away from writing and into math and science, which is what happened to me.

Fortunately, I happen to be rebellious in nature and enjoy the challenge of disproving assumptions made about me. I became an English major my first year in college, after being enrolled as pre-med. I started writing nonfiction as a freelancer the week after I was told by my former boss that writing was my worst skill and I should hone my talents toward account management.

But it wasn't until 1985 that I finally began to write fiction. And at first I wrote using what I thought to be wittily crafted sentences, sentences that would finally prove I had mastery over the English language. Here's an example from the first draft of a story that later made its way into *The Joy Luck Club*, but without this line: "That was my mental quandary in its nascent state." A terrible line, which I can barely pronounce.

Fortunately, for reasons I won't get into today, I later decided I should envision a reader for the stories I would write. And the reader I decided upon was my mother, because these were stories about mothers. So with this reader in mind—and in fact she did read my early drafts—I began to write stories using all the Englishes I grew up with: the English I spoke to my mother, which for lack of a better term might be described as "simple"; the English she used with me, which for lack of a better term might be described as "broken"; my translation of her Chinese, which could certainly be described as "watered down"; and what I imagined to be her translation of her Chinese if she could speak in perfect English, her internal language, and for that I sought to preserve the essence, but neither an English nor a Chinese structure. I wanted to capture what language ability tests can never reveal: her intent, her passion, her imagery, the rhythms of her speech and the nature of her thoughts.

Apart from what any critic had to say about my writing, I knew I had succeeded where it counted when my mother finished reading my book and gave me her verdict: "So easy to read."

• •

EXERCISE 1.1: Evaluate a Literacy Narrative

For Sultaan's or Tan's text, answer the following questions:

1. What is it? Is it a literacy narrative? Why or why not? What features does it share with Douglass's narrative?
2. What kind of person authored this literacy narrative? What can you tell about her personal history just from this story about literacy?
3. Who reads it? (List all possible audiences of this literacy narrative.)
4. What is it for? Why might the author have written this literacy narrative? What kind of message is the author trying to get across with this literacy narrative? Are there multiple messages? What are they?
5. In what ways are literacy and power connected in this literacy narrative?

GROUP ACTIVITY 1.1: Compare Literacy Narratives

Compare all three literacy narratives using the chart below:

	DOUGLASS	SULTAAN	TAN
What is it? (Describe the text.)			
Who reads it? (Name the audiences.)			
What's it for? (List the purposes and messages.)			

B. "What Is It?": Identify Shared Conventions

In the first part of this chapter, you learned how to ask the right questions in order to analyze a genre. Writers analyze genres in order to write more effectively. If you know what you need to communicate in your document and who will be reading it (and what they expect to see), you will write a better document. Asking the right questions helps you to write the most effective document.

In the rest of this chapter, we're going to delve more deeply into these three questions in order to better understand how a genre works.

Experienced writers know that any document they write has to conform—at least somewhat—to the conventions of the document's genre. Otherwise, readers may be confused by the document. Experienced writers familiarize themselves with conventions in order to know what they need to write—and where they can bend the rules.

When you compare the three preceding literacy narratives, can you identify any qualities (or conventions) that the narratives have in common? Let's make a list:

- All three literacy narratives tell a story.
- All three literacy narratives use the first-person singular pronoun "I."
- All three literacy narratives emphasize the connection between literacy and power: Douglass connects education with freedom; Sultaan connects her learning to read the Koran with power struggles with her grandmother; Tan discusses how her limited English "limit[ed] my possibilities in life."
- All three literacy narratives tell a story of transition from illiteracy and disempowerment to literacy and empowerment.

Can you think of anything else?

Although these three literacy narratives cannot fully represent the range and diversity of all existing literacy narratives, we are already getting a picture of what sorts of conventions literacy narratives tend to share.

Despite these similarities, though, the exact form a literacy narrative can take depends on a range of choices an author can make based on readers (or audience), where the document will be published (if applicable), who the author is, and so on.

Accordingly, when you are asked to compose a genre that is new to you (such as a literacy narrative), your best first step is to do a little research. This approach works for academic assignments as well as for workplace assignments. If you look at samples of an unfamiliar genre, you can figure out a lot about your audience, the format your document should take, what to include, and what kind of style to use.

You may be tempted to look for cookie-cutter templates for each genre, like the document templates that come with many word-processing programs. While there are commonalities between examples of a genre, simply filling in a template with your ideas makes writing a pretty boring process. Boring writing leads to bored readers, and bored readers do not pay attention to what they are reading. In addition, templates don't tell you much about the choices you can make to get your message across or to interest your readers.

Everyday Genres

While the literacy narratives you just read were published in books and magazines and intended for wide audiences, other genres are more common.

You may be surprised by how many genres you use for different writing tasks every day. For example, a text message is a genre, as is an email. A grocery list is also a genre, one that has a variety of conventions that a writer can choose from.

When you write these genres, you probably don't follow a template, but you probably do use some shared conventions. For example, your grocery list will obviously include the different items you plan to purchase because listing those items is the purpose of the genre. But the list may be bulleted or numbered, handwritten or typed into a smartphone, organized by supermarket section or according to the recipes you plan to make. These choices make the grocery list genre more flexible than a rigid template.

You might even ignore some of the conventions—perhaps you mix "to do" items in with your grocery list, or maybe you have your own unique way of remembering what items to get.

EXAMPLE 4: Numbered Grocery List

Groceries
1. Produce
   - Apples (4)
   - Grapes (1 lb)
   - Bananas (1 bunch)
   - Tomatoes (6)
2. Starches
   - Bread (1 loaf)
   - Tortillas (1 package of 12)
3. Meats
   - Ground beef (2 pounds)
   - Bratwurst (6)

EXAMPLE 5: Plain Grocery List

Milk
Eggs
Ice cream
Cheese
Spaghetti sauce
Penne

The next time you write something—anything—think about how many times you have written the same type of document before. Are you writing a genre with shared conventions? What conventions do you tend to follow, and what ones do you ignore? Which conventions are optional, and which ones are necessary?

EXERCISE 1.2: Discover Conventions of Everyday Genres ?

Make a list of three or four genres you write on a daily or weekly basis (such as a text message, grocery list, or journal entry). For each genre, answer the following questions:

1. What is it?
2. What conventions do you repeat every time you write this genre?
3. What conventions do you change or ignore?
4. How do you decide to change or ignore certain conventions?

MULTIMEDIA EXERCISE 1.1: Compare Written and Digital Conventions

Think of a traditional print genre (such as a letter). Next, think of a genre that is similar to the traditional print genre that only exists online or in a digital format (such as email). Answer the following questions:

1. How are the conventions of the online/digital genre different from the print genre?
2. What conventions does the digital genre share with the print genre?

C. "Who Reads It?": Identify an Audience

Experienced writers know that an effective document satisfies their audiences' expectations for that genre. For example, readers of literacy narratives expect stories that describe how an author learned a new language and simultaneously gained power (financial, political, or cultural).

Thus, when you write any genre (not just genres for school), you must always keep your audience's expectations in mind.

In the workplace, for example, you might prepare a résumé. No audience expects to read a résumé written in crayon on construction paper. Instead, because résumés are usually written by people seeking employment, readers expect résumés to present a polished and professional image. Indeed, readers expect that a résumé will provide information about the writer's work experience, education, and relevant skills in a professionally designed document. However, this does not mean that the résumé is just a template to fill out. Instead, you can creatively shape a résumé to fit within the parameters of the genre based on what your *particular* audience might want to see (Chapter 2).

For instance, you may place your work experience before your education, if your audience is interested in applicants with significant work experience. You may or may not include an "Objective" statement depending on whether résumés in your desired profession tend to use them, or whether you want to highlight a particular skill for your readers. You may include many items about yourself (and write a longer résumé) or you may select only the most persuasive elements to include (and write a shorter résumé). Employers usually expect longer résumés for more advanced positions, since applicants tend to have more work experience. All of these choices depend in part on your audience and what effect you hope to have on it.

For any writing task, you should start by considering your audience, thinking through who your readers will be.

EXERCISE 1.3: Identify the Audience

Pick one of the everyday genres that you identified in Exercise 1.2, or pick another genre that you write on a regular basis. Answer the following questions about the audiences for that genre:

1. Who will read this document? Yourself? Others? A large audience, or small?
2. What will the reader do with this document?
3. How will the reader read it? In print? Online? In a book? On a bulletin board?

MULTIMEDIA EXERCISE 1.2: Identify Your Preferences as a Reader

Think of a genre that you read online on a regular basis, such as a blog or an online newspaper. Answer the following questions from the perspective of the genre's audience:

1. Why do you enjoy reading this genre?
2. When do you usually read this genre and on what device? (For example: On a mobile phone? Tablet? Laptop or desktop computer?)
3. How do the genre's conventions make it easy and/or difficult for you to read the genre on your preferred device?

D. "What's It For?": Identify a Genre's Purpose

When analyzing examples of a genre, think explicitly about the genre's purpose or purposes. Why does this genre exist? What need does it fulfill, or what task does it accomplish?

Genres emerge when writers and readers need to address a situation that occurs over and over again. For example, one of the recurring needs met by the literacy narrative genre today is the validation of nonstandard language practices and immigrant dialects, as Amy Tan does in "Mother Tongue."

Now, think about the purposes of some everyday genres that you are familiar with. For example, the purpose of an invitation is to inform readers about the place, time, and reason for an event, and to encourage them to attend. The genre of the invitation is continually evolving to keep pace with new kinds of technology (like Evites or Facebook "events") and changing social conventions (like parties to celebrate divorces, or funerals for pets).

The purpose of another everyday genre, the restaurant menu, is to inform diners about the food options available at the restaurant and to encourage customers to purchase them. Again, dining out is a common event, so it is not surprising that the genre of the menu has developed to address that purpose and that it continues to evolve as technology evolves (for example, ordering food from an online menu to have delivered to your home).

When you are assigned to write an unfamiliar genre (either in a course or in the workplace), and you are examining samples of the genre for guidance, think about what other authors who have written the genre intended their documents to do.

EXERCISE 1.4: Identify a Genre's Purpose

Pick one of the everyday genres that you encounter often. Answer the following questions:

1. What need does this genre address? What problem does this genre seek to fix?
2. How do you know, based solely on the document you are reading?

MULTIMEDIA EXERCISE 1.3: Identify an Online Author's Purpose

Pick one of the online genres that you read every day (such as a blog or social network newsfeed). Answer the questions in Exercise 1.4.

E. Conclusion

In this chapter, we have discussed three basic questions you can use when you encounter a new genre. These three questions are the basis of the "genre toolkit."

Ask Questions

What is it?

Who reads it?

What's it for?

The three genre toolkit questions help you begin to analyze a genre. But what happens when you are in a situation where you need to write a document yourself? In Chapter 2, you will learn how to assess your own rhetorical situation and figure out where you stand.

F. Chapter Project: Write a Literacy Narrative

For this chapter project, you will write a literacy narrative. Remember, a literacy narrative is a first-person story about learning to read or write that often highlights the power the narrator gains from literacy.

Start by thinking of moments in your life when you encountered barriers posed by language. These moments might have occurred when you were a child, before you learned to read or write. They might have occurred as you learned more advanced literacy skills in school. They might have occurred when you encountered a foreign language or unfamiliar dialect.

Then, think about your audience and purpose. Who might read your narrative? What message do you want to get across?

Take another look at the examples of literacy narratives in this chapter (and perhaps search online for additional examples of literacy narratives) to determine what conventions of literacy narratives you'd like to use—and which you might like to ignore—based on your own purpose and audience for this project.

Multimedia Version

A narrative can be told using a combination of text, images, and sound. Using software that allows you to combine multimedia features, such as Microsoft PowerPoint or Prezi, tell your literacy narrative in a multimedia fashion.

Discovering Rhetorical Situations

In Chapter 1, you learned the three genre toolkit questions: "What is it?" "Who reads it?" "What's it for?" You learned how to use these three questions when you encounter an unfamiliar genre for the first time to discover a genre's conventions, audience, and purpose.

This chapter will walk you through the steps to perform before writing any genre. You will need to discover your *rhetorical situation*: your purpose, role, audience, and timing.

A. Discovering Your Rhetorical Situation

In this chapter you will learn how to identify a rhetorical situation when writing a particular document. First, read the sample student writing in Example 1, written for an English composition class, and then use the three genre toolkit questions from Chapter 1 to discover the genre.

• •

EXAMPLE 1: Aliyah's "Public Problem"

Aliyah Forsyth
English 102
Week 11

> *Prompt: What contemporary public problem do you, as a college student, feel most prepared to do something about, and why?*

As a college student, I don't have a lot of power. I don't have a lot of money, and I don't

have a job. I don't even have a car. I can't get a job that would give me money or societal

power without a college degree, so right now I have to just focus on school.

However, I am very aware of public problems such as climate change, animal abuse, domestic violence, racism/sexism/heterosexism, and others. I read about these problems online, on my favorite news sites such as Jezebel.com and through links my friends share on Facebook. I like to think that I'm a politically aware person. I just feel powerless because of my place in life.

That being said, I do think there are ways that college students can help address public problems and make the world a better place, despite our lack of power/money/transportation (ha ha). For example, even just educating our fellow students about a cause that is important is an important first step in changing things. Holding "teach-ins" in the student union, for example, about climate change, can help teach people that climate change is a real scientific fact, and not "just" a "theory" as deniers argue. Hosting screenings of documentaries on climate change and discussions afterwards would help too. We could even invite climate scientists and researchers to come give talks on campus to help educate students and the wider community further.

Basically, although I'm not prepared to spend a lot of money or use powerful influence to get things done, I can organize a relatively large community of young people—and young people have energy and the desire to shape the world to make it better for us. In many ways, this desire is the greatest power there is.

EXAMPLE 2: Aliyah's "Observations"

Aliyah Forsyth
English 102
Week 12

Prompt: Go to a place on campus that you have never visited before and observe for thirty minutes or more, taking notes. Reflect on your observations.

Today I went to the lobby of the nursing school on campus. The nursing school is a newer building, with lots of tall windows that create an atrium feeling when you first enter the lobby. There are plants all over the atrium-lobby, and benches too. I sat on one of these benches to observe.

The nursing students were easy to spot. They all wear the same green scrub uniforms with the logo of the nursing school embroidered on their chest pockets. The nursing professors were harder to spot. Some were obvious, because they wore scrubs and name-tags, but their scrubs were navy blue like the scrubs of the nurses that work in the hospital. There were also professors that were dressed in suits or other dress-clothes; these professors went into lecture halls to teach more traditional classes. Mostly, people in the lobby were coming and going from classes and other rooms in the building. But some people sat on benches and talked, or went into the snack bar area to grab cups of coffee together.

The most striking thing I noticed was the racial and gender diversity among the students. I think that most people have a preconceived notion that all nurses are older white women. But the nurses I saw were of all different races, and more surprising, they were both men and women. Yes, the women outnumbered the men, probably 60-40 if I had to guess, but for a field that has historically been dominated by women, that break-down was a surprise to me. I'd be interested in learning more about how men's entrance into the nursing profession has affected the profession in terms of public respect for nursing, but also how it has affected women's ability to get good jobs in nursing. In other words, do the male nurses tend to get the better jobs in nursing like they do in other professions?

USE THE TOOLKIT

Let's use the three genre toolkit questions from Chapter 1 to learn more about the genre of the student writing just presented.

What Is It?

These two sample texts were written by a college student, Aliyah Forsyth, for her English composition class. Aliyah labeled each piece of writing by week ("Week 11" and "Week 12"), which suggests that this kind of writing was something she did on a weekly basis for class. At the beginning of each piece is a prompt from the instructor.

The pieces themselves are relatively short (about 300 words) and are written in an informal style (Chapter 21). Aliyah uses the word "I" a lot, focusing on her own thoughts, observations, ideas, and reflections.

These two pieces of writings are *journal entries*, excerpted from Aliyah's weekly journal that she wrote for her composition class. A typical journal entry uses a two-step sequence. First, the author describes or observes something, and then the author reflects upon that description or observation.

Who Reads It?

In composition courses, typically only the author of journal entries and the author's instructor will read them. For example, Aliyah's journal will be read by Aliyah and by Aliyah's instructor. Some instructors allow students to keep their journals entirely private.

Other types of journals are more widely read, as we will see later in the chapter.

What's It For?

A journal for a composition class can have many different purposes. One purpose is to practice writing and build good writing habits. Another is to help the student to discover his or her ideas about a topic. Yet another is to prepare for longer writing projects for the class. For example, Aliyah's journal entry for Week 12 might be laying the groundwork for a research paper (Chapter 11) on gender changes in the nursing workforce.

Now that we have discovered the genre of the journal entry, let's turn to the tools that you will need in order to write one yourself.

Use the Rhetorical Situation

Every time you write a genre, you need to pay attention to your rhetorical situation. An author's rhetorical situation is made up of these four things:

1. the author's purpose (Chapter 1)
2. the author's role
3. the audience's needs
4. the document's timing

Let's say that your instructor has asked you to write a journal entry that reflects upon a reading for class. In this situation, the journal entry will only be shared with your instructor.

The author's purpose arises from the situation. The rhetorical situation helps create the purpose for a writer. A good communicator *recognizes* the rhetorical situation, *selects* the appropriate genre for the situation, and *considers* how to use that genre to fulfill his or her purpose.

Let's consider our hypothetical journal entry. While the general purpose of a journal entry is to describe and reflect upon the topic at hand (for example, a reading, an event, a current issue, or a film), you might narrow down that general purpose to fit a particular situation.

You can ask yourself, "What is my own goal for this document?"

For example, you will want to relate your journal entry to the themes, concepts, and vocabulary discussed in the particular class you are writing it for. You might use the journal entry in preparation for other, more formal writing, such as a longer essay.

Your role as an author determines the stance you take when writing. The rhetorical situation also influences your stance as a writer—the attitudes and roles you are likely to take on.

If you are asked to write a journal entry for a class, then your role is one of student. However, journals serve a variety of other purposes as well and are written by a variety of authors. Novelists, researchers, investigators, and others use journals to describe and reflect on their writing, their research progress, and their discoveries.

Depending on the subject area of your class, you might be asked to keep a research journal, a reading journal, an observation journal, or another kind of discipline-specific journal. The type of journal your teacher asks you to keep helps determine the stance you will take as the author of the journal. An observation journal for a criminal justice class might be more objective in tone, for example, whereas a reading-response journal for a world literature class might be highly reflective and opinionated.

The audience's needs impose limits on how a document is created and shared.   The rhetorical situation also suggests how your audience will respond to and use your document.

Many journal entries are only read by the author and, perhaps, the author's supervisor (or instructor). If the only reader of a journal will be the author, then the author has freedom to create a document that is meaningful only to him or her. Many authors keep journals that are only read by the author. The journal is a place where the author can generate ideas, reflect on current issues, and discover ideas that the author might want to write about. If the only audience of a journal is the author, then the author need only write in a fashion that the author can understand. Be sure that you can read your handwriting; if you use abbreviations, be sure that you will be able to understand them later when you revisit your journal entries.

If a journal entry will be shared with other readers, even with only *one* other reader, then the author has a duty to ensure that the document will be easy for an audience to understand. Write neatly, or type. Avoid abbreviations except for those that you are certain your audience will understand.

The document's timing determines what is "appropriate."   As an author, you always want to have good timing.

For example, your journal entry may have a deadline. Your professor may ask you to turn something in by a certain time so that he or she has time to read it before class.

As you will learn later in this chapter, sometimes timing is out of a writer's control.

Here is an entry from the journal of the Lewis and Clark Expedition, written by co-leader Meriwether Lewis on Monday, September 17, 1804. Keep in mind that the spelling and other "errors" in the document are original to the journals. Spelling and punctuation were less standardized in the era of this journal. The authors kept this journal as a public record of an important exploration of the North American continent.

EXAMPLE 3: Lewis and Clark Journal (excerpt)

Having for many days past confined myself to the boat, I determined to devote this day to amuse myself on shore with my gun and view the interior of the country lying between the river and the Corvus Creek—accordingly before sunrise I set out with six of my best hunters, two of whom I dispatched to the lower side of Corvus creek, two with orders to hunt the bottoms and woodland on the river, while I retained two others to acompany me in the intermediate country.

one quarter of a mile in rear of our camp which was situated in a fine open grove of cotton wood passed a grove of plumb trees loaded with fruit and now ripe. observed but little difference between this fruit and that of a similar kind common to the Atlantic States. the trees are smaller and more thickly set. this forrest of plumb trees garnish a plain about 20 feet more lelivated than that on which we were encamped; this plain extends back about a mile to the foot of the hills one mile distant and to which it is gradually ascending this plane extends with the same bredth from the creek below to the distance of near three miles above parrallel with the river, and is intirely occupied by the burrows of the *barking squril* hertefore discribed; this anamal appears here in infinite numbers, and the shortness and virdue [verdure] of grass gave the plain the appearance throughout it's whole extent of beatifull bowlinggreen in fine order. it's aspect is S. E. a great number of wolves of the small kind, halks and some pole-cats were to be seen. I presume that those anamals feed on this squirril.—

found the country in every direction for about three miles intersected with deep revenes and steep irregular hills of 100 to 200 feet high; at the tops of these hills the country breaks [off] as usual into a fine leavel plain extending as far as the eye can reach. from this plane I had an extensive view of the river below, and the irregular hills which border the opposite sides of the river and creek. the surrounding country had been birnt about a month before and young grass had now sprung up to hight of 4 Inches presenting the live green of the spring. to the West a high range of hills, strech across the country from N. to S and appeared distant about 20 Miles; they are not very extensive as I could plainly observe their rise and termination no rock appeared on them and the sides were covered with virdue similar to that of the plains this senery already rich pleasing and beatiful, was still farther hightened by immence herds of Buffaloe deer Elk and Antelopes which we saw in every direction feeding on the hills and plains. I do not think I exagerate when I estimate the number of Buffaloe which could be compreed at one view to amount to 3000.

my object was if possible to kill a female Antelope having already procured a male; I pursued my rout on this plain to the west flanked by my two hunters untill eight in the morning when I made the signal for them to come to me which they did shortly after. we rested our selves about half an hour, and regailed ourselves on half a bisquit each and some jirk of Elk which we had taken the precaution to put in our pouches in the morning before we set out, and drank of the water of a small pool which had collected on this plain from the rains which had fallen some days before. We had now after various windings in pursuit of several herds of antelopes which we had seen on our way made the distance of about eight miles from our camp.

5   we found the Antelope extreemly shye and watchfull insomuch that we had been unable to get a shot at them; when at rest they generally seelect the most elivated point in the neighbourhood, and as they are watchfull and extreemly quick of sight and their sense of smelling very accute it is almost impossible to approach them within gunshot; in short they will frequently discover and flee from you at the distance of three miles. I had this day an opportunity of witnessing the agility and superior fleetness of this anamal which was to me really astonishing. I had pursued and twice surprised a small herd of seven, in the first instance they did not discover me distinctly and therefore did not run at full speed, tho' they took care before they rested to gain an elivated point where it was impossible to approach them under cover except in one direction and that happened to be in the direction from which the wind blew towards them; bad as the chance to approach them was, I made the best of my way towards them, frequently peeping over the ridge with which I took care to conceal myself from their view

the male, of which there was but one, frequently incircled the summit of the hill on which the females stood in a group, as if to look out for the approach of danger. I got within about 200 paces of them when they smelt me and fled; I gained the top of the eminece on which they stood, as soon as possible from whence I had an extensive view of the country

the antilopes which had disappeared in a steep revesne now appeared at the distance of about three miles on the side of a ridge which passed obliquely across me and extended about four miles. so soon had these antelopes gained the distance at which they had again appeared to my view I doubted at ferst that they were the same that I had just surprised, but my doubts soon vanished when I beheld the rapidity of their flight along the ridge before me

it appeared reather the rapid flight of birds than the motion of quadrupeds. I think I can safely venture the asscertion that the speed of this anamal is equal if not superior to that of the finest blooded courser.

EXERCISE 2.1: Discover the Situation of a Journal Entry

Answer the following questions to help you figure out the rhetorical situation of Lewis's journal entry.

1. What is the author's purpose?
2. What is the author's role and potential stance?
3. Who are potential audiences? What are the audience's needs?
4. When would this document's timing be best?

MULTIMEDIA EXERCISE 2.1: Discover Other Kinds of Journals

Journals can be used in a variety of contexts. Using an Internet search engine, search for "famous diarists." ("Diary" is another word for journal.) Select an online diary or journal stored on a reliable website (such as a government, library, or university website), and read some entries.

Answer the following questions about the journal entries that you read:

1. What is the author's purpose?
2. What is the author's role and potential stance?
3. What are the audience's needs?
4. When would this document's timing be best?

B. Considering Your Purpose

In most cases, your purpose as an author will fit into one of the following categories:

- To persuade
- To argue
- To inform
- To entertain
- To explain
- To express
- To analyze

You'll find that these purposes tend to arise from different kinds of rhetorical situations and match with certain kinds of genres.

For example, what kind of document would you write if you wanted to express yourself? A journal entry, blog post, or even a status update on a social networking site would all be likely choices. You probably wouldn't write a formal report to express yourself.

When you are in a particular rhetorical situation, though, your purpose will be even more specific. Let's say you are upset that your roommate has left her dirty dishes in the sink for the fifth time this week. You might write an angry entry in your diary with the purpose of expressing your frustration at your roommate.

It is especially important to think about purpose when a college teacher gives you a writing assignment. Sometimes, the purpose may be embedded in an assignment description, and unless you can identify what that purpose is, you may miss the mark completely.

EXERCISE 2.2: Identify an Assignment's Purpose

Here are a few sample assignments. Can you identify the purpose(s) for each?

1. "Write an editorial for the school newspaper in which you support or dispute the current proposal to cut the budget for recreational sports."
2. "Write an essay in which you interpret the symbolism in *The Lord of the Flies.*"
3. "Create a cartoon that pokes fun at a stereotype of our campus."
4. "Design a brochure to inform students about a health issue they may encounter."
5. "Write a paragraph in which you describe how RNA transcription works."
6. "Write a blog post in which you share your personal experience with volunteering."
7. "Design an advertisement to encourage students to attend the health fair next week."

EXERCISE 2.3: Match the Purpose with a Likely Genre

For each of the purposes listed here, suggest one or two genres that might fit that purpose.

Purpose	Likely Genre
Persuade	
Argue	
Inform	
Entertain	
Explain	
Analyze	

C. Identifying an Author's Role

The author's role is the position an author occupies when writing. Often, in college classes, you will write in the role of "student." In other cases, both in class and out of class, you may take on a different kind of role—as an expert, a member of a particular community, a citizen, an employee, and so on. These are all different roles that shape how you write.

When you write a document, you should also think about how you want to come across to your readers. Here are three questions to ask yourself to help you identify your role as an author in any particular rhetorical situation:

1. Do I come across as likeable? Does it matter if I do?
2. Am I an expert or authority on the subject I'm writing about? (And, do I want to be perceived as one?) Do I come across as accurate, reasonable, and rational?
3. Do I come across as fair, ethical, and trustworthy?

Let's use an example to examine the kinds of choices you might make as an author. Suppose you purchased a pair of expensive sunglasses while on vacation in another state. As soon as you returned home, the frames broke during normal use. You can't return the sunglasses to the store because it is a small boutique and doesn't accept returns. Your only recourse is to write to the manufacturer to convince them to send you another pair.

This type of letter or email is often called a "product complaint" or simply a "complaint." There are different strategies that you might want to take with such a complaint, including how you want to come across as an author.

Let's look at the three author questions.

Likeability

You are writing this email complaint because the company sold you a defective product. On one hand, you have a right to be angry, or at least annoyed. On the other hand, if you come across as unlikeable in your message, then the person who receives the message may be less likely to help you.

Expertise and Reasonableness

In this situation, you will want to describe with a degree of certainty and reasonableness just how the sunglasses broke. You want to convince your reader that the breaking is not your fault. Since you are the expert in how the sunglasses broke you need to convey this information accurately to your reader.

Fairness and Trustworthiness

You want your reader to believe what you have written about their product's flaws. Therefore, you need to come across as fair and trustworthy. You don't want to be perceived as a person who would lie about how the sunglasses broke and blame the company unfairly.

As you can see, writing an effective complaint requires a lot of thought about your role as an author.

Additionally, you will need to take into account the best way to deliver your complaint to the company: via mail, via fax, or via email. Often, companies provide information for how they would prefer to receive a complaint, often on their websites. But, you might choose to bypass an online automated complaint system and send a paper letter instead, because sending a paper letter carries a certain weight, even in our digital age.

EXERCISE 2.4: Examine the Author's Role in a Cover Letter

Suppose you are writing a cover letter for an internship. Using the three author questions, think about how you would write an effective cover letter.

1. Do I come across as likeable? Does it matter if I do?
2. Am I an expert or authority on the subject I'm writing about? (And, do I want to be perceived as one?) Do I come across as reasonable and rational?
3. Do I come across as fair, ethical, and trustworthy?

D. Analyzing an Audience's Needs

Figuring out your role as an author is closely tied to your audience's needs. Before selecting an appropriate genre and creating an appropriate communication, an author must ask the following questions:

1. What level of expertise does the audience have? (Are they scientists, nonscientists, or policy makers? Managers? Executives?)
2. What attitudes does the audience have to this topic?
3. What does the audience know already? What don't they know?
4. What responsibilities do they have? How much decision-making power do they have?

Let's return to the product complaint to examine each of the audience's needs.

Expertise

Your readers will have good expertise of their sunglass product, or at least they should. In fact, in this rhetorical situation, they are the experts and you are the non-expert—at least when it comes to sunglass technology. Now, if you were an expert in high-tech plastics, you might have more expertise than your readers in that area, and you might be able to explain a weakness in their sunglass design.

Attitudes

You can probably expect that your readers will have some degree of pride in their product, and this pride might cause them to be defensive (in the worst-case scenario). Or, your readers might be very interested in keeping you happy as a customer (in the best-case scenario). You can write a more effective letter if you keep your audience's potential attitude in mind, and try to address those concerns. You might try to avoid criticizing the product in overly negative terms (call it "faulty" rather than "a piece of junk"), or you might mention your high opinion of the company in general.

Knowledge

Your readers will have good knowledge about their product in general but will not have good knowledge of how your particular pair of sunglasses broke. You can build on their expertise about their products to explain how and where the break occurred.

Responsibility and Power

If you've ever asked to "speak with someone's supervisor," you were seeking an audience with responsibility—that is, power. When writing your complaint letter, you will need to be sure to address the letter to the proper person or group—the readers with the appropriate level of responsibility and power. Ask yourself: who is capable of replacing my sunglasses? You might need to research the company's website in order to find the right audience for your letter.

EXERCISE 2.5: Analyze Your Audience

Let's return to the audience of the cover letter for the internship: the committee that is responsible for hiring you for the internship. Conduct an audience analysis for this audience.

1. What level of expertise does the committee have?
2. What attitudes do committee members have to the topic?
3. What does the committee know or not know?
4. What responsibilities does the committee have?

E. Discovering Timing

Good communication has good timing. For example, say you are an expert on hurricanes. If you publish a book on hurricanes at the same time as a major hurricane event, then your book will probably sell more copies. This is because more readers will be interested in your topic due to its timeliness.

Thus, when you are evaluating the rhetorical situation of a document, you need to examine when the communication occurs and what else is occurring at the same time. Does the communication have good timing?

Sometimes a communication has terrible timing—and often by no fault of the authors. For instance, in June 2011, the government of Northern Ireland ran a large, expensive advertisement in an issue of a national magazine in the United States encouraging tourism to Belfast. The advertisement was probably designed and arranged for publication weeks or even months before it appeared.

Then, one week before the publication of the advertisement, violent riots broke out in Belfast, making the international news. Few people would want to travel to Belfast given this risk of unpredictable violence. Thus, through no fault of its own, the advertisement had terrible timing.

This example also demonstrates how timing can be affected by place. Suppose the authors of the tourism advertisement chose to focus on another part of Northern Ireland instead of Belfast—say, Antrim or the Walled City of Derry. The audience of the advertisement would be less likely to associate the advertisement with the violence in Belfast (which is only one city in the region), and the advertisement would have had better timing.

Remember, certain rhetorical situations call for certain timely communications. Unlike the authors of the Northern Ireland advertisement, authors often have control over the timeliness of a communication. As an author, strive to have good timing—but remember that timing is not always under your control.

For example, if a friend has a birthday in two weeks, you might mail a birthday card, knowing that there is adequate time for the card to arrive before your friend's birthday. If the birthday slipped your mind and you only have one day, you might send an e-card instead, because it will arrive on time.

EXERCISE 2.6: Discover Timely Genres

Suppose that you own a stationery store. Three clients come in for assistance with each of the following wedding situations. Brainstorm any timely genres that you can imagine would be appropriate. You might list multiple answers for each situation.

- Client #1: A large wedding occurring in six months
- Client #2: A small wedding occurring in three weeks
- Client #3: An elopement that occurred last week

MULTIMEDIA EXERCISE 2.2: Discover Timely Genres Online

Scientists, contrary to popular opinion, do a lot of writing. But you might not be familiar with the type of writing that a scientist might do in the following situations. Research each of these situations, using reliable online resources, and list the types of genres that would be appropriate. Notice that each of these situations occurs at a different *time* in the research process.

- Situation #1: A scientist has a new scientific research project that needs funding.
- Situation #2: A scientist has results of a research project that need to be vetted by other experts.
- Situation #3: A scientist has findings of a research project that need to be publicly shared.

GROUP ACTIVITY 2.1: Timely Genres in Advertising

Suppose that your group owns a public relations firm. You have been approached by an ice cream shop for help launching their business. As a group, brainstorm the types of genres that you might design for your clients at different times. Use the Internet to conduct research on possible genres.

- Situation #1: The company wants a document to create interest in their ice cream shop—the month before it opens.
- Situation #2: The company wants a document to advertise a special they are having for their first week of business—next week.
- Situation #3: The company wants a document to get people to attend their Grand Opening—today.

F. Conclusion

In this chapter, you have learned that you need to take into account your rhetorical situation whenever you write a genre. You learned how to think about your purpose within a rhetorical situation, how to think about your role as an author, how to analyze an audience's needs, and how to take into account timing when writing. These four elements, along with the document's purpose, make up a rhetorical situation.

In Chapter 1, you learned about the three genre toolkit questions to ask when you encounter an unfamiliar genre for the first time. Here, you learned how to assess your rhetorical situation when sitting down to write a genre. In Chapter 3, you will learn how write a new genre with confidence.

Figure 2.1
The Genre Toolkit

G. Chapter Project: Write Journal Entries

Keeping a journal for yourself can be a good way to practice writing, to keep track of observations and research, and to generate ideas for future writing projects.

Remember, the two basic steps for writing a journal entry are these: first, describe or observe; second, reflect on your description or observation.

For the first part of this chapter project, write three journal entries about three recent movies that you have seen, three recent books that you have read, or three different songs that you have listened to. After you have written your three journal entries (each a minimum of 300 words), do the following:

- Revise your journal entries as though you were going to publish them on a blog for others to read.
- Pay attention to how your journal entries change as your audience changes.
- Assess the rhetorical situation for your journal entries using Table 2.1.

Table 2.1 Journal Entry Analysis Chart

	Private Journal Entries	**Blog Journal Entries**
What is the purpose of this journal entry?		
What is your stance as author?		
Who will your audience be?		
How can you best address your audience's needs?		
How can you make these journal entries timely?		

Writing New Genres

In the previous chapters, you have learned how to discover a new genre and to discover the rhetorical situation surrounding it, including the purpose, role, audience, and timing. In this chapter, you will learn how to study, in more detail, examples of a genre to determine its design, organization, content, and style features so that you can write that genre yourself.

A. Writing a New Genre

First, read this short essay.

• •

EXAMPLE 1: Claire Zhang, "Amy Tan Phase" (excerpt)

Sometime in the past school year, a group of Chinese tourists stopped me as I was crossing Elm Street to walk back to Old Campus. A woman asked me, in Chinese—"你会说中文吗?" *Can you speak Chinese?* I nodded vigorously and answered, "可以!" *I can!* The exclamation point is telling. That this woman recognized that I was Chinese, simply from my appearance, excited me. I was thinking *yes! Yes! I am like you! I speak your language, my language, our language!* She asked me where they could eat lunch. The moment I tried to point them in the direction of Church Street, I realized I had forgotten how to say some very basic things like *turn right*, and it took me a few seconds to remember. The words tripped out of my mouth and felt foreign and awkward on my tongue. I felt ashamed and sad, though they understood me and tottered off to where I had directed them, I suddenly noticed the rust forming on the language that had been my first. The language that is supposed to be mine. I'm losing it. I've been losing it. Little things will continue to remind me of this. I will try to write a basic sentence and find I can't remember the simplest characters. I won't recognize or be able to read some phrases in the level 1 Chinese textbook. Perhaps one of the biggest jolts is to realize that so many of my friends, who aren't Chinese—外国人 *waiguoren*, foreigner,— can speak Chinese better than I can, know more than I do. Being away from home for the year also made me realize another thing—I *miss* Chinese-ness. [. . .]

Growing up, I never felt exactly torn between two different cultures, the way characters in novels frequently described. I wasn't aware enough to notice it at the time. I naively invited all my American friends over to my home. Friends would occasionally make faces and ask what random dishes in our refrigerator might be, but it never bothered me. [. . .]

Looking back on it now, the most amazing thing is how all these events failed to make me realize that I was somewhat different from everyone else. My neighbor would ask me why I didn't wear Limited Too clothes, and I would quite candidly tell her that they were too expensive, which is what my mother told me, and hence, must be true. I marveled at the fact that my neighbor had a drawer full of at least 20 different swimsuits, when I only had two swimsuits, and how she had a room littered with Beanie Babies and Build-A-Bear bears, when I only had one Build-A-Bear bear that I got as a birthday present. But I believed it wholeheartedly and genuinely when my mother said that that was a waste of money and I didn't need it. I got into a fight with my neighbor about whether college was necessary to be successful in life, she insisting that she knew people who didn't go to college and had good jobs, and I deafly repeating the very stereotypical mantra of my Chinese parents—you have to get good grades and get into a good college. My obliviousness and naiveté saved my early childhood self-esteem.

This wouldn't last long. I slowly began to notice the differences. It came at first, when I missed pop culture references that were clearly obvious to everybody else, such as discussion about the latest Lizzie McGuire episode or when Avril Lavigne's new album was blasted at a birthday party. I would simply pretend I knew what everybody was talking about and then learn what I needed to in the privacy of my home, using the internet or television. I learned the common, socially accepted opinions about various things. I would repeat these when the subject came up. I observed how my friends or television characters interacted or acted in certain situations and mimicked them. I went on a Limited Too shopping spree before middle school with my mother. This was enough for me, and I felt that I fit in decently—though again, in retrospect, I don't think I did nearly as good a job as I felt at the time. The learning process was still very slow going. I wore tourist t-shirts and skirt ensembles with ugly sneakers to middle school, again completely unaware of how dorky I clearly was.

It was somewhere in late eighth grade, though I couldn't point to a specific moment, where I gained some sort of consciousness at realizing that I was rather socially awkward because I just didn't *know* things and wasn't comfortable with what a lot of my classmates thought was fun and cool. In middle and elementary school, I had never indulged in the weird American thing called "hanging out." No one had ever invited me, and I had always been busy and unwilling to attend even if I was invited to a birthday party. I felt uncomfortable at these things, and I preferred to spend time with my Chinese friends. I went to Chinese parties, went on vacations and trips with my Chinese friends, and played tennis with them. I felt comfortable in their presence, more confident and sure of myself. I wasn't putting on a play or mimicking anyone, in fact I was the popular and cool one. A middle school friend kept inviting me to see the Harry Potter movie with her over the summer after middle school, but I made up all sorts of excuses and then flat out ignored her until she stopped asking. 5

In high school, I made new friends, and I was invited to hang out—a lot. At first, it was foreign, but my old plan of pretending I knew what was going on and then going home to research, if necessary, worked well. I learned that movie and a meal were common ways to hang out, and that girls liked to go shopping together at the mall—a novelty considering my mother and I typically only went shopping at big discount stores like Target or Ross or JCPenny, and shopping days were only once-in-a-while planned affairs when necessary. I became more familiar with the new mall names that everybody liked to wear instead of Limited Too: American Eagle, Abercrombie, and Aeropostale. I observed my friend to understand how shopping as a teenage American girl was conducted: walk through the store, pick out clothes that look appealing, go in the dressing room to try them on, show them to your shopping partner, receive compliments and compliment your shopping partner's choice, then buy it. It was bizarre not shopping with my mom, who used to essentially pick my clothing for me, and buying clothes for fun was a strange concept—but I liked it. [. . .]

In the course of these changes, I felt myself drifting away from my old Chinese friends. I attempted to incorporate the new fun things I had learned into my time with the Chinese group. I tried to take them downtown to hang out, instead of spending time inside the house. They were bored by my desire to browse Urban Outfitters before the movie started, and were unenthused at the idea of stopping by the Cheesecake Factory after the movie to have some cheesecake and snacks and conversation—it was a waste of money. When we vacationed on a cruise together, I proposed we go to the teen dance party, but was rejected because nobody wanted to dance. I was growing increasingly bored at Chinese parties, where we mostly sat around and watched movies or talked about inane things like school and more school and school-related things. I now preferred spending time with my American friends. They were more fun, more spontaneous, more interesting. Eventually, I attended the Chinese parties less and less frequently until I stopped going altogether. I continued to indulge in more American things, going out more frequently, learning to apply makeup and paying more attention to my fashion style. When I started dating an American boy in late junior year, I felt like I had truly jumped off the deep end. [. . .]

While home had always been the more dominant place I spent my time, with the start of high school senior year and lots of American friends to hang out with every afternoon, I started skipping my mother's daily dinners and eating a lot of American food. I would leave the house and be out and about all day, returning home in the darkness when everyone in my house had gone to sleep. [. . .]

I think the most valuable thing my American friends gave me was American confidence and outspokenness, the belief in expressing and being true to yourself without caring what other people think about you—not worrying constantly about your "face." Once, I had tried to hide and pretend I didn't care about anything in an attempt to never be judged by anyone. People literally called me a robot. But I am not a robot, and I have since learned that it is okay to be more than a robot. I learned to not care so much about the judgments of others. I love and I feel and I think and I dream and I hate and I am proud of all of this—this is me, this is my identity.

10   Part of that identity, is, and forever will be, Chinese, and I don't want to forget that. Traditional Chinese values call for a balance, the yin and the yang. I am composed of two cultures—American and Chinese. It's been, and always will be, a struggle trying to juggle these two. I've spent so long trying to cultivate the American, my previously weaker side, but now it's time to embrace openly the other weakening

side too, to be true to this part of my self. This isn't my Amy Tan phase. This is who I am.

●●●

Now, take a look at the following student texts, which were written in response to an assignment for an anthropology course. What kind of documents are these?

●●●

EXAMPLE 2: Louisa Rodriguez, "Identity in Context"

Growing up in Guatemala, I never felt particularly Latina. Sure, we spoke Spanish at home and ate our share of beans and tortillas, but my parents also wanted me to leave Guatemala one day to go to America. I went to an "American" private school with courses taught in English, brought home clothes from Aeropostale and Abercrombie during our yearly trips to Miami, and was more interested in listening to Lady Gaga or Taylor Swift than the salsa and reggaeton music popular in Guatemala. But when I came to the United States last year for a high school exchange program, I suddenly found myself embracing my Latin culture. It wasn't just that my new classmates wanted me to practice Spanish with them or tell them about my country. It was that everything I'd been striving for in Guatemala—like dressing in American clothes and listening to American music—no longer made me different. Being Guatemalan made me different, and I liked that. I learned, like Claire Zhang did in her essay "Amy Tan Phase," that identity is selective. It all depends on the context. Zhang's essay suggests that identity isn't something we have, it is something we do in different situations.

While she was growing up, Zhang wanted to downplay her Chinese heritage and become more American. In grade school and high school, when she was surrounded by her family and friends from Chinese School, she desired to be more like her American classmates.

She studied American culture the way an anthropologist would. When a reference to a tv show or celebrity came up, she writes, "I would simply pretend I knew what everybody was talking about and then learn what I needed to in the privacy of my home, using the internet or television." As a child growing up in a Chinese family, she found American culture new and different. In this context, Zhang wanted to de-emphasize her Chinese culture, since she was exposed to it everyday, and learn more about the things her American classmates liked. I felt the same way as a kid growing up in Guatemala. I would pore over Seventeen magazines I bought in Miami, cutting out pictures of styles I could try or of my favorite singers and actors to put up in my room. Knowing about American culture was a way to stand out, a way to show that you were part of the "cool" group at school.

In college, Zhang began to miss her Chinese culture. Zhang writes that "Being away from home for the year also made me realize another thing—I *miss* Chinese-ness." Zhang never noticed many aspects of her Chinese culture because they were just part of her everyday life—the language she heard her mother speak, the television shows they watched, the foods they ate at home, and so on. Her food only stood out when her friends asked about unusual dishes in her refrigerator. Similarly, while I never really craved the refried black beans, plantains and tortillas that are a staple in Guatemalan cooking, when I'm faced with the endless array of pizza, pasta, barbecue, and Asian food "stations" in the dining hall, I start to crave the simple food we would eat at home.

If identity depends on the context, what does that mean for people who belong to two cultures? Zhang concludes that her identity is naturally split, like the yin and the yang of Chinese culture, and that the best solution is to find a balance between the two. If identity depends on the situation, that means making an effort to put yourself in both situations, because it is only within those situations that identity can take shape.

EXAMPLE 3: Russell Johnson, "Identity in a Material World"

When I read Claire Zhang's essay, "Amy Tan Phase," at first I could not relate. I grew up in the United States, and my family is plain, white, American. I have never felt a struggle between two ethnic cultures the way Zhang did. However, as I thought more about Zhang's essay, I realized that I could relate to her struggle between two different material cultures—one frugal and practical, the other frivolous and materialistic. Zhang's essay shows how American consumer culture provides much of the material we use to craft our "identities." The "materials" we wear, the things we consume—these are seen to be keys to American identity.

For Claire Zhang, being "American" meant shopping at certain stores, like Limited Too, or later, Aeropostale or American Eagle instead of J.C. Penney or Ross. It meant shopping for fun, too, not just for utility: "I observed my friend to understand how shopping as a teenage American girl was conducted: walk through the store, pick out clothes that look appealing, go in the dressing room to try them on, show them to your shopping partner, receive compliments and compliment your shopping partner's choice, then buy it." Zhang learned there was a protocol for shopping that other girls seemed to naturally understand. When I was growing up, I could not join the American culture Zhang describes, either. I was raised by a single father who worked two jobs to support my brother and I. Most of our clothes came from Walmart. Once or twice a year, like at the start of school, my dad would march us in and wait while we picked out a new pair of shoes, some jeans and a few shirts. Those had to last us for the school year. While guys do not care about fashion as much as girls, there were still certain things you had to have to fit in with the different social groups, like Hollister polo shirts or NBA jerseys. I could not afford either of those. This not only made me feel like I did not belong with the popular kids at school, but I've never thought about how it also makes me somewhat different from the image of the American kid.

It is not merely the quality of items one has, but the quantity that determines identity. Zhang describes how she also compared her possessions to those of her friends: "I marveled at the fact that my neighbor had a drawer full of at least 20 different swimsuits, when I only had two swimsuits, and how she had a room littered with Beanie Babies and Build-A-Bear bears, when I only had one Build-A-Bear bear that I got as a birthday present." Being American is about conspicuous consumption—owning more than you need, and being able to show it off to others. As young kids, we often use toys to form parts of our identity. There was the one kid in my elementary school who had collected every Transformer toy, or the one who had hundreds of video games in his own private game room to play them in. These kids seemed secure in knowing that the others wanted what they had. Their possessions gave them power—they could invite you to play with their toys, or they could exclude you from the group.

For Zhang to become American, she had to embrace the materialism of American culture. Buying things forms a big part of our economy and, increasingly, our identity. Does that make those of us who do not have these things less American? In a way, it does. If poor people were seen as truly American, then that would expose the lie of the American dream, in which everyone can be wealthy, everyone can buy as much stuff as they want. Not having things, or not having the right things, can mark you as not quite American.

USE THE TOOLKIT

Let's use the three genre toolkit questions to examine these texts.

What Is It?

You probably recognize these as examples of student essays that respond to a reading assignment, sometimes called reader response essays, reaction papers, or simply "response papers" or "response essays." (Here, we will call them "response essays.") And you have probably written this type of essay yourself.

Who Reads It?

Response essays may be read by your instructor, or by other students in a class. In some college courses, you might be asked to share your response essays as a way to start a group discussion. Or you might be asked to post them online and to comment on the responses posted by others in your class.

What's It For?

Response essays serve a few purposes. They help students to work through the ideas in a reading. They can lead to class discussions, or to longer writing assignments. For example, Russell might expand his ideas into a research paper (Chapter 11) exploring the history of materialism in American culture. Luisa might interview other students about how their identities change in different contexts, and then share her results in a report (Chapter 14).

Use the Rhetorical Situation

Response essays occur within a typical rhetorical situation. Your role in this rhetorical situation is that of student. The audience is usually your instructor, or maybe fellow classmates, and your purpose is usually to demonstrate to the instructor (or possibly your classmates) that you have read and engaged with the text. The timing of the document will likely be dictated by the course schedule, with a specific due date.

Using the tools in Chapter 1 and 2, then, we already know quite a bit about a response essay. But how would you go about writing one? Writing a good response essay requires more in-depth knowledge of this genre and how it works.

In this chapter, you will learn how to find out how a genre works so that you will be prepared to write it yourself. You'll dig deeper into this genre—its typical contents, style, and forms—and identify what kinds of choices you get to make as a writer of this genre.

We will use response essays as our example genre in this chapter, but the skills that you will learn in this chapter are applicable to *any* genre that you encounter. The process of learning to write a new genre can be broken down into three tasks:

1. Finding examples
2. Identifying conventions
3. Locating options

We will explore each of these steps in more detail.

B. Finding Examples

When you start to write a genre that is new to you, consider how you might locate examples from which to learn. For any unfamiliar writing task, looking at examples of the document you've been asked to write will give you a better sense of the options open to you, as well as the conventions for that genre.

To find examples, you can do one of two things: ask people you know, or look them up.

Ask People You Know

If you are asked to write a response essay in a class, the first thing to do is to ask your instructor for an example. You might also ask friends or classmates if they don't mind sharing theirs with you. For a classroom writing assignment, it is usually fair to ask friends who have taken the course already to look at their assignment to get a sense of how students have organized the genre in the past.

But, be sure to check with your professor first to be sure that you are not violating a course or college rule about plagiarism. Note, also, that under no circumstances should you copy a friend's assignment or use your friend's ideas or those from an online source without crediting them. Most colleges consider these actions to be academic dishonesty or plagiarism (Chapter 27).

In the case of the response essay, you'll need to fill in your own personal details and thoughts, anyway. But you can get a sense of how others have organized their information or written about their reactions to a text.

Look Them Up

The Internet is probably the best source for examples of genres. Try searching for the name of your genre and add the word "sample" or "example" to your search. Thus, you would type phrases like this into your search engine (such as Google): "response essay example" or "sample student response essay." In almost any case, you will be able to find plenty of hits. Your goal is not to find a template or formula for a response essay, but to learn more about the audience, purpose, and typical contents for this genre.

It is important to conduct your Internet search for samples in an organized fashion. As you search, figure out a way to keep track of your examples: (1) you can create a file on your computer to store digital files, (2) bookmark websites in your browser, (3) use electronic research tools (Chapter 24), or (4) print and save examples in a paper file. The genre examples will be useful as you are planning and drafting your own project, so you'll want to have them handy.

When looking at examples, it is important to remember that no one example represents the only way to write a type of document. It is more useful to compare a few different examples of a genre to see where they are similar and where they differ. This can help you to figure out which features of the genre seem relatively fixed, and which ones can be changed.

EXERCISE 3.1: Searching for Examples

We have included two examples of response essays in this chapter, but they were both written by students in the same college course. Try to locate more examples of response essays written for college courses. You might also locate instructions given to students about how to write this genre. Collect at least three examples to share with your classmates. Then, write down a list of observations from the materials you have collected.

C. Identifying Conventions

Once you have located examples of your genre, you can begin to identify common elements—or *conventions*—among them. If a feature recurs in many or most examples of a genre, you can consider it a convention of that genre—something readers will generally expect to see included. For instance, readers will expect to find a list of education and work experience in a résumé, because those are conventions of the résumé genre.

Take another look at the response essays at the beginning of this chapter. Let's explore the similarities that they share.

You might focus your analysis by considering the following:

- **Design:** What does the document look like? Does it include images? Special text or fonts? How are the contents arranged on the page?
- **Organization:** How are items organized in the document? Are there sections or headings? What goes in each section or part? What order do they go in?
- **Content:** What kinds of information are included in the document? What is the message or overall point? Is there a main claim or thesis (Chapter 18)? What kinds of evidence are included?
- **Style:** How is the document written? What kinds of vocabulary are used? What kinds of sentences? (Short or long sentences? Past/present/future tense verbs? Full sentences or bullet points? Statements or questions? Simple vocabulary or jargon?)

To make the task of identifying conventions easier to remember, use the acronym DOCS (Design, Organization, Content, Style).

Let's try the DOCS method to identify the conventions of the response essays provided previously.

Table 3.1 Sample DOCS Analysis

Genre	Response Essay Conventions
Design	Includes an original title and the student's name at the top; single or double-spaced; written as several paragraphs, not a single block of text; includes a works cited section
Organization	Has a definite introduction and thesis; paragraphs expand on thesis with examples drawn from the text and from personal experience; conclusion may sum up overall message or ideas gained from the text OR suggest questions to explore further.
Content	May include personal experiences and reflections/opinions, but also includes evidence from the text. Makes an argument about the text—tends to focus on a key factor or two—does not just list everything the writer noticed.
Style	Uses personal voice "I," but is still not too casual in tone. Uses academic vocabulary or terms ("metaphor," "tone," etc.).

The term "response essay" makes it seem like the genre involves casual writing, where you can simply jot down a range of ideas or opinions, as in a journal entry (Chapter 3). However, response essays actually use many of the features found in a formal academic essay. They have an introduction, body, and conclusion. They have a central thesis (Chapter 18), or main claim, that the writer supports using examples from the text and from their own experience.

The thesis usually involves more than a personal opinion or reaction. For example, neither Luisa nor Russell simply state that they like or dislike the reading, nor that they agree or disagree with the author. Instead, they each offer a thesis that is analytical and debatable.

Luisa's thesis is: "Zhang's essay suggests that identity isn't something we have, it is something we do in different situations."

Russell's thesis is: "Zhang's essay shows that today's consumer culture provides much of the material we use to craft our 'identities.' "

The thesis in each essay also does more than state the obvious. Each writer tries to say something new and interesting about the reading and what it means.

The writers also link their responses to key concepts and terms from the class in question. Luisa and Russell wrote these responses for an anthropology class focused on ethnicity and culture in America, so they tended to focus on a key concept they had been discussing in class: identity. If they were writing responses in a literature class, they might focus more on the style, imagery, or characters in the reading.

Finally, these response essays tend to be more formal and serious in tone than the term "reaction" or "response" might suggest. You might assume that a "response" could be written as a series of observations, almost like a journal entry (Chapter 2). However, a response essay is often more polished and organized than a journal entry or set of notes, since it will be read by an academic audience (your instructor or possibly your classmates).

You can use the DOCS technique to examine any genre you encounter as you plan how to write your own.

EXERCISE 3.2: Analyzing Genres

Using the materials you collected for Exercise 3.1, fill out the DOCS chart in Table 3.2. Then, compare your results to Table 3.1. Do you notice different kinds of conventions in sample essays from different kinds of courses? Do instructors from different courses have different expectations for what a response essay should look like?

TABLE 3.2 BLANK DOCS ANALYSIS CHART	
Genre	
Design	
Organization	
Content	
Style	

Be prepared to share your results with your group or class.

D. Locating Options

Some genres are more flexible than others. As you investigate examples of your genre, consider how much leeway writers seem to have. Do all of your examples look pretty standardized, or do writers have different options?

In some cases you, as a writer, can even shift the conventions of a genre. For instance, you might create a video response essay to post on your blog—a newer twist on the genre of the response essay, which usually appears in print.

As you get to know the genre you are writing, consider your options (or resources), and your limitations (or constraints).

Resources

In most cases, you will have a number of resources open to you as you begin to write, even as you conform to conventions of a genre. These resources may be internal (part of the genre itself) or external (part of the situation in which you are writing).

For instance, a response essay may be presented in print, or online, or both. It may range from a few paragraphs (for a quick in-class assignment) to many pages in length (for a more formal assignment).

Your resources for a response essay also include the different kinds of information you can include, such as the kinds of ideas and information in the text you are responding to, and the kinds of personal connections you might draw to your own experiences. Both Luisa and Russell located resources in the text they read and in their own identities and cultures, which helped them to make sense of the reading.

Your resources might also include the amount of time you have available to write the response, the expected length of the response, and so on. Length might be seen as a limitation, but it can also be a resource—it is sometimes harder to confine your ideas to a single page than it is to write a two-page response essay.

Constraints

You will also face some constraints, or factors that limit the range of options you have. The genre itself may not provide as many options to writers. For instance, a response essay keeps its focus on the text or reading assignment in question. That means that your essay should not stray from that focus to a different topic. While you might compare the reading to another text you've read or to other ideas, it is usually not okay to change the focus entirely. For example, Russell had more to say about his own opinions on why materialism is bad for American culture, but he decided not to include them so he could focus his response on the reading.

Different genres will have different types of resources and constraints. A research paper (Chapter 11), for example, requires you to discover which bibliographic style to use (MLA or APA, etc.). A film review (Chapter 9) requires you to identify criteria (such as directing, acting, or cinematographic elements) and evaluate them.

External constraints can include time, materials, and format. For example, your response essay might have to be written and submitted within two days, and you might be required to submit it as a blog post for your class website.

Internal Resources or Constraints

- Design (font, spacing, layout, color, images, bibliographic style)
- Organization (headings and sub-headings, order of items, required sections)
- Content (level of detail, technicality, types of evidence)
- Style (grammar, formality, vocabulary)

External Resources or Constraints

- Time, deadlines
- Money
- Equipment & Materials (video cameras, color printers, ink, etc.)
- Length

By looking at more examples, you can determine how much leeway you have, or the kinds of choices you get to make about your own project.

Now, examine this essay by a student writer, published at Teen Ink, a website for young writers.

Foxxy

"The Way of a Cherokee"

I don't remember much before the time I lived in Shelby, Montana, with my grandparents—which is probably why I always think I spent the first five years of my life there when in truth it was really only two. Still, even those memories have been scattered with the mountain wind and aged over the years.

I remember the hill beside my grandparents' house. (Actually it was a doublewide trailer on a plot of 20 acres that my mom used to say "could be 50 if it was stretched and rolled out flat.") I remember a time before the land was planted with trees, before it was fenced, when it was wild mountain country. Mud piled at the base of the slope, forming a wide berth of bog that was a deathtrap to any human who walked through it.

When I was six and my youngest sister, Sierra, was four, we would sit on the floor at Grandpa's feet and listen as he weaved tales about the wild prairie deer that would come across the hill if one knew when to look. Sierra and I were young tribal warriors sitting before the imaginary fires and listening to dreams that danced around the room in the smoke. The wise and mighty chieftain sat before us—ancient and proud—his eyes gleaming with youth, his words entrapping us in the world of the springing deer.

We wanted to see them.

5   Sierra and I pulled on our boots. It had rained for the past week, and the birthing liquid of the land had impregnated the Mother; she was ready to start a new life. My boots were dusty black with vivid blue trim featuring the icons of my young life— Batman and Robin. The two Gotham City saviors took my breath away, and even to this day I admire their daring and capacity to care for the people of Gotham.

Together, we marched up the hill to catch a glimpse of the white-tailed deer Grandpa had told us about. We avoided the bog at the base and bounced with pent-up excitement as we climbed without a trail to follow. In our imaginations we could already see the fluffy flags of the does, the white spots of the fawns, the towering antlers of the bucks. They danced in our minds to the beat of a drum and the song of a flute without seeing us. If they saw us, these rare and shy creatures would fly away and we would be left with only a taste of what they were like.

For a long time we kept a silent vigil, picking a spot on the crest of the hill that overlooked miles upon miles of empty wasteland to some, dreamland to us. After a half hour, most children get bored and restless, but Sierra and I were different. The only movement we made for several hours was to sit down with our legs crossed—"crisscross applesauce" my kindergarten teacher would say, "the way of a Cherokee" my grandpa called it. We liked Grandpa's way better. Cherokee was in our blood; applesauce was not.

Several hours after we began our lookout, hunger settled in our bellies like a ravenous beast craving the heart of a buffalo. We had seen no deer, none of those splendid white-tailed folk we'd heard so much about. We wanted to wait until we saw one of those graceful beings dance past, but finally we could stand it no longer. Our starvation drew us to the house as a metal trap beckons to the red fox too curious for his own good.

Sierra and I glanced at each other and without words vowed to dine on a quick lunch and dash back to resume our watch. We stood and woke our sleeping muscles, stretching tired limbs until they were ready for use. I took a quick look around, drinking it all in. The hills, the plains, the cloudless Montana sky, my home, my land: I would belong nowhere else.

10   Although Sierra and I had avoided the bog going up, we trudged right through it on our way back. It lapped at our ankles, drank in the sweet nectar of our energy, chewed us up but wouldn't spit us out. We struggled and Sierra managed to break free, but I was trapped, my foot stuck hard and fast.

The bog made sick squishing noises as I tried to pull my boot out, but it was caught and the bog wouldn't let go. Sierra laughed before she sobered up enough to fetch Grandpa. We both knew the wise man could get me loose.

So I stood and waited patiently, pondering how to get myself out of the mud. I almost fell in the process, and I recaptured my balance to discover my foot hanging above the trapped boot, the sock dirty and foot tingling.

When Sierra finally appeared with Grandpa looking like an old cowboy with his gray Western hat, dusty brown boots, work-faded jeans, and red plaid shirt, I was just coming out of the bog. With that crooked smile of his, Grandpa traversed the bog, stepping lightly in certain spots and finding balance on the mud rather than in it. He bent slowly, took hold of my boot, twisted it left once, right once, and plucked it out of the mud like a ripe apple from a wild tree.

He was a cowboy. He was a chief. He was a Cherokee. Grandpa was a wise man.

Sierra and I are older now. Grandpa left us in 2003, but something about the "Spirit Dreams" CD by Thomas Walker brought the jolt of memory back—a memory of my grandpa's tales and the adventure Sierra and I went on to discover their truth. 15

By the way, deer really are rare and shy creatures, and they do dance past quickly if you know when to look.

• •

Imagine that you are in the same anthropology class as Luisa and Russell. How would you write a response to Foxxy's essay? Your instructor has given you Luisa and Russell's examples in class, so you know something about the genre you are supposed to write. But you have to write about a different reading, and you have to be sure not to echo the kinds of claims Luisa and Russell made about culture and identity in their essays. In addition, the instructor wants you to post your response on a class blog.

You might fill out an analysis of your options and constraints as shown in Table 3.3.

Table 3.3 DOCS Analysis of Resources and Constraints for a Response Essay

	Resources	Constraints
Design	• Blog format allows for links. Can I include links to other readings or definitions? • Can I include pictures? What purpose would they serve?	• Must be under 2 pages long, or equivalent—short enough to read easily on screen. • Need to think about tags to add to my blog post so others can find it.
Organization	• How do I order different points/items? • Where does the main idea/most important one go? • How do I focus the reader on the key pieces of evidence I have?	• I have four main points, but only two pages—should I cut something?
Content	• How general/specific should my personal observations be? • How many examples should I give from the text?	• Can't fit more than a few examples into two pages, but need to provide detail. • Needs to say something new about the text—can't repeat what the teacher said or what is in the examples.
Style	• How will I describe my personal experiences—how informal or formal should I be about them? • Can I use a humorous tone, or would that be inappropriate? • What concepts from class can I use to show that I understand the text?	• Needs to be straightforward and pretty concise. • Needs to have lots of impact but in a short amount of space.

EXERCISE 3.3: Getting Started

Re-read the text "The Way of a Cherokee" and Luisa and Russell's response essays. Now, make a list of items you can use in your own response essay. You should list the following:

- Three or four possible examples from the text that you would like to use.
- Key concepts you might use. Is this essay about culture? Identity? Childhood? Education? Can you focus on the writing itself (style, imagery, characterizations)?
- Possible personal connections you can draw. Does Foxxy's experience growing up remind you of something that happened to you as a child?

GROUP ACTIVITY 3.1: Developing Theses

As a group, share your own observations from the reading "The Way of a Cherokee." In your group, come up with a list of possible thesis statements (Chapter 18) that could focus a response essay. Then, choose one or two that you think would be especially interesting to share with the class.

E. Conclusion

Reading this chapter taught you how to write a new genre by looking at examples, identifying conventions, and choosing strategies to use. You have learned how to consider issues of design, organization, content, and layout to help you compose your document.

At this stage, you have assembled three of the main "tools" for your genre toolkit.

In Chapter 1, you learned about the three genre toolkit questions you can use when you encounter a genre for the first time: "What is it?" "Who reads it?" and "What's it for?"

In Chapter 2, you learned how to assess your rhetorical situation when writing a genre.

In this chapter, you learned how to start writing a new genre by discovering how it works.

Now, whenever you are given a new writing task, you will be able to get started by asking questions, discovering situations, and examining the genre at hand. In the next chapter, we'll learn how to use the final part of the toolkit: developing a writing process.

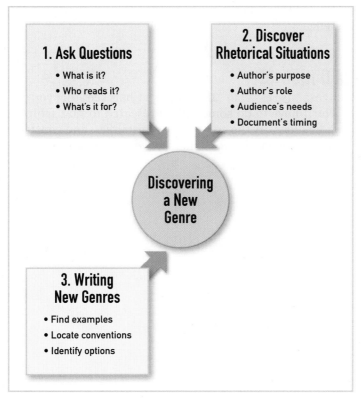

Figure 3.1
The Genre Toolkit for Chapter 3

In Part 2, you will find more specific guidelines for many of the different genres you are likely to encounter in college and the workplace—but not all of them. There are hundreds and hundreds of different genres that you may encounter, and we cannot cover all of them in one textbook. However, by using your genre toolkit, you will develop the skills you need to write any new genre you find.

F. Chapter Project: Write a Response Essay

Write a response essay to the reading "The Way of a Cherokee." You might consider how the essay deals with themes of identity, childhood, and culture. Or, you might choose to focus on the techniques the writer uses to craft the essay: the language, characterizations, descriptions, tone, etc. Be sure to organize your essay around a main thesis (Chapter 18) and to provide support from the text and from your own personal experience.

Multimedia Option

Prepare a video response essay to "The Way of a Cherokee" that you could post on a class website. You'll have to do some online research to find samples of video response essays. Then, identify the conventions, resources, and constraints available to you. Lastly, consider what choices to make given the rhetorical situation.

Developing a Writing Process

In Chapters 1, 2, and 3, you learned how to examine a genre, a genre's rhetorical situation, and the features for a genre you plan to write. In this chapter, you will learn how to write a document in that genre by developing a writing process. Usually, writing a document is more complicated than just sitting down, opening up your word processor, and typing a complete document, start to finish. This chapter describes the range of activities involved in writing a document, activities you can use to develop your own personalized approach.

A. Discovering Your Writing Process

Think about the last time you had a writing task to do—whether for a classroom assignment or for a workplace, community, or personal goal. How did you approach it? Did you plan ahead of time, and then write? Or did you just sit down and get going? Did you revise what you wrote after finishing a complete draft, or edit each sentence as you went along?

Your writing process refers to the set of actions that you used to complete your project, from the time you began thinking about the project to the time you finished it.

People who study writing often divide the writing process into five actions, as shown in Figure 4.1.

You don't necessarily need to do all of these actions in this exact order. Most writers move between different writing actions at different stages of a project. They often return to earlier actions as they go along, moving between brainstorming, drafting, revising, and editing activities until the project is finished.

Even publishing your writing—sharing it with a wider audience—might not be the end of a writing project. For example, you might post a draft to your blog, get feedback from readers, and then revise and re-publish the draft.

Instead of thinking about your writing process as a series of steps, think of the actions in Figure 4.2 as building blocks you can move around.

In Part 3 of this book, you'll learn strategies to help you streamline your writing process. But, in this chapter, we provide a quick overview so you can get started on a project right away: writing a personal essay.

Keep in mind that there is no single "correct" writing process that you must follow. As you can see in Figure 4.3, different writers use different processes. Sometimes, a

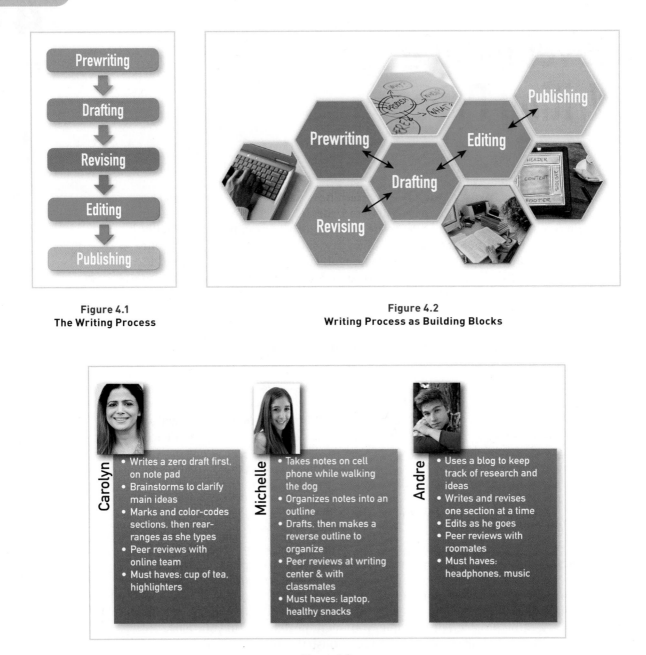

Figure 4.1
The Writing Process

Figure 4.2
Writing Process as Building Blocks

Figure 4.3
Different Writers, Different Writing Processes

writer will vary her writing process depending on the situation or genre. Writing is often more like improvising than following a routine. Our focus here is on helping you develop some different strategies you can use to plan out a writing process.

EXERCISE 4.1: What Is Your Writing Process?

Take a look at Figure 4.3, which includes brief profiles of three different writers. Then, write a profile (Chapter 5) of your own writing process. What procedures and materials do you tend to use when you write? What are your "must have" items? Where do you like to write? Do you like to be around people when you work, or do you prefer to work alone?

GROUP ACTIVITY 4.1: Come up with a Group Process

With your writing group, share your typical writing processes or strategies. Then, make a list of strategies you can use as a group to accommodate everyone's preferred writing techniques for future group projects. Will you share your work in print or online? (Consider your instructor's preferences, too.) What kinds of electronic tools will you use to share and comment on documents? Will you meet outside of class at the library or a coffee shop? What tasks will you focus on when you have group time together? How will you handle absences from team members?

　　Share your plan with the rest of the class, and then use it to keep everyone on task for the rest of the course.

B. Composing a Personal Essay

Next, let's take a look at the genre we'll be discussing in this chapter: a personal essay. In particular, we focus here on the type of personal essay that investigates core values and beliefs, one that is written for a national project called This I Believe. Thousands of people have submitted their essays to This I Believe, and each month a few are chosen to be read on National Public Radio.

EXAMPLE 1: Maisha, "Two Worlds, One Great Nation"

You may think it's simple to sum up an exact definition of what it means to be American, but it's quite difficult. Everyone has their own perception supported by a personal experience. I'm no different. My opinion changes from time to time, however there is one aspect that always remains the same. I believe that when you are allowed to be a part of multiple cultures, you are an American. What I mean by that is, yes, you belong to the American culture but you are not limited and have the freedom to join other cultures and create a whole new identity as you wish. I think that's what makes America more exceptional than other nations.

I am able to keep two different cultures that play a massive part of my life. I am American but I am also Bengali, since my parents are from Bangladesh. The Bengali culture is definitely more complicated to be a part of since I did not grow up in Bangladesh like my parents did. It is problematic for me to maintain my identity as a Bengali into my daily life as an American as well. At home, I may speak Bengali and dress in traditional clothes but once I'm out that door, I switch out of my Bengali self into my American self. However, I always somehow end up combining the two to find a definition of myself. That's the beauty. I have the choice to choose between the two but I also have the choice to mix both. I can contribute to both cultures and be able to really express who I am.

When I was younger, I was obsessed with fitting in. I wanted to be like my friends who had the image of a "true American," while I didn't. I didn't like to wear the traditional clothes from my country and I was embarrassed to bring in food of my culture for lunch. I didn't want to be Bengali. I wanted to be American. That was the time when I didn't know you had the freedom to be whoever you wanted. As I grew older and gained more knowledge and learned more about the world, I realized that no one was ever a "true American." My friends may have looked more American than me, but inside, I was just as American as they were. America is made up of all kinds of people with different races and sexes and that's why this nation is a home to people who don't feel like they don't belong. But they do. We all belong in this country because that's what the United States is all about. It's not about fitting in and trying to be American, it's about having the freedom to choose what you want.

So what is my belief about what it means to be American in simple words? To be able to be you.

EXAMPLE 2: Mark, "I Believe in the Senses"

I was born with four senses—the classic set of sight, touch, taste, and hearing. That's everything right? Well it took me a while growing up to realize that not everyone was missing the sense of smell, the one sense I was born without. Doctor's don't know why, I myself have no explanation; an early onslaught of MRI's and CATSCANS left us only guessing, and the response "wait are you serious? How is that possible?" has become almost as common in introductions as "Hi, my name is Mark." In reality though, it doesn't bother me, in fact I kind of enjoy having such a unique disorder. I have lived my whole life without it so I don't really know what I'm missing. Plus, it has caused me to consider the miracle of our senses—the beauty and wonder of such simple processes that facilitate every experience we will ever have. Our senses, which so often go unnoticed, deserve more credit, and though I only have four that is enough for me to recognize just how incredible they are.

The pleasure of taste: biting into one of my Dad's homemade biscuits. Impossibly fluffy, fragments of heaven that, when covered in the perfect amount of butter, have the power to pull me out of bed Sunday morning. It's sipping the frothy surface of a just-made mug of cocoa and feeling the glory of ideal temperatures and perfect chocolate proportions fall like world peace into my stomach. It's the wonder of tin-foil dinners on a campout, how the flavor in each bite brings the crackling of the fire, the bright stars, and solitude of being lost out in nature completely to life. I cherish taste.

The comfort of touch: sinking into a warm bathtub after a long, cold day and letting the water remind me I still have nerves (yes, I can admit I still take baths on occasion). It's hugging my Mom every day after high school and having her little arms that barely make it all the way around me dissolve every single problem for a split second. It's lying down in my soft bed when my eyes can no longer stay open and letting my blanket silence every concern about the past day while my pillow reassures me that all I need to do now is to rest. I cherish touch.

The joy of hearing: being swept away in the harmonies of a 4-minute musical masterpiece. It's the goose bumps I get from my favorite song, how the marriage of genius lyrics and heart-wrenching notes can subdue me completely for half a day. It's the tone of a familiar voice that lets me know I'm home; the relief of Friday's school bell that announces "finally, the weekend has come." It's the quiet, sacred sound of our Church choir that softly touches my spirit and connects me briefly with a higher Existence. I cherish hearing.

The beauty of sight: living my whole life in Texas and then waking up one morn- 5
ing to see the first snow of a Utah winter. It's getting inches from an original oil painting and seeing the geography of each brush stroke, realizing how every single line testifies of the artist's passion. It's making eye contact with the most beautiful girl I've ever seen—being stopped in my tracks to watch her walk by, forgetting about everything else momentarily to wonder how any one girl could look so flawless. I cherish sight.

For most people there would be another paragraph. But even though I'll never know what smelling is like, I know the greatness of the senses I do have and the fact that they make life everything I love. I believe in the senses.

USE THE TOOLKIT

Suppose you are encountering the personal essay genre for the first time. Let's use the three genre toolkit question from Chapter 1 to examine this new genre.

What Is It?
These are personal essays that appeared on the website for This I Believe, an organization that shares essays written by people of all ages and from all walks of life.

You'll notice that this type of essay draws on personal experience, that it uses the first-person voice ("I"), and that it does not rely on research or other kinds of "library sources." Each essay uses personal experience to send a message. In the first essay, Maisha draws on personal experience to highlight how important it is that America provides opportunities for individuals to integrate different cultural traditions and beliefs. The second essay has a simpler message, but uses descriptive language to really make that message—about the importance of human senses—come alive.

Who Reads It?

Anyone can visit the website for This I Believe and read these essays. Sometimes, the essays are read aloud on National Public Radio—the project began in the 1950s as a radio program—so radio listeners might also be included among the "readers" for these essays. Often, students are asked to write essays for This I Believe, so we can assume that the audience for these essays includes other students who are seeking to understand the genre itself. More broadly, personal essays similar to these may be published in magazines, or collected into books, as some of the This I Believe essays have been.

What's It For?

According to the organization's website, these essays are meant to encourage readers to share their beliefs and to learn about the beliefs of others, not to persuade readers to adopt the author's beliefs. Therefore, the purpose of a This I Believe essay is to prompt reflection on a topic, not necessarily to persuade the audience.

Use the Rhetorical Situation

The rhetorical situations that prompt personal essays can vary. You can often encounter personal essays in published books and magazines, but increasingly, people are sharing their personal stories on blogs and websites such as ThisIBelieve.org and StoryCorps.org. The essays may be actively solicited by publishers or organizations, or they may be prompted when writers feel they have something to share about their life experiences.

EXERCISE 4.2: Use the Genre Toolkit

Go to ThisIBelieve.org and find examples of two more essays that interest you. Using the DOCS method you learned in Chapter 3 (and shown below in Table 4.1), analyze the genre. List both the resources (or options) offered by the genre, and the constraints (or limitations) that seem to be present in the genre.

Table 4.1 Sample DOCS Analysis Chart

	Resources	Constraints
Design		
Organization		
Content		
Style		

What features do these personal essays seem to have in common? How much freedom do writers seem to have in this genre? Are there any constraints on this particular type of essay? Post your analysis to your course management system, or share with your writing group.

Now, let's consider how you would go about writing a personal essay for This I Believe.

C. Prewriting

A writing process usually involves prewriting, or the set of actions you do before you actually sit down to write. Prewriting actions help you to generate ideas, clarify points, or address problems you encounter. If you were writing a personal essay for This I Believe, you might start by listing things you believe in, and then jotting down notes for one or two ideas that you might write about.

You can employ a range of different techniques to help you come up with ideas. Some of them don't even involve putting pen to paper.

You can prewrite at any point in your writing process, not just when you are beginning. All of these techniques can help when you get stuck or feel like you have "writer's block" (see Figure 4.4).

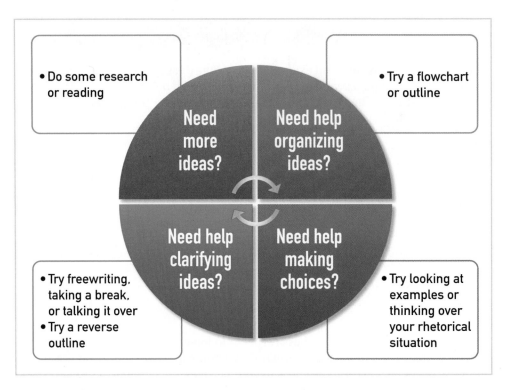

Figure 4.4
Prewriting Techniques for Writer's Block

You'll learn more about prewriting in Chapter 16, but for now, keep the following five ideas in mind.

1. Prewrite Whenever You Need Ideas or Get Stuck

As we noted earlier, there is no single "correct" writing process. This means that you don't necessarily need to start by prewriting. If you are ready to start drafting a paper, then go ahead and write. Prewriting works best when you are stuck—when you are suffering from "writer's block." Sometimes you need to clarify your ideas, or you need to organize different points you want to make.

If you find that you are stuck, you can sit down and try a few different techniques. If you are used to working on your computer, you might try writing with a pen and paper, or vice versa. Sometimes switching to a different medium can help you get out of a rut.

- Try freewriting whatever comes to mind for three minutes, without editing or erasing anything (Chapter 16).

- Try drawing a concept map or cluster chart of your paper (Chapter 16).
- Try outlining what you have written so far (called a "reverse-outline") (Chapter 20).

2. Prewrite by Reading or Doing Research

The preceding techniques tend to work when your problem relates to your own ideas—usually a problem with how to organize or clarify them. But if you don't have any ideas, it doesn't always help to wrack your brain. Instead, you might find new ideas by doing some reading and research.

Imagine you have to write an opinion paper about global warming. You could probably sit down and rattle off some of your own opinions or ideas, but you might soon get stuck, especially if you don't usually keep up on the latest discussions about global warming in science or politics.

Your best bet would be to read some recent articles about climate change. Chances are, you will disagree with some of what you read, or want to extend points others have made. Reading what others have said can often help you to discover new ideas of your own.

3. Prewrite by Thinking through Your Toolkit

The genre toolkit can also help you to brainstorm ideas. One of the best ways of coming up with ideas or solving a writing problem can be to think back over the rhetorical situation and genre for your writing task (Chapters 1 and 2). Take notes or write lists of points about your genre or rhetorical situation. Or, try using the DOCS prompts (design, organization, content, and style) to plan out your document (Chapter 3). As you write, you can return to the toolkit again and again.

Consider the case of the personal essay for This I Believe. You might develop ideas by browsing the website and thinking about what kinds of stories the organization might be looking for—stories that encourage others to think about core values and understand where other people are coming from. That gives you a clue about the kinds of things you can focus on in your essay. Has there been a time in your life when you have felt misunderstood, or when your core values have been challenged?

You might also find yourself stuck when you are not sure about the genre you are writing, or about a particular problem within a genre. Say you've started writing your personal essay, but you get stuck because you aren't sure how to conclude it. Taking a look back over your examples will give you a sense of how others have ended their essays. You might try out one of those strategies, or develop your own after seeing some of the possibilities.

4. Prewrite by Talking to Others

Sometimes the best thing you can do is talk to someone about your writing—with a classmate, a friend or family member, your dog, or even yourself (in a journal or in a voice memo). Talking over your ideas or your frustrations can often lead to new insights. For a This I Believe essay, you might ask a friend or family member to help you brainstorm some ideas drawn from experiences in your own life. Just remember to take notes so you don't forget what you've come up with.

5. Prewrite by Taking a Break

Sometimes, your brain just needs time to process ideas. Try doing something else: take a walk, do some laundry, get a coffee, or finish some errands. You may be surprised how often ideas come to when you are not thinking about a project. Some people take a notepad with them on walks and errands, or bring a cell phone with a voice memo or note-taking feature. That way, they can record ideas whenever they occur to them.

EXERCISE 4.3: Prewrite for your Personal Essay

To start, brainstorm some ideas for the kinds of core values you believe in.

1. Look at the list of themes on the This I Believe website to get you started: http://thisibelieve.org/themes/. Which of those themes seem interesting or important to you? What comes to mind when you think of those themes?
2. Choose three or four themes, and then think about what kinds of personal experiences or stories you could write about that would illustrate those themes. Which one seems to give you the best material to write about?
3. Next, choose one theme to explore in greater depth. Read some of the stories online that pertain to that theme. Make a list of conventions or choices that might be useful for you to try out, based on those examples.

Be prepared to share your brainstorming ideas in class or online, and to talk about which techniques you found most useful.

GROUP ACTIVITY 4.2: Values Inventory

With your group, brainstorm a list of "core values" that might drive a "This I Believe" essay. Then, discuss which of those values would seem most interesting to readers. Do any of those core values seem tired or clichéd? Can you come up with ideas that seem fresh and interesting? Try to find a core value for each team member to write about.

D. Drafting

Like prewriting, drafting can occur at many different stages of a writing project. You don't necessarily need to write an entire document in one sitting—especially if it is a long one. In fact, most authors alternate between prewriting, drafting, revising, and editing their work. You might write one section, then prewrite for another, then go back and revise the first one, then scrap it and rewrite it entirely.

You'll learn more about drafting techniques in Chapter 17. For now, consider the following strategies for drafting a document.

Set Goals

Drafting a writing project can seem overwhelming, especially if you are asked to write something that seems longer or more difficult than anything you've written before. Any time you sit down to write, try to set a manageable goal for yourself. Then, when you've met that goal, take a break—call a friend, go for a walk, or work on something else. Often, rewarding yourself after reaching a writing goal makes writing easier.

Your goal can be small—you might decide to write 200 words, or finish two paragraphs, or just to write for 15 minutes. Those small goals can add up to a lot of writing, especially if you write consistently.

Break It Up

In order to make the most of short writing sessions, it helps to break up writing projects into smaller sets of tasks. For example, you might decide to organize your This I Believe essay by including an opening anecdote, an explanation of the theme and how it applies to your life, an example drawn from your personal experience, and a conclusion. Each of those sections could be written separately. You might decide to write about a memory or experience first, then consider how you can link that experience to the overall message of your essay.

You do not necessarily need to write things in the order in which they'll appear in the final document. In fact, it often helps to start somewhere in the middle. If there's a section of a document that seems easiest to write, start with that. Then, you'll have some momentum going into the next section.

Go with the Flow

While setting small goals and breaking up long projects works much of the time, you'll occasionally find that you get a sudden burst of inspiration or energy. Take advantage of those moments. If you can, go with the flow and write for as long as you have that spark of energy.

Also, see if you can identify what helps you to feel inspired to write. Does doing research help? Brainstorming with friends? Focusing on something else? That way, you'll be able to develop your own strategies to help generate that spark.

Try Different Places and Different Writing Tools

A change of scenery can inspire you to write. If you've been stuck writing in your room, try going to the library or taking your laptop outside (if the weather's nice). Many students prefer to write in coffee shops populated by fellow students; others prefer the isolation of a library table or a quiet room. Find out what works for you.

Similarly, try writing with different tools. If you are used to composing on your computer, try a pen and paper, and vice-versa. Some writers even dictate their writing to a computer voice-recognition program or voice recorder because talking out loud helps them focus their ideas.

EXERCISE 4.4: Start Drafting your Personal Essay

Using the ideas that you have brainstormed, begin drafting your This I Believe essay.

As you draft, keep a time log of the different strategies you used—where did you write? What tasks did you do, when? How did you start? What seems to work best for you?

Be prepared to share your draft, and to discuss your drafting techniques, with your classmates.

E. Revising

There are two important things to understand when it comes to revising your writing.

First, revising is not the same as editing. Editing tends to be a later action in a writing process, one that focuses mainly on style and wording, and we will learn more about it in Section F of this chapter. Revising, on the other hand, is an in-depth reconsideration of your draft and its content, organization, and ideas.

Second, we equate revising with "seeking feedback" on your draft. The only way to revise successfully is to solicit useful feedback on your draft from competent readers. We do recognize, however, that there are many ways to seek feedback: from your peers (who might ask for your feedback in return), from your instructor, and, most importantly, *from yourself.*

Next, we will look at different ways to seek feedback and to revise your writing.

Seek Feedback from Others

The best way to get feedback from others is to ask someone to read your paper—a friend, classmate, co-worker, or professor. Many colleges offer writing centers where peer tutors are available to help you with any stage of the writing process, including revising.

The key to getting good feedback is to ask good questions. Don't just say, "Can you read my paper?" Instead, ask specific questions or point to specific parts you need help with. One good place to start figuring out how to ask specific questions is the assignment sheet for your writing assignment. Read your assignment sheet carefully: have you met all of your professor's expectations? (For some examples of good feedback-generating questions, see Chapter 22.)

Give Good Feedback

In most college writing classes, you'll be expected not only to seek feedback, but to give feedback to your classmates. No one likes to get a paper back from a peer workshop with just a few punctuation corrections and no substantive comments. Such poor feedback won't help the writer improve the document.

Thus, you need to learn to be a good critic as well as a good writer. Learn how to not only notice what is wrong, but also how to make suggestions for improvement.

As you read another student's draft, focus on the ideas, organization, and genre. Make suggestions to help the writer better suit the genre's conventions, make the organization clearer, or get her ideas across more clearly. Put yourself in the shoes of the intended audience. Would you find this document confusing? Convincing? Be sure to explain *why*.

Revise Your Own Work

One of the best ways to improve as a writer is to begin looking at your own writing with fresh eyes, as though you were seeing it for the first time. There are a few techniques that can make it easier to see your writing with fresh eyes:

First, it helps if you can take a break after writing and let your writing "rest" for a few days. When you return to your document to revise it, it will seem new to you and problems will be easier to spot.

Second, as you read over your work, slow down and think about (1) the rhetorical purpose for your work, (2) the genre you are writing, and (3) the audience's needs. Read through multiple times, each time taking only *one* of these challenges into account.

Third, read your document out loud. Reading out loud slows you down and forces you to consider every word on the page.

Change Things Around

Research shows that novice writers tend to revise mostly at the level of sentences, swapping out one word for another, or occasionally rewording a phrase that sounds awkward. These are good changes to make, but advanced writers tend to make larger revisions as well: scratching out whole sections, moving paragraphs around, adding new paragraphs, clarifying points, and so on.

As you are revising, ask yourself about the big picture of your document. Think about where you need to add or subtract ideas, provide more or less information, or define a term.

Key Considerations for Revision

As you revise, use the following items from your Genre Toolkit to analyze your own writing. You've already applied these considerations to examples of the genre you plan to write—now, do the same for yourself.

- Rhetorical Situation (Chapter 2)
  - Author's Role and Purpose: How do I come across to my readers? Is the document's purpose clear?
  - Audience's Needs: Does the document meet my audience's needs?
  - Document's Timing: Does this genre have good timing? Can I accomplish my writing by deadline?
- Genre: Does this look like the type of document it is meant to be? Use the DOCS method (Chapter 3).
  - Design & Layout: Is the layout and design typical of the genre? If not, should it be?
  - Organization: Does the organization suit the genre? Does the order of points or sections make sense?
  - Content: Is the type of content suitable for the genre? Should there be more examples, more evidence, more information?
  - Style: Is the style suitable for the genre? Are there sentences that are unclear, or too casual, or too formal?

EXERCISE 4.5: Revise your Own "This I Believe" Essay

Read over your essay draft. Using a highlighting tool, mark places where you might do the following:

1. Convey the rhetorical purpose for your work. Is the overall message or core value clear?
2. Emulate a convention of the genre you are writing. Are there places where you might emulate samples you've read? Where and why?
3. Modify a convention of the genre you are writing. Are there places where you might do something different from what you have seen? Where and why?
4. Meet the audience's needs or concerns. Is there anything readers might find confusing if they weren't there to experience the story you are relating? Is there anything you can do to make the story more vivid for readers?

GROUP ACTIVITY 4.3: Create Revision Questions for Your "This I Believe" Essay

1. Come up with a list of specific questions or criteria for revising your personal essay.
2. Exchange drafts with a classmate, along with revision questions to help provide good feedback.
3. Trade feedback with your classmate.
4. When you get your feedback, use it to write a revision plan, identifying at least four things you will change or improve when you revise.

F. Editing and Proofreading

At some point in the writing process, you will want to focus on the finer points of writing: word choice, sentence structure, grammar, and the like. You'll find more advice about sentence-level concerns in Chapter 22. For now, though, keep the following two principles in mind.

Plan Some Time for Editing

Leave yourself time to read over your work carefully before it is due. It is hard to catch simple errors or awkward-sounding sentences when it is four in the morning and your paper is due in five hours. Whenever possible, schedule time to read over your work when you are fresh and well rested.

Read Carefully

As you read over your work, try to slow down and focus on one thing at a time. You can try reading your paper out loud, or getting a friend to read it to you. That way, you will be less likely to skip over mistakes or funny-sounding sentences. Or, try reading with a pen or highlighter in hand, making a note whenever you notice something that needs work.

If you are reading on the screen, use your word processor's features to help you make notes. Most software programs provide tools that allow you to highlight text in different colors, add written or spoken comments, strike out words, and more. You can also use spelling- and grammar-check tools, although be careful to examine each change the program suggests carefully, as computerized tools do not always get it right.

Focus on whether your sentences sound right—do they say what you want them to say? Would they confuse a reader? If so, see if you can write things in a different way.

EXERCISE 4.6: Edit and Proofread Your "This I Believe" Essay

Edit and proofread your draft, marking your changes either on paper or on your screen. Save the edited version as a new document, then compare the edited version with your earlier version. Share your editing process with your group or post the edited version to the class discussion board.

G. Publishing

A common phrase among writers is: "Writing is never done. It's just due." You can spend hours and hours revising and tweaking your work, but in professional and academic contexts, at some point you will have to publish—"make public"—your writing.

For student writers, the writing process usually ends when an assignment is due in class. However, you may also be asked to submit your work for publication—to post it to a course website or blog, or submit it to an undergraduate journal or your student newspaper. In these cases, publishing involves a few more steps than simply printing out your essay and handing it to your professor.

Keep in mind that you should think about publishing as you work through the other actions in the writing process, not necessarily just at the end. How and where you publish your document can affect the choices you make throughout. For example, if you are publishing your writing as a blog post, you may want to include hyperlinks to other documents online. That's something you might consider as part of your brainstorming and drafting process.

Depending on what and where you are publishing, you may need to do the following:

- Change the formatting (fonts, spacing, layout) to meet the publisher's guidelines. For example, a letter to the editor for your student newspaper may be limited to 500 words, in which case you may need to edit your writing down to fit the space constraints (and possibly return to the drafting stage).
- Reconsider your audience (which may mean going back to the brainstorming phase). Perhaps you have written an essay, but want to turn it into a column for your student newspaper. This means shifting your genre and audience, so you will need to cycle back through your writing process to address those issues.
- Add additional parts to conform to a genre's conventions. An undergraduate journal might ask for an abstract or works cited list, or a short bio statement about you, or a cover letter.
- Address technical considerations or constraints. For example, you may need to submit your files in a specific electronic format or meet file size limits.

We'll address all of these issues in more detail in later chapters. For now, though, keep in mind that where and how you publish your work affects all of the decisions you make during your writing process.

Figure 4.5
The Genre Toolkit for Chapter 4

H. Conclusion

In this chapter, you have learned how to generate a flexible writing process that you can adapt to the task at hand. Keep in mind that you can use different writing actions at any time: brainstorming, drafting, revising, editing, and publishing. You do not need to use the same writing process for every assignment you write. The point is to keep in mind that writing involves different kinds of activities, and that you can develop your own favorite approaches based on what works best for you.

At this stage, you have assembled all the tools you need for your Genre Toolkit.

In Chapter 1, you learned about the three genre discovery questions that you can use when you encounter a genre for the first time.

In Chapter 2, you learned how to discover your rhetorical situation when preparing to write a genre.

In Chapter 3, you learned how to start writing a genre by determining how it works.

Finally, in Chapter 4, you have learned the tools to help you plan your writing process.

In Part 2, you will find more specific techniques for many genres that you are likely to encounter.

I. Chapter Project: Write a Personal Essay

For this assignment, you will prepare a personal essay that focuses on your own core values. Consider values related to your education, career, personal life, and or family life. Prepare a narrative essay that could be submitted to This I Believe.

With your complete essay, hand in a cover letter (a kind of business letter, Chapter 12) that explains the writing process you used to prepare your essay. Did you try any new techniques? What strategies did you find most helpful? What do you think you need to work on in this course to improve your writing?

Multimedia Option

Create an audio version of your personal essay that you could submit to StoryCorps .org.

Group Option

Prepare an audio podcast in which each member contributes a personal story that addresses a common theme or topic. You might listen to podcasts of This American Life (ThisAmericanLife.org) for examples of this type of story. Your group should work together to practice, revise, and edit each story before you record them.

PART 2

Projects

73

Profiles

A profile is a verbal portrait of a person, a group, a place, or a thing. Whereas a portrait, such as a painting or a photograph, can portray its subject with an image, a profile portrays its subject with words.

In college, you might be asked to write a profile in a variety of situations. In some cases, you will be asked to profile yourself. For instance, you might write an introduction to a portfolio of work you completed in a course. You might write a profile of a person or organization in your community for a course on social work, or of a patient with a particular mental disorder for a psychology course.

Profiles also appear in the workplace. For example, if you work for a consulting business, you might be asked to write a profile of the clients you have served. If you work for a non-profit organization, you might write a set of profiles describing the kinds of programs you offer. Journalists frequently write profile articles for magazines and newspapers. An obituary is even a profile of sorts.

In this chapter, you will learn how to write several kinds of profiles that you may encounter in your college career.

A. Profile Mini-Genre: Social Network Profile

Take a look at the following three profile pages from Facebook, the social networking site.

· ·

EXAMPLE 1: Social Network Profile of a Band

Facebook profile of a band.

· ·

EXAMPLE 2: Social Network Profile of a Company

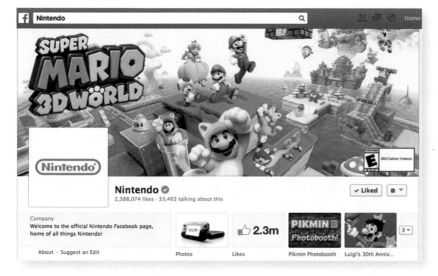

Facebook profile of gaming company Nintendo.

EXAMPLE 3: Social Network Profile of a Nonprofit Organization

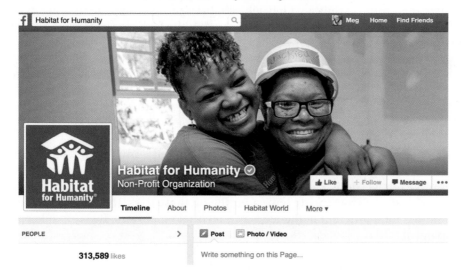

Facebook profile of nonprofit organization Habitat for Humanity.

USE THE TOOLKIT

Let's use the three genre toolkit questions from Chapter 1 to examine this genre.

What Is It?

These three profiles are short, digital snapshots or outlines of an individual, company, or group. Each profile includes photographs and text, including background information, a description, and/or links to further information.

Who Reads It?

Public Facebook profiles can be viewed by anyone with access to the Internet. In particular, users of Facebook tend to read this type of profile. Facebook readers want to learn more about the person or group whose profile they are reading.

What's It For?

Social network profiles, including profiles for Facebook, are meant to share information about a person or group. These profiles are for a band (The Most Loyal), a company (Nintendo), and a nonprofit organization (Habitat for Humanity). The Most Loyal's profile helps fans stay connected to them and their music; Nintendo's profile helps fans of their products stay up-to-date with the company and its offerings; Habitat for Humanity's profile shares information about the organization and even has a link for "Get Involved" to encourage participation by newcomers. A social network profile is thus a widely viewed, brief profile webpage that the individual or corporate author can use to present a "public face" to readers who want to learn more.

EXERCISE 5.1: Design Your Professional Social Network Profile

A social network profile helps create your online identity. You might already have a Facebook or Google+ profile or a profile on LinkedIn (a professional networking site).

For this exercise, design a networking profile for yourself for Facebook, LinkedIn, or a similar site. If you already have a profile on these sites, then you are to revise your profile for a different audience, say, potential employers. Be sure to keep the following in mind:

- Be very careful when you select what to place online. Your online identity is hard to change. Even if you delete your profile from a social network site, it remains stored (or "cached") in various locations around the web, easily accessible for years.

- Select a profile photograph of yourself that you wouldn't mind being viewed by a wide audience, including your professor and future employers.
- Think about what qualities of yourself you want to emphasize. Do you have any special skills or experiences that you want to share with friends, family, and future employers?
- Sometimes it is useful to have your résumé (Chapter 12) next to you while you are writing your social network profile. Be sure that your résumé and your social network profile are consistent (such as your education and employment history).
- Once you have designed your profile, you may decide whether you want to publish it on Facebook, LinkedIn, Google+, or all three.

GROUP ACTIVITY 5.1: Design a Social Network Profile for Your Group

Often, collaborators will use a social network group profile to coordinate their projects together. For example, a planning committee for a high school reunion might create a page for the reunion committee to keep each other posted on the events they are planning. For this activity, create a Facebook group profile for your group.

- You will need to decide what sort of profile image best represents your group: a photograph of your group sitting together? An image of a mascot? Be sure to use an image that has a Creative Commons (cc) license and not one that is protected by copyright. For a good database of (cc) images, check out the Wikimedia Commons.
- You will also need to decide how to describe your group. Look at the preceding examples for Habitat for Humanity and Nintendo. What information would you like to share with a wide audience?

B. Portfolio

Similar to a social network profile or a résumé (Chapter 12), a portfolio is a profile of a person or group that showcases the subject's experience, talents, and/or creations. What makes a portfolio unique among profiles is that it contains samples of the subject's work—music (for a band), images (for a photographer), and clips (for a journalist).

Students often create portfolios to present a collection of work and other artifacts to demonstrate a learning process that has led to mastery of a subject.

Portfolios have traditionally existed in hard copy, but more and more portfolios are appearing in online form. Here are some examples of online portfolios.

EXAMPLE 1: Online Portfolio of a Band

Online portfolio of the band Minor Stars.

EXAMPLE 2: Online Portfolio of an Artist

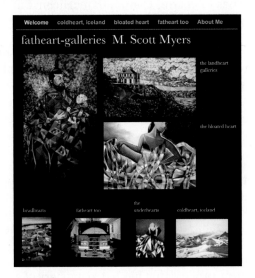

Online portfolio of an artist.

EXAMPLE 3: Online Portfolio of a Poet

Andrea Selch

Home   Works   Events

Biography

Author photo by Diane Amato

Andrea Selch has an MFA from UNC-Greensboro, and a PhD from Duke University, where she taught creative writing from 1999 until 2003. Her dissertation was a history of poetry on commercial radio in the United States from 1922 until 1945. Her poems have been published in *Calyx, Equinox, The Greensboro Review, Oyster Boy Review, Luna, The MacGuffin,* and *Prairie Schooner.* Her poetry chapbook, *Succory,* was published by Carolina Wren Press in 2000. Her full-length collection of poetry, *Startling,* was runner-up in the 2003 Turning Point competition and was published by Turning Point Press in October, 2004. [*Startling* was re-issued by Cockeyed Press in 2009.] Her most recent small collection, *Boy Returning Water to the Sea: Koans for Kelly Fearing,* was published in 2009 by Cockeyed Press. She is the winner of 2008 Hippo Award from The Monti for her spoken story, "Replacement Child." In 2001, she joined the board of Carolina Wren Press and is now President and Executive Director. She lives in rural Hillsborough, North Carolina, with her partner and their two children.

All of Selch's books may be ordered through the Carolina Wren Press website or Amazon.

Selected Works

Poetry
Startling
" ...there is nothing very quiet about Andrea Selch."
--Ron Silliman

Poetry Chapbook
Succory
Carolina Wren Press Poetry Series, #2 (2000).

Poetry/Art
Boy Returning Water to the Sea: Koans for Kelly Fearing
Poetry by Andrea Selch with illustrations by the late William Kelly Fearing. Cockeyed Press, 2009

Quick Links
E-mail the author
Authors Guild
findauthors

Online portfolio of poet Andrea Selch.

USE THE TOOLKIT

Let's use the three genre toolkit questions from Chapter 1 to examine this genre.

What Is It?

A portfolio is an in-depth profile of a person or group that provides detailed information about its subject, along with a sampling of the subject's work. All of these example portfolios provide background information, examples, and images to educate the reader about the subjects of the portfolios. The first example is the online portfolio of the band Minor Stars; the second example is the online portfolio of artist M. Scott Myers; the third example is the online portfolio of poet Andrea Selch. The primary difference between an online portfolio and a social networking page is that the portfolio provides a sampling of the subject's work. For example, on the Minor Stars website you can listen to the band's music; on Myers's website you can view images of the artist's paintings. The home page of an online portfolio usually has a menu that allows readers to view samples of the subject's work, to read a biography about the subject, and to learn how to get in touch with the subject.

Who Reads It?

Anyone with Internet access can read these portfolios, because they are published on the world wide web; but, they tend to be read by people seeking detailed information about the subjects of the portfolios. Because there are many bands, artists, and professors who have portfolio websites, chances are people will come across these portfolios by searching for the specific figures in question. However, they may also stumble upon these portfolios while browsing. Portfolios can also be prepared in print form for a more limited audience. In many writing classes, students prepare final portfolios featuring their best work from the course, and the audience is typically their instructor.

What's It For?

These three portfolios serve their readers by providing detailed information about their subjects. The fans of a band can learn more about the band's members, view the band's show dates, and listen to samples of its music. Buyers interested in art can view paintings and purchase them on an artist's website. Writers and readers can learn more about an author and the author's work.

EXERCISE 5.2: Design a Mockup of an Online Portfolio

You might want to create a portfolio to showcase your experiences and talents online, for a few purposes. Some colleges encourage students to create portfolios as a graduation requirement and to showcase what they have learned from their coursework. Other students create portfolios as a job-seeking document, something employers will see if they search the job applicant's name online.

For this assignment, design a "mock-up" of your own online portfolio, or e-portfolio. A mock-up is a plan for your design and contents.

The following steps will help you to create your mock-up:

- Describe what kind of image you want to create for yourself. This will influence everything from the contents you put up to color choices. Is this a strictly professional site, or do you want to include a sense of who you are as a person?
- Indicate what pages you want to have in your portfolio. Some portfolios include samples of previous work—while artists might include samples of their music or art, you might include samples of your writing or other projects related to your major or interests.

- Sketch out a layout for your e-portfolio (either on paper, or using PowerPoint or desktop publishing software). Look at the menus on the home pages of the e-portfolios pictured previously. What would your menu look like? You might have pages called "home," "education," "work experience," "leadership experience," or what have you. You might find it useful to have your résumé (Chapter 12) on hand while you design your e-portfolio. You should also consider the visual design of your website (Chapter 29).
- What will your home page look like? Would you include a portrait of yourself? What text would you want to include on your home page?

MULTIMEDIA EXERCISE 5.1

After you write the text and sketch out a design for each page of your e-portfolio, design and publish your page online. There are many free services that host e-portfolios, such as Wordpress.com, or your university might offer free web space and tools for e-portfolios. Research free web hosting services that provide a web platform, and select one that you would like to use to host your e-portfolio. You might need to learn more about the platform by studying tutorials they provide. Once you feel comfortable using the platform, build your e-portfolio and launch it online.

C. Program Profile

A program profile is a profile of an entity like a government program, a research institute, or a university department. Profiles can be printed in booklet form (like the "viewbook" materials published by colleges), or they can exist online. Let's take a look at some examples of online program profiles.

EXAMPLE 1: Program Profile of a Scholarship

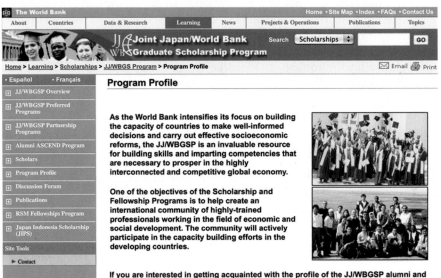

Program profile for a scholarship sponsored by the World Bank.

EXAMPLE 2: Program Profile of a Public Health Service

Program profile of a public health service.

EXAMPLE 3: Program Profile of a College Major

Durham Technical Community College

Search

ABOUT DTCC   FUTURE STUDENTS   CURRENT STUDENTS   CONTINUING EDUCATION   FACULTY & STAFF   ALUMNI & FRIENDS   HOME

Medical Assisting

Medical Assisting

➤ Explore this Career
➤ Information Sessions
➤ Essential Skills
➤ Plans of Study
➤ Course Descriptions
➤ How to Apply
➤ Contact Information

Program Requirements

Career Comparison Chart

Health Programs Home

The Medical Assisting program prepares students to become multi-skilled health care professionals qualified to perform administrative, clinical, and laboratory procedures.

Course work includes instruction in anatomy and physiology; medical terminology; scheduling appointments; coding and processing insurance accounts; billing; collections; medical transcription; computer operations; assisting with examinations and treatments; performing routine laboratory procedures; electrocardiography; supervised medication administration; and ethical/legal issues associated with patient care.

Graduates of the Medical Assisting program have employment opportunities in physicians' offices, health maintenance organizations (HMO's), health departments, and hospital clinics.

The Durham Technical Community College Medical Assisting Diploma Program is accredited by the Commission on Accreditation of Allied Health Education Programs (CAAHEP) upon the recommendation of the Medical Assisting Education Review Board (MAERB).

Program profile of a college major.

USE THE TOOLKIT

Let's use the three genre toolkit questions from Chapter 1 to examine this genre.

What Is It?

A profile of a program is related to an online portfolio, in that they both exist online and share information with a wide audience of readers about their subjects. But the nature of a program—an ongoing series of related activities and events that share a single goal—means that the program profile will need to meet different audience expectations than those met by an online portfolio. For example, the academic program in medical assisting (Example 3) has an ongoing series of courses and requirements that students and faculty will want to know about. Furthermore, the purpose of the program profile differs from a portfolio in that a portfolio showcases the subject's works, whereas a program profile does not.

Who Reads It?

Program profiles usually exist online, which means they can be read by anyone with an Internet connection. However, writers of program profiles probably have a more specific audience in mind when they design their profiles. For example, profiles of particular academic programs are meant primarily for people who are thinking of studying in those areas, while scholarship program profiles probably target people who would like to apply. In general, readers of program profiles are looking for detailed information about the programs profiled, and they have probably found the profile using a web search for that type of program.

What's It For?

Let's look at the examples. The profile of the Joint Japan/World Bank Graduate Scholars Program (Example 1) first gives a description of the program and then guides potential applicants through the process (and helps potential donors to the program learn more about the program). The profile of the child health care program (Example 2) describes the program and then gives links to contact information for those interested in participating. The profile of the Medical Assisting program at Durham Technical Community College (Example 3) describes the program and provides detailed information on the course of study for those interested in applying for the program. Thus, a program profile is a printed or online description of a program (which is an ongoing series of related activities and events that share a single goal) that provides detailed information for readers interested in the program.

EXERCISE 5.3: Write a Program Profile of a College Program

Imagine that you have been involved with a new, interdisciplinary educational program for your college that brings together students from at least two different departments to work on public service projects. For example, you might have a program that supports education majors and English majors who volunteer to teach English language skills to immigrant farm workers through a Farm Work Literacy Project.

- Your job is to design a profile of the program. You can use the example of the Farm Worker Literacy Project just described, or you can come up with a program of your own.
- Think about the kind of information that you will need to provide on the website for the program.
- Think about the two very different audiences you will need to address: students interested in participating, and donors interested in supporting the program with money.

GROUP ACTIVITY 5.2: Design a Profile of a Community Program

Imagine that you are on a committee that has developed a new public service program for your town. For example, you may have helped start a program that provides books to low-income public school libraries.

- Your job is to design a profile of the program. You can use the example of the library book program just described, or you can come up with a program of your own.
- Think about the kind of information that you will need to provide on the website for the program.
- Think about the two very different audiences you will need to address: the public whose taxes will support the program and donors interested in supporting the program with money.

D. Profile Article

A profile article describes a person, place, group, or even an event. Profile articles can be very long or very short, or anything in between. Some contain images, some do not. Let's look at some shorter profile articles.

EXAMPLE 1: Profile Article of a Dancer

Shirley Hancock

Oregon Ballet Theatre's Lucas Threefoot: Oregon Ballet Theatre's New Soloist Finds Comfort in Changing Roles

In a darkened photographer's studio on Portland's Eastbank, Lucas Threefoot is jumping so high, his torso nearly clears a tall backdrop. That athletic artistry is also vaulting his career as a ballet dancer known for his classic and contemporary hybrid style. "I'm riding a wave right now," Threefoot smiles. "A good wave."

The 23-year-old Oregon native is the new soloist with Oregon Ballet Theatre (OBT), an organization that has trained him, remarkably, since age 4. Threefoot—originally Dreyfuss, translated from German by his great, great, great grandfather who was a cobbler in Mississippi—is proof you don't need a New York City Ballet or Joffrey pedigree to succeed. You can train right here in Oregon, live ten minutes from your high school (Lincoln High) and learn to perform world-class ballet.

Threefoot's promotion to soloist comes after exemplary performances as Bluebird in Sleeping Beauty; leads in Trey McIntyre's Like a Samba; Speak, a hip-hop pas de deux; Rush at The Kennedy Center; and as Lysander in A Midsummer Night's Dream. These are the foundation for future breakout roles. "When someone like Lucas comes along—particularly a male with a classic physique—and gets a good teacher early, has drive, ambition, intelligence, coordination and musicality, well, it just doesn't happen very often," says OBT artistic director, Christopher Stowell. Threefoot grew up a kind of cultured Huckleberry Finn. His mother, a nurse, and father, a cabinet maker, encouraged their only child to excel in languages, music, even karate. He ran unfettered through the woods and fields surrounding their Beavercreek home. Then in 1992, watching the summer Olympics, Threefoot began cartwheeling through the house. "I was afraid he was going to do serious damage to his head on the brick hearth," laughs his mother, Eileen. "I had to find a way to channel that energy." She found it at OBT's Dance Movement class.

Soon enthralled, young Threefoot gave up basketball, karate, prom, even college for the rigorous demands of ballet. "There wasn't a singular moment when I said I wanted to be a ballet dancer," explains Threefoot. "If I had gone to college, I'd want to be on the cutting edge of technology, to discover something new. It's interesting because science and technology is exploring what's out there, and with dancing, you're exploring what's within—the intention behind the steps."

5   Audiences witnessed that last season when Threefoot took the male lead next to Anne Mueller in Rite of Spring, Stravinsky's provocative ballet that, in 1913, unleashed riots at Theatre des Champs-Elysees in Paris. "Oh man, so intense!" says Threefoot. "The music is just so weird and powerful. You have to match that in your intent, and Anne is just such a powerful dancer." Threefoot not only matched Mueller's level of artistry, says Stowell, but also "joined her in being a wild animal on stage," a performance Stowell likens to sprinting for fifteen minutes. Ballet as an athletic art form for both women and men, is something Threefoot and OBT want to promote. "The first thing I tell people is, 'Hey, I get to dance with beautiful women all the time,'" says Threefoot, described by a staff member as "the mischievous flirt" who charms every pretty girl walking through the door. He sees the irony that most people identify ballet with tutus and tiaras, yet King Louis the XIV was one of the world's first danseurs. And the only ballet dancer—male or female—most people can name is Mikhail Baryshnikov, Threefoot's hero. "I want his kind of power and confidence," says Threefoot.

Of course, all that confidence comes from negotiating tough life passages—like middle school, not always an easy place for a "smart, goody two shoes," let alone ballet student. "That was a formative time," reflects Threefoot. "I know how it is to be picked on, to be the odd man out, and I never want to make anyone feel that." Last season, Threefoot triumphed over a grand faux pas during the first night as Bluebird in Sleeping Beauty. "I wasn't completely comfortable in myself, and I put my hand down. That sucked," Threefoot confesses. "But it helped me be a better dancer. I realized—and it seems like a paradoxical thing—you have to overcome it in your mind before you overcome it on stage."

This fall finds Threefoot with what he calls a "comfort I've never felt before, more confident relating to people." Fresh from starring in The Nutcracker in Seoul, South Korea, and preparing for a November performance of Alex Ballard's Noesis and Noema in Lyon, France, he can't wait to translate that comfort to the Oregon stage. "My challenge this season is to bring more of my intent and personality to the audience. There are so many aspects to me. This is why ballet is not a sport. We don't dance just to show cool tricks, we dance to show what's inside us," he says. "Whatever it is you're feeling, you have to fill 3,000 seats. You have to feel it and magnify it."

EXAMPLE 2: Profile Article of a Student-Athlete

Jaime Shroeder

Goals for Life

Idaho State University women's soccer player Lanie Ward and her mother, Robyn, always enjoyed volunteering to better the lives of others.

Throughout high school, Ward and her mother were members of the National Charity League, where they won the mother-daughter service award for logging the most hours. The duo worked with young children, and donated time to organizations such as Ronald McDonald House and Road Home.

Robyn Ward took a trip to Kenya in 2006, and the pair began fundraising for RaFIKis, a charitable organization started by Ward's aunt, Sue Vanderhoof. The three women had plans to return to Kenya together, but Robyn passed away suddenly two years before the trip.

In 2011, Ward was able to make her first trip to Africa to work at a school for deaf children. Although her mother wasn't there, Ward could feel her presence, and the power of what she had accomplished through her volunteer work.

"When I got to Nakuru, all of the kids were signing my mom's name and asking where she was," Ward said. "The fact that they remembered her from six years ago was awesome. I felt like I already had a great connection with them through my mom." 5

The junior defender from Sandy, Utah, spent three weeks in Nakuru, Kenya, with a group of 20 other volunteers on behalf of RaFIKis working with children at the Ngala School for the Deaf.

"There were a couple of deaf educators and three deaf volunteers who came with us," Ward said. "We tried to pair up with one of them when we were teaching since they knew sign language and could help us communicate with the kids. We took a lot of books and math exercises with us so that is what most of the lessons were based around. We also brought some art supplies and were able to teach arts, crafts and fun projects as well."

The Ngala School for the Deaf has been in operation for more than 25 years and consists of several buildings for dormitory and educational purposes. It serves students ranging from ages 5–17 in classes from Nursery to Standard Eight and offers vocational training in carpentry and sewing to help students become employable once they have completed their education.

Deaf children are not able to attend public schools in Kenya so boarding facilities equipped to address their special needs is their only option. The Kenyan government provides minimal financial assistance and parents of deaf children are often too poor to afford boarding fees, so deaf children are often abandoned and forced to live on the streets. RaFIKis has teamed with Ngala School for the Deaf and the Rotary Club of Nakuru to help facilitate and administer sponsorships for Ngala children.

10   "It makes you take a step back and realize what you have and the little things you don't need," Ward said on the experience of meeting and working with the children in Africa. "It makes you feel incredibly grateful for everything. Those children are constantly on my mind and I think of them first. I want more people to go and experience it for themselves."

Since her trip last summer, Ward has continued her service with RaFIKis. She participated in a charity walk last October where she walked approximately four miles at Sugarhouse Park in Salt Lake City. She also volunteered at the annual tennis tournament put on as a fundraiser for the charity organization. Her brother also got involved with the fundraising activities as he donated a painting this last spring for the annual auction. These fundraisers help raise money for the RaFIKis organization and will fund a trip for Ward and several other volunteers to go back to Africa next summer.

Ward's work with the organization has also made an impact on her career aspirations.

"I am majoring in accounting and thinking about double majoring in finance," Ward said. "My goal is to become the head C.F.O. of a non-profit organization. RaFIKis is very small right now but hopefully it will grow and I could take over for my aunt, the current C.F.O."

Ward hopes that her work will inspire others to help in any way that they can and wants people to know how easy it is to make a difference.

15   "Every little bit helps, no matter how small," Ward said. "It's really easy to do and it will help and it will make a difference."

EXAMPLE 3: Profile Article of an Organization

Stephanie Gottschlich

The New Recruits: Students Answer the Call for Next Generation of Air Force Scientists

Justin Estepp describes himself as "just a bench engineer." But with a small army of student research assistants at his side in the Air Force Research Laboratory's 711th Human Performance Wing complex at Wright-Patterson Air Force Base, Estepp is grinding out game-changing research at the intersection of engineering, neuroscience, and psychology that the United States Air Force views as a new frontier for achieving military superiority.

"We hear people say 'mind reading' a lot, but that's not it exactly," Estepp says, describing his research in monitoring cognitive state. "It's a three-legged stool of applied or behavioral neuroscience: figuring out what technologies best monitor the physiology of a human, such as eye-tracking and EEG; how we can relate that physiology to their cognitive state; and then how we can augment a human's performance based on that cognitive state."

Estepp—who earned a bachelor's degree in biomedical engineering from Wright State in 2006 and is finishing his master's degree in the same field—is an associate research biomedical engineer in the wing's Human Effectiveness Directorate, Warfighter Interface Division. He is among more than a half-dozen, up-and-coming Wright State grads managing research programs inside the fence in that directorate, researching how technology can enhance a warfighter's performance in the sky, in space, or in cyberspace. Wright State grads are doing everything from researching how UAVs can fly by voice command, to evaluating new, noninvasive techniques to stimulate the brain to improve attention span, to optimizing displays so that pilots or airmen can better interpret images, among other areas.

The Air Force Research Laboratory, headquartered at WPAFB, manages the Air Force's science and technology program, a $2 billion research juggernaut employing about 9,600 people. Its eight directorates emphasize a particular area of research, and for Human Effectiveness, the key word is "human." It focuses on integrating biological and cognitive technologies to boost a warfighter's performance in instances such as operating multiple unmanned aerial vehicles, or overcoming fatigue and loss of concentration while looking at computer screens.

In designer jeans and eyeglasses and Doc Marten boots, his blazer draped across a chair, Estepp belongs to a sophisticated, postmodern generation of engineers and scientists who will move up the ranks in their various directorates to lead the Air Force research agenda in the decades to come. 5

Out of concern for a shortage of scientists and engineers, AFRL has been cultivating a cadre of young technical talent to work in government labs instead of the private sector, so that when 40 percent of its workforce retires over the next two decades, the military maintains its technological superiority.

For engineers and human factors psychologists, AFRL is an opportunity to make breakthrough discoveries in fields such as unmanned aerial vehicles, modeling and simulation, sensors, cyberspace, intelligence and reconnaissance, and human performance.

Chris Meier, a Wright State student who hopes to continue working for AFRL after completing his master's degree in biomedical engineering in 2014, is one of four Wright State engineering students working with Estepp as research assistants. "The private sector probably couldn't touch the kinds of experiences we get here, from day one," Meier said, who admits the initial attraction is in getting to play with technology's latest toys.

But for a lot of students, the base is an intimidating black box. "I really had no idea research goes on at the base until I heard about it through classmates," said Sabrina Metzger, a senior in biomedical engineering. Through contact with other Wright State students, and through faculty, Metzger found the research assistant positions in the Human Effectiveness directorate. "Once you get here, you realize it's more laid-back than you think, and you have a lot of autonomy," she says.

10   Estepp knows the value of these internships: like a lot of young professionals working at WPAFB, the Dayton native stayed in the area because of an interesting internship at the base that kept him here.

After graduating from Fairborn High School, Estepp joined the inaugural class of AFRL's Wright Scholar Research Assistant Program in 2002, the summer before his freshman year at Wright State. The program enables high school juniors and seniors to work with AFRL researchers for 10 to 12 weeks on projects including testing materials, tracking data, creating databases, charting data, and computer modeling and programming. That introduction to AFRL led to engineering internships that kept him working in the lab all the way through completion of his master's degree. In 2008, he joined AFRL as a full-time engineer.

When Estepp's lab needs student research assistants, he often taps Wright State because it offers the only biomedical engineering program in the region. From providing continuing education toward advanced degrees, to collaborations with faculty, to networking with other researchers, Wright State is "well positioned to facilitate a lot of collaborations" that would benefit the technical researchers in AFRL.

"There are a lot of us who will at some point work on advanced degrees, and Wright State is perfect for that," because of its proximity and interdisciplinary programs. "And we have access to its students, just down the street. All in all, the university is a great resource."

USE THE TOOLKIT

Let's use the three genre toolkit questions from Chapter 1 to examine this genre.

What Is It?

These profile articles are documents that present text and images describing a person (in the articles on Lucas Threefoot and Lanie Wright) or group (in the article on the Air Force Research Laboratory at Wright State). All three appear in magazines that have content posted online. They tend to include quotations from the individuals in question, provide descriptions of their accomplishments and background, and, in the cases of the Air Force Research Laboratory, connect those accomplishments to the support of the university or state. Profile articles may also appear in newspapers. A lengthier profile might turn into a biography, which is essentially a book-length profile that provides greater detail and depth.

Who Reads It?

These magazines are available online, so anyone with an Internet connection could view them. However, in all three cases the magazine addresses a particular community. The Lucas Threefoot profile appears in *1859*, a magazine that features news and profiles of interest to readers living in Oregon (or potentially those living elsewhere who want to maintain a personal connection to the state). The Air Force Research Laboratory and Lanie Ward articles appear in campus magazines, which highlight news, people, and events at a university or college—so readers might include parents, students, faculty, staff, alumni, and donors.

In general, readers of profiles are interested in learning more about the person, place, group, or event that is being profiled. Sometimes readers are conducting research and specifically search for articles about a subject. Sometimes readers simply discover a profile article that looks interesting to them and spontaneously decide to read it.

What's It For?

Profile articles describe their subjects in ways that are both entertaining and informative. Sometimes profile articles praise their subjects; sometimes they criticize their subjects; sometimes they remain neutral or objective.

In these examples, the articles take a complimentary tone, praising the individuals or groups. This is especially likely in the campus magazine profiles, which serve to advertise a college, its programs, students, and faculty to the audience (especially alumni and donors). Thus, the profiles not only inform, but also guide the reader's opinion on the subjects of the profiles.

Profiles can also present familiar subjects in a new light—that is, an article might take a new angle on a subject, or even criticize its subject. Magazines that profile political leaders, such as *Rolling Stone* or *The Economist*, often take a more critical tone.

Thus, we can see that profile articles are primarily texts—but they can feature photographs or other kinds of supporting media—that inform readers about a person, group, event, or place. Profiles can guide readers' opinions about the subjects of the profiles by striking a tone of praise or criticism.

EXERCISE 5.4: Plan a Profile

Think of a person, group, event, or place that you might want to write a profile article about. Think about how you might begin to research and write your profile by answering the following questions:

1. Do you have access to the subject of your profile? For example, is the person someone you might be able to interview, or is the person hard to reach or deceased?
2. How will you gain information about the subject of your profile? Can you visit the event? Can you do library or Internet research?

3. How long will your profile be?
4. What is the intended audience of your profile? Do you want to publish it in the campus newspaper? Put in on the Internet, say, on a blog?
5. What sort of tone do you want to take toward your subject? Is there a particular *angle* that you want to take that makes your profile special or unique?

E. Strategies for Profiles

Imagine you've been assigned to write a profile article about a member of your community. Let's look at a profile written by a student. This profile was published on the school paper's website. After reading this article, we will learn some strategies for how to write profiles.

Sarah Creek
March 10, 2014
Journalism 305: Science Writing

Profile of an Engineering Professor: Dr. Grace Yang

Dr. Grace Yang's interest in power systems began when she first learned about hybrid electric vehicles (HEV) as a college student in China. She soon decided to go to graduate school to learn more about designing power systems for HEVs, earning a Master's and a PhD at the Massachusetts Institute of Technology. Today, Dr. Yang is an assistant professor at Greenview State University, where she is part of the Center for Sustainable Energy Systems (CSES). Dr. Yang works with a team of researchers invested in designing a green energy infrastructure, or "smart grid."

Dr. Yang spends some of her time designing and testing components, but spends just as much time writing—at least fifty percent of her time, by her estimate. As a junior faculty member, Dr. Yang writes grant proposals to fund her research projects, prepares conference presentations and posters, and writes research articles. She also serves as guest

editor for a journal, so she is responsible for assigning others in her field to peer review pa-

pers considered for publication. In addition, she writes reports for government agencies or

outside agencies who want to track progress on research they have funded.

"Not many students realize that writing is especially important for science and engineer-

ing professionals," Yang stated. "But good writing will help you to advance in your career."

Oral communication is also important in Dr. Yang's job. She estimates that 20 percent of

her time involves some form of oral communication, which could mean meeting with fac-

ulty, students, or industry representatives, giving presentations at conferences, talking over

ideas with colleagues.

Prewriting (Content)

When Sarah sat down to write a profile of Dr. Yang, she began by asking herself the questions that you did in Exercise 5.4. These questions are useful when brainstorming a profile (Chapters 15 and 16).

1. Do you have access to the subject of your profile? For example, is the person someone you might be able to interview, or is the person hard to reach or deceased?

In this case, Sarah did have access to the subject: she sent a professional email to the professor and requested an interview. The professor kindly agreed. They had lunch together and Sarah asked her questions, which she had prepared in advance (Chapter 24).

2. How will you gain information about the subject of your profile? Can you visit the event? Can you do library or Internet research?

Sarah not only interviewed the professor, but she researched the professor online. Professors at universities often have online profiles or portfolios that provide basic background information about the professor's education, publications, and research and teaching interests. *Before* she interviewed Professor Yang, Sarah read her profile on the university's website. Reading the profile helped Sarah brainstorm some questions for the interview.

3. How long will your profile be?

Sarah knew that her profile would need to be relatively short in order to be published on the school paper's website. She kept this intended length in mind when she set out to write her profile.

4. What is the intended audience of your profile? Do you want to publish it in the campus newspaper? Post it online to a blog?

Sarah already had a planned venue where she would publish her profile article. Sometimes, though, you might write a profile as a classroom assignment. In that case, be sure to follow your professor's instructions carefully.

5. What sort of tone do you want to take toward your subject? Is there a particular *angle* that you want to take that makes your profile special or unique?

In this article, Sarah takes a unique angle when writing about this scientist. Rather than focusing on the professor's scientific research, she focuses on her *writing*. Often, non-scientists do not realize that scientists do a lot of writing—rather, they imagine that scientists work in a lab with machines or chemicals. This article presents Professor Yang *as a writer*, not just a scientist, which makes Sarah's perspective unique and interesting.

Drafting (Organizing)

To draft her article, Sarah started by reviewing the notes she took from her research and her interview with Professor Yang.

You might also consider a few different ways of organizing your profile:

- You might use a narrative style, telling a story about your subject. You could either include yourself in the narrative (a more personal approach), or tell your story as an outside observer.
- You might use a descriptive style, which focuses more on characteristics of your subject or elements of his or her life.

After reviewing her notes, Sarah decided to blend a narrative and descriptive organization, beginning by telling how Professor Yang started her career as a researcher in green technology, and then describing her day-to-day life as a professor.

Next, you might consider how many details to include and where to include them. For a person, you might consider:

- Physical attributes
- Personality characteristics

- Qualifications (education, job experience, etc.)
- Accomplishments (books written, art produced, etc.)
- Quotations from or about that person
- Anecdotes about that person
- History or background

You could adapt those categories if you are writing about a place, program, or some other subject. For example, for a profile of your town you might mention famous people who lived there or historic events that occurred there, or you might interview people to get quotations about that place.

Revising (Style)

Once you have a draft, focus on making your profile accessible and interesting for your audience. Sarah used the term "smart grid" to help readers connect what they might have already heard about green technology. You might also consider the following ideas:

- Terms you may need to explain or define for your reader.
- Adding "local color"—specific names of places, people, dialect, or customs.
- Figurative language, such as metaphors, similes, and the like (Chapter 21).

In her peer workshop, Sarah received suggestions from her group that helped her to adopt the neutral zone of a journalist. Had she written for another audience, such as the university's alumni magazine, she might have used a more celebratory tone. Sarah might have described Dr. Yang's tendency to dress casually in jeans, or her obsession with whitewater rafting, in order to portray a youthful, adventurous professoriate. Readers of an alumni magazine tend to be potential donors or supporters of the university, and in this case Sarah might want to encourage readers to support the university's research efforts.

Editing (Design)

You might consult examples of the type of profile you are writing to determine how to finalize your profile to suit the conventions of that genre or publication. Some profiles may include plenty of pictures, especially ones that appear online; others may include none at all. You can also pay attention to formatting—should your profile have headings and sub-headings? Should it appear in columns?

You might also consider how to refer to the sources you used for your writing. For a newspaper or magazine, you probably would not use formal citation styles such as MLA. Instead, you'd use informal citation, or possibly hyperlinks (for a digital version), to lead readers to other sources.

Finally, you might consider the limitations imposed by your genre or publication. In this case, Sarah has a strict word limit for her article, so she condensed the article to fit the parameters of her assignment.

Troubleshooting

Here are some common challenges that students face when writing profiles.

I can't find a good subject for my profile   Start by thinking about who (or what) will be easy to access. Angelina Jolie might make a good profile subject, but she might not be easy to contact (unless you have a personal connection). More local figures can be interesting to read and write about, and you may be surprised that they are often willing to speak to students. You might search for people who direct organizations on campus or in your community, people who do certain kinds of work (such as farmers, or directors of a homeless shelter), or people who have unique histories (you might find senior citizens especially interesting for this reason). The same goes for places or companies—Google might be more difficult than a local software company; the Taj Mahal (while interesting) might be less accessible than a local landmark. Look online for lists of people and places in your community, such as lists of tourist sites for your town, lists of municipal government representatives, or lists of local volunteer organizations.

I can't conduct an interview with my subject   Some people may be difficult to pin down for an interview—they may be very busy, or they may not want to be interviewed. Sometimes, your subject is deceased. In that case, you can try interviewing people who know/knew your subject—co-workers, family members, friends, and the like. Imagine you want to profile the president of your university. Chances are this person would be hard to reach, but since he or she is a major figure in your community, you would probably find plenty of other people who would have something to contribute. You can also do more research about your person—try searching for your subject online or in library databases.

You can use the same approach for an historical subject or someone who has passed away. Depending on how long ago they lived, you may still find people who can tell you about your subject. If the person lived long ago, you will need to use historical documents to tell you about them. Local figures can be good for historical profiles, because your local library or college may have archival materials you can use (such as personal letters or diaries).

My subject won't answer my questions in an interview   First, be sure that you have worded your interview questions so that they do not require simple yes/no answers. If your interview is already over, you might call or email your person and see if they mind answering a few follow-up questions. Then, you can reword your questions to see whether they can offer more details.

Example Question:	Do you find working with students interesting?
Revised Question:	What do you find most rewarding about working with students?
Follow-up Question:	When we spoke, you mentioned that you enjoyed working on undergraduate research projects with students. Can you tell me more about the kinds of projects you have worked on with some of your students?

Sometimes, people may find certain questions uncomfortable—too revealing or personal, say. In this case, you might note which questions seemed to evoke this reaction. A good interviewer will try to rephrase these questions or to ask follow-up questions to evoke a good response, but you might also consider why your subject might have found that question difficult to answer. You might mention this in your article, if you think it would interest readers or shed light on your subject.

I can't find a unique angle to take on my subject   You might need to conduct more brainstorming—even if you already have a draft—to help you determine your angle. One good technique might be to ask people what they already think of the person. Can your profile offer a new perspective? (Sarah thought it might be interesting to focus on Prof. Yang's writing, since scientists are typically portrayed as engaged in laboratory research.) You can also search for other profiles of your subject, to see if you can offer a fresh perspective. If someone is usually profiled as a professional, you might offer insight into their personal life or interests, for example.

F. Chapter Project: Write a Profile Article

Imagine you have been asked to write a profile article for a campus student magazine. Choose one of the following options:

- Profile a member of the community in which your campus is located.
- Profile a member of the faculty whose research focuses on your future profession or career field.
- Profile a place on campus or in the campus community.

You can review the profiles and advice in this chapter to help you. To recap, though, you should:

- Research your subject (using interviews, secondary sources, or both)
- Find an interesting angle
- Choose an organizational strategy (such as narrative or descriptive)
- Select interesting details
- Develop a style appropriate to the topic and genre

Group Option: Create a Profile Series

Imagine you have been asked to write a series of profiles for a campus magazine. You might profile students, instructors, majors or programs, or even places on campus. You will each write a profile to go in the magazine.

As a group, you will need to decide on:

- A focus or theme (what subjects will you choose to profile?)— you might all profile student athletes, or programs that are contributing to social problems, or places where students gather on campus.

- An appropriate format and design for your publication (such as visual elements, fonts and headings, length, etc.).
- A style guide for your publication (what kind of tone should the writers take? How formal should the writing be?).

You will be responsible for reviewing and editing the profiles, together, so that they make up a cohesive group for your publication.

Multimedia Option: Create a Profile Video

Create a video profile of a person or place in your community that will appear on a local website (your campus newspaper, say, or a community newspaper). In addition to the considerations just listed, you might consider:

- What kinds of footage should I shoot? (Interviews with people? Where should the interview be set? Should I include still or moving scenes of places and people?)
- What other elements can I add? (Text? Subtitles? Transitions between elements?)
- What kinds of audio material should I have? (Will I have music? Voiceover narration? etc.)
- What should the pacing of the video be? (Do I want lots of short shots or clips, or longer ones?)

Informative Genres

Informative genres teach people new knowledge and new skills. Informative genres range from the instructions included with a software program (usually found in the drop-down menu under "Help"), to encyclopedia entries, to procedures used in scientific laboratories. Reports (Chapter 14) might also be considered a form of informative writing, but because there are so many different kinds of reports, we treat them in a separate chapter.

In college, you might be asked to write procedures for a laboratory experiment in a biology class, compose instructions for a program you develop in a computer science class, or design a pamphlet informing students about recycling on campus for a rhetoric class.

In the workplace, much of the writing you encounter may be informative. You may need to prepare a set of instructions or procedures for a co-worker who is taking over your job while you go on vacation. If you work in marketing, you might need to prepare a factsheet highlighting the features of your company's new product. If you work in a health field, you might be asked to prepare a brochure about the benefits of getting the flu vaccine or be asked to write well-organized patient records and notes. If you are a personal trainer or physical therapist, you might prepare a set of instructions for your clients to perform exercises on their own.

All of these genres share the goal of helping readers to solve problems or perform tasks. In this chapter, you will learn how to write informative genres.

A. Informative Mini-Genre: How-To Tip

Take a look at the following three how-to tips.

EXAMPLE 1: Technology How-To Tip

This technology how-to tip is from the website Lifehacker.com.

EXAMPLE 2: Household How-To Tip

 1 **Look for areas of your house that might serve as entrances for ants.** These include cracks, holes, windows, and pet doors. These are often good locations to use one of the prevention techniques described below.

2 **Sprinkle salt on flat surfaces.** This is a great way to keep ants off of windowsills.

3 **Draw barriers using chalk.** The chalk will stick to vertical surfaces like walls and doorjambs. Ants don't like the calcium carbonate in chalk and will steer clear of it.

This household how-to tip is from the crowd-sourced website Wikihow.com.

EXAMPLE 3: Work How-To Tip

Work At Home – Stay Focused

Working at home is not for everyone. People that require daily contact with co-workers or others to provide motivation and discipline should think twice before setting up a home office. On the other side, you do not have to commute, your hours are more flexible and owning a business in the home allows tax breaks. If you have made the decision that becoming an entrepreneur is for you, here are some tips to help your success.

1. Become ultra-organized. This will increase productivity and keep you focused and on track.
2. Set up a strict structure when you 'go to your office' and when you 'leave the office'. Treat this time as if you were actually leaving the house for a job.
3. Network with other people that are working in the home. You will feel less isolated and pick up good ideas for keeping structured focus on the job.
4. Create a professional website for the business. This is not a hobby.
5. Use online communities in your business area. A wealth of ideas is available online.
6. Have the best resources you can afford. It is difficult to maintain a high business level if you are using old office equipment or dial up Internet access.
7. Keep all of your personal and professional contacts in tact. Email them regularly and call them when it is appropriate. You never know how these contacts can help you become successful in your new business.

Rating

This work how-to tip is from the website Lifetips.com.

USE THE TOOLKIT

Let's use the three genre toolkit questions from Chapter 1 to examine this genre.

What Is It?

These three informative genres are how-to tips from websites featuring informative articles and instructions as well as tips. Each of these examples includes directions for specific tasks people can perform, often presented as numbered lists. Notice that two of them (Examples 2 and 3) use an imperative, or command, verb form: "*Look* for areas" or "*Have* the best resources." This imperative form is one of the hallmarks of how-to tips and instructions.

Who Reads It?

These how-to tips are posted on websites that address users who need to solve the problem in question or who may find the tip useful. Most likely, those users have searched the web for that type of information, although they may simply be browsing a site for fun. For example, people are most likely to read up on tips for getting rid of ants if they are currently experiencing an ant infestation.

What's It For?

How-to tips are meant to help readers solve problems or improve their everyday lives. The tips for working at home, for instance, are meant to help readers in that situation to better manage their time and increase their productivity. Presumably, those who might search online for information about working at home would be people who currently have trouble staying focused while they work from home—they have a problem for which they need information or instructions.

EXERCISE 6.1: Write a Series of How–To Tips

Imagine you are starting your own website (Chapter 30) as a how-to expert in a particular area. Consider something you know about already, such as how to prepare for college courses, how to improve at a particular sport or hobby, or how to eat well on a limited budget.

Write a series of at least five how-to tips. Be sure to start by thinking about what problems people might be having that would lead them to your how-to site.

GROUP ACTIVITY 6.1: Design a How-To Website with Your Group

Imagine that your group has been asked to develop a how-to website for students at your college. You should:

- Come up with a basic outline of the kinds of sections your site will have (at least one per group member), such as healthy eating, staying fit, or getting help with courses.
- Write five how-to tips for each section.

B. Tutorial

A tutorial is simply an extended how-to tip, usually one that addresses a more complex problem or task. While a how-to tip is usually quite short, a tutorial requires a longer set of instructions. Often, tutorials use examples to walk readers through the process in question, so that they get hands-on experience performing the task. Tutorials might also be called *instructions* or *procedures*—but they are essentially all the same genre.

EXAMPLE 1: Cooking Tutorial

bon appétit

GO BACK | PRINT THIS PAGE

Tips
IN THE KITCHEN | TIPS

How to Roll out Pizza Dough

Rolling out homemade pizza dough can be tricky. The gluten in the dough makes it very elastic, so it may not be easy to stretch the dough to the size you want.

There are a couple of methods to shape either homemade or store-bought pizza dough. The most experienced pizza makers use the backs of their fists to gently stretch the dough, which keeps the dough's texture light. Most home cooks either press or stretch the dough with their fingers or use a rolling pin; the former method is slightly better because it is gentler, but both work well.

To create the perfect crust, form the dough into a round disk, then let it rest for 10 to 15 minutes so the gluten can relax. After the dough has rested, use your chosen method— pressing, stretching, or rolling—to flatten it further, dusting the dough with flour or dotting with olive oil to prevent sticking. Once the dough begins to snap back, let it rest for a few minutes again. When you start rolling again, it should be more cooperative. Keep in mind that you may need to let the dough rest several times while rolling it out.

1. Dust dough ball lightly with flour. Pat into a disk.

2. Stretch the dough into a 5- or 6-inch round. Press outward from the center, rotating the dough occasionally to form an even circle.

This step-by-step guide for rolling out pizza dough is from BonAppetit.com.

EXAMPLE 2: Computer Tutorial

Using Refworks

RefWorks is a free software program you can use to automatically create bibliographies and format research papers.

Getting Started

1. Go https://www.refworks.com/ and click on "Login to Refworks."
2. Click on "Sign up for an individual account." Enter your name, login name, password, and e-mail address, and then click on Register. You will see a screen that looks something like this:

Screenshot of RefWorks, a web-based bibliographic management service.

Now you are ready to get started with RefWorks.

Creating Your Database

Refworks enables you to create a personal database of sources—books, articles, and so on. Once you have created your database, you can use it to automatically generate a bibliography and to format your research papers.

There are two main ways to add sources to your database: you can manually enter citation information, or you can export sources directly from some databases, such as Web of Science.

EXAMPLE 3: Sewing Tutorial

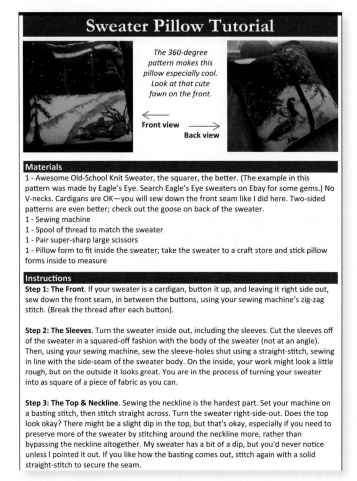

This tutorial for crafting a sweater pillow comes from KnittyProfessors.com.

USE THE TOOLKIT

Let's use the three genre toolkit questions from Chapter 1 to examine this genre.

What Is It?

Each of these three documents provides instructions to users hoping to perform a specific task: roll out pizza dough, use a new computer program, or make a pillow from a sweater. You'll notice that they provide numbered lists of instructions in the imperative or command form, such as "dust dough ball lightly with flour" or "click on Login to Refworks."

These documents also provide background information to prepare readers for the task. In some cases, a tutorial will also include information about what materials you will need—in fact, in the pizza dough case, it would be useful for readers to know what kind of pizza dough to start with, and what other items they will need (such as flour and a rolling pin).

Who Reads It?

Each of these tutorials addresses a specific audience. The pizza dough example comes from *Bon Appetit,* a cooking magazine, while the sewing example comes from a website for knitters and other fiber artists. Readers of these tutorials are likely to be interested in those specific topics, and may have done a web search or be regular visitors to those sites. The RefWorks example is an exception—it was created by a teacher for students in her writing courses.

In each case, though, the document is addressed to readers who are learning to perform the task in question, and uses language to help them accomplish those tasks.

What's It For?

These tutorials are all meant to help readers learn to do something. We might call them "reading to learn to do" genres. In each case, the writer hopes that readers will follow these instructions to learn the task at hand. Ideally, once readers perform this task a few times, they will no longer need to consult the instructions. For example, once you learn to make pizza dough using this tutorial, you should be able to do it on your own.

For this reason, tutorials tend to include features of design, organization, and style to make information memorable and easy to reference. These might include:

- Clear headings
- Short, imperative sentences
- Numbered steps
- Images that illustrate the steps performed (See Chapter 29 on designing visual elements)
- Chronological organization (according to the order of the steps to be done)
- A somewhat less formal writing style (a good strategy if you want to compensate for technical terms or complex steps) (See Chapter 21 on Style)

You can see that tutorials serve a very specific purpose: to help people to complete a task. All of the elements of this genre help to accomplish that purpose. However, keep in mind that other related genres can also be used to help people learn to do something—especially media genres such as podcasts or videos. If you've ever consulted YouTube to help you learn to do something, from learning a new dance move to unclogging a drain, then you've probably experienced what it is like to use a tutorial—and how frustrating it can be if the tutorial is not clearly designed.

EXERCISE 6.2: Create a Tutorial

Imagine you've been asked to create a tutorial specifically for students at your school or members of your community.
Here are some topic ideas:

- How to perform a specific task using your library system—for example, how to find a peer reviewed article.
- How to prepare a recipe that is unique to your region.
- How to craft something using a special skill, such as woodworking or sewing.

Write a tutorial, considering how you can use features of the genre to help readers accomplish this task.

MULTIMEDIA EXERCISE 6.1: Create an Online Tutorial

Follow the directions for Exercise 6.2, but design your tutorial for a website. Consider how you can use web features, such as links, images, or even video, to show readers what to do.

C. Factsheet

A factsheet is a genre that efficiently informs readers about a topic.

EXAMPLE 3: Factsheet about Sexual Harassment

Your Job ... Your Rights ... Your Responsibilities!

SEXUAL HARASSMENT is AGAINST the LAW

Sexual harassment is unwelcome or unwanted sexual conduct that is either very serious or occurs frequently. The harasser may be another employee, a supervisor, the company owner or even a customer. The harasser may be male or female. The sexual conduct can be verbal, physical, in writing or in pictures. Illegal sexual harassment creates a hostile or intimidating work place and interferes with an employee's job performance.

Examples of Sexual Harassment

- An employee regularly tells his co-worker that he really likes her and wants to go out with her, although she continues to say no. When he is close to her at work, he touches her. One day when they are alone, he tries to kiss her.

- A supervisor sends an employee messages on Facebook and also text messages telling the employee she will be promoted if she agrees to be his girlfriend. When she refuses, he fires her.

What You Can Do If you have been Harassed

Tell the harasser to stop. If you don't feel comfortable confronting the harasser or the conduct does not stop, tell your employer.

Report the harassment to your employer. If your company has a policy on harassment, it should identify who is responsible for handling complaints of harassment. If you are not comfortable talking to that person or your company does not have a harassment policy, talk to your manager or another manager in the company.

Talk to a parent, teacher, guidance counselor, or another trusted adult about the harassment.

Contact EEOC. Our services are free and you do not need a lawyer to file a charge.

Act promptly. Once your employer knows about the harassment, it has a responsibility to stop the harassment. Also, you may not be the only person being harassed by this individual.

Need to File a Complaint?

If you think you have been the victim of illegal job discrimination or harassment, you can file a complaint, called a charge of discrimination, with EEOC. We may mediate or investigate your charge and take legal action to stop the discrimination or harassment.

You can file a charge with EEOC if you are a job applicant, current employee or former employee; a full-time, part-time, seasonal or temporary employee, regardless of your citizenship or work authorization status.

You may file your charge in person at the nearest EEOC office or by mail. Our services are free.

Learn more about your employment rights at www.eeoc.gov
Or call EEOC at 1-800-669-4000 (TTY: 1-800-669-6820)

This sexual harassment factsheet comes from Youth at Work, a part of the U.S. Equal Employment Opportunity Commission.

USE THE TOOLKIT

Let's use the three genre toolkit questions from Chapter 1 to examine this genre.

What Is It?

A factsheet is usually a short, informative document, often distributed at information fairs, made available in offices (such as your campus health center), or posted online for readers to download. They usually appear on a single page, with blocks of text organized by questions readers might have (such as "What is shingles?") or by sub-topics (such as "Examples of Sexual Harassment"). The factsheet may define a concept or thing (Chapter 19), describe how it works or what causes it (Chapter 19), and offer solutions to address the topic (such as how to avoid getting shingles, or what to do about sexual harassment).

Who Reads It?

Factsheets usually target specific audiences. The shingles factsheet targets an audience of people over age sixty, while the sexual harassment factsheet targets an audience of young people. Both factsheets use images of people, colors, and fonts to appeal to that audience. Who do you think is the target audience for the genetic engineering factsheet?

Unlike readers of tutorials, who have sought out specific information to help them perform a task, readers of factsheets may not have an internal motivation to read the document—they are often what we might call casual readers. For example, you might pick up a factsheet while waiting in line at a pharmacy or while waiting for an appointment with your academic advisor. In some cases, though, you might be given a factsheet when you have a specific problem. Your advisor might give you a factsheet about a certificate program or new minor on campus, for instance. In this case, you'd have greater motivation to actually read it than if you just happened upon it while waiting for your appointment.

What's It For?

A factsheet, like a tutorial, is used to inform readers about a topic. While a tutorial teaches you how to do something, a factsheet provides information about an issue, topic, or problem.

You'll notice that these factsheets use different design techniques (Chapter 29) to provide that information. In particular, factsheets tend to employ bold headings, bulleted lists, and white space to make information accessible. They often use images to evoke a particular audience or message.

Increasingly, factsheets are distributed not only in print form, but also as PDF files uploaded to websites for users to either read online or download and print.

EXERCISE 6.3: Write a Factsheet for a College Program

Choose a major, minor, or certificate program at your college that interests you. Then, design a factsheet that informs students about this program and persuades them to enroll. To design your factsheet, you should do the following:

- Research the program: research its goals, its course requirements, and the kinds of careers students go into after completing the program.
- Examine other factsheets of this type, and identify what design and content features seem successful.
- Determine the type of student who would be most likely to enroll. For instance, students interested in a Spanish certificate might include international studies majors, health majors, and education majors.
- Decide what kind of information to include, and how much detail to offer.
- Consider what visual elements to use to attract students who might be interested in the program (Chapter 29).

GROUP ACTIVITY 6.2: Design a Series of Health Factsheets

Imagine that you have been asked to design a series of factsheets about health topics for students at your school. You will each design a separate factsheet, but the series as a whole should have a uniform design scheme, or template. To get started,

- Identify topics that might be of interest to students, such as healthy eating, balancing school with a job, managing stress, keeping fit, and so on.
- Identify the target audiences for each topic. Try to be specific: students interested in balancing school and a job are, evidently, students who are working and going to school at the same time; students interested in keeping fit might be those who have sacrificed exercise for studying or socializing.
- Come up with a style guide for your factsheets (Chapter 29): what fonts will you use for headings and body text? What types of colors? What kinds of images (e.g. clipart vs. photos)?
- Consider how to make each factsheet unique while sticking to the overall template. Could you use different colors while maintaining other features? Different images?
- Research appropriate content for each factsheet (see Chapter 24).

D. Informative Article

An informative article is a genre that explains, describes, and informs readers about a topic, rather than arguing for a particular personal opinion or viewpoint. You can often encounter informative articles in magazines, websites, and newspapers. For example, a newspaper article might explain and describe the results from a recent scientific study.

Like a factsheet, an informative article can take advantage of visual elements such as headings, subtitles, and images (Chapter 29). Let's examine a few informative articles using the genre toolkit questions.

EXAMPLE 1: Informative Article about Zombies (excerpt)

Zombies—A Pop Culture Resource for Public Health Awareness
Melissa Nasiruddin, Monique Halabi, Alexander Dao, Kyle Chen, and Brandon Brown

Sitting at his laboratory bench, a scientist adds mutation after mutation to a strand of rabies virus RNA, unaware that in a few short days, an outbreak of this very mutation would destroy society as we know it. It could be called "Zombie Rabies," a moniker befitting of the next Hollywood blockbuster—or, in this case, a representation of the debate over whether a zombie apocalypse, manufactured by genetically modifying one or more diseases like rabies, could be more than just fiction. Fear of the unknown has long been a psychological driving force for curiosity, and the concept of a zombie apocalypse has become popular in modern society. This article explores the utility of zombies to capitalize on the benefits of spreading public health awareness through the use of relatable popular culture tools and scientific explanations for fictional phenomena.

Although zombies are currently an integral part of our popular culture, our morbid fascination with the walking dead spans several centuries. Historians and anthropologists trace the origin of zombies to the folklore of several tribes in western Africa, from Ghana to Nigeria (1,2). During the slave trade of the late 1500s through the 1800s, persons from these regions were spirited away from their homes to till the plantations of the Caribbean and the European colonies, bringing with them the voodoo culture of magic and spells. Among some academics, zombies in the New World were thought to be wretched, half-dead creatures that reflected the bondage African-born and Caribbean slaves suffered at the hands of their masters, working to the point of exhaustion in the plantation fields while having little to no agency (2). To this day, voodoo is prominent in western Africa, Haiti, New Orleans, and parts of the Caribbean Islands (1).

Haitian voodoo folklore recognizes a dual identity of *zombis*: one form of *zombi* is an ambulatory body without a living soul, and the other, lesser-known form is a soul wandering without a body (2). This severance of a body and its soul, known as zombification, is thought to occur when a sorcerer, or *boko*, performs a combination of dark magic spells on a person to kill, enslave, or inflict illness upon him (3). *Bokos* may also use poisonous powders in which frog or toad venom and tetrodotoxin, a powerful neurotoxin secreted by puffer fish that can trigger paralysis or death-like symptoms, could be primary ingredients. Which toxins are used in the zombie powders specifically, however, is still a matter of contention among academics (*4*). Once the sorcerer has split the body and soul, he stores the *ti-bon anj*, the manifestation of awareness and memory, in a special bottle. Inside the container, that part of the soul is known as the *zombi astral*. With the *zombi astral* in his possession, the sorcerer retains complete control of the victim's spiritually dead body, now known as the *zombi cadavre*. The *zombi cadavre* remains a slave to the will of the sorcerer through continued poisoning or spell work (*1*). In fact, the only way a *zombi* can be freed from its slavery is if the spell jar containing its *ti-bon anj* is broken, or if it ingests salt or meat. The latter would usually cause the *zombi* to hunt down and kill its master before finally returning to its family or its final rest as a corpse (*1,2*).

Although most cultures would consider the zombie to be a fictional creature, zombiism (i.e., being a zombie) is rather common in Haiti, with instances of people being reported dead by loved ones, only to be spotted fully reanimated and wandering around town several weeks to several years later. In Haitian and African culture, zombification is a punishable offense on the same order of severity as murder (*1*). A person who has been zombified, or transformed into a zombie, can have a blunt affect, dull gaze, and almost stuporous behavior, characterized by a lumbering gait and simple, repetitive vocalizations and movements. Most medical evaluations would characterize victims of zombification as having mental disorders such as catatonic schizophrenia (*1*). The aforementioned traits have been incorporated into the current interpretation of zombies found in modern film and media.

History of Zombies in the Media

Zombie folklore made its appearance in modern media in *Das Cabinet des Dr. Caligari,* [5] a silent horror film directed by Robert Wiene, which debuted in Germany in 1921. The film's depiction of zombies paralleled Haitian lore: a sleepwalker under the control of another individual. The notion of a zombie was primarily defined by the control an individual had over another, and the main character in this film had the characteristic attributes of the early zombie: the unique lumbering gait, lack of higher cognitive ability, and obedience to another individual.

Drawing inspiration from Richard Matheson's 1954 novel *I Am Legend*, George A. Romero spawned the more modern film manifestation of the undead zombie and the notion of a zombie apocalypse in *The Night of the Living Dead*. These zombies were the corporeal expression of strife, a mechanism to demonstrate rising social tension in response to a ruinous threat. Subsequent media have continued to use adaptations of Romero's zombie. The film adaptation for *I Am Legend* depicts humans who have undergone physiologic changes, developing intolerance for the sun and a unique form of communication while maintaining the ability to learn through mimicry and form social hierarchies. In the film *28 Days Later,* infected humans transform into creatures characterized by preserved intellect and tremendously aggressive behavior. However, this expansion of aptitude is not uniform in modern media: *Shaun of the Dead* portrays zombies as very slow-moving, with incredible strength but no intelligence—they are fooled by normal humans who mimic their gait and groans. In addition, *Juan of the Dead* includes zombies dismissed by the Castro government as dissidents, and

Warm Bodies depicts zombies as human protectors once they begin to transform back into humans. *Land of the Dead* revolves around the zombie siege of a noninfected gated community and sees the leader of the zombies gain class consciousness toward the end of the film. None of these interpretations are necessarily out of step with the use of zombie movies as a useful public health messaging tool.

Though most popular in film, zombies are present in other forms of media as well. They can be found in print, with novelizations such as *Zombies for Zombies: Advice and Etiquette for the Living Dead* and the popular comic book series *Marvel Zombies*. Increasingly, however, these flesh-eating monsters have found themselves in videogames, feasting upon unwary protagonists since the introduction of *Zombie Zombie* in 1984 (*5*). Zombies have since spread to the more general population in games such as *Plants versus Zombies* and *Resident Evil*, available on several different platforms of accessible technology.

A brief look through the history of the zombie's evolution within media unearths their progressing ability to serve as a vehicle to reach greater audiences. Frank Darabont's award-winning theatrical adaptation of *The Walking Dead* comic books has proven that zombies maintain television prominence even when serving as the backdrop to a character-driven television drama. In his critically acclaimed novel *World War Z: An Oral History of the Zombie War*, Max Brooks explores social issues surrounding zombie apocalypse, such as the efficacy of government. These popular and varied manifestations of zombies elucidate the potential for a comprehensive dissemination of knowledge, from identifying traits indicating infection to explaining the significance of public health infrastructure. Zombies are a unique medium that allow for the audience's suspension of disbelief and for intellectual engagement.

Zombies and Parallels with Other Public Health Issues

Although zombies are certainly not the only favored supernatural creatures in modern times, they appear to be the best conduit to educate the layman about re-emerging infectious diseases such as rabies. The current popular interpretation of vampires, for instance, has shifted away from the classic grotesque undead creature that voluntarily dines on the vein and sires new vampire progeny and instead has embraced the idea of vampirism as the paragon of human existence, alive or undead. The interpretation of zombies has been diverse, but at its core, zombiism remains an existence in which the victim has been stripped of any higher consciousness or agency. The reimagining of zombiism as a virulent, incurable disease makes it an effective analogy for understanding of and interest in other infectious diseases.

10   Zombie popularity may be a perfect opportunity to increase awareness of rabies. The most prominent resemblance between those afflicted with rabies and zombiism begins at the mouth; both ailments are primarily transmitted through biting (see Table). While the pathogenesis for zombification is less consistent, rabies spreads through infected saliva entering the body (*6*). In addition, victims indicate infected status with increased production of fluid from the mouth; in the case of rabies, increased salivation occurs to improve chances of transmission (*6*). Rabies control in practice may be similar to hypothetical control of zombie outbreaks. For example, in 2008, Indonesian officials in Bali killed roughly 50,000 dogs in 5 days after an

outbreak of rabies (7). This sparked a great deal of controversy, leading to the primary alternative of mass vaccination. If a zombie apocalypse were to occur, surviving humans might not have the capacity for mass vaccination. The sole option may be to kill the undead for human survival; however, the ethics of destroying something that was once human might be called into question.

Table

A comparison of zombie folklore and rabies epidemiology

Characteristics	Zombies	Rabies
Susceptibility	Human infection requires fictional apocalyptic environment	Requires environment with infected animals, such as dogs or bats
Cause	Tyrant virus, other viruses, unknown pathogens	Mononegavirales
Virus transmission	Bites and scratches; unknown pathogen; spread human to human; 100% effectiveness	Bites; saliva infected with rabies virus; spread animal to human
Virulence	Victims die and become "walking dead"	Victims die and stay dead
Symptoms	Fever, chills, loss of hair and pigmentation, hobbling gait	Delirium, anxiety, stress, hallucinations, muscle spasms, convulsions
Control methods	Avoiding bites from existing zombies; intervention includes destroying brain of zombies	Avoiding bites from dogs and bats; postexposure prophylaxis
Exposure in popular culture		
Nonscientific media	Movies, books, television shows	Movies, books, television shows
Scientific media	Zombie web sites, CDC*, Nature	Academic journals, global health Web sites, NIH*, CDC, Nature

*CDC, Centers for Disease Control and Prevention; NIH, National Institutes of Health.

Additional physical characteristics of rabies and zombiism are similar (see Figure). Once infected, victims display overall weakness and low-grade fever (6,8). In the case of zombiism, the advent of fever typically indicates the transition from human into zombie. When affected by rabies, human movement is irregular; muscle spasms and convulsions accompany numbness and loss of muscle function (6). Although their physical ability varies in media, the zombies we are familiar with generally have a distinctive, hobbling gait. Rabies causes difficulty swallowing because drinking causes spasms of the voice box; zombies largely lack the ability to produce any sound other than a deep groan, although they have been capable of speaking the word "brains" in classic zombie cinema.

Shared characteristics are not limited to physical attributes. A person with rabies will experience several changes in mental state, such as increased anxiety, stress, restlessness, delirium, abnormal behavior, and even hallucinations (9,10). Zombies will also typically display a limited level of cognitive function, with aggressive behaviors strengthening as cognitive function declines (8). However, there have been several exceptions. For example, in *I Am Legend*, the monsters were able to emulate a hunting trap made earlier by the protagonist. In the films *28 Days Later* and *28 Weeks Later*, zombies had vastly amplified rage and slightly mitigated planning and judgment, while still mostly preserving other cognitive functions.

The numerous parallels between zombies and rabies, as well as other infectious diseases that are a threat to public health, enable the use of a popular media creature to promote the prevention and control of a public health problem. Pending specific training in public health or medicine, the layperson may gain substantial interest and understanding of rabies with our comparison and utility of zombies. In the media, protagonists always find a way to fight back against the zombies and try to maintain their survival. The attack on infectious diseases is similar to this fight against a new menace, in that new ways will be discovered along with those already known to prevent, treat, and control infections. The use of the zombie analogy can provide food for thought, thus providing inspiration for persons to be prepared for and prevent infectious disease outbreaks. . . .

Conclusions

Zombies can be used as a powerful tool for increasing awareness of issues of public health significance. The popularity of the Center for Disease Control (CDC) piece on preparing for a zombie apocalypse has been instrumental in teaching how to prepare for disasters like the Tohoku Earthquake in Japan. We propose continuing these efforts, building on the popularity of zombies to increase public health awareness in the general public, and explore additional issues that may have not been considered in the past, such as infection control, mental health issues, ethics of disease, and

Comparison of Physical Characteristics of Zombies and of an Animal with Rabies.

bioterrorism potential. These issues can be explored by taking advantage of various forms of media, including 1) distributing informational pamphlets, books, and other printed media explaining the similarities between zombie infestations and lesser-known outbreaks and how to protect oneself and others; 2) creating satirical or dramatic public service announcements to promote defensive community strategies against infectious disease outbreaks by using zombiism as an analogy; 3) using interactive games, computer programs, and smartphone applications to enable the public to safely experience the natural progression of real epidemics on different levels of aggregation (e.g., individuals, communities, policymakers, medical and public health officials, both infected and uninfected), with and without intervention strategies such as vaccination, quarantine, or extermination; and 4) and facilitating the creation of clubs, societies, blogs, and even magazine articles across age ranges, academic institutions, and internet interest groups to share the excitement of applying what we can learn about zombies to more applicable avenues of life, such as public health and epidemiology. We must also consider the possibility—no matter how remote—that zombies could very well be replaced by other popular culture icons in the future. To that end, we must continue to adapt and use these pop culture tools to increase interest in and awareness of notable public health issues affecting the world.

References

1. Littlewood R, Douyon C. Clinical findings in three cases of zombification. *Lancet*. 1997;350:1094–6.
2. Ackermann HW, Gauthier J. The ways and nature of the zombi. *J Am Folk*. 1991;104:466–94.
3. McAlister E. A sorcerer's bottle: the visual art of magic in Haiti. In: Cosentino DJ, ed. *Sacred arts of Haitian vodou*. Los Angeles: UCLA Fowler Museum of Cultural History; 1995. p. 304–21.
4. Davis EW. The ethnobiology of the Haitian zombie. *J Ethnopharmacol*. 1983;9:85–104.
5. Shaw P. A history of zombies in video games. *PC World*. 2010 [cited 2012 May 28]. http://www.pcworld.com/article/206769/history_zombies_video_games.html
6. Rabies. *PubMed Health A.D.A.M. Medical Encyclopedia*. 2012 [cited 2012 May 28]. http://www.ncbi.nlm.nih.gov/pubmedhealth/PMH0002310/
7. Chinese county clubs to death 50,000 dogs: Campaign against rabies prompts mass slaughter in southwestern China. *Associated Press*. 2012 [cited 2012 Dec 19]. http://www.nbcnews.com/id/14139027/ns/health-pet_health/t/chinese-county-clubs-%20death-dogs/#.URibxVqjdms
8. Centers for Disease Control and Prevention. Rabies. 2012 [cited 2012 May 3]. http://www.cdc.gov/rabies/
9. Wilson T. How zombies work: zombies in popular culture. *How Stuff Works*. 2005 [cited 2012 May 28]. http://science.howstuffworks.com/science-vs-myth/strange-creatures/zombie3.htm
10. Resident Evil. T-virus. *Resident Evil Wiki*. 2012 [cited 2012 May 18]. http://residentevil.wikia.com/Tyrant_virus

. . . .

EXAMPLE 2: Informative Article about Dental Care

Dental Anxiety in Children and What to Do about It
Karla Rankoff

Last week, Amandine Diop brought her son, Gaspar, age 5, to the dentist for a regular check-up. When they entered the waiting room, Gaspar seemed fine, heading immediately to the toys in the children's corner. But when the dental hygienist came out to show Gaspar to the exam room, he suddenly had a complete meltdown—screaming, crying, and crumpling to the floor. Gaspar had visited the dentist before with no problem. So why was he suddenly so afraid?

Parents know that good dental care is an important part of growing up. They also know that the dentist does not exactly rank number one on most kids' lists of fun destinations. But that doesn't mean that kids can't get through a dentist visit without a tantrum. To alleviate fear of the dentist, you first need to figure out where that anxiety is coming from.

Where Dental Anxiety Comes From
Studies show that your own attitudes toward dental care might influence your children. A study published in the *International Journal of Pediatric Dentistry* in May 2004 found a strong correlation between parents' levels of anxiety about dental care and their child's anxiety levels. And evidence shows that this makes a big difference in a child's overall oral health.

In one study, researchers found that children whose mothers were anxious about visiting the dentist were more likely to have cavities, perhaps because these mothers were likely to avoid going to the dentist—and bringing their kids with them. According to the study, published in *Caries Research* in February 2012, over 44 percent of children whose mothers had medium or high levels of anxiety about visiting the dentist had cavities, compared with 34 percent of children whose mothers had low anxiety levels.

5   Does this mean you should blame yourself if your child drags her feet on the way into the dentist office? Not necessarily. Some research shows that children who have had a bad experience at the dentist in the past are more likely to be anxious—which makes sense. Researchers at the University of Glasgow found in a 2000 study that a traumatic event at the dentist, like getting a tooth pulled, made children more anxious, especially if the event happened at a young age. But, the study (published in the journal *Behavior Research and Therapy*) indicated that a positive visit to the dentist could do a lot to prevent anxiety later on.

This fact might explain why older children (8–11 year olds) were actually *more likely* than younger children to be nervous about the dentist—their past experience may have made them fearful. In a study published in *Child: Care, Health, and Development* in 2009, researchers found that older children had already experienced the two scariest items in the dentists' arsenal: the drill and the needle. Those experiences made them more wary than their younger counterparts.

Your dentist and their staff can also affect your child's anxiety level. A review of research on this topic by UK researchers found that dental professionals who demonstrated empathy and used both verbal and physical reassurance could help to put their young patients at ease. In contrast, when dental staff used coercion, insults, physical restraints, or threats, children were more likely to show anxiety about the dentist. The review, published in October 2011 in *Patient Education and Counseling*, also found it important for dental professionals to clearly explain to children what steps they would be taking, so that children knew what to expect.

What to Do

If your child is anxious or fearful about the dentist, try to figure out which factors might be causing it. Is it your own attitudes? Negative experiences in the past? The attitude and approach used by your dentist and her staff?

When Amandine thought over what might have been causing Gaspar's anxiety, she realized that it was not due to her own attitudes or those of her dentist. She knew she had been positive about visiting the dentist, and that Gaspar's dentist was extraordinarily patient, explaining each step of the process and letting Gaspar practice brushing and flossing on a puppet. Gaspar's own experiences at the dentist had been pleasant before this one visit. But then Amandine remembered that Gaspar had recently stayed with his grandparents for the weekend. Gaspar's grandpa had shown Gaspar how he could remove his dentures, joking with Gaspar that his teeth were gone because a mean dentist had pulled them all out. Gaspar must have taken his grandpa's story seriously, Amandine realized. Once she reassured Gaspar that grandpa was only joking, Gaspar was able to put his fears behind him.

Following these tips can help you and your child to have a more pleasant time at the dentist: 10

- Be careful not to share your own fears or anxieties with your child—and make sure family members don't, either. To put your child at ease, you can role play a dentist visit ahead of time using dolls or puppets, or simply explain what to expect.
- Select your dentist carefully—find someone used to working with children, who shows empathy, and who does not use punitive measures (threats, put-downs, or physical restraints). Try to get a referral from a trusted friend who also has children.
- Ask your dentist to explain each step of the examination (or any procedures) clearly using a model or doll, so that your child knows what to expect.
- Make sure young children have a few positive, routine visits under their belt before any more traumatic procedures (such as teeth pulling or fillings) are needed. If possible, try to delay major treatments until the child is ready. Ask your dentist if a sealant or fluoride treatment can help to postpone any more invasive procedures.

· ·

EXAMPLE 3: Informative Article about Mass Shootings (excerpt)

What Happened in the Newtown School Shooting: There's No Explaining Such a Horrific Act, but Here's Important Background Information

MotherJones.com

By Asawin Suebsaeng, Deanna Pan, and Gavin Aronsen. Friday, Dec. 14, 2012 1:52 PM PST

On Friday morning, 27 people were killed in a shooting rampage at an elementary school in Newtown, Connecticut. Among the fatalities are 20 children, six adults, and the shooter. [**Update:** Authorities told AP the gunman killed his mother before driving to the school in her car, where he targeted two classrooms in one section of the building.] Sandy Hook Elementary is secure and the alleged gunman is dead, Connecticut State Lt. Paul Vance told reporters at a press conference Friday afternoon. Authorities reportedly recovered three guns—a Glock and SIG Sauer, both pistols, inside the school and a Bushmaster .223-caliber rifle ~~in the shooter's car~~. [**Update:** On Saturday, officials including the state's chief medical examiner said that the rifle was the primary weapon used in the shooting.] At least 100 rounds were fired. Officials have checked the suspect's home for evidence.

A spokesperson for Connecticut Gov. Dannel Malloy said President Obama called the governor to express his condolences and offer any federal resources to assist in the ongoing investigation....

Here's what we know:

What do we know about the shooter? Despite earlier media reports which misidentified the alleged shooter as Ryan Lanza, of Hoboken, New Jersey, AP confirmed the suspected gunman is Adam Lanza, 20, Ryan Lanza's brother. Adam Lanza reportedly shot and killed his mother, Nancy Lanza, ~~who reportedly worked at Sandy Hook Elementary School~~, before attacking the school. A law enforcement official told AP Adam Lanza died from an apparent self-inflicted gunshot wound. He was found dead inside the school. [**Update:** It appears Nancy Lanza did not work at school, but Adam had had an altercation with staff there a day prior to the shooting.]

5   According to AP, Ryan Lanza told law enforcement officials his brother may suffer from a personality disorder.

What are the gun laws like in Connecticut? According to the NRA, Connecticut requires permits for handguns, but not for shotguns or rifles. It's illegal to possess a handgun if you've been convicted of a felony or a "serious juvenile offense."

How does the Newtown shooting compare to other mass shootings in this country? This year alone there had already been six mass shootings—and a record number of casualties, with 110 people injured and killed prior to today's incident. (An FBI crime classification report identifies an individual as a mass murderer—as opposed to a spree killer or a serial killer—if he kills four or more people in a single incident, not including himself, and typically in a single location.) The shooting at Sandy Hook Elementary School is also the 12th mass shooting at a school in the United States in the past 30 years, according to our research; it is the second deadliest shooting behind the Virginia Tech massacre in 2007 that killed 33 and injured 23.

USE THE TOOLKIT

Let's use the three genre toolkit questions from Chapter 1 to examine this genre.

What Is It?

These documents are all informative articles: documents that provide information about a topic, including plenty of facts and details drawn from research, for a popular (non-scholarly) audience. You might consider an informative article to be a longer, more elaborate factsheet. For example, Karla's article provides facts about the causes of dental anxiety in children, but presents them in paragraph form, rather than simply listing the causes and effects she had uncovered through research (Chapter 24).

Who Reads It?

These articles all are written for popular websites, magazines, or newspapers. Some readers might find these articles by searching for specific information, such as "how Zombies work" or "what happened in the Newtown shooting?" Karla, a student writer, designed her article to be read by parents, using *Parenting* magazine as her model. Unlike factsheets, which target readers in search of specific information, these articles are also meant for casual readers, those reading for entertainment as well as information.

What's It For?

Informative articles often serve two purposes: to inform and to entertain. Readers of informative articles are probably not seeking to master a particular skill, as in a tutorial. While factsheets are primarily informative, informative articles often add elements to entertain readers. Karla meant her article to be informative, but she included an anecdote about a mother and her child in the introduction to draw readers in. Readers of the informative article about the Newtown shooting might be seeking out information, rather than entertainment, since the events in question are horrific. However, since the article appeared on *MotherJones.com,* the website for a popular magazine, readers may also have begun by browsing the magazine for entertainment when they encountered this article.

EXERCISE 6.4: Plan an Informative Article

Think of a topic that readers might want to know more about, either for their own research or just for fun. Consider popular trends, ideas, or topics you've heard about recently that people might want to know more about, and search the news for terms or ideas. For example, has there been a natural disaster in your area recently? Perhaps readers would like to know more about how tornadoes or hurricanes work. Is the government proposing a new round of economic reforms, such as quantitative easing? You could write an article explaining what quantitative easing is and how it works. Is there an election coming up? You could write an article explaining how campaign financing functions.

Share your list of ideas with your group. Together, determine which topics seem most interesting for an informative article.

E. Strategies for Informative Genres

Let's see how one student, Karla (Example 2), put together an informative article.

Prewriting (Content)

Karla brainstormed her topic using a list. Her instructor assigned her to write an informative article related to her major or area of interest. As a science major with an interest in becoming a dentist, Karla wanted a topic that would reflect those interests.

After browsing some online sources, such as ScienceDaily.com, for research topics (Chapter 23), she developed the following list of potential topics:

- Effects of poor oral health on school performance
- Links between obesity and poor oral health
- Causes/effects of dental anxiety in children; what to do about it
- Whether herbs and supplements (coconut oil, vitamin D) can prevent tooth decay

Karla decided that the third topic would be worth exploring more, since she had been interning at a dentist's office and had noticed that many children were severely anxious about dental visits.

Next, Karla considered the audience for her article (Chapter 2). She used the following questions to brainstorm her approach:

1. Who, in particular, might read this article?
   - Dentists and dental professionals who want to know how they can help children feel at ease
   - Parents who want to know how to help their children get over fear or how to prevent fear
   - Child psychologists
   - Teachers

2. Which audience do I want to reach, and how?
   - Primarily parents—so I should shoot for a magazine like *Parenting*
   - Other audiences might be secondary—for example, parents might show the article to their dentist, teacher, etc.

3. What do they already know about this topic?
   - Readers might know a fair amount about dental health (either from reading or from general experience/knowledge), but they might not know much about dental anxiety in particular, its causes, effects, etc.
   - Some readers will have more scientific knowledge than others.

4. What attitudes do they have toward this topic?
   - Audience members want to help their children to avoid or overcome dental anxiety.
   - I can appeal to the aspirations of readers to help children.
   - Readers will have generally positive attitudes—although some parents might feel resistant if article seems to blame them for children's anxiety.

5. How motivated will they be to read the article?
   - Some might be reading for information AND action—they'll want to know what they can do to help their children.
   - Others might just be reading casually (*Parenting* is often in doctors' and dentists' offices; or they may have a subscription and read for general entertainment/curiosity).

Finally, Karla used her campus library to locate information for her article. She searched for articles about dental anxiety in children, using library databases (Chapter 24), evaluated her sources to help determine what information to include in the article (Chapter 25), and then considered how to integrate sources into her article (Chapter 26). She also interviewed a friend of hers, Amandine, whose son had recently had a bad visit at the dentist.

Drafting (Organizing)

To draft this article, Karla started by organizing the main findings from her research. She had two main kinds of sources, research articles reporting on single studies, and reviews of multiple studies (Chapter 11). Karla carefully read each source, highlighting key information to include in her article, and then grouped that information by the main causes of dental anxiety.

She started with a concept map (Chapter 16). The concept map (Figure 6.1) helped her to identify the main causes of dental anxiety in children that she could address in her article: parental attitudes, past experience, and actions of dental professionals.

Next, after examining some informative articles in *Parenting* for inspiration, Karla organized her main ideas into a rough outline (Chapter 20). She decided to frame her research with an anecdote from her interview with Amandine. Then, she decided, she would explore the main causes of dental anxiety, using evidence from her research sources, and wrap up by showing how Amandine had addressed her son's anxiety. Since some *Parenting* articles included bulleted or boxed lists of

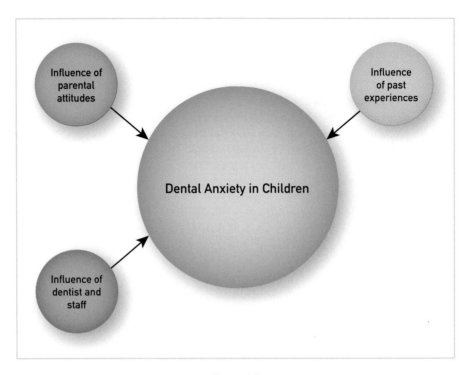

Figure 6.1
This concept map demonstrates the many causes of dental anxiety in children.

suggestions, she decided to include one listing concrete steps parents could take to address dental anxiety with their children.

1. Anecdote from interview with Amandine
2. Main causes:
   a. Parental attitudes:
      i. Correlate with children's attitudes
      ii. Correlate with dental health outcomes (cavities)
   b. Past experiences
      i. Experience with fillings, pullings, etc. = more anxiety
      ii. Older children actually more anxious—more exposure to bad experiences
   c. Dentist & staff approaches
      i. Verbal and physical reassurance, explaining each step, etc.
      ii. Avoiding negatives (restraint, putdowns, etc.)
3. What to do about it:
   a. Wrap up anecdote—what Amandine did
   b. Bulleted list/box—main suggestions

Then, Karla wrote a first draft based on this outline. She realized that she had or-ganized her article primarily by concepts or themes (Chapter 20). You might also organize an informative article using the "Five W and an H" questions: *Who? What? Where? When? Why?* and *How?* (Chapter 16), or by another organizational scheme (Chapter 20), depending on your topic, audience, and purpose.

Revising (Style)

Karla shared her rough draft with her writing group on the class discussion board. Her group members felt that while the draft presented interesting information, it was sometimes presented in more scientific language, like the sources Karla consulted. They suggested revising the document to better suit non-scientific readers.

For example, Karla originally wrote this sentence:

> In one study, researchers found that children of mothers with dental anxiety were more likely to have dental caries, perhaps because these mothers' reluctance led to reduced dental visits for their children.

After her peer workshop, she revised it to include more suitable vocabulary and level of formality (Chapter 21):

> In one study, researchers found that children whose mothers were anxious about visiting the dentist were more likely to have cavities, perhaps because these mothers were likely to avoid going to the dentist—and bringing their kids with them.

Karla also worked on introducing information about her sources in the text, rather than just dropping in information. She used signals to indicate where she got her research, which not only made it possible for readers to locate that information, but also made her article seem more credible (Chapter 26). For example, in her original draft, she had written this:

> This fact might explain why older children (8–11 year olds) were actually *more likely* than younger children to be nervous about the dentist—their past experience may have made them fearful. Older children have already experienced the two scariest items in the dentists' arsenal: the drill and the needle.

She changed that sentence to indicate where this information came from:

> This fact might explain why older children (8–11 year olds) were actually *more likely* than younger children to be nervous about the dentist—their past experience may have made them fearful. In a study published in *Child: Care, Health, and Development* in 2009, researchers found that older children had already experienced the two scariest items in the dentists' arsenal: the drill and the needle.

Because informative articles published in magazines do not use formal academic citations, Karla used these more informal cues to show where the information came from. However, she handed in a separate works cited list so that her instructor could see where she had found information.

Editing (Design)

To finalize her article, Karla considered how to use formatting and design elements to her advantage. She decided to include a headline and subsections like those in the sample articles she read. Thinking more about the document's design (Chapter 29), she later added a copyright-free image from Wikimedia Commons (not shown) that she thought evoked the themes in the article.

She also proofread her article twice, correcting any word choices that still sounded too technical for her audience.

Troubleshooting

Here are some common challenges that students face when writing informative genres.

I can't find a good topic for my informative genre.   The Internet is full of examples of how-to and informative genres. In fact, aside from social networking and media-viewing, looking up information constitutes one of the most common uses of the Internet. Thus, finding a good topic might seem difficult—it can seem like every-thing you want to know is already there!

To start with, think about unique skills or knowledge you possess. Can you cook a special dish that is unique to your family or heritage, or one that requires a specific technique? Perhaps you could write an informative article about the food traditions of your community.

Or, think about topics that have always fascinated you. You might already have expertise about a topic related to your major or one of your hobbies that you can share with your audience.

You might also think about everyday things or phenomena that you usually take for granted. Where did the milk carton come from? Who designed it, when, and why? Where does ketchup come from, and how did it come to be such a popular condiment? What actually happens when you do an ATM or debit transaction?

I don't know what kind of information to include.   Start by considering your audi-ence. What will they want to know about your topic? What kinds of questions will they have? What will they find most interesting? For example, say you are writing an informative article about crime scene investigators. Readers might not want to read all about the specific techniques used to do forensic analysis at a crime scene, but they may want to know what kinds of things investigators look for, including some of the strangest clues that they have uncovered, and how those clues can lead to a conviction.

I can't find any good information.   Locating the kind of information you need for an informative text can be difficult. For a tutorial, you might actually need to do the task you are describing, stopping to write down each step.

For a factsheet or informative article, there are a number of possible sources for information. It can be good to start with general reference sources, such as dictionaries, encyclopedias, or textbooks. You might also use more specialized sources, such as books and articles (Chapter 24). Consult your campus librarian for assistance. You might also do some original research of your own, perhaps by interviewing an expert.

I can't tell if my information is too difficult for readers.   The best way to determine how well your informative text works is to ask someone to read your document. Ask your reader to note places where she got confused or had trouble following your writing. For example, you might ask someone to read your informative article and highlight any term that you need to define, where she had difficulty understanding you, and so on. For a tutorial, you could ask someone to actually try to perform the task in question using your instructions. Professional writers call this stage *usability testing*. Usability testing helps you to identify not only whether your writing is correct, but whether it is useful for readers.

F. Chapter Project: Write an Informative Article

Create an informative article for students on your campus. Design your article to suit an online news source with students as the primary audience. You can follow the steps taken in the preceding example. You should

- Consider your audience's needs and interests.
- Conduct some research.
- Draft, revise, and edit your document.

Group Option: Create an Article Series

With your group, create a series of articles for incoming first-year college students, informing them about topics that will help them survive the first year, such as "what first-year students need to know about procrastination" or "what first-year students need to know about living on campus." (Other topics could include campus life, specific college traditions, signing up for classes, etc.) Your articles will appear in a magazine given to next year's incoming class.

First, come up with a list of topics. Think back to your time preparing for college and your first few weeks. What did you find difficult? What did you want to know more about?

Then, identify strategies for research, which could include interviewing more advanced students, doing library research, or even conducting a field observation.

As a group, you will need to decide:

- What topics will you address?
- What are the most important things readers need to know about each topic?
- How will you write your articles for a cohesive tone and design?

You will collectively be responsible for reviewing and editing all of your articles so that they meet a common standard for style and content.

Multimedia Option: Make an Informative Video

Follow the preceding directions, but now consider how you would provide information in a video format. Consider the following:

- What kinds of sounds should I record? (Narration? Music? Dialog?)
- What kinds of images or video recordings can I include?
- How should I organize the video? (An overview? A list of contents? A story format?)
- What should the pacing of the video be?

Write a rough timeline for your video. To get feedback on your draft, have a group member read through it and write down how they see the video proceeding, and what kinds of scenes or contents they would include. That way, you can see whether your content and pacing are clear. Finally, record your video and upload it to your course management system.

Inquiries

An inquiry is an informal investigation into or a record of anything you encounter in the world. Examples of inquiries are wide ranging, and include a food journal, an exercise diary, a sleep diary, a baby diary, a gardening planner, and many others. Once the data gathered in an inquiry takes on a more formal shape, it can become a report (Chapter 14), an analysis (Chapter 8), even a proposal (Chapter 13).

In the classroom, an inquiry can be used as prewriting for other, more formal genres. For example, class notes taken by a student can form the groundwork for a research paper later in a semester. Reading notes on an assigned reading can later become part of a book review for a class assignment.

In a professional setting, observation notes taken by an ethnographer might later be used to write a field report about a culture. A journalist takes reading notes when conducting research and later uses those notes to write a news report (Chapter 14).

In this chapter, you will learn about a variety of written inquiries that you might encounter in an academic setting.

A. Inquiry Mini-Genre: Student Class Notes

Class notes are a type of inquiry students use to investigate what they are learning.

EXAMPLE 1: Student Notes from an English Class

Josephine Perry: St. Augustine on Love
English 316: 2/18/14

AD 354–430
Bishop of Hippo (now in Algeria). Born in Algeria (then part of Roman Empire).
Studied rhetoric in Carthage, during which time he lived a hedonistic lifestyle (girls girls girls);
taught rhetoric in Carthage for 9 years, then in Rome, then in Milan.
Love life: had a son with a woman in Carthage; dumped her to get engaged; dumped his young bride as well as another concubine.

Later wrote: "By love I mean the impulse of one's mind to enjoy God on his own account and to enjoy oneself and one's neighbor on account of God, and by lust I mean the impulse of one's mind to enjoy oneself and one's neighbor and any corporeal thing not on account of God."

AD 386—religious conversion; gives up teaching rhetoric, swears off marriage, becomes a priest. Moved back to Africa & became a famous preacher. Goal was to convert people in Hippo to Christianity.

Lisa asked a good question: What relationship did Augustine's mistreatment of women have with his decision to convert and become a priest? Did he feel guilty?

EXAMPLE 2: Student Notes from an Engineering Class

Patrick Lam's notes for a Component Based Software Engineering course.

EXAMPLE 3: Student Notes from a Psychology Class

Class: Psych 209
Date: October 2, 2011
Chapter/Topic: Chapter 1
Page: 4 of

Notice that I left this blank. I don't fill it in until I am finished with the chapter.

Lecture Notes Oct 2/5	Questions	Textbook Notes
D. Measurement—looking for some certain things. Example: Student who is weighed on scale.	Monitor in Psychology (Magazine)	3. Possible limits of "free choices"
1. Reliability: consistency of a measure.	I titled this section "Questions," but I often write other misc things that I want to remember here. I think of it as a multi-purpose column	B. Science makes systematic observations • Scientists systematic observations include: a. precise definition of phenomena being observed b. reliable + valid measuring tools that yield useful + interpretable data. c. generally accepted methodologies d. System of logic for drawing conclusion and fitting those into general theories.
2. Validity: does a measure truly assess quality that it is claimed to measure? Truthfulness of a measure.		
3. Accuracy: Agreement with a known standard (process of calibration).		C. Science produces public knowledge. • An objective observation isn't someone who is completely objective (like Peirce thought). It just means something that can be verified by more than 1 observer.
Focus remains with those two because the 3rd will often be disputed.	I didn't hear the last name of someone the professor mentioned during lecture so I left a blank space. If I think the name is important I can fill it in later if its mentioned or I know what to ask the prof later on.	—Done through replication: where someone redoes another's study and gets same results. • Replication can only be done if they know precisely what was done. This is done by rules that are found in Publication Manual of APA.
E. Testable Questions— • Can hypothesis/claim be falsified at least in principle (Notion of Falsifiability) by Carl		
F. Public Reporting: Many places they can publish.	Psychological Science (Peer Reviewed journal)	• Introspection: a form of precise self-report.
—Peer Reviewed journals (most esteemed).		—The problem w/ introspect is that its subjective and not verifiable.
—Sci are proud and want to get it out	When I take a break from reading, I like to leave a note to remind me where I left off.	—John B. Watson concluded that something can only be "scientific" if its directly observable and can be verified
—Way you establish reputation		
—We have to be aware of knowledge in order to		

Jenna Shrewsbury's notes for a psychology course. She annotated her own notes to demonstrate her study process.

USE THE TOOLKIT

Let's use the three genre toolkit questions from Chapter 1 to examine this genre.

What Is It?

These class notes were all written by college students. You'll see that most students list the course title and date at the top of each page. Possibly, the students wrote that information before class began, in order to keep notes organized.

The notes are not always written in complete sentences. Some are funny asides that the author wrote to herself to help her remember important points (e.g., "girls, girls, girls" in Josephine's English class notes in Example 1).

The students have written down notes from what the professor said in class as well as notes from class discussion. Josephine, in Example 1, wrote down a question that another student asked that she found important. In this way, the student has engaged in discussion by listening closely to what others are saying. Jenna, in Example 3, has included a column for questions that she might need later on when she is working on a paper.

You'll see that each student has developed his or her own note-taking system. Josephine, in Example 1, takes notes on her computer, while Patrick in Example 2 and Jenna in Example 3 feature handwritten notes. Jenna, in Example 3, has developed a template that she prints out and uses for all of her classes.

Who Reads It?

Each student wrote these notes primarily for his or her own use. They need to take good notes because these notes are important to their grades. For example, one student might use his notes later in the semester to prepare an essay for the course, while another might use her notes to study for a final exam.

Sometimes, though, students share their class notes with each other—for example, to help a student who missed class get caught up.

What's It For?

Class notes help a student learn the material. By taking notes, the student summarizes, in her own words, the readings, lectures, and class discussions of a course. Putting course material in one's own words is essential to this type of inquiry—and all inquiries—because using one's own words forces a writer to formulate her own ideas about a subject. Later in the semester, these ideas might become the content of an essay, a presentation, or an exam answer.

EXERCISE 7.1: Evaluate Your Class Notes

Review your class notes for two of your classes last week: one class you really enjoy, and one class that you enjoy a little less.

Compare these notes. Write your answers to the following questions:

- Do you write more notes in the class you enjoy, or more in the class you don't enjoy? Why do you think that is?
- Would someone else be able to read your class notes and understand them? Does this hold true for both classes? Why or why not?

- Do you have a system for note-taking? What is it? If not, should you develop one?
- Do you write down ideas that you come up with when you take notes? Do you write down ideas that come from other students? Why or why not?

GROUP ACTIVITY 7.1: Exchange and Evaluate Class Notes

In your small group, trade your class notes with each other. Read your classmate's notes. Write your answers to the following questions, and be prepared to share your answers with your classmates.

- Can you understand what your classmate has written? Why or why not?
- Would these notes be helpful to you if you needed them in a crunch? Why or why not?
- Does the note-taker write down ideas that he or she has come up with? Does he write down ideas that come from other students? Why do you think he or she did/didn't do these things?

B. Blog Entry

Blogs are an online collections of writings, sketches, images, and other media that the authors have written (or gathered) to reflect on their lives, on events that have occurred, on media, or on their thoughts or dreams.

EXAMPLE 1: Blog Entry for a Mass Communications Class

Disappointment: *Rizzoli & Isles*

By Brandy

As a fan of Tess Gerritsen's books, when I learned TNT was giving Gerritsen's central characters a show of their own, I was excited, and set my dvr accordingly. Then, I set about waiting to see who had been cast in the titular roles. Don't ask, it never really occurs to me that I could, you know, use the internet to find out stuff like that in advance. It was obvious from the first commercials I saw that whatever TNT's *Rizzoli & Isles* was going to be, it wasn't going to be too much like the books. For about 7 books I'd imagined Rizzoli, as she is described, with a mop of unruly dark curls, and as good looking, but in an unconventional way; Dr. Isles was, as she is often described, the queen of the dead, a little goth, with red lipstick and straight black hair cut in a bob with straight bangs—which is, as it turns out, how Ms. Gerritsen looks (well, not exactly goth, but you get the idea). While there was never any doubt in my mind these women would be beautiful in their own ways, um . . . Angie Harmon and Sasha Anderson were not exactly the faces that leapt into my mind as I read these books. . . .

Like I said, although I'd initially hoped for something a little different, this review isn't about comparing the television show to the books. The characters, stories, and tone of each is distinct enough that a real comparison is impossible. The books are detective fiction, pure and simple. The television show walks the genre lines between serious police procedural and comedy. It is almost as if the producers really wanted an hour long comedy, and knew stretching a sit com that long would grow tedious, so they decided to incorporate a police procedural to bump up the story. I've never seen an episode, so I could be wrong, but *Rizzoli & Isles* makes me think it is like a female Nash Bridges.

It might surprise you, but the light nature of the show is not really what bothers me. A lot of police procedurals err in the opposite way, taking themselves too seriously. What bothers me about *Rizzoli & Isles* is that the light tone is achieved at the expense of the title characters. At every turn the show undermines the power of two strong women working together, and becoming friends by making every second conversation between the two about getting, or having, a relationship, every third conversation about the case—as if their jobs are an afterthought, and the remaining conversations about clothes and shoes. There has to be some sort of heterosexual romance for at least one of the women in nearly every episode because the writers are working overtime to ensure that it is clear Rizzoli & Isles are not lesbians. (Well, except for those episodes where they pretend to be lesbians— you know, for laughs.) As a viewer it is impossible to take either Rizzoli or Isles seriously because at every turn we are reminded that Rizzoli can't get a man because she is not feminine enough, and that despite looking like a fashion plate Isles can't function socially because she is just too smart.

EXAMPLE 2: Blog Entry for a Sociology of Gender Class

CARSON'S SOCIOLOGY OF GENDER BLOG

TEENAGE YEARS
(11-16 years old)

RELATIONSHIPS

FASHION

HOME
EC.
VS.
SHOP

SPORTS

A visual blog by Carson McDonald.

EXAMPLE 3: Blog Entry for a Political Science Class

Straw-Man Fallacy and the "Anti-Antiterror Left"
By Lucia Gonzalez Hernandez

In a column titled "The 'Al-Qaeda Seven': The Anti-Antiterror Left and Legal Standards," the editorial staff at the *Wall Street Journal* agreed that the insinuations made by Lynn Cheney and her colleagues at Keep America Safe about the seven Justice Department lawyers who defended Guantanamo Bay terror suspects were "unfortunate." (Essentially, in dubbing the lawyers the "Al-Qaeda Seven," Lynn Cheney implied that these attorneys, who worked *pro bono* to provide representation guaranteed by our Constitution, worked on behalf of Al-Qaeda.)

But the WSJ also criticized many on the left who they find hypocritical: "Many liberals seem to believe that while it was a war crime to agree with [former VP] Dick Cheney's antiterror methods, it is somehow a lawyer's patriotic duty to defend terrorists. This is the mindset that these columns describe as that of the anti-antiterror left."

When I first read this phrase, "the anti-antiterror left," it struck me as the typical hawk-right hyperbole used to create a straw-man. The straw-man fallacy is a favorite of those who participate in political discourse, both in the media and in Washington (or Raleigh, for that matter). The fallacy works like this: you exaggerate (through overstatement, for example) the position of your opponents in order to make their positions easier to refute. Hawks on the right have often criticized pro-peace Americans as weak or unamerican.

For example, Lynn Cheney's KAS writes in its mission statement: "Amidst the great challenges to America's security and prosperity, the current administration too often seems uncertain, wishful, irresolute, and unwilling to stand up for America, our allies and our interests." For KAS, then, the Obama administration won't "stand up for America"—an exaggeration used for persuasive effect.

5   So: labeling folks who think Gitmo should close and that former VP Cheney's prewar tactics were misleading as "the anti-antiterror left" first appeared to me as a straw-man fallacy, ripe with hyperbole.

But then I thought about it. What does the term "antiterror" mean? It seems to refer to a set of principles, such as those espoused by former VP Cheney and his daughter, such as rendition, waterboarding, and the like. Had the WSJ used the term "pro-terror," they would have committed the straw-man fallacy, and probably many other fallacies as well. But they did not.

I wonder, should those on the left who disagree with the Cheneys, the WSJ, and KAS, disagree with the label of "anti-antiterror"? Perhaps, rather than disagreeing, their strongest rhetorical move would be to claim the label as their own.

USE THE TOOLKIT

Let's use the three genre toolkit questions from Chapter 1 to examine this genre.

What Is It?

All three of these blog entries have a few things in common. They gather together ideas in an informal fashion. They reflect upon events in the author's life: a television show watched, the experience of being a teen, an article read in a newspaper. The verbal blog entries include phrases such as "I wonder," "I'd hoped," and "I thought," indicating the reflective nature of a blog. All three demonstrate how the blog entry is a form of inquiry: each explores a topic, using words, images, and hyperlinks to investigate and record ideas. Brandy's blog entry about the television show *Rizzoli & Isles*, for example, is less formal than a review essay (Chapter 9), but it still explores the strengths and weaknesses of the show. Indeed, Brandy might build upon the blog entry later in the semester to write a review essay of contemporary television shows.

Who Reads It?

Blogs can be very private, written only for the eyes of the author. These blog entries, and most blogs written for school or published online, are meant to be shared with others. For example, Lucia wrote her blog entry, Example 3, in response to a prompt from her political science teacher to write about a current event. While blog entries remain reflective and informal, they are written in a fashion that is easy for others to understand.

What's It For?

Carson put together his visual blog entry, Example 2, in preparation for writing a paper on gender differences. Brandy wrote her blog post, Example 1, because her professor asked her to reflect on a new television show. All of these blog entries are meant to influence readers' opinions on current cultural events. Blog entries, then, can be written with a more formal project in mind, or for their own sakes, that is, for reflection and generating ideas.

EXERCISE 7.2: Keep a Blog for One Week

For one week, write every day as though you were writing for a blog. Write for a minimum of ten minutes each session. Each session, pick a topic to write about. You can pick a topic from one of your classes (brainstorm for an assignment, for example), or from a book you've read, or a television show or movie you've watched.

MULTIMEDIA EXERCISE 7.1: Create a Visual Blog Entry

Pick one of the following topics. Using PowerPoint or similar software, create a visual blog. You can download pictures from the Internet and insert text to reflect upon the images. You can even record audio (an "audio PowerPoint") to accompany your visual blog entry.

- Friendship
- Romance and love
- Adventure
- Travel
- The environment

C. Reading Notes

Reading notes are reflective pieces written in response to texts. Students write reading notes to prepare for classes, for exams, or for writing papers about books. They are an informal version of reading response essays (Chapter 3). Reading notes are a kind of inquiry because they record the reader's informal investigation of a text.

●●●

EXAMPLE 1: Reading Notes for a Rhetoric Course

> *Mei-Lin*
>
> **Aristotle, On Rhetoric** 8/24/14
>
> Persuasion
>
> —*necessary when auditors are faced with a choice*
>
> —*the "probable"*
>
> ★—*Are there any circumstances that don't involve interpretive constructions? Are there truths?*
>
>   → *Aristotle: all is persuasion*
>
>   → *Plato: "Truth" does exist.*
>
> 3 Species of Rhetoric
>
>   —*Judicial/Deliberative/Epideitic. (Speech acts)*
>
>   —*Persuasion relies on ethos, pathos and logos—an interaction of the three.*
>
>   ↓
>
> *Ethos: a sense of the speaker, how S feels about the topic & the subject matter*
>
>   • *Phronesis: Common sense or practical wisdom. Important in American rhetoric.*
>   *(Politicians being "too smart")*
>
>   • *Arete: Moral virtue*
>
>   • *Eunoia: good will towards the audience*
>
>   → *all 3 are situationally determined*

●●●

EXAMPLE 2: Reading Notes for a Research Paper

Terrence B.

Notes on Pamela Lewis Reading

Pamela Lewis, "Behind the Glass Wall: Barriers that Incarcerated Parents Face Regarding the Care, Custody and Control of their Children" (2004)

Lewis's arguments:
  • Lewis suggests that visitation is a legal right.
  • Legal barriers and prison rules unjustly prevent visitation.
  • Limited access to legal services makes hearings problematic for incarcerated parents.
  • Legal services often given only when parental rights are being terminated.

My thoughts:
  • In what ways can visitation be construed as a "legal right"? Under the U.S. Constitution? At the state level? Is it a fundamental right under the Due Process Clause?

- If felons can be stripped of their fundamental right to vote, can they also be stripped of their right to parent? Draw an analogy with voting and the movement to restore the franchise to felons?
- If parenting is a fundamental right, should there also be a right to counsel in situations where parental visitation is challenged?

EXAMPLE 3: Reading Notes for a Literature Course

Michael M.

Elizabeth Barrett Browning Response: "The Cry of the Children"

I am interested in discussing the types of accusations EBB makes in "The Cry of the Children." This is not a mere woe-and-pity poem meant to demonstrate the plight of the helpless. She makes accusations and threats, that are both gendered and political.

In the first stanza, Browning writes, "Do ye hear the children weeping, O my brothers / Ere the sorrow comes with years? / They are leaning their young heads against their mothers / And *that* cannot stop their tears." Here she makes what appears to be an emotional appeal to her fellow countrymen, her "brothers." She emphasizes the children's misery by showing that even their mothers' care does not bring them solace. Although these may appear to be gender-neutral, in particular the invocation of "brothers," I argue that she makes a specific accusation towards men, and men in power—government, industry—to do something. The mothers, in contrast, are helpless to help their own children. Browning repeats the call to "brothers" in line 9.

The call for help is also directed at the nation as a whole, but even this is a gendered call and accusation. At the end of the first stanza she refers to "the country of the free" (12), but later, at the end of the second stanza, she refers to Britain ironically as "our happy Fatherland" (24). The nation, and its political powers, are the father-figure of this poem, in contrast with the helpless mother-figures.

The children living in poverty, laboring in mines and workhouses, wish for death as an escape from misery. Their lives spent in the dark mines and factories contrast with the sunshine and vegetation outside. In stanza five, Browning writes, "Sing out, children, as the little thrushes do; / Pluck you handfuls of the meadow cowslips pretty." In response, the children compare this natural beauty with "the weeds anear the mine" and reject the speaker's offer of comfort in natural beauty: "Leave us quiet in the dark of the coal-shadows." The natural world, often associated with the feminine, contrasts starkly in the masculine world of industry.

USE THE TOOLKIT

Let's use the three genre toolkit questions from Chapter 1 to examine this genre.

What Is It?

All three examples of reading notes just presented discuss a particular text in detail. Mei-Lin, in Example 1, examines *Rhetoric* by Aristotle; Terrence, in Example 2, examines a legal article by Pamela Lewis; Michael, in Example 3, examines "Cry of the Children" by Elizabeth Barrett Browning. Terrence's research paper is examined in greater detail in Part 3 of this book.

All three students note the name of the text and the name of the author. Mei-Lin's notes on Aristotle resemble an outline of the ideas in Aristotle's text. Terrence's notes are more of a quick summary of the arguments of the article and his reflections on those arguments. Michael's notes on Browning are highly reflective and resemble a journal entry (Chapter 2). Thus, reading notes and journal entries can overlap as genres.

Who Reads It?

Reading notes are typically written for the note-taker to read. Sometimes, though, a note-taker will share the notes with classmates or a teacher.

What's It For?

By recording the reader's informal investigation of a text, reading notes accomplish many things. First, they help the note-taker better understand and recall the reading material. Second, reading notes can be the beginning stages of research, helping the note-taker assemble research material in preparation of writing an outline or a paper (Chapter 24).

EXERCISE 7.3: Write Reading Notes

Look through your school newspaper (either the print version or the online version) and select a short article or opinion piece to read. Once you have finished reading, write some reading notes by answering the questions below:

- Who is the author? What can you learn about the author from the article? How does the author's identity affect your feelings toward the text?
- What do you believe is the main purpose of the article? Find a quotation from the article that supports your belief.

- In what ways does the author accomplish this main purpose? By giving examples? By conducting research and sharing it with readers?
- How does this text make you feel? Angry? Hopeful? Why?

GROUP ACTIVITY 7.2

Look through your school newspaper (either the print version or the online version) and select a short article or opinion piece to read. Once everyone in your group has finished reading the piece, discuss how you would answer the questions in Exercise 7.3. How would these questions help each of you better understand the text that you have read?

D. Observation Notes

Observation notes are notes taken by writers to record events that they have witnessed. Like they do with reading notes, writers record observation notes to prepare for classes, for exams, or for writing papers about what they have witnessed.

EXAMPLE 1: Observation Notes for an Anthropology Assignment

Name of Observer: Zachary Fitzgerald
Location: Campus Courtyard
Date: April 18, 2014
Time: 12:30 p.m.–1:00 p.m.

Observations of the Campus Courtyard

I observed student interactions at the Campus Courtyard, a popular outdoor "hangout" spot located between the library and the student union. The courtyard is a shady, rectangular area paved in brick, with built in benches. It is surrounded by trees and azalea bushes (which were in full bloom). There is a large, round fountain in the center.

At the start of the observation period, there were two main groups of students who were hanging out in the courtyard: a group of skateboarders surrounding the fountain, and a group of students clustered in the southwest corner. Other students walked through the courtyard on their way to the Student Union, the library, or classes, but I focused on those who were sitting or standing in the courtyard for most of the observation period (thirty minutes).

The skateboarding group consisted of three male and two female students. There were three skateboards between them. One of the male students was showing a female student a trick, and then encouraging her to practice it. The remaining two males were standing with the other female, talking. Occasionally, they would take one of the skateboards and do a lap around the paved area. The students were dressed in similar styles: tight jeans (usually black), t-shirts, and sneakers.

The students in the southwest corner included four women and two men. At the start of the observation period, one of the women was speaking, glancing at a notebook, and gesturing frequently. After she spoke, the other students cheered and applauded briefly. Then, a few students seemed to offer comments. Next, a male student began to speak—also referring to a notebook. The group proceeded to go around the circle, with each student speaking and the rest listening and applauding, followed by a short period in which different students spoke. Some of the students had food with them—one was eating an apple, another a sandwich.

Reflections:

The skateboarding group and "speaking" groups both seem to represent different sub-cultures found on our campus. The skateboarding group shared a style of dress, common interest, and set of bodily habits. As we have been learning in class, these are some of the components sociologists study when they study culture. The "speaking" group's sub-culture was less obvious, but my interpretation was that perhaps they were practicing for the upcoming campus poetry slam. The students seemed to share a particular style of emphatic, rhythmic speaking, and a particular way of responding to each poem with encouragement. My observation supports the idea that sub-cultures exist on a college campus, and that they share certain, observable traits (dress, style of speech, interests, etc.).

EXAMPLE 2: Observation Notes for an Education Course

Student-Observer: Belinda W.
Student-Teacher: Sierra M.
11th Grade English, 9:00am Friday
May 7, 2014

Peer Classroom Observations: Sierra M.

1. Students were all on time, and many were early.
   Conclusion: They were obviously excited for the class and ready to begin.
2. The one student that was late apologized directly to Sierra after class and explained that he was held up for a class related errand.
   Conclusion: It was clear he respected her and the rest of the class.
3. The banter and conversation at the beginning of class was not that much different than the conversation during class.

Conclusion: The atmosphere was extremely comfortable. The students weren't intimidated by the dynamic of class and so felt comfortable to share their ideas.

4. The students did not talk over one another but almost all of them spoke.

Conclusion: They all seemed extremely respectful of one another and of Sierra, and they were invested in the group discussion.

5. They were all leaning forward over their desks.

Conclusion: All were engaged and wanted to be there.

6. Most of them did not raise their hands before they spoke.

Conclusion: The classroom dynamic resembled a conversation rather than Sierra wielding the power and directing discussion. The conversation also never dove off topic into an unproductive tangent.

7. Several students would refer to the previous student when they spoke, either disagreeing or agreeing with them.

Acknowledging that the dialogue was with the students and not necessarily with Sierra, they engaged respectfully with each other. It was very exciting to see students conversing with each other in such a positive way.

8. When one student was searching for the answer to a question posed the others chimed in to help him.

Conclusion: The students seemed to have solidarity with each other and Sierra.

9. Students would praise other students.

Conclusion: Sierra built a supportive atmosphere in the classroom.

10. Students stayed on topic the entire time.

Conclusion: Although Sierra was not necessarily directing discussion per se, the students understood that they were there to discuss language and rhetoric. Although the topic varied from song lyrics to advertisements to a short story they related it all to language and rhetoric.

11. The students disagreed with one another.

Conclusion: Students felt comfortable enough to engage and take opposing stances to the topics under discussion and allowed that one was not right or better than another.

12. The students were taking pictures with a camera that Sierra had brought in since this was the last class period that they had.

Conclusion: At first I thought this would be very distracting but it was actually a great way for the students to express themselves. Again, they were respectful with it and it turned out to be a bonding experience instead of a disruption.

13. The students participated in group discussion for the majority of the class period stemming from individual student's presentations on songs or advertisements.

Conclusion: Again, while there were several students that clearly felt more comfortable talking than others, I didn't notice any of them acting like they felt shut down. This was also a great way for students to have the center of attention if they wanted it while not losing the positive momentum of the group discussion.

14. They moved quickly from each student presentation to the next.

Conclusion: Once the conversation began to slow down about each topic, Sierra would suggest a new presenter. This had the effect of moving the class forward without shutting any one off too quickly or exhausting the conversation past productivity. It also allowed several students to have a few moments to speak about what they had brought in and many were clearly excited to share their song or advertisement with the rest of the class.

Final Thoughts: I was most surprised at the insightful comments that these students were making. They seemed far beyond the 11th Grade level, and I think that stemmed from the expectation of the class. Sierra expects a lot from the students, and they gladly rise to the occasion and beyond. I also found it to be an incredibly positive environment even while students were disagreeing with each other and bringing up controversial political subjects. I appreciated Sierra's frank conversation with her students. Her interaction with them was as respectful as her interaction with her peers, and, as a result, she has a class full of students that respect her back. I also appreciated Sierra's bold move to draw the attention to herself as a feminist at one point to make a point about audience. I think students could benefit from more interaction like this.

End: 9:50am

EXAMPLE 3: Observation Notes for a Chemistry Course

Observation notes for a chemistry course.

USE THE TOOLKIT

Let's use the three genre toolkit questions from Chapter 1 to examine this genre.

What Is It?

Like reading notes, observation notes are informal investigations—only they are investigations of *events* the writer has witnessed, rather than investigations of texts. The preceding examples provide observations of three different events or locations: students hanging out at a campus location, an English class meeting, and a scientific experiment. All three documents share similar qualities: (1) they are informal in tone and presentation; (2) they all have a title of some sort at the top, recording when and where the observations took place; and (3) they all record the author's investigations as they took place, usually in a chronological fashion.

Who Reads It?

Often, observation notes are only meant to be read by their author. Sometimes, though, students share their observation notes with their teacher or group mates. Zachary's observations were written as a sociology assignment. Belinda's student-teacher observation notes were written for her professor in her education course. Lab notes would be shared with a lab partner.

What's It For?

Students who write observation notes often must prepare a more formal project, such as a paper or a lab report, using the field notes as a primary source of data (Chapter 23). In Example 2, Belinda's notes serve two purposes: to provide feedback to a fellow student-teacher, Sierra, and to show Belinda's own knowledge about teaching to Belinda's professor.

EXERCISE 7.4: Conduct a Field Observation

Choose a location on or near your college campus. Plan to spend one hour observing a particular facet of social interactions at that location. For example, you might observe how often students are on their cell phones while ordering at the coffee shop, or whether or not people wipe off the gym equipment after using it. Take notes during your observation, and then write a one-page summary of your observations.

E. Strategies for Inquiries

Review Belinda's classroom observation of Sierra's student-teaching (Example 2). Imagine that you have been asked to write observation notes in a similar fashion, with a list of observations and then a list of conclusions to follow. This "double-entry" strategy is a great way to structure observation notes if you haven't been given a structure by your instructor. You can write your observations first, then reflect upon them later. Let's go step-by-step through this writing process.

Prewriting (Content)

When writing field notes, you will either be assigned a group or location to observe, or your instructor will allow you to choose what to observe.

If you are allowed to choose the group or location that you will observe, be sure to choose with care. You will be examining it very closely and spending a lot of time with the subject. You can select a location that is familiar to you, such as the student gym, but if you do, try to observe a specific action that you haven't noticed before. You can also select a location that is unfamiliar to you; in this case, try to record as much detail as possible about the people and the locale.

Check with your instructor to ensure that you are following best practices for informing your subjects about your observation and that you are not violating anyone's privacy or intruding on private space.

In Belinda's case, she was assigned a specific group to observe: Sierra's high school classroom. Belinda knew that she could not name any student names in her observation notes because naming names would violate the students' privacy.

Drafting (Organizing)

Be sure to put a heading at the beginning of your field notes. In the heading, identify the location or group of people that you observed. Record the date and time as well. Provide as many details as feasible about the observations in your heading.

Provide a title for your observations. Belinda titled her field notes "Peer Classroom Observations: Sierra M." This title informed readers about exactly what is contained in the field notes. (Example 3, the lab notes, is titled "Preparation of Salicylic Acid," another accurate and helpful title.)

Belinda initially took her field notes by hand. She drew a line down the center of a piece of notebook paper. She wrote observations on the left side of the line, and she wrote her conclusions based on those observations on the right side of the line. This kind of note-taking is called "double-entry" note-taking. Table 7.1 is an excerpt of her original notes.

Table 7.1 Belinda's Double-Entry Notes

OBSERVATIONS	CONCLUSIONS
Students were all on time, many early	Excited for class to begin
The one student that was late apologized directly to Sierra after class and explained that he was held up for a class-related errand	Respect
The banter and conversation at the beginning of class was not that much different than the conversation during class	Comfortable, not intimidated, relaxed dynamic

Revising (Style)

Although field notes are informal in style, if someone besides the note-taker will be reading them, they must be revised carefully. Be sure to use complete sentences in your revision, even if you wrote your original notes in fragments.

Belinda revised her double-entry notes into an organized list of observations. After each observation, she wrote a conclusion. She labeled her conclusions with the word "conclusion" so that her professor would understand the structure of her notes. She typed her notes neatly on her computer rather than turning them in handwritten.

Editing (Design)

Your heading and your time notations should be easy to read. You can type them in boldface or underline them if your notes are hand-written. These headings and notations are the structural bones of your observation notes.

Belinda's notes have two time markers: the start time and the end time of the class period. Because a class period is already well structured, the time markers are not as crucial. If you are observing a less structured event, such as a party or a similar informal gathering, time markers help your reader understand how much time has passed between each of your observations.

Troubleshooting

Here are some common challenges that students face when writing inquiries.

What if people want to talk to me?   Although your role is more of an observer than a participant, if someone wants to talk to you, record that conversation as part of your field notes. If your teacher agrees, you should explain what you are doing there and ask them if it's OK with that person for you to observe and take notes.

What if I can't think of an interesting place to observe?   Every potential location can be an interesting place to observe—you are responsible for making the observation interesting. Even if you are in a familiar place, like a coffee shop, start paying close attention to all of the people there. What are they doing, exactly? What kinds of conversations are going on? Eavesdrop a little bit. Stand by the counter and really watch what the baristas are doing back there. What sorts of jobs do the workers do? Why? When examined closely, even your regular coffee shop can appear as a whole new world.

You should discuss with your instructor whether you should get the permission of the baristas or the manager to stand there and observe. You don't want to get in the way or cause other inconvenience!

F. Chapter Project: Write Observation Notes

Conduct a field observation of a location on your campus to evaluate how well campus resources are utilized by students. Any location on campus is open to your observation. For example, you might observe how often students stopped to pay attention to the artwork on display in the Student Union, or how many students used a video game room in the Student Union over the course of an hour.

Spend one hour at the location, keeping track of how many people come and go, recording what they do and whatever else you notice. (What kinds of games were played in the video room? Were there more men or women?) Revise your notes and type them up so that you can share them with the student affairs office.

Group Option: Comparative Field Observations

As a group, conduct the field observation requested by the student affairs representative in the Chapter Project (Section F of the chapter). Each group member should record his or her own field notes at a different time of day.

Once the observations have been gathered, compare your field notes to those of the other observers in your group. How similar are these notes? How different?

As a group, compile your notes into one "master" version that you can share with your student affairs representative.

Multimedia Option: Presentation of Findings

Put together a presentation, such as a PowerPoint, presenting your findings (Chapter 29). Be prepared to deliver a talk on your findings (Chapter 30).

Analyses

An analysis is a document that helps readers to interpret information. The goal of an analysis is to break down complex information into its components. For example, during a football game you might see an expert analyzing a play in slow motion, showing the blocking, the quarterback's motion, the receivers' routes, and so on. They might then offer an interpretation of why that play was effective (or not).

In college, analyses are common assignments. You are probably familiar with some types of analyses already, such as a literary analysis. In humanities courses, analysis is often used to interpret texts—a short story, a work of art, or a speech, for example. In other courses, though, you may be asked to analyze information, such as the latest trends in consumer preferences for a business class (a market analysis) or common themes in a series of interviews you conducted for a sociology class (a content analysis). In a film class, you might write a scene analysis. In each case, the goal is to take something complex (a data set, a series of transcribed interviews, a film) and break it into simpler terms by identifying common features or patterns.

In the workplace, you may be asked to write an analysis for a number of reasons. If you work for a library, you might be asked to analyze the needs of community members (community analysis). If you work for a retail company, you might be asked to analyze demographic information about customers (customer analysis). An engineer might analyze the energy efficiency of a building (building analysis). Business consultants analyze the performance and goals for companies using a SWOT analysis, which stands for "strengths, weaknesses, opportunities, and threats." In the health sciences, lab technicians perform various kinds of analyses, such as a blood type analysis or an analysis of an x-ray or image. In all of these cases, the writer's goal is to process complex information for the audience, using key concepts or patterns to make that information manageable.

In this chapter, you will learn to write several kinds of analyses. We will focus on the types of analyses you will be most likely to encounter in college humanities courses, but keep in mind that the genre toolkit can help you to discover other kinds of analyses that you may encounter in the future.

A. Analysis Mini-Genre: Keyword Analysis

Take a look at the following images.

EXAMPLE 1: Keyword Analysis of a Speech

President Barack Obama's speech announcing the death of Osama bin Laden.

EXAMPLE 2: Keyword Analysis of a Court Opinion

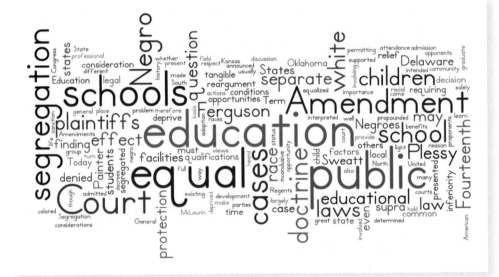

Brown v. Board of Education, U.S. Supreme Court, handed down in 1954.

EXAMPLE 3: Keyword Analysis of a Government Document

The Declaration of Independence, drafted by Thomas Jefferson, delivered July 4, 1776.

USE THE TOOLKIT

Let's use the three genre toolkit questions from Chapter 1 to examine this genre.

What Is It?

All of these images provide fodder for a kind of analysis, called a *keyword analysis,* in which a long text is broken down by the words it contains most often, or its keywords. The size of the words in a word or tag "cloud" indicates their frequency in a text—the bigger the word, the more often it is used. You may have seen similar kinds of keywords analyses—often called *word clouds* or *tag clouds*—on blogs and websites. Sometimes, bloggers will post a keyword analysis showing the categories they post about most often.

The keyword analysis examples shown here were made using a service called Wordle (http://www.wordle.net), which allows users to make these images and post them in a public web gallery.

As the reader, you can then examine the keyword analysis and *interpret* what it means. The keyword analysis shown in Example 1 analyzes President Obama's May 2011 speech announcing the killing of Osama bin Laden. Example 2 analyzes the Supreme Court opinion for *Brown v. Board of Education,* the 1954 decision that led to desegregation of American schools. Example 3 analyzes the text of the Declaration of Independence from Britain of the American Colonies. In each case, the most common words tell you something about the text. For example, the word "children" figures prominently in Example 2, which you might interpret to mean that the Supreme Court justified their decision in part by appealing to the audience's concern for children.

Who Reads It?

Keyword analyses are usually read by visitors to websites, where they may be posted, or by scholars who study language and rhetoric. For example, a scholar hoping to analyze the language used in the Declaration of Independence might include a keyword analysis in a research paper (Chapter 11).

What's It For?

Keyword analyses can give you a sense of what a text is about. They provide a visual tool to help you interpret the text, giving insight into its main themes and ideas. For instance, in Example 3, you might notice that the word "powers" figures prominently. Why is this the case? You might look at instances of the word "powers" to determine why the word is so central to the Declaration of Independence.

Or, in Example 1, you might consider why the words "country" and "people" appear more prominently in the speech than such words as "justice" and "security." What effects do these kinds of words have on an audience? If you wanted to say more about Obama's speech, you might write a longer analysis using some of the tools of rhetoric. In fact, you could write a rhetorical analysis, an analysis genre that you will learn about later in this chapter.

EXERCISE 8.1: Do a Keyword Analysis

Choose a speech or text that you find interesting. You might go to AmericanRhetoric .com for a long list of famous speeches. Then, use a keyword analysis tool, such as Wordle (http://www.wordle.net) or TagCloud (http://www.tagcloud.com), to do your own keyword analysis.

Next, write a paragraph or two in which you interpret your findings. What words were used most often in your sample? What might that say about the rhetorical situation for the speech—its effect on an audience, how it reflects the speaker, or what it has to do with the timing for the speech? Did the frequency of certain words—or their infrequency—surprise you? Did you find what you expected? (See Chapter 2 for more on rhetorical situations.)

MULTIMEDIA EXERCISE 8.1: Customize a Keyword Analysis for Particular Audiences

Keyword analysis tools give you a range of options for formatting your keyword analysis. You can choose fonts, colors, orientation (whether words are primarily vertical or horizontal), and so on. Create a keyword analysis based on a text, as in the preceding exercise, but then consider how you can customize it for a specific audience. To create your keyword analysis, you should:

- Select two different audiences who might be interested in your keyword analysis—such as readers of a particular blog, students at your university, experts on that topic, and so on. Consider how you might format your keyword analysis for two different audiences.
- Create a keyword analysis. Then, use formatting features to customize it for each audience.
- In a paragraph or two, explain how you altered the keyword analysis for each audience.
- Post your keyword analyses and your explanation to your course management system.

B. Literary Analysis

A keyword analysis is a simple tool for analyzing a text or document, but as we have seen it does not by itself provide much room for you to explain or interpret the analysis. Nor does it enable you to analyze a text using other kinds of tools or concepts. The genre of literary analysis is, in some ways, similar to a keyword analysis, but it involves analyzing a text using a range of concepts drawn from the study of literature.

● ●

EXAMPLE 1: Literary Analysis of a Novel

Morris Green
Assignment #3
Professor Burke
March 17, 2014

Christopher Boone as an Unreliable Narrator

In Mark's Haddon's novel, *The Curious Incident of the Dog in the Night-Time,* the main character is Christopher Boone, a boy who has Asperger's Syndrome. Asperger's Syndrome, a variant of autism, is a psychological condition characterized by difficulties with communication and social behavior. A person with Asperger's syndrome may have trouble interpreting what other people say or how they act, and may therefore seek refuge in special interests and rituals. According to this definition, Christopher Boone is an "unreliable narrator" (Booth 339), a narrator whose version of the facts is called into question either due to personality flaws or, in this case, a psychological condition. Yet, despite (or perhaps because of) his condition, Christopher is a remarkably observant narrator, one who does not lie, questions metaphorical thinking and favors literalness, and focuses on details that a neurotypical person might not see. The plot of *The Curious Incident of the Dog in the Night-Time* shapes the reader's gradual recognition that Christopher is, in fact, a reliable narrator and an unusually sharp observer of the world, despite his autism.

Readers of *The Curious Incident* might first notice Christopher's detailed observations of the world around him. At the start of the story, we learned that Christopher has been detained by the police—but we do not yet know why. If one has read the jacket cover, and knows that Christopher is meant to be a character with Asperger's syndrome, we might

> To shape his thesis, this writer first sets up a contradiction or paradox: Christopher is both unreliable and reliable at the same time. Then, he addresses this paradox with his argument: that the narrator, Christopher, represents a remarkably reliable storyteller.

wonder whether he has done something wrong, or wonder whether he is confused about what is happening to him. However, Christopher provides a detailed description of the police cell, noting that it is "almost a perfect cube, 2 meters long by 2 meters wide by 2 meters high" and that it "contained approximately 8 cubic meters of air." Christopher describes the "small window with bars" and the "metal door with a long, thin hatch near the floor . . . and a sliding hatch higher up" (16). All of these details create a vivid picture for the reader, but they also create credibility for the narrator. An unreliable narrator might relate details that do not seem to match what a police cell might be like. Hence, Christopher's credibility as a narrator increases.

> The writer uses quotations from the text as evidence.

    As Christopher works backward in time, telling his story beginning with the death of the neighbor's dog, we also learn that he does not lie: "A lie is when you say something happened which didn't happen," he explains. When Christopher tries to lie, he begins thinking about all of the other things that did not happen:

> For example, this morning for breakfast I had Ready Brek and some hot raspberry milkshake. But if I say that I actually had Shreddies and a mug of tea I start thinking about Coco-Pops and lemonade and Porridge and Dr Pepper and how I wasn't eating my breakfast in Egypt and there wasn't a rhinoceros in the room and Father wasn't wearing a diving suit and so on and even writing this makes me feel shaky and scared. (23)

Christopher dislikes this shaky and scared feeling, and avoids it at all costs. Christopher writes, "this is why everything I have written here is true." By relating his own opinions on lying, Christopher generates even more credibility as a narrator. If the reader takes his statements at face value, he or she will likely accept the truth of his story.

> The writer follows quotations with explanations and interpretations, showing why they are important.

Finally, one might question whether Christopher is using metaphorical language when he writes about key events. Is the neighbor's dog symbolic in some way? Did it actually die, or is the death of the dog meant to stand in for the loss of Christopher's mother? Again, Christopher's writing reassures the reader that a literal interpretation is to be used. Christopher insists that "people do not have skeletons in their cupboards" and that when "imagining an apple in someone's eye doesn't have anything to do with liking someone a lot and makes you forget what the person was talking about" (18). Here again, the reader learns that Christopher is unlikely to use metaphorical or symbolic language, and that we should take his story at face value.

In conclusion, Christopher comes across as a reliable narrator because of three key traits: his vivid observations, his insistence on not lying, and his avoidance of metaphorical languages. All of these traits are aspects of Asperger's syndrome, at least as it is portrayed in the book, and these very traits make Christopher come across not as unreliable, as one might suspect, but as more reliable than a person who does not have Asperger's syndrome. After all, the neurotypical person is likely to embellish their tale for greater effect, or to use symbolic language to emphasize the themes of a story. By avoiding these strategies, Christopher becomes an ultra-reliable narrator, one who draws the reader in with his candid voice and unique point of view on the world.

Works Cited

Booth, Wayne. *The Rhetoric of Fiction*. Chicago: University of Chicago Press, 1983. Print.

Haddon, Mark. *The Curious Incident of the Dog in the Night-Time*. New York: Random House, 2003. Print.

EXAMPLE 2: Literary Analysis of a Play

Ellen Chapman
21 February 2014

Women's Roles in Elizabeth Cary's *The Tragedy of Mariam*

"Are Hebrew women now transformed into men?" Constabarus asks his wife, Salome,
when she informs him that she will seek a divorce against him, a right legally guaranteed to
men only. This notion of gender-role reversal, explicitly stated in Act I, reemerges themat-
ically throughout the remainder of Elizabeth Cary's play, *The Tragedy of Mariam*. On the
surface, the play seems ambivalent in its presentation of opinions on women's appropriate
roles in society. For instance, Salome cannot gain a divorce from Constabarus because the
law forbids it, but she can manipulate her brother, King Herod, to have him killed. Upon
closer examination, however, this ambivalence is itself consistent throughout the play: although women do not step out of the bounds of their legally inscribed gender roles, they do
exercise immense (life and death) power from those restricted roles.

Salome's great influence is illustrated when she makes a deal with her other brother,
Pheroras, in Act III, Scene 1 (107, Ferguson Text). Pheroras has married Graphina without
Herod's consent. Now that Herod has returned, he is afraid that Herod will force him to
divorce his love. Salome, sensing Pheroras's fear, turns it to her advantage:

Salome. Well, brother, cease your moans. On one condition

I'll undertake to win the King's consent:

Graphina still shall be in your tuition,

And her with you be ne'er the less content.

Pheroras. What's the condition? Let me quickly know,

That I as quickly your command may act . . .

Salome. 'Tis [not] so hard a task: It is no more

But tell the King that Constabarus hid

The sons of Babas . . .

Salome exercises great power over Pheroras because she has great influence over Herod. She convinces her brother to betray her husband Constabarus for her, and ensures Constabarus's death. Pheroras explicitly states that he will follow Salome's "command"—control over the family lies in Salome's hands.

Indeed, control over the kingdom appears to lie in the hands of women. Once Mariam is betrayed, her son Alexander is threatened by Doris, Herod's first wife, who wishes her own son by Herod, Antipater, to take the throne after Herod's death. Salome and Doris ensure that the line of the Maccabean / Hasmonean Dynasty ends with Mariam's death. Although Doris was set aside by King Herod when he wished to secure his claim via marriage to Mariam, she remains an important voice in the play, conniving with her son to regain her former place of power. That her voice remains in the text suggests that association with a man—in this instance, Herod—does not dictate the force that a woman may exert upon public events.

The only character in the play that does not exercise influence over men appears to be the title character, Mariam herself. While other women in the court are conniving and exerting influence, Mariam refuses to lie: "I cannot frame disguise, nor never taught / My face a look dissenting from my thought." Despite being the title character, Mariam plays a small role in the play; her story is told—and her fate sealed—largely through the words and actions of other characters, further demonstrating her lack of influence and inability to exercise agency. For her refusal to woo herself back into Herod's good graces, Mariam loses her life.

Thus, two of the main female characters in the play, Salome and Doris, each exercise some power over men, albeit within the bounds of societal constraints. It is difficult to discern where Cary herself would fall in this debate from the words actually spoken by characters. However, the existence of this play—a tragedy named for a woman, with a tragic hero that is a woman and a hero's nemesis that is a woman, in which the men are merely pawns that women use to accomplish their own ends, in which women's speech comprises most of the actual text—suggests that Cary intends to show that women possess important power indeed, perhaps even *manly* power.

EXAMPLE 3: Literary Analysis of a Diary

Mark Washington
March 12, 2014

Household Battles in 1616 as Shown in Anne Clifford's Diary

The diary of Anne Clifford reveals that she was pressed between powerful men on all sides: her uncle, who would inherit her father's estate; her husband; the Archbishop of Canterbury; the King of England. Clifford's husband and the government wished her to renounce her claim to the estate in return for a cash settlement. Clifford and her mother argued that her father's barony should descend to the nearest heir, Clifford herself. It would be easy to read her diary and focus on the more public aspects of her texts. Her rebellion against the Archbishop and the King appears heroic, especially since the cause she stands for is her right to inherit, as a woman, her father's property. Clifford indeed demonstrates great bravery in the face of the public pressure applied upon her by powerful men. However, I argue that the tenacity that she demonstrates in private, at home with her family, shows even greater courage. For Clifford, it was at home that she took the greatest risks.

Throughout this text Clifford is pressured by men of public stature to relinquish her claim to her father's estate. Clifford seems to place her duty to her birth family above the obligation to obey her husband or even the King. Early in the text, Clifford is visited by the powerful Archbishop of Canterbury. They speak privately for "one hour and a half" (64). The Archbishop attempts to persuade Clifford, "both by divine and human means." Clifford states that she must confer with her mother before she can decide. Clifford's insistence on seeing her mother seems to suggest that the pressure she feels from her family outweighs the pressure from the powerful man. Perhaps her duty to care for her mother held more significance for Clifford: as a widow, Clifford's mother did not have a natural claim to her husband's estate. If her daughter were to inherit, then she would have greater access to her former property.

Clifford too has a daughter; by refusing to relinquish her claim she risks losing her. The diary suggests that Clifford's husband Sackville tries every method to coerce Clifford to sign over her rights. He wants to gain control over the funds from the settlement. Although Clifford demonstrates great bravery by refusing the wishes of the King, I argue that she feared even greater consequences by refusing her husband. The text suggests that she fears her husband more than she fears the King. Compare the language she uses to describe her husband's threats with the language she uses to describe the situation with the King. Clifford writes that Sackville "would come down and see me once more, which would be the last time that I should see him again" (67). With these words, Sackville threatens to abandon her. Sackville then calls to have their daughter Margaret taken away from Clifford. Clifford writes that this was "somewhat grievous to me, but when I considered that it would both make my Lord more angry with me and be worse for the child, I resolved to let her go" (67). Here, Sackville pressures Clifford by taking away her child. Compare Clifford's distress here with her descriptions of her interactions with the King.

After Clifford is locked into the King's visiting room with her husband and other powerful men, the King asks "whether we would submit to his judgement in this case" (80). All of the men agree. Clifford refuses and says she will not give up her property, "at which the King grew in a great chaffe." However, Clifford herself does not express much concern; rather, Sackville fears that Clifford will be in a "public disgrace" and appeases the King to save face. I argue that Clifford's language suggests a greater concern with the "private" consequences of her actions than with those of the "public" realm. She is devoted to her mother and her daughter; she fears her husband's power over her even more than she fears the King.

Overall, Clifford's diary offers snippets of a life hemmed in by male power, but one in which Clifford did show persuasive power, especially in private. Her tenacity in the face of attempts by men to disinherit her of her noble position is strongest in private, when the wellbeing of her mother and daughter are at risk. In this way, the diary exemplifies how women in the seventeenth century worked within their conscripted roles, exercising influence in private even when such power was denied to them in public.

USE THE TOOLKIT

Let's use the three genre toolkit questions from Chapter 1 to examine this genre.

What Is It?

A literary analysis breaks down a work of literature (a novel, poem, short story, etc.) into its component parts. In Example 1, Morris analyzes a novel, *The Curious Incident of the Dog in the Night-Time,* by examining how its main character is constructed. In Example 2, Ellen examines the roles of three female characters in a play.

A literary analysis usually takes the form of an essay, although it can also appear as a blog post or published article. The examples included here were all written for college courses in English literature. Example 3, for instance, was written for a sophomore-level literature course called Renaissance Women in Literature.

To analyze the text, writers use key tools for literary analysis (Box 8.1). For instance, both Morris (Example 1) and Ellen (Example 2) focus on characters. You can see that Morris used the concept of the "unreliable narrator" for his framework, while Ellen focused on how female characters were able to exercise influence within a constrained society.

Who Reads It?

A literary analysis may be written as a classroom genre, for students to write and teachers to read, but it is modeled after the kind of writing that literature professors do. Literary scholars value textual evidence—quotations from the original source— that are then interpreted by the writer. You can see that each of the student writers here includes quotations drawn from the source text. For example, Ellen includes a passage of dialogue from the play, while Mark includes quotations from Clifford's diary. Each writer then interprets those quotations, explaining their significance in the text.

A literary analysis may become a research paper (Chapter 11), which a literature professor would publish in a scholarly journal. You may also see a literary analysis on a blog or website. Often, readers of literature post their own analyses to share with other readers on their personal blogs.

What's It For?

The goal of a literary analysis is to interpret a particular literary work by breaking the literary work into parts and examining these parts. A writer of a literary analysis will examine features such as these: how the literary work affects readers; what the work means; how the work is crafted by the author; how the language functions; and how the author develops characters or plot.

A literary analysis tends to make an overall claim or thesis about the literary work in question. That is, a literary analysis makes an argument (Chapter 18) for a particular interpretation of a work of literature. Literary texts are open to many different interpretations, so your task as a writer is to convince your readers to agree with, or at least consider, your account of how the text works. For example, while Ellen argues that the female characters in the play were able to influence male characters, at least to some extent, another analysis might argue the opposite, drawing on other points of evidence in the text to make the case that women's attempts at influence were futile.

For any tool of literary analysis (Box 8.1) then, you can ask yourself these three questions:

- What is it? (Identify the feature)
- How does it work in the text? (Exemplify through quotations)
- Why does it matter? (Interpret the quotation)

Box 8.1   Tools for Literary Analysis

- **Character:** Who are the key characters? What traits do they have, and how does the writer show this? How do those characters develop or change over the course of the story?
- **Plot:** What are the key plot events? How does the plot drive the characters (or vice versa) or theme?
- **Setting:** Where does the story take place? How does the author convey the details of the setting? Why does the setting matter—how does it support the character development, plot, or theme?
- **Themes:** What are the main themes in the story? (e.g., secrecy, trauma, death, love?) How do those themes work their way into the character, plot, setting, and so on?
- **Imagery:** How does the author's language evoke images for readers? What kinds of images are created? Why do those images matter? How do those images support the character, plot, themes, and so on?
- **Symbolism:** Do any of the key images in the text "stand for" something else? Can they be understood as metaphors for key themes or ideas in the

text? Why do those symbols matter? Do they support the character, plot, themes, and so on?

- **Style:** What kinds of words, sentences, and patterns does the author use? What effect do those choices have? (See Chapter 21 for more on style.) Why do they matter—do they support the character, plot, themes, and so on?
- **Genre:** What type of literary genre is this (short story, poem, novel, etc.)? Does it fit into a sub-genre (e.g., romance novel, sentimental novel, mystery, suspense, etc.)? What are the typical elements of that genre, and how does the author use them?

EXERCISE 8.2: Write a Literary Analysis

Mark Haddon's *The Curious Incident of the Dog in the Night-Time* evoked controversy over its portrayal of an autistic character. Different writers have used literary analysis to weigh in on that controversy, paying close attention to how the text is written.

Choose another literary text that has proven controversial among readers in the last decade or so. Here are some examples:

- Kathryn Stockett's *The Help.* Controversy emerged in 2011 over its depiction of African American domestic servants and the white protagonist who tells their stories.
- Stephanie Meyer's *The Twilight Saga.* Readers debated the appropriateness of a love story between teenaged Bella Swan and Edward Cullen, a vampire who spies on his love interest while she sleeps and seems to control his girlfriend's behavior and friendships.
- Ellen Hopkins's *Crank.* This book narrates the story of a teenager's addiction to crystal meth and was challenged for being inappropriate for young adult readers given its realistic account of drug abuse.
- Stephen Chbosky's *The Perks of Being a Wallflower* or Jeffrey Eugenides's *The Virgin Suicides.* These books were often challenged for how they dealt with the reality of suicide.
- James Frey's *A Million Little Pieces.* This faux-memoir was controversial for its exaggerations of real-life events.

First, do some research on the controversy surrounding your text. Then, imagine you have been asked to contribute a piece to a national magazine explaining why your text is controversial. What elements in the text are controversial, and how do they work? For example, you might analyze the dialogue in *The Help* or the characters in *The Twilight Saga.* Write a literary analysis that breaks down your text, showing how it works and why it might be controversial.

GROUP ACTIVITY 8.1: Roundtable Presentations

As a group, stage a presentation (Chapter 30) about a controversial novel. Imagine your novel has been challenged by some parents in your local school district, and the school board is considering banning the book. Each of you will make a presentation at the next school board meeting. (See the list in Exercise 8.2 for ideas of books that might be banned.) Each of you will choose a different role: literary scholar, school teacher, concerned parent, student, and so on. Try to choose roles that might represent different viewpoints on the book's value for students.

Each group member should prepare a four-minute speech in which you use literary analysis to explain the merit (or lack thereof) of your novel. Your classmates can then ask you questions about your analysis and vote on a course of action (to ban the book or not).

MULTIMEDIA EXERCISE 8.2: Podcast of a Literary Controversy

Follow the guidelines for Group Activity 8.1. Instead of presenting your roundtable to the class, prepare a ten-minute podcast to be aired on your local public radio station or posted to a local news website. You can appoint one person to be the moderator or narrator for your podcast. Your podcast should include different analytical perspectives on the novel in question.

C. Scene Analysis

While a literary analysis takes a text as its object of analysis, a scene analysis takes a film as its object of analysis. For a scene analysis, you use the concepts drawn from the study of film to analyze a particular part from that film.

A scene is usually defined as a unit of the film that occurs within a single location and continuous time. A scene ends when the action shifts to a different location or time.

EXAMPLE 1: Scene Analysis of *Brokeback Mountain* (excerpt)

Kerri Zuiker

Brokeback Mountain Reunion Scene

In director Ang Lee's 2005 film, *Brokeback Mountain,* two cowboys meet one summer

for a sheep herding job on Brokeback Mountain and fall in love. Because of the time period—their initial encounter is set in 1963—they have to keep their relationship a se-cret, and spend the next twenty years trying to balance having wives and families with continuing their relationship. The tagline of the film, "Love is a force of nature," suggests that these two men are drawn together by something powerful and natural. The physical location of Brokeback Mountain is also an integral part of their relationship, as it is only on that mountain that they can truly be free and express their love for one another without society closing in on them.

In the scene of their first reunion since working together on Brokeback, Jack Twist and Ennis del Mar have not seen each other for four years. During this time, they've both got-ten married and had children. One day, Jack sends a postcard to Ennis, telling him he'll be in the area. Ennis writes back accepting the invitation to meet up again, and the next scene shows Ennis waiting anxiously at the window of his apartment for hours for Jack to arrive.

The scene starts off with a close-up of Ennis waiting anxiously at the window, smoking a cigarette and flicking the top of his lighter open and shut as he stares out. There is some non-diegetic music in the very beginning of this scene, being a sound bridge over from the previous scene, and it consists of a single guitar playing single chords slowly.

The next shot is an eyeline match of Ennis's view of the parking lot and street outside his apartment. This shot helps to establish the setting. We see the drab parking lot, a cloudy gray sky, and pale buildings. There is very little green in the immediate area except for a few trees on the far side of the lot and the mountains far off in the distance. This is in stark contrast to the beautiful landscapes of Brokeback Mountain. Also in contrast to the stun-ning colors of the mountain is the setting of the apartment. The walls are all yellow and brown, pale in comparison to the greens and blues of Brokeback. The furniture is close together and cramped in contrast with the wide open spaces of the mountain. The lighting is also very dark, with most of the lighting in the apartment being what sunlight comes in from the window. Even later in the evening, when there are lights on in the house, the apartment still seems very drab and dull-looking, nowhere near the brilliance of the sunlight that was present on the mountain.

After Ennis and his wife Alma have a short chat, and Ennis shoots down her idea of taking Jack out for dinner, he goes back to the window, opening another beer bottle and lighting another cigarette to wait for Jack. There is a shot that parallels the first in the scene, a close-up of Ennis sitting at the same place near the window. He repeats the motions of lighting up another cigarette and smoking it as he stares out the window. This shows his anxiety about Jack's arrival, and that his mind is on nothing else besides seeing Jack again.

The next shot cuts to Ennis sitting on the couch, with Alma and one of their daughters sitting at the kitchen table in the background. Ennis's posture reflects the fact that he's almost given up on Jack showing up. He's slouching on the couch, his forehead resting on one hand and his eyes closed. Around him are six beer bottles, which clues the audience in to about how long he's been waiting for Jack. Ennis only moves when he hears the sound of a truck offscreen pulling into the parking lot. He looks up then stands up and goes over to the window, where we see him smile for the first time in the scene. There is another eyeline match that shows a long shot of Jack getting out of his truck in the parking lot.

Ennis rushes out of the apartment to greet Jack, and for the first time in the scene we see Ennis happy and smiling, instead of muttering and with a somber look on his face. This shows the audience that even after four years, the two characters still have affection for each other, and that for Ennis, his relationship with Jack might be more satisfying than his relationship with Alma. He runs down the stairs and they embrace each other fiercely. During this interaction, they are shot mostly in close-ups, always showing the two of them and never just one person.

EXAMPLE 2: Scene Analysis of *Chinatown*

Kevin Mikkelson
Scene Analysis: *Chinatown*
Director: Roman Polanski
Starring: Faye Dunaway, John Huston, Jack Nicholson
Year Made: 1974

The first scene of the film opens with a close-up shot of black-and-white photographs of a couple making love in a field. A person is off-camera, flipping through them. Each image is more sordid than the last. A man's voice is making painful squawking noises as he sees each one. The camera slowly pans out from the photographs to reveal the full scene: a rumpled man viewing the photographs, standing in front of a desk in a neat office. Another man, private investigator J. J. Gittes (Nicholson) is seated behind the desk, watching the man, presumably his client and the husband of the woman in the photographs. The client is rumpled looking, his hair standing on end. In contrast, Gittes is dressed in a crisp white suit, its cleanliness belying the "dirtiness" of the work he does: catching cheating spouses with a camera lens. Gittes does not seem to be enjoying his client's suffering, in fact, his facial expression reveals disgust at the whole situation.

The client throws the photographs in the air, punches the wall, leans against the window blinds, and cries, his body hunched over. The camera films him from the back, revealing his portly body and wooden blinds and beige drapes. Gittes's office is well kept; he is presumably a successful P.I. Gittes says to his client, "Enough's enough. You can't eat the Venetian blinds; I just had 'em installed on Wednesday." Gittes pours a cup of liquor from a bottle stored in a glass cabinet behind his desk and hands it to his client, saying, "Down the hatch."

His client says, "She's no good."

Gittes replies, "What can I tell you kid? You're right. When you're right, you're right. And you're right!"

The camera cuts to the exterior of the office, where a young, pretty secretary in a gray flowered dress stands and files papers in a filing cabinet. A metal fan blows, indicating that the weather is warm. The window behind her is filled with glass bricks, and the light fixture is early twentieth century: altogether, the scene fixtures indicate a warm climate and an era earlier than the date the film was made, perhaps the 1930s or 1940s.

Gittes and his client enter from behind camera left, Gittes with his arm draped reassuringly over his client's shoulder as he ushers him from the office. We hear muffled conversation as they approach, and then these final words from Jake to his client: "I don't want your last dime. What kind of a guy do you think I am? [*some words of thanks from the client*] Call me Jake." Jake's demeanor belies his words here, though. He seems like just the kind of guy who would take your last dime. He preys on the emotionally weak and vulnerable, makes his living on their pain—a good enough living to buy a fancy white suit and new blinds for his office. This opening scene creates a character portrait, then, of

Gittes. And, as his character is challenged during the course of the movie (beginning with his very next client, the fake Mrs. Mulray), he grows less mercenary, gaining empathy and a moral compass.

EXAMPLE 3: Scene Analysis of *Apocalypse Now*

Leo Cooper
February 16, 2014

Mr. Clean's Death and Use of Sound in *Apocalypse Now*

Apocalypse Now is well known as a visual masterpiece. The film, produced and directed by Francis Ford Coppola, includes breathtaking scenes of the Vietnamese jungle, memorable shots, in near darkness, of Captain Willard's encounters with the renegade Colonel Kurtz, and eerie close-ups of Willard's eyes. However, one should not overlook the masterful use of sound in the film. In particular, the scene of Mr. Clean's death on the Nung River demonstrates how the film employs sound—music, sound effects, and narration—to convey the mood of the film.

This particular scene is a study in contrasts. It opens peacefully, with a shot of the water trailing behind the boat as it sails down the Nung River. Calm flute music plays and birds chirp as one of the crewmen hands out the mail. The shots cut from crewman to crewman, each opening and reading a letter. Yet, there is a note of foreboding as we hear a voiceover in which Willard reads a letter he has just received from on high. We see an over-the-shoulder shot, with the camera focused on the letter, as Willard reads the note that the last person sent out to track Kurtz has gone over to the other side. The music gets a little slower and more ominous in tone, in a minor key.

The ominous tone in the music builds to a crescendo as a purple flare is set off, shrouding the boat in a violet haze. Dialog continues, with the men joking around and reading from their letters, when suddenly we hear the sounds of shots being fired from the bank of the river. We hear shots pinging off the metal of the boat, the men screaming war cries, and the metallic sounds of the crewmen shooting back. The camera angles get more and more chaotic, with shots of the men shooting from different perspectives. Finally, when they emerge from the haze of smoke and out of the fire, the men realize that Clean has been shot in the maelstrom.

Suddenly it is quiet—the music stops—as Charles is called to check out Clean. The music starts again, this time the sound of a lonely flute, as the men come to realize what has happened. Meanwhile, we hear a woman speak in a voiceover from the letter Clean had presumably been reading prior to the attack: "Anyhow, do the right thing, stay out of the way of the bullets, and bring your heinie home all in one piece, 'cuz we love you very much. Love, Mama." The woman's voice conveys the sadness of the situation, and one of the men begins to cry. Meanwhile, the music shifts into a more surreal mood, accompanying the slow motion shots of the camera.

The scene is a masterful display of sound as well as cinematography. Indeed, while the images convey the chaos of the attack, it is the sound that conveys the mood of the scene, which shifts from calm to panic to a surreal kind of despair. This particular scene shows how the sound editor uses voiceovers, music, and sound effects to create this mood, contributing greatly to the overall power and significance of the scene in building dramatic tension as the men head further into the jungle.

USE THE TOOLKIT

Let's use the three genre toolkit questions from Chapter 1 to examine this genre.

What Is It?

These three examples are scene analyses. A scene analysis shares many features of a literary analysis and may even refer to some of the same concepts, such as character, plot, and setting. However, a scene analysis tends to focus on a discrete unit of a film—a single scene—and it uses concepts specific to filmmaking, such as lighting, sound, and camera movement. For instance, Kerri's analysis of *Brokeback Mountain* explains why the choice of lighting and set design matters, in terms of how it differs from earlier scenes, set outdoors in the mountains, and contributes to the central plot of the film, a love story between two cowboys. In Example 2, Kevin focuses mainly on elements of the setting, including the sets, props, and character's dress. In Example 3, Leo focuses primarily on the sounds in a particular scene from *Apocalypse Now,* including voiceovers, music, and sound effects. By narrowing their focus to certain elements, the writers create more coherent analyses—otherwise, they might have ended up with disjointed lists of observations.

Who Reads It?

A scene analysis is a common assignment for students in classes focused on film, including courses in literature, film studies, and foreign languages. Leo wrote his scene analysis (Example 3) for a literature course, where students read Joseph Conrad's *Heart of Darkness* before viewing and analyzing *Apocalypse Now,* an adaptation of Conrad's novella. Kevin's analysis was written for a film course taught in his college's Department of Art and Design. Film scholars use these same elements of scene analysis in their own research and writing. However, you may also find scene analyses written for a broader audience, such as on blogs or websites for fans of a particular movie or genre of movie.

One major difference between a scene analysis and a literary analysis is that it can be much easier to give examples in a literary analysis, because readers can read quotes from the text. For a scene analysis, you will need to convey details from the film instead, using descriptive language (Chapter 19). You can use several different types of evidence (Chapter 18): quotations from the dialogue of the film, still photographs from the film itself, or descriptions of the scene. You might even embed a clip from the film, or a link to an online clip, in your analysis. That way, readers could see the scene for themselves. If you are writing a scene analysis, consider how you can best convey the scene to your readers.

What's It For?

A scene analysis is used to show readers what decisions went into making a film, from the elements of the set design to the particular camera angles and shots used.

By examining these choices, the writer can then make an argument about the quality of the filmmaker's technique, or the screenwriter's script, or the actor's performance. For instance, Leo used his analysis to argue for the importance of the film's sound, not just its visual effects.

When writing a scene analysis, you can use analytical tools for Scene Analysis (Box 8.2). Be sure to ask these three questions:

- What is it? (Identify)
- How does it work in the scene? (Exemplify)
- Why does it matter for the film as a whole? (Interpret)

Box 8.2   Tools for Scene Analysis

- Lighting
- Sound: Sound effects, music, voiceovers, narration, etc.
- Camera angles and movement
- Perspective
- Space
- Foreground/background
- Set design

- Props
- Colors
- Dialogue or script
- Characterization: Actors' body language, movement, expression
- Blocking: Actors' positions on the screen
- Costumes, hairstyles, make-up

EXERCISE 8.3: Write a Scene Analysis

Imagine that you have been asked to contribute an essay to a special issue of an undergraduate literary journal on adaptations of literature for film.

Choose a story that has been made into a film. Identify a key scene from this story, and then locate it in the film. Here are some ideas:

- *Taming of the Shrew* (William Shakespeare) and *10 Things I Hate About You*
- *Emma* (Jane Austen) and *Clueless*
- *Romeo and Juliet* (William Shakespeare) and *Romeo + Juliet*
- *Othello* (William Shakespeare) and *O*
- *Heart of Darkness* (Joseph Conrad) and *Apocalypse Now*
- *The Help* (Kathryn Stockett) and *The Help* (film)

Analyze how your scene plays out in the original text and in the film version. If you'd like, you can compare multiple film versions (for instance, there have been a number of screen adaptations of *Romeo and Juliet*). What choices are made in the film scene to convey essential features of the plot, character development, and so on? How do the choices made by different filmmakers affect your overall impressions?

GROUP ACTIVITY 8.2: **Group Scene Analysis**

As a group, do Exercise 8.3. Have each member of your group select a different scene from the same literary work and write an analysis of how it functions in the film. Imagine that you are also contributing to a special issue of a journal on the film you have chosen. As a group, write the introduction to that special issue, highlighting the main themes or commonalities you uncovered in your individual analyses.

MULTIMEDIA EXERCISE 8.3: **Video Scene Analysis**

Do Exercise 8.3, but prepare a video presentation for your scene analysis. Imagine that your analysis will be submitted to a web-based undergraduate literary journal for a special issue on adaptations of literature for the screen.

   To get ideas, you can search for examples of student scene analyses on YouTube. You can use still shots and clips from your films, voiceovers, and text to explain how your scene functions.

D. **Rhetorical Analysis**

A rhetorical analysis can take as its object a film or work of literature, and it can consider many of the same elements. However, the central goal of a rhetorical analysis is to account for the effect of a work on readers or viewers. Rhetorical analysis can be applied to a variety of texts and even objects: speeches, editorials, articles, books, websites, and even works of art.

EXAMPLE 1: Rhetorical Analysis of a Government Document

Cody M. Poplin
English 102i

Rhetorical Strategies and Effectiveness
in the Declaration of Independence

   It is a document enshrined in America's foundation. It speaks of liberty, pursuing

dreams, and the annihilation of an oppressive government. It accomplished every goal conceived for it and is still studied today because of its historical impact. The Declaration of Independence is more than a letter from one vehement aristocrat to a King; it is what it was meant to be, a rallying cry of the soul and a standard for freedom. Through its resolute tone and formal style, the writers of the Declaration forged a rhetorical piece with various strategies, and ultimately changed the shape of the world.

Historians accredit the transcription of the Declaration to Thomas Jefferson. The future president of the United States held a powerful position in the Virginia House of Burgesses, and he was influential in the crafting of American ideals of Republicanism and the expansion of this new Nation. But to credit the entire document to one man would not do it justice. Fifty-six men signed the Declaration that affirmed war with Great Britain was inevitable and obligatory. While every one of them played a commanding role in the formation of the document, one must believe that Jefferson spoke for more voices than those of a few men when he penned, "We hold these truths to be self-evident, that all men are created equal."

Jefferson proclaimed without fear that King George III, the named audience of the text, must suffer the consequences of his tyrannical actions. He enumerates the "usurpations" of the British Crown, such as taxation without consent, and the amassing of troops in the Colonies. The document begins by stating that decent respect for the "Law of Natures God" calls the revolutionaries to "declare [that] which impel them to separation." This statement conjures up ideas of a greater cause than merely human desires that should be granted, and this theme is carried throughout the manuscript as justification for the Colonist's actions. Another intended audience of the Declaration of Independence was the citizens of America themselves. The intrepid assertions would cause one to rise to bravery and rally to join one's fellow compatriots.

   Jefferson's primary goal, and that of the signers of the Declaration, was to bind themselves to their resolution, list out the grievances of the people, and inspire others to fight. These goals were accomplished through listing of facts, persuasive wording, expounding on the offenses of the monarchy, and claiming that the revolution was of a higher calling. By employing a variety of rhetorical strategies, the writers of the Declaration of Independence created the first document that was truly for the people, by the people.

- -

EXAMPLE 2: Rhetorical Analysis of a Novel

Kelly's Blog
Kairos, Violence, and *The Hunger Games*
Posted by Kelly Simpson

In an interview, Suzanne Collins, author of the bestselling book series *The Hunger Games,* shares what prompted her to write about a dystopian society in which children compete in televised war games:

> there is so much programming, and I worry that we're all getting a little desensitized to the images on our televisions. If you're watching a sit-com, that's fine. But if there's a real-life tragedy unfolding, you should not be thinking of yourself as an audience member. Because those are real people on the screen, and they're not going away when the commercials start to roll.

Collins herself suggests that *The Hunger Games* is more than a novel—it is an argument. The book seeks to persuade readers that our media culture inappropriately glamorizes violence and desensitizes us to the human costs of war. That argument gains force through the timing, or *kairos,* of the book and the cultural events from the 2000s that made it relevant to readers.
   The timing of *The Hunger Games* helps to explain why it can be read as an argument against media violence. The book was published in 2008, seven years after the United States declared war in Afghanistan, and five years after the Iraq War began. Both wars were prominently featured on television, with live footage being broadcast

around the world. However, until 2009 the United States had a ban on portraying images of fallen soldiers from that war, so viewers did not generally see the human toll of those wars. Images of dead soldiers or citizens in Afghanistan and Iraq were seldom shown, either.

At the same time, American viewers were inundated with a variety of reality television shows that seemed to celebrate violence, from Ultimate Fighting Championships (a no-holds-barred style of fighting with few rules) to reality shows such as *Jackass* and *The Real World*, which featured various forms of drunken debauchery and violence.

Concerns were raised about violence in music and other media after the 1999 Columbine massacre and a string of other school shootings throughout the following decade. In 2001, the United States Surgeon General released a report on youth violence, citing the Columbine massacre as its exigence, and in 2003, the American Psychological Association released a major report citing media exposure to violence as a key cause of aggressive behavior in youths. Youth violence was a major topic of discussion in the years leading up to the novel's release.

Thus, after a decade of war, reality television, and real life violence, the topic of children, war, and violence was timely, or kairotic, in 2008, when *The Hunger Games* was issued.   5

EXAMPLE 3: Rhetorical Analysis of a Public Controversy

Carlos Fernandez-Smith
English 112
October 31, 2013

Appraising *The Help*: *Ethos* and *Logos* in Critical Accounts

In 2011, the film *The Help* was released to great fanfare. An adaptation of the bestselling

book by Kathryn Stockett, the film version boasted a star-studded cast, including Emma

Stone, Viola Davis, Octavia Spencer, Bryce Dallas Howard, Jessica Chastain, and Cicely

Tyson, and it generated buzz early in the award season, later garnering four Academy

Award nominations. Yet, not everyone was enamored with the film, which tells the story of

a young white woman in the segregated Mississippi of the early 1960s, a woman who sets

out to tell the stories of the black women who served as maids in white women's homes.

While praised by some as an insightful portrayal of the struggles black women faced, others heavily criticized the film. In their assessments of the film, critics relied on the rhetorical appeals of *logos* (or logic) and *ethos* (or credibility). In fact, I argue that the combination of these two appeals is what made these criticisms persuasive.

Critics of the film tended to employ three main logical arguments: that the film was historically inaccurate, that it relied on threadbare racial stereotypes and stock characters, and that it misrepresented African American speech patterns. Perhaps the most prominent critics of the film's historical accuracy were members of the Association of Black Women Historians (ABWH). They issued a public statement about the film in 2011, arguing that it included many historical inaccuracies. For instance, members of the association claimed that the film overlooks historical evidence showing that many African American domestic workers were subjected to sexual harassment, exploitation and physical abuse at the hands of their employers. The ABWH states further that the film ignores the context of the Civil Rights movement in Mississippi, aside from a nod to the assassination of Medgar Evers in 1963. The film does not portray how Mississippi residents organized demonstrations in protest of his death, showing instead street scenes of "utter chaos and disorganized confusion." Indeed, Roxane Gay notes in her article that the film portrays the main African American characters, the maids, as oblivious to or uninterested in Civil Rights, even though the Civil Rights movement would have been in full bloom at the time the film is set. These claims rely on logos, or an appeal to the reader's sense of logic. By citing historical facts, the writers hope to shift readers' opinions about the film.

As many film scholars have noted, contemporary movies continue to offer limited roles to African Americans. Often, these roles depend upon stereotypes, such as the "magical negro," which sociologist Matthew W. Hughey describes as a "stock character that often appears as a lower class, uneducated black person" who helps to "save and transform disheveled, uncultured, lost, or broken whites . . . into competent, successful, and content people" (544). Critics argued that, in *The Help,* the main African American characters are "magical negroes," inspiring the white protagonist to complete her book about "the help." In an article in *The Rumpus,* author Roxane Gay notes that *The Help* contains "not one but twelve or thirteen magical negroes who use their mystical negritude to make the world a better place by sharing their stories of servitude and helping Eugenia 'Skeeter' Phelan grow out of her awkwardness and insecurity." By casting the characters in *The Help* as stereotypes, Gay makes a logical argument: in short, the film should be considered negatively because it traffics in stereotypes, and stereotypes are bad.

Critics also protested the use of another stock character, the Mammy, who is perhaps best exemplified by the character played by Hattie McDaniel in the film adaptation of *Gone With the Wind.* Until the 1960s, the Mammy character was one of the only ones African American actresses could hope to play. As scholar of African and Afro-American Studies Charlene Regester writes, such roles meant that African American female characters would remain "an indistinct figure, a shadow, in a film's background" (3), even if some actresses, like McDaniel, were able to "reform" the stereotypical role into one of power and agency (161). In the case of *The Help*, the Association of Black Women Historians noted that the Mammy character "allowed mainstream America to ignore the systemic racism that bound black women to back-breaking, low paying jobs" by representing domestic servants as "asexual, loyal, and contented caretakers of whites." For the ABWH, these roles did not provide actresses such as Octavia Butler or Viola Davis (who played two of the main roles) with an opportunity to reform the stereotyped roles. Although they are describing characters here, these claims are fundamentally part of the writers' use of logos: they make claims and support them by reasons. In this case, the writers use examples to support their claim that the characters in the film represent racial stereotypes.

In addition, both Gay and the ABWH members criticized the language used by the characters in the film. Gay argued that "The over-exaggerated dialect spoken by the maids evokes cowed black folk shuffling through their miserable lives singing Negro spirituals," while the ABWH argued that the dialect made a regional linguistic variation into a "child-like, over-exaggerated 'black' dialect." It is notable that both critics use the term "over-exaggerated." In doing so, they portray the film not only as inaccurate, but also suggest that the inaccuracy was intentional, molding the characters into stock caricatures rather than granting them a more realistic (and perhaps less comforting) role.

All of these logical claims work, in great part, because the writers of these critiques possess external ethos. The ABWH's members are all professors of history at major universities in the United States. Their statement appears on the ABWH home page, which includes the logo of the organization, and is signed by five of its members. Each member lists their affiliation with a university and the ABWH organization. The statement also starts off by invoking the title of the organization in the first line. In this way, the statement establishes the ethos of its authors, and we are to trust their arguments in part because they are made by scholars who have studied African American history extensively. This makes their claims that the film is historically and culturally inaccurate more compelling.

Likewise, Gay's article relies on different forms of external ethos. The end of the article includes a short biographical statement, which tells us that Gay is herself an accomplished author, who has published stories in *Salon*, *Brevity*, *Ninth Letter*, and other literary magazines, and a co-editor of a literary magazine, *PANK*. Yet, Gay also generates ethos within the text by identifying herself as an African American woman, by relating her own personal responses to the film, and by referring to her own views, as a writer, about the challenges of writing "across race." For instance, Gay begins her article by describing how reading and viewing representations of African American history can be "painful," "frustrating and infuriating," since such representations make her realize that, if born at a different time, "I too could have been picking cotton or raising a white woman's babies for less than minimum wage or enduring any number of intolerable circumstances far beyond my control." By invoking her own identity, Gay builds credibility. Her own racial background matters because she is discussing a film that purports to represent her history. Later, by detailing her own struggles as a writer to "get it right" when writing about another ethnic group, she builds credibility by portraying herself as fair minded and at least somewhat sympathetic to the creators of *The Help*.

Thus, critics of *The Help* tend to rely primarily on logical claims, or *logos*, but the success of those claims depends in great part on their ethos, both internal and external. Their criticisms likely hold sway with readers who trust that, as credible, informed speakers, the ABWH and Gay have viewpoints that should be valued. Despite the criticism lobbed by Gay, the ABWH, and others, though, *The Help* went on to box office success and at least some critical acclaim. Does this mean that critics were unsuccessful in their rhetoric? By raising these important issues, the ABHW and Gay were successful, at least, in creating awareness among some viewers that the film should be viewed critically.

Works Cited

Gay, Roxane. "The Solace of Preparing Fried Foods and Other Quaint Remembrances from 1960s Mississippi: Thoughts on *The Help*." *The Rumpus.* August 17, 2011. Web. October 23, 2013.

Hughey, Matthew W. "Cinethetic Racism: White Redemption and Black Stereotypes in 'Magical Negro' Films." *Social Problems* 56.3 (2009): 543–77. Print.

Jones, Ida El, Daina Ramey Berry, Tiffany M. Gill, Kali Nicole Gross, and Janice Sumler-Edmond. "An Open Statement to the Fans of *The Help*." Association of Black Women Historians. Web. October 21, 2013.

Regester, Charlene B. *African American Actresses: The Struggle for Visibility, 1900–1960.* Bloomington, IN: Indiana University Press, 2010. Print.

USE THE TOOLKIT

Let's use the three genre toolkit questions from Chapter 1 to examine this genre.

What Is It?

Like a literary or scene analysis, a rhetorical analysis identifies key concepts or features of its chosen text and then gives examples and interprets those examples. The rhetorical analyses presented here take different texts as their focus. Example 1 uses a government document, the Declaration of Independence. Example 2 focuses on a novel, *The Hunger Games,* and Example 3 focuses on opinion pieces (Chapter 10) written about a film, *The Help.* Unlike a literary or scene analysis, these rhetorical analyses focus not only on the quality of the texts, but how they are used to persuade an audience. In order to persuade, a text (or film) needs to make an argument and try to convince readers to accept it.

Notice that each writer chooses a different set of rhetorical tools for analysis. In Example 1, Cody focuses on tone and style. In Example 2, Kelly focuses on the timing of *The Hunger Games* (Chapter 2). In Example 3, Carlos focuses on the rhetorical appeals to logic (*logos*) and credibility (*ethos*) (Chapter 18).

If you are writing a rhetorical analysis, you might choose to focus on rhetorical concepts such as those listed in Box 8.3. In fact, you might consider some of the same concepts you are learning to think about in your own writing.

Who Reads It?

A rhetorical analysis may be written by students in a writing or rhetoric class, but it is also modeled after the kind of writing that rhetoric scholars produce. You may also see a rhetorical analysis in a news blog, magazine, or website. Kelly posted her rhetorical analysis of *The Hunger Games* on her course blog. Increasingly, experts use rhetorical analysis to explain the effectiveness of key speeches, such as the president's State of the Union address.

What's It For?

The goal of a rhetorical analysis is to explain how a text affects readers—why it persuades them, and what kinds of arguments it makes. In Example 1, Cody considers why style choices in the Declaration of Independence would have appealed to audiences in the 1770s. In Example 3, Carlos tries to account for why some readers found criticisms of *The Help* persuasive—even though the film went on to great success. Thus, the point of a rhetorical analysis is not simply to list out rhetorical features of a text, but to interpret them in terms of how they might affect readers.

Once again, you can use these three questions to guide your rhetorical analysis:

- What is it? (Identify the rhetorical strategy)
- How does it work in the text? (Exemplify)
- Why does it matter? How would it affect readers? (Interpret)

Box 8.3   Tools for Rhetorical Analysis

- *Ethos* (credibility) (Chapter 18)
- *Pathos* (emotions and values) (Chapter 18)
- *Logos* (reason and logic) (Chapter 18)
- Style (Chapter 21)

- Arrangement (organization) (Chapter 20)
- Delivery (presentation) (Chapter 29)
- Rhetorical figures (metaphor, simile, antithesis, etc.) (Chapter 21)
- Audience (Chapter 1)
- Timing (*kairos*) (Chapter 2)
- Purpose (Chapter 1)
- Genre (Chapter 1)
- Argument or claim (Chapter 18)
- Evidence (Chapter 18)
- Rhetorical situation (Chapter 2)

EXERCISE 8.4: Plan a Rhetorical Analysis

Step 1. Identify a current controversy. For example, identify something that is happening on your campus or something that is in the news.

Step 2. Compile a list of sources that pertain to this controversy. Check the editorial page of the newspaper or search online for blogs or other sources.

Step 3. As you read or listen to these sources, see if you notice patterns in the arguments that people are making about this controversy. Do the arguments tend to center around *timing* ("This isn't the right time to act.")? Do the arguments tend to center around appeals to *ethics* ("We should act because it is the right or moral thing to do.")? Use the Tools for Rhetorical Analysis (see Box 8.3) to help you identify five common rhetorical strategies in the texts surrounding your selected controversy.

Step 4. Compile a list of rhetorical strategies and the examples of each strategy that you have located in your texts.

E. Strategies for Analyses

Imagine you have been asked to write an analysis that will help people to understand a text, film, speech, or controversy. We'll take as our example a project one student, Carlos, worked on: a rhetorical analysis of the controversy surrounding the film *The Help*. Let's see how Carlos got started.

Prewriting (Content)

Carlos began by collecting his sources, for empirical research (Chapter 24), or primary sources. This included opinion articles from online newspapers and magazines, an official statement by the Association of Black Women Historians (ABWH), and database sources (Chapter 24), such as a scholarly article about stereotypes in film.

Carlos read each of his sources, making notes on his observations. For example, here is how he marked up the statement by the ABWH.

<hr />

EXAMPLE: An Open Statement to the Fans of *The Help* (excerpt)

On behalf of the Association of Black Women Historians (ABWH), this statement provides historical context to address widespread stereotyping presented in both the film and novel version of *The Help*. The book has sold over three million copies, and heavy promotion of the movie will ensure its success at the box office. Despite efforts to market the book and the film as a progressive story of triumph over racial injustice, *The Help* distorts, ignores, and trivializes the experiences of black domestic workers. We are specifically concerned about the representations of black life and the lack of attention given to sexual harassment and civil rights activism.

> *This is the main claim of the Statement.*

During the 1960s, the era covered in *The Help,* legal segregation and economic inequalities limited black women's employment opportunities. Up to 90 per cent of working black women in the South labored as domestic servants in white homes. *The Help*'s representation of these women is a disappointing resurrection of Mammy—a mythical stereotype of black women who were compelled, either by slavery or segregation, to serve white families. Portrayed as asexual, loyal, and contented caretakers of whites, the caricature of Mammy allowed mainstream America to ignore the systemic racism that bound black women to back-breaking, low paying jobs where employers routinely exploited them. The popularity of this most recent iteration is troubling because it reveals a contemporary nostalgia for the days when a black woman could only hope to clean the White House rather than reside in it.

> *Logos / facts: This paragraph provides one reason to support the main claim, that the film glorifies domestic servants using the Mammy figure.*

Both versions of *The Help* also misrepresent African American speech and culture. Set in the South, the appropriate regional accent gives way to a child-like, over-exaggerated *"black"* dialect. In the film, for example, the primary character, Aibileen, reassures a young white child that, "You is smat, you is kind, you is important." In the book, black women refer to the Lord as the "Law," an irreverent depiction of black vernacular. For centuries, black women and men have drawn strength from their community institutions. The black family, in particular provided support and the validation of personhood necessary to stand against adversity. We do not recognize the black community described in *The Help* where most of the black male characters are depicted as drunkards, abusive, or absent. Such distorted images are misleading and do not represent the historical realities of black masculinity and manhood.

Furthermore, African American domestic workers often suffered sexual harassment as well as physical and verbal abuse in the homes of white employers. For example, a recently discovered letter written by Civil Rights activist Rosa Parks indicates that she, like many black domestic workers, lived under the threat and sometimes reality of sexual assault. The film, on the other hand, makes light of black women's fears and vulnerabilities turning them into moments of comic relief.

Similarly, the film is woefully silent on the rich and vibrant history of black Civil   5
Rights activists in Mississippi. Granted, the assassination of Medgar Evers, the first Mississippi based field secretary of the NAACP, gets some attention. However, Evers'

assassination sends Jackson's black community frantically scurrying into the streets in utter chaos and disorganized confusion—a far cry from the courage demonstrated by the black men and women who continued his fight. Portraying the most dangerous racists in 1960s Mississippi as a group of attractive, well dressed, society women, while ignoring the reign of terror perpetuated by the Ku Klux Klan and the White Citizens Council, limits racial injustice to individual acts of meanness.

We respect the stellar performances of the African American actresses in this film. Indeed, this statement is in no way a criticism of their talent. It is, however, an attempt to provide context for this popular rendition of black life in the Jim Crow South. In the end, *The Help* is not a story about the millions of hardworking and dignified black women who labored in white homes to support their families and communities. Rather, it is the coming-of-age story of a white protagonist, who uses myths about the lives of black women to make sense of her own. The Association of Black Women Historians finds it unacceptable for either this book or this film to strip black women's lives of historical accuracy for the sake of entertainment. . . .

When brainstorming for an analysis, first focus your attention on the text, like Carlos does. Your ideas should come from carefully reading or observing your object—whether it is a literary text, a speech, image, or film. You should read or examine your object several times, making notes about what seems interesting or significant to you.

Use tools for rhetorical analysis to guide you. As Carlos read his text, he focused first on the logic, or *logos,* of the piece, and then on *ethos* (Chapter 18).

Make notes on the text itself—often, highlighting and marking up a text can help you to deepen your analysis. You can do the same for an image or shot from a film—use digital tools to circle or mark key elements.

As you take notes, consider which of the key concepts or questions stands out for you, as a reader or analyst of your key object. Usually, an analysis focuses on a small set of concepts available, not all of them. If you simply run through every possible concept (say, *ethos, pathos, logos,* timing, and style for a rhetorical analysis), then your essay might end up rather disjointed—more like a list of observations than a coherent interpretation.

In his notes on the ABWH statement, Carlos seems to have noted the presence of *logos* and *ethos* several times. This became the focus of his essay.

Developing a Claim

Once you have noticed patterns in your notes, you might begin to formulate a key claim or thesis.

Take a look at the examples in this chapter. What kinds of claims do authors make?

If you think back to the purpose of an analysis—to explain how something works—that should tell you about the kinds of claims that are expected. An analysis is not like a review (Chapter 9), which evaluates whether something is good or bad. While you might mention which particular elements of your text are effective or ineffective, your primary focus is on explaining *why* this is the case, using the tools and concepts of the field you are studying (such as literature, film, or rhetoric).

Carlos tried out a few different claims, or thesis statements, based on his subject:

- Critics of the film *The Help* were persuasive largely because of their *ethos*.
- Criticisms made of the film *The Help* draws on the *ethos* of the writers as well as logical arguments; readers might trust the logical arguments because of the *ethos* of the writers.

Carlos decided that the second option would give him a more interesting angle for his analysis, because he could discuss the strategies used in the statement and also write about how they are connected.

You might also formulate a thesis that responds to what others have said about your object of analysis (Chapter 18). Perhaps you have read other analyses of your object that tend to overlook a key factor or offer an interpretation with which you disagree. For instance, Carlos saw that some bloggers and online magazines recast criticisms as "slamming" the movie or as "blasting" the film. These viewpoints, Carlos might argue, make the statement seem more like a rant or tirade, not the kind of measured response he interprets in their language.

Of course, you might also develop or modify your claim after you have begun drafting your essay and organizing your notes.

Drafting (Organizing)

When you are ready to draft your analysis, you can, of course, use any of the drafting strategies you find useful (Chapter 17). There is no one, correct way to draft an analysis. However, writers of analyses tend to use some of the following strategies:

- **Begin with your evidence**. You might start by grouping together the evidence you'd like to use for your analysis: quotations or passages (in a text) or key images (for a film). Then, consider how you might order those pieces of evidence. Do they fit into any patterns or groups? Writers often organize their evidence first, and then write the parts that introduce that evidence and interpret it. Carlos began by jotting down the main logical claims that he found in criticisms of *The Help* and then writing a section explaining how those claims worked. He then did the same for a section on *ethos,* showing how each source drew upon the credibility of its author.
- **Provide information your audience will need before they can get to the analysis.** Does your audience have the background information needed to go straight to the analysis? Or do they need to know something before they get started? For a work of literature or a film, the reader might need to know the overall plot before they can focus on the analysis. For a rhetorical analysis, your reader might need historical context: where was a speech given, or when was a text published? Your answers to these questions will help you draft

material for the first part of your analysis. Carlos began his analysis by briefly describing the film—when it came out, how it was received, and what it was about—before introducing the controversy he would analyze.

- **Frame your analysis in terms of popular or critical reception.** For this particular genre, you might consider introducing and/or concluding your analysis with a discussion or summation of scholarly or popular interpretations of your subject. For instance, Carlos started by discussing the critical reception of *The Help* by popular media critics, but he might have also begun by summarizing what scholars have said about the portrayal of domestic servants in film.

Revising (Style)

Keep in mind the following style tips when revising your analysis.

Use Appropriate Terminology.   Once you have a draft, focus on using the language of the discipline in question. For example, for a literary analysis (see Box 8.1), you should draw on terms related to literature, including the key concepts you may have discussed in class. Similarly, for a film analysis (see Box 8.2) you should employ terminology related to film. Pay attention to the terms your instructor uses in class, and try to work those into your essay. Carlos not only used the terms *logos* and *ethos* (Chapter 18), which he had learned in class, but also distinguished between "external" and "internal" *ethos,* to refer to *ethos* already possessed by the writer and to *ethos* generated within a text, respectively.

Introduce and Interpret Quotations.   You should also consider what language you use to introduce and interpret quotations and examples. If you look at the sample papers included in this chapter, you will see that writers often introduce quotations using phrases such as the following:

- "Christopher provides a detailed description of the police cell, noting that . . . " (Morris)
- "Gay argued that . . . " (Carlos)

You'll see they also follow quotations with sentences such as these:

- "This shows his anxiety about Jack's arrival." (Kerri)
- "By invoking her own identity, Gay builds credibility." (Carlos)

Each quotation is introduced and then interpreted. You should never insert a quote or example without framing it with your own language in this way.

Use Descriptive Language.   Keep in mind that your reader may not have read the text (or seen the film) you are talking about. Accordingly, you should use descriptive language where necessary (Chapter 19) to help the reader understand or picture what you are discussing. Notice how Kerri refers to the "drab parking lot, cloudy gray sky, and pale buildings" in the scene she analyzes from *Brokeback Mountain*.

Editing (Design)

As you edit and format your paper, keep in mind the formatting your audience expects. For a formal scholarly paper, you'll use citations and follow the paper format of a particular citation style. Because he was writing his paper for an English class, Carlos used MLA style (Chapter 28).

For an online format (such as a blog post or online article) you can use hyperlinks, embed video, and use highlighting or different colors for emphasis.

Troubleshooting

Here are some common challenges that students face when writing analyses.

I can't come up with a thesis.   Generating a thesis or claim for an analysis can be quite difficult, especially if you think of your essay merely as an exercise or assignment written for the teacher. Instead, think about how you can respond to what others might think about your subject, or what others have said about it. Then, you have an occasion to make an argument. Do some critics find that your favorite film is shallow or fluffy, but you think it actually has depth? Can you argue that those who focus on the style of your author overlook how she uses logical appeals? Do some research to get a sense of what others have said, and remember to correctly quote, paraphrase, summarize, and cite their arguments (Chapter 28).

I can't find any . . . (*pathos*, imagery, etc.).   Sometimes, students go down the list of concepts available for analysis as though it were a scavenger hunt and are then surprised when they come up empty-handed. "Why is there no symbolism in this paragraph?" they wonder. "Why is there nothing remarkable about the camera angles in this scene?"

Not every concept will be relevant to your analysis in every case. If a certain concept does not seem to apply to your object, that is fine. In fact, the lack of a concept may in itself be noteworthy. Why might a filmmaker choose to use a single, static camera angle for a scene? Why might a speaker avoid making overly emotional appeals? You might be able to come up with an interesting interpretation to explain why this is the case.

My analysis is boring.   Your goal as an analyst of a literary, rhetorical, or artistic text is to identify something interesting about it—something other people have not noticed. The most obvious observations are not always the most interesting. In Carlos's case, simply noting the presence of *ethos* and *logos* seemed less interesting than considering how these rhetorical appeals interacted. Focusing his attention in this way gave Carlos an interesting angle on his topic.

When you review your own notes, you might look for elements that seem surprising to you—for example, unexpected for the genre or rhetorical situation, or unusual for the author in question. You might also do some secondary research about your subject—the speaker or author, the rhetorical situation, timing, and so on—in order to develop a deeper understanding of how the text you're analyzing functions.

F. Chapter Project: Write a Rhetorical Analysis

Write a rhetorical analysis of a current controversy. Your task is to compose an analysis of one or more key texts involved in that controversy. To do so, you must undertake the following steps:

- Identify an object of analysis.
- Identify rhetorical concepts you will use for your analysis.
- Find examples to support your analysis.
- Interpret the significance of your findings for the controversy you are addressing.

If you get stuck, read over the section on *Strategies for Rhetorical Analysis.*

Group Option: Prepare a Networked Rhetorical Analysis

As a group, follow the assignment guidelines for the Chapter Project. Each member of your group will work on a different object of analysis networked to the same controversy. For example, if you wanted to analyze the controversy surrounding climate change (and what to do about it), you could each choose a key text—a speech by the president, a statement by scientists, an opinion piece by a politician, and so on. Then, you would each prepare an analysis of your text(s).

Collect your analyses together. As a group, write an introduction to your rhetorical analyses that identifies the key issues at stake in your controversy and provides an overview of the rhetorical strategies it entails. Make sure that your introduction also shows how the texts you analyze relate as a network.

Multimedia Option: Prepare a Digital Rhetorical Analysis

Complete the Chapter Project, but instead of preparing a traditional print document, compose your rhetorical analysis in an alternate format: a video analysis, screencast, podcast, or website. You should consider which media formats will allow you to provide evidence and interpretation of your object. (For example, a video format is a natural fit for a rhetorical analysis of a speech or film, but might not lend itself as well to the analysis of a text; a podcast might be a good fit for an analysis of a speech.)

Reviews

A review is a critical appraisal of something based on criteria by which the reviewed item is measured. Review genres include book reviews, film reviews, theater reviews, music reviews, concert reviews, and basically any other review of an event, publication, or performance.

In college, you will encounter a variety of review genres. For example, you might be asked to write a paper that uses elements of a book review. Your professor might ask you to compare two books by the same author with one another, or to compare a book with its film adaptation. In these scenarios, you might begin the essay by evaluating the books or films using review criteria you learn in this chapter. Then, you might move on to a literary analysis or scene analysis (Chapter 8). You might combine these strategies to put together a research paper (Chapter 11).

In professional settings, reviews serve an important purpose. Some reviews are journalistic, such as film or book reviews published in newspapers or magazines. These reviews guide moviegoers and readers. Still other reviews are written for the purpose of assessing and suggesting improvements, such as product reviews or website reviews. In business, you might be asked to write a review of an employee's performance or of the effectiveness of a particular department, policy, or program within a company.

In this chapter, you will learn how to investigate different types of review genres, including how to determine the criteria that authors use to evaluate the different items that they are reviewing. Criteria are simply the standards by which *anything* is judged (the design features of a car, the taste/texture/appearance of food). Before you can review something, you must get a sense of what criteria your readers will care about. For example, readers of car reviews care a lot about gas mileage and top speed, but less about the color of the oil cap.

Similarly, when you review a book, film, theatrical performance, or concert, you must read other reviews to discover what criteria readers of these reviews care about. Thus, part of understanding the genre of reviews is understanding the criteria as well.

A. Review Mini-Genre: Online Product Review

An online product review is a short evaluation of a product, posted by a consumer or user, on either an e-commerce site or a consumer information site.

EXAMPLE 1: Product Review of a Coffee Grinder

200 of 217 people found the following review helpful:

★ ★ ★   **So-so coffee, grinder stops working!,** August 11, 2013

By **Petra V.**— See all my reviews

This review is from: **JavaExpress Dual Coffee Maker & Grinder, Stainless Steel (Kitchen)**

I received this coffee maker and grinder as a wedding gift in 2012. I registered for this item after a fair amount of research: I wanted an all-in-one machine that would grind and then brew, and I wanted a burr grinder since I'd read it produces better coffee.

First, the good. It makes pretty good coffee, especially if you put it on the strongest setting. The coffee comes out plenty hot, and you can set it to grind and brew your coffee on a timer and wake up to fresh coffee. For a 12-cup coffee machine, it is fairly compact and doesn't take up too much room on my counter.

Now, the bad: For one, the plastic seems cheap. Also, the burr grinder gets clogged with beans and stops working. Then you have to try to fish out the beans, which is hard to do since the machine is big and bulky and you can't just dump them out.

Overall, though, this is a good machine if you want a burr grinder and coffee maker in one for a reasonable price. Just be careful to keep the grinder cleaned out!

EXAMPLE 2: Product Review of Computer Software

Does what it does, well. ★ ★ ★ ★ ★ by Keno—Jun 11, 2013, The Diptic app provides a simple interface for creating layouts of multiple photographs, while allowing customization of each photograph within the layout. I have two small kids that never want to sit next to each other for a photograph, so I use Diptic to create collages of photographs of my kids to share with family and friends. The application is simple and straightforward, with an easy learning curve. Highly recommended.

EXAMPLE 3: Product Review of an eBook Reader

USER jojo23 ★ ★ ★ ★ ★ **This is a great eReader for indoors and out!**

Posted August 3, 2013

I had my doubts about an e-ink ebook reader, because I really like my tablet. But now I carry both with me! This reader is great for reading outside in the sun, but the LED light makes it perfect for reading at night, too, and I don't wake my partner in bed when I want to stay up with a good book. The battery life is incredible, too.

USE THE TOOLKIT

Let's use the three genre toolkit questions from Chapter 1 to examine this genre.

What Is It?

These reviews are short documents that evaluate products that are for sale online. They all contain praise and criticisms of the products reviewed. All three sites share a five-star rating system, a space for a title for the review, and a space for the review itself.

The criteria that reviewers employ are commonly used standards by which we, as consumers, judge products: Is the product useful? Well made? Priced appropriately? Aesthetically pleasing? Durable? Functional?

Example 1, for instance, closely examines how well made the product is, in this case a coffee grinder. The reviewer discusses the materials and effectiveness of the product: the "plastic seems cheap" and "[t]he burr grinder gets clogged with beans." Example 2 is a review of computer software for laying out photographs; the reviewer discusses a specific purpose that she uses the software for, and that the software serves this purpose well: creating photo-collages of her children. Thus, for the reviewer in Example 2, the software is useful.

Who Reads It?

The primary audience for product reviews are people interested in buying the products, who read the reviews to determine if the products will meet their needs. A secondary audience includes the makers of the products, who read the reviews and update their products based on the feedback reviewers provide.

What's It For?

Interested buyers use consumer reviews to help them decide whether to purchase the product. The makers of the products use the reviews to help create better products in the future.

EXERCISE 9.1: Write a Product Review

Select a product that you have recently purchased and write a review of the product. Keep in mind the necessary elements of the review: a title for your review, a numerical rating system (such as zero to five stars), and an honest assessment of the product's strengths and weaknesses.

MULTIMEDIA EXERCISE 9.1: Write an Online Product Review

Select a product that you have recently purchased (for example, a book from Amazon.com) and review the product for a website that sells it. You do not necessarily need to have purchased the item from the website where you are writing your review. Keep in mind the necessary elements of the review: a title of the review, a numerical rating (if available), and an honest assessment of the product's strengths and weaknesses.

B. Film, Art, or Performance Review

Authors often write film, art, or performance reviews for newspapers or magazines. Students of film, art, or performance also write reviews for classes.

●●●

EXAMPLE 1: **Art Review Essay for a Composition Course**

Jacob Clayton
English 102i

Contrast, Art, and Justice

Contrast. This is the order of the day as one observes two pieces of art; one is a photograph showing a group of men trading livestock, and the other is John Wilson's "Native Son." The first image, showing the treatment of another creature as property, invokes thoughts of the dehumanization of African American's, and, in fact, the challenge facing all people who's skin tone separates them from society's status quo. On the other hand, "Native Son" depicts an African American as unmistakably human; the large, expressive eyes and thoughtful tilt of the head suggest that this is a man with hopes and dreams.

The dehumanization of minorities is a key player in the continuation of the death penalty; society is less hesitant to exterminate those deemed "less equal than others". The majority of those subjected to capital punishment are part of a racial minority, and this disproportionate distribution allows the public at large to keep their consciences burden-free. Like the pig in the picture, African Americans are often perceived as inferior to their white counterparts. Animal imagery has been related to African-Americans throughout much of Western literature, as demonstrated in Shakespeare's "Othello", where the Moorish General is characterized as an "old black ram".

This negative perception is unacceptable in a nation characterized by diversity, and America has made real progress against it. While the Dred Scott decision cast slaves as property, decisions like *Brown v. Board of Education* and *Plessy v. Ferguson* helped African-Americans gain the rights and respect due to human beings. Unfortunately, racism cannot be combated on only a grand scale; it is a personal decision that individuals are called to make. When we can fully embrace the diversity our nation offers, we will realize that it is beyond our moral qualifications to judge another human being in matters of life and death.

EXAMPLE 2: Katie's Album Review from Student Newspaper

Katie Fennelly

Of Montreal's New Album: A Mix of Weird Sounds and Intrigue

You're not supposed to judge a book by its cover, but sometimes you just have to. And sometimes that judgment is right.

The same goes when you first look at the cover of Of Montreal's newest album, "Paralytic Stalks." You're not really sure what's going on, but you're intrigued. It's colorful and exciting; it also kind of makes you uncomfortable.

The album's art reinforces what you'll hear on the band's eleventh album: a whole lot of weird.

Of Montreal is a band that's hard to explain. Not because its sound keeps changing, but because it is so different. Think a very theatrical, glam-pop version of The Shins or Queen, but probably on lots of psychedelic drugs.

5   "Paralytic Stalks" isn't necessarily a concept album. The band is primarily one man, Kevin Barnes, and the music is more of his personal opus than a record and for that reason, needs to play from beginning to end.

And although Of Montreal released the jazz flute-heavy "Dour Percentage" as the album's first single, "Paralytic Stalks" isn't full of songs that will find a home on your iPod's shuffle. While that can be frustrating for the casual listener, the creation of a complete album is something that needs to be celebrated.

"Paralytic Stalks" isn't necessarily easy on the ears, but that's probably the point. It's nearly an hour of thorny and extravagant psychedelic pop. The album blurs the line between music and art, which really is a line that should never have been drawn in the first place—I'm looking at you, LMFAO.

But if you can embrace the weird, this album is worth it.

EXAMPLE 3: Film Review

Film Review: "Epic"

Though visually gorgeous, animated film "Epic" disappoints with lackluster plot and performances.

Written by Nathan Cook
23 May 2013

Director Chris Wedge's ("Ice Age") new animated film "Epic" is a visually spectacular movie. It's easily one of the most gorgeous films so far this year: The trees sway in the wind, the light filters through branches and when magical things happen in the film, they look magical. Even the characters are beautiful. If "A Bug's Life" had fashion models, these tiny creatures would be them. (Hello, Beyonce.) Blue Sky Studios—the people who brought you the "Ice Age" franchise—have crafted something that is aesthetically stunning.

However, "Epic" feels a bit like a remake of 1992's "FernGully," albeit slightly more interesting and, well, epic than that. A city girl, Mary-Katherine (voiced by Amanda Seyfried, of "Dear John" and "Mamma Mia" fame), goes to reconnect with her estranged father, who spends his time trying to prove the existence of the tiny forest folk. It turns out that her father, voiced by Jason Sudeikis ("Saturday Night Live"), isn't crazy after all, proven when Mary-Katherine accidentally gets shrunken down to the size of these "leaf men." What follows is a fairly standard adventure that involves saving both the forest and Mary-Katherine's broken relationship with her father. There's a fairly ineffectual villain played by Christoph Waltz ("Django Unchained") who tries to turn the forest into rot, a foolhardy flying ace, Mary-Katherine's love interest, Nod (played by Josh Hutcherson of "The Hunger Games") and, of course, incredibly annoying sidekicks of the post-"Shrek" era trope who pipe up with cliched, misappropriated modern slang.

The actors are serviceable, although perhaps the only standout character is Colin Farrell ("Alexander," "In Bruges") as the stalwart General Ronin. He's so much more capable than our protagonists as a seasoned Leafmen warrior that you wonder why a Tinkerbell-sized teen and her cohorts are really necessary at all. In addition, the bumbling father character and his three-legged dog provide a good amount of both heartstring-tugging and comedic relief. Otherwise, everyone turns in an enjoyable performance, especially when it looks as lush and life-like as it does.

The design work is great—the Leafmen wear armor that is part-samurai, part-Celtic warrior and sit atop hummingbirds with tiny saddles. The locations all look nearly photorealistic; where most 3-D feels as if it turns the characters into cutouts on an otherwise flat plane (when it does anything at all), with "Epic" the audience feels like they could actually walk into the enormous forest on display. If given the chance to see this in the 3-D format, take it.

5   Aside from a bland story, perhaps the other major fault that the filmmakers stumble into is talking down to their audience. It's frustrating to find that many animated filmmakers believe younger viewers aren't smart enough to connect plot points, or, worse, assume that adults don't make up a part of their audience. [. . .] There's one scene in the first part of the film that features a mother literally explaining to her child what's going on in the scene, even though the film itself has already told the audience the story.

While it has its faults, "Epic" is a solid adventure film. Visually, it's Academy Award material. While it has a relatively bland plot, it sprinkles the proceedings with enough honesty, laughs and flourish that it's worth a watch. It's miles above many other animated films that have come out in recent years, and it's much better for families than films like "Escape from Planet Earth" and "The Smurfs 2" that somehow keep popping up in theaters. If you're looking to see some of the most stunning animation this side of Pixar, then you're in for a treat.

USE THE TOOLKIT

Let's use the three genre toolkit questions from Chapter 1 to examine this genre.

What Is It?

All three reviews are relatively short texts that assess an aesthetic production (a film, work of art, or performance). Each review begins with a "hook" to capture the reader's attention and also the details (such as the title) of the subject. Then the authors provides a basic description of the subject, and offer their evaluation of it.

As Jacob's art review, Example 1, is an essay, rather than a journalistic piece, it also provides the author's reflections upon the subject and connections with subject matter beyond the scope of the artwork. The second two reviews are more traditional reviews written for university newspapers. They provide assessment of the quality of the subject the authors reviewed.

The criteria the authors use depends on the media. For example, in Nathan's film review, he focuses on the plot, acting, visual effects, and animation, which are important criteria for evaluating a film.

Who Reads It?

Reviews published in magazines or newspapers may be read by the general public, but especially those interested in seeing a film, performance, or art show. A review essay written for your class may only be read by your classmates and teacher.

What's It For?

The main purpose of a review is to help readers to decide whether or not to see the production for themselves—whether to go see the film or attend a performance or art show. Sometimes, reviewers may explicitly recommend readers to do so (as in Nathan's review of the film *Epic*), while in other cases the recommendation is implicit.

EXERCISE 9.2: Write a Movie or Performance Review

Suppose you are a journalist writing reviews for your college paper. Your assignment is to write a movie or performance (play or concert) review.

Remember to include all of the facets of a review: a hook, a summary of the performance or movie, and an evaluation of strengths and weaknesses using criteria for the medium you have chosen to review.

Before you write your review, then, you need to examine reviews of the medium and determine the criteria that reviewers tend to focus on. Once you have a list of the criteria that you can use to evaluate the movie or performance you are reviewing, compose your review.

MULTIMEDIA EXERCISE 9.2

After you write your review, share it online through a service such as RottenTomatoes .com (a website where users can submit their movie reviews).

C. Book Review

A book review describes, analyzes, and evaluates a book or books. Book reviews often share qualities of movie reviews. However, some book reviews take on longer, essay-style qualities (as does the third review, following).

EXAMPLE 1: Book Review for a Blog

Brian Braden

Top Pick! Brian's 99 Cents: Review of *The Quill Pen* by Michelle Isenhoff

Like most of the books I review here on the Underground, I found Michelle Isenhoff's *The Quill Pen* in Amazon's discount slush pile. I didn't look at the cover, and I skipped the description. I just dove right into the sample and was immediately hooked.

The Quill Pen is the story of Micah, a boy on the cusp of manhood living in an east coast harbor village in the early 1800s. He dreams of life on the western frontier but cannot escape the shadow of his stern merchant father. Life is a series of mundane drudgeries for Micah until he discovers a mysterious quill pen while cleaning an old widow's attic. Not only can it write without ink, whatever one writes with it comes true. Micah eventually discovers the pen's dark secret, but not before it exacts a terrible price.

As I flew through the book, I kept thinking to myself how much my kids would love this. Then it dawned on me—this must be a middle grade or young adult novel. I usually don't read MG, or even YA, but I didn't care. I had to find out what happened next.

The young protagonist and supporting characters clearly put this novel in the MG/YA category. However, *The Quill Pen* is one of those rare books that defy being pigeon-holed because it is so well written. Isenhoff's quality prose, well-crafted dialogue, and richness of the historical setting make *The Quill Pen* entertaining for adults as well. She paints the characters with masterful strokes. Micah's post-colonial village comes alive with detail older readers will appreciate while keeping the plot clipping forward for kids. Isenhoff's prose is smooth, effortless, and sucks readers in immediately. Combined, these strengths give *The Quill Pen* a classic, almost Twain-like feel. This book is so well edited it could have come out of any major publishing house, a worthy feat for any indie author.

5   *Quill*'s only fault is it slows slightly in the middle, which might lose some MG readers. For older readers, this won't be an issue. It could also use a snappier cover worthy of the content inside.

The Quill Pen is suitable for any age capable of understanding the subject matter. Nothing here should concern parents.

The Quill Pen is delightful on every level. Isenhoff is an indie author worth keeping an eye on. This entertaining story of adventure, magic, and history is one of those gems of self-publishing that make this job so enjoyable.

This magical pen writes itself into my Top Picks with a score of 94 out of 99 cents.

• •

EXAMPLE 2: Book Review for a Website

Risa Applegarth

Review of *The Changeover* by Margaret Mahy

Another odd, interesting, tension-filled book from Margaret Mahy, with a frankness about sex that marks this book as coming from both another time and another place (New Zealand, 1974). The cover design and even the fonts in the Scholastic/Point copy I read take me right back to the rack of Christopher Pike and Lois Duncan books I worked my way through at the public library in the early 90s. The elements of menace, imagination, and romance came together more satisfyingly for me in *The Tricksters* than they did here, but I still enjoyed this thoroughly. Both of the Mahy books I've read so far play quite explicitly with the romance genre and its expectations—Harry is writing "a torrid romance" in *The Tricksters*, and Sorry reads romances by the dozen that Laura scorns—so I'm curious to see if that's a characteristic that runs throughout Mahy's work.

• •

EXAMPLE 3: Book Review Essay for an English Class

Adriana Lorenzini
March 2010

Gertruda's Oath by Ram Oren and *Habibi* by Naomi Shihab Nye:

A Book Review Essay

Every story has a thousand different perspectives. Every retelling of a story can be what

the storyteller honestly believes, yet two versions of the same story can sound completely

different. *Gertruda's Oath* and *Habibi* are both about the Palestinian-Israeli conflict, but

these books are very different. *Gertruda's Oath* recounts the tale of Michael, a Jewish boy,

and his nanny, Gertruda, and their escape from Nazi Poland to Israel. *Habibi* documents

Liyana and Rafik's adventures when they move to Palestine. Reading these two books as companion novels will impact the reader's perspective on the Palestinian-Israeli conflict differently than reading one book by itself. Reading these books together will represent both sides of the conflict, and provide insight into the causes and effects of the conflict as perceived by both sides. In this review I will start by writing two mini-reviews, about *Habibi* and *Gertruda's Oath*. I will summarize the books, discuss the authors, and analyze their structures (both books have uncommon structures). Then I will compare the two books, and discuss reading them together.

Naomi Shihab Nye was born in 1952, to a Palestinian father and an American mother (Wikipedia, "Naomi Shihab Nye: Wikipedia"). She grew up in St. Louis and later moved to San Antonio. She also spent part of her youth in Jerusalem, with her Palestinian family (The Steven Barclay Agency, "Naomi Shihab Nye"). She is the author of many novels and poetry collections (The Steven Barclay Agency, "Naomi Shihab Nye"). In 1997, Nye wrote *Habibi,* a novel about an American-Palestinian girl named Liyana who moves from St. Louis to Palestine. As you can see, *Habibi* is part memoir.

Habibi has an episodic structure which means that the book is a series of stories with the same characters. This structure makes it easy for Nye to keep the reader interested in the story, but work in several different aspects of the Palestinian-Israeli conflict. Rather than talk about one part of Liyana's life in Israel, Nye focuses on those of Liyana's adventures that highlight the Palestinian-Israeli conflict in an average civilian's daily life.

At the beginning of the story, Liyana and her brother Rafik live with their Palestinian dad and American mother in St. Louis (p.1). Then, their father announces that the family is moving to Palestine (p.3). "Poppy" wants his children to meet his Palestinian family and experience a different culture. Poppy's children have always lived in America, so they are hesitant at first. But after a month or so, Rafik and Liyana grow to love their new homeland (p.75). They go to school, make friends, see landmarks, and spend time with family (p.75). But now and then, among the engaging tales of pranks pulled and curious peoples encountered, the reader sees the conflict that prevails in Israel. The two children meet Khaled and Nadine, young refugees from a camp near Liyana's apartment (p.138). Nye makes the quartet's escapades the main story. But occasionally Nye pulls Khaled and Nadine's refugee status back into the spotlight (p.226). She does this to remind the reader of the terrible plight of refugees in Israel, and the circumstances that caused Khaled and Nadine to become refugees. Later, Liyana befriends a boy, Omer, and thinks he is Arab, then realizes he is Jewish (p.150). Liyana cherishes her friendship, but does not mention Omer to her family, because she fears they will disapprove of him and his religion (p.158). *Habibi* has many mini-climaxes, all showing different aspects of the Palestinian-Israeli conflict. Each provides a unique insight into the conflict.

Habibi is an amazing read, offering a new perspective on the Palestinian-Israeli conflict. The book highlights the Palestinian side of the conflict, and through the voices of Liyana, her family, and the people they encounter, the reader is able to better understand the Palestinian side of the conflict's motivations. Because the reader likes Liyana and Rafik, they are more open to listening to the Palestinian opinion and situation, because Liyana and Rafik are describing it. The book was entertaining and well-written. I would recommend it to anyone who enjoys novels about overcoming obstacles in a modern-day setting.

Ram Oren was born in Tel Aviv Israel in 1936 and is Jewish. He has lived in Israel for most of his life and has sold an unprecedented one million books in Hebrew. In 2008, Ram

Oren wrote *Gertruda's Oath,* and in 2009, the book was translated into English. *Gertruda's Oath* is a true story of the survival of a young Jewish boy, Michael Stolowitzky, and his nanny, Gertruda, during World War II. Ram Oren wrote the book because Michael Stolowitzky asked him to. It was written " . . . with Michael Stolowitzky's own extensive participation" (Ram Oren, *"Gertruda's Oath"*).

Gertruda's Oath has a disjunctive structure, which means that the book follows the stories of several different unrelated characters that now and then encounter each other. This allows Oren not only to tell a story, but also to develop and describe the different characters involved. The book opens with three story lines (those of S.S. officer Karl Rink, the Polish Stolowitzky family, and Gertruda Babalinski the nanny), and slowly they merge into one plot. This structure shows just how many different people, of different backgrounds, were dragged into WWII.

Michael Stolowitzky (a young Jewish boy), his family, and his Catholic nanny, Gertruda, live in a mansion in Warsaw, Poland (p.40). *Gertruda's Oath* is the story of what happens when these characters are separated by World War II. The book also tells the story of Nazi officer Karl Rink, and how Rink helps to save Michael and Gertruda (p.14). When the Nazis try and commandeer his factory, Mr. Stolowitzky goes to Berlin (p.72). While he is away, the Nazis invade Poland. Mr. Stolowitzky tries to get his family out of Poland, but fails (p.96). Michael, his mother, and Gertruda flee to Vilna, a village the Nazis have not occupied yet near Warsaw (p.112). There Michael's mother dies of a stroke (p.121). So Gertruda and Michael are alone in the world. Gertruda pledges to take care of Michael as though he were her own son, and when the war is over, to take him to live in Israel (p.122).

Karl Rink is also in Vilna, where he is stationed. He encounters Michael and Gertruda and saves their lives on one occasion (p.187). The book is a tragic tale of WWII, one of compassion and survival against all odds. *Gertruda's Oath* chronicles Michael and Gertruda's adventures as they flee death and the Nazis. In this amazing true story, Michael and Gertruda finally make it to Israel. But the book is about the journey, and all of the people who made it possible.

Where *Habibi* discusses the impact of the Palestinian-Israeli conflict, *Gertruda's Oath* is about the historical roots of the Israeli-Palestinian conflict. Jews consider Israel to be their holy land, and were already immigrating there before and during the war. After the war, the state of Israel was established to give displaced Jews a place to call home. Israel is holy above all other places to Jews, and many survived hell thinking that one day they would get there. These books helped me realize that the Palestinian-Israeli conflict is not just about land, it is about a country sacred to many people.

Reading *Gertruda's Oath* and *Habibi* as companion novels really helps the reader understand the Palestinian-Israeli conflict. I read *Habibi* first, and I immediately understood the Palestinian side of the conflict better. As a grandchild of Jewish grandparents, I have always been more exposed to the Israeli side of the conflict than the Palestinian side. When I read *Habibi*, I realized that not only is Israel sacred to the Palestinians for religious reasons, it is also sacred because it is their homeland. *Habibi* is about family and friendship in the midst of a conflict. Liyana and her family feel just as strongly about Israel as any Jew does. And reading *Gertruda's Oath*, I saw how important Israel is to the Jews. I can see how, now, when the Jews have lived in Israel for seventy years, they do not want to pack up and leave.

But reading *Gertruda's Oath* helped me realize that even before the establishment of Israel, Jews saw Israel as their original homeland, the land that they would one day return to. No side of the conflict will surrender, and reading *Habibi* and *Gertruda's Oath* together helped me realize why. Both sides of the conflict cherish Israel, and for the same reasons: Israel is sacred to them because of their religion, and special to them because it is their homeland. Both books are incredible. They tell stories of compassion and humanity in situations that seem to lack these qualities. Pairing these books together represents both sides of the conflict, and expresses the sensitivity and magnitude in a way that no one book can.

Works Cited

Oren, Ram. *Gertruda's Oath: A Child, A Promise, A Heroic Escape During World War II.* New York: Doubleday, 2009. Print.

"Naomi Shihab Nye." *The Steven Barclay Agency.* Web. 24 May 2011. http://www.barclay agency.com/nye.html.

"Naomi Shihab Nye." *Wikipedia.* Web. 24 May 2011. http://en.wikipedia.org/wiki/ Naomi_Shihab_Nye.

Nye, Naomi Shihab. *Habibi.* New York: Simon Pulse, 1997. Print.

"Ram Oren." *RamOren.com.* Web. 24 May 2011. http://www.ram-oren.com/biography.htm.

USE THE TOOLKIT

Let's use the three genre toolkit questions from Chapter 1 to examine this genre.

What Is It?

A book review is a text that summarizes and evaluates a book. A book review, whether short or long, contains two important qualities. First, the review provides an overview of the plot and characters of the book. Second, the review evaluates the book's strengths and weaknesses. A book review essay, a longer form of book review, might compare the book to other books; delve deeply into the characters and themes of the story; or connect the story to contemporary or historical events.

   The criteria that reviewers use to evaluate books include character development, plot, structure, dialogue, description, and the quality of the prose or writing itself.

Who Reads It?

People interested in buying books read book reviews. Book review essays sometimes attract a larger audience, as they are often read for their own sake, as essays. For example, some book review essays cover a broader topic (such as a current event, or an artist's life), and so attract an audience beyond readers who simply want to know whether to read a specific title.

What's It For?

The primary purpose of a book review is to summarize and evaluate a book so that readers can decide whether to read the book. Book reviews can also provide entertainment in and of themselves, by providing a biography of the writer's life or a comparative study of many books on the same topic.

EXERCISE 9.3: Write a Book Review

Suppose you have been asked to write a book review for your local newspaper. Think of a book that you have recently read, and write a short review. Be sure to include a brief summary of the plot and characters, as well as an evaluation of the strengths and weaknesses of the book. Use the criteria you discovered earlier in this chapter when you evaluate the book.

MULTIMEDIA EXERCISE 9.3: Write an Online Book Review

After you have written your book review, share it on a website such as Google Books, Amazon.com, GoodReads.com, or Barnes & Noble's website, sites where the public can post reviews of books.

D. Website Review

A website review describes, assesses, and makes recommendations for improving a website.

EXAMPLE 1: Website Review for an Online Forum

Forum: Redesign Critiques
Posted by Megan M.

Hello,
Sorry for the delay in releasing this post. I just didn't see it for some reason.

I wouldn't have realized that button did something until you pointed it out. You could try making it bigger or making it animate a little bit, like a pulse action.

There are a few things that I find disorienting about this site. The first is that you're advertising complete IT solutions but you seem to be mainly offering web design and development. I don't know, maybe it's just me, but I would think it would be easier to target the clients you're looking for by emphasizing web development instead (thinking of SEO). Or maybe this is just a regional terminology thing too—to me "IT solutions" means more hardware, networking, servers, things like that.

5   The other thing I find disorienting is that the words in the logo don't match the words in the domain (pdgroup.co vs. Prima DG in the logo). Even writing out the full company name in the logo might be better. What DG stands for might not be immediately obvious either.

Also, I find the font size used for the body area to be very small and hard to read. The descriptions of the services you offer are very, very, brief and quite vague. I would expect to see more there, including samples of previous work.

I hope that helps. Overall the site looks really good. I like the drawing, it gives a lot of character and uniqueness to the site. And I think it gives the impression that there are 6 people busy working away on my project.

● ●

EXAMPLE 2: Website Review for a Computer Course (excerpt)

Hester Cho
Engl 318: Composition and Multimedia Design

Healthcare.gov: Website Review

Since its launch in 2013, Healthcare.gov has proven controversial. Designed by a Canadian firm, the website immediately experienced functionality problems due to coding errors and bugs. However, less attention has been paid to the visual design, usability and layout of the site. Viewing the website from this perspective reveals additional problems; namely, a failure to consider users' needs and to simplify content.

Navigation

The landing page for Healthcare.gov provides three main options: "See plans before I apply," "Apply now for health coverage," and "See if I can get lower costs." These options appear in colorful circles on the center of the screen. However, the user can also click on additional options using a navigation bar at the top of the screen: "Learn" (with secondary headings for "individuals and families," "Small Businesses," and "All Topics"); "Get Insurance" (which leads to a different page, the Healthcare Marketplace); and Log In. The items on the navigation bar represent different types of actions—one provides additional information, another leads to a separate site, and a third leads to a log in page. Thus, the page suffers from an unclear hierarchy. Should one click on the circles or the navigation bar? The two navigation options compete with one another and may end up confusing the user.

Aesthetics

The site uses a color scheme of blue, orange, and white. On the main page, two of the circles are a darker shade of blue on a lighter blue background, and one circle is orange. The text is white. Each circle features an icon to help distinguish it further. The orange "Apply Now" circle is slightly larger than the other two. Overall, the front page is neat and visually appealing.

Accessibility

The lack of a clear hierarchical navigation scheme would make this website difficult for someone to navigate using a text reader or other assistive technologies. In addition, the three main circles are images, not text, so they might also prose problems for those users. In addition, the design may not provide enough contrast for users with visual impairments: the white text on a blue background, and the lighter blue circles on a darker blue background may pose problems. It is, however, possible to navigate the site using only a keyboard, so that is a plus.

Summary

Overall, Healthcare.gov suffers from design flaws that may compound the problems users have been having with the site's functionality. The unclear navigation scheme may dissuade users from signing up for healthcare, and may make use for people with disabilities especially problematic. This is especially disheartening since, presumably, people with disabilities might represent a large part of the audience for the site—people who lack health insurance and/or have been denied coverage before. Given the site's important role in enacting part of the Affordable Care Act, it is unfortunate that greater care was not taken in its design.

EXAMPLE 3: Website Review for a Composition Course

Jonas Webber
English 101

Website Review of Ravelry.com

Overview

Ravelry.com is a social networking site for knitters and crocheters. It contains a database of

patterns and other tools to help crafters.

Appearance

The home page features the Ravelry logo: a red ball of yarn with the site name. There is

also a tagline, "Where my stitches at?" which is a trendy play on words and gives the site

a youthful flair. Down the left, main column is the Ravelry blog, with the latest news and

updates about the site. Down the right column are widgets, such as a search window and a

short help menu.

User Interface

The site is easy to navigate. Across the top of every page is the same menu, no matter what

page you're on. The first option is "My Notebook," which is like a Ravelry member's "Face-

book" page. (Ravelry members are called "Ravelers.")

   The fonts are easy to read and the pages are laid out in a predictable fashion. Because the

site echoes other social networking sites, people who are familiar with social networks will

understand how this site works. For example, you can add other Ravelers as "friends" and

keep up-to-date on knitting topics in the forums.

Product/Service Enticement

The service this site offers is fortunately free. But even if it weren't free, as an avid knitter

I'd be willing to pay a nominal subscription fee, like ten dollars a year, for access to the site.

Suggestions for Improvement

The main flaw of Ravelry is that when you get a message on the site, the site is incapable of

emailing you a notification. Therefore, if you get a message but don't check your Ravelry

inbox all the time, you might not get the message in a timely fashion. Integrating external

notification would make Ravelry a better site.

Final Thoughts and Rating

On a scale of 100 points, Ravelry.com earns 95, because of the lack of external notification.

Otherwise, I highly recommend this site to knitters and crocheters.

USE THE TOOLKIT

Let's use the three genre toolkit questions from Chapter 1 to examine this genre.

What Is It?

A website review is a document that describes and evaluates the strengths and weaknesses of a website and makes recommendations for improvement, if any improvements are needed. These reviews usually feature several criteria, such as appearance, interface (how well the website interacts with users), and functionality (how well the website performs the task it is meant to perform). In Example 1, the reviewer pointed out many aspects of the website's appearance that could be improved on: a button's appearance, a confusing logo, and a font size that was "very small and hard to read."

Who Reads It?

Website reviews are often read by website owners or developers. Sometimes website owners commission reviews of their sites so that they can improve them. Teachers also assign students to write website reviews as part of class assignments, as in Examples 2 and 3.

What's It For?

Website developers and owners read reviews in order to learn how to improve their websites. For this reason, getting reviews from a variety of types of users is valuable. Website reviews can also help web designers, even student web designers, figure out what a good website looks like, so that they can design good websites in the future. In fact, only a few months after Jonas wrote his review of Ravelry .com shown in Example 3, the website added the feature that he suggested (email notification of messages received). Other reviewers of the website had made similar observations, and the web developers listened to those reviews and improved the site.

EXERCISE 9.4: Compare Three Websites

Pick three websites that sell similar products (for example, Nike, Adidas, and Asics; or Amazon, Barnes & Noble, and Kobo).

Using Table 9.1, the Website Comparison Chart, compare the strengths and weaknesses of the three websites. You don't need to write complete sentences.

Table 9.1 Website Comparison Chart

QUESTION	1.	2.	3.
Do you understand what the site is about?			
Is it easy to use? Can you find what you're looking for?			
Is the content strong?			
Do you understand what the text is saying? Do you notice any spelling or grammar mistakes?			
If this site is offering a product or service, would you sign up or buy it?			
Is the site attractive to you?			

GROUP ACTIVITY 9.1: Test and Review a Website

As a group, select an e-commerce website to test and review, such as Amazon.com or BestBuy.com. Separately, attempt to navigate the site, testing as many features as you can. Keep notes on how easy or difficult it is to use the website. Use the chart in Table 9.1 to help you keep notes, if you wish.

Come together and compare your experiences. Were there certain parts of the site that were easier to navigate than others? Did more experienced computer users have an easier time with certain aspects of the website, or was the site accessible to users of all computer skill levels? After you have compared notes, as a group fill out the chart in Table 9.1, taking into account everyone's experiences on the site.

E. Strategies for Reviews

Suppose you've been asked to write a website review, similar to Jonas's review in Example 3, on behalf of an academic department at your school. You would begin by familiarizing yourself with the department's website: read all the content, check to be sure all links work, and assess the quality and usefulness of both its content and its design using the criteria for website reviews.

To learn more about strategies for writing website reviews, we'll look at how Jonas composed his review of Ravelry.com.

Prewriting (Content)

Jonas used the following questions to get started with his review. He answered each question for Ravelry.com using the chart in Table 9.2. He didn't worry about writing in a formal fashion on this chart. He just took notes as he navigated the site.

Table 9.2 Website Review Prewriting Chart

Website Review Questions	Ravelry.com
Do you understand what the site is about?	Yes. The site is very straightforward about its purpose as a social networking and resource site for knitters and crocheters.
Is the site easy to use? Can you find what you're looking for?	The site is very easy to use and intuitive, at least for a basic user. I haven't tried to add patterns or serve as an "editor," but as a basic user, the projects page, the pattern search, and the forums are a breeze.

Is the content strong?	The content is user generated: users add patterns to the pattern database and yarns to the yarn database. I was surprised to find that the online knitting community was so strong and computer-savvy. The staff of volunteer editors keeps the databases accurate and up-to-date. The content is thus very impressive, and probably the best reason to join.
Do you understand what the text is saying? Do you notice any spelling or grammar mistakes?	Considering how much of the site is user-generated there are rarely any errors in the formal pattern or yarn pages. There are errors in the forums, of course, but those are informal areas of the site and no one expects them to be well written.
If this site is offering a service, would you sign up for it?	I'm not a knitter or crocheter, so Ravelry isn't for me. I surveyed some of my friends, though, to see if they would be interested in joining. Amazingly, all of my friends who do knitting or crocheting are already members! I was so surprised because I had never heard of Ravelry before signing up for this project.
Is the site attractive to you?	The visual design of the site is one of its strongest points. Their logo is a cartoon drawing of the company owner's Boston Terrier and a ball of yarn. The colors are saturated (not pastel or country-fied). This site definitely appeals to the younger, hipper knitter—which I didn't really know existed until I did this project.
What's the number one weakness?	I asked my friends, and they all said the same thing: They wish the website would email them when they received a PM (private message). After using the site for a while, I can see how it would be annoying to not know when someone sent you a message.

Drafting (Organizing)

Once you have brainstormed your review, you can begin to turn your answers to those questions into a document that you can share with others. Turn your notes into complete sentences. Be sure that you've included enough detail to help your reader understand what you are describing. Don't forget to evaluate the strengths and weaknesses of the site, and to make suggestions for improvement.

Jonas's chart, as you can see, contains a lot of what would become his final website review. The more prewriting you can do, the easier your drafting will be.

Revising (Style)

Because your review will be read by website designers, your review must be written in a straightforward and easily understood fashion. Consider using short sentences. Prefer the active voice. If your review will be read by the website owner, you can even use a tone of command, especially when making suggestions (e.g., "To increase readability, you should consider changing the font color from gray to black.").

Editing (Design)

Make your review easy to read by using headings to separate material into chunks. Jonas used useful headings to break up the sections of his review: "overview," "appearance," "user interface," "product/service enticement," "suggestions for improvement," and "final thoughts and rating." Craft headings that make sense for your review.

Troubleshooting

Here are some common challenges that students face when writing reviews.

What if I don't know anything about website design?
You don't need to know anything about design to write a strong website review. Some computer users are more experienced than others, but websites must serve users of all different computer skill levels. As a non-expert, you'll be in a better position to evaluate how well a website works for the average user. Focus on your own experience, and what would have made your experience better.

What if I can't find anything that needs improvement?
If you can't find any aspect of the website that needs improvement, then you can praise the website designers for doing a great job. Be specific about what the website does well. For example, "This interface makes it easy for users to find information about courses. The search engine works well. I searched for three courses and was able to find information for all of them." Knowing what works is just as useful as knowing what needs improvement. When web designers need to add new features in the future, they'll be sure to add features that are similar to the effective ones they've created in the past.

F. Chapter Project: Write a Website Review

Write a review of a website commonly used by college students (such as your college's library website, the student affairs website, etc.). Assume that your audience is the web developer or webmaster for the site, and your goal is to provide feedback specifically about how this website can be improved for student users.

Here are some questions to help get you started with your review. Remember to make suggestions for improvement.

- Is the site visually attractive to you? Why or why not?
- Is it easy to use? Can you find what you're looking for?
- Do you understand what the site is about?
- If this site is offering a product or service, would you sign up for or buy it?
- If you were interested in this site's content, would you come back? Why or why not? If the site has a forum community, would you sign up for it and post? Why or why not?
- Is the content strong? Do you understand what the text is saying? Do you notice any spelling or grammar mistakes?

Group Option: Compare Website Reviews

Have each person in your group write a review of the same website. After each of you has finished reviewing the site, come together and compare your reviews. How are they similar? How are they different?

Rate yourselves as Internet users—are you beginners? Experts? Programmers? Also rate your level of interest and experience with the topic or product whose website you are reviewing. How does your status as an Internet user affect how you evaluated the website?

Argumentative Genres

Argumentative genres are genres that aim to persuade. Writers of arguments use logic, evidence, emotions, and other means of persuasion to encourage an audience to agree with a claim or thesis. While the term "argument," in everyday use, describes a quarrel, here we use it not as a negative term, but to describe any genre in which the main goal is persuasion.

In college, you may be asked to compose arguments in any number of courses. Argumentative genres you may encounter in college include an editorial, letter to the editor, persuasive essay, persuasive speech, or the like. For example, in a history class you might be asked to take a position in a class debate on the causes of the Civil War. In a biology class, you might be asked to compose a persuasive essay arguing for or against stem cell research. In other situations, an argumentative genre might be hidden in the prompt for a traditional essay or "paper." For example, in an education class, you might be asked to write a paper that argues for or against instituting same-sex education in your state. To identify argumentative genres in a writing prompt, look out for words like "defend," "take a stance," "argue," "persuade," "take a position," and so on. In some cases, though, you will encounter arguments in other genres as well. For example, a film review (Chapter 9) might seek to persuade readers whether to go see a movie, and you are often asked to develop a claim or argument to support academic writing. (For more on argument as a strategy that crosses genres, see Chapter 18.)

In the workplace, arguments appear in a variety of settings. The most familiar examples of workplace arguments might be the "opening arguments" and "closing arguments" lawyers present in trials. These arguments are not quarrels, but attempts to persuade the jury to support one side of the case. In business, you may be asked to design a sales pitch to present to potential clients or investors. Journalists compose editorials and opinion pieces. Even the sermons composed by clergy members can be considered arguments, since they seek to persuade members of a religious group to abide by that group's doctrine.

In this chapter, you will learn how to compose a range of argumentative genres, genres whose main purpose is to persuade an audience. However, arguments tend to appear in other genres, as well—a recommendation report (Chapter 14) argues for a particular course of action, and a rhetorical analysis (Chapter 8) argues for a particular interpretation of a text. For this reason, you may also consult Chapter 18 on argumentative strategies that work in any genre.

A. Argumentative Mini-Genre: Print Advertisement

Perhaps the most common argumentative genre that you encounter in everyday life is an advertisement. Take a look at the following advertisements. Using the three genre toolkit questions, see if you can identify how this genre works.

EXAMPLE 1: Army Advertisement from 1985

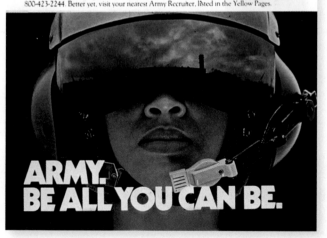

Army recruiting poster from 1985.

EXAMPLE 2: Army Advertisement from 2000

Army recruiting poster from 2000.

USE THE TOOLKIT

Let's use the three genre toolkit questions from Chapter 1 to examine this genre.

What Is It?

These are advertisements for the U.S. Army. They appeared in print magazines in the United States over the last four decades. All of these advertisements have the same underlying claim: you should consider joining the Army. (For more on making claims, see Chapter 18.)

EXAMPLE 3: Army Advertisement from 2010

Army recruiting poster from 2010.

Who Reads It?

While anyone might encounter an advertisement such as these in a magazine, chances are the Army's marketing firm had a more particular audience in mind when they designed these ads. Their primary audience probably includes those who are most likely to consider joining the army—typically, young men and women who are looking for a career path.

However, each of these advertisements makes different assumptions about who the army is seeking to recruit. Example 2 addresses an audience who is considering college, and makes the argument that joining the army will help to defray college costs. Notice that the ad addresses the reader directly, using the second person ("you"). Those "you" statements help to construct a reader as someone who fits the image the Army Reserve is trying to create.

In comparison, how does Example 1 appeal to—or construct—an audience? You might notice that the ad features an image of a person. Considering that the army has traditionally been composed of men, it is notable that the person pictured is a woman. Why was the army trying to recruit more women to join? Why would focusing on an individual person, rather than the kind of image shown in the second ad, help to persuade women to join?

Finally, the last image does not include images of things or people, but a simple word, "STRONG," spelled out with the first letters of the names of six key battles in American history. It might be less obvious who is intended to read this ad, but we might surmise that the audience is expected to know about these battles, and to identify with them as part of a tradition. According to the Army itself, this campaign was developed "to specifically address the interests and motivations of those considering a career in the U.S. military," and was included mainly in media targeting young adults.

What's It For?

The Army advertises mainly to recruit soldiers. The needs for Army recruitment change over time. In the 1980s, when the first of these advertisements was published, the United States was not engaged in any major wars, although it maintained military outposts and engaged in various operations around the world. Accordingly, the goal at that point might have been to recruit members to join the reserves, who would train on weekends but would probably not be deployed abroad. This changed in the 2000s, when the wars in Iraq and Afghanistan drew soldiers not just from the full-time Army, but also from the Reserves. The third advertisement comes from this period, when the United States needed individuals who would be willing to serve in those wars. You can see that the Army tried two different strategies to persuade readers to join—first appealing to individual pride and purpose in the "Army of One" campaign, and then trying appeals to patriotism and history in the "Army Strong" campaign. These are examples of appeals to emotions and values, or *pathos* (Chapter 18).

EXERCISE 10.1: Create an Advertisement

Choose a product you use often or with which you are familiar. Then, imagine that you work for an ad agency that is designing a new campaign for that product. The company hopes to attract a new audience to their product—one that has not traditionally been targeted in their advertising.

Write an email (Chapter 12) to your manager explaining who the new target audience should be, and how you think an advertisement can appeal to that audience.

MULTIMEDIA EXERCISE 10.1: Design a Social Media Campaign

Choose a product you use often or are familiar with. Then, imagine that you work for an ad agency that is designing a new campaign for that product. The company hopes to use social media to create interest in their product. Design a social media campaign to generate "buzz" about your product. Submit an email (Chapter 12) to your manager explaining what audience you tried to appeal to with your advertisement, and what choices you made to attract that audience.

B. Column, Op-Ed, or Letter to the Editor

Advertisements are argument genres that usually share a single, fundamental argument: to recruit people. In the Army case, the goal is to enlist new recruits, but also, perhaps, to recruit other Americans as supporters of the Army. Other organizations and corporations may use advertising to "recruit" viewers or readers in other ways—as consumers of a product or service, or as believers in the image the company is trying to create for itself.

However, advertisements are not the only genres that "recruit" an audience. If you want to get people to agree with an idea, support a proposal, vote for or against something, or take a specific action, you might also write a more extended piece, such as an opinion column, op-ed, or letter to the editor. All three are genres that appear in newspapers and magazines, and all three seek to recruit readers to support an argument.

EXAMPLE 1: Opinion Column for a Student Newspaper

Nate Rushing

UF's Meatless Mondays Are Ridiculous

"Mmm, tofu."

That will soon be a more common phrase thanks to Meatless Monday and several other well-intentioned organizations. From now on there will be more vegan options in UF's feeding troughs.

Of course, we can only hope that soon UF will cease to see any point in keeping meat on the menu on Mondays.

I mean, sure, vegan food sucks, but there's countless benefits to counterbalance this fact, right?

First, meat is unhealthy. It's full of fat and other animal byproducts and bacteria. 5
No chance of mad cow without the cow, right? Sure, salmonella can be spread through peanut butter, but it's meat that is the real problem, right? And, sure, you

can easily purchase super-lean cuts of both pork and beef, but that would require personal responsibility and discernment. And sure, we get vitamin B-12 almost exclusively through meat, and, more specifically, the bacteria in meat, but let's cling to that easy view of all bacteria being harmful.

Second, meat is unnecessary. What do we need meat for, anyway? Yes, it contains B-12, which, unless we take multivitamins or eat feces, we won't get without meat, but what's one essential vitamin? And yes, meat has complete proteins that contain all the essential amino acids all in one place, but hey, it's probably more efficient to spend time, money and effort getting together all the essential amino acids piecemeal. Yeah, I'm almost positive it makes sense to figure out exactly what plants contain—which of the twenty essential amino acids—and make sure that you eat enough of them on a regular enough basis to ensure you won't be malnourished.

Third, meat is inefficient. Surely the huge carbon meatprint I hear about is avoidable. It makes sense that, if cows eat corn to produce the meat we take from them, we can just cut the middleman and eat the corn ourselves. Never mind the fact that a huge portion of their diet is grass. Maybe grass is the next cilantro. Or we could just take the farmland that's currently being used for livestock and grow corn on it, right? This is a perfect solution, disregarding the immense amount of development and unnatural measures it would take to convert current livestock land to crop land, rendering the trade-off basically pointless.

For all these reasons and others, it's more than apparent that Meatless Monday has the right idea. My question is, why aren't we going to fully meatless Monday? Or meatless UF, for that matter. If meat really is this bad and pointless, why are we allowing this scourge on our campus at all?

Shouldn't we be looking out for our students, protecting them from the bad choices they may make?

10   Sure, we want college students to feel like they're adults, but we can't really trust them to make the right decisions—even the most basic ones like what to eat.

So, to the Meatless Monday folks, I say: Press on, fight the good fight for making other people's decisions for them under the assumption that the average layman doesn't have the time or wherewithal to truly know what's best for himself or herself.

I mean, really, where would we be if we let people truly exercise personal freedom? Nowhere good, that's for sure.

EXAMPLE 2: Letter to the Editor of a Student Newspaper

Dear Editor:

In response to your article "Meatless Mondays Marches to the Tune of Trayless Fridays" (20 Apr. 2011), I would like to compliment Kalamazoo College for joining the exciting campaign that is introducing thousands of students to vegetarian cuisine. Demand for meatless options on college campuses is growing every day, and students across the country are adopting Meatless Mondays as a result. A recent study by ARAMARK, a leading food-service provider, concluded that one in four college students are actively seeking out vegan options when they sit down to eat.

In fact, United Nations scientists have determined that raising chickens, pigs, and other animals for slaughter generates about 40 percent more greenhouse gasses than all the cars, SUVs, trucks, and planes in the world *combined*. Most students are also horrified to discover that chickens have their beaks cut off when they're only days old and that cows and pigs are often skinned and dismembered while still conscious. If these kinds of abuses were inflicted upon cats or dogs, it would result in felony cruelty-to-animals charges. Yet these practices are standard in an industry that refuses to make even the most basic improvements in the way that animals are treated.

Luckily, not only is going vegetarian the single greatest action you can take for animals and the environment, it's also the best choice that you can make for your health. Both the U.S. Department of Agriculture (USDA) and the American Dietetic Association have endorsed vegetarian diets. Don't forget that people can get all the protein that they need from nuts, seeds, yeast, grains, beans, and other legumes. Going vegetarian has never been easier or tastier, with so many delicious and cruelty-free dishes, such as vegan barbecue riblets and vegan pizza. For more information, visit peta2.com to request a free vegetarian/vegan starter kit.

Sincerely,
Amelia Jensen, College Campaigns Assistant

EXAMPLE 3: Op-Ed for a Student Newspaper

Rini Sampath

Insults against Disabled People Must Be Eradicated

In 2004, when 17-year-old Adam Holland cheerfully smiled for a photograph in his art class, he had no idea that the image would later re-surface as a popular meme.

Perhaps you've even seen it. No, it's not the iconic Bad Luck Brian or Scumbag Steve images that provide some giggles at the expense of another individual's dignity.

It's actually worse. And sickeningly offensive.

With one look at this recent meme, it's clear that Holland's physical features and cognitive ability are distinct from others. That's because Adam Holland has Down syndrome.

According to ABC News, a radio station in Florida re-purposed the original photograph of Holland at the Vanderbilt Kennedy Center into one in which he clutches a sign reading "Retarded News." This photo was used as promotion for its "Retarded News" segment, where talk jockeys would discuss odd news. 5

After learning of the photo's usage, Holland's family filed a lawsuit earlier this week against Cox Media, the owner of the Tampa, Fla., radio station WHPT-FM.

Unfortunately, this is not the first time a mentally disabled person has been mocked on the Internet. A quick Google search reveals that the Internet hosts a plethora of other tasteless graphics. This demonstrates a terrible epidemic in our nation—an epidemic of insensitivity toward the entire disabled community.

This isn't an isolated incident. It's actually a daily occurrence. For one, people constantly pepper everything from film dialogues to daily conversations with insulting uses of the word "retarded" to mean stupid or unintelligent. Even T-shirts and bumper stickers bare various forms of the word.

The Holland family might very well lose its battle in the courts since tort liability has protected the perpetrators of similar defamatory actions in the past. The Hollands' request of $18 million in compensatory and punitive damages might even seem unreasonable.

10   Yet, this hefty punishment could deter others from denigrating helpless individuals such as Adam Holland in the future.

Though the outcome of the actual case is unclear, this does not mean the Holland cause should lose in the eyes of the average American. Even if the law does not side in his favor, we ought to help him.

In fact, every individual can support Holland and stand up for the millions of others in the disabled community by eliminating the word "retard" from daily usage.

"When [it is] used as a synonym for 'dumb' or 'stupid' by people without disabilities, it only reinforces painful stereotypes of people with intellectual disabilities being less valued members of humanity," notes The Joseph P. Kennedy Jr. Foundation, a foundation created to help those with intellectual disabilities.

The first step to eradicating insensitivity toward disabled persons is to recognize the existence of these harmful words in our vernacular. Freedom of speech, after all, does not entitle any person to degrade another group of individuals.

15   Surely, disposing this word from common usage might seem unreasonable. To some, political correctness is a last priority when their lives are inundated by other concerns.

But this isn't just about political correctness. This is about being human. Every time someone uses this word, it trivializes the integrity of the disabled community. To create a world accepting of people from all walks of life, this change to word choice must occur.

In the end, able-bodied people can only say so much about the use of the word "retard."

But hearing it from someone who experiences mental disability? Now that creates an impact.

"I'm a 30-year-old man with Down syndrome who has struggled with the public's perception that an intellectual disability means that I am dumb and shallow," wrote Special Olympics athlete John Franklin Stephens. "Being compared to people like me should be considered a badge of honor. No one overcomes more than we do and still loves life so much."

USE THE TOOLKIT

Let's use the three genre toolkit questions from Chapter 1 to examine this genre.

What Is It?

A column, op-ed, or letter to the editor is a short, persuasive genre that appears in the opinion section of an online or print newspaper, in which the author argues a position about a current event or issue. Nate and Rini wrote columns or op-eds (also called "opinion pieces"), while Amelia wrote a letter to the editor.

Do you see any other differences between the two types of opinion pieces? You'll notice that Amelia begins her letter by referring to another piece of writing that had already appeared in the same newspaper, and that her text is slightly shorter than Nate's. We might conclude that a letter to the editor is usually a sort of response or follow-up to a longer news item, often a longer editorial or article. Most newspapers will print several letters to the editor in a single issue, and since space is at a premium, they tend to be short and concise. While online news sites don't need to worry as much about space, they still tend to encourage readers to respond in short, concise ways, often in short comments readers can post on an opinion column.

Who Reads It?

The audience for an op-ed or letter to the editor is partly determined by the newspaper in which it appears. College newspapers, for instance, tend to appeal mainly to students (who write the articles, too), but are also read by faculty, college alumni, and even members of the surrounding town or community.

Yet a more specific audience is also invoked by the writing itself. Take another look at Nate's editorial. Who do you think he is speaking to, specifically, among those who are readers of the University of Florida's college newspaper? You'll notice that Nate refers a couple of times to "students" or "college students," but he also uses the third person plural "we." While anyone could find Nate's column online, then, it seems that he is addressing students at his college. Meanwhile, Rini invokes a broader audience in her piece, which addresses an issue not confined to the college she attends, but one of larger scope: the importance of avoiding language that denigrates people with disabilities.

What's It For?

Just as the Army posters were trying to recruit people to join the military, these documents are trying to recruit people to support a particular position or argument. They use a variety of strategies to do so—providing reasons to support the claim, elaborating on those reasons with facts and other forms of evidence. (Turn to Chapter 18 for more on the structure of logical arguments.)

Let's take a closer look at the structure of Amelia's argument.

What is Amelia's main claim? You'll see that she does not quite state it explicitly, but that she supports Meatless Mondays and wants readers to do so as well. So, we might translate her claim as "You should support Meatless Mondays" or "Meatless Mondays are a good thing."

What reasons does she give? The first reason she provides is that Meatless Mondays are already garnering support from students, many of whom choose vegetarian and vegan meals. The second reason is that eating animals contributes to environmental problems, and the third is that eating animals often entails cruel and inhumane practices. Finally, Amelia states that eating a vegetarian diet is beneficial to your health.

Amelia, Nate, and Rini also appeal to the readers' emotions and values (Chapter 18), by choosing specific language and vocabulary to set the right tone (Chapter 21). For example, Rini chooses terms such as "mocked," "tasteless," and "offensive" to describe how Adam Holland was portrayed, terms that evoke the audience's sympathy for Adam and dislike for the radio station that used his picture.

EXERCISE 10.2: Join a Debate

Read the opinion section of your local newspaper, and identify a current issue or debate you find intriguing. Write a letter to the editor in response to an article or editorial. Note that you do not necessarily have to argue "for" or "against" the issue—you may also extend what others have said, provide a different angle on the debate, or argue for a "middle ground" between two extremes.

GROUP ACTIVITY 10.1: Letters to the Editor

As a group, choose a recent op-ed column in your local newspaper. Then, as individuals, write a letter to the editor in response to that column. Next, compare your responses by answering the following questions:

1. What claims did each of you make?
2. What reasons did you use to support your arguments?
3. Do any arguments seem to be supported by weak evidence? How can you make those weak arguments stronger?

(See Chapter 18 for more on the structure of arguments.)

C. Candidate Speech

Argument genres are also composed to be delivered orally, not just to be read in print. One of the most common types of oral argument proliferates around the time of elections, when candidates are trying to persuade people to vote for them.

EXAMPLE 1: Candidate Campaign Announcement Speech

Speech by Barack Obama
February 2007, Springfield, IL

Let me begin by saying thanks to all you who've traveled, from far and wide, to brave the cold today.

We all made this journey for a reason. It's humbling, but in my heart I know you didn't come here just for me, you came here because you believe in what this country can be. In the face of war, you believe there can be peace. In the face of despair, you believe there can be hope. In the face of a politics that's shut you out, that's told you to settle, that's divided us for too long, you believe we can be one people, reaching for what's possible, building that more perfect union.

That's the journey we're on today. But let me tell you how I came to be here. As most of you know, I am not a native of this great state. I moved to Illinois over two decades ago. I was a young man then, just a year out of college; I knew no one in Chicago, was without money or family connections. But a group of churches had offered me a job as a community organizer for $13,000 a year. And I accepted the job, sight unseen, motivated then by a single, simple, powerful idea—that I might play a small part in building a better America.

My work took me to some of Chicago's poorest neighborhoods. I joined with pastors and lay-people to deal with communities that had been ravaged by plant closings. I saw that the problems people faced weren't simply local in nature—that the decision to close a steel mill was made by distant executives; that the lack of textbooks and computers in schools could be traced to the skewed priorities of politicians a thousand miles away; and that when a child turns to violence, there's a hole in his heart no government could ever fill.

It was in these neighborhoods that I received the best education I ever had, and where I learned the true meaning of my Christian faith. After three years of this work, I went to law school, because I wanted to understand how the law should work for those in need. I became a civil rights lawyer, and taught constitutional law, and after a time, I came to understand that our cherished rights of liberty and equality depend on the active participation of an awakened electorate. It was with these ideas in mind that I arrived in this capital city as a state Senator.

It was here, in Springfield, where I saw all that is America converge—farmers and teachers, businessmen and laborers, all of them with a story to tell, all of them

Obama is careful to show that he is seeking the presidential nomination not out of a desire for personal power, but out of a desire to help his country. In this way, he portrays himself as someone who possesses humility.

Here, Obama appeals to those immediately present at the speech, but also paints himself as a down-to-earth, average American. During this first part of his speech, Obama focuses on establishing his character as a speaker, or *ethos*. He wants listeners to understand who he is, where he came from, and what kind of leader he will be.

seeking a seat at the table, all of them clamoring to be heard. I made lasting friendships here—friends that I see in the audience today.

It was here we learned to disagree without being disagreeable—that it's possible to compromise so long as you know those principles that can never be compromised; and that so long as we're willing to listen to each other, we can assume the best in people instead of the worst.

That's why we were able to reform a death penalty system that was broken. That's why we were able to give health insurance to children in need. That's why we made the tax system more fair and just for working families, and that's why we passed ethics reforms that the cynics said could never, ever be passed.

It was here, in Springfield, where North, South, East and West come together that I was reminded of the essential decency of the American people—where I came to believe that through this decency, we can build a more hopeful America.

10   And that is why, in the shadow of the Old State Capitol, where Lincoln once called on a divided house to stand together, where common hopes and common dreams still live, I stand before you today to announce my candidacy for President of the United States. I recognize there is a certain presumptuousness—a certain audacity—to this announcement. I know I haven't spent a lot of time learning the ways of Washington. But I've been there long enough to know that the ways of Washington must change.

The genius of our founders is that they designed a system of government that can be changed. And we should take heart, because we've changed this country before. In the face of tyranny, a band of patriots brought an Empire to its knees. In the face of secession, we unified a nation and set the captives free. In the face of Depression, we put people back to work and lifted millions out of poverty. We welcomed immigrants to our shores, we opened railroads to the west, we landed a man on the moon, and we heard a King's call to let justice roll down like water, and righteousness like a mighty stream.

Each and every time, a new generation has risen up and done what's needed to be done. Today we are called once more—and it is time for our generation to answer that call.

For that is our unyielding faith—that in the face of impossible odds, people who love their country can change it.

That's what Abraham Lincoln understood. He had his doubts. He had his defeats. He had his setbacks. But through his will and his words, he moved a nation and helped free a people. It is because of the millions who rallied to his cause that we are no longer divided, North and South, slave and free. It is because men and women of every race, from every walk of life, continued to march for freedom long after Lincoln was laid to rest, that today we have the chance to face the challenges of this millennium together, as one people—as Americans.

15   All of us know what those challenges are today—a war with no end, a dependence on oil that threatens our future, schools where too many children aren't learning, and families struggling paycheck to paycheck despite working as hard as they can. We know the challenges. We've heard them. We've talked about them for years.

What's stopped us from meeting these challenges is not the absence of sound policies and sensible plans. What's stopped us is the failure of leadership, the smallness of our politics—the ease with which we're distracted by the petty and trivial, our

---

Obama shifts to a focus on common values he shares with potential voters— compromise, good faith, fair taxes, and family.

Here is where Obama outlines the thesis of his campaign speech: I am running for President because I want to change Washington.

Here Obama appeals to America's national mythology and history, again invoking common values the voters will share.

chronic avoidance of tough decisions, our preference for scoring cheap political points instead of rolling up our sleeves and building a working consensus to tackle big problems.

For the last six years we've been told that our mounting debts don't matter, we've been told that the anxiety Americans feel about rising health care costs and stagnant wages are an illusion, we've been told that climate change is a hoax, and that tough talk and an ill-conceived war can replace diplomacy, and strategy, and foresight. And when all else fails, when Katrina happens, or the death toll in Iraq mounts, we've been told that our crises are somebody else's fault. We're distracted from our real failures, and told to blame the other party, or gay people, or immigrants.

And as people have looked away in disillusionment and frustration, we know what's filled the void. The cynics, and the lobbyists, and the special interests who've turned our government into a game only they can afford to play. They write the checks and you get stuck with the bills, they get the access while you get to write a letter, they think they own this government, but we're here today to take it back. The time for that politics is over. It's time to turn the page.

We've made some progress already. I was proud to help lead the fight in Congress that led to the most sweeping ethics reform since Watergate.

But Washington has a long way to go. And it won't be easy. That's why we'll have to   20
set priorities. We'll have to make hard choices. And although government will play a crucial role in bringing about the changes we need, more money and programs alone will not get us where we need to go. Each of us, in our own lives, will have to accept responsibility—for instilling an ethic of achievement in our children, for adapting to a more competitive economy, for strengthening our communities, and sharing some measure of sacrifice. So let us begin. Let us begin this hard work together. Let us transform this nation.

Let us be the generation that reshapes our economy to compete in the digital age. ←
Let's set high standards for our schools and give them the resources they need to succeed. Let's recruit a new army of teachers, and give them better pay and more support in exchange for more accountability. Let's make college more affordable, and let's invest in scientific research, and let's lay down broadband lines through the heart of inner cities and rural towns all across America.

And as our economy changes, let's be the generation that ensures our nation's workers are sharing in our prosperity. Let's protect the hard-earned benefits their companies have promised. Let's make it possible for hardworking Americans to save for retirement. And let's allow our unions and their organizers to lift up this country's middle class again.

Let's be the generation that ends poverty in America. Every single person willing to work should be able to get job training that leads to a job, and earn a living wage that can pay the bills, and afford child care so their kids have a safe place to go when they work. Let's do this.

Let's be the generation that finally tackles our health care crisis. We can control costs by focusing on prevention, by providing better treatment to the chronically ill, and using technology to cut the bureaucracy. Let's be the generation that says right here, right now, that we will have universal health care in America by the end of the next president's first term.

> Obama begins to outline a policy platform or set of goals. Note that they are pretty unspecific—instead, they appeal to the audience's idealized vision of policies. Obama does not say how he will reshape the economy or make college more affordable, for instance.

25   Let's be the generation that finally frees America from the tyranny of oil. We can harness homegrown, alternative fuels like ethanol and spur the production of more fuel-efficient cars. We can set up a system for capping greenhouse gases. We can turn this crisis of global warming into a moment of opportunity for innovation, and job creation, and an incentive for businesses that will serve as a model for the world.

Let's be the generation that makes future generations proud of what we did here.

Most of all, let's be the generation that never forgets what happened on that September day and confront the terrorists with everything we've got. Politics doesn't have to divide us on this anymore—we can work together to keep our country safe. I've worked with Republican Senator Dick Lugar to pass a law that will secure and destroy some of the world's deadliest, unguarded weapons. We can work together to track terrorists down with a stronger military, we can tighten the net around their finances, and we can improve our intelligence capabilities. But let us also understand that ultimate victory against our enemies will come only by rebuilding our alliances and exporting those ideals that bring hope and opportunity to millions around the globe.

But all of this cannot come to pass until we bring an end to this war in Iraq. Most of you know I opposed this war from the start. I thought it was a tragic mistake. Today we grieve for the families who have lost loved ones, the hearts that have been broken, and the young lives that could have been. America, it's time to start bringing our troops home. It's time to admit that no amount of American lives can resolve the political disagreement that lies at the heart of someone else's civil war. That's why I have a plan that will bring our combat troops home by March of 2008. Letting the Iraqis know that we will not be there forever is our last, best hope to pressure the Sunni and Shia to come to the table and find peace.

Finally, there is one other thing that is not too late to get right about this war—and that is the homecoming of the men and women—our veterans—who have sacrificed the most. Let us honor their valor by providing the care they need and rebuilding the military they love. Let us be the generation that begins this work.

Here, Obama addresses counter-arguments or objections. One of the main objections he faced was that his campaign and its focus on change was naïve or unrealistic, so he seeks to allay that concern here.

30   I know there are those who don't believe we can do all these things. I understand the skepticism. After all, every four years, candidates from both parties make similar promises, and I expect this year will be no different. All of us running for president will travel around the country offering ten-point plans and making grand speeches; all of us will trumpet those qualities we believe make us uniquely qualified to lead the country. But too many times, after the election is over, and the confetti is swept away, all those promises fade from memory, and the lobbyists and the special interests move in, and people turn away, disappointed as before, left to struggle on their own.

That is why this campaign can't only be about me. It must be about us—it must be about what we can do together. This campaign must be the occasion, the vehicle, of your hopes, and your dreams. It will take your time, your energy, and your advice—to push us forward when we're doing right, and to let us know when we're not. This campaign has to be about reclaiming the meaning of citizenship, restoring our sense of common purpose, and realizing that few obstacles can withstand the power of millions of voices calling for change.

By ourselves, this change will not happen. Divided, we are bound to fail.

But the life of a tall, gangly, self-made Springfield lawyer tells us that a different future is possible.

He tells us that there is power in words.

He tells us that there is power in conviction. 35

That beneath all the differences of race and region, faith and station, we are one people.

He tells us that there is power in hope.

As Lincoln organized the forces arrayed against slavery, he was heard to say: "Of strange, discordant, and even hostile elements, we gathered from the four winds, and formed and fought to battle through."

That is our purpose here today.

That's why I'm in this race. 40

Not just to hold an office, but to gather with you to transform a nation.

I want to win that next battle—for justice and opportunity.

I want to win that next battle—for better schools, and better jobs, and health care for all.

I want us to take up the unfinished business of perfecting our union, and building a better America.

And if you will join me in this improbable quest, if you feel destiny calling, and see 45 as I see, a future of endless possibility stretching before us; if you sense, as I sense, that the time is now to shake off our slumber, and slough off our fear, and make good on the debt we owe past and future generations, then I'm ready to take up the cause, and march with you, and work with you.

Together, starting today, let us finish the work that needs to be done, and usher in a new birth of freedom on this Earth.

> The speech ends with more overt appeals to emotions.

EXAMPLE 2: Candidate Campaign Speech

Madison Peace

Student Body President Speech

Every Student Body President Candidate claims that the College is at a crossroads, that next year represents a pivotal time for our institution and that the most important decisions in the College's history will be made next year.

The truth is that next year's challenges are not any more difficult than this year's challenges or last year's challenges. They're just different. We don't need to view each year as a turning point. Rather, we should strive for continual improvement for our institution.

In Principles of Management and Organization, we talk about the principle of kaizen. Kaizen is the idea of continual improvement. Organizations that practice kaizen don't view every situation as a crisis. Instead, they analyze challenges as potential opportunities for growth.

Growth requires leadership. And leadership is more than delegation. Leadership is more than vision-casting. Leadership is more than expressing an opinion or creating a venue for opinions to be expressed. A leader has to do all of these things, but a leader also needs a substantial strategy for moving our institution forward. Otherwise, we'll be reacting to every crisis instead of cultivating kaizen. We'll be passively responding, instead of actively seeking to improve the way our student government works. A leader is someone who sees a problem, develops a solution, garners support for his or her plan, and efficiently executes it. Being a leader requires not only the ability to listen, but also the foresight to understand where you want to go. Leadership is about more than just building bridges; it's about crossing those bridges, and fording onto a future of new challenges and new opportunities.

5   This election is about how you want your student body president to represent you. In my campaign, I've presented you a portrait of where I want to lead our College. I've painted a picture of what the Honor Code, Student Life, and Student Government could be. I've done this, because I believe we need to move beyond speaking in abstractions. We talk too much about vision and community and don't do enough of the things that actually create community or enhance vision. Student Government should be committed to tangible action, not merely idle speculation. As Student Body President, I'd be more than an opinion gatherer; I'd be a problem solver.

But I can't solve all of our problems alone. I can't even solve one of them by myself. I need you to offer more than your opinions; I need you to work towards solutions. I need to hear more than your voice; I need you to participate in student life and government. I need you not only to speak up, but to stand up.

I need you to stand up and take ownership of student life. If you stand up, I will support you. I want to support Student Organization Leaders by offering a summit like executive teams receive. Organization Leaders will be equipped for success. Their leaders would have training in expense reports, budget forecasting, marketing, and succession planning.

I need you to stand up and support City Engagement. City Engagement is a pivotal part of the identity of the college. We should not only be serving our school. We should be serving our city. As Student Body President, I will support City Engagement financially and have City Engagement coordinators for each House in place at the start of next year with projects ready to go. This will help City Engagement become part of each House's identity.

I want to help you believe in student government as well. The Council isn't an effective system if students don't know they're being represented.

10   We ask a lot of our House Presidents. We ask them to manage the finances of their house, promote honor, develop community, and represent students on the Council. I want to make sure we respect the time of our House Presidents, as well as other student leaders. I'm committed to improving the way our school supports student leaders and I'll take the lead in making sure their opinions are heard and represented to the administration. Student leaders can't support you, if they aren't supported. Fixing our representation problems starts by communicating what the structure we have for solving problems is, and supporting that structure so that it is able to do its job.

Our current structure, The King's Council, relies on consideration from the administration to accomplish its objectives. The administration has no inherent reason to take the opinion of the Council seriously. The only way that our government can earn credibility with the administration is by using the only currency that is universally accepted—ideas. If we present compelling ideas to the administration, the administration will come to respect our student government. An effective student body president must not only relay complaints, but devise and pitch a solution to solve them to the 15th floor.

I know many of you have concerns about academics at King's. This year your House Scholars have been meeting with the Provost's office and I think that's started some great conversations. Next year, I want to formalize this process by putting the full weight of the Council and the Office of the student body president behind this initiative. I want to create an Academic Concerns Committee composed of House Scholars, faculty members, and Provost office representatives. This vehicle of communication will allow us to represent the concerns of students in a respectful and effective way. King's is first and foremost a College and I want you involved in the conversation about academics here. We say we're an academically rigorous, elite institution. Let's match our rhetoric with a plan of action that shows the administration that we care deeply about what is happening in the classroom.

You need to stand up for the most important issue facing students at King's: the honor code. The code of responsibility I proposed in my platform is designed to help eliminate the ambiguities of our current honor code system. By providing clear expectations for how students should conduct themselves, we'll make the honor code something our community can believe in. But just developing a code of responsibility isn't enough. If all we do is adopt a code, we won't have made any progress. I think we need to adopt a code, but we also need to adopt an attitude. I want to see Houses develop their own honor cultures. I love the way the House of Reagan created an oath that holds their members to a higher standard than the honor code requires. If you start initiatives like this in your House, I'll work with the administration to ensure that we communicate honor to students in a coherent fashion. If we do this, together we can restore dignity to honor.

I'm running for Student Body President because I want to help our College start to implement its vision. My platform is designed to do exactly that. When dealing with tough issues like the Honor Code, spiritual life, and academic consistency, I want to apply our College's best values, like giving students the freedom, and responsibility, to be adults, and develop a solution that reflects these value commitments in a meaningful way. This will allow King's students to do more than talk about the vision; we'll be living it.

Today, I ask for your vote not because we are faced with a crisis and I think I can fix   15
it, but because we're presented with an opportunity that I think we need to take. You're being presented with the chance to strengthen student government by making it more efficient and professional. Next year, I offer you vision and action, grace and truth, experience and fresh ideas.

I hope you'll give me the opportunity to lead, not as one above you, but as one of you. Together, let's refine honor, let's strengthen our voice, and let's flourish.

EXAMPLE 3: Candidate Acceptance Speech

Mayor Michael R. Bloomberg's Victory Speech
November 4, 2009

> Following is the text of Mayor Michael R. Bloomberg's victory speech, delivered at the Sheraton New York Hotel and Towers in Midtown Manhattan, as transcribed by *The New York Times*.

Thank you. Gracias. What a week this is turning out to be. Tonight, a hard-fought victory in a very difficult year, and—who knows?—maybe in a few days, the biggest victory parade that Broadway has ever seen. [. . .]

Today voters from every borough and every background and every neighborhood and every nationality, from every party and every persuasion, went to the polls and they chose progress.

More progress in our schools, more progress fighting crime and poverty, more progress creating jobs and affordable housing. And more progress building a greener and healthier city.

The voters have spoken, and now, it's up to us to deliver. Can we do it?

5   I know we can. And I know we will.

Our city and our country, as we all know, are going through some very difficult times. We're in the midst of the worst national recession we've had in decades, and these are tough times, even for our tough town. Tonight, throughout the nation, the public has been very clear, and some incumbents have learned that they are tired of politics as usual.

The public wants their leaders from both parties to get things done. They want more independence, and less partisanship, and a government that is free of the special interests.

And that's what we've done in New York City. And that's why New Yorkers have defied tonight's trend and said yes, instead of no.

Now, a little while ago, I received a very gracious call from Comptroller Bill Thompson. Come on—Bill is a good man, who I've always enjoyed working with, and in all fairness, he ran a spirited campaign and he put up a tough fight. He deserves a round of applause. Come on.

10   And I thank Bill Thompson for his service to the city, and I also want to congratulate our new comptroller, the first Asian-American elected to citywide office, John Liu. And our new public advocate, Bill de Blasio.

I look forward to working with them and all of Bill Thompson's supporters, because at the end of the day, we all agree on a heck of a lot more than we disagree on, especially our love of New York City.

Now, we've come so far in these past few years by staying united, and that's how we're going to climb out of this national recession together. Over the past year, in the subway and in diners all around the city, I've talked with men and women who are struggling to get by. Some have lost their jobs, others fight every month to pay the rent or the mortgage. I know it's not easy out there. But I also know this: while we can't fix the national recession, we can and we will get our city through these tough times. And we'll come out stronger than ever.

And I'm committed to working twice as hard, in the next four years, as I did in the past eight. And during the good times, we showed that New York City could outperform the nation in creating jobs, improving schools, fighting climate change, even extending life expectancy. And now in these tough times, we're going to show that we can keep outperforming the rest of the country.

Over the next four years we're going to make the safest big city in the country even safer. We've driven crime down so low the experts are now wondering if it can go any lower. Well let me tell you something: We're determined to find out.

We're also going to keep improving what is far and away the best public school system of any big city in the country. We've made amazing progress these last eight years, and we're just getting started. We're also going to make New York the most environmentally friendly city in the country. And more trees in every neighborhood: one million trees. 15

We're going to have the most ambitious job-creation strategy in the country, with new jobs and small business from the South Bronx to Coney Island.

We'll extend the most ambitious public health agenda in the country and complete the largest affordable-housing plan in the country. We'll offer more immigrant adults English-language classes so they can fully contribute to our economy. And we'll continue to fight for real immigration reform in Washington because *Nueva York es una ciudad donde adoremos todos las culturas.*

We'll do all of this and a lot more. If you think you've seen progress over the last eight years, I've got news for you: You ain't seen nothing yet.

Well, conventional wisdom says historically third terms haven't been too successful. But we've spent the last eight years defying conventional wisdom. If you remember, after 9/11, when the pundits said it would take decades for us to recover, we proved them wrong. When they said crime could only go up, not down, we proved them wrong. When they said nothing could be done to close the ethnic achievement gap in the schools, we proved them wrong. We've proven the experts wrong again and again and again and we're not stopping now.

We're going to make the next four years the best yet and we're going to do it with the same independent approach we've always taken: making decisions based on the facts, not the politics. Doing the right thing, not the easy thing. And taking the best ideas, no matter where they come from. That's what being independent is all about. 20

I couldn't be more honored to be the first independent to be elected mayor in the city's modern history. New Yorkers want a mayor who can stretch across the aisle and bring people together. That's what we've done over the past eight years and that's what we did in this election. We've built the most diverse coalition of supporters this city has ever seen: thousands and thousands of people who gave their time and energy to this campaign: college students and seniors, union members and small-business owners, New Yorkers from every community, speaking just about every imaginable language, reaching out to every single voter in every neighborhood. Handing out literature, making phone calls, stuffing envelopes and, up to this evening, knocking on more than two million doors. Make no mistake: you make this happen. Actually, this is the first time I've seen any of you standing still. None of this, none of this would have been possible without all of you. And I thank you from the bottom of my heart.

I've also had the single best campaign staff ever assembled, led by the tireless and talented Bradley Tusk. Bradley did an amazing job as our campaign manager, and I know he would be the first to say that it was a total team effort.

Day after day, they work literally around the clock to get our message of progress out there, and they did it with tremendous integrity and passion, and I am forever grateful and finally, finally I want to thank the women in my life, who have always given me their love and support, both on and off the campaign trail: my daughters, Emma and Georgina; my sister, Marjorie, and her two daughters; Diana, of course; and my mother, Charlotte, who is celebrating our victory. My mother is celebrating our victory at home in Medford tonight. When I talked to her on the phone I said, "Just one glass of Champagne," but she told me to mind my own business.

Tonight we're going to enjoy this celebration. We've earned it. But tomorrow, you have my word. I'll be back at work bright and early. I can't wait. I love this city. I love it for all the reasons that you do: the energy, the excitement, the people, but I think I love it most because this is the place where no matter who you are, no matter where you come from, if you work hard enough and have a little luck along the way, nothing can stop you from your greatest dreams. Don't let anyone tell you it's not possible, because I know it is.

25   And working together, I have no doubt that our best days are still ahead. Our best years are still ahead. Now, can we do it? Will you help me? Will you help make the greatest city in the world even better? Will the Yankees win Game 6? You better believe it. God bless. Enjoy the night. Or, as we say in Gaelic, *Disfruta la noche*. Thank you, and God bless New York City.

∙∙

USE THE TOOLKIT

Let's use the three genre toolkit questions from Chapter 1 to examine this genre.

What Is It?

These three documents are examples of speeches at three different stages of a political campaign. The speech in Example 1 was delivered by Barack Obama, when he was seeking the nomination for U.S. President from the Democratic Party. This is the speech he gave to kick off his campaign. The speech in Example 2 was delivered by a college student to campaign for student body president. The speech in Example 3 was delivered by Mayor Michael Bloomberg when he won the election for Mayor of New York City. Thus, each speech was delivered at a different stage in the political process: at the beginning of a campaign, during a campaign, and after victory.

Each of these speeches offers an overview of the campaigner's goals, invokes common values, and makes an argument: that listeners should support the candidate.

Who Reads It?

The immediate audience of any campaign speech are those who are present for the speech and are hearing it live. If the speech is also broadcast live over television or radio, then the immediate audience can expand to include listeners all over the world. If a speech is reprinted and published on the Internet, as these speeches were, then they can be read by anyone interested in learning more about the candidate's campaign.

Some of these speeches would have a broad, national scope, such as Obama's speech, since he was seeking election as president of an entire country. In contrast, Madison's student body president speech would have a smaller primary audience, mainly students at her college who might be voting for her. Bloomberg's speech would be somewhere in the middle. His speech would not only reach New Yorkers, but also some listeners across the country, given the influence and size of New York City and the fact that Bloomberg was already well known as a business magnate (owner of a company famous for its global financial products).

What's It For?

The goal of all three campaign speeches is to get listeners on the candidate's side. Even after an election, a candidate wants to win over those who have not voted for him or her, as Bloomberg did. Once he became mayor, he was mayor of all New Yorkers—not just those who voted for him. The goal of the victory speech, then, is to thank his supporters but also to draw in those who had not supported him.

Let's take a closer look at Obama's speech to learn about the goals of a campaign speech and how a speaker accomplishes those goals.

Obama's speech occurred at the beginning of his campaign; he was just getting started. The Democratic primary process was beginning, and Obama had already garnered a base of supporters. In order to win the nomination, though, he would need to get more Democratic Party members behind him—he needed to recruit them.

How does he try to get people on his side? You can see that Obama does not say much about the specific steps he would take as President. The first part of his speech establishes his character, or *ethos*, as a potential presidential candidate, providing information about his life, family, and career.

The second part of his speech focuses on celebrating the values he shares with those he hopes to recruit—people who are unhappy with the current political situation, people who feel the government needs to change, people who, in his words, want to "transform this nation."

In other words, the speech uses organization to its advantage by first trying to create an impression of Obama as a person, and then trying to connect that persona to the values of his audience.

Obama's example suggests that campaign speeches tend to work by drawing on and reinforcing common values and ideals, and less on the concrete actions a politician will take. Campaigns also focus heavily on the character and background, or *ethos*, of each candidate (Chapter 18).

Often, practical actions become relevant later in a political campaign, once the presidential candidates have been chosen and have established themselves in the public's mind. You'll notice that the campaign speech by Madison focuses more specifically on concrete actions—perhaps because the vote was set to happen immediately after the speech. At that stage in her campaign, Madison had presumably already established her *ethos* among students on her campus, and could then focus on the actions she would take.

You'll also see that the language used in a campaign speech differs somewhat from that used in written genres. Political campaign speeches tend to use a variety of rhetorical devices to get audiences amped up, as in the closing lines of these speeches:

- Barack Obama: "Together, starting today, let us finish the work that needs to be done, and usher in a new birth of freedom on this Earth."
- Madison Peace: "I hope you'll give me the opportunity to lead, not as one above you, but as one of you. Together, let's refine honor, let's strengthen our voice, and let's flourish."
- Michael Bloomberg: "I love this city. I love it for all the reasons that you do: the energy, the excitement, the people, but I think I love it most because this is the place where no matter who you are, no matter where you come from, if you work hard enough and have a little luck along the way, nothing can stop you from your greatest dreams."

All three speakers use rhetorical devices (Chapters 8 and 18) to urge the audience to join them and embark on a new endeavor, seeking to generate an emotional response that will lead to action.

Of course, the oral delivery of a speech also makes a big difference. If you watch videos of campaign speeches, you'll note that speakers alter their pacing, voice, gestures, and facial expressions throughout their speeches. (For more on elements of oral delivery, see Chapter 30.)

EXERCISE 10.3: Write a Campaign Speech

Imagine you are seeking a nomination for student government at your college. To get on the ballot, you will need signatures from 300 students who are willing to support you. These students will form your political base should you make it on the ballot.

First, identify two different constituencies or groups of students who might support you. (They might be students in your academic year vs. those in other years, students who commute vs. students who live on campus, students in different major areas, etc.)

Then, write two short campaign speeches (approximately 2 minutes long), for two different groups of students. Consider how you can appeal to the values you share with those students, and how you can portray your character in a way that meets their expectations.

Practice your speech, and then be prepared to deliver both versions of your speech in class. See if your classmates can correctly identify what kinds of students you aimed to recruit.

MULTIMEDIA EXERCISE 10.2: Create a Campaign Website

Imagine you are seeking a nomination for student government at your college. To get on the ballot, you will need signatures from 300 students who are willing to support you. These students will form your political base should you make it on the ballot.

Create a rough sketch (or mock-up) for a website that will provide information about your campaign and recruit supporters. Consider how you will appeal to the values of voters, and how you will develop your character or *ethos*. Check out some websites that candidates have used for different political campaigns to get an idea of how they tend to look.

Use a desktop program (such as PowerPoint or Word) or draw a sketch of your mock-up—a non-functioning image of what your website will look like. Your mock-up should include the sections you will include, how they will be laid out on your site, your choices of colors and images, and any text you plan to include.

GROUP ACTIVITY 10.2: Launch a Political Campaign

While we often focus solely on the candidates in an election, it actually takes a team to get someone into office. Most campaigns include a number of advisors and other team members. For this assignment, your group will act as a campaign team. First, decide who will act as the political candidate for your group. Then, as a team, develop an overall message: How will you portray your candidate's *ethos*, and how will you appeal to the values of your student electorate?

Next, choose a role and task for each group member from those listed here:

- Candidate: deliver a 4-minute campaign speech
- Speechwriter: write and coach candidate on speech
- Public relations consultant: prepare a press release announcing the speech
- Graphic designer: prepare a political campaign poster for your candidate
- Social network consultant: design a web campaign using social media tools

As a group, you will introduce your campaign to the class in a 15-minute oral presentation.

D. Satire

So far, we have examined arguments that work in visual, written, and oral genres, and we have examined a number of strategies writers use in those genres, including logic (claims, reasons, and evidence), appeals to the emotions and values, arrangement (or organization), and style. While these genres share a focus on persuading an audience, they have different conventions, in part because each one appears in a different type of rhetorical situation. Different kinds of argument genres appear in magazines, in newspapers, and at political rallies.

We turn now to another genre of argument, one that uses irony as its main rhetorical device. If you watch late night television shows, such as *The Daily Show with Jon Stewart*, you are probably familiar with this genre: satire.

EXAMPLE 1: Satire for a Student Newspaper

Pia DiGiulio

Uncontrolled Study Orgies Break Out in Gender-Neutral Dorm

The University Administration and certain parent groups have shown appropriate concern about the proposed, so-called "gender-neutral" housing situation that would allow male and female university students to live in the same dorm rooms.

Indeed, as the term "gender-neutral housing" is actually a euphemism that hides the dangers inherent in such living arrangements, I will not deign to use the term in this article. Rather, I will call a spade a spade and use the term "boy-girl sexy-time housing."

And it's not like I don't have evidence to back up my coinage. One dorm on campus has been experimenting (now *there's* an appropriate term!) with boy-girl sexy-time housing for a full semester now, and the results are in. There are orgies happening everywhere in Garner Hall. This evidence should be adequate to squash this proposed housing plan for good.

Specifically, there have been documented, wanton, uncontrolled, study orgies breaking out at all times of the day and night in Garner Hall. According to my sources, alcohol may or may not have played a role in these study orgies. Susan Day, a resident of Garner who asked me not to use her middle name out of concern for her privacy, bore witness to this travesty: "The orgies were everywhere you turned, in every room. Students had books strewn all over their rooms. Pens of every color, and notebooks—these fancy composition books from places like France and Japan. And they were *writing* in them. Shudder."

Dan Merkel, a senior and a Resident Advisor in Garner, fears for the safety of his residents now that the boy-girl sexy-time housing plan is in effect: "They just can't control themselves. They're too young to know any better. Adults have to use their judgment to protect these students from themselves. I worry that they're just not going to get enough sleep because of all this studying. I worry what these intense conversations are going to do to their still-developing bodies. I just can't stop worrying. Someone needs to step in."

There you have it, readers. Under the best of circumstances, students can barely think for themselves. And now that they live in boy-girl sexy-time housing, they clearly can't think at all. Administrators, parents—it's up to you to do what you can to put a stop to the debauchery of boy-girl sexy-time housing.

(Author's Note: If you do write in to oppose the housing proposal, be sure to refer to the proposal as "Gender-Neutral Housing" to ensure that the Administration knows what you are talking about.)

EXAMPLE 2: Satire Pamphlet (excerpt)

Jonathan Swift

A Modest Proposal: For preventing the children of poor people in Ireland, from being a burden on their parents or country, and for making them beneficial to the publick.
First published: 1729

It is a melancholy object to those, who walk through this great town, or travel in the country, when they see the streets, the roads and cabbin-doors crowded with beggars of the female sex, followed by three, four, or six children, all in rags, and importuning every passenger for an alms. These mothers instead of being able to work for their honest livelihood, are forced to employ all their time in stroling to beg sustenance for their helpless infants who, as they grow up, either turn thieves for want of work, or leave their dear native country, to fight for the Pretender in Spain, or sell themselves to the Barbadoes.

I think it is agreed by all parties, that this prodigious number of children in the arms, or on the backs, or at the heels of their mothers, and frequently of their fathers, is in the present deplorable state of the kingdom, a very great additional grievance; and therefore whoever could find out a fair, cheap and easy method of making these children sound and useful members of the common-wealth, would deserve so well of the publick, as to have his statue set up for a preserver of the nation.

But my intention is very far from being confined to provide only for the children of professed beggars: it is of a much greater extent, and shall take in the whole number of infants at a certain age, who are born of parents in effect as little able to support them, as those who demand our charity in the streets.

As to my own part, having turned my thoughts for many years, upon this important subject, and maturely weighed the several schemes of our projectors, I have always found them grossly mistaken in their computation. It is true, a child just dropt from its dam, may be supported by her milk, for a solar year, with little other nourishment: at most not above the value of two shillings, which the mother may certainly get, or the value in scraps, by her lawful occupation of begging; and it is exactly at one year old that I propose to provide for them in such a manner, as, instead of being a charge upon their parents, or the parish, or wanting food and raiment for the rest of their lives, they shall, on the contrary, contribute to the feeding, and partly to the cloathing of many thousands.

5   There is likewise another great advantage in my scheme, that it will prevent those voluntary abortions, and that horrid practice of women murdering their bastard children, alas! too frequent among us, sacrificing the poor innocent babes, I doubt, more to avoid the expence than the shame, which would move tears and pity in the most savage and inhuman breast.

The number of souls in this kingdom being usually reckoned one million and a half, of these I calculate there may be about two hundred thousand couple whose wives are breeders; from which number I subtract thirty thousand couple, who are able to maintain their own children, (although I apprehend there cannot be so many, under the present distresses of the kingdom) but this being granted, there will remain an hundred and seventy thousand breeders. I again subtract fifty thousand, for those women who miscarry, or whose children die by accident or disease within the year. There only remain an hundred and twenty thousand children of poor parents annually born. The question therefore is, How this number shall be reared, and provided for? which, as I have already said, under the present situation of affairs, is utterly impossible by all the methods hitherto proposed. For we can neither employ them in handicraft or agriculture; we neither build houses, (I mean in the country) nor cultivate land: they can very seldom pick up a livelihood by stealing till they arrive at six years old; except where they are of towardly parts, although I confess they learn the rudiments much earlier; during which time they can however be properly looked upon only as probationers: As I have been informed by a principal gentleman in the county of Cavan, who protested to me, that he never knew above one or two instances under the age of six, even in a part of the kingdom so renowned for the quickest proficiency in that art.

I am assured by our merchants, that a boy or a girl before twelve years old, is no saleable commodity, and even when they come to this age, they will not yield above three pounds, or three pounds and half a crown at most, on the exchange; which cannot turn to account either to the parents or kingdom, the charge of nutriments and rags having been at least four times that value.

I shall now therefore humbly propose my own thoughts, which I hope will not be liable to the least objection.

I have been assured by a very knowing American of my acquaintance in London, that a young healthy child well nursed, is, at a year old, a most delicious nourishing and wholesome food, whether stewed, roasted, baked, or boiled; and I make no doubt that it will equally serve in a fricasie, or a ragout.

I do therefore humbly offer it to publick consideration, that of the hundred and 10 twenty thousand children, already computed, twenty thousand may be reserved for breed, whereof only one fourth part to be males; which is more than we allow to sheep, black cattle, or swine, and my reason is, that these children are seldom the fruits of marriage, a circumstance not much regarded by our savages, therefore, one male will be sufficient to serve four females. That the remaining hundred thousand may, at a year old, be offered in sale to the persons of quality and fortune, through the kingdom, always advising the mother to let them suck plentifully in the last month, so as to render them plump, and fat for a good table. A child will make two dishes at an entertainment for friends, and when the family dines alone, the fore or hind quarter will make a reasonable dish, and seasoned with a little pepper or salt, will be very good boiled on the fourth day, especially in winter.

I have reckoned upon a medium, that a child just born will weigh 12 pounds, and in a solar year, if tolerably nursed, encreaseth to 28 pounds.

I grant this food will be somewhat dear, and therefore very proper for landlords, who, as they have already devoured most of the parents, seem to have the best title to the children.

Infant's flesh will be in season throughout the year, but more plentiful in March, and a little before and after; for we are told by a grave author, an eminent French physician, that fish being a prolifick dyet, there are more children born in Roman Catholick countries about nine months after Lent, the markets will be more glutted than usual, because the number of Popish infants, is at least three to one in this kingdom, and therefore it will have one other collateral advantage, by lessening the number of Papists among us.

I have already computed the charge of nursing a beggar's child (in which list I reckon all cottagers, labourers, and four-fifths of the farmers) to be about two shillings per annum, rags included; and I believe no gentleman would repine to give ten shillings for the carcass of a good fat child, which, as I have said, will make four dishes of excellent nutritive meat, when he hath only some particular friend, or his own family to dine with him. Thus the squire will learn to be a good landlord, and grow popular among his tenants, the mother will have eight shillings neat profit, and be fit for work till she produces another child.

15   Those who are more thrifty (as I must confess the times require) may flea the car-cass; the skin of which, artificially dressed, will make admirable gloves for ladies, and summer boots for fine gentlemen.

As to our City of Dublin, shambles may be appointed for this purpose, in the most convenient parts of it, and butchers we may be assured will not be wanting; although I rather recommend buying the children alive, and dressing them hot from the knife, as we do roasting pigs.

A very worthy person, a true lover of his country, and whose virtues I highly es-teem, was lately pleased, in discoursing on this matter, to offer a refinement upon my scheme. He said, that many gentlemen of this kingdom, having of late destroyed their deer, he conceived that the want of venison might be well supply'd by the bod-ies of young lads and maidens, not exceeding fourteen years of age, nor under twelve; so great a number of both sexes in every country being now ready to starve for want of work and service: And these to be disposed of by their parents if alive, or other-wise by their nearest relations. But with due deference to so excellent a friend, and so deserving a patriot, I cannot be altogether in his sentiments; for as to the males, my American acquaintance assured me from frequent experience, that their flesh was generally tough and lean, like that of our school-boys, by continual exercise, and their taste disagreeable, and to fatten them would not answer the charge. Then as to the females, it would, I think, with humble submission, be a loss to the publick, because they soon would become breeders themselves: And besides, it is not im-probable that some scrupulous people might be apt to censure such a practice, (al-though indeed very unjustly) as a little bordering upon cruelty, which, I confess, hath always been with me the strongest objection against any project, how well so-ever intended.

But in order to justify my friend, he confessed, that this expedient was put into his head by the famous Salmanaazor, a native of the island Formosa, who came from thence to London, above twenty years ago, and in conversation told my friend, that in his country, when any young person happened to be put to death, the executioner sold the carcass to persons of quality, as a prime dainty; and that, in his time, the body of a plump girl of fifteen, who was crucified for an attempt to poison the Em-peror, was sold to his imperial majesty's prime minister of state, and other great mandarins of the court in joints from the gibbet, at four hundred crowns. Neither indeed can I deny, that if the same use were made of several plump young girls in this town, who without one single groat to their fortunes, cannot stir abroad without a chair, and appear at a play-house and assemblies in foreign fineries which they never will pay for; the kingdom would not be the worse.

Some persons of a desponding spirit are in great concern about that vast number of poor people, who are aged, diseased, or maimed; and I have been desired to em-ploy my thoughts what course may be taken, to ease the nation of so grievous an in-cumbrance. But I am not in the least pain upon that matter, because it is very well known, that they are every day dying, and rotting, by cold and famine, and filth, and vermin, as fast as can be reasonably expected. And as to the young labourers, they are now in almost as hopeful a condition. They cannot get work, and consequently pine away from want of nourishment, to a degree, that if at any time they are accidentally hired to common labour, they have not strength to perform it, and thus the country and themselves are happily delivered from the evils to come.

I have too long digressed, and therefore shall return to my subject. I think the advantages by the proposal which I have made are obvious and many, as well as of the highest importance.

For first, as I have already observed, it would greatly lessen the number of Papists, with whom we are yearly over-run, being the principal breeders of the nation, as well as our most dangerous enemies, and who stay at home on purpose with a design to deliver the kingdom to the Pretender, hoping to take their advantage by the absence of so many good Protestants, who have chosen rather to leave their country, than stay at home and pay tithes against their conscience to an episcopal curate.

Secondly, The poorer tenants will have something valuable of their own, which by law may be made liable to a distress, and help to pay their landlord's rent, their corn and cattle being already seized, and money a thing unknown.

Thirdly, Whereas the maintainance of an hundred thousand children, from two years old, and upwards, cannot be computed at less than ten shillings a piece per annum, the nation's stock will be thereby encreased fifty thousand pounds per annum, besides the profit of a new dish, introduced to the tables of all gentlemen of fortune in the kingdom, who have any refinement in taste. And the money will circulate among our selves, the goods being entirely of our own growth and manufacture.

Fourthly, The constant breeders, besides the gain of eight shillings sterling per annum by the sale of their children, will be rid of the charge of maintaining them after the first year.

Fifthly, This food would likewise bring great custom to taverns, where the vintners will certainly be so prudent as to procure the best receipts for dressing it to perfection; and consequently have their houses frequented by all the fine gentlemen, who justly value themselves upon their knowledge in good eating; and a skilful cook, who understands how to oblige his guests, will contrive to make it as expensive as they please.

Sixthly, This would be a great inducement to marriage, which all wise nations have either encouraged by rewards, or enforced by laws and penalties. It would encrease the care and tenderness of mothers towards their children, when they were sure of a settlement for life to the poor babes, provided in some sort by the publick, to their annual profit instead of expence. We should soon see an honest emulation among the married women, which of them could bring the fattest child to the market. Men would become as fond of their wives, during the time of their pregnancy, as they are now of their mares in foal, their cows in calf, or sow when they are ready to farrow; nor offer to beat or kick them (as is too frequent a practice) for fear of a miscarriage.

Many other advantages might be enumerated. For instance, the addition of some thousand carcasses in our exportation of barrel'd beef: the propagation of swine's flesh, and improvement in the art of making good bacon, so much wanted among us by the great destruction of pigs, too frequent at our tables; which are no way comparable in taste or magnificence to a well grown, fat yearly child, which roasted whole

20

25

will make a considerable figure at a Lord Mayor's feast, or any other publick entertainment. But this, and many others, I omit, being studious of brevity.

Supposing that one thousand families in this city, would be constant customers for infants flesh, besides others who might have it at merry meetings, particularly at weddings and christenings, I compute that Dublin would take off annually about twenty thousand carcasses; and the rest of the kingdom (where probably they will be sold somewhat cheaper) the remaining eighty thousand.

I can think of no one objection, that will possibly be raised against this proposal, unless it should be urged, that the number of people will be thereby much lessened in the kingdom. This I freely own, and 'twas indeed one principal design in offering it to the world. I desire the reader will observe, that I calculate my remedy for this one individual Kingdom of Ireland, and for no other that ever was, is, or, I think, ever can be upon Earth. Therefore let no man talk to me of other expedients: Of taxing our absentees at five shillings a pound: Of using neither cloaths, nor houshold furniture, except what is of our own growth and manufacture: Of utterly rejecting the materials and instruments that promote foreign luxury: Of curing the expensiveness of pride, vanity, idleness, and gaming in our women: Of introducing a vein of parsimony, prudence and temperance: Of learning to love our country, wherein we differ even from Laplanders, and the inhabitants of Topinamboo: Of quitting our animosities and factions, nor acting any longer like the Jews, who were murdering one another at the very moment their city was taken: Of being a little cautious not to sell our country and consciences for nothing: Of teaching landlords to have at least one degree of mercy towards their tenants. Lastly, of putting a spirit of honesty, industry, and skill into our shop-keepers, who, if a resolution could now be taken to buy only our native goods, would immediately unite to cheat and exact upon us in the price, the measure, and the goodness, nor could ever yet be brought to make one fair proposal of just dealing, though often and earnestly invited to it.

30   Therefore I repeat, let no man talk to me of these and the like expedients, 'till he hath at least some glympse of hope, that there will ever be some hearty and sincere attempt to put them into practice.

But, as to my self, having been wearied out for many years with offering vain, idle, visionary thoughts, and at length utterly despairing of success, I fortunately fell upon this proposal, which, as it is wholly new, so it hath something solid and real, of no expence and little trouble, full in our own power, and whereby we can incur no danger in disobliging England. For this kind of commodity will not bear exportation, and flesh being of too tender a consistence, to admit a long continuance in salt, although perhaps I could name a country, which would be glad to eat up our whole nation without it.

After all, I am not so violently bent upon my own opinion, as to reject any offer, proposed by wise men, which shall be found equally innocent, cheap, easy, and effectual. But before something of that kind shall be advanced in contradiction to my scheme, and offering a better, I desire the author or authors will be pleased maturely to consider two points. First, As things now stand, how they will be able to find food and raiment for a hundred thousand useless mouths and backs. And secondly, There being a round million of creatures in humane figure throughout this kingdom, whose whole subsistence put into a common stock, would leave them in debt two million of pounds sterling, adding those who are beggars by profession, to the bulk of farmers, cottagers and labourers, with their wives and children, who are beggars in effect; I desire those politicians who dislike my overture, and may perhaps be so bold to attempt an answer, that they will first ask the parents of these mortals, whether they would not at this day think it a great happiness to have been sold for food at a year old, in the manner I prescribe, and thereby have avoided such a perpetual scene of misfortunes, as they have since gone through, by the oppression of landlords, the impossibility of paying rent without money or trade, the want of common sustenance, with neither house nor cloaths to cover them from the inclemencies of the weather, and the most inevitable prospect of intailing the like, or greater miseries, upon their breed for ever.

I profess, in the sincerity of my heart, that I have not the least personal interest in endeavouring to promote this necessary work, having no other motive than the publick good of my country, by advancing our trade, providing for infants, relieving the poor, and giving some pleasure to the rich. I have no children, by which I can propose to get a single penny; the youngest being nine years old, and my wife past child-bearing.

EXAMPLE 3: Satire News Article

The Onion

Professor Deeply Hurt by Student's Evaluation

Leon Rothberg, Ph.D., a 58-year-old professor of English Literature at Ohio State University, was shocked and saddened Monday after receiving a sub-par mid-semester evaluation from freshman student Chad Berner. The circles labeled 4 and 5 on the Scan-Tron form were predominantly filled in, placing Rothberg's teaching skill in the "below average" to "poor" range.

Although the evaluation has deeply hurt Rothberg's feelings, Berner defended his judgment at a press conference yesterday.

"That class is totally boring," said Berner, one of 342 students in Rothberg's introductory English 161 class. "When I go, I have to read the school paper to keep from falling asleep. One of my brothers does a comic strip called 'The Booze Brothers.' It's awesome."

The poor rating has left Rothberg, a Rhodes Scholar, distraught and doubting his ability to teach effectively at the university level.

"Maybe I'm just no good at this job," said Rothberg, recipient of the 1993 Jean-Foucault Lacan award from the University of Chicago for his paper on public/private feminist deconstructive discourse in the early narratives of Catherine of Siena. "Chad's right. I am totally boring."

In the wake of the evaluation, Rothberg is considering canceling his fall sabbatical to the University of Geneva, where he is slated to serve as a Henri Bynum-Derridas Visiting Scholar. Instead, Rothberg may take a rudimentary public speaking course as well as offer his services to students like Berner, should they desire personal tutoring.

"The needs of my first-year students come well before any prestigious personal awards offered to me by international academic assemblies," Rothberg said. "After all, I have dedicated my life to the pursuit of knowledge, and to imparting it to those who are coming after me. I know that's why these students are here, so I owe it to them."

Though Rothberg, noted author of *The Violent Body: Marxist Roots of Postmodern Homoerotic Mysticism and the Feminine Form in St. Augustine's Confessions*, has attempted to contact Berner numerous times by telephone, Berner has not returned his calls, leading Rothberg to believe that Berner is serious in his condemnation of the professor.

"I'm always stoned when he calls, so I let the answering machine pick it up," said Berner, who maintains a steady 2.3 GPA. "My roommate just got this new bong that totally kicks ass. We call it Sky Lab."

10   Those close to Rothberg agree that the negative evaluation is difficult to overcome.

"Richard is trying to keep a stiff upper lip around his colleagues, but I know he's taking it very hard," said Susan Feinstein-Rothberg, a fellow English professor and Rothberg's wife of 29 years. "He knows that students like Chad deserve better."

When told of Rothberg's thoughts of quitting, Berner became angry.

"He'd better finish up the class," Berner said. "I need those three humanities credits to be eligible to apply to the business school next year."

The English Department administration at Ohio State is taking a hard look at Rothberg's performance in the wake of Berner's poor evaluation.

15   "Students and the enormous revenue they bring in to our institution are a more valued commodity to us than faculty," Dean James Hewitt said. "Although Rothberg is a distinguished, tenured professor with countless academic credentials and knowledge of 21 modern and ancient languages, there is absolutely no excuse for his boring Chad with his lectures. Chad must be entertained at all costs."

USE THE TOOLKIT

Let's use the three genre toolkit questions from Chapter 1 to examine this genre.

What Is It?

These are examples of satirical arguments, or satire. A satirical argument works by arguing the opposite case in an exaggerated way, or by using irony to point out the inconsistencies or absurdity of another argument. While it may come across as funny, satire also has a deeper purpose: to criticize problems in a social structure, institution, or government.

Example 1 criticized what the author perceived to be unreasonable fears of gender-neutral housing held by the university administration—that the housing policy would cause students to behave promiscuously. In Example 2, Jonathan Swift was criticizing the cruel attitudes of his contemporaries toward the poor in Ireland. In Example 3, the writers of the piece criticized the tendency for universities to use student satisfaction as an increasingly important criterion for decisions, including evaluations of professors.

Satire also tends to use a common set of rhetorical features. For example, word play and style choices are very important.

Who Reads It?

These satires are all directed primarily at members of a specific community—those who belong to the social institution being critiqued, but also those who might be entertained by the satire.

For instance, Swift published his satire anonymously in 1729, as a pamphlet meant to support the cause of the Irish, who were exploited by the English, dealing with famine, poverty, and the unscrupulous absentee landlords that Swift mentions in his "proposal." Swift's satire was meant to be read not only by the Irish who were suffering these conditions, but also by the British, who had the potential to change those conditions. Pia's satire mocks the administrators and parents who, she would argue, infantilize college students with their fears about gender-neutral housing.

What's It For?

The goal of a satire is to argue a point or lodge a criticism in a humorous way, often by pointing out the absurdities in news events, politics, and the like. Authors of satire use exaggerated appeals to emotions to make their points, seeking to persuade through indirect means. Readers must be able to figure out that the piece is not to be taken seriously in order to be persuaded by it. In some cases, readers may not realize that a satirical column such as this one is not meant to be taken literally. Some readers of "A Modest Proposal," for instance, have thought that Swift was actually advocating for infanticide and cannibalism! Thus, it is important for writers of satire to take into account the possibility that some readers may get the wrong idea.

EXERCISE 10.3: Analyze a Satire

Locate several examples of satire: either "fake news," such as *The Onion*, advertisements, or editorials in a newspaper or magazine (print or online). Take note of what strategies seem effective and funny, and what pieces miss the mark (either by being offensive or simply being unfunny). Then, come up with a set of criteria for an effective satire piece.

> ## MULTIMEDIA EXERCISE 10.3: Analyze Satire across Media Forms
>
> Locate several examples of satire from different media formats—videos, blogs, news columns, or visual advertisements. Come up with a list of strategies used in these different examples, and sort them into two groups: features that occur across different formats, and features that are unique to one format. For example, you might find that the tendency to distort a familiar logo or image occurs mainly in advertisements, while the tendency to use wordplay (such as "The Daily Voice" becoming the "Daily Vice") tends to appear in multiple formats.

E. Strategies for Argumentative Genres

So far, we have examined several different kinds of argumentative genres, starting with a visual example (an advertisement), and then considering written examples (letters to the editor and editorial), and then oral examples (a campaign speech). We then examined satire as a kind of argumentative genre that can appear in any of those types. In the process, we have identified a number of features that argumentative genres share, including appeals to logic, emotion, and character. (You'll find more information about arguments, in general, in Chapter 18.)

In this chapter, then, we'll examine how you might go about writing one of these genres. Imagine that you have been asked to contribute a satire for your college newspaper.

Let's see how one student, Pia, went about this assignment.

Prewriting (Content)

First, Pia looked at some recent articles in the newspaper (online and in print) to determine what kinds of topics seemed timely, and to identify what kinds of topics might be appropriate for a good satire. She also brainstormed a list of recent events and issues in her campus and in her local community:

- *student council elections*
- *proposal for gender-neutral housing on campus*
- *town-gown relations*
- *student parking*
- *cutting the physical education requirement*

Next, Pia tried writing out different claims (sometimes called thesis statements—see Chapter 18). Since she was writing a satire, she considered claims that she could exaggerate for effect, making a few notes about possible ideas or points she might make for satirical effect.

- *student council elections*
  - *Your posters and annoying chants totally make me want to vote for you.*
- *proposal for gender-neutral housing on campus*
  - *We should just call gender-neutral housing on campus "boy girl sexy time" housing since that's what everyone's afraid of*
- *town-gown relations*
- *student parking*
  - *Parking lots totally beautify campus landscape so we should have more of them.*
- *Cutting the physical education requirement*
  - *"Life fit" classes are too rigorous—I couldn't finish my Melville paper because I had to study for my walking class.*

Next, Pia brainstormed more ideas for the issue she finds most compelling from her list—gender-neutral housing. She thought this issue would give her the most fodder for her satire. Here's a snippet from her notes:

- *Gender neutral housing on campus = "boy girl sexy time" housing.*
  - *"Orgies" of student studying break out late night—parody of a party (books strewn everywhere, writing indiscriminately in notebooks, etc.)*
  - *Could include interviews from students living in Garner Hall*

Of course, Pia also did research (Chapter 24) to see what others were saying about her topic.

Pia also planned her satire to address the counter-arguments (Chapter 18) that people had made against gender-neutral housing. She also framed a rebuttal.

Counter-Argument against Gender-Neutral Housing

- *What people are saying: Gender neutral housing will lead to inappropriate sexual activity. → Use idea of "orgies" and "boy-girl sexy-time housing" to lampoon this idea.*

Rebuttal

- *Implies we are children who cannot be responsible for ourselves—use a quote to parody this point?*

Drafting (Organizing)

When drafting an argument, it is important to consider how your opening will draw readers in. If you are addressing an audience that opposes your position, for example, you may want to create an introduction that first addresses their concerns, before stating your own opinion.

In the case of a satire, the opening often reads like a typical argument—that is, it poses as a serious case for or against something. The reader should gradually realize that you are writing satirically, not in earnest. Pia started out with a paragraph that might read as a serious argument:

> The University Administration and certain parent groups have shown appropriate concern about the proposed, so-called "gender-neutral" housing situation that would allow male and female university students to live in the same dorm rooms.

The reader would gradually realize that Pia was speaking satirically—that she was not actually opposing gender-neutral housing—in the next paragraph, when she introduces the term "boy-girl sexy-time housing."

The rest of the article serves to amplify the claim through additional examples and details. Pia added quotations as evidence, but for a serious argument you might also build up evidence in the form of facts, statistics, or reason chains (Chapter 18).

Revising (Style)

When you seek feedback on your draft, ask readers to highlight phrases or terms that might alienate your readers, such as inflammatory language that might seem fine for people who already agree with you, but that might turn off readers who do not agree. You should pay close attention to your tone. Sometimes, weighted language (Chapter 21) can be used selectively to emphasize your points, but you should be careful to avoid overly emotional wording.

In a satire, it is important not to take things too far. Often, there is a fine line between poking fun at an issue and offending readers, especially if you are writing about a topic that can come across as racist, sexist, homophobic, or narrow-minded.

Pia originally wrote the following quote from Susan Day (a fictional resident of Garner Hall).

> Susan Day, a resident of Garner who asked me not to use her middle name out of concern for her privacy, bore witness to this travesty: "The orgies were everywhere you turned, in every room. Some girls are studying promiscuously—they are off studying every night in a different guy's room. Then we get to watch them stumble home in the morning, still in their disheveled study clothes from the night before."

During peer review, Pia's classmates mentioned that this passage seemed over the top and that it might be drawing on sexist stereotypes. So Pia revised this quotation to read as follows:

> Susan Day, a resident of Garner who asked me not to use her middle name out of concern for her privacy, bore witness to this travesty: "The orgies were everywhere you turned, in every room. Students had books strewn all over their rooms. Pens of every color, and notebooks—these fancy composition books from places like France and Japan. And they were *writing* in them. Shudder."

Also, be careful about writing in the first person ("I think . . ."). While your personal opinions may be valid, focusing too much on yourself can make you come across as self-centered or ill-tempered. Instead, support your position with evidence drawn from other sources as well, from interviews with fellow students to facts and statistics (Chapter 24).

You might also watch out for logical fallacies, which are claims that may mislead or manipulate an audience (Chapter 18). Note that a satire, however, might actually work by drawing on fallacies, such as exaggerated appeals to pity or fear.

Editing (Design)

When you write for a newspaper or other print or online news publication, the editorial staff will exercise a lot of control over the design of your document. They will also edit your work, sometimes changing entire words or sentences that you wrote. They may also give your work a title. This is normal for a print newspaper as well as the newspaper's website.

In Pia's case, the newspaper editor suggested a new title, "Uncontrolled Study Orgies Break Out in Gender-Neutral Dorm," instead of her original title, "Let's Call Gender-Neutral Housing What it Is: Boy-Girl Sexy Time." The editor also shortened her article slightly to fit with the newspaper's standard length for opinion pieces.

If you would like to exercise more control over the final appearance of your editorial or article, you should publish it yourself, on a blog, for example, or on a flier.

Troubleshooting

Here are some common challenges that students face when writing argumentative genres.

I need help formulating my claim.   When writing an argument, you can start with the arguments of others. For a satire, you can take an opinion that you think is incorrect, and then satirize it by exaggerating the original claim. For a letter to the editor, find an article in the paper that you disagree with and start from there. (See Chapter 18 for more on how to develop claims.)

I can't find any evidence to support my argument.   A lack of evidence may mean that you need to reconsider your claim. It is unethical to argue a point just because you believe in it despite all evidence to the contrary. It is highly unethical to argue a point that requires you to ignore or twist the facts. (See Chapter 18 for more on how to locate evidence through research, personal experience, and rhetorical invention.)

I need help organizing my argument.   You can look carefully at examples of the genre you are writing, including the selections in this chapter. Pay attention to how writers tend to begin, how they order their sections or points, and how they conclude. Then, try out some of those strategies for your own document. (See Chapter 20 for more on how to organize your argument.)

My argument seems self-centered.   Sometimes, relying too heavily on your own experience can lead to an argument that seems self-centered. For example, if you are writing a letter to the editor for your college newspaper about a problem affecting you personally (say, lack of air conditioning in your dorm room), you might feel tempted to describe your own personal suffering.

However, your argument might seem more compelling if you also include the perspectives of others in your dorm. You could interview friends and use quotes to support your claims, or you could do some research to determine the prevalence of the problem and its possible effects. (How many students lack air conditioning?)

Also, consider the perspective of your audience—what aspects of the issue will they care about? School administrators might care more about the air conditioning problem if you can connect it to students' overall performance in school or their satisfaction with the university.

My argument seems boring.   Sometimes, when students write argumentative genres, they tend to get stuck in "student mode," and they end up producing something that reads more like an essay or five-paragraph theme than the genre they have been asked to write. Watch out for features of the essay genre that you use automatically, such as formal transitional words and phrases to start each paragraph (such as "In conclusion," or "Moreover,").

Often, argumentative genres use different strategies to focus each paragraph, such as providing a statistic, example, short sentence, or rhetorical question. You might also alter your tone or level of formality (see Chapter 21) to liven up your prose and make it more suitable for the genre.

F. Chapter Project: Write a Satire

Write a satirical op-ed column or letter to the editor for your college newspaper. Think about your audience (members of the college community) and your purpose (to persuade your readers to agree with your point of view).

Group Option

Put together an issue for the April Fool's issue of your campus magazine or newspaper. With your group, brainstorm topics for satirical news stories, opinion columns, and letters to the editor. Then, write at least two pieces each. If you get stumped, look for examples from satire publications such as *The Onion*. Make sure to vet each piece carefully with your group, making sure that your documents are humorous, not offensive.

Multimedia Option

With your group, prepare a segment of a satirical news show, in the style of Jon Stewart or Stephen Colbert. You should each take on a speaking role (you can be reporters, experts, the host, or an invited guest, for example). You might choose a recent current event or controversy to focus your segments. Record your segments with a video camera, and be prepared to share them with the class.

Academic Research Genres

Academic research genres are the means through which scholars share their research with other scholars and the world. A scholar is a researcher who contributes to an academic field. While specific academic fields sometimes use specific genres (such as field reports in anthropology), many academic fields share the genres featured here.

In college, many of the assignments you will write will be academic research genres. In almost any course, you may be asked to write a research paper, article, or review. When an instructor asks for a research genre, that means you are expected to do outside research, drawing on sources besides the ones you have read in class and your own ideas. (For more on doing research, see Part 4.) For example, in a political science class you might be asked to research how education and income levels influence voter participation in your state and compose a research paper that demonstrates your findings. For a sociology class, you might be asked to interview someone you know from a different ethnic background to yours, and then use research on assimilation and ethnic identity to interpret the interview results.

In the workplace, academic research genres are written primarily by scholars. Professors at large universities are typically required to publish research in order to get promoted. They write articles and literature reviews for scholarly journals. However, academic research genres are similar to a variety of other kinds of writing that you might encounter outside universities and colleges. Many types of reports (Chapter 4) include findings from research and may include a literature review section.

In this chapter, you will learn how to compose several of the most common academic research genres: abstracts, annotated bibliographies, literature reviews, and research papers.

A. Academic Research Mini-Genre: Abstract

An abstract is a short document, usually a single paragraph, that accompanies a research article or student research paper. The abstract summarizes the main research questions and findings. Researchers often need to write abstracts before they publish their results.

For example, when submitting a proposal for a conference presentation, a researcher may need to include an abstract of their presentation—in some cases before they have even finished their research! In this case, the abstract summarizes the research project and what the researcher anticipates she will find.

EXAMPLE 1: Abstract for a Biology Article

M. Navarrete, G. Perea, D. Fernandez de Sevilla, M. Gómez-Gonzalo, A. Núñez, et al. (2012), "Astrocytes Mediate In Vivo Cholinergic-Induced Synaptic Plasticity," PLoS Biology 10(2) doi:10.1371/journal.pbio.1001259.

When we learn associations between items or ideas, such as the value of currency used in a foreign country, the connections between certain brain cells become stronger. In the cellular process thought to underlie learning and memory—long-term potentiation (LTP)—the simultaneous activation of two connected neurons causes one cell to respond more robustly to signals from the other one. "Neurons that fire together wire together" is a phrase commonly used to describe this phenomenon.

Recent studies suggest that neuronal communication and LTP are influenced by star-shaped glial cells called astrocytes, which are known to provide nutrients to neurons and support their basic functions. However, because much of this evidence was collected from brain slices and different research groups have produced conflicting results, scientists have questioned the involvement of astrocytes in learning.

This week in *PLoS Biology*, neuroscientist Alfonso Araque of the Cajal Institute in Madrid, Spain, and his collaborators report novel evidence of LTP regulation by astrocytes in living rats and propose a new cellular mechanism of learning and memory. Because this study suggests that astrocytes play an integral role in storing information in the brain, it resolves an important and high-profile debate in the field.

In the study, Araque and his team focused on pairs of neurons in the hippocampus, a brain region that is crucial for learning and memory. They generated LTP either by pinching the rat's tail or through direct electrical stimulation of the neurons.

Using in vivo imaging techniques, the researchers also found that these manipulations boosted calcium levels in astrocytes, causing them to release the neurotransmitter glutamate. This chemical signal binds to and activates proteins called metabotropic glutamate receptors (mGluRs) located on the surface of nearby neurons, thereby enhancing LTP. Consistent with this chain of events, the team found that elevated calcium levels in astrocytes triggered an increase in neurotransmitter release from the neurons.

The researchers further determined that LTP only occurred when mGluRs were functional and when neuronal responses and calcium signaling in astrocytes were simultaneously evoked by stimulation. By regulating LTP through the activation of mGluRs, which are prevalent in the hippocampus, astrocytes may support learning in a range of situations and could be an important target for treating Alzheimer's disease and other memory disorders.

5

EXAMPLE 2: Abstract for a Rhetoric Article

Mike Duncan, "Polemical Ambiguity and the Composite Audience: Bush's 20 September 2001 Speech to Congress and the Epistle of 1 John," *Rhetoric Society Quarterly,* **Fall 2011, 41:5, 455–471.**

George W. Bush's September 20, 2001, address to Congress and the first-century CE early Christian text of 1 John both exhibit a form of rhetorical ambiguity, called here "polemical ambiguity," that does not fit within Eisenberg's concept of strategic ambiguity, but rather serves as its argumentative doppelgänger. Polemical ambiguity allows a rhetor to leave real and potential allies in a composite audience in doubt as to the exact parameters of the rhetor's message, while an alienated section of the composite audience perceives a stark and wholly unambiguous message. The following analysis explores how Bush's speech and 1 John, faced with composite audiences, pursue similar goals through the use of polemical ambiguity, as well as how this particular maneuver is closely linked to religious rhetoric.

EXAMPLE 3: Abstract for a Political Science Article

Jessica Ross, "Closing Guantanamo Bay: The Future of Detainees," *NeoAmericanist,* **2010, 5:1.**

At the start of his presidency, Barack Obama issued an Executive Order to shut down the naval base at Guantanamo Bay and halt all detainees' trial proceedings pending the creation of a review process. Legal scholars and White House advisors made suggestions regarding how to shut the prison down and what to do with its occupants. In this paper, I will argue that detainees should be tried in federal courts and sent home or transferred to prisons within the United States. I will examine the nature of the President's Executive Order and documents outlining traditional protections granted to detainees including the Geneva Conventions, the Uniform Code of Military Justice, and Supreme Court rulings. An analysis of how to proceed with the adjudication of detainees will follow. My findings illustrate that the most efficient solution to these problems is to implement domestic parole programs and try detainees in US federal courts.

USE THE TOOLKIT

Let's use the three genre toolkit questions from Chapter 1 to examine this genre.

What Is It?

The preceding three documents are all examples of abstracts. Each one provides a short summary of an academic research article. Abstracts usually contain the title of the article, the author's name(s), the main claims of the article, the research methods, and the methods of analysis. You'll also see that abstracts sometimes include a set of keywords that go along with the article—these are search terms readers might use to find similar articles. You will notice that abstracts use specialized vocabulary from the field in question: the first abstract refers to the "in vivo imaging techniques," while the second one refers to terminology from rhetoric studies, such as "strategic ambiguity."

Who Reads It?

Abstracts often appear before a full article. Researchers may read the abstract first, and then decide whether to read the entire article. Students also find abstracts useful when conducting research, since the abstract will tell them whether articles are relevant to their projects. Abstracts may also be read by other audiences; for example, a journalist may use an abstract to write a news article about a new scientific finding.

What's It For?

An abstract provides a brief overview of the article, helping potential readers to decide whether or not to read the article. You'll also notice that abstracts tend to give away the main claim or findings—that is, an abstract does not leave readers guessing about what an article contains.

EXERCISE 11.1

Imagine that you have been asked to submit a proposal for an undergraduate research conference happening on your campus. Your proposal will include an abstract of the research you plan to present.

- Choose a topic related to your major field of interest (Chapter 23) .
- Then, determine a primary research method (Chapter 24).
- Prepare an abstract describing your topic, the methods you hope to use, and the results you expect from your research.
- As an alternative, if you are writing a research paper for your course, begin by writing an abstract to help you plan your research paper.

GROUP ACTIVITY 11.1

Imagine that your group is putting together a panel presentation for an undergraduate research conference happening on your campus. You will share an overall topic, but each of you will present research from the perspective of a different academic discipline. For example, if you choose to present on HIV/AIDS, you might have an education student research teachers' attitudes toward teaching HIV/AIDS awareness, a film major study how AIDS patients are represented in film, a nursing major research students' awareness of HIV/AIDS prevention, and a pre-law student study the restrictions in immigration laws pertaining to HIV/AIDS.

Each group member will:

- Choose a topic related to your major field of interest (Chapter 23).
- Then, determine a primary research method (Chapter 24).
- Prepare an abstract describing your topic, the methods you hope to use, and the results you expect from your research.

B. Annotated Bibliography

While an abstract summarizes one article or source, an annotated bibliography is a list of many sources with short summaries of each. The summaries, or annotations, are similar to abstracts, only they may also include an evaluation of each source—how credible or sound it is, or how relevant it may be for a specific project.

EXAMPLE 1: Annotated Bibliography for a Student Research Paper (excerpt)

Chris Clayman

Annotated Bibliography

Primary:

U.S. House. Subcommittee on Foreign Operations and Government Information, Committee on Government Operations. *U.S. Government Information Policies and Practices: The Pentagon Papers (Part 1) (Witness Panel #2)* Hearing, 92nd Cong., 32, 1971. (testimony of Joseph Bishop). Print.

Professor at Yale Law School speaks of the constitutional problems of using Executive Privilege for prior restraint, in the context of NYT's release of the Pentagon Papers. His insights will help address constitutional questions in the censorship of leaks.

Secondary:

Cohen, Henry. "Press Restrictions in the Persian Gulf War: First Amendment Implications," *U.S. Congressional Research Service* Publication No 91-316 A (1991). Print.

Analyzes press restrictions during the Persian Gulf War and implications for the First Amendment's guarantee of free speech and press. Reviews content of press restrictions, pro and con arguments, restrictions in prior wars, lawsuits, and first amendment principles on prior restraint and right of access. This gives my paper the ability to compare leak practices now with leaks during the first Gulf War.

EXAMPLE 2: Annotated Bibliography for a Dissertation (excerpt)

"Resisting the Apocalypse: Telling Time in American Novels about AIDS, 1982–1992" (Doctoral Dissertation by Lisa Garmire, UCSB 1996)

COMPREHENSIVE ANNOTATED BIBLIOGRAPHY OF AMERICAN AIDS NOVELS: 1982–1992

PRIMARY AIDS NOVELS

The experience of living with AIDS lies at the center of the narratives of these contemporary American novels.

Bishop, Michael. *Unicorn Mountain*. New York: Arbor House, 1988.

This novel interweaves Native American and unicorn mythologies to trace parallels between a virus that plagues a herd of mysterious unicorns in the Rockies and AIDS, which assails and ultimately kills Bo, one of the novel's main characters. Though ending with Bo's death, the novel moves beyond death by incorporating Ute mythology about spiritual afterlife and depicts Bo's journey to "Over There."

Black, Jeff. *Gardy and Erin*. Stamford, CT: Knights Press, 1989.

Gardy and Erin tells the story of a successful businessman, Gardy, and his experiences during the course of a year. The narrative is framed by two AIDS-related suicides: early on, Gardy's lover commits suicide following an HIV+ diagnosis, and toward the end of the book, Gardy witnesses his friend Stan commit suicide and die with dignity rather than suffer any longer from AIDS. Gardy ultimately copes with these losses by assuming fatherhood over a neglected little girl, Erin. AIDS and death are linked by suicide in this novel.

Bourjaily, Vance. *Old Soldier: A Novel*. New York: Donald I. Fine, 1990.

This novel describes a fishing trip that the old soldier, 60-year-old and just divorced Joe makes with his younger brother and musician, Tommy, whose AIDS prevents his lungs from working well enough to play bagpipes. The novel culminates in a shootout, when AIDSphobic nearby campers burn their camper and fire weapons on Tommy. Tommy drowns himself in the river rather than subject Joe and "little Joe" (Tommy's son) to a slow death. The novel ends with Joe telling his grandson that Tommy died a "clean death."

Bram, Christopher. *In Memory of Angel Clare*. New York: Fine, 1988.

This novel traces how a group of friends copes with the loss of their mutual friend, Clarence, who has died of AIDS. Interspersed within this narrative is the recollection of Clarence's life with his lover, Michael, and Clarence's developing illness and then death from AIDS. This secondary narrative tracks the apocalyptic trajectory of AIDS but is somewhat alleviated by the primary narrative's depiction of the surviving characters' emotional growth beyond mourning.

EXAMPLE 3: Annotated Bibliography Published in a Journal (excerpt)

Annotated Bibliography:

Women and Literacy

Sandra Kerka and Susan Imel

Books, Articles, and Reports

Breen, M. J., & Hall, L. (1999). *So many changes: Women, health, and midlife.* Toronto, Canada: Lawrence Heights Community Health Centre Press. The thoughts, ideas, feelings, and experiences of 35 women interviewed by the authors are woven throughout the text, which is written at a fifth-grade reading level. Chapters on stress, menopause, and relationships will appeal to midlife and older women and will serve as a springboard for discussion. Appropriate for group or one-on-one instruction.

Castle, J., Attwood, G., & Smythe, S. (2001, June). Are women-targeted programs women-positive? In R. O. Smith et al. (Eds.) *Proceedings of the Adult Education Research Conference, Michigan State University, East Lansing.* Full text available at http://www.edst.educ.ubc.ca/aerc/2001/2001castle.htm. The authors distinguish between women-targeted and women-positive programs, citing examples of unsuccessful education programs in South Africa that were targeted at women. They question the educational and political aims of these initiatives and suggest that women-positive programs foreground gender within a broader context of transformation involving both men and women.

Cottingham, S., Metcalf, K., & Phnuyal, B. (1998, July). The REFLECT approach to literacy and social change: A gender perspective. *Gender and Development,* 6(2), 27–34. The authors look at the opportunities offered by REFLECT, a participatory approach to adult literacy and social change, to promote women's rights and gender equality, outlining the principles on which the REFLECT process is based and analyzing the learning points arising from an evaluation of three pilot projects using the approach.

Cuban, S. (2001, April). "Oh, so lucky to be like that, somebody care": Five case studies of selected midlife women learners seeking care in a literacy program. Paper presented at the Annual Meeting of the American Educational Research Association, Seattle, WA. The author reports on a study that problematizes the role of caring in

Annotated bibliography published in a journal.

USE THE TOOLKIT

Let's use the three genre toolkit questions from Chapter 1 to examine this genre.

What Is It?

From the preceding examples, you can see that an annotated bibliography is a list of sources on a given topic, accompanied by short summaries. Each annotated bibliography uses the citation style appropriate for the academic field in question: the first two use MLA format (Chapter 28), while the third one uses APA format (Chapter 28).

You'll notice that, for each source, the author has provided a brief description. You might consult the abstract for a source (if it has one) to help write this summary, but the goal of an annotated bibliography is to provide your own assessment of the research and its usefulness.

The annotation may address some of the following questions:

- What is this source about?
- Who wrote it?
- How will it be useful for researchers or for your own research?

Who Reads It?

Annotated bibliographies are usually read by other researchers. The second example was published on a website, so readers are probably researchers who have searched for information about AIDS and novels. The third example was published in the journal *Women's Studies Quarterly*, so readers are likely to be scholars in Women's Studies who are searching for information about literacy. The first example is a student assignment, so the readers likely include the professor and classmates.

What's It For?

Annotated bibliographies help scholars to find out what research has been done on a particular topic. For researchers, annotated bibliographies are great timesavers—they collect relevant information in one place and give readers a sense of its importance. Sometimes, annotated bibliographies will also evaluate the information included, so readers get a sense of how credible or authoritative each source may be. As a student, you might also write an annotated bibliography to help you get started on a larger research project. You'll be able to refer back to your annotated bibliography as you conduct further research or write a research paper, article, or presentation.

EXERCISE 11.2: Prepare an Annotated Bibliography

Using the topic you chose in Exercise 11.1, prepare an annotated bibliography of sources pertinent to your topic. For each source, summarize the main research finding, and then indicate how this study relates to your proposed research. For example, does the method used give you ideas for your own research methods (Chapter 24)? Does this research open up a new line of inquiry for you to pursue? Identify at least six relevant sources, using library databases (Chapter 24).

GROUP ACTIVITY 11.2: Prepare a Group Annotated Bibliography

Do Exercise 11.2, as before, only with the goal of assembling a bibliography that will be useful for researchers doing interdisciplinary research (or research across several disciplines). You will each look for specialized sources from your area to include in the group bibliography. Aim for at least six sources each.

MULTIMEDIA EXERCISE 11.1

Create an online annotated bibliography for your research topic. Consider how you can make use of online features to make your bibliography more useful for others. Can you provide links? Images? A way to navigate through the list?

C. Literature Review

Like an annotated bibliography, a literature review is a summary of previous research. However, while an annotated bibliography is a list of sources, a literature review presents a group of sources in essay form and interprets their significance in a given field. A literature review helps an audience find out what research has been done in a field, and often, helps them evaluate that research.

EXAMPLE 1: Literature Review for an Environmental Science Course

Kirby Diamaduros

Tropical Rainforest Deforestation: Effects, Mitigation, and Solutions

Introduction to Deforestation

Each year, more than two billion tons of carbon dioxide and other greenhouse gases are liberated into the atmosphere as a result of deforestation (*1*). Earth's atmosphere is entirely composed of a medley of elements and gases including carbon dioxide, oxygen, and nitrogen. These gases play a vital role in the Earth's ability to sustain life. However, in the past century, increased rates of deforestation have caused some of these gases to greatly increase their presence in the atmosphere. Gases such as carbon dioxide and methane, known as greenhouse gases, have increased by as much as 145% in the atmosphere, causing the world's natural warming process to accelerate quickly (*2*). An accumulation of greenhouse gases in the atmosphere has amplified the greenhouse effect and can be partially attributed to the destruction of tropical rainforests around the world.

Deforestation is the destruction of forests and rainforests resulting in the permanent loss of vegetation. Tropical deforestation is acknowledged as one of the most socio-economically threatening problems facing the world today (*3*). The destruction of rainforests results from myriad causes including the clearing of forests for farm and pasture land, misguided government policies, and commercial exploitation of tropical forest resources (*4*). This article will focus on the global and local ramifications of tropical rainforest destruction, government policies regarding deforestation, and possible solutions to deforestation. If deforestation is more closely researched, its effects will be better understood and movements towards repression and methods for reforestation and afforestation can be applied.

Local and Global Effects of Deforestation

Deforestation accounts for nearly 25% of all human-induced emissions of atmospheric carbon dioxide (1). Tropical rainforests are typically destroyed and cleared to facilitate land used for agricultural or residential purposes. The profound effects of tropical deforestation can adversely influence the Earth and its inhabitants on both local and global levels. Studies by Houghton (1990) and Fearnside (2005) concluded that as tropical rainforests are cleared, the wood from these forests is either combusted, used for the production of wood products, or left at the site to decay. Continued research proves that each of these processes liberates substantial amounts of carbon dioxide and other greenhouse gases into the atmosphere.

Locally, the destruction of tropical rainforests can cause an augmentation in the rate of soil erosion, a decline in the amount of rainfall in surrounding areas, reduction of the water-holding capacity of soils, and an increase in the frequency and severity of floods (5). Consequently, the effects of soil erosion and nutrient depletion combine to cause infertility and a decline in the sustainability and productivity of the land. In order to counter soil degradation, inputs of nutrients, manure, and lime may be utilized; however, limited quantities of resources render this method ineffective for large areas (6).

Perhaps one of the most significant and obvious effects of deforestation, global warming has been in the spotlight of nearly every conservationist for over two decades. Global effects resulting from the destruction of tropical rainforests include the irreversible loss of entire species of fauna, alterations in the hydrological cycle, and variations in the climate of the Earth. Fearnside (2005) and Houghton (1990) both acknowledged that deforestation results in an increase in the emission of greenhouse gases and, therefore, an amplification of the greenhouse effect. Carbon dioxide and other greenhouse gases such as nitrous oxide and methane are released from the combustion of wood and destruction of forests. These gases also play a critical role in increasing the rate of global warming. In order to better understand the effects of tropical deforestation on the Earth, research needs to be conducted to quantitatively assess the amount of carbon dioxide released into the atmosphere annually due to the destruction of tropical rainforests.

Government Policies Regarding Global Warming

With more than two billion tons of carbon dioxide and other greenhouse gases being released into the atmosphere each year, the effects of deforestation are becoming more evident to government agencies around the world, forcing them to look for new ideas to halt deforestation. There are two main strategies which governments are using to approach the mitigation of deforestation. One such approach is through the passing of international reforms and protocols and the other is through the enforcement of local mitigation policies.

In 1992, more than 150 nations met in Rio de Janeiro at the United Nations Framework Convention on Climate Change in order to discuss policies regarding climate change and deforestation. The meeting in Rio de Janeiro gave birth to another conference which was held in Kyoto, Japan in 1997. Since then, countries throughout the world have pushed for the destruction of forests to be included in limitations on greenhouse-gas emissions in the Kyoto Protocol. Implications such as these have received much opposition from some European countries and, surprisingly, Brazil, which has fought to keep the inclusion of forest protection out of the Kyoto Protocol for unjustified reasons (6). The United States has also refused to ratify the Kyoto Protocol because it claims that the protocol is flawed in allowing China, the second largest emitter of greenhouse gases, to be entirely exempted from the requirements of the Kyoto Protocol simply because it is considered a developing country (7).

While some international reforms have greatly influenced the push for the repression of deforestation, many countries with significant areas of tropical rainforests have a tendency to mitigate deforestation on their own terms. In order to restrict deforestation, countries such as Brazil launch campaigns against deforestation using inspections and fines annually. Since the first campaign in 1989, the implementation of these repression methods has proven ineffective. Studies show that deforestation rates appear to fluctuate and dissipate independently of repression campaigns (6). It is evident that methods for repressing deforestation are in need of reform. However, before international organizations and local governments can implement reforms, the effects and potential solutions of deforestation must be better understood.

Solutions to Counteract the Effects of Deforestation

Deforestation is constantly proceeding in more than fifteen nations worldwide including Brazil, Madagascar, and Tanzania (3). Individual nations and organizations worldwide have begun looking at the potentially beneficial effects of reforestation and afforestation as a solution to tropical rainforest deforestation. The most common practice implemented to combat the effects of deforestation is reforestation, the re-establishment of new vegetation where forests once existed but were destroyed by human processes (8). Reforestation is being used as a method to offset carbon emissions in areas such as the Sichuan Province in China (*9, 10*). Studies in China indicate that reforestation thoroughly reduces the effects of deforestation in tropical areas by increasing concentrations of soil carbon, increasing the amounts of nutrients such as nitrogen in the soil, and by decelerating soil erosion (*10*). Reforestation also allows vegetation being grown in these areas to sequester carbon from the atmosphere, thus reducing levels of carbon and reversing the effects of deforestation on global warming (*9*).

The articles of the Kyoto Protocol not only discuss the mitigation of deforestation through reforestation, but also through the promotion of afforestation projects. Afforestation is the conversion of land into forested areas (*8*). Countries such as the United States and Vietnam have begun experimenting with the practice of afforestation as a means to increase rates of carbon sequestration (*11, 12*). The testing of afforestation has provided positive results of increased rates of carbon sequestration in many tropical areas of East Asia (*11*). Afforestation also shares many of the effects of reforestation including the reduction of soil erosion and increases in soil carbon concentrations (*13*). Continued research needs to be conducted on the quantitative effects of afforestation and reforestation on carbon sequestration in tropical rainforests. These conclusions will aid in discovering which methods of afforestation or reforestation will prove most effective in heavily deforested tropical areas.

Conclusions

Even with recent advancements towards the repression of tropical rainforest deforestation, the problem is still prominent throughout the world. This article explored the local and global effects of deforestation, local and international policies regarding deforestation mitigation, and solutions to counteract the effects of deforestation. The evidence presented in this article supports the hypothesis that, as research continues, deforestation and its effects are becoming better understood and, consequently, methods for the repression of the destruction of tropical forests are also becoming more effective. Mitigation policies are also becoming more sufficient as research concerning tropical rainforest deforestation is completed.

While much research concerning the causes and effects of tropical deforestation has been completed, there is still much research to be performed. The effects of restoration methods in deforested areas are still in need of quantification, as are the effects of afforestation in tropical areas around the world. Also, there is still much debate and much research to be accomplished over the total area of tropical rainforest which has been destroyed as well as the effect of this destruction on atmospheric greenhouse gas levels. As the world begins to address the serious effects of deforestation as a global rather than a regional problem, continued research will be able to generate more environmentally effective reforms on mitigating tropical rainforest destruction.

References

1. Kourous, G. (Food and Agriculture Organization). (2005, December 9). *Incentives to curb deforestation needed to counter climate change.* Retrieved from http://www.fao.org/newsroom/en/news/2005/1000176/index.html

2. Sierra Club. Global Population and Environment Program. Retrieved from http://www.sierraclub.org/population/reports/globalwarming.asp

3. CIDA Forestry Advisors Network.(2003, August 31). *DEFORESTATION: Tropical forests in decline*. Retrieved from http://www.rcfa-cfan.org/english/issues.12-1.html

4. World Rainforest Movement. (n.d.). *Causes of deforestation*. Retrieved from http://www.wrm.org.uy/deforestation/

5. Houghton, R. A. (Environmental Science & Technology). (1990). The global effects of tropical deforestation. Retrieved from http://pubs3.acs.org/acs/journals/doilookup?in_doi=10.1021/es00074a001

6. Fearnside, P. M. (2005, June). Deforestation in Brazilian Amazonia: History, rates, and consequences. *Conservation Biology 19*(3). Retrieved from http://www.blackwell-synergy.com/doi/full/10.1111/j.1523-1739.2005.00697.x?cookieSet=1

7. Barrett, S. (1998). Political economy of the Kyoto Protocol. *Oxford Review of Economic Policy 14*(4). Retrieved from http://oxrep.oxfordjournals.org/cgi/content/abstract/14/4/20

8. FAO Corporate Document Repository. (2000). *FRA 2000: On definitions of forest and forest change* (FRAP Working Paper 33). Retrieved from http://www.fao.org/docrep/006/ad665e/ad665e04.htm

9. Silver, W. L., Lugo, A. E., & Ostertag, R. (2000). The potential for carbon sequestration through reforestation of abandoned tropical agricultural and pasture lands. *Restoration Ecology 8*(4). Retrieved from http://www.blackwell-synergy.com/links/doi/10.1046/j.1526-100x.2000.80054.x

10. Liu, S. L., Chen, L. D., Fu, B. J., & Lu, Y. H. (2002). Effects of reforestation and deforestation on soil properties in humid mountainous areas: A case study in Wolong Nature

Reserve, Sichuan province, China. *Soil Use and Management 18*(4). Retrieved from

http://www.ingentaconnect.com/content/cabi/sum/2002/00000018/00000004/art00010

11. Foley, J. A. et al. (2005). Global consequences of land use. *Science 309*(5734). Retrieved

from http://www.sciencemag.org/cgi/content/full/309/5734/570

12. Nguyen, H. T., Adger, W. N., & Kelly, P. M. (1998). Natural resource management in

mitigating climate impacts: The example of mangrove restoration in Vietnam. *Global

Environmental Change, 8*(1). Retrieved from http://www.uea.ac.uk/env/cserge/pub/wp/

gec/gec_1996_06.htm

13. Nilsson, S., & Schopfhauser, W. (1995). The carbon-sequestration potential

of a global afforestation program. *Climate Change, 30*. Retrieved from http://

www-ca2.csa.com/ids70/view_record.php?id=2&recnum=0&SID=eee65f

e6b2174578d34bc8d6a6e219e7&mark_id=search%3A2%3A0%2C0%2C1

EXAMPLE 2: Literature Review for a Medical Journal (excerpt)

Internet-Based Physical Activity Interventions: A Systematic Review of the Literature

Marleen H van den Berg, PhD, Johannes W Schoones, BA, and Theodora PM Vliet Vlieland, MD, PhD

Introduction

Regular physical activity is associated with lower morbidity and mortality rates from cardiovascular disease [1–4], diabetes mellitus [5], cancer [6], and osteoporosis [7]. Despite these proven health benefits, the majority of the adult population in Western nations does not meet the public health recommendations for physical activity [8-12]. Therefore, there is a need for the delivery of effective interventions aimed at positively influencing physical activity behavior.

Traditionally, most physical activity interventions use face-to-face modes of delivery (eg, individual consultations or group meetings). [. . .] With the number of people having access to and using the Internet rapidly increasing [19], the Internet is more and more used as a mode of delivery for physical activity programs. The strength of Internet-based physical activity interventions lies in the fact that with this mode of delivery large numbers of individuals can be reached at lower costs than with face-to-face interventions [20]. Moreover, by using the Internet, participants can access large amounts of information, and they can choose the time when they would like to interact and receive information [21]. Previous reviews on the effectiveness of Web-based physical activity interventions have indicated that the Internet can indeed serve as a promising mode of delivering physical activity interventions [20-24]. However, most of these reviews need to be updated as they comprised studies that were conducted between 2000 and 2003. This is all the more important as previous reviews included mainly observational and anecdotal studies, whereas a number of randomized controlled trials have been published over recent years. Moreover, specific methodological characteristics of studies on physical activity interventions, such as the measurement of physical activity, have not yet been addressed in reviews that were exclusively aimed at Internet-based interventions.

The aim of this review is therefore to systematically assess both the methodological quality and the effectiveness of interventions designed to promote physical activity by means of the Internet as evaluated by randomized controlled trials.

Methods

Search Strategy

In cooperation with a trained librarian (JS), a search strategy was composed. The following databases were searched: PubMed (1949 to July 2006), Web of Science (1945 to July 2006), EMBASE (OVID-version, 1980 to July 2006), PsycINFO (1887 to July 2006), and Cochrane Library (1990 to July 2006). The search strategy consisted of the AND combination of three main concepts: Internet, physical activity, and intervention. [. . .] To be included, articles had to describe an intervention in which one of the primary goals was the promotion of physical activity among adults (18 years or older). Furthermore, the intervention had to be delivered predominantly by means of the Internet in one of the following ways: (1) exchange of information via the World Wide Web between a health care setting and an individual (eg, between a clinic and a participant's home or workplace), (2) use of email for communication between a therapist or health care professional and a patient (or patient group). Internet-based physical activity interventions that promoted physical activity in order to achieve a secondary goal, such as weight reduction, were also included. [. . .]

Results

5   [. . .] The physical activity outcome measures of both the intervention and control groups are expressed as pretest and posttest results. [. . .] Four studies included one physical activity outcome parameter [32,35,36,41], five studies included two physical activity parameters [34,39,40,42,43], and one study reported more than two

physical activity parameters [37]. Five of the 10 selected studies reported additional physical fitness-related outcome measures such as cardiorespiratory fitness, flexibility, and body weight [32,35-37,43]. In three of these five studies [32,35,36], the reported changes in physical activity level were considered a secondary outcome; primary outcomes in these studies were changes in body weight and waist circumference [35,36], cardiorespiratory fitness, and walking speed [32].

Regarding the four studies [. . .] in which Internet-based interventions were compared with a waiting list, two studies reported significant differences between the intervention and control groups [39,42]. With respect to the four studies [. . .] in which the intensity of contact in two types of Internet-based physical activity intervention varied, one study reported significant differences between the intervention and control groups with respect to change in physical activity level [37]. Two of the four studies [35,36] [. . .] were not primarily aimed at increasing physical activity level, but rather to decrease body weight and waist circumference.

The changes in physical activity level were all nonsignificant in the three studies in which the applied treatment procedures of two Internet-based physical activity interventions varied. [. . .] This section comprised one study in which physical activity was not the primary outcome measure [32].

[. . .]

Discussion

On the basis of the above-mentioned results of this review, we conclude that there is indicative evidence that Internet-based physical activity interventions are more effective than a waiting list group. With respect to which components serve as the key components (i.e., amount of contact or type of treatment procedure), the evidence is scanty.

Several factors may have contributed to the limited evidence of effectiveness. First, the number of eligible studies was limited. [. . .] Second, this review comprised mainly short-term physical activity interventions. Only three studies incorporated interventions of 6 months or longer. [. . .] Third, the baseline physical activity levels of the participants differed, making it difficult to report on the overall effectiveness of these interventions. Moreover, four studies in this review did not report any baseline physical activity levels. Since physically active persons in general are better able to comply with physical activity interventions and maintain a healthy lifestyle than sedentary persons [49-51], incomplete or inconsistent information about baseline physical activity levels may have influenced our results. [. . .]

In conclusion, the methodological quality as well as the type of physical activity outcome measure of Internet-based physical activity interventions varied. However, Internet-based physical activity interventions appear to be more effective when compared to a waiting list strategy. Whether or not adding specific components to Internet-based physical activity interventions will result in greater effectiveness compared to Internet-based interventions in which these components are missing or offered less intensely remains to be established. An important advantage of Internet-based interventions is that they can reach large numbers of people at relatively low cost. However, more cost-effectiveness studies should be done in order to establish the exact surplus value of this delivery method when compared with more traditional methods such as face-to-face sessions. Moreover, future research should properly define the control groups and incorporate both long-term as well as uniform and objective physical activity outcome measures.

References

1. Berlin JA, Colditz GA. A meta-analysis of physical activity in the prevention of coronary heart disease. *Am J Epidemiol.* 1990;Oct 1;132(4):612–28. [PubMed: 2144946]

2. Kaplan GA, Strawbridge WJ, Cohen RD, Hungerford LR. Natural history of leisure-time physical activity and its correlates: associations with mortality from all causes and cardiovascular disease over 28 years. *Am J Epidemiol.* 1996 Oct 15;144(8):793–7. http://aje.oxfordjournals.org/cgi/pmidlookup?view=long&pmid=8857828. [PubMed: 8857828]

3. Sesso HD, Paffenbarger RS, Lee IM. Physical activity and coronary heart disease in men: The Harvard Alumni Health Study. *Circulation.* 2000;Aug 29;102(9):975–80. http://circ.ahajournals.org/cgi/pmidlookup?view=long&pmid=10961960. [PubMed: 10961960]

4. Lee IM, Rexrode KM, Cook NR, Manson JE, Buring JE. Physical activity and coronary heart disease in women: is "no pain, no gain" passé? *JAMA.* 2001 Mar 21;285(11):1447–54. doi: 10.1001/jama.285.11.1447. http://jama.ama-assn.org/cgi/pmidlookup?view=long&pmid=11255420.joc01451 [PubMed: 11255420]

5. Helmrich SP, Ragland DR, Leung RW, Paffenbarger RS. Physical activity and reduced occurrence of non-insulin-dependent diabetes mellitus. *N Engl J Med.* 1991;Jul 18;325(3):147–52. [PubMed: 2052059]

6. Giovannucci E, Ascherio A, Rimm EB, Colditz GA, Stampfer MJ, Willett WC. Physical activity, obesity, and risk for colon cancer and adenoma in men. *Ann Intern Med.* 1995;Mar 1;122(5):327–34. http://www.annals.org/cgi/pmidlookup?view=long&pmid=7847643. [PubMed: 7847643]

7. Bravo G, Gauthier P, Roy PM, Payette H, Gaulin P, Harvey M, Péloquin L, Dubois MF. Impact of a 12-month exercise program on the physical and psychological health of osteopenic women. *J Am Geriatr Soc.* 1996 Jul;44(7):756–62. [PubMed: 8675921]

8. Jones DA, Ainsworth BE, Croft JB, Macera CA, Lloyd EE, Yusuf HR. Moderate leisure-time physical activity: who is meeting the public health recommendations? A national cross-sectional study. *Arch Fam Med.* 1998;7(3):285–9. doi: 10.1001/archfami.7.3.285. http://archfami.ama-assn.org/cgi/pmidlookup?view=long&pmid=9596466. [PubMed: 9596466]

9. Centers for Disease Control and Prevention (CDC). Physical activity trends—United States, 1990–1998. *MMWR Morb Mortal Wkly Rep.* 2001;Mar 9;50(9):166–9. http://www.cdc.gov/mmwr/preview/mmwrhtml/mm5009a3.htm. [PubMed: 11393487]

10. Hootman JM, Macera CA, Ham SA, Helmick CG, Sniezek JE. Physical activity levels among the general US adult population and in adults with and without

arthritis. *Arthritis Rheum.* 2003;Feb 15;49(1):129–35. doi: 10.1002/art.10911. http://dx.doi.org/10.1002/art.10911. [PubMed: 12579604]

11. Fontaine KR, Heo M. Changes in the prevalence of US adults with arthritis who meet physical activity recommendations, 2001–2003. *J Clin Rheumatol.* 2005 Feb;11(1):13–6. doi: 10.1097/01.rhu.0000152143.25357.fe.00124743-200502000-00004 [PubMed: 16357691]

12. Ooijendijk W, Hildebrandt V. Physical activity in the Netherlands 2000: first results from the monitoring study Physical Activity and Health [in Dutch]. In: Ooijendijk W, Hildebrandt V, Stiggelbout M, eds. *Trendrapport Bewegen en Gezondheid 2000/2001.* Heerhugowaard, The Netherlands: PlantijnCasparie; 2002:7–23.

[. . .]

19. World Internet Users and Population Statistics 2006. *Internet World Stats. Web site* http://www.internetworldstats.com/stats.htm. Accessed August 16, 2007.

20. Marcus BH, Nigg CR, Riebe D, Forsyth LH. Interactive communication strategies: implications for population-based physical-activity promotion. *Am J Prev Med.* 2000 Aug;19(2):121–6. doi: 10.1016/S0749-3797(00)00186-0.S0749-3797(00)00186-0 [PubMed: 10913903]

21. Napolitano MA, Marcus BH. Targeting and tailoring physical activity information using print and information technologies. *Exerc Sport Sci Rev.* 2002 Jul;30(3):122–8. doi: 10.1097/00003677-200207000-00006. [PubMed: 12150571]

22. Marcus BH, Owen N, Forsyth LH, Cavill NA, Fridinger F. Physical activity interventions using mass media, print media, and information technology. *Am J Prev Med.* 1998 Nov;15(4):362–78. doi: 10.1016/S0749-3797(98)00079-8. S0749379798000798 [PubMed: 9838978]

23. Marshall AL, Owen N, Bauman AE. Mediated approaches for influencing physical activity: update of the evidence on mass media, print, telephone and website delivery of interventions. *J Sci Med Sport.* 2004 Apr;7(1 Suppl):74–80. doi: 10.1016/S1440-2440(04)80281-0. [PubMed: 15214605]

24. Winett RA, Tate DF, Anderson ES, Wojcik JR, Winett SG. Long-term weight gain prevention: a theoretically based internet approach. *Prev Med.* 2005 Aug;41(2):629–41. doi: 10.1016/j.ypmed.2004.12.005.S0091-7435(05)00037-X [PubMed: 15917062]

[. . .]

32. Rovniak LS, Hovell MF, Wojcik JR, Winett RA, Martinez-Donate AP. Enhancing theoretical fidelity: an e-mail-based walking program demonstration. *Am J Health Promot.* 2005;20(2):85–95. [PubMed: 16295700]

[. . .]

34. Marshall AL, Leslie ER, Bauman AE, Marcus BH, Owen N. Print versus website physical activity programs: a randomized trial. *Am J Prev Med.* 2003 Aug;25(2):88–94. doi: 10.1016/S0749-3797(03)00111-9.S0749379703001119 [PubMed: 12880874]

35. Tate DF, Wing RR, Winett RA. Using internet technology to deliver a behavioral weight loss program. *JAMA.* 2001 Mar 7;285(9):1172–7. doi: 10.1001/jama.285.9.1172. http://jama.ama-assn.org/cgi/pmidlookup?view=long&pmid=11231746.joc01569 [PubMed: 11231746]

36. Tate DF, Jackvony EH, Wing RR. Effects of internet behavioral counseling on weight loss in adults at risk for type 2 diabetes: a randomized trial. *JAMA.* 2003 Apr 9;289(14):1833–6. doi: 10.1001/jama.289.14.1833. http://jama.ama-assn.org/cgi/pmidlookup?view=long&pmid=12684363.289/14/1833[PubMed: 12684363]

37. Van Den Berg MH, Ronday HK, Peeters AJ, Le Cessie S, Van Der Giesen FJ, Breedveld FC, Vliet Vlieland TPM. Using internet technology to deliver a home-based physical activity intervention for patients with rheumatoid arthritis: a randomized controlled trial. *Arthritis Rheum.* 2006 Dec 15;55(6):935–45. doi: 10.1002/art.22339. [PubMed: 17139640]
[. . .]

39. Napolitano MA, Fotheringham M, Tate D, Sciamanna C, Leslie E, Owen N, Bauman A, Marcus B. Evaluation of an internet-based physical activity intervention: a preliminary investigation. *Ann Behav Med.* 2003;25(2):92–9. doi: 10.1207/S15324796ABM2502_04.[PubMed: 12704010]

40. Mckay HG, King D, Eakin EG, Seeley JR, Glasgow RE. The diabetes network internet-based physical activity intervention: a randomized pilot study. *Diabetes Care.* 2001 Aug;24(8):1328–34. doi: 10.2337/diacare.24.8.1328. http://care.diabetesjournals.org/cgi/pmidlookup?view=long&pmid=11473065. [PubMed: 11473065]

41. Kosma M, Cardinal BJ, Mccubbin JeA. A pilot study of a web-based physical activity motivational program for adults with physical disabilities. *Disabil Rehabil.* 2005 Dec 15;27(23):1435–42. doi: 10.1080/09638280500242713. L51X290818153558 [PubMed: 16418058]

42. Plotnikoff RC, Mccargar LJ, Wilson PM, Loucaides CA. Efficacy of an E-mail intervention for the promotion of physical activity and nutrition behavior in the workplace context. *Am J Health Promot.* 2005;19(6):422–9. [PubMed: 16022206]

43. Hageman PA, Walker SN, Pullen CH. Tailored versus standard internet-delivered interventions to promote physical activity in older women. *J Geriatr Phys Ther.* 2005;28(1):28–33. [PubMed: 16236225]
[. . .]

49. King AC, Kiernan M, Oman RF, Kraemer HC, Hull M, Ahn D. Can we identify who will adhere to long-term physical activity? Signal detection methodology as a potential aid to clinical decision making. *Health Psychol.* 1997 Jul;16(4):380–9. doi: 10.1037/0278-6133.16.4.380. [PubMed: 9237091]

50. Worcester MUC, Murphy BM, Mee VK, Roberts SB, Goble AJ. Cardiac rehabilitation programmes: predictors of non-attendance and drop-out. *Eur J Cardiovasc Prev Rehabil.* 2004 Aug;11(4):328–35. doi: 10.1097/01.hjr.0000137083.20844.54.00149831-200408000-00010 [PubMed: 15292767]

51. Bock BC, Marcus BH, Pinto BM, Forsyth LH. Maintenance of physical activity following an individualized motivationally tailored intervention. *Ann Behav Med.* 2001;23(2):79–87. doi: 10.1207/S15324796ABM2302_2. [PubMed: 11394558]

● ●

EXAMPLE 3: Literature Review for a Scientific Blog

Agustín Fuentes

Get Over It: Men and Women Are from the Same Planet

Recent publication in PLoS ONE by psychologist Del Giudici and colleagues [i] has reignited the debate about just how "naturally" different men and women are. Del Giudici et al. state that their findings of a "pattern of global sex differences . . . may help elucidate the meaning and generality of the broad dimension of individual differences known as 'masculinity-femininity'."

In a commentary, psychologist Dario Maestripieri [ii] gushes that this study has finally demonstrated that "when it comes to personality men and women belong to two different species." In spite of the hoopla and pronouncements that men are indeed from Mars and women from Venus this study, and the commentaries, ignore that trying to assess and explain similarities and differences between human genders and sexes is very complicated and quite messy. Apparently, it also makes people act a little silly.

There are three major problems with the conclusions being drawn from study: a) "gender" and "sex" are used interchangeably, b) evolved differences in men and women are not being measured, and c) relevant biological and anthropological datasets are ignored. Let me just review these problems and leave you with a plea for a bit of sanity and some scientific integrity when it comes to thinking and talking about men and women.

"Sex" and "Gender" are not the same thing. Sex is a biological state that is measured via chromosomal content and a variety of physiological and developmental measures. Gender is the roles, expectations and perceptions that a given society has for the sexes. Most societies have two genders on a masculinity-femininity continuum, some have more. The two are interconnected, but not the same thing. We are born with a sex, but acquire gender and there is great inter-individual diversity within societies and sexes in regards to how sex and gender play out in behavior and personality. There is an extensive body of literature demonstrating this, but many researchers interested only in definitive distinctions between men and women choose to disregard it.

To measure evolutionary differences in behavior within a species is extremely difficult, but there are at least two basic methodological approaches that are required. First, assessments must be comparative across more than one population of the species of interest. Second, the traits being measured must have some way of being linked or connected with heritable aspects of human physiology or behavior that has an effect on overall fitness, and they must be assessed via measures that are accessible, and replicable, across different populations in the species. Del Giudici et al. used a large questionnaire sample of mostly white, educated Americans. Relative to the global diversity in cultural structure, this is a limited sample and not a comparative evolutionary one for the species. 5

Their data come from assessments of 15 personality variables using scales such as "reserved vs. warm," "serious vs. lively," "tolerates disorder vs. perfectionistic," and "shy vs. socially bold." These are indeed personality assessments but they are mired in cultural contexts and meanings, not easily transferable across human societies in time and space, and extremely difficult, if not impossible, to connect, quantitatively, to any aspect of human physiology, neurology, or other structured, identifiable, target for natural selection to act on. Also, these are most likely not static traits of individuals, but rather dynamic states that are fluid over the lifetime.

[. . .] There are no consistent brain differences between the sexes [iii], there is incredible overlap in our physiological function [iv], we engage in sexual activity in more or less the same patterns [v], and we overlap extensively in most other behavior as well. There are some interesting re-occurring differences, particularly in patterns of aggression and certain physiological correlates of reproduction, muscle density, and body size. However, anthropological datasets show enormous complexity in how and why men and women behave the ways that they do [vi]. Studies in human biology and anthropology regularly demonstrate a dynamic flexibility and complex biocultural context for all human behavior, and this is especially true for gender.

Del Giudici et al. and Maestripieri are trying to counter Janet Shibley-Hyde's "gender similarities hypothesis" [vii] because they "know" that men and women are more different than similar. There are many valid points of contention in regards to Shibley-Hyde's seminal paper and Del Giudici et al. bring up an important methodological one, but do not provide an actual assessment and analysis of the overall data set and meta-analyses that Shibley-Hyde used [viii]. My concern is not so much with some good back and forth in the peer reviewed literature, rather it is with the blogospheres' and the public's response to the article and to yet another flare-up in over simplistic assertions about the way that men and women "are" by nature.

There is something about avidly trying to prove men and women are different, or the same, that makes people lose their mind a bit. No matter how much some want it to be true, it is just not that simple; there are no clear cut and easy answers to why we do what we do, and why men and women sometimes have problems getting along. To ignore the enormous wealth of data on how men and women are similar AND different and to try to tackle this enormously complex reality via one-dimensional approaches is just poor science.

[i]   Del Giudice M., Booth, T., and Irwing P. The distance between Mars and Venus: Measuring global sex differences in personality. *PLoS ONE. 2012;*7(1): e29265.

[ii] http://www.psychologytoday.com/blog/games-primates-play/201201/ gender-differences-in-personality-are-larger-previously-thought

[iii] Eliot L. *Pink brain, blue brain.* Houghton Mifflin Harcourt; 2009., Wood JL, Heitmiller D, Andreasen NC, Nopoulos P. Morphology of the ventral frontal cortex: relationship to femininity and social cognition. *Cerebral Cortex. 2008;*18, 534–40.; Bishop K, Wahlsten D. Sex differences in the human corpus callosum: myth or reality? *Neuroscience and Biobehavioral Reviews. 1997;*21(5):581–601.

[iv] Fausto-Sterling A. *Sexing the body: gender politics and the construction of sexuality.* Basic Books; 2000., Ellison, PT, Gray PB, Eds. *The endocrinology of social relationships.* Harvard University Press; 2009:270–93.

 [v] Herbenick D, Reece M, Schick V, Sanders SA., Dodge B, Fortenberry JD. Sexual behavior in the United States: results form a national probability sample of men and women ages 14–94. *J. Sex Med.* 2010;7(suppl. 5):255–65.

[vi] Nanda S. *Gender diversity: cross-cultural variations.* Waveland Press; 2000., Donnan H, Magowan F. *The anthropology of sex.* Berg Publishers; 2010.

[vii] Hyde JS. The gender similarities hypothesis. *Am Psychol.* 2005;60: 581–92.

[viii] See Shibley-Hyde's comments at http://www.plosone.org/annotation/ listThread.action?inReplyTo=info%3Adoi%2F10.1371%2Fannotation %2F2aa4d091-db7a-4789-95ae-b47be9480338&root=info%3Adoi %2F10.1371%2Fannotation%2F2aa4d091-db7a-4789-95ae-b47be9480338

USE THE TOOLKIT

Let's use the three genre toolkit questions from Chapter 1 to examine this genre.

What Is It?

A literature review is a survey of the existing research on a topic in a certain field (or discipline). By conducting the review, a researcher gets a sense of where gaps lie in the field's knowledge of a topic, what approaches others have used to examine a topic, and what researchers already know about a topic. A writer may use the review to get started on an original research project, or she may publish the review so that other researchers can read it. The student writer in Example 1, Kirby, was reviewing studies of deforestation and its environmental effects. In Example 2, the writers are reviewing studies of Internet-based programs to encourage physical activity, and in Example 3, the writer reviews studies of sex differences.

Literature reviews may vary considerably between disciplines and even journals. In general, though, you can expect that literature reviews will do the following:

- Be organized according to sub-topics, themes, questions, or methods at issue, *not* by the individual sources included. For example, Kirby divided his literature review into three main categories: local and global effects of deforestation, government policies, and solutions; while the published example is organized like a report, with an introduction, methods, results and discussion (Chapter 14).
- Use detailed evidence from research articles (Chapter 24).
- Use the citation style common to the journal or discipline (Chapter 28).
- Employ technical, discipline-specific vocabulary, but define key terms for readers who may be new to the discipline in question.
- Employ a formal style, sometimes balanced with less formal elements to make the review more accessible (Chapter 21).

Who Reads It?

Literature reviews are read by other researchers. They may be meant for individuals who are new to a field and want to find out about the latest research, or they may be written for specialists who want to know what areas or methods are most promising for future research. For instance, readers of Example 2 might be designing their own study of Internet programs to increase physical activity, and might want to know what other studies have been done so that they can design a more effective study. In some cases, they may be written for a broader audience. Example 3 appeared on a blog linked to the website for the print magazine *Scientific American*, which publishes articles about science for a general readership.

What's It For?

A literature review does more than just summarize current research: it often makes an argument for why that research is or is not important, or it may argue for a particular direction for research in that field. In Example 2, the authors conclude that more long-term research studies need to be done, to see how well Internet-based programs work over time. In Example 1, Kirby argues that more research needs to be conducted in order to quantify the effects of reforestation on carbon dioxide levels.

EXERCISE 11.3: Write a Literature Review

Using the sources you identified in Exercise 11.2, write a literature review. You can choose to direct your literature review to an academic audience (as in Example 1) or to a broader public audience (as in Example 3).

D. Research Paper

While a literature review reports on previous research, a research paper is a report on original research. Original research can include a new reading of a literary text, archival research that includes something new about an historical figure, or scientific research in a laboratory, to give a few examples. However, you might include material from a literature review in your research paper to establish what scholars have already published about your topic. Research papers also typically include an abstract to key readers into the main contents and findings.

EXAMPLE 1: Research Article for an Undergraduate Journal (excerpt)

Kristine Thompson
Psychology
Class of 2014

Wait, You Stormed Franklin Street?
The Social and Psychological Motivations of UNC Sports Fans

Introduction

Sports are captivating spectacles that possess the capacity to affect the lives of millions of Americans, the ability to entertain people of all ages, and the unique power to blur the lines that divide our society. From the iconic images and famous radio broadcasts to the modern day heroics that captivate the nation, sports make up a vast and diverse subculture in the United States. Sports are an undeniable staple of American society, generating a total of $17.7 billion from commercial sports and an additional $21.4 billion from recreational activities, and also appearing in daily headlines of the country's most popular media corporations (Washington and Karen 187). Sports are often referred to as a microcosm of society, and in 1988 ranked ahead of the automobile, petroleum, and airline industries in gross national income (Frey and Eitzen 508). The centerpiece that allows for sports to make such a tremendous economic impact on society is the fan. A fan is defined as an "enthusiastic devotee of some particular sports object"; that is, in economic terms, fans are the consumers of sports when they purchase tickets or merchandise affiliated with a particular team (Hunt et al. 440). According to a study conducted by Murrell and Dietz, fans view themselves as an integral part of the game and a driving force behind the economic and social power of sport (28). Yet, as of 1995, only four percent of published research in sport psychology and sociology focused on the fan (Wann "Preliminary Validation" 377). Though this focus has increased in recent years, there remains a lack of understanding and investigation into the motivations of sports fans (Wann "Preliminary Validation" 377). This study focuses on the social and psychological factors that promote sports fandom and analyzes nine key motivations of sports fans at the University of North Carolina at Chapel Hill.

College athletics is a primary area of sports culture that exemplifies the extreme enthusiasm and passion of sports fans. According to Beyer and Hannah, "in no other country [than the U.S.] is college sports taken so seriously, given such large budgets, or so embedded within the structure of universities" (105). At UNC, which is widely recognized for its historic basketball program, students have been known to stand in line for hours to purchase tickets, take road trips to away games, and in one of the more famous displays of fanatic behavior, storm the main road on campus when the basketball team defeats archrival Duke. Sports at UNC comprise an important role in the larger framework of the university. For example, sports merchandise sales fund grants and financial aid packages awarded to students through contractual obligations, such as the ten-year, $37.7 million deal signed with Nike in 2008 (UNC General Alumni Association 1). Yet, even while serving as a crucial aspect of the university and eliciting such extreme behavior, sports are often uncritically accepted as part of the university culture without careful consideration of the complex ways sports culture is woven into the lives of the community members. The purpose of this study is to investigate the vast and diverse sports culture at the University of North Carolina–Chapel Hill in order to provide a more complete understanding of the motivations of Carolina fans.

Background

Previous studies aimed at identifying and understanding fan motivation helped to guide this study towards an investigation of North Carolina sports fans. The motivations given in this study were determined from current published research focused on the various factors and motivations of sports fans, namely the Sport Fan Motivation Scale model developed by Daniel Wann ("Preliminary Validation" 377–96). Using a variety of study methods, including a survey of gender and demographic fan information, Wann was able to identify and validate nine common motivations found among a diverse fan population ("Preliminary Validation" 377–96). The nine motivations identified in Wann's study were eustress, self-esteem, escape, entertainment, economic, aesthetic, group affiliation, family, and tradition. Eustress is defined as the positive form of stress involved in sport that energizes the fan, such as a last second shot to win the game or the gut-wrenching nervousness a fan experiences when winning and losing hangs in the balance (Wann "Preliminary Validation" 377). Self-esteem is a psychological influence in which a fan's own self-esteem is improved when the team is successful (Wann "Preliminary Validation" 378). Escape is a fairly common explanation of sport fandom, where fans use sports as a way to escape reality and gain temporary relief from daily stress. Entertainment involves the theatrical aspect of sport, because just like movies or TV shows, sports are entertaining and are built primarily around this entity. Economic refers to motivations regarding the economic success of the fan, for example gambling and other activities that involve monetary rewards for team achievement (Wann "Preliminary Validation" 378). Aesthetic appeal refers to the attraction of fans to the beauty and grace of athletic performance (Wann "Preliminary Validation" 378). Arguably, the most well-known motivation is group affiliation, which describes the desire to be part of something bigger than oneself and the human desire of group interaction that play a large role in fandom. The final motivation in Wann's study is family, in which fans relate sports to spending time with their family. These motives provided the lens through which the fan culture of UNC was viewed. Additionally, the Sport Fan Motivation Scale has been used by numerous researchers to further investigate sport fandom in the United States (Armstrong 309; James and Ridinger 260; Kwon and Trail 147; Wann et. al "Motivational Profiles" 6).

Methods

To study the main fan motivations at the University of North Carolina, a survey of UNC students (n = 111) was conducted to assess various levels of fan involvement and perceived motivations. [. . .] Surveys were distributed among the UNC population using an online survey, with no emphasis or data collection on demographics such as gender, age, etc. Participants were asked three questions and responses were automatically recorded using online qualtrics software provided by the Odum Institute of Research in Social Science at UNC. Participants were first asked to rank their level of involvement with NCAA athletics at UNC, including attending games, playing sports, etc., by choosing one of the following responses: never, rarely, sometimes, quite often, and very often. This assessment of fan involvement was incorporated for two purposes. The first was to provide an accurate gauge in the trends of sport involvement at UNC and to analyze basic sport involvement of the UNC community. The second was to limit bias as much as possible and ensure a diverse population of sports fans was studied, not merely those who are "die-hard" sports fans or who regularly attend games.

In the second question, which served as the main data collection aspect of the   5
current study, participants were presented with a list of nine possible motivations and asked to rank them in order of most important to least important. As stated previously, the motivations indentified by Daniel Wann in the Sport Fan Motivation Scale served as the framework of this study. Additionally, a ninth motivation was added to include the tradition of Carolina athletics. Subsequent studies by Wann have shown that tradition may also influence fan and team behavior (Wann "Understanding the Positive Social" 275). Tradition proved to be a worthwhile motivation to include in a study of collegiate athletics.

The third and final question presented in the current study was an open response in which participants were given the option of stating any other reasons they had for their level of sports involvement. Free responses were compared with quantitative data from previous questions to identify trends on data.

Results

Statistical analysis of 111 participant responses was used to determine the results presented in this study and to identify the overall ranking of each motivation. Results for question one, regarding participant's level of fan involvement, are reported as a straight value corresponding to the number of participants that choose each response. Analysis shows the majority of participants report being quite involved with sports at UNC (n = 39). The responses of each participant are shown (see Table 1) and graphically represented (see Figure 1) to provide a complete depiction of the distribution of responses for question one.

Table 1   Participant Level of Sport Involvement at UNC

#	Question	Never	Rarely	Sometimes	Quite Often	Very Often	Responses	Mean
1	I am involved with sports at UNC...	11	17	28	39	26	121	3.43

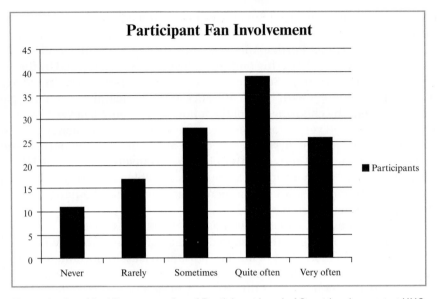

Figure 1   Graphical Representation of Participant Level of Sport Involvement at UNC

Results for question two, regarding the motivations of UNC sports fans, are reported as calculated numerical responses of each participant. In the survey, participants were asked to rank each motivation from 1 to 9, with 1 being the most and 9 being the least important. Responses showing the ranking of each motivation given by each participant were recorded. That is, the number of participants that ranked each motivation number one, number two, number three, and so on were recorded. This raw data is shown in Table 2. To determine the overall ranking of each motivation and take into account average ranking, not simply the motivation with the most "1" responses, individual responses were multiplied by a predetermined constant. For each motivation, the number of participants that ranked the motivation number 1 was multiplied by 9, the number of participants that ranked the motivation number 2 was multiplied by 8, so on and so forth, with the number of participants that ranked the motivation number 9 being multiplied by 1. For example, as shown in Table 2, 27 participants ranked eustress the most important motivation, which was multiplied by 9, 29 participants ranked it the second motivation, which was multiplied by 8, and so on. The manipulated values of each motivation were then added together to determine the final overall ranking of the nine motivations. The calculated rankings are shown in Figure 2. Results show the most important motivation for sport fandom at the University of North Carolina–Chapel Hill is entertainment, followed by eustress, escape, and group affiliation. Data show the least important motivation for sport involvement is economic concern; with 75 of the total 111 participants ranking economic the least reason for being involved with sports at UNC.

Table 2   Raw Data of Participant Rankings of Nine Motivations

#	Answer	1	2	3	4	5	6	7	8	9	Responses
1	I enjoy the tension and anxiety when my team is involved in a close game and winning and losing comes down to one play	27	29	16	10	10	6	6	5	2	111
2	I feel better about myself when I watch sports and I enjoy increased self-esteem after my team wins	1	11	14	10	15	13	14	24	9	111
3	Going to games or playing sports relieves stress and helps me forget about reality for a moment	15	18	23	19	11	9	7	8	1	111
4	Sports are a form of entertainment and I enjoy watching the game itself	32	23	12	19	12	8	4	0	1	111
5	I am a sports fan because I like gambling or betting on games	1	0	1	0	7	6	9	12	75	111
6	I enjoy the beauty and grace of athletics	4	2	11	13	15	16	19	21	10	111
7	I enjoy watching sports with large groups of people and I like feeling like I am part of something bigger than myself	16	14	17	17	16	10	14	7	0	111
8	Watching games gives me an opportunity to be with my family	7	6	10	9	10	17	23	22	7	111
9	I like Carolina sports because of the rich sports history and tradition	9	8	8	14	15	26	14	11	6	111
	Total	112	111	112	111	111	111	110	110	111	111

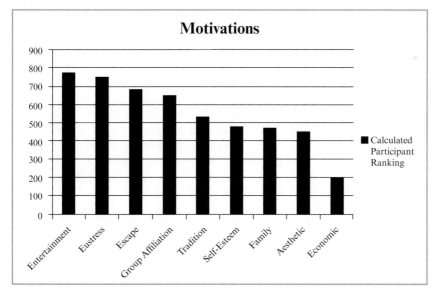

Figure 2 Calculated Participant Rankings of Nine Motivations

The free responses of participants from question three provided additional information about the sports culture at UNC. A number of participants cited sports as an important part of their identity, or they have played sports or have been sports fan their whole life, or sports provide unique opportunities to be involved with other people at Carolina.

Discussion

10   The results of this study show several interesting trends that can be used to better understand the sports culture at North Carolina. According to the data presented in this study, the most important motivation for students and members of the UNC community is the entertainment value of sports. Simply put, sports are fun and provide people with entertainment; like watching television or listening to music, sports are a leisure activity (Wann et. al "Sport Fan Motivation" 115). This finding in the UNC community comes as no surprise and is consistent with numerous findings in other studies. In one such study, Funk and James determined fans are often motivated by the prospect of hedonic, or pleasurable, experiences (139). While this result may seem intuitive, it can be attributed to the physiological desire to be involved with things we are interested in and may help explain the enormous revenues generated by sports. And, going one step farther, if an individual finds the behaviors associated with sport fandom—such as storming Franklin Street—entertaining, s/he is more likely to engage in those behaviors than someone who finds no entertainment value in sports. Interestingly, another study conducted by Frey and Eitzen proposed the idea that increased media surrounding sports has created an emphasis on display and entertainment value, altering the nature of sports (Frey and Eitzen 508). Frey and Eitzen call this change in the production of sports entertainmentization, where sports media has made a concerted effort to enhance the appeal of their sport product consistent with the commercial and entertainment agendas of media and sport establishments (509-10). Therefore, it only makes sense that when fed a more entertaining product, albeit often unconsciously, people are motivated to engage in sports to fulfill their desire for entertainment.

Another finding in relation to the entertainment motivation of sports at UNC is the similarity to the results of a study conducted by Daniel Wann, Frederick Grieve, Ryan Zapalac and Dale Pease that examined motives as they related to specific sports. Wann et. al examined differences in motivational profiles of fans of 13 different sports, including college basketball, professional football, boxing, tennis, etc. ("Motivational Profiles" 6). For college basketball, in which Wann et. al surveyed 138 participants, the motivations were ranked in the following order from high to low motivation: entertainment, eustress, group affiliation, self-esteem, family, aesthetic, escape, and economic ("Motivational Profiles" 11). These findings are strikingly similar to those presented in the current study and provide valuable insight into the responses of UNC students. Given the replicated findings of fans of college basketball coupled with the well-known historical relationship between North Carolina and college basketball, the motivations of sports fan at UNC may be a direct result of the most popular sport. Confounding variables may be present in this study and limitations of the survey conducted do not allow for a causal relationship to be determined. It could be that students who identify themselves as sports fans are attracted to UNC in the first place because of the fact that UNC is a traditional basketball school, which simply leads to more fans who are motivated by entertainment to attend UNC. Yet, even with possible confounding factors, it is clear that an interesting connection exists between the profile of sports fans at UNC and the most popular sport on campus. Further investigation into this relationship may reveal more about the motivations and behaviors of UNC fans and of college basketball fans in general.

The second ranked motivation identified in the current study is eustress. Studies have shown that fans experience physiological responses, such as increased heart rate, and emotional responses as a result of close, thrilling games (Murrell and Dietz 28). It has long been accepted in the field of psychology that positive emotional and rewarding experiences can stimulate the release of dopamine in an area of the brain known as the nucleus accumbens, which is involved in the reward pathway of the human brain (Kalat 76). Dopamine and the reward pathway are part of the biological mechanism responsible for pleasures that arise from food, drugs, and other addictions. If an individual finds sports to be an emotional and positive experience, these physiological factors can increase their desire to participate in that event. This would suggest that the emotional experiences many fans associate with sports reinforce a biological connection to the game, making it no surprise that many fans enjoy the emotional, heart wrenching aspect of sports. It should be clear that this study did not explicitly test neurotransmitter release and is not suggesting a definite release of dopamine in sports fans, but given the previous research it is a plausible explanation.

The third most important motivation found in the current study is escape. Logic would most likely support this motivation, as many would agree with the proposition that people engage in many activities to escape reality. Many previous studies have shown sports can serve as an escape from the "daily routine" and may provide a unique experience outside the realm of daily life (Funk and James 128). Another explanation for this motivation is the fact that sports, according to Margaret Duncan, symbolize recurring themes in life (30). Duncan argues sports appeal to people because they dramatize the spectator's everyday existence and they provide an escape mechanism for people to transcend reality (30). However, while it is clear that escape is an established motivation for sport fandom, an interesting trend in this study is how highly ranked escape was among the nine motivations. Recall that this study showed striking similarities to a study of college basketball fans conducted by Daniel Wann and others in 2008. The only major variation between Wann's study and the current study is the ranking of escape. In Wann's study, escape was ranked seventh, whereas in this study escape is ranked in a much higher third. A possible explanation for the increased importance of the escape motivation is the environment in which this study was conducted. UNC—a large, public campus—is a unique environment that consists of thousands of college students whose daily lives include a plethora of stressful situations. Furthermore, as reported in the Daily Tar Heel on March 30th, 2011, a survey conducted by the UNC Counseling and Wellness Services reported 80% of UNC freshman reported feeling overwhelmed at some point in the past 12 months, four times the national average of 20.5% (Smialek 1). Given the academic rigor associated with UNC, it is not surprising that escape ranks higher among the UNC community because sports provide an outlet from daily stresses for students and other members of the UNC population, allowing them to relax and enjoy a fun activity. This is also supported by scientists that have found that being involved with sports fandom results in a more mentally healthy individual (Wann "Understanding the Positive Social" 272). These factors, along with the traditional influences of the escape motivations, may explain why escape serves as a main motivation for students at UNC.

The fourth highest ranked motivation of sports fans at UNC is group affiliation, arguably the most well-known and understood of the motivations discussed in the current study. Recall group identification refers to the psychological desire to be socially involved. Group identification has long been a focus of sport motivation research, even dating back to research conducted in the 1960s that suggested urban dwellers attach themselves to various sports teams to feel a sense of belonging and identity (Murrell and Dietz 29). Research into human psychology has long revealed humans are social beings, with a vital, inherent need to associate with others in order to maintain individual mental health. Thus, it is not surprising that sport scientists agree that due to the social nature of sport, fandom is likely related to the desire to maintain psychological well-being (Wann "Understanding the Positive Social" 272–73). At UNC, it would seem these explanations for sport fandom are supported in both quantitative response in the survey and subsequent action. Although ranked behind entertainment, eustress, and escape in the current study, results show that out of 111 participants, none ranked group affiliation as the least important motivation. Group affiliation was the only motivation that revealed such results; all other motivations were ranked last by at least one participant. Further, careful analysis of free responses by participants reveal group affiliation is manifested in nearly every aspect of fan involvement.

15   Although family, self-esteem, and tradition were studied separately in this investigation, they are often considered to be directly related to the idea of group affiliation and will be discussed as an extension of social motivation. This is supported by the results of the current study that rank tradition, self-esteem, and family directly behind group affiliation. Yet the most interesting result of this study is not the quantitative ranking of these motivations, but rather the responses given by some participants that directly relate to these motivations. Several participants explicitly stated that sports provide an opportunity to be connected to the Carolina community. The following are selected responses that exemplify the idea of group affiliation, tradition, self-esteem, and family at UNC:

> "Carolina sports brings the whole campus together"
> "Being involved in Carolina athletics gives me a sense of being a part of the UNC community"
> "School pride"
> ". . . Because it's my school and I am a part of it"
> "It's part of the Carolina experience"
> "Social connectivity; enthusiasm and atmosphere"
> "Carolina has a history of being really good at most sports"
> ". . . UNC sports are part of me and how I identify myself"
> "I go to UNC Chapel Hill . . . not being involved in UNC athletics and the tradition of being a Tar Heel would be a waste of my time here"

These responses show a personal and intimate connection to not only the game itself but also the idea that sports create a sense of belonging and self-worth that comes with being connected to a large, historic community. It is known that individuals derive personal strength and a sense of identity from connection to social groups, often motivated by the positive effects on psychological well-being discussed previously (Fisher and Wakefield 25). Furthermore, these motivations have a direct impact on the behaviors displayed by many UNC fans. A fan's loyalty and involvement with a specific team will often guide their behavior; the stronger these connections the more likely the fan is to engage in behaviors beneficial to the group (Hunt et al. 442). This may explain why so many students and other fans are willing to stand in line outside the Dean Dome for hours to get the opportunity to see their beloved Tar Heel basketball team, or why they exhibit such seemingly crazed behavior as they storm Franklin Street after marquee wins. The strong relationship between sports and the UNC community promotes the upholding of university tradition and increases the willingness of individual group members to engage in behaviors that are viewed as part of the larger group (Fisher and Wakefield 24). Not to mention, storming Franklin Street may connect to the top motivation in this study, entertainment, as the behavior is most likely fun for many college students.

The final motivation in this study was economic, which refers to the potential monetary gain of a fan through gambling on sports. In the current study, economic was ranked the least important motivation by an overwhelming majority of participants. 75 of the 111 participants ranked economics as the least important motivation for being involved with sports at UNC. Given the population studied and focus on student fans of collegiate athletics, this result is not surprising. Seemingly, college students are highly motivated by factors that do not involve monetary personal gains. However, it should be noted that in the larger context of sport fandom in the United States, gambling has been shown to be a large part of the sports market and should not be discredited in studies of the larger sports culture in America (Frey and Eitzen 510–11).

Conclusion

The results of this study show sport fandom at the University of North Carolina is more than a simple, erroneous activity, but rather a strong connection that stems from a variety of psychological and social factors. The innate human desire for entertainment motivates a considerable number of sports fans, both at UNC and in the overall context of sport fandom, and may represent a shift in the production and culture of sports in America.

Environmental factors associated with college also trigger psychological and social connections to sport. Students that are under the constant stress of daily life use sports as a way to bring entertainment into their lives, and while it may be unknown to the fans themselves, sports help to enhance psychological health. Furthermore, potential biological changes in the brain support the notion that sport involvement is not simply motivated by outside factors but stems from the interworking of human physiology. This, coupled with the numerous social factors promoting group identification and enhanced self-identity, supports the idea that sport fandom is inherently a positive experience for many members of the population. As a result, many of the behaviors that arise from sport related activities are extensions of these psychological and social factors and work to further enhance the overall effects of sport fandom.

20   While this study presents an array of potential motivations, continued research into the field of sport psychology is highly recommended to further enhance the understanding of sport fandom. Future studies into the motivations of sports fans should attempt to replicate the findings presented in this study and possibly present new motivations that further explain sport fandom. Further empirical analysis of additional college populations or populations that represent the larger context of sport fandom in America will continue to provide a more complete understanding of fan involvement and behavior. When viewed through the lens of psychological and social motivating factors, sport involvement can be more clearly understood. The continued investigation of the ideas presented in this study will help to shed new light upon an activity that has long been a part of human society.

[. . .]

Works Cited

Armstrong, Ketra. "Race and Sport Consumption Motivations: A Preliminary Investigation of a Black Consumers' Sport Motivation Scale." *Journal of Sport Behavior* 25.4 (2002): 309–30. Web.

Beyer, Janice, and David Hannah. "The Cultural Significance of Athletics in US Higher Education." *Journal of Sport Management* 14.2 (2000): 105–32. Web.

Duncan, Margaret. "The Symbolic Dimensions of Spectator Sport." *Quest* 35.1 (1983): 29–36. Web.

Fisher, Robert, and Kirk Wakefield. "Factors Leading to Group Identification: A Field Study of Winners and Losers." *Psychology and Marketing* 15.1 (1998): 23–40. Web.

Frey, James, and Stanley Eitzen "Sport and Society." *Annual Review of Sociology* 17.1 (1991): 503–22. Web.

Funk, Daniel, and Jeff James. "The Psychological Continuum Model: A Conceptual Framework for Understanding an Individual's Psychological Connection to Sport." *Sport Management Review* 4.2 (2001): 119–50. Web.

Hunt, Kenneth, Terry Bristol, and R. Edward Bashaw. "A Conceptual Approach to Classifying Sports Fans." *Journal of Services Marketing* 13.6 (1999): 439–52. Web.

James, Jeffrey and Lynn Ridinger. "Female and Male Sport Fans: A Comparison of Sport Consumption Motives." *Journal of Sport Behavior* 25.3 (2002): 260–78. Web.

Kalat, James. *Biological Psychology.* 10 ed. Belmont: Wadsworth, 2009. Print.

Kwon, Hyungil, and Galen Trail. "Sport Fan Motivation: A Comparison of American Students and International Students." *Sport Marketing Quarterly* 10.3 (2001): 147–55. Web.

Murrell, Audrey, and Beth Dietz. "Fan Support of Sport Teams: The Effect of a Common Group Identity." *Journal of Sport and Exercise Psychology* 14.1 (1992): 28–39. Web.

Smialek, Jeanna. "UNC Looks to Combat Mental Health Issues." *Daily Tar Heel* [Chapel Hill] 30 Mar. 2011: n. pag. *Daily Tar Heel*. Web. 18 Apr. 2011.

UNC General Alumni Association. "UNC, Nike Sign New 10-Year Contract." UNC General Alumni Association. N.p., n.d. Web. 17 Apr. 2011. http://alumni.unc.edu/article.aspx?sid=6840

Wann, Daniel. "Understanding the Positive Social Psychological Benefits of Sport Team Identification: The Team Identification-Social Psychological Health Model." *Group Dynamics* 10.4 (2006): 272–96. Web.

———. "Preliminary Validation of the Sport Fan Motivation Scale." *Journal of Sport and Social Issues* 19.4 (1995): 377–96. Web.

Wann, Daniel, Michael Schrader, and Anthony Wilson. "Sport Fan Motivation: Questionnaire Validation, Comparisons by Sport, and Relationship to Athletic Motivation." *Journal of Sport Behavior* 22.1 (1999): 114–39. Web.

Wann, Daniel, Frederick Grieve, Ryan Zapalac, and Dale Pease. "Motivational Profiles of Sport Fans of Different Sports." *Sport Marketing Quarterly* 17.1 (2008): 6–19. Web.

Washington, Robert R. E., and David Karen. "Sport and Society." *Annual Review of Sociology* 27.1 (2001): 187–212. Web.

EXAMPLE 2: Conference Paper by an Undergraduate

Rick Ingram
Conference Paper

Gender Discrimination and the Movement towards Equality in the Workforce

On January 29, 2009, President Obama signed into law the Lilly Ledbetter Equal Pay Act, which took a major step towards eliminating gender discrimination in the United States labor system. From the earliest establishment of America as a nation, up until the Civil Rights movement in the 1960's, the struggle to find a place for women workers in our nation has been a persistent problem. Do acts such as the Ledbetter Act indicate that our system is becoming less discriminatory? While there is some debate, many scholars agree that the road to equality in the labor system has been a long one, but through increasing government regulation, gender discrimination is narrowing. Although gender discrimination has long been tolerated in our labor system, in the society that we live in today there is no room for such discrimination, as it not only limits productivity, but also violates a basic principle of equality that has been established by our nation through legislation such as the Civil Rights Acts, Equal Rights Acts, and more recently, The Lilly Ledbetter Fair Pay Act. In this paper, I argue that the gender discrimination that has plagued the U.S labor system is becoming less prevalent through government regulation, and thereby leading to a more equal, efficient labor system.

To identify how legal acts have lessened gender discrimination in the workplace, I first examined the history of gender discrimination in our nation, drawing on research from political science and legal scholarship. Next, I examined the implications of the government regulations that have been set in place, primarily in the last 50 years, in order to stifle gender discrimination in the workforce. These acts suggest that, due to the multiple regulations set in place by the government, gender discrimination is slowly moving towards a problem of the past.

Before I discuss how government regulation limits gender discrimination in the labor system, I must first explain the history of gender discrimination. In the early 1940's, as World War II was beginning, the United States labor system took a major turn—it started employing women by the masses. With multitudes of men going overseas to war, the production in the United States fell on women workers, and by the height of the war women accounted for around 19,170,000 people in the labor force (Hartmann 78). Marie Bussing-Burks, a lecturer in economics at the University of Southern Indiana, believes that this incredible increase in the percent of women in the labor force substantially raised inequality (Bussing-Burks).

Bussing-Burks asserts that, "Increases in female labor supply decreased both female and male wages, but had a stronger effect on women" (Bussing-Burks). In making this comment, Bussing-Burks attempts to suggest that the increase in female workers was not a major success for women, but rather, the increase hurt them. Her statement points out the gender discrimination in the 1940's labor system. The essence of Bussing-Burks' argument is this—with the substantial increase in women workers during the 1940's, women provided competition to those male counterparts, and would work for cheaper wages than those males who had to support a family. In a situation much like our current immigration condition, women would do a high-quality job for a cheaper price than males, which created a discriminatory measure that was widely instituted into businesses. Although women were being welcomed into the labor system, the discrimination they faced came in the form of unfair wages. After the war, however, when those male soldiers came home, gender discrimination manifested itself in more than just wage discrepancies.

At this point in time, the battle to keep women in the labor system became a long and arduous struggle. Susan Hartmann, a history professor who specializes in 20th century women's history at Oklahoma State University, claims that "Between 1943 and 1945, polls indicated that 61 to 85 percent of women workers wanted to keep their jobs after the war" (82). Here, Hartmann delves into the very essence of the problem after the war; women had adapted to being an integral part of the working world, and they would not easily be shoved to the side for men.

In order to perceive the movement away from gender discrimination in the labor system, I must first present a number of regulations that have been set in place in the post-World

War II era. In the 1960's, the United States began to make the first serious moves towards eliminating gender discrimination in the labor system. By establishing the Equal Pay Act of 1963, this law effectively amended the Fair Labor Standards Act, and was designed to primarily abolish wage discrepancies based on sex (EPA). The law states that:

> No employer having employees subject to any provisions of this section shall discriminate, within any establishment in which such employees are employed, between employees on the basis of sex by paying wages to employees in such establishment at a rate less than the rate at which he pays wages to employees of the opposite sex in such establishment for equal work on jobs the performance of which requires equal skill, effort, and responsibility, and which are performed under similar working conditions. (EPA)

This law is the first concrete example of a regulation being set in place specifically to stifle gender discrimination. One court case that strengthened the passage of the Equal Pay Act of 1963 was *Corning Glass Works v. Brennan (1974).* In this case, Justice Thurgood Marshall upheld questionable parts of the Equal Pay Act of 1963 as he ruled that it was against the law for Corning to refuse equal pay to women simply because men would not work at a lower wage (Corning 189). The idea that men should be given higher wages for the same job violated the basic premise of the Equal Pay Act of 1963. According to Casandra Butts, a Harvard Law graduate and Vice President of Domestic Policy at the Center for American progress, by ruling against Corning, Justice Marshall's decision greatly strengthened the validity and credibility of the Equal Pay Act of 1963 (Butts). This example of further government regulation was simply another step towards narrowing gender discrimination in the workplace.

To fully grasp the elimination of gender discrimination, I must speak on Title VII of the Civil Rights Act of 1964. As part of the Civil Rights Act of 1964, Title VII effectively prohibits employment discrimination based on race, color, religion, sex and national origin (CRA). Jo Freeman, a history professor at Yale University, touches on the significance of Title VII when she states, "Although no one really took seriously the NWP's efforts to equate sex and race discrimination, ERA opponents were of two minds. They acknowledged that women experienced discrimination in employment and argued that specific anti-discrimination measures would be preferable to the ERA" (Freeman 163–184). In making this statement, Freeman argues that although "sex" was added into Title VII, its effects were not taken as seriously as they should have been. The idea that women would not be discriminated against at all was a concept that had never been taken seriously in the United States, until an abundance of government regulation made it a topic of focus. Freeman maintains that "At a time when the division between 'men's jobs' and 'women's jobs' was still taken for granted, the implications of prohibiting discrimination in employment on the basis of sex had not been fully explored. If they had been, so revolutionary a proposal is unlikely to have passed" (Freeman 163–184). This statement is a representation of the underlying feelings of many legislators at the time—while government regulations were being set in place to eliminate gender discrimination, many did not believe that the regulations would be meaningful. Many scholars, such as Jo Freeman, saw Title VII of the Civil Rights Act of 1964 as something that was pushed through Congress in the wake of John F. Kennedy's death. Because of his death, there was a sense among legislators that regulations which had been set into motion by JFK, such as the Civil Rights Act of 1964 and the Equal Pay Act of 1963, should have an automatic pass, and be implemented by those in power. Freeman's statement that some legislators had not explored "the implications of prohibiting discrimination in employment on the basis of sex" serves to show that even while discriminatory government regulation was being passed, there was still an overwhelming sense of discriminatory feelings. These feelings are representative of the strenuous journey to change personal feelings on gender discrimination.

While regulations over the last 50 years have muffled gender discrimination, even more regulations, such as the Lilly Ledbetter Fair Pay Act (2009), have been put into action to continue eliminating this problem. On May 29th, 2007, the Supreme Court of the United States of America formally denied Lilly Ledbetter her right to sue her employer, Goodyear Tire and Rubber Co. (Ledbetter 622). As a 19 year employee of the company, Ledbetter discovered pay discrepancies between her and her fellow male counterparts paychecks in March of 1998. When Ledbetter filed her suit against Goodyear initially, the district court ruled in favor of her, and awarded her $3,841,041.93 for back pay, punitive damage, and mental anguish (Grundvig 199). Unfortunately, for Ledbetter, Goodyear appealed for, and was granted, a remittur, which cut Ledbetter's award to $360,000, and they were also granted a new trial. This trial that took place in the Eleventh circuit reversed the initial decision made by the courts, and instead only reviewed Ledbetter's case on the 180 days before Ledbetter filed her claim. Adam L. Grundvig, a J.D candidate, and a Senior Staff Member the *Journal of Law & Family Studies*, explains the ludicrous nature of the controversial 180 day statute of limitations as he writes, "I have never liked women, much less women in the workplace. I feel it is my duty to discourage them from working, so I have consistently paid them twenty-five percent less than their similarly-situated male counterparts. I have absolutely no intention of changing this practice; your pay will remain where it is" (Grundvig 206). This outrageous statement, while it would never be said by a manager, simulates what would have to be said for a female worker to legitimately file a claim with the EEOC within the 180 day statute of limitations if she had discovered a discrepancy in her pay after 180 days of receiving her first pay check. In explaining the complexity of the 180 day law, Grundvig states that the women would have exactly 180 days to:

> Allege that the manager's continued application of a sex-based discriminatory
>
> pay policy is the "discrete" act of discrimination in violation of Title VII, and,
>
> if she prevailed, recover damages for both the disparate pay she received from
>
> paychecks issued subsequent to the date of her EEOC charge and up to two
>
> years of backpay. (Grundvig 199)

Grundvig uses this outlandish example of what a manager would have to say to point out the flaws in the, at the time, current 180 day statute. As the trial continued, after an appeal of the Eleventh court district's ruling at the Supreme Court, Justice Alito followed suit as the other courts, and ruled against Ledbetter, leaving the flawed 180 day system of the EEOC in place. The first act of legislation signed into law when Barack Obama entered office was the Lilly Ledbetter Fair Pay Act. This law effectively overruled the prior decision of the Supreme Court in *Ledbetter v. Goodyear Tire and Rubber Co.(2007)*, as well as amended the Civil Rights Act of 1964, which "states that the 180-day statute of limitations for filing an equal-pay lawsuit regarding pay discrimination resets with each new discriminatory paycheck" (CRA). Barack Obama's act of legislation shows how through government regulation, our nation is moving towards a labor system with less gender discrimination. The fact that, even today in our more gender friendly society, it still took so long to eliminate such a discriminatory measure shows that the road towards gender equality in the labor force has been a very long one.

The signing into law of the Lilly Ledbetter act is proof of narrowing gender discrimination in the U.S. In this paper, I argued that the gender discrimination that has plagued the U.S labor system is becoming less prevalent through government regulation, and thereby leading to a more equal, efficient labor system. In arguing my point, I examined the history of gender discrimination in our nation. Scholars such as Marie Bussing-Burks and Susan Hartmann provide accounts on how the history of gender discrimination has set into place a flurry of government regulations. Next, I examined the implications of the government regulations that have been set in place, primarily in the last 50 years, in order to stifle gender discrimination in the workforce. With acts such as Title VII of the Civil Rights Act of 1964, and the Equal Pay Act of 1963 being implemented into America society, the movement towards eliminating gender discrimination began. As Freeman suggests, regulations not only legally started to change gender discrimination, but also the societal mindset of gender equality. Finally, I showed that due to the multiple regulations set in place by the government, gender discrimination is slowly moving towards a problem of the past. When assessing the large number of regulations set in place on the subject of gender discrimination, the overwhelming numbers show a narrowing of gender discrimination.

While the battle for equality continues, so many of the regulations set into place build off of prior ones, and therefore the system is constantly becoming more efficient and thorough. Future research might assess the effects of the Ledbetter Act, including its economic effects as well as societal ones. Researchers might also assess whether other policies, such as family leave or work-life balance initiatives, can improve gender equality in the workplace, or whether they can lead to deleterious effects, such as discrimination against those taking advantage of such initiatives. As time continues, we as a nation will continue to perfect our labor system until the day when gender discrimination is indeed a problem of the past.

Works Cited

Bussing-Burks, Marie. "Women and Post-WWII Wages." *The National Bureau of Economic Research Digest.* November 2002. http://www.nber.org/digest/nov02/w9013.html. Web. 7 April 2009.

Butts, Cassandra. "Marching On for Equal Pay." *Center for American Progress.* 7 May 2004. Web. 7 April 2009. http://www.americanprogress.org/issues/2004/05/b68060.html. Web.

Civil Rights Act of 1964. Pub. L. 88-352. 78 Stat. 241. 2 July, 1964. Print.

Corning Glass Works v. Brennan. 417 U.S. 188. Supreme Court of the United States. 1974.

Equal Pay Act of 1963. Pub. L. 88-38. 29 Stat. 56. 10 June, 1963.

Freeman, Jo. *We Will Be Heard: Women's Struggles for Political Power in the United States.* Lanham, MD: Rowman & Littlefield, 2008. Print.

Grundvig, Adam L. "*Ledbetter v. Goodyear*: The U.S. Supreme Court Rubs Salt in Plaintiffs' Disparate Pay Title VII Wounds." *Journal of Law and Family Studies* 10 (2007): 199–212. Print.

Hartmann, Susan M. *The Home Front and Beyond: American Women in the 1940s.* Boston: Twayne Publishers, 1982. Print.

Ledbetter v. Goodyear Tire and Rubber Co. 550 U.S 618. Supreme Court of the United States. 2007.

EXAMPLE 3: Conference Paper by an Undergraduate

Penelope Edwards
English 432: Literature of Slavery
Professor Adriano

Purity and Corruption: Reading Harriet Jacobs through
the Lens of the Bathsheba Tale

Throughout the first half of her story, *Incidents in the Life of a Slave Girl*, Harriet Jacobs

writes much about the "corruption" of female slaves' "purity" by slaveowners. Although

she hints at the complete physical subjugation of slave women to their masters' whims

(sexual and otherwise), never does she discuss explicitly the brutality of rape. Instead, she

talks of the "degradation" of slave girls by the slaveowners, and of how this system in turn

corrupts all people of the south:

> No matter whether the slave girl be as black as ebony or as fair as her mistress.
>
> In either case, there is no shadow of law to protect her from insult, from vio-
>
> lence, or even from death; all these are inflicted by fiends who bear the shape of
>
> men. The mistress, who ought to protect the helpless victim, has no other feel-
>
> ings towards her but those of jealousy and rage. The degradation, the wrongs,
>
> the vices, that grow out of slavery, are more than I can describe. They are
>
> greater than you would willingly believe. (26)

Jacobs writes about the corruption of purity, and not the violence associated with it. Surely

she does not fear corruption more than she fears rape and other forms of sexual violence.

No—Jacobs was a savvy author. She knew who would be reading her book, she always kept this audience in the front of her mind. The target audience of *Incidents in the Life* was white, northern, middle-to-upper-class women who were probably not part of the abolitionist movement. But Jacobs, with her persuasive tale, hoped to sway them to join her cause.

"Identification," as described by Kenneth Burke, is a method of creating, via persuasion, a joining of interests in a cause (20). Burke writes: "A is not identical with his colleague, B. But insofar as their interests are joined, A is *identified* with B" (20). Identification, then, might be necessary for coalition-building, especially when those one might want to bring over to one's cause have trouble understanding the life experiences of those they are being asked to support.

Such was the challenge faced by Jacobs and her white readers. For many reasons, Jacob's purity argument must have seemed more likely to arouse sympathy in these white female readers than the discussion of rape. Furthermore, while rape was a wrong suffered by each black, enslaved woman alone, corruption was a wrong that could infect an entire community, a community composed of whites and blacks, men and women, adults and children. By naming a wrong that could harm white women as well, Jacobs created a means by which her readers could identify with enslaved black women. Jacobs brilliantly tread a delicate line in her narrative: revealing the horrors of slavery while creating a world that her audience could sympathize, even empathize, with. She created this world through a variety of small narratives that enabled her readers to identify with her as she told her narrative.

For example, early in the narrative, Jacobs describes her desire to have a marriage and a home, a near-impossibility under slavery. Instead of marrying, she succumbed to her mortal weaknesses, and exercised her only option under slavery by having a sexual affair with a white man, Mr. Sands:

> If slavery had been abolished, I, also, could have married the man of my
>
> choice; I could have had a home shielded by the laws . . . but all my prospects
>
> had been blighted by slavery. I wanted to keep myself pure; and, under the
>
> most adverse circumstances, I tried hard to preserve my self-respect; but I was
>
> struggling alone in the powerful grasp of the demon Slavery; and the monster
>
> proved too strong for me. (46)

Jacobs was very savvy in her presentation of the sexual abuse suffered by female slaves, including her own abuse. Here, for example, she blamed "the demon Slavery" for her abuse at the hands of Mr. Sands, rather than Mr. Sands himself. Furthermore, rather than discussing the grim details of her relationship with him, she bemoans the loss of her purity.

At least two important ends were served by the "purity" approach, rather than the rape approach. First, Jacobs was fighting against the rampant, destructive stereotype of black women, slave women in particular, as hypersexual beings (a stereotype that persists today). That Linda (Jacobs's pseudonym in the narrative) was so concerned about her purity and saving herself for marriage combatted these stereotypes. Moreover, these concerns over purity would have been ones that wealthy, white, northern women could relate to much more easily than they could to a constant fear of rape.

Rape of middle-to-upper-class women in those days was considered by society not so much a violent crime against the woman as it was a financial crime against the woman's family. It ruined the woman's prospects of marriage if she were unmarried, and it risked bringing a bastard into the family if she were married—how could her husband be sure whose child she bore, and therefore whose child would inherit the family property? Often, the rapist was forced to marry the woman in order to preserve honor and property. Although rape of slave women was a horrific epidemic, it would not have evoked the identification that Jacobs aimed for with her narrative.

In order to garner even greater identification with her audience, Jacobs also writes about the sexual degradation of white families in the south. This degradation was due to, according to Jacobs, the forced degradation of female slaves:

> The white daughters early hear their parents quarreling about some female slave. Their curiosity is excited, and they soon learn the cause. They are attended by the young slave girls whom their father has corrupted; and they hear such talk as should never meet youthful ears, or any other ears . . . . Slavery is a curse to the whites as well as to the blacks. It makes the white fathers cruel and sensual; the sons violent and licentious; it contaminates the daughters, and makes the wives wretched. (44-5)

Jacobs write about how slavery hurts whites because many people in the north would have been more moved to hear about how slavery harmed white people—they would not have cared about black peoples' suffering. Or, if they did care, they would have had an easier time identifying with the suffering of white people. In the end, Jacobs's motivations must have been practical: describing the harmful effects of slavery on whites was more likely to evoke the sympathy of white readers who were not abolitionists and who did not feel any sympathy for black people.

More than once, Jacobs tells of the greater suffering of female slaves who possess physical beauty: "If God has bestowed beauty upon her, it will prove her greatest curse. That which commands admiration in the white woman only hastens the degradation of the female slave" (26). After Jacobs has begun her affair with Mr. Sands, the man comes to her grandmother's house:

> I returned to my good grandmother's house. She had an interview with Mr.
>
> Sands. When she asked him why he could not have left her one ewe lamb—
>
> whether there were not plenty of slaves who did not care about character—he
>
> made no answer . . . . (49)

The note to the text suggests that this line is "[p]erhaps a reference to the Old Testament practice of sacrifice, in which the sacrificial animal was generally male." I suggest that the editor is mistaken in this reference. Jacobs here refers to the biblical story of David and Bathsheba, from the Old Testament Christian Bible book of Samuel.

From the roof of his castle, King David saw Bathsheba bathing through her window; he thought she was very beautiful (Sam. 11.2). Knowing she was married to a soldier named Uriah, who was off fighting at war, he had her brought to the castle "and he slept with her" (Sam. 11.3-4). She got pregnant (Sam. 11.5), and David had Uriah sent to the front lines of battle, and then ordered all other soldiers to withdraw from around him "so he will be struck down and die" (Sam. 11.15). Then David brought Bathsheba to the castle to live with him, and they married (Sam. 11.27).

Shortly thereafter, the prophet Nathan came and told David a story about a man and his "one little ewe lamb" (Sam. 12.2). The man was very poor and all he had was the one ewe lamb and he loved her very much; she lived in his house and slept in his bed; "It was like a daughter to him" (Sam. 12.3). One day, his wealthy neighbor was having company to dinner, and instead of slaughtering one of his many sheep, he slaughtered the poor man's ewe to feed to his company (Sam. 12.4). David "burned with anger against the man," and said that the man "deserved to die" (Sam. 11.5). Nathan said, "You are the man!" (Sam. 12.7).

In many ways, the sufferings of the slave girls that Jacobs recounts parallel the sufferings of Bathsheba: beauty is a curse; the slave woman's life does not belong to her, but to the whim of powerful men. This is a biblical reference that is explicit enough to have been identified by her readers at the time. By drawing this biblical parallel, chastising a white slave owner the way Kind David himself was chastised, Jacobs makes it even easier for her white readers to relate to the sufferings of a slave.

Works Cited

Burke, Kenneth. *A Rhetoric of Motives.* Berkeley: University of California Press, 1969. Print.

Holy Bible: New International Version. Grand Rapids, MI: Zondervan Bible Publishers, 1978. Print.

Jacobs, Harriet. *Incidents in the Life of a Slave Girl.* New York: W.W. Norton & Company, 2000. Print.

USE THE TOOLKIT

Let's use the three genre toolkit questions from Chapter 1 to examine this genre.

What Is It?

A research paper refers to any document that presents original research to an academic audience. There are several sub-types of research papers:

- If you present your research in the form of a written text and submit it to a journal, you write a research article, as Kristine did in Example 1.

- If you present your research at a conference, you write a conference paper or prepare a conference presentation, as Rick and Penelope did in Examples 2 and 3.
- You can also present your research in a visual format, such as a conference poster (Chapter 30).
- If you prepare your research for a course assignment, you may write a research paper (see Terrence's example in Chapter 28).

While these genres differ in format, they tend to share common features. In scientific and social science fields, they are often organized with an abstract, introduction, literature review, methods, results, and discussion or conclusions. These sections are indicated by sub-headings, as shown in Example 1. In humanities fields, the organization may or may not include headings—Rick's conference paper, written for a political science course, does not. However, notice that Rick still structures his paper around a description of his methods, results, and conclusions.

Each of these research genres uses detailed evidence from the research, which may be numerical data, excerpts from interviews, quotations from source texts, etc. (Chapter 24). In her article, Kristine presented numerical data and quotes from her survey, while Rick relied on database research (Chapter 24) to find legal statutes and scholarly articles about his topic.

These research genres also use the citation style common to the journal or discipline (Chapter 28) in question, employ technical, discipline-specific vocabulary, and use a formal style, although that style may vary by discipline (Chapter 21).

Who Reads It?

While these sub-genres differ somewhat in format, they are all meant for academic audiences—usually other researchers in a particular field. When you write a research genre for a course, you are usually imagining an audience of scholars in that field.

In some cases, though, research articles reach audiences from different disciplines, or an interdisciplinary audience. Undergraduate research journals and conferences often include students writing about many different fields. Kristine's research article (Example 1) was published in an undergraduate research journal, so it was likely read by other students and faculty interested in the topic—not just those interested in sports psychology. Yet, Kristine wanted to demonstrate that she was learning the discipline of sports psychology, so she included terms like "eustress," a term she encountered in her research that refers to the positive kind of stress one feels at an exciting sports game.

Rick's conference paper (Example 2) and Penelope's conference paper (Example 3) were both presented at undergraduate research conferences at their colleges. Usually, those conferences are attended by students and faculty from all different departments.

What's It For?

The main purpose of a research paper is to share the results of a study with other researchers. Researchers find research most interesting if it contributes something new to the field, so the goal of a research paper is not only to demonstrate that you have done sound research, but to show how that research adds to the field. In Example 1, Kristine identified a gap (Chapter 23) in research on sports psychology: there were relatively few studies of the psychological motivations of sports fans. She also identified a local population that would make good participants for her study: sports fans at her own college, who were known for their wild behavior after basketball games. By surveying these sports fans and identifying the factors driving their behavior, Kristine made a genuine contribution to what we know about sports fans. In Example 2, Rick discusses a recent development in the law. In Example 3, Penelope provides a new, unique reading of an older literary text.

EXERCISE 11.4: Plan a Research Paper

Pull together the abstract, annotated bibliography, and literature review that you wrote for exercises 11.1, 11.2, and 11.3. Using these documents, identify a gap in the research that you are investigating.

Start drafting ideas for how you might contribute to the field of research. Could you do original, primary research, such as archival work (Chapter 24), a survey (Chapter 24), or ethnographic observations (Chapter 7)?

E. Strategies for Academic Research Genres

Imagine you've been assigned to write an academic research paper to submit to an undergraduate research journal or conference. You've already written an abstract, annotated bibliography, and literature review.

Now, you need to draft your paper. Let's see how one student worked through the writing process, using as our example the paper in Example 2 by Rick Ingram, "Gender Discrimination and the Movement towards Equality in the Workforce."

Prewriting (Content)

Much of your content will come from research. You will need to do some preliminary research about your topic (Chapter 23), and then identify a research question. If you do not have a topic in mind, or if one has not been assigned, you can browse for topics (Chapter 23) using web-based sources, your course readings, or even discussions with friends.

Rick knew that he was interested in gender discrimination, so he did some initial research on the main legal cases and statutes related to his issue. Then, he drafted a research question:

Is gender discrimination becoming more or less prevalent? How is government regulation affecting gender relations in the labor system?

Once you have researched an area, you will need to figure out what research you can do to answer this question. Rick realized that he would need to search library databases (Chapter 24) to uncover the history of gender in the labor system and the laws that have been passed to address it.

Drafting (Organizing)

Research papers are often organized according to the basic pattern of introduction, methods, results, and discussion—either explicitly, as in Kristine's example, or implicitly, as in Rick's case. In Rick's genre and field, section headings are not always used. If you are writing a research article for a scientific or social scientific field, like Kristine was, you can use those sections to help you start drafting your paper.

Rick was writing a genre that did not call for those section headings, but Rick still organized his paper using those four sections. He started by organizing his findings—the results from his research into the history of gender discrimination, labor systems, and the law. He wrote that section first, since he had all the information at hand.

Next, he wrote an introduction that gave an overview of the topic at hand, his research question, and his main claim. He gave an overview of the methods he used to address this question. Finally, he wrote the conclusion to his conference paper, considering what his study had shown and what areas of future research scholars might address.

Revising (Style)

Research genres should be written in the style of the discipline in question. To show that you are a member of that discipline, you should use the vocabulary, level of formality, and even sentence structures typical of that field.

For example, Rick used the technical term "remittur" in his paper, since he was writing for a political science class. This term refers to when a legal judge lowers the amount of damages a jury has granted. Since Rick's audience included other scholars familiar with the law, he did not need to define the term, but if he had been writing a different genre, such as an op-ed (Chapter 10), he would probably not use that term at all.

During peer review sessions, Rick revised his paper to employ the more formal style typical of a conference presentation. Here is his original draft:

Although women were being welcomed into the labor system, they still got cheated out of equal wages. After the war, moreover, when Johnny came marching home, they started to see more than just a smaller paycheck.

During peer review, Rick's classmates remarked that his writing seemed too infor-mal for a scholarly audience. So Rick revised this passage, as follows:

> Although women were being welcomed into the labor system, the discrimina-tion they faced came in the form of unfair wages. After the war, however, when those male soldiers came home, gender discrimination manifested itself in more than just wage discrepancies.

Editing (Design)

In general, for academic courses, research papers should be written in a simple typeface using the conventions of the research style that you are using: MLA, APA, or what have you. These research styles often dictate the margin size and recom-mended font sizes. Be sure to design your paper by following these guidelines (Chap-ter 28). Be sure to proofread carefully (Chapter 22), since your credibility as a researcher is in part affected by your attention to detail.

Since Rick was delivering his conference paper in public, he needed to focus on oral presentation (Chapter 30). Rick practiced his paper several times, and even re-corded himself using his laptop's camera so he could eliminate any nervous habits.

If you are publishing your research in an undergraduate journal, like Kristine did, you might have a different set of submission guidelines to address. Check the web-site for the journal in question to see what guidelines to use.

Troubleshooting

Here are some common challenges that students face when writing academic re-search genres.

I don't know what genre to write.   If you are being asked to examine, report on, summarize, critique, or review what other researchers have published on a topic, chances are the literature review is an appropriate genre for you to use. From Part 1, you'll remember that what we *call* a genre is less important than the purpose of the genre, audience the genre speaks to, and message that document conveys. When-ever you are reviewing and commenting on previous research, you are writing the genre of the literature review.

If you are being asked to conduct original research of your own (surveys, inter-views, field observations, experiments, analysis of archival documents, etc.), then you may be writing a different genre, such as a research article or conference paper. These, too, might be called "research paper" or "research essay," but the purpose of the genre is different. In this case, you will be expected to present results from some kind of original study. A brief literature review might appear toward the start of this kind of document, where you situate your project in relation to what other scholars have done, but the review does not make up the whole document.

I can't come up with a good topic.   Good research topics often come not out of thin air, but from reading what other researchers have written. As you read other studies in your field, consider what gaps or limitations others have noted. These can be good starting places for future research. See Chapter 23 for more on finding a topic.

I don't know what research method to use.   Your research method will depend in part on the genre and discipline you are writing for. If you are writing a research paper in psychology, for instance, you might use an experiment, survey, or interview. If you are writing a research paper in a history class, you might use an oral history interview or work with archival documents. (See Chapter 24 for more on research methods and how they are used in different disciplines.)

F. Chapter Project: Write a Research Paper

Following the guidelines in this chapter, write a research paper about your chosen topic. Consult Part IV of this textbook for more on developing a topic, choosing research methods, and finding sources. Be sure to include a list of works cited at the end (Chapter 28) in order to avoid plagiarism (Chapter 27).

Multimedia Option: Design a Conference Poster

After you have conducted your research, design a conference poster to accompany your research paper. See Chapters 29 and 30 for more assistance.

Workplace Genres

Workplace genres include the variety of genres that writers compose in professional or formal settings, including emails, letters, proposals, plans, and résumés. Although these genres are typically found in the workplace, students use these genres all the time: they compose emails to professors; they write letters to scholarship committees; and they design résumés for summer internships. In business courses, students write professional letters, proposals, and plans regularly, but workplace genres might also appear in other courses that stress entrepreneurship or professional development. The ability to write workplace genres is an essential skill for success in college.

These skills are essential outside the classroom as well. For example, in the workplace, the ability to compose a professional email is essential, since the genre conveys authority and competence. Workplace genres perform much of the work of organizations, from documenting what work has been done to securing new contracts or clients.

In this chapter, we will discover three workplace genres that students encounter most often: emails, letters, and résumés. Because this family of genres shares a similar audience—professional readers in the workplace—we will keep this audience in mind as we discover the genres in this chapter.

A. Workplace Mini-Genre: Company Slogan

A company slogan is a short phrase or sentence that companies and other organizations use to capture the public's notice and draw attention to their brands.

EXAMPLE 1: Slogan for a University

Fresno State slogan.

EXAMPLE 2: Slogan for a Radio Station

KCRW IS MORE THAN JUST A RADIO STATION.

KCRW IS THE FUTURE OF PUBLIC MEDIA.

Slogan for public radio station KCRW.

EXAMPLE 3: Slogan for a Government Agency

SM

SNAP Supplemental Nutrition Assistance Program

Putting Healthy Food Within Reach

Slogan for a United States Department of Agriculture program.

USE THE TOOLKIT

Let's use the three genre toolkit questions from Chapter 1 to examine this genre.

What Is It?

A slogan is a short, catchy phrase that companies use to capture consumer attention. These three examples illustrate how short slogans can be. In Example 1, for California State University, Fresno, the slogan is only three words long: "Discovery. Diversity. Distinction." Slogans tend to be presented in bold, colorful type to catch the eye.

Who Reads It?

Companies and organizations intend their slogans to be read by a wide, popular audience—the wider, the better. They hope their slogans will be instantly recognizable. Therefore, slogans need to be as simple and clear as possible. Some companies and organizations may aim for a smaller market, or niche, in which case they craft their slogans to appeal to that particular audience. The organization featured in Example 2, KCRW, is a public radio station in Santa Monica, California. It serves Los Angeles and its surrounding areas. Its target audience, then, is composed of people who live in that geographical region.

What's It For?

Slogans capture popular attention and create brand recognition. Ideally, they entice people to purchase products sold by a company or to otherwise support an organization. They also create goodwill toward a company, even among those who do not buy the company's products on a regular basis. For example, a person might not need to participate in the federal government food stamps program (Example 3), but the government would like to encourage wide support of the program among all U.S. citizens.

EXERCISE 12.1: Craft a Slogan

Suppose you are starting a public awareness campaign to address a need on your campus or in your town. Design a slogan for your campaign that helps raise awareness of the issue you are addressing.

GROUP ACTIVITY 12.1: Pitch a Slogan

Suppose your group is a marketing company hired to design a public awareness campaign to address a need on your campus or in your town. Have each person in your group pitch a slogan for the campaign; then, have the group as a whole vet each slogan. Which slogan best generates wide support for the campaign? Why?

B. Email

Email is a crucial form of communication. In the workplace, you might send dozens of emails every day. Even though email is often a casual kind of communication, certain conventions still apply when writing emails.

EXAMPLE 1: Student's Reference Request Email

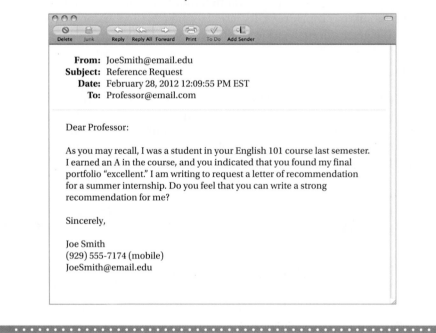

EXAMPLE 2: Club Meeting Email

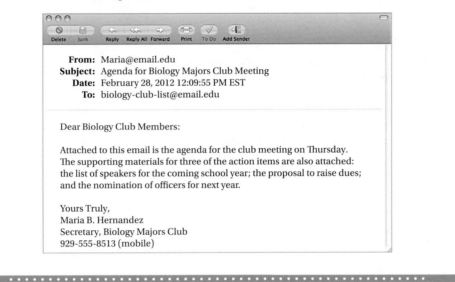

Delete Junk Reply Reply All Forward Print To Do Add Sender

From: Maria@email.edu
Subject: Agenda for Biology Majors Club Meeting
Date: February 28, 2012 12:09:55 PM EST
To: biology-club-list@email.edu

Dear Biology Club Members:

Attached to this email is the agenda for the club meeting on Thursday.
The supporting materials for three of the action items are also attached:
the list of speakers for the coming school year; the proposal to raise dues;
and the nomination of officers for next year.

Yours Truly,
Maria B. Hernandez
Secretary, Biology Majors Club
929-555-8513 (mobile)

EXAMPLE 3: Article Rejection Email

Delete Junk Reply Reply All Forward Print To Do Add Sender

From: Journal@email.edu
Subject: Journal decision declining to publish your article
Date: February 28, 2012 12:09:55 PM EST
To: Marshall@email.com

Dear Marshall:

After editorial review, we regret to inform you that your paper, "Call It What
It Is: Why 'Student' Athletes Should Be Paid to Play," has not been accepted
for publication.

Your paper addresses a topic which is potentially engaging and relevant.
However, your lack of a significant original contribution makes the paper
unsuitable for publication.

Thank you very much for your submission. We wish you luck on your future
academic endeavors.

Sincerely,
Editorial Staff
Undergraduate Research Journal
Journal@email.edu
777.555.5432 (phone)

USE THE TOOLKIT

Let's use the three genre toolkit questions from Chapter 1 to examine this genre.

What Is It?

An email is an electronic letter. The documents in the preceding examples are all emails sent by students regarding important business in students' lives. The emails share a few important qualities. First, the subject line of each email explicitly states what the email is about. Second, each email is short, limited to one to three paragraphs. Each paragraph is also concise, sometimes only including one sentence. Lastly, each email includes an email signature, information that appears after the email closing ("Sincerely" or "Yours Truly") and provides contact information about the sender of the email. This signature is the equivalent of the return address in a print letter.

Who Reads It?

Emails are read by many different audiences. In the workplace, emails are read by clients, co-workers, bosses, etc. In college, emails might be read by professors, teaching assistants, friends, group members, and family members. Remember, too, that because of the nature of email, they are easily forwarded to unintended recipients by the person that you sent the email to, so be very careful what you write in an email.

Each of the emails in the preceding examples has a different audience. The first was sent from a student to a professor, and therefore the tone is deferential. The second was sent from a student to members of a club that the student works for, and the tone is more casual. The third was sent from the student editors of an undergraduate journal to a student who had submitted an article for publication. The tone is one of explanation and kindness, to soften the blow of rejection.

What's It For?

Emails usually serve a clear purpose: they may be used to convey information, make a request, or inquire about something. While the primary purpose is informative, a secondary purpose is to maintain the goodwill of the audience. Like the slogans earlier in this chapter, these emails seek to create and maintain a positive impression of the individual or organization—even when conveying bad news, as in the rejection email in Example 3.

EXERCISE 12.2: Compose an Email Requesting a Letter of Reference

One of the most important emails you will send as a student is an email requesting a letter of reference from a professor. Suppose you need a letter of reference for a job or internship—or perhaps you actually do need such a letter. Compose an email requesting this letter from a professor. Be sure to explain how the professor knows you and why the professor should write you a letter—all while striking a respectful tone to maintain the professor's goodwill.

C. Business Letter

A business letter is a formal, printed letter used to conduct workplace affairs.

EXAMPLE 1: Cover Letter for a Student Job Application

Jessica Wang
44 Market Street, Jefferson, MO 44999
JWang@email.edu | 777.555.2354

5 May 2013

Marty C. Jones
Hiring Partner
Smith and Jones LLP
332 Main St.
Townville, NC 27899

Dear Mr. Jones:

I am writing to apply for an internship with your law firm this summer. Your firm has indicated that it is interested in hiring an undergraduate pre-law student to help with paralegal duties. I believe that I am an excellent fit for this position.

As you can see from my résumé (attached), I have excellent grades and leadership experience. You have requested a student with a professional demeanor and responsibility; my duties as the President of the pre-law club at my college have taught me both professionalism and responsibility. Your job listing notes that the paralegal will have a lot of contact with clients; my experience working as a receptionist for a local non-profit has given me experience working with the public, experience that will enable me to serve your clients.

Thank you for considering my application.

Yours Truly,

Jessica Wang
Jessica Wang

. . . .

EXAMPLE 2: Acceptance Letter from a Graduate Program

Evergreen State University
College of Arts & Sciences

Gerry A. Sampson
Director, Graduate Studies
Department of Political Science
Evergreen State University
363 Tinny St., Greenville, NY 12083

May 5, 2013

Joe A. Smith
347 Franklin Ln.
Chesterfield, MO 63006

Dear Mr. Smith:

I am pleased to inform you that your application for admission to the Political Science graduate program at State University has been accepted for the school term commencing Fall of 2013.

Your application has given us some insight into your skill and ability. You have proven to have consistently above average grades, and your recent coursework has shown that you are a determined and devoted student. We believe that you will be a welcome asset to our program.

Enclosed are the necessary forms to finalize your acceptance. This paperwork, along with your deposit, is due by June 1, 2013.

Thank you for taking an interest in the Political Science Department at College University, and we look forward to beginning the new term with you.

Yours Sincerely,

G. A. Sampson
Gerry A. Sampson
Director of Graduate Studies

Enclosures
cc: Prof. B. Simmons, Dept. Chair

EXAMPLE 3: Thank-you Letter to a Professor

Joe A. Smith
347 Franklin Ln., Chesterfield, MO 63006
JoeSmith@email.edu | (929) 555-2345

March 10, 2013

Professor Jackie Turner
Department of Political Science
Maple State College
111 College Way
Mapleville, VT 05474

Dear Professor Turner:

I am writing to thank you for your support of my application to the graduate program in Political Science at Evergreen State University. Because of your strong letter of recommendation and your phone call to your former mentor at the school, I have been offered a position in the fall incoming class of graduate students.

Thank you for your strong mentorship of me during my time here at Maple State College, and I hope we can stay in touch in the coming years.

Best Wishes,

Joe A. Smith
Joe A. Smith

USE THE TOOLKIT

Let's use the three genre toolkit questions from Chapter 1 to examine this genre.

What Is It?

A business letter is a formal, hard-copy communication. It first contains information about the sender (sometimes in formal letterhead), then the date sent, and then information about the recipient. The salutation includes the word "Dear" with the formal name of the recipient, followed by a colon (not a comma). The body of the letter is usually single-spaced with an extra space between paragraphs. It concludes with a complimentary closing, such as "Yours Truly," (in Example 1), "Yours Sincerely," (in Example 2), or "Best Wishes," (in Example 3) followed by the sender's name. Some letters, such as Example 2, include additional details, such as a list of enclosures, or a "cc:" line (meaning "carbon copy") to indicate who else is receiving a copy of the letter.

Who Reads It?

Letter writers intend their letters to be read by the letter recipient, usually a professional contact. However, as with any piece of writing, you should expect that a letter might be shared with others. For example, Example 3, sent by a student to a professor, might be shared by the professor with colleagues in order to show what a thoughtful student the letter-writer is. In the case of Example 2, the graduate school acceptance letter, the writer has indicated that the chair of the department will also receive a copy, by listing her as "cc:"

What's It For?

Like an email, a letter serves many purposes: to inform, inquire, request, and maintain goodwill with an audience. Business letters usually make that purpose explicit very early on, in the first paragraph. In Example 3, the letter-writer Joe makes his purpose clear in the very first sentence: "I am writing to thank you."

In the age of email, letters have taken on a higher level of formality. Thus, you should write a letter when you want to make a strong impression on the recipient by demonstrating that you have taken the time to write a letter instead of an email.

EXERCISE 12.3: Write a Rejection Letter

Suppose you are hiring someone to serve as a graphic designer for a small business you have started. Write a rejection letter to an applicant who has applied to join your company. Try to put yourself in the recipient's shoes. Consider how you can maintain the reader's goodwill, while clearly indicating that the applicant has not been chosen.

D. Résumé

A résumé is a short document that job seekers prepare to share their work experience and qualifications with potential employers.

EXAMPLE 1: Résumé for an Occupational Therapy Major

JAELYN GARCIA JOHNSON

2010 Morris Ct. | Austin, Texas 78748 | 512.555.3425 | jaeyln.johnson@email.edu

OBJECTIVE
To start my career as a nursing aide at a local rehabilitation center

EDUCATION

Austin Community College   Expected June 2016
Austin, Texas

- Associate of Applied Science Degree in Occupational Therapy
- Related course work: Mind-Body Systems, Human Movement and Environmental Effects, Psychosocial Evaluation and Intervention, Research Methods, and Field Work (at St. David's Rehabilitation Center)

EXPERIENCE & SKILLS

Rehabilitation and Physical Education

- Shadowed Dr. Borges at St. David's Rehabilitation Center; cleaned patient living areas, fed, exercised, and interacted with patients, as instructed; helped maintain patient records (3 months.)
- Taught physical education activities to children in grades K-3; interacted with students and teachers; supervised class activities; designed lesson plans. (5 hours per week.)

Office Management Skills

- Office Assistant at Vanguard Corporation (2010 – Present). Package and ship software; track and compile client contact data; manage client relationships
- Proprietor of Pet Sitting Business (2003 – Present). Care for clients' pets while they are out of town; interact with clients in person and over the phone; develop print and email advertising.

Language Skills

- Proficient in Spanish with strengths in reading and writing. Experience with written translation.

Computer Skills

- Experience in Microsoft Windows; Microsoft Office suite including Word, PowerPoint, and Excel.
- Social media skills including Facebook, Twitter, and blogging

ACHIEVEMENTS

- Athletic Accomplishments: Four-Year Varsity Letter Winner, Indoor Track & Field; Captain of the Cross Country Team
- Vision Award Recipient: Given to two outstanding and committed freshmen athletes on the Cross Country team. Sponsored by the SHS Sports Booster Club.

EXAMPLE 2: Résumé for a History Major

JONATHAN MARCUS STONE

OBJECTIVE

To launch my career in computing with an entry-level sales position

EXPERIENCE

2009 – Present Oxford Taekwondo America   Oxford, NC

Taekwondo Instructor
- Taught group and private lessons to children and adults, including some autistic students
- Managed client contracts at gym facility
- Nationally certified by Taekwondo America in 2009

EDUCATION

2010 – 2014   University of Mississippi   Oxford, MS

- B.A. in History

INTERESTS

- Two-sport Varsity Letter Winner: Basketball and Track and Field. Scholar-Athlete recognition for being a varsity athlete with a high GPA.
- Beta Club President. Organized community service events for this academic club, ran meetings, and attended summer workshops.
- Northwest Oxford High School Representative to the Town of Oxford Youth Council chartered by the Town Council. Planned events attended by all citizens of Oxford

AWARDS

- Financial Scholarships Earned: Town of Oxford Youth Council
- Scholarship, and Mississippi Agricultural Fair Scholarship.
- National Merit Scholarship Commended Student

JONATHANSTONE@EMAIL.EDU

755 OXFORD CIRCLE, OXFORD, MS 38655 • 662.555.4435

EXAMPLE 3: Résumé for a Recent College Graduate

4000 Maple Station, Mapleview, NH 603-555-6772 ptb3@maple.edu

Phillip T. Beckett

Objective	To leverage my experience and education into a entry-level position with a lobbying firm

Professional Highlights

Speaker of the House
- Leader of Maple University Student Government Houses of Representatives
- Chair of Policy Committee
- Co-chair of Safety Committee

Research Assistant
- Research Assistant for 2 years, for Dr. Margo Cummings, at Maple University
- Designed and directed research experiments on directed forgetting
- Managed participant enrollment and stipends

Vice-President of Young Democrats
- Organized and lead various projects for Maple University Young Democrats
- Served as Public Relations Director before becoming Vice-President

Tutor
- Provided peer tutoring at Maple University Writing Center
- Tutored fellow students in Psychology and French

Skills
- Leadership
- Debate and argumentation
- Communications and writing skills
- Student organization and mobilization
- Social media and computer skills
- Fluent in French
- Canvassing and cold-calling
- Type 85 words per minute
- Classical Pianist

Education   B.A. in Psychology   Maple University, Mapleview, NH   May 2012

Achievements   Dean's List, GPA 3.73 in major, 3.34 overall   Elliot Smith Peabody Academic Scholarship

References   References are available on request.

USE THE TOOLKIT

Let's use the three genre toolkit questions from Chapter 1 to examine this genre.

What Is It?

Looking at the preceding documents, we see that a résumé is a short document—often as short as one page—that shows the writer's education, work experience, and other job qualifications, such as computer skills or foreign language abilities. In Example 1, Jaelyn highlighted her athletic accomplishments because her vocation as an occupational therapist is one that draws upon athleticism. In Example 2, Jonathan highlighted his extensive computer software experience to show that he can be useful on the job in an office that uses any of a variety of different computer systems.

Who Reads It?

Résumés are read by people who hire other people for jobs. In large companies, hiring is done by human resources specialists. In smaller companies, a supervisor might do the hiring personally. Sometimes, your résumé may be read by many people at one company before you will be invited to interview for a job. For this reason, your résumé will need to be tailored to a specific job, but it will also need to be general enough to appeal to multiple people at one company. In Example 3, Phillip, who recently graduated from college and is now looking for a job, figures that employers reading his résumé will be most concerned with whether or not he has a record of work experience. For this reason, Phillip grouped all of his experience—paid or not—under the heading "Professional Experience," creating a long and impressive list.

What's It For?

A résumé is a tool to help you get a job, an internship, or another type of employment. It communicates your qualifications quickly and clearly in a fashion that your reader expects to see. As you can see from the preceding résumés, résumés follow a fairly predictable structure (even as their surface appearances might vary). This structure contains subheadings that make the document easy to skim and typefaces that are easy to read. Remember: an effective résumé is one that gets you the job that you applied for.

EXERCISE 12.4: Analyze Résumés Using DOCS

In Chapter 3 of this book, you learned the DOCS method for analyzing new genres, which teaches you to look at (1) design, (2) organization, (3) content, and (4) style when considering a new genre.

Using the DOCS chart in Table 12.1, conduct a DOCS analysis of the preceding sample résumés.

Table 12.1   DOCS Résumé Analysis Chart

Genre	*Résumé Conventions*
Design	
Organization	
Content	
Style	

E. Strategies for Résumés

Imagine you've been asked by a potential employer to submit your résumé for an internship, a volunteer opportunity, or for a paid job. How would you go about writing this document? Let's look at how Jaelyn (Example 1) prepared her résumé to apply for jobs as an occupational therapist.

Prewriting (Content)

Before you can write your résumé, you need to brainstorm the material that you will put in each section of your résumé. For example, you might draw three columns on a piece of paper: one for education, one for experience, and one for skills. Under each column, you could start listing *all* possible items that you could put under each heading. For education, list every club you belonged to, every activity you participated in. For experience, list every job and internship.

Here's Jaelyn's prewriting list for her experience section of her résumé. Notice how she listed more items than she actually put on her résumé. (The ones she ended up putting on her résumé she marked with a star.)

> *Office Assistant at Vanguard Corporation**
> *Nanny for a professor in my department*
> *Proprietor of Pet Sitting Business**
> *Physical Education Instructor**
> *Lifeguard at neighborhood swimming pool in high school*
> *Volunteer at Second Chance Pet Adoptions*

As you prewrite, try to get everything down on paper, even experiences that you don't think are relevant for your résumé. You want to have a wealth of options to choose from. Later, when you are writing your résumé, you can select the activities that are most persuasive to potential readers. Jaelyn eventually selected the starred items because those were the ones that seemed most important to potential employers. For example, working as a physical education instructor seemed like good experience for someone who eventually wanted to work as an occupational therapist (who provides physical therapy to clients who have injuries or disabilities).

Drafting (Organizing)

There are many different ways to organize a résumé. You should get a feel for the variety of résumés out there before you start writing your own. The first thing to do is ask friends or classmates if they don't mind sharing theirs with you. That way, you can get a sense of how others have organized their information or written about their experiences with school and work. Your campus career center is also an excellent resource for guidance on writing a résumé.

The Internet is another great source for examples of genres. Try searching for the name of your genre and add the word "sample" or "example" to your search. Thus, you would type phrases like this into your search engine (such as Google): "résumé example" or "sample student résumé." In almost any case, you will be able to find plenty of hits.

Based on your set of samples, you will see that there is no standard format for a résumé. While it is typical to begin with your name and address, then education, then professional experience, you will notice that other sections may vary (such as Computer Skills, Awards, and so on). You can choose sections like these to highlight your unique skills.

Once you have a résumé outline that you like, you can begin arranging the information that you gathered while brainstorming within your résumé design. Jaelyn settled on three headings: Education, Experience & Skills, and Achievements. She grouped together Experience & Skills to make her list of experience look more impressive; as a student, she just did not have much work experience under her belt.

Revising (Style)

Notice how descriptions are written in the best résumés. For examples, strong résumés don't always use full sentences; instead, they use lots of action words ("volunteered," "taught," etc.). Furthermore, the level of formality tends to be high (Chapter 21).

Descriptions focus on accomplishments that the writer hopes to highlight; there are lists under each category and each item that provide details and explanations. Thus, it isn't enough to simply state that you were a Research Assistant. You must provide a list of details using action words to describe what you did as a research assistant.

Ideally, you should tailor the descriptions of your experiences to match job advertisements in your field. Study job ads: what sorts of keywords tend to pop up?

Jaelyn used keywords like "supervised," "patients," and "designed" to emphasize her experience with working with people; her job as an occupational therapist will require her to work closely with clients and other staff members in a therapy clinic.

Editing (Design)

Keep in mind that a résumé must be easy to skim. It also must be short, ideally just one page for someone just starting out in his or her career. Your headings should be emphasized using boldface or other font choices to make them easy to find. Be sure to make these headings consistent throughout. Jaelyn opted for a more modern style of résumé because her field, occupational therapy, views itself as cutting-edge and savvy with technology. Employers would welcome a résumé that embraced a modern style.

Use bullets or other strategies to make your lists easy to read. Be sure that you follow any specific formatting requests made by a potential employer, such as specific subheadings or descriptions of certain types of duties.

Lastly, be sure to proofread carefully. Any typos or errors at all will hurt your professional *ethos* (Chapter 18).

Troubleshooting

Here are some common challenges that students face when writing workplace genres.

I don't have any "real" work experience, or my work experience is lame.
Work experience isn't necessarily experience that you received a paycheck for. Think about any work—volunteer work included—that you performed that might be relevant to the job you are applying for. If you are applying to work in a fundraising office, your volunteer experience gathering signatures for a petition means that you have experience approaching strangers and are comfortable asking for their support for a cause. Those are skills that you need to work in fundraising.

If you worked as a server in a restaurant, you might think that your work experience isn't worthy of respect. But the skills you learned on the job may be very valuable to your future employer. You just need to describe them well on your résumé. Were you responsible for large sums of cash in a cash register? That's a great responsibility. Note that on your résumé. Did you supervise other workers? Note that as well, because management experience is very valuable. Don't downplay your experience; instead, couch your experience in terms that your future employer will understand.

Study sample résumés to see how others have described their work experience that is similar to yours.

I don't have any special "skills."
Often, the last section of a résumé is reserved for special abilities that might set you apart from other candidates for a job. Sometimes

these skills are work-related (language skills, computer skills, typing ability). Other times, these skills reveal a little bit about your personality (musical ability, athletic ability). When thinking about what to put in your "skills" section, think first about your audience. What do you know about the person who will be reading your résumé? Will this person be impressed by your ability to train cattle horses, or by your ability to repair automotive engines? These special skills, although unrelated to the work you may be applying for, reveal that you are a well-rounded person with an interesting background. That interesting background means that you will be *interesting to have around the workplace*, and potentially fun to work with.

F. Chapter Project: Write a Résumé

Prepare a résumé that you could use to apply for a job, internship, or volunteer opportunity.

We've already examined the genre of the résumé in some detail in this chapter. Now, think about connecting that genre to a particular rhetorical situation.

1. Locate an advertisement for a job, internship, or volunteer opportunity you would like to have. Use the advertisement to help you investigate the rhetorical situation: the purpose, the audience's needs, your role, and the timing. Find keywords that you can work into the résumé, such as "communication" or "teamwork."
2. Write a résumé that is appropriate for that rhetorical situation. Using your analysis of possible resources and constraints, make your own choices to craft a persuasive résumé.

Multimedia Option: Create a Résumé Website

Prepare a résumé that you could use on a personal website. In this case, you will not be applying for a particular job—people post résumés online so that they can be accessed at any time. For example, a freelancer who is seeking new clients might post their résumé and link to it from their social networking profile. You'll have to do some exploration to find samples of online résumés; identify the conventions, resources, and constraints available to you, and then consider what choices to make given the rhetorical situation. Your campus career center is an excellent place to begin your research.

Proposals

A proposal is a genre that asks for something from someone. For example, in a wedding proposal, the proposer asks someone to marry him/her. The audience (the girlfriend or boyfriend) has the power to agree to the proposal—or to reject it. Proposals are characterized by this unequal relationship between the writer/speaker and the audience: the audience has the power to say yes or no.

In college, you might be asked to write a proposal to start a new student organization or to enroll in an independent study course you have designed with a professor. Or, you might write a marketing proposal for a business class. In a city and regional planning course, you might be asked to come up with a proposal for a new redevelopment project in your town.

In the workplace, proposals are a very common genre. In a number of fields, potential clients will put out a request for proposals (RFP), and businesses write proposals hoping to get the job. For example, a company might request advertising proposals for a new ad campaign. A contractor might write a building proposal for a client seeking to build a new home or office. A caterer might put together a proposal for someone seeking to host an event like a wedding or retirement celebration.

In this chapter, you will learn how to write several of the proposals that you might encounter as a college student.

A. Proposal Mini-Genre: Elevator Pitch

An elevator pitch is a short speech (usually 30 seconds to two minutes long) that you prepare in order to quickly summarize a proposal. You might prepare an elevator pitch if you are working in sales and want to be prepared for potential customers, or if you are an entrepreneur and want to be prepared in case you meet a potential investor. The term "elevator pitch" refers to the idea that you could complete your proposal during an elevator ride, in case you happen to be riding the elevator with someone who could say yes to your proposal.

EXAMPLE 1: Elevator Pitch to an Employer

"Professor Lee? I'm a first-year biology major. I'm experienced in gel electrophoresis and Matlab, and I'm really interested in learning more about genetic research. Would you be willing to consider me for a position as lab assistant next year? I can send you my résumé and references."

EXAMPLE 2: Elevator Pitch to an Investor

"Bananarama will be Springfield's first full-service banana stand. We'll sell fresh, hand-dipped bananas in 34 enticing flavors. The frozen fruit market is among the fastest growing in our state, since it offers a health-conscious alternative to ice cream and frozen yogurt. Would you be interested in being part of an enterprise with projected $1 million in sales over the next five years? I can send you my business plan by email."

EXAMPLE 3: Elevator Pitch to a Customer

"Hi, would you like a free sample of our Hungerfree energy bars? With each sale, we donate fifty percent of our proceeds to UNICEF to fight child hunger. Plus, the peanuts, whole grains, and honey will help you get through your next college class Hungerfree. If you like the sample, you can buy a bar for just $2."

USE THE TOOLKIT

Let's use the three genre toolkit questions from Chapter 1 to examine this genre.

What Is It?

An elevator pitch is a short request. Each one begins with an introduction—either of a person, of a business, or of a product. Then, each pitch provides a very short description—of the person's qualifications, the business's value, or the product's qualities. Each pitch also includes a request. You may begin or end with the request. You can see that in Examples 1 and 2, the request comes last, after the explanation. In Example 3, the request comes first, and the explanation second.

Who Reads It?

Elevator pitches are usually delivered orally, so instead of a reader, they have a listening audience. For each of these examples, you can imagine a different audience and situation. In Example 1, you might imagine that a student has run into a professor in the hallway or waited to speak to him after class. In Example 2, you can imagine that Bananarama's owner has met a wealthy investor at a business fair or at an event for alumni of the owner's college. And, in Example 3, we can guess that a student may have set up a display in a high-traffic area on campus. In each example, the audience is a potential employer, investor, or client, someone who has the power to grant the request.

What's It For?

An elevator pitch is primarily a persuasive genre: the goal is to convince someone to grant your request, or at least to consider it. For that reason, you can consider an elevator pitch a very short argument. In some cases, it is also an opening for further conversation or writing. You might follow up an elevator pitch with a résumé, as in Example 1, or with a longer print proposal, as the Bananarama owner did (Example 2).

EXERCISE 13.1: Write an Elevator Pitch

Prepare a short (30-second) elevator pitch for a job you would like. Imagine you are meeting a recruiter for your ideal employer at a campus job fair. How would you pitch yourself to that person? Practice your pitch several times, and then deliver it to your classmates or group.

GROUP ACTIVITY 13.1: Adjust Elevator Pitches for Various Audiences

With your group, decide on a product or service for your local community. Determine how you would make that product or service available. Then, each of you will prepare a 30-second elevator pitch for a different target audience:

- A potential investor
- A potential customer
- A potential employee
- A reporter for the business section of the local newspaper

Adjust your tone and message for each audience's concerns. Practice your pitches, then deliver them to the class.

B. TV, Book, or Film Pitch

A TV, book, or film pitch is a short document intended to sell a TV show, book, or film to producers/publishers.

EXAMPLE 1: TV Pitch

Genre: Documentary
Title: *Mixed in America*
Logline: *African American Lives* for teens of mixed racial heritage. Five teens from mixed race backgrounds investigate the history of interracial relationships, ethnicity, and identity in America. In the process, each teen learns something about themselves, their family history, and their country.
Synopsis:
(Themes: Reality-based, documentary, history)

In a middle class black neighborhood in Chicago, a sixteen-year-old girl raised primarily by her African American mother wonders about the Caucasian father she never knew. A fifteen-year-old boy in rural, small-town Wisconsin thinks his great-great-grandfather was Native American, but doesn't know for sure. In suburban North Carolina, a Chinese and Latin American high-schooler wants to know more about her family's roots.

What happens when these students get a chance to find out where they come from? In this series, each teen starts off on a quest, assisted by a team of historians, archivists, and geneticists, to find out more about themselves and about America. It's a fascinating look at the melting pot in America, through the perspective of five teens.

Five episodes:

1. Meet the teenagers and their families. Get to know each teen and find out about how their mixed-race heritage has shaped their life. We'll see one teen talk about the peer pressure she faces to "choose" between her African American and Caucasian identities, how another family blends Chinese and Latino American traditions, and how other teenagers view students of mixed-race backgrounds. We'll also hear each student's questions about his or her heritage.

2. Brianna—The episode begins in Chicago, where Brianna lives with her mother in a townhouse in Lincoln Park. We see her examining the few photographs she has of her Caucasian father. A librarian helps her to track down information on microfilm; we learn Brianna's father was a marine and is probably living in Texas. An historian traces Brianna's father's heritage back to the 1700s in colonial America—and we see he lived in the same county in Georgia where Brianna's mother's family lived as enslaved workers.

3. Edward—Edward shares the stories he heard from his grandfather about his Native-American great-grandfather. With an anthropologist, Edward travels to

speak with elders of the Dakota Sioux tribe in Wisconsin. Then, a geneticist helps Edward to interpret results from DNA sequencing, and we learn the truth about Edward's grandfather's claims.

4. Katya—In Charlotte, North Carolina, we met Katya, whose father is Chinese and whose mother is Mexican. We travel to Mexico to meet Katya's extended family and to Jamaica, where Katya's Chinese family members settled in the 1880s.

5. Ramon—In Orlando, Florida, we meet Ramon, who wants to know more about his Cuban father. With an historian in tow, we travel to Cuba and track down Ramon's father, who lives in Centro Habana. Ramon learns about Afro-Cuban religion and dance, and meets his father and six brothers and sisters for the first time.

EXAMPLE 2: Book Pitch

There's a difference between book smarts and street smarts—and not everyone has both in ENTANGLEMENT.

Awkward Greta Donovan, the fiercely intelligent daughter of a philandering physics professor, can't relate to people. If you ask her the temperature, she'll say nineteen degrees when it's actually sixty-six. Her father taught her that Fahrenheit is for dummies.

No wonder she can't see it coming when someone tries to kill her.

One year before she's attacked, a naive Greta moves to Los Angeles with her college roommate Daphne Saito, a troubled girl with an abusive past. The charismatic Daphne teaches Greta how to buy stilettos, wear lip gloss, and navigate 1990s Hollywood nightlife.

But Daphne's own insecurities make betrayal her modus operandi.

The girls toy with the men in their lives, recklessly racing through relationships. One night, Daphne twists a man up too tight and then turns him loose. Greta ends up in the wrong place at the wrong time.

Daphne's careless malice puts Greta's life on the line. Now Greta must save herself from Daphne before it's too late.

ENTANGLEMENT, a completed manuscript of 75,000 words, is Tana French meets the Los Angeles underbelly of Bret Easton Ellis's LESS THAN ZERO.

EXAMPLE 3: Film Pitch

Working Title: PUSHOVER

Thirty-one-year-old Anna Edmonds made a big mistake. Eight years ago, she turned down the dashing yet impecunious Craig Wentworth, persuaded by her wealthy parents that Craig, an enlisted marine, wasn't good enough for her. She thought she could do better. But now she's single, fending off extra pounds, and zealously applying wrinkle cream.

Now, Craig is back in small-town Virginia. He's now a military hero evading flirtatious advances from all the local girls, and Anna is stuck taking care of her sister's kids in her free time and working at her dad's law firm. Craig is ready to settle down, but this time he wants someone different—someone strong-willed and resolute, who won't be swayed by what other people think.

Enter Layla, Anna's co-worker, a 20-year-old bubbly flirt. Craig thinks he may have met his match—until Layla's strong will gets her in trouble. Will Craig realize Anna has been the one all along? Or will his sense of duty make him stay with Layla?

In this modern-day adaptation of Jane Austen's *Persuasion,* we learn that a steadfast heart is more important than a resolute mind, and that true love doesn't always happen the way we expect it to—but it does happen.

Logline: Will the hero find the strength to take back the girl who broke his heart?
Target Audience: 18–40 year old females
Genre: Romantic Comedy
Actors: Alexis Bledel (Anna); Theo James (Craig); Miranda Cosgrove (Layla)
Similar Films: *Clueless, Bridget Jones' Diary*

USE THE TOOLKIT

Let's use the three genre toolkit questions from Chapter 1 to examine this genre.

What Is It?

A TV, book, or film pitch is a type of short proposal. The pitch usually begins with a short summary intended to capture the reader's attention. In Example 3, the pitch for the movie "Pushover" begins with this line: "Thirty-one-year-old Anna Edmonds made a big mistake." Readers are left wondering what mistake she has made, and will hopefully move on. This "hook" is followed by a longer description or synopsis of the proposed project, including the main plot lines, characters, and, in the case of the television show, "Mixed in America," episodes.

Who Reads It?

These pitches are submitted to readers who can actually help to bring the project into being. This may be an agent, producer, or editor. In Example 2, the book pitch would be read by an agent that the author hopes will represent him and negotiate a book deal. In each case, the reader is looking for the next "hit"—a book, TV show, or movie that will appeal to an audience. They might turn down pitches that represent great ideas but have limited marketability. For this reason, the pitches include comparisons to similar projects that have been successful: the television pitch (Example 1) compares "Mixed in America" to the successful program *African American Lives*, which aired on PBS; the book pitch (Example 2) compares the novel to the work of novelist Tana French and the novel *Less Than Zero*; while the film pitch (Example 3) compares "Pushover" to the films *Bridget Jones' Diary* and *Clueless*, which were also modern adaptations of Jane Austen novels. Since these readers receive many proposals of this type, the proposals must be written so that they stand out in some way. They must clearly describe the project and show what makes it different, exciting, and appealing to an audience.

What's It For?

The goal of a pitch is to get support for a project. In the case of a book, an agent may agree to help you market your project to a press, while an editor (who works for a press) may agree to publish your book. In the case of a TV or film pitch, the goal is to get a producer to sign on. The producer will provide the funds necessary to actually put the TV show or film into production. Thus, these pitches are all persuasive in nature—the goal is to get readers on board with the project.

EXERCISE 13.2: Write a Pitch

Start with an idea for a TV show, book, or film you would be interested in producing. Then, write a pitch in which you persuade an audience to support that project. You will need to do research on existing projects so that you can show how your proposed project (your book, show, or film) is unique.

C. Student Proposal

A student proposal is a document that requests approval for a new campus organization, event, course, or activity. At most universities, students can request approval (and sometimes funding) for these endeavors, but they must first complete a proposal that is approved by college administrators.

EXAMPLE 1: Student Event Proposal

Student Event Proposal Form

General Information

Name of Organization(s): <u>International Student Club</u>

Person Completing Request: <u>Victor Egbukichi</u>   **E-mail:** <u>victore@uca.edu</u>

Event Description

Description of Event: _____

Place and time: <u>Mondays, 2:30-3:30 pm; Student Union Room 2010b</u>

Expected attendance <u>25 students (undergraduate)</u>

Describe how this event will benefit the UCA community: International students now make up 8% of the student body at UCA, in accordance with the university's global mission. However, international students often struggle to make American friends. Many end up socializing mainly with other students from their home country, which can prevent international students from improving their language skills or learning about American culture. While international students can interact with American students in classrooms, these are high stakes situations where they may feel shy about speaking up. The weekly coffee hour will give these students a chance to meet American students in a friendly, low pressure situation.

American students who are learning a foreign language can also practice their language skills with international students, and learn more about their culture.

Describe other activities and events your student organization has held this year:

The International Student Club has thus far hosted four International Days in the cafeteria, highlighting the food and culture of China, India, Nigeria, and Russia. We plan to host four more International Days in the Spring semester (for Mexico, Ethiopia, Brazil, and Spain).

We have also participated in the Student Organization Carnival and sponsored three members in the Dance Marathon.

Describe how your student organization will publicize this event:

We have designed the attached poster, which we will put up in the Student Union, cafeteria, and in the Language & Literature buildings.

Describe how this event is unique:

This activity will help us to recruit new members who are not necessarily international students, but who would like to participate in our organizational mission. This is the first activity we know of that will specifically address the communication gap between international and American students.

EXAMPLE 2: Student Organization Proposal

Student Organization Council

Proposal for Student Organization

Name of Organization: Campus Community Garden

Name of Organizer: Leticia Garcia-Rodriguez

Contact Phone Number: 222-222-2222

Email Address: Leticia@gsu.edu

Name of Advisor: Professor Peabody

Contact Phone Number: 222-222-2224

Email Address: p.peabody@gsu.edu

Please answer the following questions as completely as possible in the space provided.

> **1. Describe the mission of your organization:**
> The Campus Community Garden will encourage sustainable food at GSU by providing classes, hands-on workshops, and fresh fruits and vegetables for students, faculty, and staff.
>
> **2. Describe how your organization is unique or new:**
> To date, no student organization at GSU focuses on growing fresh food and teaching gardening skills. Other food-related organizations, such as Local Food GSU, focus on advocating for purchasing food locally, but do not promote gardening.
>
> **3. Describe how your organization will benefit the GSU community:**
> Any student will be able to apply for a plot in the community garden, purchase fresh food at our weekly garden market, or volunteer for bi-weekly garden work days. Students can also sign up for free courses on topics such as composting or planting a windowsill garden.
>
> **4. Describe how your organization fulfills GSU's mission:**
> Sustainability is one of the key terms in GSU's mission statement. This organization will help students and faculty to promote sustainability and make a direct impact on the college's ecological footprint.

EXAMPLE 3: Independent Study Proposal

Independent Study Proposal Outline

Semester and Year	Spring 2016
Student Name	Tyler Williamson
Instructor Name	Professor Molly Johnson
Date Proposal Written	September 15, 2015

Project Description:

In her 1995 speech to the United Nations Fourth World Conference on Women, Hillary Clinton said: "And let us heed the call so that we can create a world in which every woman is treated with respect and dignity, every boy and girl is loved and cared for equally, and every family has the hope of a strong and stable future." Clinton has modeled her world-wide call for women's rights upon the United Nations' protection of human rights, and many others have followed. But the question remains: is she guilty of cultural solipsism when she outlines standards of women's rights based upon the lifestyle of bourgeois western women? Who decides what it means to be "treated with respect and dignity"?

This independent study will examine the call for universal women's rights: is such a goal possible, and if so, what would these "rights" look like? Throughout the semester, I will work to shed my resistance to cultural perspectives from beyond the West, through readings, documentary screenings, discussions and reflections, research and presentations, and interviews with women in our community who have left their native countries to make new lives in America.

Assignments:

1. Documentary film rhetorical analysis (5 pages)
2. Interview series of immigrant women in America (5 interviews)
3. Final research paper on international women's rights (20 pages)

USE THE TOOLKIT

Let's use the three genre toolkit questions from Chapter 1 to examine this genre.

What Is It?

These proposals all relate to aspects of student life, whether it is planning an event, starting a student organization, or proposing an independent study. Like the elevator pitch, each of these proposals "pitches" something—an event, organization, or course of study. To do so, the proposal describes the goals of the activity, explains why it is unique, and outlines how it will contribute to the campus community or to the student's education. In Example 1, Victor writes that the activity will promote communication between international and U.S. students, helping international student make friends. In Example 2, Leticia writes that the garden "will encourage sustainable food" on the university campus.

All of these proposals are forms that writers download from a website and fill out. These forms give writers a clear idea of what to include, but the writers must still make rhetorical choices in order to create a persuasive case.

Who Reads It?

These proposals are read by decision makers who decide which proposals to approve or fund. The audience may be other student leaders (such as members of the Student Organization Committee), college administrators, or professors. The audience for Example 3, Tyler's independent study proposal, would include the professor whom he has asked to advise the project and the director of undergraduate studies of the political science department. The readers of the proposals decide which proposals to approve based on how persuasive the writer has been. They may prioritize proposals that are likely to help the greatest number of students, or proposals that are the most unique, or those that seem most feasible to implement.

What's It For?

The purpose of a student proposal is to persuade readers to grant the request for approval. Often, approval may entail funding. Thus, a proposal is essentially an argument: you provide good reasons for readers to support your request (Chapter 18). In Example 2, Leticia shows how her proposed organization will promote sustainability, a key goal at her university.

EXERCISE 13.3: Propose a Student Organization or Event

First, determine how students can go about proposing a new organization or event on your campus. If there is a form, download and save it to your computer. Then, write a persuasive proposal for your organization or event.

D. Grant Proposal

A grant proposal, like an elevator pitch, a TV/film/book pitch, and a student life proposal, seeks support for a project. In the case of a grant proposal, the support is money. The examples that follow demonstrate that a grant proposal requires you to show that you are doing something new, unique, and important.

EXAMPLE 1: Grant Proposal for an Outreach Project

Vincent Abiona

Technology Education in Nigerian Hospitals

Each year, 30% of procedures performed in Nigerian hospitals are unsuccessful. This isn't due to poor doctors or nurses, but instead, a lack of technological resources; the inability to access vast medical information over the internet, and the inability to efficiently keep track of patients through spread sheets. In a study conducted on Nigerian doctors in 2004, results showed that only 26% of respondents owned a computer and of those, only 18.9 percent demonstrated a high skill level (Bello et al., 2004). As technological advances are made, traditional methods of treating cases change, and these changes could be considered vital to the treatment of a patient. Through advancements in technology doctors can communicate their findings on how to treat cases more efficiently. Computer literacy has been proven to be a vital skill in the medical field, whether as a means of communication, organization of data, or access to doctors' and researchers' findings. Without this skill, important medical resources become inaccessible. When interviewed, Dr. Ronke Oyelaja stated that during her time of working in Nigerian hospitals, computers were not a resource, instead, books and journals were looked into.

A study of Nigerian medical students showed that when tested, 57.4% of a group of medical students were computer illiterate, deprived of a now critical resource in medical education (Ajuwon, 2003). It is clear that the problem stems early in the training process. Improved efforts such as inclusion of computer education in medical and nursing curriculum and establishment of computer laboratories are required to increase the student's access to computers and the internet. With these resources set in place, Nigerian doctors are going to become more computer literate. With computer skills, Nigerian doctors and nurses would have access to the current medical knowledge that has been refined over many years by doctors and researchers. With access to such knowledge, cases and conditions that may be unfamiliar to a doctor can be researched to see past effective treatments, increasing a clinic's ability to treat a patient.

As a child growing up in Nigeria, I experienced the trial and error method of Nigerian clinics and hospitals first hand. As I began my career path of becoming a doctor, I made improving Nigerian hospitals and clinics one of my lifetime goals. Doctors and Nurses did what they could to the best of their knowledge, but many times, diagnosis and treatment were lacking due to information and technology limitations. I propose to start a small computer training program in a clinic or hospital in Lagos, Nigeria, where medical students can learn the fundamentals of computers and their use in the medical field, specifically researching medical cases. First, the skill level of participating medical students will be assessed prior to the training program. Basic knowledge, such as navigation of the desktop and launching and using applications like Microsoft Word and Excel, will be tested. These skills are useful for keeping a database of patients, and creating documents and letters of findings to share in the medical world. Then students' ability to use web browsers such as Mozilla Firefox and Internet Explorer, and accurately search for medical information as well as the use of creditable sources will be accessed. Once their computer literacy level has been established, participants will undergo the training program which has a curriculum that will focus on the use of Microsoft applications, and how to research credible medical information over the internet, as well as basic navigation and use of computers (which will be tailored based on their test results).

To teach the Nigerian medical students, medical students from Mountain State University (MSU) with skill levels high enough to teach the materials will be assembled. I also hope to recruit students from Mountain State campus organizations like the Pre-med association. Mountain State University promotes students gaining experience abroad and making an influence both in and outside of their community. This program would give multiple medical students the ability to give to a foreign community by exercising and teaching the skills that they have acquired, providing an enriching experience for both MSU and Nigerian medical students. This opportunity could also be available to undergraduate students on a pre-med track or to show strength in the computer sciences. I will head the team of student teachers, as I am familiar with both cultures and hold enough qualifications to teach the material, such as: The Mountain State Most Technologically Savvy Student (for 4 consecutive years) as well as certificates of completion for numerous high school and university level computer courses. All of my previous experience in technology as well as health sciences will enable me to be an efficient teacher for the Nigerian Medical students. I can also speak one of the three main tribal languages of Nigeria on a skill level high enough to communicate with locals.

The program will begin in the first week of June 2012. During this time, we will set ⁵ up a small computer lab in the clinic for students to use. The skill assessment test will be administered during the second week. Two to three days will be taken to fully develop a four to six week curriculum based on the assessment test. The first two to three weeks will focus on teaching students the basics of how to use a computer; start up, launching software, saving and opening documents, using web browsers, etc. The remaining two to three weeks will focus on using Microsoft Word and Excel for practical purposes (documenting findings, creating informational flyers for patients) and researching over the internet. During the final week, students will be assessed again to determine their progress through the program.

It will cost an estimate of $2,400 per person for a plane ticket from the Mountain Regional Airport to Lagos Airport and back. At most, a total of two students' airfare will be covered by the Burch Fellowship Grant, totaling airfare to $4,800. I am applying for other grants to reduce the cost for other students to travel. In terms of housing, students will live in my father's house in Nigeria. It is a large enough living space for up to five people. Living expenses will only cover food and transportation, a total of $1,000 ($500 for each person covered in airfare), a total of $5,800. One of the most important essentials of this program is the computers and internet access needed for training. I am going to apply for a Center for Faculty Excellence (CFE) Instructional Innovation Grant. The CFE has set aside a portion of an awarded gift by computer maker Lenovo as one of four Lenovo Innovation Centers worldwide for instructional grants that are being used to promote innovation in specific areas of focus: collaborative learning, global education, and engaging large class sections. I will apply under the Global Education Track, which is awarded for promoting new learning opportunities across international boundaries. Innovative technology use under this track will be used to connect MSU students and faculty with peers and educational partners around the world.

This program could be the start of a major change in hospitals and clinics in Nigeria. Computer education could become part of the standard curriculum for medical students, and I need the help of the Mountain State Fellowship Fellows Program to make it possible.

References

Ajuwon, G. (2003). Computer and internet use by first year clinical and nursing students in a Nigerian teaching hospital. *BMC Medical Informatics and Decision Making, 3*(1), 10.

Bello, I. S., Arogundade, F. A., Sanusi, A. A., Ezeoma, I. T., Abioye-Kuteyi, E. A., & Akinsola, A. (2004). Knowledge and utilization of information technology among health care professionals and students in Ile-Ife, Nigeria: A case study of a university teaching hospital. *Journal of Medical Internet Research, 6*(4), e45. doi:10.2196/jmir.6.4.e45

EXAMPLE 2: **Grant Proposal for an Undergraduate Research Project**

Janelle Markham

Closing the Gap in Dental Care:

Dental Anxiety in Children in Bertie County

North Carolina lags behind many other states in quality and access to dental care. In 2010,

32% of adults in North Carolina had not visited a dentist in the past year (North Carolina

Department of Health and Human Services, 2004). As of 2010, 18% of North Carolina children had not seen a dentist in the past year, and 12% had never seen a dentist at all (North Carolina Child Health Assessment and Monitoring Program, 2010).

Given these conditions, many children enter kindergarten in North Carolina with a history of dental disease. In one study, 40% of kindergarteners had a history of dental disease, and 23% had not been treated for their dental problems (North Carolina Department of Health and Human Services, 2004). Children living in rural areas and children from low income families are more likely to lack access to dental care and to have poor dental health (Hartsock, Hall, and Connor, 2006; Lee, 2012). Not only can poor dental health lead to pain and discomfort, it can also contribute to school absences, speech dysfunction, and nutritional deficiencies (Hartsock, Hall, and Connor, 2006).

Many barriers prevent rural and low-income children from getting dental care, including financial constraints, travel required to get to a dental provider, and lack of information about the importance of dental health (Lee, 2012). Among adults, dental anxiety is also a factor: adults with low dental anxiety tended to receive more regular dental care than did adults who feared dentist visits (Arcury et al., 2012). However, it is unclear whether parental anxiety about dental care affects children's own attitudes toward dental care. Is dental anxiety passed on from parent to child? Since dental anxiety is a predisposing factor for poor dental health outcomes, it is important to determine how it develops and what can be done to reduce dental anxiety in children.

The goal of this research project will be to study parents' attitudes toward dental care in a rural, low-income North Carolina population, and to determine whether those attitudes correlate with children's attitudes to dental care.

Project Goals and Methods

My proposal is to develop a two-pronged research study during the summer of 2014. In the first phase, I will seek Internal Review Board (IRB) approval for my project, recruit participants from Bertie County who have children entering kindergarten in public schools, and complete the study design. After getting IRB approval, I will recruit participants at the orientation and enrollment sessions for incoming kindergarten students at three Bertie County public schools: East Bertie Elementary, Peabody Elementary, and Westgate Elementary. The goal is to enroll 60 parents, total, in the study, or 20 from each school.

The study will consist of two sets of interviews: one with parents and one with their children. The parents will complete the Dental Anxiety Scale (Corah, Gale, and Illig, 1978), and then meet with an interviewer to discuss their responses. Interviews will be designed for approximately 20 minutes each and will allow participants to elaborate on their own attitudes toward dental care, whether they think they pass on those attitudes to their children, and information about their children's dental health (such as how often they see a dental health provider). Interviews with children will last 10 minutes, and will involve a simple set of questions, such as "Have you been to a dentist before?" and "How did you feel about going to the dentist?" A set of simple facial expressions (smily face, frown, tears, etc.) will be used to help children identify their feelings.

Results will be used for a report on dental anxiety in kindergarten children, which I will submit to the Bertie County Public Health Department. I also plan to publish my results as an article in a dental health research journal.

Personal Statement

While volunteering in a kindergarten classroom in Bertie County, NC, [I noticed that] many of the children expressed fear of dental care. During a visit from a public health nurse, most of the children said that they brushed their teeth regularly, but many indicated that they feared going to the dentist. This led me to question why such young children already feared the dentist, and whether their parents' attitudes played a role. In addition to addressing this need, this project contributes directly to my academic goals as a pre-dentistry major.

References

Arcury, T. A., Savoca, M. R., Anderson, A. M., Chen, H., Gilbert, G. H., Bell, R. A., . . . Quandt., S. A. (2012). Dental care utilization among North Carolina Rural Older Adults. *Journal of Public Health Dentistry*, 72: 190–197. Doi: 10.1111/j.1752-7325.2012.00329.x

Corah N. L., Gale E. N., & Illig S. J. (1978). Assessment of dental anxiety scale. *Journal of the American Dental Association*, 97, 816–819.

Hartsock, L., Hall, M. B., & Connor, A. M. (2006). Informing the policy agenda: The community voices experience on dental health for children in North Carolina's rural communities. *Journal of Health Care for the Poor and Underserved, 17,* 111–123. Doi: 10.1353/hpu.2006.0005

Lee, J. Y. (2012). Access to dental health care for children in North Carolina. *North Carolina Medical Journal, 73,* 115–116.

North Carolina Department of Health and Human Services (NC DHHS) Oral Health Sec-

tion. (2004). *Community Oral Health Assessment, Epidemiological Survey (2003–2004).*

Raleigh, NC: Author.

North Carolina Child Health Assessment and Monitoring Program (CHAMP), State Cen-

ter for Health Statistics (2010). *Annual Survey Results.* Retrieved from http://www.schs

.state.nc.us/SCHS/champ/2010/dentist.html

EXAMPLE 3: Grant Proposal for a Study Abroad Project

Grace McDermott

Nutritional Access and Awareness for the Children of Burmese Migrant Workers in Mae Sot, Thailand

Background Information

In 2009, *The Economist* estimated that 120,000 migrant workers from Burma currently reside in the border town of Mae Sot, Thailand. These workers of varying ethnic backgrounds flee from Burma primarily because of the disastrous economic situation, widespread human rights violations by the Burmese military, and/or loss of property to the Burmese government. As roughly half of these workers are undocumented, they are often exploited by employers and many receive less than half of the official Thai minimum wage, leading to high poverty rates among this segment of the population ("Myanmar's Overflow," 2009). The children of these workers also represent a sensitive population with low access to healthcare, nutritional awareness, and general education (Amnesty International, 2005).

In order to promote education for the children in these growing communities of migrant workers, independent organizations such as the Burma Labor Solidarity Organization (BLSO) have constructed schools to specifically address the needs of these transient, often undocumented populations (Union Aid Abroad, 2008). However, in many of these schools, the curriculum focuses primarily on language skills, computer literacy, history, and math. Nutritional education is lacking at best and a nutritionally balanced diet is practically inaccessible for many of these students and their families. The results of a recent study regarding the nutritional condition of school children in rural China suggested that poor nutrition is strongly associated with low socioeconomic status. The results of this study further discern a strong correlation between poor nutrition and lower school performance (Yu and Hannum, 2011). As many of the migrant families from Burma living in Thailand are subsisting on a less-than-minimum-wage salary, malnutrition is a frequently observed malady. According to an article published in 2010 by the Foundation for Education and Development, 31% of migrant workers from Burma living in southern Thailand report frequently not having access to adequate quantities of food. 66% report rarely eating meats or proteins in general. Even more astoundingly, 71% of the population sampled in that study reported regularly experiencing days in which they would eat nothing but rice (Ellis, 2011).

Understanding these conditions, I would like to implement a two-part project in one of the BLSO-sponsored schools to investigate the students' nutritional access and to foster awareness about nutrition and general health.

Personal Interest and Experience

As one of the co-presidents of the Southeast Asia Interest Association (SEAIA) at UNC, I have become very interested in these issues. For the past 5 years, SEAIA has contributed financially to a BLSO-sponsored school in Mae Sot, Thailand, and spread awareness to the UNC campus community regarding the issues of the governance of Burma, the refugee situation both in Thailand and the United States, and the rights of both refugees and migrant workers from Burma. We have also worked extensively as mentors and English as a second language tutors for refugee families who have been resettled in the Chapel Hill-Carrboro area. I am currently volunteering for a third year as a mentor.

Project Description and Methods

According to the Mae Sot school's coordinator and our organization's primary contact at the school, one of the Mae Sot School's future goals is to ensure the proper nourishment for all of the students at the school. Considering this goal, I would like to focus my research on two target areas: dietary needs assessment research and a nutritional education program.

Dietary Needs Assessment Research

In order to conduct this fundamental aspect of my project, I would devise a strict set of interview questions to survey the overall nutritional situation of the children at the Mae Sot School. This survey would be verbally administered by me with the aid of a hired translator and recorded on a tape recording device. The questions would focus primarily on both access to different components of a healthy diet (fruits, vegetables, proteins, clean water, and vitamins) for students and also parental and student opinions of the current lunch program provided by the school. Lastly, as a follow up to this research, I would like to consult with one or two nutrition professors at UNC's school for Public Health after my project has been completed in order to review my findings and determine what could be feasibly added to the current lunch program to help the school reach its goal of providing adequate nutrition for all of its students. In order to investigate nutrition in this population through personal interviews, I would need to receive IRB approval before the beginning of my project.

Basic Nutritional Education Program

In the past, members from SEAIA at UNC have traveled to the Mae Sot School and taught temporary English language classes for the students there. In a similar way, I would like to provide a basic nutrition seminar for the students during my stay in Mae Sot in order to provide them with the awareness of how to make healthy food choices in the future and how dietary choices affect overall health. In order to implement this portion of my project, I would plan to do some preliminary research with local school system health educators in order to devise a lesson plan before my project start date. Some major topics I would like to focus on would include balanced daily food choices, exercise, and health problems associated with poor nutrition. I would also plan to create picture-based learning tools and an interactive teaching plan in order to engage the students of all different age groups and English language capabilities.

Project Importance

While SEAIA's monetary donations to the BLSO school in Mae Sot have supported several different projects there in previous years, our proceeds primarily help to support the school lunch program. As our organization has been instrumental in providing food for the students at this school for almost half of the past decade, I believe that it is imperative for us to assess the effectiveness of our contributions and learn how we can increase the efficacy of our impact. Research based on a population of Bhutanese refugees found a high prevalence of vitamin B deficiency-related conditions including "hematologic and neurological" disorders in this specific population despite a highly regulated diet provided by UN Refugee Agency consisting of "rice, lentils, chickpeas, vegetable oil, sugar, salt, and fresh vegetables" (Centers for Disease Control and Prevention, 2011). This demonstrates the importance of balanced diets, especially in populations with low access to diverse nutritional options.

Furthermore, while health and physical education are key structural components of elementary, middle, and high school curricula in the United States, the Mae Sot School in Thailand does not currently provide a nutritional or health education program. I think that implementing such a program will enhance the student's awareness of their personal control over different aspects of their health and hopefully inspire them to make educated, healthy choices about food and exercise in their daily lives now and in the future.

Community-Based Research Statement

10   By bringing the knowledge of local health educators and nutrition experts to this small school on the Thai-Burma border, I hope to engage our local community with an international issue and nourish an awareness for the similarities between our communal needs despite our cultural differences.

Works Cited

Amnesty International. (2005). *Thailand: The plight of Burmese migrant workers.* New York, NY: Amnesty International. Retrieved from http://www.amnesty.org/en/library/asset/ASA39/001/2005/en/7003d6fd-d4e2-11dd-8a23-d58a49c0d652/asa390012005en.pdf

Centers for Disease Control and Prevention. Vitamin B12 deficiency in resettled Bhutanese refugees—United States 2008-2011. (2011). *Morbidity and Mortality Weekly Report, 60*(11), 343–346.

Ellis, Mark. (2010). Foundation for Education and Development (FED): Maternal and child health survey. Takuapa, Thailand: Foundation for Education and Development. Retrieved from http://www.slideshare.net/Zsantander/family-planning-child-health-survey

Myanmar's overflow: Migrant workers battled by the slump. (2009, March 19). *Economist.com*. Retrieved from http://www.economist.com/node/13334070.

United Aid Abroad. (2008). *Report to donors 2007-2008: The Thai Burma border*. Sydney, AU: Author. Retrieved from http://www.apheda.org.au/projects/thaiburma/pages/files/Donor_Report_07-08_ThaiBurma_BLSOMaeSot.pdf

Yu, Shengchao, and Emily Hannum. (2007). Food for thought: Poverty, family, nutritional environment, and children's educational performance in rural China. *Sociological Perspectives, 50*(1): 53–77. doi: 10.1525/sop.2007.50.1.53

USE THE TOOLKIT

Let's use the three genre toolkit questions from Chapter 1 to examine this genre.

What Is It?

A grant proposal is another type of pitch. Instead of pitching a product or media project, though, a grant proposal usually pitches a research, artistic, or outreach project. Grant proposals vary in length and organization, but they tend to include (1) a project summary or overview, (2) a detailed description of the project goals or methods, and (3) a rationale for why the project will benefit researchers or community members. However, there is no standard format for a grant proposal—often it varies according to the grant you are applying for. Grace was applying for a grant that provided a specific set of subsections to include, so she structured her proposal accordingly. However, Vincent and Janelle applied for a program that only asked for a "project narrative," so they had to develop their own organization schemes. You'll notice that these three examples also include lists of references—grant proposals tend to require research in order to show how the proposed project is new and original.

Who Reads It?

Writers prepare grant proposals for funding agencies. Committees of qualified reviewers read the proposals. In the preceding examples, students were applying for sources of funding available on campus. The reviewers were likely professors, administrators, and possibly other students with an interest in the granting agency. Grace was applying for a grant made available through a campus center for global studies, so she determined that her audience would include professors and students involved in international studies. Janelle was applying for a grant that supported research and outreach in her state, so she surmised that reviewers of her proposal might be faculty involved in those activities.

What's It For?

The goal of a grant proposal is to demonstrate that the proposed project is new, original, important, and feasible. Writers must carefully explain how their project contributes to an important need in the community. For example, Janelle hoped that using statistics about the problems with dental care in her state would convince readers that she was addressing an important problem. Writers of grant proposals must also show that the project is feasible—that it can be done by an undergraduate student. In the third example, for instance, Grace shows that the project is feasible by describing existing relationships between the Southeast Asia Interest Association and the Mae Sot School in Thailand.

EXERCISE 13.4: Plan a Grant Proposal

To get started on a grant proposal, you need to conduct research about grants and fellowships available at your school or in your community. For example, maybe a large business with headquarters in your state offers grants for community projects. Your college may offer grants for student research or outreach projects. A local arts council may offer grants for artistic projects.

Once you have located a potential grant, see if there is an outline or form that you must submit. Sometimes, you will find a detailed description or outline of what to include; in other cases, you will receive very little guidance and will need to write a "project narrative" or "project description." Write a list of components that you will need to include, and what research you will need to do in order to write those components.

E. Strategies for Proposals

Imagine you've been assigned to write a grant proposal for an outreach project in your community. Let's see how Janelle proposed her project to help students in her community with dental anxiety.

Prewriting (Content)

Janelle began by researching the requirements for her grant. As she began, Janelle wrote this in her notes:

> For this unit, I am applying to the Chatham Fellowship. The purpose of this organization is to give grant money to students who want to make a difference in their community or other communities in the world. On their website, they say they want students that are passionate about their proposals and dedicated to seeing it be successful. So in my proposal I need to explain why I'm so invested in seeing this project take off—I don't want to spend too much time explaining why I need the money, but I want them to see that if they gave me the money it'd be put to good use.
>
> I'll also need to do some research to show that students in my community have lower dental health outcomes, especially in children, to justify the need for this program. I'll need to research dental health issues among rural and low income North Carolinians.
>
> They don't give much information about the proposal contents, so I'll have to come up with my own organization scheme.
>
> Also, the website for the grant suggests a proposal of approximately 1,000 words.

Following Janelle's lead, then, you should consider the following questions about your proposal:

- What is my rhetorical purpose? What information does the grant agency give about what they are looking for, and how can I meet those requirements?
- How can I show that my project is unique? Important? New?
- What kinds of research will I need?
- What contents should I include?
- How should I organize the proposal?
- How long should it be? Are there any additional formatting guidelines?

Drafting (Organizing)

In some cases, a granting agency will provide an outline or even a form for you to fill out. In that case, your task is simply to draft and organize your proposal according to those guidelines.

In Janelle's case, the granting agency only requested a 1,000-word "project narrative." Janelle used genre discovery to help her figure out how to structure her narrative. She looked up examples of other grant proposals and determined that her grant should include an overview, a description of the need for her project, a project outline, a budget, and sections connecting her personal investment in the project and the project's significance for the community.

In addition to her personal experiences, Janelle used a library database to find sources (Chapter 24) reporting on dental health outcomes in North Carolina.

Revising (Style)

One of the challenges of writing grant proposals is striking an appropriate tone and level of formality (Chapter 21).

In her peer review sessions, Janelle's classmates remarked that her writing style seemed overly impersonal. In her revision, she focused on incorporating her personal experience without over-emphasizing it. Here's how the new section turned out:

Personal Statement

While volunteering in a kindergarten classroom in Bertie County, NC, I noticed that many of the children expressed fear of dental care. During a visit from a public health nurse, most of the children said that they brushed their teeth regularly, but many indicated that they were afraid of going to the dentist. This led me to question why such young children already feared the dentist, and whether their parents' attitudes played a role.

Since I hope to pursue a career in dental health, this project contributes directly to my academic goals. On a personal level, I am invested in this project because I was born in Bertie County and care deeply about my community. If selected as a grant recipient I will be fully committed to seeing this project through to completion.

Editing (Design)

As she was editing her grant proposal, Janelle realized that readers would probably be reading many proposals at once. She decided that anything she could do to make her text easier to read would increase her chances. For this reason, she decided to include headings and sub-headings that would help readers find what they were looking for as they read.

She also made sure to use consistent page numbering and to format her references in a consistent format, in this case APA (Chapter 28).

Troubleshooting

Here are some common challenges that students face when writing proposals.

I can't figure out how to show my project is unique or important.   The uniqueness and importance of your project, in the end, comes from you, the grant writer. If you are having trouble explaining to someone else why your project is unique or important, start by describing it to yourself. Use a brainstorming technique, such as a free-write (Chapter 16), and describe all of the reasons that the grant is unique or important *to you*. Once you have figured that out, you can begin to explain these reasons to an external reader.

I can't find any research on my topic.   If you can't find research on your topic, you need to start by asking a research librarian for assistance. Research librarians in your library are experts at helping students who have hit dead ends. It is possible that you just aren't asking the right research questions.

F. Chapter Project: Write a Research or Grant Proposal

Take the grant that you planned in Exercise 13.4. Following the preceding guidelines, write your grant proposal. Be prepared to submit your proposal to the group that decides whether to award the grant. If necessary, read more about developing a topic (Chapter 23) and conducting research (Chapter 24).

Group Option: Write a Proposal Together

Work with your team to write a grant proposal. Grant proposals are often written by teams of researchers who plan to carry out the project together. You might choose a topic that one of you considered for Exercise 13.4, or you might choose another topic together.

Reports

A report is a communication that answers these questions: What is happening? What happened? Sometimes, reports answer these questions as well: Why is this happening? What should we do about it? The report may provide the results of an activity, investigation, or study. Reports sometimes take these results and formulate recommendations.

In college, you might be asked to write a report on the results of your research. Perhaps the most common type of report is a lab report, which is a genre common to many scientific disciplines. You may also be asked to write progress reports that update your instructor on your progress on a research or group project. For a political science class, you might be asked to write a policy report, in which you research and evaluate a possible solution to a problem (such as whether your state should require police officers to detain suspected illegal immigrants).

In the workplace, reports are a very common genre. In many workplaces, reports help to create a history of events and work performed—and they also provide evidence of what you have accomplished. In business fields, writers may produce progress reports, updating their team leader on the status of a project. Police officers write accident reports and incident reports. If you work as an emergency medical technician (EMT), you will be required to write patient care reports detailing what happened at each call: what the main problem was, how you treated the patient, and so on. Publicly traded companies (and many non-profit organizations) publish an annual report each year, informing stakeholders about how the organization has performed.

In this chapter, you will learn how to write some of the report genres you are most likely to encounter as an undergraduate student.

A. Report Mini-Genre: Social Networking Status Update

Social networking websites such as Twitter and Facebook give users the opportunity to write brief status reports about themselves throughout the day.

EXAMPLE 1: **Social Network Status Update**

"We won the game! Headed to the pub to celebrate."

EXAMPLE 2: **Work Network Status Update**

"Just got promoted to brand manager!"

EXAMPLE 3: **Academic Network Status Update**

"Just received my acceptance to study abroad. Can't wait to see Hong Kong!"

USE THE TOOLKIT

Let's use the three genre toolkit questions from Chapter 1 to examine this genre.

What Is It?
The status updates are short reports on recent events in the writer's life. They are usually one or two short sentences or sentence fragments. The updates can also include photographs, links, and videos. In Example 2, the writer posts the good news about a recent event: a promotion at work.

Who Reads It?
Social networking status updates are usually read by the friends and contacts of the writer. They are semi-public announcements, depending on the social network service, so writers should expect them to be viewed by many people (potentially beyond the writers' friends or contacts).

What's It For?
Status updates report the current state of the writer: location, attitudes, or beliefs. In Example 1, the writer conveys excitement over a sporting event and location—the pub. In Example 3, the writer conveys excitement about an upcoming study abroad program and posts the location of the program—Hong Kong.

EXERCISE 14.1: Write Status Updates

For an entire day, write a status update every hour, on the hour, starting when you wake in the morning and ending when you go to bed. You can post your status updates on a social networking site, or write them privately in your journal.

The next day, write a paragraph reflecting on your status updates. Do they provide an accurate portrait of your day? Why or why not?

B. News Report

A news report is an article in a newspaper or magazine—or on a news show on television—that reports on current or past events.

....

EXAMPLE 1: College Sports News Report

Chris Eckard, *Diamondback Online*

Men's Basketball's Stoglin Named Second-team All-ACC

Two Terrapins men's basketball guards earned recognition from the ACC yesterday for their play during the regular season.

Terrell Stoglin earned second-team All-ACC honors and Nick Faust made the All-Freshman team, the conference announced yesterday. The two guards were the Terps' lone representatives on the five teams selected by the conference's media members.

"I'm really happy for both our guys, this honor is well-deserved," coach Mark Turgeon said in a release. "They both have had great years for us so far."

Stoglin became the first player to lead the conference in scoring (21.2 points per game) and not make the first team since 1999.

5   "Will never forget this," Stoglin tweeted yesterday afternoon about the perceived snub.

Stoglin, who made the All-Freshman team a year ago, also averaged 3.4 rebounds and 1.9 assists per game. He hit more 3-pointers than anyone in the conference and ranked third in 3-point percentage (38 percent).

The sophomore was joined on the second team by North Carolina's Kendall Marshall, Florida State's Michael Snaer, N.C. State's C.J. Leslie and Virginia Tech's Erick Green. If Stoglin stays atop the ACC scoring list—he's currently more than three points ahead of the league's second leading scorer—he would become the sixth Terp to lead the conference in scoring.

Faust, meanwhile, came on strong after a rocky start to his career. He has averaged 13 points, five rebounds, 2.4 assists and 1.4 steals in the past seven games as a starter, filling in for injured point guard Pe'Shon Howard.

Along with Faust, the ACC honored Duke's Austin Rivers, Boston College's Ryan Anderson, Virginia Tech's Dorian Finney-Smith and Miami's Shane Larkin on the All-Freshman team.

The ACC First Team included Rivers, along with the entire North Carolina starting   10
frontcourt—forwards Tyler Zeller, John Henson and Harrison Barnes—as well as Virginia forward Mike Scott and Duke guard Austin Rivers.

···

EXAMPLE 2: Science News Report

Daniel Wheaton, *The Daily Nebraskan*

UNL Psychology Study Finds College-Aged Men Struggle with Image, Objectification

Social pressures to look good and be sexy might be crushing college-aged men's hopes of finding a significant other.

A recent study completed by several University of Nebraska–Lincoln psychology faculty members found young men are beginning to show signs of objectification and body shame.

"You see objectified images of women everywhere," said Sarah Gervais, a professor of psychology. "But, the truth is, if you walk through the grocery store lines, you're going to see that there are body builders on magazines and a lot of really attractive men there as well. That has to be having some sort of impact on men, too."

Brian Cole, a psychology graduate student, Meghan Davidson, assistant professor of educational psychology, and Sarah Gervais, assistant professor of psychology, collaborated on the project.

The study, "Body Surveillance and Body Shame in College Men: Are Men Who   5
Self-Objectify Less Hopeful?" was published in the April edition of the research journal "Sex Roles."

The team recruited 227 UNL students, of which the majority were white and heterosexual, and asked them to complete a survey about their appearance and how they felt about their ability to maintain and pursue relationships.

Simply put, men who don't have chiseled abs and toned arms are more likely to feel body shame, which damages their hope to create and sustain relationships.

"Hope can play a major role in improving outcomes," Cole said. "It is not only focused on the hope that things can be better, but that the individual can do something to make it better."

Cole said the relationship issues had the largest impact on romantic relationships, but social relationships were affected as well.

He said the study was inspired by older scholarship looking at the objectification   10
of women, and by his previous work, looking at hope theory.

While women have suffered the effects of objectification through various forms of media, men are beginning to deal with similar images. The societal definition of masculinity has shifted to focus on male body image.

"I think the stereotypes of the past that men don't care about their appearance or that men are judged only by what they can accomplish are even less true than they used to be," said Jan Deeds, director of the UNL Women's Center. "Ten years ago media images showed a wider range of what was considered an attractive man, but now all men are supposed to have Ryan Gosling's abs."

As part of the Women's Center, Deeds organizes several workshops that discuss how objectification affects relationships. In the "Reconstructing Barbie and Ken," workshop, she discusses the importance of non-physical attributes in attraction.

"When we do workshops about relationships both men and women make lists of what they want in a romantic partner, and the top items are always someone they can trust, who makes them laugh, who treats them with respect and who supports their goals," Deeds said.

15   The researchers plan on expanding the study by looking at a broader spectrum of men. They said they believe similar findings will come from gay men, but not in older men. Cole said he would like to do more tests in an actual lab to obtain more data on body shame "in the moment."

Cole said he hopes men will start having conversations about body image but he speculated that it would be difficult, saying "men are taught to restrict their emotions when it comes to shame."

EXAMPLE 3: Art News Report

Esteban Cortez, *The Collegian at Fresno State*

Grad Student Explores African-American Culture in Art

Some people called Vanessa Addison-Wilson's artwork "enlightening" at her solo exhibit Thursday night at the Fresno State Conley Art Gallery. Fresno State student Tara Wren enjoyed it because it provides viewers with a different point of view regarding African-American culture.

"[The collection] is a very different element of African-American people throughout history and how society views us and sometimes how we view ourselves," Wren said Thursday night at Addison-Wilson's opening reception. "It's very creative and thought-provoking."

These are the thoughts and emotions Addison-Wilson hoped to evoke in viewers through her pieces.

In her first solo exhibit titled "Signifyin'," Fresno State graduate student and assistant professor Addison-Wilson explores the themes of religion, family and her African-American culture. Through the use of collage, painting and animation, Addison-Wilson created a vibrant 11-piece collection that comments on society's views of African-Americans.

5   "The body of the collection is reflective of African-American culture," Addison-Wilson said. "It shows what African-Americans see of their self and what society sees."

In her "Strange Fruit" piece, the artist placed printed paper images, magazine cut outs, colored tissue paper, fabric and acrylic paint to form a face on a giant canvas.

Addison-Wilson carefully selected the images in "Strange Fruit" to comment on the public's perception of African-American culture. A small portion of the collage, for example, features a magazine cut out with the portrait of an African-American child with the text "Don't shoot. I want life." To the right, an image of an African-American man forming gang hand signs with a bandana covering his face is placed.

Every symbol in the collection is a piece of social commentary, Addison-Wilson explained.

While some gallery viewers praised the collection for its bold statements, others praised it for aesthetic reasons.

"It's very unique and the patterns are all very different," Fresno State student Lilian   10
Leon said.

Addison-Wilson has always been interested in art, she said, but she just recently began to create art pieces in a formal way. Her focus is graphic design, which she teaches at Fresno State parttime.

She plans to create new pieces for the 2013 San Francisco Bay Area exhibit "The Art of Living Black," which features regional artists of African descent. She was invited to feature existing and new pieces in the 17th annual exhibit, and if she shows next year, she might be the first artist to feature animation art.

With her Fresno State exhibit closing this week, Addison-Wilson is happy that she was able to show her work to her family and the Fresno State community.

"It was nice to show to family who hadn't seen my work," she said. "It's such a privilege to show as a solo artist because it doesn't always happen as a grad student."

USE THE TOOLKIT

Let's use the three genre toolkit questions from Chapter 1 to examine this genre.

What Is It?

A news report is an account of a recent event. Although the topics are very different from one another—sports, science, art—they are all reports. Each one answers key journalistic questions: Who? What? Where? When? Why? How? Then, they provide additional information to interest readers or to fill in details. Example 1 reports on the perceived snubbing of a member of the university's basketball team. Example 2, published in the University of Nebraska's student newspaper, reports on a scientific study conducted by members of the psychology department at the university. Example 3 reports on the work of a student artist.

Who Reads It?

News reports are meant to be read by the public, specifically members of a community, whether that's a college, city or town, state, or nation. For example, student newspapers have as their primary audience the students and other community members of their college or university. However, as many student newspapers are also published online, student newspapers now have a much broader potential audience, one that is national or even international in scope. Reports tend to be read by readers interested in the topic covered. Examples 1, 2, and 3 were all published in university newspapers from around the country—from Maryland, Nebraska, and California. Most readers will browse a newspaper or news website, scan the headlines, and then read the articles that most interest them.

What's It For?

A news report conveys information about a recent event. In the preceding examples, the events include the selection of an all-conference basketball team (Example 1); the findings of a recent scientific study (Example 2); and the opening of an art exhibit (Example 3). The information is factual, rather than opinionated, in nature. In Example 3, the writer reports on how others interpret an art exhibit, but not on the author's own interpretation or opinions.

EXERCISE 14.2: Write a News Report

Select a current event on campus or even beyond your campus. Write a short news report conveying the details of the event. Use the examples above as your models. You might need to interview a professor or student to research your report, or conduct research online.

MULTIMEDIA EXERCISE 14.1: Write a Multimedia News Report

Write a news report about a current event on campus. Bring along your camera so that you can photograph the event as well. Using word processing software, put together a news report using words and pictures. See Chapter 29 for guidance on using visual elements, layout, and design.

C. Progress Report

A progress report is a detailed status update on a project. Like a news report and a status update, it answers the question, "What is happening?"

EXAMPLE 1: Progress Report on a Student Project

From: Marshall@email.edu
Subject: Update on my poetry collection
Date: January 3, 2013 12:15:55 PM EST
To: ProfessorJames@email.com

Dear Professor James:

As requested, I'm writing you to provide a midpoint progress report on my capstone project in creative writing.

You are advising me on a poetry collection, to be written across the course of two semesters. As we agreed at the beginning of the fall semester, the collection will contain 36 individual poems that have gone through multiple revisions. I am to turn in a draft of the completed collection to you no later than March 1, and I am to revise this draft by no later than May 1, at which point I will turn in the final collection to you for grading.

At this time, I have written 24 poems. Of these 24, 14 are in a "final" stage of revision (pending your March comments, of course). This means that I have 10 poems to revise and 12 more poems to compose and revise.

I have encountered only one major hurdle during this process. The archival material I needed to consult for historical context for several poems was on loan to another institution. However, I contacted a curator at that institution who was able to send me scans of the material.

Thus, I now feel like I am on track to complete the 36 poems by the March 1 deadline.

Sincerely,

Marshall McLaughlin

EXAMPLE 2: **Progress Report on a Research Assistant's Project**

From: Mary Wu
Subject: Progress on War on Terror research
Date: January 3, 2013 12:15:55 PM EST
To: ProfessorJames@email.com

Dear Professor:

I'm writing to update you on my work as your research assistant on the article that you are writing on the rhetoric of the War on Terror.

Currently I am researching news articles that mention the War on Terror since 2005, as you requested. I have found many articles on news databases such as LexisNexis. I have sorted the articles based on various criteria, such as straight news articles, opinion pieces, and pieces that mention the term "rhetoric." I thought this sorting might be helpful to you.

I have encountered few problems during the course of this research. The main problem is the vast quantity of articles that are out there. It would be helpful if you provided me some parameters to help limit my search.

Currently, I have no work scheduled to complete after I finish this project. I anticipate spending another five hours on this. After that, I will need a new assignment.

Thanks,

Mary Wu

EXAMPLE 3: **Progress Report on a Class Project**

From: Lily Pearson, John Chao, Carolyn Wax, Anita Simmons
Subject: Class Project: Progress Report
Date: March 29, 2014 9:08 am
To: SHS@email.edu

Student Health Gets Real: Student Opinions of Student Health Services Progress Report

Scope
Our project is to survey 250 students on campus about the student health services that they have received and the quality of those services. Then we will write a report on the survey results and share the report with a representative of student health services.

Work Completed
After two weeks of work, we have completed our interviews of students. There are five members in our group, and we surveyed 50 students each, for a sample of 250, about 1/10th of the student body of our college. We believe this to be a strong representative sample.

Challenges
We faced the small challenge of encouraging our classmates to participate in the survey. At first students didn't seem to want to take the time to answer the questions. Once we told them that we would be sharing the survey results with student health, they were more willing to take the time to complete the interviews. For this reason, we are slightly behind schedule, since the surveys took longer to complete than anticipated.

Work Remaining
In the remaining part of the semester, we must compile the results using a spreadsheet, and then write a narrative report of what these results mean for student health on campus. Lastly, we need to share the report with a Student Health Services representative in a meeting. We believe that the four weeks remaining to complete this project give us ample time to do these tasks, despite the delays we faced.

USE THE TOOLKIT

Let's use the three genre toolkit questions from Chapter 1 to examine this genre.

What Is It?

A progress report is an update of the writer's accomplishments on an ongoing project. Each of these progress reports conveys the same basic information in basically the same order: (1) background on the project; (2) work accomplished since the last update; (3) any problems encountered; (4) work remaining to be done; and (5) an assessment on whether that work will be done on time and as expected.

Who Reads It?

The intended recipient of the report is often a supervisor—whether a manager or a professor. In Example 2, the writer Mary is a research assistant to Professor James, a manager who is also a professor. However, if your supervisor changes for any reason, the old supervisor might share your progress report(s) with your new supervisor.

What's It For?

A progress report informs your reader about the status of your project; warns your reader about potential problems; and either reassures your reader that the project can be completed as expected, or informs your reader that it cannot. The goal is to maintain the good will of the reader—which can be a challenge if you are behind schedule, as was the case in Example 3. In Example 2, Mary noted that she was having trouble narrowing down the research articles that she had found.

EXERCISE 14.3: Write a Progress Report

For any large project that you have been assigned in any class this semester, write a report informing your professor of your progress. Consider which of these five main parts of a progress report might work for your rhetorical situation:

1. background on the project;
2. work accomplished since the last update;
3. any problems encountered;
4. work remaining to be done; and
5. an assessment on whether that work will be done on time and as expected.

GROUP ACTIVITY 14.1: Write a Group Report

For any large group project that you have been assigned in this class, write a report informing your professor of your group's progress. Include the five main parts of a progress report just listed.

D. Recommendation Report

A recommendation report is a document that reports on an investigation: what happened? It then provides evidence to support a course of action: what should be done about it?

. . . .

EXAMPLE 1: Health Sciences Recommendation Report (excerpt)

National Transportation Safety Board

Safety Report
Reaching Zero: Actions to Eliminate Alcohol-Impaired Driving

Executive Summary

The National Transportation Safety Board (NTSB) has long been concerned about alcohol-impaired driving, which accounts for approximately one-third of all US highway fatalities. In the past several decades, awareness of the dangers of alcohol-impaired driving has increased. Public and private entities focusing on this safety issue have changed social perceptions concerning alcohol-impaired driving; they have also achieved important legislative actions to help reduce it. Due to these efforts, the number of lives lost annually in alcohol-impaired-driver-related crashes declined 53 percent, from 21,113 in 1982 to 9,878 in 2011; and the percentage of highway fatalities resulting from alcohol-involved crashes is down from 48 percent in 1982 to about 31 percent today.

In recent years, however, US success in addressing this safety issue has plateaued. Since 1995, although the annual number of fatalities has declined, nearly one in three of all highway deaths still involves an alcohol-impaired driver. The cause of these deaths is well understood and preventable, yet even the most concerted efforts have not kept thousands of lives from being lost each year. If traditional methods are no longer reducing the problem, new—and possibly challenging—initiatives must be considered.

In this safety report, the NTSB—

- Describes the scope of the impaired driving problem; [. . .]
- Examines the effect of alcohol consumption on an individual's ability to operate a motor vehicle and on the risk of being involved in a crash; and
- Evaluates the effectiveness of current and emerging alcohol-impaired driving countermeasures and identifies new approaches and actions needed to reduce and ultimately eliminate alcohol-impaired driving.

[. . .] This safety report addresses the necessity of providing all the following elements to achieve meaningful reductions in alcohol-impaired driving crashes: stronger laws, improved enforcement strategies, innovative adjudication programs, and accelerated development of new in-vehicle alcohol detection technologies. Moreover, the report recognizes the need for states to identify specific and measurable goals for reducing impaired driving fatalities and injuries, and to evaluate the effectiveness of implemented countermeasures on an ongoing basis.

5   Specifically, the report makes recommendations to the states in the following safety issue areas:

- Reducing the per se blood alcohol concentration (BAC) limit for all drivers,
- Conducting high-visibility enforcement of impaired driving laws and incorporating passive alcohol sensing technology into enforcement efforts, [. . .]
- Establishing measurable goals for reducing impaired driving and tracking progress toward those goals.

Introduction

Twenty-five years ago, on May 14, 1988, one of the deadliest highway accidents in US history took place in Carrollton, Kentucky, when the driver of a pickup truck traveling the wrong way on Interstate 71 drove his truck into a church activity bus (NTSB 1989). The bus was occupied by a driver, 3 adults, and 63 children, ranging in age from 10 to 18. The church bus's fuel tank was punctured during the collision sequence and a fire ensued, which engulfed the entire bus. The bus driver and 26 bus passengers died as a result of this accident, and 34 bus passengers sustained minor-to-critical injuries. Toxicology tests for the pickup truck driver, who survived the crash with serious injuries, showed that he was severely intoxicated at the time of the accident. Test results indicated that he had a blood alcohol concentration (BAC) of 0.26 about 1.5 hours after the collision, indicating that his BAC would have been even higher at the time of the accident.

Since the Carrollton accident, much progress has been made in reducing alcohol-impaired driving, but the problem remains. Thousands continue to die on US roads each year due to this single safety issue. When, in 2012, the National Transportation Safety Board (NTSB) began to evaluate the effectiveness of current and emerging alcohol-impaired driving countermeasures, and to identify possible new approaches and actions, it determined that the ultimate goal of the effort was to find a way to reach zero fatalities, injuries, and accidents involving alcohol-impaired driving.

This is an ambitious goal. But the NTSB believes that over time it can be achieved if federal and state authorities, as well as local communities, commit to the concept that reaching zero is both possible and necessary. In the European Union (EU), which has had such a commitment for more than 10 years, road deaths attributed to alcohol have declined by more than 50 percent (Podda 2012). The EU has renewed its commitment and has set the goal of again halving fatalities by 2020. US states that have enacted similar programs are experiencing greater reductions in fatality rates than those states that have not (Munnich and others 2012). Programs that achieve significant results are comprehensive efforts that set a high bar for reducing fatality rates, require interaction and cooperation among jurisdictions and authorities, and incorporate strategies that are data-driven and based on measurable results. Moreover, they demand constant review and reassessment to determine which efforts are most successful and then to target resources to expand and enhance those efforts. Although major collisions caused by alcohol-impaired driving, such as the Carrollton accident, capture public attention, every day individuals die on US highways because of alcohol-impaired driving. Hundreds of thousands of people have died in the past 25 years due to this issue. Today, if localities, states, and federal entities dedicate their resources to developing comprehensive programs to eliminate highway accidents caused by alcohol, the goal of reaching zero deaths from alcohol-impaired driving in the United States is achievable. This report is intended to identify which efforts should be elements of such programs.

[...]

Scope of the Impaired Driving Problem

Alcohol-Impaired Driving Fatalities

According to the National Highway Traffic Safety Administration (NHTSA) Fatality Analysis Reporting System (FARS), in 2011, there were 32,367 highway fatalities in the United States.[1] NHTSA defines an alcohol-impaired driving fatality as one that involves a driver with a BAC of 0.08 g/dL or higher.[2] According to FARS estimates, in 2011, there were 9,878 alcohol-impaired driving fatalities, which represented 31 percent of all highway fatalities. Although the FARS database has limitations, such as variability in how well states report their driver BAC levels, it is generally considered the most comprehensive source for national data on fatal traffic crashes.[3] NHTSA compiles traffic safety facts based on the FARS data for a number of highway safety issues.

[...] Between 1982 and 2011, annual impaired driving fatalities went from 21,113 to 9,878, a 53 percent reduction. During that same period, there was a 74 percent decline in the fatality rate.

Incidence of Drinking and Driving

Despite decades of public campaigns and other efforts to discourage driving after drinking, survey and observational data show that many people continue to do so. In 2010, about 1.8 percent of respondents to the Centers for Disease Control and Prevention (CDC) Behavioral Risk Factor Surveillance System survey[4] reported one or more episodes of alcohol-impaired driving in the past 30 days.[5] By extrapolating those data to the general population, researchers estimated there were 4 million individuals who drove impaired and approximately 112 million alcohol-impaired driving episodes that year (Bergen, Shults, and Rudd 2011, 1351–56). Although this represented a decline since 2006, the numbers are still high. Rates of drinking and driving were disproportionately high among young men, binge drinkers,[6] and individuals who do not regularly wear seat belts. [...]

Based on its review of impaired driving fatality and injury data, the NTSB concludes that although impaired driving injuries, fatalities, and fatality rates in the United States have significantly decreased over the past several decades, the pace of these reductions has slowed since the mid-1990s; and alcohol-impaired driving continues to contribute to thousands of fatalities and tens of thousands of serious injuries each year. Based on its review of research tracking impaired driving behaviors and attitudes, the NTSB concludes that the public generally believes that driving after drinking alcohol poses a significant threat to safety; however, many people continue to drive after drinking.

Countermeasures to Reduce Alcohol-Impaired Driving

Reducing the Per Se BAC Limit

Since 2004, all states have had a per se BAC limit of 0.08 for noncommercial drivers age 21 and over. Since 1988, federal regulations have set a 0.04 per se BAC limit for commercial drivers (49 Code of Federal Regulations [CFR] 382.201), and all states have "zero tolerance" laws that specify per se BAC limits between 0.00 and 0.02 for drivers under 21. In a few states, different per se BAC limits apply to school bus drivers or convicted DWI offenders (NHTSA 2012).

15   [. . .] [L]aboratory studies have shown that driving-related performance is degraded at BAC levels as low as 0.01, and epidemiological studies employing crash data have shown significantly elevated crash risk at BAC levels near 0.05. Lowering per se BAC limits has been associated with reductions in impaired driving crashes and fatalities. For example, 14 independent studies conducted in the United States found that lowering the BAC limit from 0.10 to 0.08 resulted in reductions in alcohol-related crashes, fatalities, or injuries of 5–16 percent (Fell and Voas 2006, 233–43). Other studies have found similar results (for example, Dee 2001, 111–28; Shults and others 2001, 66–88; Voas, Tippetts, and Fell 2000, 483–92). In 2012, the CDC listed 0.08 per se BAC laws among the "top 20 violence and injury practice innovations since 1992" (Kress and others 2012, 257–63).

[. . .] The NTSB concludes that changing legal per se BAC limits from 0.08 to 0.05 or lower would lead to meaningful reductions in crashes, injuries, and fatalities caused by alcohol-impaired driving. Therefore, the NTSB recommends that the 50 states, the Commonwealth of Puerto Rico, and the District of Columbia establish a per se BAC limit of 0.05 or lower for all drivers who are not already required to adhere to lower BAC limits.

Providing High-Visibility Enforcement of DWI Laws

Law enforcement influences driver behavior through both specific and general deterrence. Specific deterrence refers to the effects of the legal consequences experienced by drivers who are apprehended for breaking a law. General deterrence refers to countermeasures that discourage unlawful behaviors. Based on arrest data, as well as drivers' self-reports of driving after drinking, it has been estimated that alcohol-impaired drivers make an average of 80 impaired driving trips before being detected and arrested (Ferguson 2012, 427–41). Because such a small proportion of impaired driving trips results in detection and arrest, countermeasures that foster general deterrence of impaired driving are likely to have a positive safety impact.

[. . .] HVE has been successful not only in reducing the incidence of crashes and fatalities related to alcohol-impaired driving but also in other safety efforts, such as encouraging seat belt use and discouraging distracted driving (Solomon, Ulmer, and Preusser 2002; Cosgrove, Chaudhary, and Reagan 2011). The NTSB has historically supported elements of impaired driving HVE. For example, in 1968, the NTSB asked the FHWA to develop a program incorporating media to support law enforcement efforts targeting impaired drivers. In the 1980s and 1990s, the NTSB recommended that states develop coordinated statewide programs for selective alcohol enforcement operations and include sobriety checkpoints as a part of their comprehensive alcohol and highway safety programs. In 2000, the NTSB called on states to establish a comprehensive program to address hard core drinking driving that included several components consistent with HVE. The NTSB concludes that HVE is an effective countermeasure to deter alcohol-impaired driving. [. . .]

Reaching Zero

Although there has been substantial progress in reducing crashes due to alcohol impairment since the 1980s, impaired driving continues to represent one of the largest and most persistent sources of traffic injuries and fatalities. Over the years, numerous approaches have been taken around the world to reduce the toll taken by impaired driving, with varying levels of success. In preparing this report, NTSB staff reviewed hundreds of peer-reviewed research reports, meta-analyses, and systematic reviews that evaluated the effectiveness of impaired driving countermeasures to identify those most likely to result in significant reductions of impaired driving injuries and fatalities.

The best hope for meeting the goal of eliminating alcohol-impaired driving will come when states and communities adopt those practices that have been empirically demonstrated to be effective. In this report, the NTSB has described several countermeasures that meet this standard, including the following:

- Reducing per se BAC limits,
- Conducting HVE that incorporates passive alcohol sensing,
- Increasing use of ALS/ALR laws and providing for use of interlocks in conjunction with license suspensions,
- Requiring interlocks for all DWI offenders, accompanied by consistent and effective programs to ensure compliance, and
- Continuing efforts to reduce recidivism among DWI repeat offenders.

Endnotes

[1] The NHTSA 2011 FARS data are the most current available.

[2] BAC is measured as a mass of alcohol per volume of blood. In the United States, the standard measurement is represented as grams per deciliter (g/dL).

[3] For example, in 2011, FARS reported that 39 percent of all drivers were not tested for BAC and that BAC test data were missing for an additional 10 percent of drivers. Since 1982, NHTSA has used a statistical procedure known as imputation to replace missing values. In 2012, the NTSB made several recommendations to NHTSA and the states to improve BAC reporting rates.

[4] The CDC Behavioral Risk Factor Surveillance System completes more than 400,000 adult interviews each year. It is the largest continuously conducted multi-mode (mail and telephone) health survey system in the world.

[5] This is based on the response to the survey question, "During the past 30 days, how many times have you driven when you've had perhaps too much to drink?"

[6] "Binge drinking" was defined by the authors as four or more drinks on one occasion for women and five or more for men.

References

Bergen, G., R. A. Shults, and R. A. Rudd. 2011. "Vital Signs: Alcohol-Impaired Driving Among Adults—United States, 2010." *Morbidity and Mortality Weekly Report* 60(39): 1351–56.

Cosgrove, Linda, Neil Chaudhary, and Ian Reagan. 2011. *Four High-Visibility Enforcement Demonstration Waves in Connecticut and New York Reduce Hand-Held Phone Use.* DOT HS 811 845. Washington DC: National Highway Traffic Safety Administration.

Dee, T. S. 2001. "Does Setting Limits Save Lives? The Case of 0.08 BAC Laws." *Journal of Policy Analysis and Management* 20(1): 111–28.

Fell, J. C., and R. B. Voas. 2006. "The Effectiveness of Reducing Illegal Blood Alcohol Concentration (BAC) Limits for Driving: Evidence for Lowering the Limit to .05 BAC." *Journal of Safety Research* 37(3): 233–43.

Ferguson, S. A. 2012. "Alcohol-Impaired Driving in the United States: Contributors to the Problem and Effective Countermeasures." *Traffic Injury Prevention* 13(5): 427–41.

Kress, H. C., R. Noonan, K. Freire, A. Marr, and A. Olson. 2012. "Top 20 Violence and Injury Practice Innovations since 1992." *Journal of Safety Research* 43(4): 257–63.

Munnich, Lee W., Frank Douma, Xiao Qin, J. David Thorpe, and Kai Wang. 2012. *Evaluating Effectiveness of States' Toward-Zero-Deaths Programs.* CTS 12-39T. Minneapolis, MN: Center for Transportation Studies.

NHTSA (National Highway Traffic Safety Administration). 2012. *Digest of Impaired Driving and Selected Beverage Control Laws, 26th edition.* DOT HS 811 673. Washington, DC: NHTSA.

NTSB (National Transportation Safety Board). 1989. *Pickup Truck/Church Activity Bus Head-On Collision and Fire Near Carrollton, Kentucky, May 14, 1988.* NTSB/HAR-89/01. Washington, DC: NTSB.

Podda, F. 2012. *Drink Driving: Towards Zero Tolerance.* Brussels: European Transport Safety Council. Accessed January 23, 2013 at http://www.etsc.eu/documents/Drink_Driving_Towards_Zero_Tolerance.pdf.

Shults, R. A., R. W. Elder, D. A. Sleet, and J. L. Nichols. 2001. "Reviews of Evidence Regarding Interventions to Reduce Alcohol-Impaired Driving." *American Journal of Preventive Medicine* 21(4S): 66–88.

Solomon, Mark G., Robert G. Ulmer, and David F. Preusser. 2002. *Evaluation of Click It or Ticket Model Programs.* DOT HS 809 498. Washington DC: National Highway Traffic Safety Administration.

Voas, R. B., A. S. Tippetts, and J. C. Fell. 2000. "The Relationship of Alcohol Safety Laws to Drinking Drivers in Fatal Crashes." *Accident Analysis and Prevention* 32(4): 483–92.

EXAMPLE 2: Recommendation Report for a Chemistry Course

THE HEALTH RISKS AND COST EFFECTIVENESS OF CHLORINE
AS A POOL WATER SANITIZER
Prepared By: Bradley J. Kinnison

EXECUTIVE SUMMARY

A number of health risks are commonly associated with exposure to chlorine in swimming pools, but is chlorine the true cause of these risks? Swimmers frequently attribute rashes, acne outbreaks and asthma to their over-exposure to chlorine. This has led to large amounts of research being conducted on the three main chlorine variants—gaseous Cl_2, liquid Sodium hypochlorite (NaOCl) and solid calcium hypochlorite ($Ca(OCl_2)_2$) (Nemery et al., 2002)—in order to determine whether they cause these harmful health impacts, and if so to what degree they are a causal factor. This report examines the research in an attempt to answer whether chlorine or an alternative option is the best method of sanitizing pool water. This is accomplished primarily by studying the long and short term health impacts of chlorine on the body of a swimmer. The cost effectiveness of chlorine is also analyzed against two popular alternative sanitization methods, but the primary focus is on the negative health effects of chlorine due to its impact on the well-being of the swimmers.

It has been determined that the harmful nature of chlorine is caused by its reaction with organic matter in the water to form what are known as disinfection by-products (DBPs). These DBPs are volatile and highly reactive molecules that are responsible for most of the harmful health impacts of chlorine (Weaver et al, 2009). The studies show that these chlorine DBPs are linked to the short term effects of rashes, acne outbreak, hair damage and eye inflammation, but they are merely aggravating factors and not the primary causes of these harms. Studies regarding the long term effects of chlorine linked it as an increasing risk factor for asthma and cancer. Sufficient evidence was not provided to adequately link chlorine exposure to cancer later on in life. In the case of asthma, studies did show a clear connection between swimmers' frequent exposure to chorine and latent onset asthma in the future. While this connection is clear, the degree to which chlorine actually causes asthma is not known. It is safest to say that it is a contributing factor, and one that should be avoided if it is possible.

Next, two alternative sanitization methods were examined: a saltwater chlorine regeneration system and an ozone generator system. Both of these systems reduce the concentration of chlorine to safe levels and effectively sanitize bacteria in pool water at the same time. The saltwater chlorine generation system has been found to be a more effective disinfectant that creates a water composition more comfortable to swimmers than chlorine.

The short and long term cost efficiency of each of the five sanitization methods were then evaluated and compared against one another. Liquid sodium hypochlorite is the cheapest disinfecting agent and thus the most cost efficient in the short run, but the saltwater chlorine regeneration system was found to be the most cost efficient choice in the long run despite high initial expenses for the equipment (Mendioroz, 2009). This data is summarized in Figure 1 in the Cost Evaluation section.

It is concluded then that research shows that chlorine is not a sufficient cause of the health risks examined, but that it is merely a contributing factor. It is clear that chlorine does have some harmful impacts on the body, but these mostly stem from a combination of other factors. Research has not yet been able to link chlorine to these detrimental health effects with any solid degree of sufficient causal authority. On the other hand, studies have shown that there are better alternative methods of sanitizing pools. Ozone purification and saltwater chlorine generation systems are two of these alternatives that provide clean water that is more comfortable to the swimmers, and are even more cost efficient in the long term for the pool administrator.

From these conclusions, the following recommendations have been made in response to the initial question of whether chlorine is the most effective and safe pool sanitization agent:

Replace chlorine sanitization with a saltwater chlorine generation system if it is at all financially viable.

Do more research to determine the degree to which chlorine actually causes its attributed long term effects of asthma and cancer.

Do more research on the vulnerability of children under the age of 15 to early onset asthma.

Post signs detailing the possible health risks of chlorine at all pools operated by the UNC Campus Recreation department.

INTRODUCTION

Is chlorine in swimming pools dangerous to the health of swimmers? This question has been raised by the UNC Campus Recreation department because of an increasing trend of acne outbreak, rashes, and asthma in UNC club swimmers. The UNC Campus Recreation department commissioned this report in order to learn more about the causal relationship between chlorine and these health risks. This study is important to them because they have responsibility for the health of the student athletes that use their facilities, and it is also important to the athletes themselves who may experience some of these harmful health impacts. While the health of student athletes is their primary concern, the Campus Recreation department also requested that this report briefly research the cost effectiveness of chlorine in comparison to some other pool water sanitization methods. The goal of this report is to determine if pool chlorine is a sufficient cause of the above health risks reported in UNC club swimmers, and thus whether or not the UNC Campus Recreation department should find another method of sanitizing the pools on campus. This will be addressed by first examining research on the short and long term physiological health impacts of chlorine on swimmers. Next the cost effectiveness of chlorine in comparison to some alternative sanitization methods will be discussed. After all the research has been weighed, a list of professional recommendations will be made to the Campus Recreation department as to how they should proceed.

Chlorine is the most common pool water sanitization agent, which is primarily due to the fact that it is highly reactive and thus kills bacterial microorganisms in the water quickly and thoroughly. Its high reactivity is also its primary disadvantage; after killing bacteria, it then enters into secondary reactions which can produce substances that are harmful to the human body. Chlorine may be applied to pool water as a sanitization agent in a variety of forms, the most popular of which are gaseous Cl_2, liquid Sodium hypochlorite (NaOCl) and solid calcium hypochlorite ($Ca(OCl_2)_2$). This study will focus directly on the effects of the chlorine molecule and not on the effects of the compound it may be administered with. Before examining the effects of chlorine, it is first important to understand how the bodies of swimmers are exposed to it. Pool workers pour a certain mass and concentration of chlorine into the water in pools in order to sanitize it. The chlorine then comes into contact with the skin when the swimmer enters the pool. It first interacts with the epidermal surface of the skin, and then small amounts diffuse through the dermis and into the cardiovascular system (blood-circulatory system). This can cause moderate to severe dryness, rashes, and acne outbreaks. Chlorine may also dehydrate the cornea of the eye, causing a burning and itchy sensation. Chlorine can also enter the body through the respiratory cavities while swimming, primarily through the mouth. It may either enter in liquid form (swimmers frequently swallow pool water by accident) or in gaseous form through the inhalation of chlorinated water vapor hanging over the pool (Pool Water Chemistry, 2010).

RESULTS

Health Impact on Swimmers

Chlorine as a sanitization agent in pool water has been purported to be harmful to the health of swimmers. It is associated with both short and long term detrimental health effects. While it has been associated with negative health impacts, it is not clear as to what degree chlorine is directly responsible for them. In some cases chlorine may merely be a contributing factor that merely compounds the effects of other chemicals, whereas in other cases chlorine may have sufficient harmful health impacts in and of itself. The degree to which chlorine harms swimmers will be evaluated below in relation to its most commonly attributed short and long term effects.

Before the short and long term health effects are discussed, it is important to understand why chlorine causes these effects. The primary reason is that chlorine is an extremely reactive element due to its need for one more valence electron and its high electronegativity (3.16 on the Pauling scale); only oxygen (3.44) and fluorine (3.98) have higher electronegativity values (WebElements, 2010). This high reactivity causes chlorine to react with other substances in pool water, forming what are called chlorinated disinfection by-products (DBPs). The most common and volatile DBPs form when chlorine reacts with organic molecules in the water to produce chloramines (Weaver et al., 2009). The reaction of these chloramines with the human body is the primary cause of the detrimental health effects listed below.

Short Term Effects

The most commonly reported short term harmful effects of chlorine on swimmers are rashes, acne outbreaks, hair damage and inflammation of the eye. The chlorine molecule dehydrates the epidermal surface of the skin and hair, leading to inflammation, outbreaks and short term surface damage. It does this by removing the sebum (oil layer) on the surface of the skin and hair. The sebum is produced by the sebaceous glands of the dermis in order to waterproof and protect the skin (Pool Water Chemistry, 2010). The skin is left directly exposed to the chlorine with almost no protection. Chlorine removes a similar sebum layer in hair, leading to dry and damaged hair. It is important to note that chlorine is not the only cause of skin, hair and eye dehydration; pure pool water without chlorine will begin to dehydrate the skin on its own. Chlorine significantly escalates this process though (Erdinger et al., 1998), making it a significant contributing factor that must be taken into account when thinking about which sanitization agents to use in pools.

Swimmers often attribute eye inflammation to chlorine as well. While chlorine can contribute to burning, itchy eyes—especially at pH levels below 7 or above 8, which are standard pool pH levels—it is not as strong a cause as most people think it is. In a study on the irritating effects of chlorine DBPs, Erdinger et al. indicated that chlorine concentrations alone could not explain eye irritation people experience after swimming in a pool. Erdinger et al. went on to say that the irritating effect of chlorine on the conjunctiva is small in comparison to the effects of many other chemicals acting on the eye at the same time (1998). Chlorine induced inflammation of the eye has not been proven to be a factor of serious consequence. While chlorine may not be a sufficient cause of all of these short term health impacts, it is at the very least an aggravating factor that should be counteracted where possible.

Long Term Effects

The most frequently reported long term effects of pool chlorine on swimmers are an increased risk of developing asthma and cancer. The development of cancer has been correlated with pool chlorine, but it there is not sufficient evidence to prove a direct link between the two. DBPs may be the cause, but that mechanism has not been verified yet (Zwiener et al., 2007). Pool chlorine, on the other hand, is more strongly linked as a cause of asthma developing later on in swimmers. When high concentrations of chlorine diffuse through the skin and into the bloodstream, it can cause pulmonary damage over time. A buildup of chlorine in the alveoli of the lung due to direct inhalation of chlorine rich water or water vapor can also cause long term respiratory damage. These are two primary causes of a latent onset of asthma (Nemery et al., 2002). A European study, conducted on hundreds of children between the ages of 10–13, showed that kids have an even higher risk of developing asthma from exposure to swimming pool chlorine than adults do (Bernard et al., 2006). Swimming has been established as one of the best exercises for those with asthma due to the warm moist environment (Goodman and Hays, 2008), but chlorine has adverse effects on the respiratory system that act in opposition to those benefits. Studies are in opposition as to whether or not the benefits outweigh the harms, or vice versa. While the degree of chlorine's impact on asthma is not fully known, it has been recognized as an aggravating factor, and thus finding a safer alternative would be ideal.

Alternative Sanitization Methods

There are alternatives to using chlorine as the primary sanitization agent in cleaning pools. Some of these alternatives use chlorine, but they do so in a much lower concentration. The reason that they still use chlorine is because they are not quite as strong of disinfectants as chemical sanitizers are. Two of the most common alternatives are listed below:

Saltwater Chlorine Generation System—This is virtually a chemical free alternative to chlorine sanitizers. Salt water (which is comprised of basic table salt, $NaCl$, in water), which is non-volatile, is poured into the pool. A salt generator then causes the $NaCl$ to dissociate, thus allowing the reactive chlorine molecule to kill bacterial microorganisms. The generator then converts the separate sodium and chlorine ions back into the non-volatile

NaCl molecule. This system produces pool water that is less reactive and has a more comfortable feel than chlorine rich water (Mendioroz, 2009).

Ozone Generator—This system produces the ozone gas (O_3) and pumps it into the pool water. Once in the pool water, this gas oxidates and reacts with the bacteria in the water, thus purifying it. Small amounts of chlorine are added to the water to aid in killing residual bacteria. This system can reduce the presence of bather contaminants by up to 20% more than chlorine filtration does. This system is used extensively in European countries. The primary disadvantage to the system is that ozone itself is toxic if left unfiltered from the water, and it creates a significant amount of volatile DBPs. Since ozone must be filtered from the water before swimmers may re-enter, bacteria then begins to reproduce more quickly. The ozone treatment method is highly effective for disinfecting pool water over short periods, but it must be applied frequently in order to maintain homeostasis. This is often an inconvenience to swimmers (Wojtowicz, 2004).

Cost Evaluation

The cost effectiveness of each of these sanitization methods will be considered without factoring in their previously discussed sanitization effectiveness or health impacts. Five primary methods of sanitization have been surveyed: the three chlorine variants—gaseous Cl_2, liquid Sodium hypochlorite (NaOCl) and solid calcium hypochlorite ($Ca(OCl_2)_2$)—, the saltwater chlorine generation system, and the ozone generator. The overall short and long term cost evaluation results are summarized in Figure 1 below the individual cost analyses.

Gaseous Cl_2—While the substance itself is the cheapest sanitization agent (approximately $1.00 per pound in 2009), system construction—tanks, valves and generators—and the safety equipment that must be purchased with it are very expensive. The short term expenses are much higher than the liquid or tablet chlorine agents (Mendioroz, 2009).

Liquid Sodium hypochlorite (NaOCl)—As of 2009 the average cost of this agent in the United States was $1.44 per pound. This agent is cheap, and it does not require high initial payments on expensive equipment as gaseous Cl_2 does. The downside to liquid sodium hypochlorite is that it cannot be stored for long. It degrades much quicker than solid calcium hypochlorite. This is the most cost-efficient sanitization agent over the short term, so long as it is used before it begins to degrade (Mendioroz, 2009).

Solid calcium hypochlorite $(Ca(OCl_2)_2)$—As of 2009 the average cost of this agent in the United States was $2.29 per pound. While this agent is not as cheap as liquid sodium hypochlorite, its advantage is that it can be stored for much longer periods of time without degrading. This allows it to be bought in bulk for a slightly cheaper price (it is still more expensive than liquid sodium hypochlorite), whereas liquid sodium hypochlorite cannot be bought due to its degradable composition (Mendioroz, 2009).

Saltwater Chlorine Generation System—This system eliminates the need to buy regular quantities of a sanitization agent, which significantly cuts recurring costs. The drawback of this alternative is that it costs a large amount of money up front, usually between $1500 and $4000 (Precision Pool Construction Inc., 2010). This system is more cost efficient in the long term since a chlorine agent does not have to be purchased regularly and in large quantities. Maintenance and replacement parts for the generator are expensive, but they are not required often (Wojtowicz, 2004).

Ozone Generator—This system also reduces recurring costs by eliminating the need to regularly purchase large quantities of chlorine. This system necessitates a large initial payment as well—approximately $800 to $2500—which is significantly cheaper than the saltwater chlorine generation system. The drawback to this system is that maintenance and replacement parts for this generator are also expensive, and they are required more frequently than for the saltwater chlorine generation system (Wojtowicz, 2004).

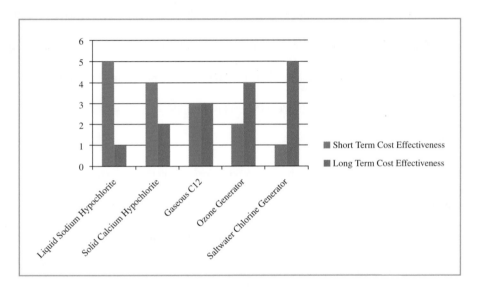

Figure 1. Short and long term cost evaluation of five sanitization methods on scale of 1–5.

It can be seen from Figure 1 above that the short term cost effectiveness decreases across the table, and the long term cost effectiveness increases across the table. This shows that even though the initial cost of the saltwater chlorine generation system is higher than the others, it will lead to saving money in the long run.

CONCLUSION

The research shows that chlorine is not a sufficient cause of the health risks examined, but that it is merely a contributing factor. It is clear that chlorine does have some harmful impacts on the body, but these mostly stem from a combination of other factors. Research has not yet been able to link chlorine to these detrimental health effects with any solid degree of causal authority. On the other hand, studies have shown that there are better alternative methods of sanitizing pools. Ozone purification and saltwater chlorine generation systems are two of these alternatives that provide clean water that is more comfortable to the swimmers, and are even more cost efficient in the long term for the pool administrator.

RECOMMENDATIONS

For UNC Pool Services:

Replace chlorine sanitization with a saltwater chlorine generation system if it is at all financially viable.

Post signs detailing the possible health risks of chlorine at all pools operated by the UNC Campus Recreation department.

For UNC Researchers:

Do more research to determine the degree to which chlorine actually causes its attributed long term effects of asthma and cancer.

Conduct more research on the vulnerability of children under the age of 15 to early onset asthma.

REFERENCES

Bernard A, Carbonnelle S, de Burbure C, Michel O, Nickmilder M. 2006. Chlorinated pool attendance, atopy, and the risk of asthma during childhood. *Environmental Health Perspectives 114(10):*1567–1573.

Erdinger L, Kirsch F, Sonntag HG. 1998. Irritating effects of disinfection by-products in swimming pools. *Zentralbl Hyg Umweltmed 200(5-6)*:491–503.

Goodman M., and Hays S. 2008. Asthma and swimming: A meta-analysis. *Journal of Asthma 45(8)*:639–47.

Mendioroz, Randy. 2009. A Closer Look-Pool Water Sanitizers. Park and Recreation Business. PRG1009_Mendioroz_Pool.pdf [Internet] [cited 2010 10/26/2010]. Available from: http://www.aquaticdesigngroup.com/images/press/PRG1009_Mendioroz_Pool.pdf.

Nemery B, Hoet PH, Nowak D. 2002. Indoor swimming pools, water chlorination and respiratory health. *European Respiratory Journal 19(5):*790–3.

"Pool Water Chemistry." [Internet] [cited 2010 10/5/2010]. Available from: http://www.deh .enr.state.nc.us/ehs/quality/wph.htm.

Precision Pool Construction Inc. | Salt water chlorine generator's for in-ground pools. [Internet] [cited 2010 10/26/2010]. Available from: http://precisionpool.net/2010/04/ salt-water-chlorine-generators-for-in-ground-pools/.

Weaver WA, Li J, Wen Y, Johnston J, Blatchley MR, Blatchley ER III. 2009. Volatile disinfection by-product analysis from chlorinated indoor swimming pools. *Water Research 43(13)*:3308–18.

WebElements Periodic Table of the Elements | Periodicity | Electronegativity (Pauling) |

periodicity [Internet] [cited 2010 10/18/2010]. Available from: http://www.webelements

.com/periodicity/electronegativity_pauling/index.html.

Wojtowicz, J. A. 2004. Water Treatment of Swimming Pools, Spas, and Hot Tubs.

Kirk-Othmer Encyclopedia of Chemical Technology.

Zwiener C, Richardson SD, De Marini DM, Grummt T, Glauner T, Frimmel FH. 2007.

Drowning in disinfection byproducts? Assessing swimming pool water. *Environmental

Science & Technology 41(2):*363–72.

EXAMPLE 3: Medical Recommendation Report (excerpt)

Centers for Disease Control and Prevention

**Prevention and Control of Meningococcal Disease: Recommendations
of the Advisory Committee on Immunization Practices (ACIP)**

Summary

Meningococcal disease describes the spectrum of infections caused by Neisseria meningitidis, including meningitis, bacteremia, and bacteremic pneumonia. Two . . . vaccines that provide protection against meningococcal serogroups A, C, W, and Y . . . are licensed in the United States for use among persons aged 2 through 55 years. [. . .] This report compiles and summarizes all recommendations from CDC's Advisory Committee on Immunization Practices (ACIP) regarding prevention and control of meningococcal disease in the United States, specifically the changes in the recommendations published since 2005. . . . ACIP recommends routine vaccination with a quadrivalent meningococcal conjugate vaccine (Men-ACWY) for adolescents aged 11 or 12 years, with a booster dose at age 16 years. ACIP also recommends routine vaccination for persons at increased risk for meningococcal disease. [. . .]

Introduction

This report compiles and summarizes all recommendations from CDC's Advisory Committee on Immunization Practices (ACIP) regarding prevention and control of meningococcal disease in the United States, specifically the changes in the recommendations published since 2005 (1), and describes the process undertaken and the rationale used in support of these recommendations. [. . .]

Meningococcal disease describes the spectrum of infections caused by Neisseria meningitidis, including meningitis, bacteremia, and bacteremic pneumonia. Meningococcal disease develops rapidly, typically among previously healthy children and adolescents, and results in high morbidity and mortality. For unknown reasons, incidence has declined since the peak of disease in the late 1990s, and approximately 800–1,200 cases are reported annually in the United States. This decline began before implementation of routine use of meningococcal vaccines in adolescents and have occurred in all serogroups. [. . .]

Methods

ACIP's Meningococcal Vaccines Work Group* (the Work Group) revised the meningococcal vaccine recommendations on the basis of the most current data on safety, efficacy, and immunogenicity of meningococcal vaccines. The Work Group comprises a diverse group of health-care providers and public health officials, including professionals from academic medicine (pediatrics, family practice, internal medicine, and infectious disease specialists), federal and state public health professionals, and representatives of provider organizations. [. . .]

The Work Group considers published, peer-reviewed studies as the primary source   5 of data in making recommendations for the prevention and control of meningococcal disease. In addition, unpublished data (e.g., immunogenicity and safety data in age groups outside the licensed indication) that are relevant to issues under discussion also were considered. [. . .] In addition, because rare adverse events might not be observed in prelicensure clinical trials because of the limited number of subjects enrolled, postlicensure observational data also were used in the assessment of meningococcal vaccines.

Background

Meningococcal Disease among College Students

Studies conducted in the 1990s that focused on quantifying the risk for meningococcal disease among college students demonstrated that the overall incidence among college students was similar to or somewhat lower than that observed among persons of approximately the same age in the general population (43). However, in a case control study involving 50 cases among college students (44), multivariate analysis indicated that first-year college students living in residence halls were at higher risk for meningococcal disease than other students (matched odds ratio [OR]: 3.6; CI = 1.6 – 8.5). Other studies in the 1990s yielded similar results (45,46).

In 2000, before licensure of meningococcal conjugate vaccines, ACIP recommended that first-year college students living in residence halls consider vaccination with the quadrivalent meningococcal polysaccharide vaccine (MPSV4), which was licensed in 1981 (47). Since the 2000 ACIP recommendation, many colleges have required all matriculating students to be vaccinated. Thirty-six states and the District of Columbia have mandates requiring education of college students about meningococcal vaccines or proof of meningococcal vaccination for attendance (a list of these states is available at http://www.immunize.org/laws/menin.asp). When the first meningococcal conjugate vaccine was licensed in 2005, ACIP recommended that all first-year college students living in residence halls be vaccinated with Men-ACWY-D (1). [. . .]

Cost-Effectiveness Analyses

As part of the evaluation of the adolescent vaccination program, a cost-effectiveness analysis was performed to compare the cost-effectiveness of the following three vaccination strategies: 1) a single dose at age 11 years, 2) a single dose at age 15 years, and 3) a dose at age 11 years with a booster dose at age 16 years (ACIP, unpublished data, 2010). The economic costs and benefits of these meningococcal vaccination strategies in adolescents were assessed from a societal perspective (99,100).

A multivariable analysis was performed with a Monte Carlo simulation in which multiple parameters were varied simultaneously over specified probability distributions. These parameters included disease incidence (46%–120% of the 10-year average), case-fatality ratio (34%–131% of the 10-year average), rates of long-term sequelae, acute meningococcal disease costs (i.e., inpatient care, parents' work loss, public health response, and premature mortality costs), lifetime direct and indirect costs of meningococcal disease sequelae (i.e., long-term special education and reduced productivity), and cost of vaccine and vaccine administration (range: $64–$114). Vaccination coverage (37%–90%) and initial vaccine efficacy (39%–99%) also were varied for evaluation purposes. The vaccine was assumed to be 93% effective in the first year, and then waning immunity was modeled as a linear decline over the next 9 years unless a booster dose was administered. The vaccine effectiveness of the second dose was assumed to be higher with a slower rate of waning immunity. The results of the cost-effectiveness analysis indicate that a 2-dose series at ages 11 years and 16 years has a similar cost-effectiveness compared with moving the single dose to age 15 years or maintaining the single dose at 11 years. However, the number of cases and deaths prevented is substantially higher with the 2-dose strategy. [. . .]

Recommendations for Use of Meningococcal Vaccines

Routine Vaccination of Adolescents

10   ACIP recommends routine administration of a MenACWY vaccine for all persons aged 11 through 18 years. A single dose of vaccine should be administered at age 11 or 12 years, and a booster dose should be administered at age 16 years. Adolescents who receive their first dose at age 13 through 15 years should receive a booster dose at age 16 through18 years. The minimum interval between doses of MenACWY is 8 weeks. Adolescents who receive a first dose after their 16th birthday do not need a booster dose unless they become at increased risk for meningococcal disease. Persons aged 19 through 21 years are not recommended routinely to receive MenACWY. MenACWY may be administered up to age 21 years as catch-up vaccination for those who have not received a dose after their 16th birthday. Health-care personnel

should use every opportunity to provide the booster dose when indicated, regardless of the vaccine brand used for the previous dose or doses. [...]

First-Year College Students Living in Residence Halls

First-year college students living in residence halls should receive at least 1 dose of MenACWY before college entry. The preferred timing of the most recent dose is on or after their 16th birthday. If only 1 dose of vaccine was administered before the 16th birthday, a booster dose should be administered before enrollment. Some schools, colleges, and universities have policies requiring vaccination against meningococcal disease as a condition of enrollment for either incoming first-year students living in residence halls or all incoming first-year students. For ease of program implementation, persons aged ≤21 years should have documentation of receipt of meningococcal conjugate vaccine not more than 5 years before enrollment.

References

1. CDC. Prevention and control of meningococcal disease: recommendations of the Advisory Committee on Immunization Practices (ACIP). *MMWR* 2005;54(No. RR-7).

[...]

43. Harrison LH, Dwyer DM, Maples CT, Billmann L. Risk of meningococcal infection in college students. *JAMA* 1999;281:1906–10.

44. Bruce M, Rosenstein NE, Capparella J, Perkins BA, Collins MJ. Meningococcal disease in college students. In: *Abstracts of the 39th Annual Meeting of the Infectious Diseases Society of America.* Philadelphia, PA: Infectious Diseases Society of America; 1999:276.

45. Neal KR, Nguyen-Van-Tam J, Monk P, O'Brien SJ, Stuart J, Ramsay. M. Invasive meningococcal disease among university undergraduates: association with universities providing relatively large amounts of catered hall accommodations. *Epidemiol Infect* 1999;122:351–7.

46. Froeschle J. Meningococcal disease in college students. *Clin Infect Dis* 1999;29:215–6.

47. CDC. Meningococcal disease and college students: recommendations of the Advisory Committee on Immunization Practices (ACIP). *MMWR* 2000;49(No. RR-7):13–20.

[...]

99. Ortega-Sanchez IR, Meltzer MI, Shepard C, et al. Economics of an adolescent meningococcal conjugate vaccination catch-up campaign in the United States. *Clin Infect Dis* 2008;46:1–13.

100. Shepard CW, Ortega-Sanchez IR, Scott RD II, Rosenstein NE. Cost-effectiveness of conjugate meningococcal vaccination strategies in the United States. *Pediatrics* 2005;115:1220–32.

USE THE TOOLKIT

Let's use the three genre toolkit questions from Chapter 1 to examine this genre.

What Is It?

As the preceding examples demonstrate, a recommendation report is a long document that researches the current status of something and provides recommendations for future courses of action. In Example 1, the report researches current trends in drunk driving and recommends three action steps to reduce drunk driving (including reducing the legal blood alcohol concentration limit). Recommendation reports tend to contain subsections, including (1) an Executive Summary; (2) an Introduction; (3) a description of Methods; (4) a list of Results; (5) Conclusions; (6) Recommendations; and (7) References. However, report writers can also generate section headings based on different criteria or subtopics as required by their rhetorical situations. Example 3 includes a heading titled "Cost-Effectiveness Analyses" to emphasize the importance of cost to the implementation of the vaccine under review.

Who Reads It?

Recommendation reports are meant to be read by whomever can put the recommended course into action, such as an organization or government agency. In many cases, public audiences may not read the original report (although government reports are usually posted online) but a version of that report modified for a nonspecialist audience, such as a factsheet (Chapter 6).

What's It For?

Authors of recommendation reports intend their reports to bring about change. For example, the author of the report in Example 1 hopes to eliminate drunk driving. In some cases, however, a recommendation report may conclude that no action is necessary. It is still important to write the report, though, since it provides evidence that may be useful for others in the future.

EXERCISE 14.4: **Plan a Recommendation Report**

Identify a problem on your campus or in your community, such as overcrowding of the gymnasium, lack of vegetarian food options at the dining hall, or poor scheduling of public buses. To get started on your plan, take the following steps:

- Write a research question. For a recommendation report, your question is usually something like this:
  - Is it feasible to do _____? (e.g., open a vegetarian food kiosk on campus)
  - Is it better to do _____ or _____? (e.g., run more buses on route A or route B?)
  - What causes _____, and how can we improve _____? (e.g., What causes overcrowding at the gym, and how can we lessen it?)
- Identify the types of research that you will need to conduct. Will you need to conduct interviews, observations, surveys, library research, or a combination of these (Chapter 24)?
- Choose criteria for decision-making, such as technical requirements, cost, and moral considerations. For example, you might study the feasibility of a vegetarian food kiosk based on availability of separate food preparation facilities, cost of vegetarian ingredients, and the ethical obligations of the college to provide for different dietary needs.

E. Strategies for Reports

Imagine you've been assigned to write a recommendation report on a problem on your campus. Your audience will be university administrators, who will use your report to decide on an appropriate course of action. Let's see how Brad (Example 2) approached his report.

Prewriting (Content)

First, Brad rewrote his question until he was happy with how it would focus his report.

Topic: Dangers of chlorine in the campus pool and possible alternatives
Question: Is it feasible to switch from chlorine to saline sanitization methods?
Which is better, chlorine or saline? (Pretty much same as above . . . only this one emphasizes quality, not feasibility…)
Possible research tactics:

1. Interview the pool facilities manager
2. Research alternatives to chlorine, such as saline

What criteria should I use to evaluate my research?

1. Cost: how much do chlorine alternatives cost?
2. Moral issues: are we endangering children by chlorinating pool water? Are warnings adequate?

Health Effects—long term, short term

Drafting (Organizing)

When you are assigned a longer writing project, it can be helpful to divide the project into sections, and write one at a time. As Brad began to draft his report, he started with Methods, since he had already completed his research and found it easy to write about that. Then, he drafted the results, conclusions, and recommendations. He left the introduction and executive summary for last, since those were hardest for him to write.

Revising (Style)

Recommendation reports are written in a formal style (Chapter 21). Avoid using the word "I," and maintain a professional tone. Pay close attention to how the recommendations are organized. In a written report, they are usually written in the imperative or command form, in a bulleted list. In his first-year composition course, Brad was assigned to write a recommendation report that would address a public health problem on his college campus.

Here's how Brad rewrote his recommendations, which he originally drafted in paragraph form:

The Pool Services Manager should replace chlorine sanitization with a saltwater chlorine generation system if it is at all financially viable. There should also be signs placed detailing the possible health risks of chlorine at all pools operated by the UNC Campus Recreation department. UNC researchers might consider doing more research to determine the degree to which chlorine actually causes its attributed long term effects of asthma and cancer. In particular, they should do more research on the vulnerability of children under the age of 15 to early onset asthma.

Here is the revised version:

For UNC Pool Services:

1. Replace chlorine sanitization with a saltwater chlorine generation system if it is at

   all financially viable.

2. Post signs detailing the possible health risks of chlorine at all pools operated by

   the UNC Campus Recreation department.

For UNC Researchers:

1. Do more research to determine the degree to which chlorine actually causes its

   attributed long term effects of asthma and cancer.

2. Conduct more research on the vulnerability of children under the age of 15 to early

   onset asthma.

Editing (Design)

Visual elements can strengthen recommendation reports, as they lend interest and support to your words. If you create charts to bolster your data, your report will have a stronger impact on your reader. Brad also considered how to convey key information in visual form, and decided to use graphs to illustrate his findings (Chapter 29). In Brad's report, Figure 1 shows the relative costs of different types of water sanitation methods.

Troubleshooting

Here are some common challenges that students face when writing reports.

My research suggests this is not a good idea. The goal of a recommendation report is not necessarily to argue for a course of action you personally support. Instead, your goal is to show what is best, based on the evidence and a careful weighing of criteria. If your evidence clearly shows that it is not a good idea to pursue a course of action, that is okay. You can still write the report—that way, your readers will know why it is not a good idea.

My criteria have conflicting results.   Let's say that a certain course of action, such as a new vegetarian kiosk on campus, has strong support from students and fits the university's goals and mission—but it will be expensive. You can still recommend that the college go forward with the plan, if you think the two other criteria outweigh the cost criterion. In other words, you can weigh the criteria and recommend a decision accordingly. In the real world, recommendations are seldom clear-cut, but usually require decision makers to choose among multiple options.

I can't come up with any recommendations.   Your recommendations can be as simple as saying, "Yes, go ahead with this idea," or "No, do not go ahead with this idea." However, in government and business settings, reports often recommend more research, or a trial run, or an experiment. Consider what additional information could be gathered, or what additional steps could be taken to put a project into practice.

F. Chapter Project: Write a Report

Using the topic you selected earlier in this chapter, write a recommendation report. Using the examples in this chapter, design an organization scheme to suit your topic and purpose. Consider what kinds of research (Chapter 24) you will need, and how to weigh the evidence you gather to make reasoned recommendations.

Group Option: Group Recommendation Report

Complete the chapter project as a group. Choose a significant problem on campus that will require different types of research. You can divide up your tasks based on research method (e.g., survey, library research, etc.), and then divide up the sections of the report to write.

Multimedia Option: Podcast Report

Complete the chapter project, but then imagine you have been asked to speak on your local public radio station or a campus station about the recommendation report. Prepare a script of your online report, and then record it using a software program such as Audacity. Be sure that you consider how the audience of this podcast report is different from the original audience of your recommendation report.

PART **3**

Writing Process

397

Developing a Topic

A. Genre Toolkit: What Are You Writing?

Before you can select a topic or subject for writing, you need to figure out what kind of document you are writing. A topic is different from a thesis (Chapter 18). While a thesis refers to what you will say when you write (what claim or argument you will make), your topic simply refers to what you will be writing about. For example, if you are assigned to write a film review (Chapter 9), your topic will be the movie you have chosen to write about. Your thesis will relate to your actual evaluation of that movie—whether it was good or bad, and why.

Let's see how one student, Terrence, used the three genre toolkit questions (Chapter 1) to determine what kinds of topics were appropriate for his writing project.

USE THE TOOLKIT

What Is It?

First, Terrence figured out what kind of document he was writing. Was it an op-ed or letter to the editor? A report? A research paper?

Terrence's professor assigned him to write a research paper. He read Chapter 11, "Academic Research Genres," to learn more about the genre of the research paper. He learned that a research paper presents new, interesting research on a timely topic in a particular academic field. Thus, a research paper's topic is constrained by the genre: if Terrence wanted to write a social psychology research paper, then he needed to write on a topic that is *of interest to others in the field of social psychology.*

Who Reads It?

Next, Terrence needed to figure out who was going to read his research paper. Was his research paper merely an assignment for class—and therefore to be read only by his teacher? Or was he going to present it at a conference to other students or researchers? Would it be possible to use his paper as a writing sample for a summer internship or other job application? Was it possible that he would submit the paper to a journal that publishes research by undergraduates?

Terrence identified his professor as the primary audience of his research paper, but he also thought that he might want to present his paper at the undergraduate research conference that his college hosted every year. Thus, he knew he needed to keep in mind that his research paper might have an audience beyond just his professor.

However, his professor remained his primary audience. He therefore knew that *his topic needed to satisfy his primary audience's needs*. In Terrence's case, his professor said that students' research topics needed to tie in somehow to the students' life experiences.

What's It For?

Lastly, Terrence needed to figure out what his document would *do*—that is, the document's purpose. Was it to inform? To persuade? To inquire? In the case of a research paper, the purpose is both *to inform a reader and to make an argument about the research and its significance*.

Once Terrence identified his document's purpose, he felt that he was ready to begin searching for topics. Before he began searching, he listed the answers to the three genre toolkit questions to help him stay on track:

What is it? A research paper on a topic of interest to others in the field of social psychology.

Who reads it? Primary: My professor. Secondary: Undergraduate research conference. My professor limited my topic to something I have personal experience with.

What's it for? To inform my readers (professor and conference audience) about my research and why my research is important.

B. Browse for Topics

There are many places where you can begin to find timely and important topics for documents that you need to write. Here are some places where Terrence looked to find possible topics for his research paper.

What Are You Studying?

The first place you might look for topic ideas is in your reading assignments for your classes. Look in your textbook and also at other assigned or suggested readings on your syllabus. Your class readings are useful because you've already read and likely discussed them, which means that you've already conducted some research. Class readings are useful for another reason as well: they clue you into what your professor thinks is important. You might even find that a course reading from another class gives you an idea.

In Terrence's case, his reading on parental separation from children in his child psychology course gave him inspiration for a paper on incarcerated parents being separated from their children.

What Are You Talking About?

After Terrence came up with his idea to write about incarcerated parents being separated from their children, he opened up his Twitter account and posed a question to all of his followers. Here is what he tweeted:

> What do y'all think about kids visiting their moms in prison? Helpful to kids? Too scary? For research. Pls RT.

"Pls RT" means "please retweet"—Terrence asked his friends to share his query with all of their own followers as well. Terrence received many replies to his tweeted query, some from people whom he had never met before. He even heard back from a professor at his university's law school who researches prisoner's rights. The law professor emailed Terrence some recommended reading that helped him get started with research.

What Are You Reading About?

Another strategy would be to look through online sources to see what topics seem timely or interesting. Search online news aggregators such as Google News; a web-based aggregator like Reddit or Digg; or a specialized news source (such as Science Daily.com for science). Terrence searched these online outlets for any recent events that dealt with incarcerated parents, child visitation, or other prisoner's rights issues. Terrence searched the keywords "jail and psychology" and "prisoners and psychology." He came up with a variety of news items that told him the trending topics in his area, such as the psychology of death-row inmates and the psychological ill effects of solitary confinement.

His topic, which dealt with children and their incarcerated parents, was not currently in the headlines, but many other topics were. He shared some of the other topics that he found with his classmates to help them get started with their papers. One of his classmates decided to write about the timely topic of the psychological effects of solitary confinement.

C. Narrow Topics with Initial Research

It comes as a surprise to many students that you can do research *before* finalizing a topic. In fact, doing some preliminary research often helps you to select a strong topic. Getting started with research (Chapter 23) and developing a topic work hand-in-hand. If you are writing a research paper, *before you settle on a topic*, you need to first figure out what kind of research has already been done in your area of interest.

Terrence had already decided he wanted to write about incarcerated parents being separated from their children, but he didn't know how to narrow his topic so that he could write a paper of the appropriate length for his class assignment. He turned to scholarly sources, to research articles that are of a similar genre to what Terrence himself would be writing, to figure out just what he wanted to say.

Scholarly texts are articles and books published *by* experts in a field, *for* experts in a field (Chapter 25). You can find scholarly journals through your school's library website. Many scholarly articles are available online through databases that your school subscribes to. You can also use Google Scholar, which confines your searches to scholarly sources rather than the entire Internet.

Search scholarly texts for articles about your topic using keywords. Terrence searched "parents and prison," for example. You should ask a librarian to help you narrow your search terms if your initial search returns too many results to be useful. You will want to search in journals that are in your area of study—in Terrence's case, policy journals, law journals, and psychology journals.

Suppose Terrence's initial research revealed that many states have laws that prevent children from visiting their parents in prison. But, he also found that new research was revealing that there are psychological benefits to allowing children to visit incarcerated parents—benefits to both children and parents. He would now be on his way to having a topic: the psychological benefits to both children and parents that come from allowing children to visit their incarcerated parents in prison.

Terrence still had a little more work to do. He needed to figure out what he could say that was *new* or *special* about his topic. He didn't want to simply replicate the work that another researcher had done. Terrence needed to find a gap to fill. Terrence believed, as many students do, that the notion that he might have something new or original to say seems unlikely. He is a student, after all. What could he possibly have to say that some important professor or researcher hasn't already written? Chapter 23 discusses in detail how to craft your research to fill a gap.

Prewriting

When you have a good idea of your topic, you can begin prewriting. Prewriting refers to a series of techniques that writers use to help them develop ideas. Prewriting can help you find out more about your topic—including what you *already* know (you might be surprised!). As you learn more about your topic, you will be able to narrow it down to one that is more manageable. Prewriting can also help you figure out a way to state your thesis or claim (Chapter 18) and to come up with ideas to support it. Finally, prewriting can also help you break through writer's block, by helping you get your ideas flowing again, and by helping you get those ideas from your brain and onto the page.

The point is, there are many ways that prewriting techniques can help you get your writing started and keep it moving.

A. Freewriting

Most of us have an internal editor that bogs us down when we try to write. It can be hard to free ourselves of the internal editor that tells us to correct our wording or fiddle with our sentences. Freewriting is one technique that will free you from your internal editor.

Freewriting, in some ways, is the easiest thing in the world to do. It is also very difficult to get used to. In order to freewrite, *you simply sit down and start writing*. Resist the urge to revise. Don't worry about word choice, grammar, or where you are going with your ideas.

Here are some tips for successful freewriting.

Do Not Read What You Have Written

Resist the temptation to even look at the words you have just written until you are finished freewriting. Looking at what you have written can tempt you into editing, when what you should be doing is writing.

If you can't resist rereading what you've written as you freewrite, there is a strategy that can help break this habit. When you sit down to freewrite at your computer, *turn off the monitor* before you begin. You can also change your text color to white, making it invisible. These techniques can help you focus on writing itself, the *process*, rather than focusing on what you have just typed, the *product*.

Time Yourself

Some people prefer to set a timer to limit their freewriting. This is called timed free-writing. By setting a timer—for, say, two minutes or five minutes—you can create a short period of time free of your internal editor. Keep your flow of words coming, and do not stop until the time is up.

Keep Going

The most important strategy for successful freewriting is this: *do not stop writing.* If you get to a word or concept that has you stumped, simply draw (or type) a blank line, or write the words "Come back to this," or write "What here?" And then *keep going.* It is much easier to go back later and fill in those blanks once you have a body of writing to draw from. Often, you will end up writing the words that go in the blanks later in the same freewrite.

Ask a Question

Sometimes it is easier to start freewriting if you write a question at the top of your page. Your freewriting then becomes an attempt to answer that question. Remember, though, that there is no "right" or "wrong" answer to your question—and you're not going to be graded on the answers that you *do* come up with.

For example, let's return to Terrence's proposed research paper topic on psychology and prisons (Chapter 15). He decided to focus his research on the benefits and drawbacks of allowing young children to visit their incarcerated mothers. He might begin his freewrite by typing this question at the top of a page: "Why would it be good for young children to visit their mothers in prison?" Then, using the information that he remembered from his initial research, combined with his own creativity, he might begin jotting down everything he can come up with. Those ideas may become the basis of his research plan (Chapter 23).

Looping

You can "loop" your freewriting in order to stay on track. Looping simply means freewriting for a short period of time, perhaps three minutes. At the end of the time period, read what you have written and select the most promising ideas. Use those ideas to launch into another freewrite that focuses on those ideas. Repeat this process until your freewrite is intensely focused on your topic.

B. Question–Dialogue

Sometimes, it is easier to point out all of the things you *wish* you knew. In a question-dialogue prewrite, you first write a list of questions. For example, Terrence might write:

- "What are the risks to children who visit their mothers in prison?"
- "What sorts of accommodations do prisons need to make to keep kids safe?"
- "How often should kids be allowed to visit their mothers? For how long?"

In the question-dialogue process, keep writing all of the questions that you wish you knew the answers to.

Then, go back and start writing answers. Use the freewriting techniques discussed earlier in this chapter. This kind of prewriting can help you start making notes about ideas that you need to research further. Jot down research ideas, research search terms that might be useful (Chapter 23), books and other resources you might want to look at, etc.

By the time you are finished, you might have the makings of a powerful research plan and a basic outline for your research paper.

Try the Journalist Questions

If you don't know where to start when writing down your questions, you can use the journalist questions—the five-Ws and one-H. These questions can help you get started. You'll find that they are easy to expand upon.

1. Who?
2. What?
3. When?
4. Where?
5. Why?
6. How?

Here's how Terrence wrote out the journalist questions to help his prewriting process:

Who would benefit from allowing children to visit their mothers in prison?

What is the purpose of allowing children to visit their mothers in prison? What benefits would follow from this?

When did we start imprisoning women in Western society? When did we start separating women from their children?

Where has this type of policy been implemented?

Why do people oppose this policy? Why is it a good idea?

How would this be implemented?

Try the Stasis Questions

Another set of questions that you might find useful are the stasis questions (Chapter 18). These questions help you identify the context and the conflicts in a given situation and develop a solution. You can use these questions to help start a question-dialogue prewrite.

1. What is it? (Facts)
2. How do we define it? (Definition)
3. Is it good or bad? (Evaluation)
4. What caused it? (Cause)
5. What are its effects? (Consequences)
6. What should we do about it? (Proposal)

Here's how Terrence used the stasis question to frame questions about his topic:

Facts: What is the current policy for imprisoned mothers of young children?

Definition: Would this policy count as a parental rights issue or a criminal justice issue?

Evaluation: Would this policy be fair or unfair for the children involved?

Cause: What brought about the existing policy in the first place?

Consequences: What would the effects of this policy entail for children? Mothers?

Proposal: Should this policy be enacted?

C. Audio-Brainstorming

Some people have an easy time *talking* about complicated subjects but find it difficult to *write* about them. Luckily, we are living in an age when recording our voices is easy to do. Cell phones and other mobile devices as well as computers have microphones and recording software built right in. There are many mobile apps and software programs that transcribe as you speak, creating a written transcript that you can edit later.

An audio brainstorm is basically a freewrite that you do out loud, instead of on paper. Later, you can transcribe what you have said. But for now, don't edit—just think out loud.

Just Start Talking

One way to do an audio brainstorm is to just start talking about your subject. Try using phrases like "What I'm trying to say is . . . ," or "I wish I knew more about . . . ," and then just see what comes.

Write a List of Questions First

You might find it helpful to write a list of questions to ask yourself before you start your audio brainstorm. When you run out of things to say, move on to the next question. Use the guidelines from question-dialogue to help come up with your questions. You can use the journalist questions, or the stasis questions, or both.

Post to a Social Media Network

You can always draw on the wisdom of your online networks to help you with paper ideas. If you belong to a social network such as Facebook or Twitter, you can post a question to your friends or contacts. This can be a good way to get plenty of ideas in a short amount of time. When he was researching his topic, Terrence posted messages to his followers on Twitter, such as this one: "What do you think of letting kids see their moms in #prison?" He received a lot of great responses to his tweets, including one from a law professor at his school who received a retweet from a friend of Terrence.

Bring in a Friend

Sometimes writers need to bounce ideas off friends. Find a friend who doesn't mind allowing you to record his or her voice. Say, "I just need to explain my ideas to you to see if they make sense." Then start talking. Allow your friend to point out places where your ideas do not make sense, or places where your friend wishes you could explain an idea with more depth. Later, you can go back through the recording and make notes of those places that need more research and more thought. You can even have your friend "interview" you by asking you a list of questions that you have written.

D. Concept Mapping

Concept mapping, also called clustering or even flow-charting, is a visual way to freewrite. Concept mapping allows you to connect your ideas visually, so that you can see how they relate. Generally speaking, a concept map is *a diagram or sketch of a brainstorm.*

Concept-mapping is two-dimensional. Ordinarily, we use writing in a one-dimensional way: putting ideas end to end in a one-direction line. Concept-mapping allows you to branch out in many directions to find relationships between thoughts, questions, and ideas. If you are a visual thinker, you might prefer to sketch out your ideas using a concept map, instead of using freewriting. Terrence used a concept map (Figure 16.1) to help him plan ideas for his research paper on child visitation and incarcerated mothers.

A concept map looks like circles or boxes connected by lines, and inside these shapes are sentences, phrases, or single words that represent an idea. The lines represent the relationships between these ideas.

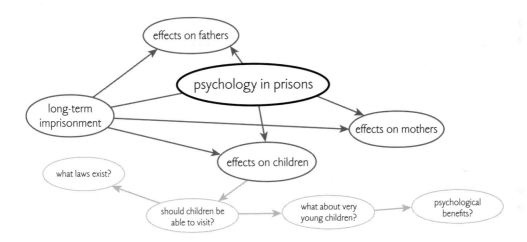

Figure 16.1. Terrence's Concept Map

You might find it helpful to include simple headings for each idea included in the map. You can even color-code the circles (or boxes) around the ideas to indicate the type of idea it represents.

One way to color-code or label your concept map might be to use some of the following:

- Question—what is the main question you will address?
- Issue—what is the broad issue at stake?
- Undisputed fact—what do we know already about this issue? What has been established by previous research?
- Disputed fact—what facts are disputed or uncertain based on existing research or opinions? (This is often where you can find a gap for your own writing.)

We included these headings in Figure 16.2.

Figure 16.2. Terrence's Concept Map with Color Codes and Headings

Here are some steps to follow for creating a concept map:

1. Figure out what medium you will use to draw your map. A large piece of paper (16″ × 20″) works well and gives you more space to work. A whiteboard also works really well, if you have access to one. Computer software provides another choice.
2. Start with one or more key topics or issues. Write these in the center of the page and draw separate circles around each idea. You might use some of the other invention strategies provided in this chapter to help you get started.
3. As you think of ideas that relate to the key topic(s), write them down and draw circles around them.
4. Draw lines between the circles to show relationships. Get creative, and go in all directions from the key topic.
5. Use colors and headings to indicate priority or other types of categorization.
6. Try not to worry about neatness or organization—those things come later, after you have developed your ideas.

Depth and Breadth

Keep both *depth* and *breadth* in mind while you map your ideas. *Depth* refers to how far you can take each of these initial ideas. *Breadth* refers to how many initial ideas you can invent from the original issue. If you are trying to maximize the number of ideas you can come up with, try for both.

Technology

Some software companies have caught on to the usefulness of concept mapping and have created software just for this process. Using this software is especially useful if more than one person is working on a project—the document can be emailed from user to user until the concept map is complete.

You might find online apps to create cluster maps, such as Mindmeister.com or Bubbl.us. These tools allow groups to map across the Internet. Microsoft Word and PowerPoint both include tools that you can use for concept mapping. Give it a try the next time you brainstorm arguments for a case.

Drafting

While "drafting" refers to the action of putting words on paper or screen, it also involves organizing ideas so that you can start putting them down in the first place. In most cases, you will have some pre-writing (Chapter 16) to help you, whether that includes notes from your research, a formal outline, or just some ideas you have jotted down. When you start drafting, you begin to organize this pre-writing into sentences and paragraphs (for traditional documents) or into images, sounds, and other media (for multimedia documents). In this chapter, you will learn different drafting strategies that can help you to compose effectively.

A. Try Out Different Drafting Strategies

A strong writer has a number of different drafting strategies at his or her disposal. Here are a few to get you started.

Sketch out the Genre

Your analysis of the genre you are writing should help you to begin drafting. Some genres will give you a pretty clear set of sections and even content to include. For example, a résumé (Chapter 12) typically includes a number of relatively standard sections (although you have some control over how the sections are ordered). To start writing a résumé, you can outline those sections first, and then fill in the information you have planned to include.

Other genres, such as a film review (Chapter 9) or literary analysis (Chapter 8), might be somewhat less structured—but you will still have an introduction, some kind of body, and a conclusion of sorts. If you get stuck, go back and look at more examples of the genre you are writing, and determine what kinds of sections you might use to organize your document.

As he was writing his paper, Terrence began with an outline based on articles he read in undergraduate research journals:

Terrence's Outline

- Abstract
- Introduction—begin with the conversation scholars are having about this issue and how I will add to it—what a psychological perspective adds to the issue of visitation for children of incarcerated mothers

- Body—take up main arguments against visitation advanced by scholars/barriers preventing visitation, then show how psychological research contradicts it
  - Include personal experience??
- Conclude with implications for law or policy
- Works cited list

Write around Your Evidence

One common strategy for writers is to begin by ordering the main pieces of evidence you will be using (Chapters 24 and 26). Scientists typically plan out the visual evidence they will include in a scientific article, such as graphs or tables displaying numerical data. Then, they write explanatory texts to accompany those visual representations of their results. You can do something similar even if your main pieces of evidence are textual, such as quotations from a novel or a set of interviews. Try ordering your evidence, and then writing text that introduces, explains, and evaluates that evidence. Terrence began by sketching in some of his evidence within the body section of his paper, being careful to include citation information (Chapter 28) so that he would avoid inadvertent plagiarism (Chapter 27).

Terrence's Evidence

> Best interest of the child standard (article)
>
> Costa (2003): prison "it epitomizes all that is unhealthy and dangerous." unfair for children to visit a "very bad place"; "Prison is not an atmosphere appropriate for the growth maturation of our youth. 'Ah what childhood memories these kids will have' "
>
> Pamela Lewis (2004) on legal barriers: "the Kentucky Court of Appeals held that incarceration does not preclude or interfere with the parent's right to a hearing on the matter of visitation"; but hearing process is complicated

After listing his main pieces of evidence, he added text to elaborate on or explain key pieces of evidence. For instance, he expanded on the third point of evidence as follows:

Terrence's Elaboration

Incarcerated parents often long to maintain or mend their relationship with their children. Many mothers would want nothing more than to get the chance to see their child, and try to comfort them with love and an explanation. Yet, even if the family wants to participate in visitation, the process is not easy. Pamela Lewis (2004), a family lawyer, argues that although courts have indeed agreed that visitation is a fundamental right for people in prison to have, numerous legal barriers and prison regulations are preventing visitation from occurring as much as needed. She points out several legal factors that prohibit child visitation. First she cites the case *Alexander v. Alexander,* in which "the Kentucky Court of Appeals held that incarceration does not preclude or interfere with the parent's right to a hearing on the matter of visitation." This means that regardless of a parent's incarceration, she still has a right to petition the court for visitation. However, as Lewis describes, the hearing usually proves to be problematic, as there is limited access to legal services involving domestic issues for incarcerated parents.

Go Section by Section

It can be daunting to start a long writing project from scratch. One helpful strategy is to divide your project into different sections, such as the introduction, conclusion, and body sections, and draft one at a time. You do not necessarily need to start with the introduction. In fact, for many genres it can be easier to start in the middle, with the "meat" of the document.

Terrence began by working on the body of his paper, since he had done his research and knew how to get started with that. He was less sure about how to introduce or conclude his paper, so he left those tasks for later.

Move Things Around

Learn how to use your word processor to highlight, cut, and paste blocks of text. Do not be afraid to take advantage of those tools. You can cut sentences and paragraphs and move them around to see where they fit best in the structure of your document. When dealing with a longer draft, some writers use the highlight tool to color code common topics or ideas. Then, you can simply move similar ideas so that they are together in the text.

While Terrence was drafting the body paragraphs for his essay, he realized that his original outline did not work for the argument he was making. As he looked over his draft, he highlighted information that needed to be moved earlier in the paper. Then, he used the cut-and-paste tool to move information around.

Terrence's Cut-and-Paste

The main legal factor that prevents child visitation for incarcerated mothers is the "best interest of the child standard,". . . .

In regards to the visitation rights of incarcerated parents, especially mothers, there has been a cold stance taken that avoids the true needs of the parent's rehabilitation and the child's development. Many believe that visiting an inmate is detrimental to the child. Costa (2003), a legal scholar, discusses how prison is not a healthy environment for children as "it epitomizes all that is unhealthy and dangerous." She asserts that it is unfair for an innocent child to have to attempt to understand that her parent did something "bad" and has to stay at that "very bad place." The constant tension of visiting an incarcerated mother and the emotional trauma of having to say "goodbye" is detrimental to the child's development, Costa argues. "Prison is not an atmosphere appropriate for the growth maturation of our youth. 'Ah what childhood memories these kids will have'" (Costa, 2003).

Costa exemplifies the blanket bias that is present in our society, which in turn is re-flected in the laws. As an individual who spent a large portion of my childhood visiting my incarcerated father, I could not agree more with scholars. Although I understand that

everyone has his or her own unique experiences, I always looked forward to these visits

rather than having any feeling of anguish or anxiety. If more research is conducted, maybe

it would be discovered that I was indeed the norm, and not the exception.

Incarcerated parents often long to maintain or mend their relationship with their chil-

dren. Many mothers would want nothing more than to get the chance to see their child,

and try to comfort them with love and an explanation. Yet, even if the family wants to par-

ticipate in visitation, the process is not easy. Pamela Lewis (2004), a family lawyer, argues

that although courts have indeed agreed that visitation is a fundamental right for people

in prison to have, numerous legal barriers and prison regulations are preventing visitation

from occurring as much as needed *[explain this better]*. She points out several legal factors

that prohibit child visitation. First she cites the case *Alexander v. Alexander,* in which "the

Kentucky Court of Appeals held that incarceration does not preclude or interfere with

the parent's right to a hearing on the matter of visitation." This means that regardless of a

parent's incarceration, she still has a right to petition the court for visitation. However, as

Lewis describes, the hearing usually proves to be problematic, as there is limited access to

legal services involving domestic issues for incarcerated parents.

Re-read, Then Write

If you get stuck, try re-reading what you have written so far. This often works best if
you take a little break from writing and go back to your text with fresh eyes. By
re-reading your draft, you may come up with new ideas or simply get into the mood
to add more. Terrence added notes to himself (shown in bold) when he reread what
he wrote, to remind himself what he should do next.

Terrence's Rough Draft

Title . . . ? Moms Behind Bars? DRAFT

[Intro—start with general topic—how many mothers are incarcerated, etc., and why legal system makes it that way . . . *Fill this in later*]

Incarcerated parents often long to maintain or mend their relationship with their children. Many mothers would want nothing more than to get the chance to see their child, and try to comfort them with love and an explanation. Yet, even if the family wants to participate in visitation, the process is not easy. Pamela Lewis (2004), a family lawyer, argues that although courts have indeed agreed that visitation is a fundamental right for people in prison to have, numerous legal barriers and prison regulations are preventing visitation from occurring as much as needed *[explain this better].* She points out several legal factors that prohibit child visitation. First she cites the case *Alexander v. Alexander,* in which "the Kentucky Court of Appeals held that incarceration does not preclude or interfere with the parent's right to a hearing on the matter of visitation." This means that regardless of a parent's incarceration, she still has a right to petition the court for visitation. However, as Lewis describes, the hearing usually proves to be problematic, as there is limited access to legal services involving domestic issues for incarcerated parents.

Another legal factor that prevents child visitation for incarcerated mothers is the "best interest of the child standard," **[. . . *expand on this using Lewis . . .*]**

In regards to the visitation rights of incarcerated parents, especially mothers, there has been a cold stance taken that avoids the true needs of the parent's rehabilitation and the child's development. Many believe that visiting an inmate is detrimental to the child. Costa

(2003), a legal scholar, discusses how prison is not a healthy environment for children as "it epitomizes all that is unhealthy and dangerous." She asserts that it is unfair for an innocent child to have to attempt to understand that her parent did something "bad" and has to stay at that "very bad place." The constant tension of visiting an incarcerated mother and the emotional trauma of having to say "goodbye" is detrimental to the child's development, Costa argues. "Prison is not an atmosphere appropriate for the growth maturation of our youth. 'Ah what childhood memories these kids will have'" (Costa, 2003). *[Perhaps include an image of a visiting room to contrast with this point?]*

Costa exemplifies the blanket bias that is present in our society, which in turn is reflected in the laws. *[get more research on this].* As an individual who spent a large portion of my childhood visiting my incarcerated father, I could not agree more with scholars *[Who?].* Although I understand that everyone has his or her own unique experiences, I always looked forward to these visits rather than having any feeling of anguish or anxiety. If more research is conducted, maybe it would be discovered that I was indeed the norm, and not the exception. *[should I include this? Say more about it?]*

B. Digital Composing: Find Tools that Work for You

Writers today employ a range of tools to help them write, whether they are preparing a traditional print document or a multimedia text that incorporates images, sounds, or video. Using different digital tools can help you to compose more efficiently and to open up new possibilities for the kinds of things you can compose. Keep in mind, though, that your goal should be to make the tools work for you—try to figure out how each tool (whether it is pen and paper or a web design program) can help you to accomplish your own writing goals.

Paper and Pens Are Tools, Too

We might not think of pens and paper as technologies for writing. In fact, many students prefer to compose documents on a computer, and only use pen and paper for jotting down notes and ideas. However, it is worth trying to write out a document (or sketch out a website or plans for a video) on paper. Sometimes, switching from one medium to another can get your creative juices flowing. Writing by hand can feel very different from typing, so you might try it sometime to see how it works for you.

Many writers employ other low-tech tools, from notebooks and notecards to highlighters and Post-it notes. For example, some students write down their ideas and notes on index cards and then put them in order, moving from a set of ordered cards to a written draft. Others use Post-it notes to flag important information in books or articles. Remember that you can experiment with these kinds of tools to see what works best for your own writing process.

Terrence wrote down quotes from his research on index cards.

Terrence's Notecards

(1) Lewis, Pamela. Title: "Behind the Glass Wall: Barriers that Incarcerated Parents Face Regarding the Care, Custody, and Control of Their Children." Year: 2004 Journal of the American Academy of Matrimonial Lawyers Vol. 19 Pg. 97-116
→ visitation is a legal right.
→ legal barriers prevent visitation + prison rules (97)

(2) Lewis—"Behind the Glass Wall"
• Alexander v. Alexander—"the Kentucky Court of Appeals held that incarceration does not preclude or interfere with the parent's right to a hearing on the matter of visitation."

(3) Lewis—"Behind the Glass Wall"
→ limited access to legal services makes hearings problematic for incarcerated parents.
→ legal services often given only when parental rights are being terminated.

He rearranged them in the order he thought would work best, and then rearranged them again when he got stuck.

Terrence also wrote out some of his draft by hand. After drafting the body section, he was stuck on his introduction, so he decided to switch from his computer to a notebook to see if that would help—and it did! Here's his handwritten introduction draft:

Terrence's Handwritten Introduction

Millions of children are torn away from their mothers every day, and its perfectly legal—and not because of some loophole in the law. Over 1.5 million children in the US have ~~a parent in jail~~ an incarcerated parent, & our legal system is preventing these children from visitation with their incarcerated parents, especially mothers. Many argue that children should not visit not be exposed to prison, and that any visitation is emotionally unhealthy. True, prison is a cold and awful life situation for anyone . . . But, regardless of what their parents have done, they still have children who depend on them. The law ignores this fact, since courts can deny visitation if they find it would be ~~bad~~ detrimental for the child. But what factors determine that? Often, these factors are not based on <u>actual evidence</u>, but on the stigma surrounding "detriment."

Make Your Word Processing Program Work for You

Today, most writers use a word processing program such as Microsoft Word to compose texts, although there are many other programs and apps (some of them free) to try out. Most of these programs offer tools that can help you to compose more effectively. For instance, if you assign heading styles to your section headings (in Word, located under Styles), you can then tell the software program to generate a Table of Contents or to show you the Document Map (basically, a list of your main headings and sub-headings). That tool allows you to see your document at a glance.

Many of the features in a word processing program can mimic other tools: consider the actions of cutting, pasting, notes (under Review in Word) and highlighting, which all have non-digital parallels. Marking up your text using those tools can help you to keep track of your ideas and re-organize your writing as you go.

You can also use the Track Changes tool if you want a record of the changes you have made. This can be useful if you want to try out a new idea, without losing your original work in case you change your mind. Terrence did this as he was working on his introduction. He wanted to experiment with the order of his ideas, and so he used Track Changes so that he could easily see what he had changed, and remove it if he wanted to go back to the old version. He could see that everything underlined and in red was a change, and he could choose to "accept" or "reject" those changes as needed.

Terrence's Tracked Changes

Over 1.5 million children in the United States have an incarcerated parent. Millions of these children are torn away from their mothers everyday, and it's perfectly legal—not because of some loophole in the law. Our legal system is preventing these children from visitation with their incarcerated parents, especially mothers. True, prison is a cold and awful life situation for anyone, let alone a child. Many argue that children should not be exposed to prison, and that any visitation is emotionally unhealthy. But, regardless of what their parents have done, they still have children who depend on them. The law ignores this fact, since courts can deny visitation if they find it would be detrimental. But what factors determine that visitation would be detrimental? Often, these factors are not based on actual evidence, but on the stigma surrounding "detriment."

Try Different Software

A number of alternatives to traditional word processing programs are now available, and you might find some of them useful to you. One program, Scrivener, allows you to focus on writing without worrying about the formatting of your text. Scientists and mathematicians often compose with a program called LaTeX, which combines features of a word processor with computer code. Like Scrivener, LaTeX encourages writers to focus first on the content of their writing, and on layout and design second.

Another set of tools includes Google Docs and Adobe Buzzword, which are free, online word processors. One advantage of these tools is that you can access your documents from any computer, and they are automatically stored for you—no worrying about losing your files. Google Docs also allows multiple writers to work on a document at once, so it is great for working with a team. In fact, we composed much of this textbook using Google Docs, since it allowed both of us to write and revise simultaneously.

Since Terrence liked to work on his paper from the computer lab in the library as well as from home, he used a cloud computing storage service, Dropbox. This allowed him to open his files from any computer, without worrying about a flash drive that he might lose.

Try Audio

If you are composing an audio text, such as a podcast, you will obviously want to take advantage of audio recording and editing software. A number of free programs, such as Audacity (audacity.sourceforge.net), can help you to record and edit sounds, including music and voice recordings. However, even if you are not composing an audio text, you might like to try composing orally. A number of applications for your smartphone, tablet, or computer will allow you to speak your ideas out loud and will then transcribe them in a written document. Composing orally sometimes works well if you are stuck at a certain part of a draft, or if you have trouble typing as quickly as you'd like.

Since Terrence sometimes came up with ideas for his paper while he was walking home from campus, he used his cellphone to record reading notes (Chapter 7) and even compose sentences that he could enter into his draft later. After he read one article in the library, for example, he recorded this message to himself:

- *"That Costa article really bugs me. It's another example of . . . of a blanket bias in society against people who go to prison and their children."*

Terrence decided he liked the term "blanket bias," and included it in his essay:

- *"Costa exemplifies the blanket bias that is present in our society, which in turn is reflected in the laws"*

Audio materials might also form part of the evidence or data for a more traditional written text. For instance, imagine you were writing a rhetorical analysis (Chapter 8) of the chants and slogans used at a student protest event. You might embed an audio clip you took of those chants into a web document in order to give readers a sense of what those chants sounded like.

Try Video

As is the case with audio, you might use video for a few different reasons. Most computers now come with video recorders that allow you to use your built-in camera to record yourself. Of course, for a multimedia project you might also use the video camera on your smartphone, tablet, or a more hi-tech camera, to record scenes. Video may provide the evidence or data within a web text. For example, in a natural science class you might videotape the behavior of birds at a bird feeder, code what you see, and embed a video clip (or a still from the video) in your document to provide evidence for your claims. Terrence thought about recording a video interview with the child of an incarcerated mother, but decided that his target genre and audience did not allow for video. Or, you might compose a project that is entirely in video form, such as a public service announcement for a local organization.

Try Screencasting

One additional composing tool, screencasting, can involve audio, video, and text. A screencast uses special software to record what happens on your desktop. You can open documents and type, play videos or music clips, navigate around the web, and more. A screencast might provide a good way to create a tutorial or set of instructions (Chapter 6). But it can also be put to more experimental uses. Try out a program such as Camtasia or Jing to get started with screencasting.

C. Writing Collaboratively

In college courses, you will sometimes be asked to write a document as a team. In fact, in this textbook we have included team writing tasks in every project chapter. Writing as a team can be challenging, since you will want to make sure everyone contributes to the task and that everyone has input into the decisions you make. Here are some strategies to help you compose a document as a group:

Divide and Conquer

One way to compose with a group is to divide up your document into sections. Each person takes a shot at drafting a section. Then, you can put together your sections and edit it (Chapter 22) to make it consistent in style and tone (Chapter 21).

Co-writing

Another option is to actually sit down with your group and compose your text together, line by line. While this does not always work for a longer document, it can be effective for shorter genres, especially when you need to pay careful attention to the words you use. For example, if you are designing a brochure together as a group, it might make more sense to come up with ideas together. Appoint one person to be the recorder—that person will take charge of writing down what everyone says. Then, you can each look over the draft and finalize the language. Digital tools can also help you with co-writing. Google Docs allows multiple users to work on a document at the same time, and to see what each person is typing.

Re-writing

For some documents, it might make sense to have one person write a first draft of the whole text (or a section, as in "Divide and Conquer," mentioned previously). The next step in re-writing is for a second person to take over that section, revising and rewriting it to clarify the meaning or add ideas. You can take turns re-writing the same section as many times as you would like. When you do re-writing, you'll find that it soon becomes hard to tell who actually wrote what—each person's words will be mixed up with everyone else's.

Assign Roles

In professional writing contexts, people usually take on different roles, all of which go into producing a finalized document. For example, a website might have a content developer (the person who writes the main content), a content editor (the person who revises that writing for effective style), a layout and design editor (who fixes the text so that it appears properly on the web page), and a technical editor (who checks to ensure the accuracy of the information presented). For some genres, such as a tutorial (Chapter 6), it might make sense to assign each person in your group a different role along those lines. This way, you can draw on each group member's strengths. Someone who is good at grammar and editing can take on the role of content editor, while someone with technical knowledge can edit for accuracy, and so on.

Generating Arguments

A. What Is an Argument?

An argument makes a particular kind of claim or thesis. Both "claim" and "thesis" refer to a main point of a document. However, the term "claim" emphasizes that a main point should be argumentative—it should seek to persuade someone to adopt a new way of thinking or acting. This applies not only to argumentative genres (Chapter 10), but even to academic research genres (Chapter 11). In a research paper, you are arguing for a specific idea, interpretation, or finding. For example, a history research paper might argue for a specific interpretation of how a government policy came into being.

Here are some examples of main points that Terrence might make for his research paper:

- Prisons should provide visitation rights to incarcerated mothers because it will benefit children psychologically to maintain bonds with their mothers.
- Prisons should not provide visitation rights to incarcerated mothers because children are likely to be psychologically damaged by visiting a prison.

If you look closer, you'll see that each of these comments takes a stand on the issue of visitation rights for mothers in prison—they each make an argument.

You'll also see that each of these statements offers a reason to support the claim. The first statement argues that visitation rights should be granted *because* children will benefit psychologically, while the second argues that visitation rights should not be granted *because* children will be damaged psychologically by visiting prisons. You can think of reasons as "because-statements" that support a main claim or thesis.

In its simplest form, then, an argument consists of a claim supported by one or more reasons.

How to Recognize an Argument Genre

Much of the writing you do for your college courses will be argumentative in nature. Most academic writing includes an argument or thesis—but not always. In some genres, your claim may be more like a research question or statement of purpose, as in a scientific research report or a business memo. In other genres, your claim may be implicit rather than explicitly stated, as in a personal narrative or résumé. Only some genres, such as the ones featured in Chapter 10 (Argumentative Genres), are usually framed explicitly as arguments. But that does not mean they do not require you to make a claim and support it with good reasons.

Look for common terms for argument.

You may find that arguments get called different things by different professors or in different fields. When you get a writing assignment, look out for these words:

- Claim
- Stance
- Thesis
- Main point
- Angle

- Persuade/persuasive/persuasion
- Convince
- Argument/argue
- Editorial/opinion
- Assert/assertion

These words usually indicate that your task is to construct an argument.

Look for the word "thesis."

You may be accustomed to thinking about writing as being organized around a thesis. In fact, you might be given a writing assignment in a college course that requires you to use a thesis and support it.

You may have been taught that good writing should expand upon a statement that expresses the main point of the paper. Typically, the thesis is then supported by several "points." When you think about a thesis in this manner, the thesis is not necessarily an argument—you aren't necessarily trying to convince someone to think in a new way or to take a course of action.

A thesis that simply expresses your main point is merely a statement that sums up your ideas.

In college writing, though, it is more accurate to consider your thesis as a *claim that you must support with reasons.* Your professor will expect you to make points, yes, but also to use those points to prove a claim with well-reasoned, researched reasons. For that reason, when you see or hear the word "thesis," think "argument."

Look for opinions.

Opinions and arguments are not the same thing. We all have opinions, about everything from politics to popular culture, sports to school policy. Sometimes, we back up our opinions with arguments—but not always. Opinions tend to be more like subjective beliefs, and we often share them without trying to argue for them or persuade others to support them.

In a college course, however, if you are asked to give an opinion on something (such as a reading in a literature class or an issue in a political science class), you will usually be expected to support your opinion with good reasons—basically, you will be expected to make an argument. For example, if you are asked to write a response essay (Chapter 3) giving your opinion or thoughts on a text, think "I need make an argument about this text."

Newspapers and magazines often publish arguments under a section called "Opinion" or "Commentary." This is tricky wording, because these kinds of texts are not simply statements of what someone thinks about an issue—they are arguments that seek to persuade others to agree. By posting your opinion—plus reasons to support it—on a public forum, by writing a letter to the editor, or by starting a debate with a friend, you've entered the realm of argument.

Now that we've clarified what we mean by argument, let's consider how you can go about writing one.

B. Examining the Topic

Any argument you generate should respond to an ongoing debate or controversy surrounding your topic (Chapter 15).

When you've been assigned to write an argumentative genre, or develop a claim or thesis, it can be tempting to come up with your claim first. You may already have an opinion about this issue, so you might write up your claim first, and then set out to find reasons and evidence to support your claim.

However, a good argument should do more than set out to prove an opinion you already hold. As a college student, you will be expected to show that you've studied the topic at hand, read about it from different viewpoints, and then generated your own argument. Taking the time to research the topic at hand will also help you to make a stronger argument, since it will help you to develop better reasons and find more evidence.

It is important that you research your area of interest *before* you settle on an argument or thesis. Here are some reasons why.

Good Arguments Contribute to a Current Debate or Controversy

Imagine you are writing about child visitation rights for mothers who are in prison. You'd be unlikely to just sit down and write an article on this topic out of the blue. However, you might write a research article about this topic if it were an issue being debated in scholarly or legal circles. In that situation, you'd have a reason to write your article, and you'd be able to respond to the specific claims others have made about it. For his research paper (Chapter 11), Terrence chose to respond to a scholarly controversy over whether or not children of incarcerated parents should be allowed to visit their parents in prison.

Good Arguments Respond to What Others Have Said

Good arguments contribute to current debates in part by responding to what others have said—by agreeing, disagreeing, extending key points, or making counterarguments. Scholars tend to write articles that contribute to an ongoing research program or "conversation." In Terrence's case, legal scholars have published articles recently about child visitation rights, which means it is a topic of interest to researchers in that field.

Good Arguments Stake Out New Ground

It may seem counter-intuitive, but reading what others have said can actually help you to come up with your own claims and reasons. You'll probably find that you came up with more ideas after reading what others have written. It may seem paradoxical, but by exposing yourself to other opinions and viewpoints, you can often generate more of your own ideas—counter-arguments, extensions, and alternatives to what others have said. Terrence was able to stake out new ground by drawing on psychological studies of child visitation to address legal scholars, who had not yet considered the psychological research.

C. Researching Arguments

Reading up on an issue should help you to find new things to say, to refine your own claims, and to address your argument to a specific rhetorical situation. As you prepare to enter the conversation with your own argument, you should also do two different kinds of research:

- Researching what others have argued about your issue
- Researching the facts and evidence that support your argument about the issue

Researching what others have argued means reading up on what others have written on your topic. To find out about what others have written, you might check out the opinion pieces in newspapers and blogs, find articles about the latest developments, or even look up transcripts of speeches given at rallies or meetings. In the case of a local issue, you might check to see whether your college or town has issued official statements or policies, read editorials in the student newspaper, and perhaps also check out websites and articles beyond your own community to see what is happening elsewhere.

Researching the facts and evidence that support your argument means tracking down the data to support the arguments *that you will eventually make* on your issue, such as information from books, articles, and newspapers. (See Chapter 24 for information about how to locate these kinds of research.) It may be tempting to do this research *after* you've made up your mind about your argument—but doing so might bias your research. (Bias means a particular slant or stance on an issue to color how you interpret the evidence, which can make you less objective.) If you do some preliminary research beforehand, you'll be able to make a more valid claim in the end, one that reflects the evidence uncolored by your personal opinion.

Note that you can use the same process when you are assigned most academic writing projects. Let's see how Terrence approached his writing assignment, a research paper on child visitation rights for incarcerated mothers, once he had conducted his research. (For more on conducting research, refer to Part 4.)

D. Developing a Thesis (or Claim)

Once you have researched your issue, you can begin to determine what type of claim to make. One useful strategy can be to brainstorm many different claims before settling on one.

Using Stasis Questions

You might try an ancient technique called stasis questions to help you sort through the research you have done and to develop a claim. Stasis questions help you to pinpoint the key arguments at stake in any issue. They can also help you to identify the kind of claim you would like to make.

The stasis questions are:

- What is it? (Facts)
- How do we define it? (Definition)
- Is it good or bad? (Evaluation)
- What caused it? (Cause)
- What are its effects? (Consequences)
- What should we do about it? (Proposal)

Let's take up an example. What are some arguments Terrence might have made based on research about the psychological effects of visitations for children of mothers who are in prison? This type of question is likely to result in either a consequence claim or a proposal claim:

Consequence claim: Granting visitation rights to incarcerated mothers would (or would not) improve the lives of their children.

Proposal claim: Prisons should (or should not) grant visitation rights to incarcerated mothers.

You could build an argument around either of those questions. In fact, the consequence claim might turn into a reason to support the main proposal claim.

Working through the stasis questions can help you to identify a range of possibilities. Then, you can figure out which claim you'd like to choose.

Responding to Other Arguments

In addition to the stasis questions, you can also use argument templates, which usually work by responding to or extending what others have said.

For example, while conducting research for his paper, Terrence wrote reading notes (Chapter 7) about an article by a legal scholar:

Terrence's reading notes

Costa discusses how prison is not a healthy environment for children as "it epitomizes all that is unhealthy and dangerous." She asserts that it is unfair for an innocent child to have to attempt to understand that her parent did something "bad" and has to stay at that "very bad place." The constant tension of visiting an incarcerated mother and the emotional trauma of having to say "goodbye" is detrimental to the child's development, Costa argues. "Prison is not an atmosphere appropriate for the growth maturation of our youth. 'Ah what childhood memories these kids will have.'"

Terrence has a few options here. He could agree, disagree, question, or extend Costa's claims in different ways:

- **[agree] I agree that** visitation may be traumatic for some children, **but** I argue that children should be able to visit their parents as long as they do not show signs of trauma or distress.

- **[question] While Costa claims psychological** risks are associated with visitations in prisons, in this paper I question her views, investigating whether or not **psychological research supports her claim that** children may receive significant harm from visiting their parents.

- **[extend] In addition to** the effects on children Costa identifies, I argue that visitation produces negative effects for mothers as well.

- **[disagree] I disagree with** Costa's argument, and argue that research supports visitation rights for imprisoned mothers. For this reason, prisons should enforce regular visitations for children of incarcerated mothers.

You can try this strategy in your own writing: start by identifying some of the claims you've identified in your examination of the case or issue. Then, try out some of the patterns shown in the preceding list.

Making a Claim

Once you have generated some possible claims, take some time to weigh your options before choosing which one to pursue.

Your choice of which claim to pursue might depend on your analysis of the issue. You might consider some of these factors:

- Are people arguing this point, or have they moved on to a different point or claim? Do you want to take the debate in a new direction, or take up an issue already being discussed?
- Which claim does the evidence support best?
- Which claim seems most interesting or novel?
- Which claim will be most persuasive to your audience?

In Terrence's case, a review of psychological studies led him to choose the fourth option from his previous list, staging his argument as a refutation of Costa's claims. Note that the second option might have led to a similar response, only one framed in a slightly less straightforward manner. (The questioning approach may be a good one to use in highly controversial debates, if you want to maintain the good will of the audience before refuting their argument.)

Of course, you can always revise and sharpen your claim as you start writing. Sometimes, you'll find yourself wanting to change your claim once you've written a draft. Revision is a good thing, and it is also nearly inevitable; do not worry too much about finding the perfect argument ahead of time.

E. Finding Good Reasons

Once you have chosen a claim, work on brainstorming reasons to support your claim. Here again, you can draw on your research for ideas (Chapter 24), but once you have gathered research you can use stasis theory to help you organize them.

Using the stasis questions, try to come up with a series of potential reasons, or because-statements, that support your claim. Terrence sat down and came up with the following reasons to support his claim.

Terrence's Reasons

Children should be able to visit their mothers in prison:

- fact—**because** children of incarcerated parents are at higher risk for depression.

- definition—**because** visitation rights are human rights.

- evaluation—**because** the current system is unethical.

- cause/consequence—**because** the current system punishes children, not just their parents, leading to psychological damage.

- proposal—**because** prisons should work to support families.

This is just a starting point, of course. Terrence could generate plenty of different arguments for any of these points, especially as he continued his research.

Once again, try to come up with many more reasons than you will eventually need for your document. To make a strong argument, you should generate many reasons, and then select only the very best ones. As is the case with your main claim, you should consider:

- Which of these reasons will be most persuasive to my audience?
- Which of these reasons can I support with good evidence?
- Which of these reasons seem most, well, reasonable? Which seem far-fetched?

You can always change your reasons around once you begin drafting. As you write, you might come up with new reasons, or find out that some seem less strong than you originally thought.

F. Locating Evidence through Research

When you need to locate evidence through research, you mine published sources for evidence you can use to support your argument. Let's see how Terrence began gathering evidence for his paper. First, he searched for information using his library's website, identifying books and articles on his topic. (For more on finding sources, see Part 4.)

Once he gathered this information and began reading through it, Terrence looked for different kinds of information, including statistics or numerical data, research findings, and testimony by authoritative figures, such as legal scholars or psychologists. All of these forms of evidence could be useful for supporting his claim.

Statistical or numerical data is often used to support public arguments, but it appears in academic writing as well, especially in the sciences and some social sciences. In these fields, it may be called quantitative data. In either case, writers tend to prefer quantitative information taken from reputable sources—often research studies conducted at universities or by government agencies. In some cases, survey results are also used, and these, too, may come from academic research or from some polling centers, such as the Pew Research center or Gallup polls. These are all examples of research findings that might support an argument.

Terrence found one source that showed that over 1.5 million children in the United States have at least one incarcerated parent—a fact he planned to use in his research paper.

Note that research findings can also involve descriptive data, or qualitative data, not just numbers. For instance, you might cite the results of a series of observations, interviews, or the like. Terrence found one study showing that the effects of a parent's incarceration (such as anxiety, depression, and anger) were lessened in the case of children who could regularly visit their mothers.

Another choice is to refer to or quote from an expert of some kind. If you simply refer to the expert, you are drawing on authority. If you quote from an expert, or someone otherwise involved in the issue, you are employing testimony. Terrence carefully noted not only the names of the authors of sources he found, but also their credentials—were they legal scholars? Psychologists? Then, he planned to mention those individuals directly in his paper.

A related form of evidence involves citing information from texts. Textual evidence can include quotations from literary texts, historical documents, legal cases or statutes, philosophical treatises, speeches, and so on. In some academic disciplines, especially the humanities (literature, history, philosophy, etc.), arguments are made by drawing heavily on textual evidence. Other disciplines tend to prefer quantitative evidence, especially the sciences and many social sciences (psychology, sociology, linguistics, etc.). In Terrence's case, textual evidence included material from legal cases related to visitation rights, which he planned to include in his paper.

In other cases, you might provide audiovisual evidence to support your claims: photographs, diagrams, graphs, charts, video or audio clips, and so on. In a scientific article, technical tables and diagrams may support much of the argument. For instance, a neuroscientists' argument for the significance of research findings may rest heavily on images taken from brain scans. In legal arguments, visual evidence might include material objects, such as a bullet casing or a bloody shirt shown at a murder trial. Terrence decided that his genre, a research paper for an undergraduate law journal, did not usually feature visual evidence, but he later adapted his paper into a factsheet, using visual and design elements. (You can see his factsheet in Chapter 29.)

Types of Evidence

- statistics or numerical data
- research findings
- testimony
- textual evidence
- audiovisual evidence: images, video, audio, objects

As always, you'll need to observe how these forms of evidence are used in the genre you plan to write.

G. Rhetorical Appeals: *Ethos, Pathos, and Logos*

While you can always find evidence through research, you can also develop evidence based on your analysis of the case at hand. To do so, you use the rhetorical appeals to *ethos* (credibility), *pathos* (emotion), and *logos* (logic).

Ethos

Ethos refers to the credibility and authority of the writer. *Ethos* can work in two ways: you can possess it, or you can earn it. For example, if you are an expert in your field, say a legal scholar or a scientist, you would possess *ethos* by virtue of your education and experience. Likewise, if a speaker has a reputation for being reasonable, honest, and reliable, he or she has *ethos*.

However, if you do not already possess *ethos*, you can earn it. In academic writing, you can earn *ethos* by doing careful research (Chapter 24), consulting credible sources (Chapter 25), and citing your sources properly (Chapter 28). You can also earn *ethos* by demonstrating that you are reasonable, honest, and reliable.

It is easier to maintain *ethos* if you take a fair position on an issue than if you are arguing a view that might be seen as radical. For example, it would be harder for Terrence to argue that mothers should be acquitted of all but the most violent crimes than to argue that mothers should be allowed monthly visitations with their children. The former argument might seem unreasonable, leading to less *ethos* on the part of the writer.

Pathos

Pathos refers to appeals to the emotions or values of the audience. In some genres, emotional appeals can be overt. In fact, we expect emotional appeals when we hear speeches at a political rally or read opinion columns about controversial issues. If you are writing a speech or op-ed (Chapter 10), you can consider how you'd like your audience to feel when they are listening or reading. You can also think about what values they might share, such as fairness, equality, or freedom.

In academic research genres (Chapter 11), we may expect fewer emotional appeals, but that does not mean you cannot appeal to the values of an audience. In our student example, the audience includes law students and scholars. What are some of the key values for that audience? A legal audience might value justice, fairness, and consistency with legal precedent. Accordingly, the writer might consider how to frame his proposal as just, fair, and consistent with legal precedent.

Logos

Much of the advice in this chapter about locating a claim, reasons, and evidence has to do with *logos*, or logic. In addition, though, rhetorical handbooks include the following logical tools. Let's see how Terrence might think about using these tools for his research paper.

Analogies   Analogies are useful because they help readers to understand a new problem or situation in terms of a more familiar one. Terrence could potentially compare depriving a child of his mother to some other type of deprivation: "Depriving a child from his mother is like depriving a fish of water. Children need their mothers to survive."

Examples   Examples are cases or instances that you use to illustrate a point. In Terrence's case, he could use an example of a particular child who was not able to visit his mother in prison. Or, he might give an example of a particular legal case.

Anecdotes   Another way to provide logical reasoning can be to use an anecdote. An anecdote is an extended example, usually told as a story or real incident. Terrence could tell a story about a time when a child visited his or her mother in prison.

Reason chains   In some cases, you may find it effective to construct a series of reasons that build on each other. We can call a series of reasons a reason chain.
   Here's an example of a reason chain Terrence might use:

- Psychological evidence shows negative effects when a child cannot visit his incarcerated mother.
- Visitation yields positive effects on a child's self-esteem, lowers anxiety, and decreases risk of depression.
- Those positive effects might lead to less delinquency, higher school performance, and lower rates of incarceration among children.

H. Addressing Counter-Arguments

A good argument attempts to anticipate and address opposing claims (or counter-arguments) that readers might have. If you can address the audience's concerns, or make what is called a rebuttal, you head off disagreement and make it more likely for readers to be persuaded.

To identify likely sources of opposition, take a close look at your claim and reasons, and consider how someone might counter those claims or reasons. Or, you can also look at opposing claims that you have seen in your research.

For example, here's how Terrence anticipated counter-arguments for his argument chain:

- Counter-argument: Psychological evidence shows negative effects when a child cannot visit his mother.

  - Rebuttal: Psychological evidence that claims visitations are traumatic.

- Counter-argument: Visitation yields positive effects on self-esteem, anxiety, and depression.

  - Rebuttal: Visitation decreases self-esteem, increases anxiety and depression.

- Counter-argument: Those positive effects might lead to less delinquency, higher school performance, and lower rates of incarceration among children.

  - Rebuttal: Children of imprisoned parents are more likely to go to prison themselves.

Next, Terrence should identify strategies to address those counter-arguments in his paper. Here are a number of strategies you can use to address arguments.

Anticipating:	**Some will argue that** a prison is no place for a child. I hope readers will first consider the facts.
Acknowledging:	**Although** children of imprisoned parents are more likely to go to prison themselves, studies show that children allowed to visit their parents are more likely to break the cycle of violence.
Refuting:	**Some have claimed that** visitations are traumatic for children. **However**, those claims reflect a bias present in our society that is not supported by research.

I. Arguing Ethically: Avoiding Fallacies

As a college writer, you will be expected not just to argue effectively, but to argue ethically. There's a difference. Sometimes, arguments can be very persuasive because they manipulate us to think in a certain way. As a reader and writer, you should be on the lookout for these kinds of manipulative arguments—often called fallacies—in your own writing and in the sources you read.

We have categorized these fallacies according to the three rhetorical appeals: *pathos*, *logos*, and *ethos*. Some fallacies work by manipulating the reader's emotions (*pathos*), others through faulty or misleading reasoning (*logos*), and others through inappropriate appeals to authority or character (*ethos*).

Emotional/Values Manipulation

Appeals to emotions can be considered fallacies when they seem to distract from the main point, seem excessive or overly charged, or when they invoke prejudices. People tend to find appeals to pity, fear, and bigotry especially manipulative.

Here are some fallacies that Terrence might have encountered in his own research (Chapter 24) and writing for his academic research paper (Chapter 11). These fallacies serve to manipulate readers' emotional responses or values:

Tradition: An appeal to tradition argues that something should or should not be done because we have always done it that way. This can be a fallacy because not every tradition is worth upholding. For example, discrimination on the basis of gender or race is a societal tradition that should not be upheld.

> *Example*: We've never allowed children into prisons so we shouldn't start now.

Here, there is no reason why one should uphold the tradition that children have not previously been allowed in prisons simply because it is tradition.

Pity: An appeal to pity inappropriately preys on the reader's emotions to sway them. While not all appeals to emotions are fallacies, they can become fallacies if taken to the extreme.

> *Example*: One child never got to see her father for 10 years. She was so depressed that she ended up committing suicide.

Here, the case taken is an extreme case, ending in suicide rather than, say, disappointment or depression.

Fear: An appeal to fear, like an appeal to pity, inappropriately manipulates readers' emotions.

> *Example*: If we allow children to visit their parents in prison, we will be allowing a new generation of criminals to endanger our society.

Here, the example seeks to sway readers by appealing to their fear of criminals, but this appeal is inappropriate because it assumes (without evidence) that children will become criminals by visiting their parents in prison.

Prejudice: An appeal to prejudice relies on readers' stereotyped assumptions, or readers' pre-existing negative beliefs about a type or group of people.

> *Example*: We should limit visitation rights for incarcerated parents be-
> cause they do not make good role models.

In this case, the assumption is that prisoners are poor role models—a prejudice or stereotype not supported by evidence.

Logical Manipulation

Logical fallacies depend on errors of reasoning. Either the main claim is not supported by the reasons or evidence, or reasons and evidence are taken too far, to an inappropriate or extreme conclusion.

Here are some logical fallacies that Terrence might have encountered in his own research and writing for his paper (Chapter 11). These fallacies rely on readers' failure to locate flaws in logical reasoning:

Slippery Slope: A slippery slope argument works by assuming that an initial step (which may be true) leads to a chain of events that is not necessarily true, or is not substantiated by evidence.

> *Example*: Allowing children to visit their parents in prison would lead to
> greater self-esteem, which would lead to decreased crime rates,
> which would ultimately break the cycle of violence in American
> society.
>
> *Example*: Allowing children to visit their parents in prison would lead to
> exposure to the prison lifestyle, which would lead to increased
> crime rates, which would ultimately lead to an epidemic of vio-
> lence in American society.

Here, while the first steps may be true, it is not necessarily the case that the latter chains of events will take place. One cannot take these chains of events as valid reasons to support (or not support) parental visitations in prison.

False Analogy: A false analogy occurs when an inappropriate or unsuitable analogy is given as a reason to support a claim.

> *Example*: Depriving a child of his mother is like depriving a fish of water.

Here, the analogy is false because a fish will literally die without water, while a child will not necessarily die without his mother.

Hasty Generalization: A hasty generalization occurs when a specific fact or reason is used to support a much broader, more general claim.

> *Example*:   An attempt at establishing regular visitations for children of imprisoned mothers failed. So, visitations do not work.

In this case, the conclusion "visitations do not work" is a fallacy because one example is taken as a sufficient reason to support a broad, general claim. The fact that one such program did not work does not necessarily mean that no visitation programs will work.

False Cause: A false cause fallacy occurs when a reason or fact is inappropriately assumed to be the cause of a given outcome. Usually, this involves mistaking a correlation (the co-existence of two things) with the assumption that one thing causes another.

> *Example*:   Crime rates have actually gone down in areas where visitations are not allowed. Thus, visitations increase crime rates.

Here, we have a false cause fallacy because the claim ("visitations increase crime rates") is not necessarily supported by the facts. While crime rates may have gone down in those areas without visitation programs, there is no evidence to show that disallowing visitation programs caused the decrease in crime.

Straw Man: A straw man argument distorts the opponent's position, and then refutes that position.

> *Example*:   Those who support visitation rights for parents in prison want to turn the prison system into a joke, where there is no accountability for illegal actions. That would be like living in a third world country. So, we shouldn't allow prison visits for children.

Here, the argument is a straw man because opponents of child visitation programs do not really "want to turn the prison system into a joke." This is a fallacy because it does not appropriately present the opposite argument.

Ignorance: An argument from ignorance assumes that lack of information or evidence about something justifies a claim.

> *Example*:   There is no evidence that allowing visitations is effective, so they should not be allowed.

In this case, the argument is a fallacy because it assumes that a lack of study on child visitations necessarily means they should not be implemented.

Red Herring: A red herring argument works by distracting readers by introducing a separate topic or claim into a debate.

> *Example*:   Parents who are in prison are obviously criminals. So, we should not allow them to see their children.

Here, the writer assumes that it is easier to persuade readers that prisoners are criminals, and criminals are bad, distracting them from the real issue of whether those parents have a right to see their children.

Circular Reasoning or Begging the Question: Circular reasoning (also called begging the question) happens when the main claim and reasons in an argument are essentially saying the same thing.

> *Example*:   Allowing visitations for children will make them happier. Thus, depression will be reduced if children can spend time with their parents.

Here, the claim or conclusion ("depression will be reduced . . .") is basically the same as the reason offered, "Allowing visitations for children will make them happier."

False Dichotomy: A false dichotomy occurs when readers are given a choice between only two options, when more options exist.

> *Example*:   Either we allow visitation rights for children of incarcerated parents, or we prepare to pay for an epidemic of delinquency.

In this example, readers are unfairly presented two options (visitation rights or "an epidemic of delinquency"), when more possibilities exist.

Ethical Manipulations

Ethical manipulations or fallacies involve inappropriate appeals to character and authority. They can be considered fallacies when they distract from the issue at hand, when they assume that what has always been done or thought must be correct, or when they unfairly malign individuals and groups.

Here are some logical fallacies that Terrence might have encountered in his own research and writing for his paper (Chapter 11):

Character Appeal or Ad Hominem Attack: A character appeal casts an individual or group in an inappropriately negative light, instead of addressing the issue at hand.

> *Example*:   Those who argue for visitation rights are usually children of imprisoned parents. These children have clearly been raised by criminals and have a vested interest in the issue. So, we should not listen to them.

In this case, proponents of visitation rights are unfairly maligned, and their credibility called into question.

Appeal to Authority: An appeal to authority occurs when something is taken to be true just because an authoritative person says it is so—especially if that person has no special knowledge or expertise of the issue.

Example: We should allow visitation rights in prison because Oprah Winfrey has said it is a good idea, and she is one of the most respected people in the world.

Here, the appeal to authority is a fallacy because Oprah Winfrey does not necessarily have special insight into child psychology, the law, or criminal justice.

Note that in academic writing, appeals to authority are commonly used, and are not necessarily fallacies. When you cite the claims of an established scholar in a field, who is speaking about a topic she has researched, then you can accept her claim as true—especially if other authorities agree.

Bandwagon Appeal: A bandwagon appeal is used when the actions of an admired or prestigious individual or group is used to justify a course of action for a different individual or group.

Example: Other industrialized nations allow visitation for children of imprisoned parents. It is becoming a widespread trend. So, the United States should implement it.

In this case, the example of "other industrialized nations" adopting visitation programs does not necessarily support the claim that the United States should follow suit. There may be important differences between the United States and these other countries that do not factor into this argument.

However, note that this type of appeal can be effective and appropriate in some cases. For example, colleges and universities regularly adopt programs and standards used at what they consider "peer institutions," other colleges and universities like them, if the evidence shows that such programs have been effective elsewhere.

J. Argument Troubleshooting

I Can't Find a Thesis or Claim

You can either try some brainstorming strategies (Chapter 16) or do some more reading. In the first case, you might try freewriting, concept mapping, stasis questions, or even just taking a walk to get your gears moving. In the second case, try reading some more arguments or research on your topic. You might find a jumping off point—a claim you want to counter, extend, or qualify.

I'm Not Sure How to Organize My Argument

Think about arranging your claims and reasons based on what you think will be most effective for your audience:

- Will your audience be pre-disposed against your claim? If so, you might need to address their objections first, before moving on to your own arguments.

- Will your audience be pre-disposed against you? If so, you might need to spend some time cultivating your *ethos* first. How can you show them you are a reliable person to write about this issue?
- Will your audience be confused about the issue? If so, you might need to address their misconceptions or confusion first, and then put forward your own claims.
- Will your audience lack information (key terms, definitions, knowledge) about this issue? In this case, you might want to start by giving them the background knowledge they'll need to understand your argument.
- Is your audience already predisposed to support your claim—but needs extra encouragement to act? In this case, you might summarize the issue briefly, but then move on to providing the extra impetus the audience needs to take action—perhaps in the form of emotional appeals, or *pathos*.

I Can't Find Any Evidence

You may need to look harder, in different places. Turn to Chapter 24 for more help finding research. Remember that your campus librarians are good resources for research questions. You can also ask your writing group or your instructor for help.

If you have searched for evidence to support your claim and still can't find any, that may mean that you need to revise your claim. Say you want to argue that unhealthy food causes college students to gain significant amounts of weight. However, research studies show that students, on average, only gain a few pounds during college. In order to argue fairly, you will have to adjust your claim. Perhaps you can argue that unhealthy food leads to inattention, sleepiness, or some other kind of problem—but you will need to see if the research supports it. You may end up arguing the opposite side of the case!

Using Rhetorical Modes

Writers use certain strategies, or modes, for different kinds of writing. These modes tend to work at the level of the paragraph or section, and certain modes tend to be used in certain genres.

As you are drafting a document, rhetorical modes can help you develop your ideas. Try using rhetorical modes as a form of invention—a way to come up with things to say or a way of framing your ideas. You can use Table 19.1 to help you consider how each mode might help you generate ideas based on your analysis of your audience, purpose, and genre.

Let's see how Terrence used rhetorical modes as he revised the first draft of his essay.

A. What Happened? Narration

Narration involves recounting events that have happened in the past, often using lively, descriptive language. You might use a narrative to provide support for a key point, usually by drawing on your personal experience or on experiences of others.

In his original draft, Terrence briefly related events from his own childhood in order to support his point that visiting a prison is not necessarily traumatic for a child.

Terrence's Narration

As an individual who spent a large portion of my childhood visiting my incarcerated fa-

ther, I could not agree more with Stewart. Although I understand that everyone has his or

her own unique experiences, I always looked forward to these visits rather than having any

feeling of anguish or anxiety.

In his peer workshop, one of Terrence's group members suggested that he elaborate on this point using narration to provide a detailed account of an event that he

Table 19.1 Modes and Their Uses

	A. Narration	**B. Description**	**C. Definition**
Audience (Who Reads It?)	Would my audience find my document more interesting if I included a story? Would it help them to identify with me or the topic?	Does my audience need details in order to picture an event, person, place, or thing?	Does my audience already know this term? Do they need a definition? How detailed of a definition? Do they need a more specialized definition, or a more general one?
Purpose (What Is It For?)	Would a narrative help to support one of my points or claims?	Would detailed descriptions help me to get my point across?	Does the audience need to understand a term in order to understand my point?
Genre (What Is It?)	Are narratives usually included in this genre?	Does this genre usually feature detailed, descriptive language? What kinds of descriptions are appropriate for this genre?	What kinds of definitions are usually given in this genre? Should I provide a more specialized definition (i.e., for a research article or grant proposal)? Should I provide a more general definition (i.e., for a profile essay or news report)?

experienced personally. Terrence liked the idea and used narrative as an invention strategy to see if it would strengthen his essay.

Terrence's Revised Narration

When I was six years old, I visited my father for the first time. As my mom and I pulled

up to the building, my heart was pounding in my throat, but it wasn't from fear—my

heart pounded in anticipation. I couldn't wait to see my dad again—to gaze into his eyes

D. Classification	E. Compare/Contrast	F. Cause/Effect
Does my audience need to know these types of things, and how they differ?	Can I help my audience understand something by comparing it to something else that they are already familiar with?	Does my audience need to know the causes or effects of a phenomenon? Do they agree about these causes/effects, or do I need to prove it to them?
Do I need to explain these types of things to make my point?	Does my audience need a comparison in order to understand my claim?	Does describing causes or effects support my main claim or thesis?
Do classifications usually appear in this genre?	Do comparisons usually appear in this genre?	Do cause or effect elements typically appear in this genre?

and hear his chuckle. When the prison gate opened, I walked into the room and into my dad's arms. That night, I fell asleep thinking about my dad, and I could hardly wait for our next visit. Visiting my dad did not have negative effects for me—instead, it was a positive experience.

Terrence's narrative includes a chain of events—arriving at the prison, meeting his dad, and then coming back home—and ends with a short summary of what the narrative means.

You might see this type of narration in genres that appear in magazines or newspaper writing, such as a profile article (Chapter 5).

Narration can also appear in other genres where you might recount something that happened. You might consider the methods section of a research article (Chapter 11) or report (Chapter 14) to be a sort of narration, or the observation notes from a field study (Chapter 7). These narratives might be told in more formal language, but they are still narratives because they recount an event and have a beginning, middle, and end.

B. What Is It Like? Description

Description involves portraying people, places, and things in concrete language. Your goal is to get readers to picture these items, to feel that they are in on the action. Using description can make your writing more lively and interesting for readers. Terrence decided to revise his narrative to include more description.

Terrence's Description

When I was six years old, I visited my father for the first time. As my mom and I pulled up to the gray, cement block of a building, my heart was pounding in my throat, but it wasn't from fear—my heart pounded in anticipation. I couldn't wait to see my dad again—to gaze into his deep brown eyes and hear his hearty chuckle. When the prison gate clanked opened, I practically skipped walked into the room, ignoring the fetid smell of cigarettes, urine and bleach. That night, I fell asleep thinking about my dad, the warm touch of his hand on my shoulder, the taste of the warm orange drink we shared. Clearly, visiting my dad did not have negative effects for me—instead, it was a positive experience.

By adding sensory details (highlighted), Terrence has made it much easier for readers to picture the scene. We can now imagine what it must have been like for Terrence to visit his father.

Here are some sensory details you can add:

- Sights
- Sounds
- Smells
- Touch
- Taste

You can see that Terrence tried out a different writing style here. He used more adjectives (his dad's "deep brown" eyes and "hearty" chuckle) as opposed to the more objective language in most of his essay.

Terrence also used onomatopoeia, or a word that sounds like the thing being described, when he wrote that the prison door "clanked" open.

Descriptions tend to occur in narrative genres, such as personal essays (Chapter 4), profile articles (Chapter 5), and the like, but they might also appear in an op-ed (Chapter 10), and even in some academic research (Chapter 11). For example, an anthropologist might write a detailed description of a person she encountered while conducting research in Nepal, while a paleontologist might write a detailed description of a fossil.

C. What Is It? Definition

Definition can be useful whenever you use a term that your audience might not already understand, or when you are using a general term in a specific way. You should decide whether to define terms—and in how much detail—based on your audience, purpose, and genre.

Terrence's audience included students interested in political science, law, and public policy. Terrence thought these readers may not have familiarity with the legal term "best interest of the child standard," so he needed to provide a definition in his paper.

Dictionary Definition

The most common way of defining a term is to look it up in a dictionary, and then quote that definition.

Chances are "best interests of the child standard" will not appear in a standard college dictionary. Terrence consulted a specialized legal source to find a written definition, but its language was too complex for his purposes. Instead, he decided to use a definition on a government website intended for a more general audience. Here's the definition of the standard that he found through his research:

Terrence's Dictionary Definition

"[T]he deliberation that courts undertake when deciding what type of services, actions, and orders will best serve a child as well as who is best suited to take care of a child" (http://www.childwelfare.gov/systemwide/laws_policies/statutes/best_interest.cfm)

To find a specialized dictionary for your topic or field, consult your library website or a reference librarian.

Functional Definition

Terrence used a functional definition, defining the "best interests of the child standard" according to what it does or what it is used for.

Terrence's Functional Definition

Another legal factor that prevents child visitation for incarcerated mothers is the "best interest of the child standard," the test used in most jurisdictions when deciding on issues of visitation and custody (Lewis, 2004). This test allows visitation to be determined solely by the opinion of the court.

A functional definition is useful when readers will be more concerned with what something *does* than what it *is*. In this case, readers did not need a lengthy discussion of the legal concept, because Terrence's purpose was to show how the statute was used in this specific instance, not what it is in general.

Negative Definition

A negative definition defines something in terms of what it is *not*. A negative definition of "the best interests of the child standard" would note that it is not a federal mandate, but a state-by-state standard. This may be important for readers to know, and it would help them to better understand what it is.

Synonyms

In some cases, you can provide a short, quick definition by providing a synonym. If there is another term commonly used for the term you seek to define, you can provide that term as well. For instance, Terrence considered defining the term "detriment," using the synonyms "harm" or "damage." You can find synonyms in a thesaurus.

E. How Is It Similar/Different? Comparison/Contrast

447

Example

Sometimes, the best way to help readers to understand a term is to give an example. To define "best interests," Terrence gave an example of a case where the doctrine might be used.

Terrence's Example

> For instance, a court might rule that a child should live with his adoptive parents, not his biological parents, based on the logic that the adoptive parents provided a more stable home environment. That decision would rest on the doctrine of "best interests."

Definitions occur in almost every genre, but the type of definition given can vary. In a biology textbook, for example, you are likely to read dictionary or functional definitions, since the goal is to provide students with in-depth understanding of biological terms and concepts. In an informative newspaper article (Chapter 6) about the same concept, though, you might find a synonym or an example, since readers do not need to have a detailed understanding, just a working knowledge of the concept.

D. What Kind Is It? Classification

Classification involves placing something in a category, or sorting categories into various subcategories. For instance, Terrence might classify "best interests of the child" as a type of legal standard.

Classification often appears in textbooks, for example, where students need to learn about different types of things, such as the parts of speech in a language course, or the cultures of Nigeria in an African studies course.

E. How Is It Similar/Different? Comparison/Contrast

Use comparison or contrast to explain how two or more things are similar or different. Comparison and contrast can help you to pin down the meaning and importance of something—an event, idea, person, or thing.

In Terrence's essay, he contrasted how legal scholars view child visitation in prisons with how psychology scholars view it. In fact, he decided to organize his paper roughly by outlining, first, how legal scholars view the issue, and second, how psychology scholars offer contrasting evidence.

The comparison/contrast mode appears in a wide variety of genres. For example, in a profile (Chapter 5) of a politician, a writer might contrast the politician with another politician who holds different views.

F. What Causes It? What Are Its Effects? Cause/Effect

The mode of cause and effect involves explaining either what factors lead to a particular event or outcome (cause) or what factors result from a particular event or outcome (effects). Your analysis of your audience, purpose, and genre can help you to decide whether and when to use the cause and effect modes.

In Terrence's case, cause and effect were very important to his main claim—that children should be able to visit their parents in prison. Much of his argument has to do with the effects of these visitations on children and their mothers. While some scholars claim the effects are primarily negative, Terrence claims that there can be many positive effects if children can visit their parents in prison. Much of Terrence's essay is devoted to explaining the *effects* of visitation.

Terrence's Cause/Effect

Increased visitation will help the reunification process between mother and child. During the stressful and seemingly never-ending process of regaining custody of one's child, visitation can help motivate the incarcerated mother and encourage her not to give up her battle.

However, Terrence also devoted some attention to the *causes* of current attitudes toward visitation when he says that "Costa exemplifies the blanket bias that is present in our society, which in turn is reflected in the laws." Here, Terrence argued that a bias against incarcerated person *causes* or brings about laws against visitation for children of imprisoned parents.

A variety of genres use the mode of cause and effect. For example, in a political speech (Chapter 10), a candidate might argue that certain negative effects in society are caused by the political actions of her opponents.

Organization

Organization refers to the order in which you present the contents of a document. Different genres tend to use different types of organization. In other words, they order information in different ways.

A. Discovering Organization through Genre

The best way to determine how to organize a document that you need to write is to discover the genre itself. Often, particular genres have particular organization strategies that writers tend to follow. For example, a recommendation report tends to include a fairly standard set of sections, including an executive summary, introduction, methods, sections based on criteria or sub-topics, conclusion, and recommendation (Chapter 14).

A research paper (Chapter 11) may also have a fairly standard organization scheme, although the way the paper is organized varies by discipline. The first thing you should do is ask your teacher about the organization and structure that your teacher expects you to follow.

You can also discover how professionals write research papers in your field. If you are writing a research paper in the sciences, you should read articles in scientific journals to discover the organizational strategies that science writers employ. If you are writing in political science, then you should read political science journals. The point is, the more you study the type of document that you need to write, the easier it will be to organize that document.

In some cases, though, a genre may be more flexible in its organization, which means you can develop your own set of sections. For instance, an application to graduate school may simply require a "personal statement." Based on your study of samples and the rhetorical situation, you could develop your own organization scheme for a personal statement.

B. Outlining before Writing

Once you have studied the genre you will be writing, you can use a variety of organization strategies to help you get your thoughts in order. Outlines, flowcharts, and digital tools such as mindmaps provide ways to organize your ideas. As we study these organization strategies, we will use a political science research paper as our example.

An outline is a text-based list of the ideas that you will include in your research paper.

Let's examine Terrence's outline for the body section of his paper, "Being Mommy Behind Bars: The Psychological Benefits of Child Visitation with Incarcerated Mothers" (Chapter 28).

Terrence starts his outline by providing his thesis (Chapter 18). When using any organization strategy listed here, you will find it useful to put your topic or thesis at the top of the page (or screen) to help keep yourself on track. Here is Terrence's thesis:

Terrence's Thesis

Thesis: Child visitation for incarcerated mothers has positive psychological effects on both child and mother. The legal field has been narrow-minded in its policies toward incarcerated parents, and according to psychological research visitation should change to increase the amount of time mother and child spend together.

Terrence then listed the reasons that support his thesis, each of them numbered.

Terrence's Reasons

Thesis: Child visitation for incarcerated mothers has positive psychological effects on both child and mother. The legal field has been narrow-minded in its policies toward incarcerated parents, and according to psychological research visitation should change to increase the amount of time mother and child spend together.

Reason 1. Some of the barriers to visitation are difficult to overcome.

Reason 2. More attention needs to be paid to the psychological effects of maternal incarceration and child visitation.

Reason 3. Children visiting their incarcerated mothers is beneficial.

Then, he listed supporting evidence for each of these main arguments, such as these for Reason 1.

Terrence's Supporting Evidence

Reason 1. Some of the barriers to visitation are difficult to overcome.

1-A. Incarcerated parents often long most to maintain or mend their relationship with their children. Even if the family wants to participate in visitation, the process is not easy.

Evidence

Lewis, P. (2004). "Behind the glass wall: Barriers that incarcerated parents face regarding the care, custody and control of their children." *Journal of the American Academy of Matrimonial Lawyers, 19*, 97–116.

Lewis explains that visitation by children should be a fundamental right for incarcerated parents. Some legal factors preventing visitation are the fact that many incarcerated parents are unaware that they have a right to a hearing before their visitation can be denied; limited access to legal service for domestic issues; and the "best interest standard" of the child that is usually upheld on an argument without extensive analysis. Prison administrations prevent visitation so long as they are "rationally related to a legitimate penological interest."

He numbers these supporting reasons (such as "1-A") to indicate that they support Reason 1. Next, Terrence could begin drafting his paper based on this outline.

In the next section, we will see how Terrence uses his outline to strengthen his reasons and his research.

C. Using Outlines as You Write

Not everyone likes to start with an outline. Many people prefer to start drafting first, and use an outline later. There are many points in the writing process at which outlining can help you. For example, you should begin organizing your thoughts—in writing—long before you actually are finished with all of your research. Your research will stay better organized if you do.

Writing and organizing are complementary processes—you can work on them at the same time. Outlines keep your ideas organized, which can help you strengthen your writing. Here are some ways that outlines can make your paper better as you go along.

To Find Holes in Your Research

If you use an outline as you write, you might find that some sections of your paper are weaker than others. If you find you do not have enough to say about some of your reasons, it might be because you need more evidence. This is a sign that you need to go back to your research, either reading your existing sources more carefully, or looking for more sources.

To Find Weak Arguments

You can also use your outline to find weak arguments. In his outline, Terrence not only listed the arguments that supported his position, but also the arguments that went against his position: the counter-arguments (Chapter 18). After he provided a counter-argument, however, he also provided a rebuttal, or a counter-counter-argument (along with support from evidence). Here is an excerpt from a later part of Terrence's outline that demonstrates how to outline counter-arguments and rebuttals, along with their evidence.

Terrence's Counter-Arguments and Rebuttals

2-B. Counter-Argument

Many believe that visiting an inmate is detrimental to the child.

Evidence

Costa, R. D (2003). "Now I lay me down to sleep: A look at overnight visitation rights available to incarcerated mothers." *New England Journal on Criminal & Civil Confinement, 29,* 67–97.

Costa discusses how prison is not a healthy environment for children: "it epitomizes all that is unhealthy and dangerous." She argues that it is unfair for an innocent child to have to attempt to understand that their parent did something "bad" and has to stay at that "very bad place." The constant tension of visiting an incarcerated mother and the emotional trauma of having to say "goodbye" is detrimental to the child's development. "Prison is not an atmosphere appropriate for the growth maturation of our youth. 'Ah what childhood memories these kids will have.'"

2-C. Rebuttal

Costa exemplifies the blanket bias that is present in our society, which in turn is reflected in the laws. These facts are simply not supported by research. More attention must be paid to psychological studies, because these studies take a less biased stance on incarceration than do other fields of research.

Evidence

Stewart, B. G (2002). "When should a court order visitation between a child and an incarcerated parent?" *University of Chicago Law School Roundtable* 9, 165–178.

Stewart argues that more psychological research needs to be done to continue assessing the effects of child visitation to their incarcerated mothers. In addition, he concludes that: (1) there is no reason to believe that visitation in prison is more harmful to children than other types of visitation with a non-custodial parent and (2) there is no evidence that mere exposure to the prison environment leads to long term harm in children.

To Revise a Draft

You may also use an outline to help you revise a draft. If you have written a draft (Chapter 17) but find that your ideas seem confusing, you might try reverse outlining. In a reverse outline, you write down the topic or purpose for each section you have written. Then, you can look over your outline and see if it makes sense. A reverse outline can help you to decide how to shift things around in your draft for a clearer organization.

To Narrow or Broaden Your Topic

Outlines can also help you see where you need to narrow or broaden your topic. Once you write a detailed outline like the one Terrence has written here, you can see if you have too many or too few reasons. If you have too many reasons, you may need to edit them down to choose the strongest ones (Chapter 18). If you don't have enough reasons, you probably need to do more research (Chapter 24).

Here is a long excerpt from Terrence's finished outline. Examine how all of the parts fit together.

Terrence's Outline

Thesis: Child visitation for incarcerated mothers has positive psychological effects on both child and mother. The legal field has been narrow-minded in its policies toward incarcerated parents, and according to psychological research visitation should change to increase the amount of time mother and child spend together.

1. Some of the barriers to visitation are difficult to overcome.

1-A. Incarcerated parents often long most to maintain or mend their relationship with their children. Even if the family wants to participate in visitation, the process is not easy.

1-B. Courts have agreed that visitation is a right that incarcerated individuals should have. However there are numerous legal barriers and prison regulations that prevent visitation from occurring as much as it is needed.

Evidence

Lewis, P. (2004). "Behind the glass wall: Barriers that incarcerated parents face regarding the care, custody and control of their children." *Journal of the American Academy of Matrimonial Lawyers, 19*, 97–116.

Lewis explains that visitation by children should be a fundamental right for incarcerated parents. Some legal factors preventing visitation are the fact that many incarcerated parents are unaware that they have a right to a hearing before their visitation can be denied; limited access to legal service for domestic issues; and the "best interest standard" of the child that is usually upheld on an argument without extensive analysis. Prison administrations prevent visitation so long as they are "rationally related to a legitimate penological interest."

2. More attention needs to be paid to the psychological effects of maternal incarceration and child visitation.

2-A. Far too often the legal community places emphasis only on the legal factors of a particular case, law, statute, or even their interpretation of the Constitution.

2-B. When it comes to the visitation rights of incarcerated parents, especially mothers, there has been a cold stance taken that avoids the true needs of the parent's rehabilitation and the child's development.

2-B Counter-Argument

Many believe that visiting an inmate is detrimental to the child.

Evidence

Costa, R. D (2003). "Now I lay me down to sleep: A look at overnight visitation rights available to incarcerated mothers." *New England Journal on Criminal & Civil Confinement, 29*, 67–97.

Costa discusses how prison is not a healthy environment for children: "it epitomizes all that is unhealthy and dangerous." She argues that it is unfair for an innocent child to have to attempt to understand that their parent did something "bad" and has to stay at that "very bad place." The constant tension of visiting an incarcerated mother and the emotional trauma of having to say "goodbye" is detrimental to the child's development. "Prison is not an atmosphere appropriate for the growth maturation of our youth. 'Ah what childhood memories these kids will have.' "

2-C. Rebuttal

Costa exemplifies the blanket bias that is present in our society, which in turn is reflected in the laws. These facts are simply not supported by research. More attention must be paid to psychological studies, because these studies take a less biased stance on incarceration than do other fields of research.

Evidence

Stewart, B. G (2002). "When should a court order visitation between a child and an incarcerated parent?" *University of Chicago Law School Roundtable* 9, 165–178.

Stewart argues that more psychological research needs to be done to continue assessing the effects of child visitation to their incarcerated mothers. In addition, he concludes that: (1) there is no reason to believe that visitation in prison is more harmful to children than other types of visitation with a non-custodial parent and (2) there is no evidence that mere exposure to the prison environment leads to long term harm in children.

3. Children visiting their incarcerated mothers is beneficial to the child.

When a child is withheld from visiting their mother negative side effects occur. However, when visitation is allowed there are numerous positive implications.

Evidence

Snyder, Z. K (2001). "Parenting from prison: An examination of children's visitation program at a women's correctional facility." *Marriage & Family Review, 32*, 33–61.

Snyder's research finds that when a parent is incarcerated the child has an increased risk to suffer from anxiety, depression, sleeplessness, anger, and attention deficiencies. Her research goes on to show that children's visitation programs and parenting classes can im-

prove the relationship between incarcerated mothers and their children.

   3-B. Long-term effects of having an incarcerated parent can ensue. However if visitation

is allowed, then the problem may be prevented earlier and the child's future will be more

promising as a result.

   Once he had prepared this outline, Terrence was ready to put his organized ideas into paragraphs.

D. Paragraphing

Paragraphs are the framework of many different written genres, including the research paper. In many written genres, writing strong paragraphs is essential for strong organization. For example, when writing a cover letter for a job application (Chapter 12), ensuring that each paragraph accomplishes a specific goal (describing your purpose in writing, describing why you are a good fit for the position, etc.) is essential to meeting your reader's needs.

   Paragraphs in a research paper must accomplish many tasks, and so they can be difficult to write. We have broken this difficult task down into four steps.

   First, read this sample paragraph from Terrence's paper, built upon the arguments discussed previously.

Terrence's Paragraph

   Costa exemplifies the blanket bias that is present in our society, which in turn is reflected

in the laws; however, the "facts" Costa describes are simply not supported by research.

More attention must be given to psychological research, which takes a less biased stance

on incarceration. Benjamin Stewart (2002), a legal scholar, argues that more psychologi-

cal research needs to be done to continue assessing the positive effects on development of

child visitation with incarcerated mothers. In his analysis of several studies and programs, including Project H.I.P. ("Helping Incarcerated Parents"), Stewart concludes that: (1) there is no reason to believe that visitation in prison is more harmful to children than other types of visitation with a non-custodial parent and (2) there is no evidence that mere exposure to the prison environment leads to long-term harm in children. As an individual who spent a large portion of my childhood visiting my incarcerated father, I could not agree more with Stewart. Although I understand that everyone has his or her own unique experiences, I always looked forward to these visits rather than having any feeling of anguish or anxiety. If more research is conducted, maybe it would be discovered that I was indeed the norm, and not the exception. Following Stewart's suggestion, I will next move on to the psychological outcomes of child visitation or denial thereof.

Step 1. Use a Strong Topic Sentence

Terrence's paragraph has a strong topic sentence: "Costa exemplifies the blanket bias that is present in our society, which in turn is reflected in the laws; however, the 'facts' Costa describes are simply not supported by research."

This topic sentence tells us what the paragraph will be about: debunking bias against child visitation of incarcerated parents.

A strong topic sentence tells your reader what the paragraph is about, but it also anchors the paragraph in the context of your paper. In this case, the topic sentence refers back to the previous paragraph, which outlined Costa's viewpoints in detail.

Step 2. Support Your Point with Evidence

Once you have a strong topic sentence, you can move on to the argument that the paragraph intends to make. Provide your supporting argument, and then provide the evidence that supports your argument.

In this sample paragraph, Terrence provides two types of evidence: evidence from a respected researcher, a legal scholar named Benjamin Stewart, and evidence from his own life experience as a child with an incarcerated parent. Both types of evidence work to rebut Costa's argument.

Step 3. Explain the Evidence

Once you have provided the evidence that supports your point, you need to explain how the evidence works. You can't expect your readers to make all of the connections between your arguments and your evidence on their own. You have to draw those connections.

Notice that Terrence interprets or explains the evidence. He does not expect it to stand on its own, but helps readers to understand why it is important or relevant to his argument.

Step 4. Transition to the Next Paragraph

Transitions are words, phrases, or sentences that connect one part of a document to another part of a document. Transitions in a paragraph usually occur at the end to help a paragraph dovetail with the paragraph that follows. (Transitions can also be used at the beginning of a paragraph [or section] to dovetail with what came before.)

At the end of his paragraph, Terrence makes a smooth transition into the next paragraph by using a transition sentence. The transition sentence clues in the reader that the writer is about to shift topics. "Following Stewart's suggestion, I will next move on to the psychological outcomes of child visitation or denial thereof."

Common Transition Words and Phrases

In addition	Additionally	Furthermore
Alternatively	On the contrary	Rarely
In general	Generally	Usually
As a result	Consequently	In conclusion

E. Ordering Sections or Topics

For his paper, Terrence came up with an outline, or order of ideas, that was based on the logic of his argument. Each section built on the previous one to lead the reader to support his thesis. We call this type of organization logical organization.

However, there are other kinds of organization you might try, depending on your genre and purpose. Be sure to pay close attention to the kinds of organizations used in examples of your genre.

- General to specific
- Simple to complex
- Chronological

- Methodological (organized around different research methods)
- Conceptual (organized around theories or concepts)
- Problem-solution
- Compare/contrast—organize around key points of similarity or difference
- From strongest to weakest point (or weakest to strongest)
- From most to least interesting
- From least to most interesting (climactic organization)
- Put the weakest (or the bad news) in the middle
- From good news to bad news (or positive to negative)

When selecting one of these organizational structures, remember the genre toolkit questions, and use them to guide your choice: What is it? Who reads it? What's it for?

For example, a newspaper article leads with the most interesting information and progresses to the least interesting. Newspaper editors and writers know that most people aren't patient enough to read the entire article.

F. Introductions

Many genres require some form of introductory text. For example, business letters and emails require greetings (Chapter 12). Journalistic genres, such as news articles (Chapter 6) or op-eds (Chapter 10), require catchy first sentences, called "ledes." These introductory texts often serve the purpose of catching a reader's attention and clearly stating the writer's purpose.

When writing a research paper, introductory paragraphs are arguably the most important paragraphs that you write. Many readers decide whether to finish reading a research paper simply on the basis of the introduction. You want to catch your reader's interest, and earn your reader's respect, by writing a strong introduction.

Introductions to research papers typically start with an opening statement to establish why a topic is important. This statement can be an anecdote, a striking observation, a quotation, a statistic, or a statement of how the topic is of current research interest. Your opening statement announces your topic and its importance. It should rarely be gimmicky, unless that's what your genre calls for.

Terrence's Introduction

Terrence follows up this dramatic opening statement, supported by a statistic that also explains the importance of his topic.

Today in America millions of children are being torn away from their mothers, and it is

perfectly legal. Over 1.5 million children in the United States have at least one incarcerated

parent, and our legal system is prohibiting these children from being able to have visitation with their incarcerated parents, specifically mothers. Many argue that children should in no way be exposed to prison, and that any visitation of an incarcerated parent is both emotionally unhealthy and detrimental to a child. It is true; prison is a cold and awful life situation for anyone to experience. But, regardless of what incarcerated parents may have done, they still have children who depend on them. The law has ignored this fact, stating that the courts have the ability to deny visitation if they find it would be detrimental to the child. But what factors exactly determine detriment? Often, the factors used to prove detriment are not based on any actual evidence; the stigma surrounding incarceration is all that is needed to establish "detriment." The field of psychology has taken a different perspective on incarceration than that taken by the legal system. Psychological experts understand that withholding a child from her mother is often more detrimental than exposing her to the world of prison. By denying visitation, the legal field has simply been narrow-minded in its policies and perspectives on incarcerated parents. This dichotomy between the psychological and legal fields is what inspired my research. In this paper, I argue that child visitation with an incarcerated mother has positive psychological effects on both the child and the mother. First, I will examine the current barriers for incarcerated mothers to gain visitation of their children. Second, I will analyze how child visitation of incarcerated mothers affects the development of the child, parental strain, and the mother-child relationship. Lastly, I will discuss the future implications on society of the increased child visitation for incarcerated mothers and the children themselves.

Terrence points to both the popular and the scholarly conversations that he hopes to join with his paper.

Readers now have a sense that Terrence is going to respond to these critics, and indeed he does in the sentence that follows.

After establishing his area of research, Terrence provides his thesis (look for the word "argue").

He then turns to his own angle that he will use in this research paper, the "field of psychology."

After providing his thesis, Terrence describes the methods he will use to prove his thesis.

In a later chapter, you can read Terrence's paper in full (Chapter 28). These rhetorical moves—opening statement, conversation, thesis, methods, and forecast—are the core moves for the introduction in many research papers in many different fields.

However, before you write your introduction, you should read the introductions of a few samples of your genre to get the feel for how introductions work in that genre.

G. Conclusions

Conclusions are notoriously difficult to write. For a research paper, writers typically begin by summarizing the main findings. However, a good conclusion does more than just restate what you have already written.

You can go beyond summary to tell your reader the implications of your research: what does your research *mean*? Ask yourself, "Now what?"

In Terrence's conclusion paragraph, he describes how "Our Children's Place" (a program that allows young children to live with their incarcerated mothers if the mothers' offenses are non-violent) offers one possible solution to the problems he has discussed in the body of his paper.

Terrence's Conclusion

Our Children's Place shows great promise and has had nothing but great results. It is these types of ground-breaking initiatives that have really been able to grasp the true effects of incarceration on the parent and the child. Unfortunately, current policies have generally disregarded the subject and have allowed societal perceptions of crime, rather than true academic research, to influence legislation. In recent years, the field of psychology has made great strides in assessing the true effects of incarceration on children. Experts have proven that child visitation is positive for both the parent and the child. Child visitation must be increased in order to alleviate the psychological strains that take place during incarceration. Better-informed visitation policies may even break the relentless cycle of crime.

His final two sentences draw to a close the summary of his findings. They also tie his findings to the bigger picture: how to break the cycle of crime. When you are writing a conclusion, then, consider the implications of your findings. What do they mean? Why should we care?

Conclusions may work differently in different genres. In some genres, such as a recommendation report (Chapter 14), the implications might be concrete actions readers should perform. In others, such as a literature review (Chapter 9), they may refer to future research readers should undertake. Your analysis of examples of your genre should give you a sense of how to approach the conclusion.

Developing Style

Style refers to the myriad writing choices that you make as you compose a document. Word choice, sentence length, language complexity—all of these elements make up style.

We often think of style as something you "have," not something you do. For example, you might think, "My writing style is unique or idiosyncratic." But good writers can vary their style for different genres, audiences, and purposes.

In this chapter, you will learn how to address writing style after you already have a draft. Remember: style comprises all of the writing choices that you make as you compose. Keep those choices in mind as you work.

When you begin focusing on style, first consider whether your style is appropriate for the writing task at hand. Appropriateness refers not to whether stylistic choices are grammatically correct, but to whether or not they fit the genre, audience, and purpose for your document. Again, use the three genre discovery questions from Chapter 1 to help you focus on appropriate style.

A. Matching Style to Genre, Audience, and Purpose

When working on style, your first considerations should be your genre, audience, and purpose. If you closely examine sentences in some examples of the genre you are writing, you will start to notice certain patterns or features.

Let's take a look at excerpts from some of the sources Terrence came across while doing research for his article:

EXAMPLE 1: Article in an Online Magazine (excerpt)

Maya Schenwar

The Prison System Welcomes My Newborn Niece to This World

Truthout.org

My niece—the first baby of my family's newest generation—was born last Wednesday morning at 10:52 AM. She is a superhero, although she probably doesn't realize it yet. Her path into this world was a rough, rough haul.

Here's how it went: At 4:30 a.m. Tuesday, my sister was called out of bed in the state prison where she's incarcerated with the news that she'd be heading to the hospital. Her water hadn't broken, and she hadn't started contractions. But this was the time slot in which she was scheduled to give birth. The labor would be induced.

During and after the birth, my sister was allowed no family or friends at her bedside, or even in the hospital. She endured labor alone, except for medical personnel and two prison guards, who rotated shifts, watching her at all times.

After 26 hours, my niece finally pushed her way out—7 pounds, 5 ounces, and crying like crazy. (Wouldn't you?)

Following the birth, a guard immediately shackled my sister's ankles to the bedpost. "It made it hard to pick up the baby from the basket next to the bed," she told us afterward. "I was afraid I was going to drop her."

Our state has anti-shackling laws in place, preventing women from being chained to their hospital beds during labor. But that doesn't mean they can't be chained afterward.

The ritual my sister underwent Tuesday and Wednesday wasn't an unusual occurrence. In prison, 4 percent to 7 percent of women are pregnant on arrival.

The vast majority of women in prison are incarcerated for nonviolent offenses. (Plus, even those incarcerated for violent offenses aren't likely to pull a fast one while they're in labor.) Virtually none are "flight risks." In The Root, advocate Malika Saada Saar writes, "Anyone who has given birth, indeed, any person who has witnessed the birthing process, knows that the prospect of a woman in childbirth trying to run away or tackle a corrections officer is almost comical." Yet because during the wildly tumultuous hours of labor and birth, these women are outside of prison walls, they're tightly restricted, permitted virtually no contact with their loved ones.

> The author uses informal language ("crying like crazy") to make the text accessible for readers.

> The author uses reported speech to dramatize the scene.

> Many of the sentences in this example are short.

· ·

In the preceding example, we see short sentences, descriptive language, dialogue, and a lower level of formality. We might conclude that the genre of the online magazine article employs these features for this type of story. If we think about the audience and purpose of an online magazine article, these choices begin to make sense. Readers are likely to read such sites primarily for entertainment, and they are likely to browse the magazine for interesting stories. The writer's goal is to attract and keep the reader's attention so that the serious message of the article comes across—that current practices for pregnant inmates are unacceptable.

· ·

EXAMPLE 2: Article in a Research Journal (excerpt)

Ann Booker Loper and Elena Hontoria Tuerk

Improving the Emotional Adjustment and Communication Patterns of Incarcerated Mothers: Effectiveness of a Prison Parenting Intervention

Journal of Child and Family Studies

The author uses words that derive from the Latin roots of the English language. These words tend to be more formal.

For most inmate mothers, the most difficult prison stressors are concerns about their children's wellbeing and sadness about separation (Clark 1995; Harris 1993; Kazura 2001). Moreover, many incarcerated mothers maintain ineffective parenting styles that were developed prior to their imprisonment and struggle to communicate appropriately with their children's caregivers (Clark). Conflict with a child's caregiver can undermine a mother's interest in her child by limiting her involvement in decisions about her child's care. Although most mothers expect to resume custody of their children after incarceration (Banauch 1985; Gaudin and Sutphen 1993), lack of contact disrupts the parent–child relationship and diminishes a mother's authority to make legal and educational decisions for her child from prison (Clark 1995; Johnston and Gabel 1995).

The author avoids weighted language in describing mothers' parenting (i.e. "ineffective" instead of "awful").

The preceding research article features denser (not necessarily longer) sentences, with more formal vocabulary. The author seems to be striving for objectivity in this text, and we do not see much vivid description or dialogue. Again, the audience and purpose for this genre help us to understand the style choices: the goal is to inform readers from a specialized field, and the writer chooses language that creates a formal, academic tone and conveys authority.

EXAMPLE 3: Article in Target Journal (excerpt)

Ashley McAlarney

Access for All: Federal Funding and Regulation of For-Profit Higher Education

Dialectics

Profit-seeking companies can provide opportunities for education that are traditionally unavailable to many citizens. However, at times, some engage in shadowy business practices that can harm students and demonstrate a misuse of public funds. The entanglement of private education and public money, associated with the for-profit sector of higher education, grows more controversial when misrepresentations of programs and inadequate training leave students unable to find employment and pay back federal loans. Recent efforts have been made by the Department of Education to impose regulations on for-profit schools to ensure that they are using fair business practices. Under these rules, if a school is not preparing students for gainful employment after graduation, it is deemed ineligible for federal funding, and attendees cannot receive federal loans and grants to pay for their education.

The preceding excerpt is from Terrence's target journal, *Dialectics*. Since Terrence hopes to publish his work in this journal, he takes a close look at this sample article. For instance, the writer uses formal verbs ("impose," "deemed," "ensure"), just like the research article in Example 2. However, Terrence notices that the writer also uses some word choices to take a stance on the issue—for example, she describes the "shadowy business practices" used by for-profit schools.

Again, the audience and purpose for this journal help to explain the style choices. As in Example 2, the author seeks an objective, academic persona, and style choices help the writer to convey authority. However, as an undergraduate journal, *Dialectics* may also seek to attract student readers. Using a more critical tone may allow the writer to attract readers by generating controversy.

Based on his analysis of the genre, audience, and purpose, Terrence decides he might be able to dramatize the issue he is writing about with some descriptive language, but that he should probably not go overboard. He incorporates more narrative elements in part of his paper (Chapter 19) to engage readers' attention, but he maintains the more objective style of a researcher in much of the paper.

Let's take a look at some specific elements to keep in mind when selecting an appropriate style.

B. Choosing a Persona

In writing, persona refers to how writers present themselves with relation to the subject or topic and audience. (Do not confuse persona with tone, which refers to the attitude the writer takes toward the subject or topic.)

It is important to note that the persona an author uses in a text is not necessarily the persona he or she uses in real life, and that you may have several different personas for different contexts. For instance, in your classes (and often, classroom writing), you take on the persona of a student, but at your job you take on the persona of an employee. In writing, persona is a rhetorical decision. For example, the persona you use to write a scientific lab report will be different from the persona you use in a profile article.

Think of your persona as connected to the role you take on as a writer. If you are writing a lab report, you will take on the persona of a scientist. Imagine yourself as a scientist—how would you write if you were in that role? In contrast, if you are writing a profile article (Chapter 5), you might imagine yourself as a freelance writer for a magazine. Picture yourself in that role. What kind of persona should you take on in this case?

Most writing that is based on research (such as research articles, reports, and grant proposals) tends toward an objective persona. That is, the writer seeks to distance himself or herself from the research, so that the research findings speak for themselves. In the sciences, especially, researchers try to write themselves out of the picture, because they want the focus to be on the results of their experiments or research. In contrast, in some genres writers strive to emphasize their involvement in the text. A magazine writer might write herself into the text, making her persona stand out, because a profile article is often a "human interest" piece—the writer can be part of the action of the text, or take a closer stance.

In Terrence's case, he thought it would be appropriate to mention his own connection to the issue of parental visitations in prisons, and to dramatize it with descriptive language (Chapter 19).

C. Choosing Tone

Tone refers to the attitude the writer takes. Is it critical? Sarcastic? Enthusiastic? Supportive? Note that for some genres, the tone is mainly neutral, as in a research article or report. In other genres, you have more room to choose a positive or negative tone, as in an op-ed piece (Chapter 10).

Terrence was careful to strike a neutral tone in his article. While he strongly disagreed with some of the studies he quoted, he was careful not to appear critical of the researchers themselves. However, he did include some elements of drama. Consider his introduction:

> Today in America millions of children are being torn away from their mothers,
>
> and it is perfectly legal. Over 1.5 million children in the United States have at
>
> least one incarcerated parent, and our legal system is prohibiting these chil-
>
> dren from being able to have visitation with their incarcerated parents, specifi-
>
> cally mothers.

Here, Terrence strikes a slightly ominous tone in the first sentence, but balances it with an objective statistic. He considered this tone to be appropriate for his target audience and the genre he was writing.

D. Making Vocabulary Choices

Your choice of vocabulary should also fit with your audience, genre, and purpose.

One element of vocabulary choice involves the kinds of words chosen. In English, we often have two (or more) words that say basically the same thing, but some of those words sound more formal than others. Pay attention especially to verbs (action words) and nouns (words for persons, places, and things).

Compare the following two passages:

Version 1: Anglo-Saxon Verbs

> Child visitation will help **ease** parental stress while incarcerated. Being arrested
>
> can be one of the most tragic and confusing events that can occur in one's life,
>
> and having a child will certainly **make** that experience **harder** for most.

Version 2: Latinate Verbs

> Child visitation will help to **alleviate** parental stress while in prison. Being ar-
>
> rested can be one of the most tragic and confusing events that can occur in
>
> one's life, and having a child will certainly **complicate** that experience.

In English, verbs that come from the Latin roots of the language tend to seem more formal and scholarly than those that come from the Anglo-Saxon roots of the language. Table 21.1 shows some examples.

Table 21.1 Latinate and Anglo-Saxon Verbs

Latinate Verbs	Anglo-Saxon Verbs
Cogitate	Think
Maintain	Keep
Impose	Force
Ascertain	Learn
Receive	Get
Purchase	Buy
Accumulate	Gather

Notice that the words on the left side sound fancier, or more formal, than the words on the right. The Anglo-Saxon words tend to be shorter and to seem more casual.

The same goes for nouns. Compare the following passages:

Version 1: Anglo-Saxon Nouns

> I argue that each of these issues can increase the amount of stress surrounding the **jailing** of a mother, and perhaps delay her release by slowing the rehabilitation process. A mother's **drive** can quickly evaporate while her **child** is withheld.

Version 2: Latinate Nouns

> I argue that each of these issues can increase the amount of stress surrounding the **incarceration** of a mother, and perhaps delay her release by slowing the rehabilitation process. A mother's **motivation** can quickly evaporate while her **progeny** is withheld.

As with nouns, verbs come across as more technical and formal in their Latinate form than in their simpler Anglo-Saxon form.

Table 21.2 Latinate and Anglo-Saxon Nouns

Latinate Nouns	Anglo-Saxon Nouns
Festival	Party
Conflict	Fight
Impression	Feeling
Obstacle	Hurdle
Object	Thing

By analyzing your genre, you can determine which kinds of words seem to be appropriate. In the examples of research articles he read, Terrence noticed a preference for the more formal Latinate vocabulary, so he tried to use those kinds of words in his writing, as well.

Terminology

You should also pay attention to the specific terms used in the field or discourse community in which you are participating. If you are writing for a specific academic field (such as anthropology, sociology, biology, etc.), you will find that writers employ specific words that either do not appear in other fields or are used differently in other fields. Employing the terminology of your field shows your membership in that community.

Terrence used the term "best interests of the child" because he was writing for an audience of legal and political science scholars who would likely understand the concept. However, if he were writing about a magazine article for a general audience, not members of the community, then he would have to either define that term or choose less specific synonyms (Chapter 19).

E. Choosing a Level of Formality

Vocabulary is one element of formality, or the overall style of a text. Consider how clothing choices convey formality. If you are invited to a formal event such as a prom or wedding, you might wear your most formal clothing: a suit or gown, maybe even a tuxedo. For a professional event, such as a job interview, you would wear professional clothing: a suit and tie for men, and a skirt or pantsuit for women—not quite so formal as a prom or graduation ceremony, but not casual either. And for a casual event, like a company picnic or college party, you would likely wear something more informal—khakis, jeans, a shirt or blouse.

Similarly, you can clothe your writing in different styles, depending on the genre, audience, and purpose. You might use a high level of formality with a very formal audience, such as lawyers or scientists (picture a judge in robes, or a scientist in a lab coat). Most academic fields, such as law, sciences, and medicine, tend toward formal writing, especially for research genres.

Most business writing and persuasive writing actually functions in the middle level, mixing formal elements with a few casual elements. You might use casual writing for blogs, personal emails, personal letters—such as thank-you letters—and posts to social networking sites.

Table 21.3 demonstrates some style changes you can make to increase or decrease formality.

Table 21.3 Levels of Formality

	High	Middle	Low
Vocabulary	Technical, scientific terms, jargon specific to a discourse community or field	Balances technical terminology with everyday terms	"Everyday" terms
	Latinate vocabulary	Mixes Latinate with Anglo-Saxon vocabulary	Prefers Anglo-Saxon vocabulary
Examples	"Best interests"	"Best interests of the child, a doctrine used to..."	"what's best for the child"
	"Deoxyribonucleic acid (DNA)"	"DNA, or genetic material..."	"Genetics," "Heredity"
	"Cogitation"	"Thought"	"Thinking"
	"Appears"	"Seems"	"Looks like"
Contractions	No	Sometimes	Yes
	It is not . . .	It is not . . . or It isn't . . .	It isn't . . .
Personal Voice ("I" or "We")	No	Sometimes	Yes
	The court finds . . . The results indicated . . .	I argue that . . . We surveyed 100 students . . .	I think . . . I believe . . . You should
Grammatical Voice	Tends toward passive voice	Mixes active and passive voice	Prefers active voice
	Results were found . . .	Results were found . . . or We found results . . .	We found results . . .

F. Using Rhetorical Figures

Rhetorical figures are special language patterns you can use to express an idea in an original, eloquent, or persuasive way. You are probably familiar with some rhetorical figures already, such as metaphor, simile, and analogy. You might think about using a rhetorical figure whenever you'd like to emphasize a point in your writing.

Again, consider your genre, audience, and purpose first. Some genres are especially laden with rhetorical figures. You might expect to hear this kind of language in a presidential campaign speech, or a eulogy given at a funeral, or in a profile article.

Genres used in professional and academic language may feature fewer rhetorical figures, but you can still use them in those genres for effect.

Repetition

Repetition creates emphasis. Repetition also helps to keep an audience interested, to create memorable phrases, and to increase the emphasis or force of your statements. Here is an example of repetition of words and phrases for emphasis from the "I Have a Dream" speech by Martin Luther King, Jr., delivered in Washington, DC, in 1963.

> But one hundred years later, the Negro still is not free. One hundred years later, the life of the Negro is still sadly crippled by the manacles of segregation and the chains of discrimination. One hundred years later, the Negro lives on a lonely island of poverty in the midst of a vast ocean of material prosperity. One hundred years later, the Negro is still languished in the corners of American society and finds himself an exile in his own land. And so we've come here today to dramatize a shameful condition.

Here's how Terrence tried to work repetition into his draft. He decided the conclusion might be a good place for repetition, because he wanted to emphasize his main ideas.

First Draft

> Experts have proven that child visitation is positive for both the parent and the child. Child visitation must be increased in order to alleviate the psychological strains that take place during incarceration. Better-informed visitation policies may even break the relentless cycle of crime.

Revision

> Experts have proven that child visitation is positive for both the parent and the child. Child visitation must be increased in order to alleviate the psychological strains that take place during incarceration. **Better-informed visitation**

> policies may even break the relentless cycle of crime, a cycle whose costs for society are much too high, a cycle that reduces children's potential, a cycle that must be broken.

Parallelism

Repetition also functions on the level of grammatical structures, rather than words and phrases. By constructing parallel phrases or sentences, you create a rhythm that makes information easier for an audience to grasp, while simultaneously increasing emphasis. Here is another example from King's speech:

> We cannot walk alone.
>
> And as we walk, we must make the pledge that we shall always march ahead.
>
> We cannot turn back.

As he continued to work on his conclusion, Terrence noticed places where he could improve parallelism:

First Draft

> Unfortunately, current policies have generally disregarded the subject and have allowed societal perceptions of crime, rather than true academic research, to influence legislation.

Revision

> Unfortunately, current policies have generally disregarded the subject, have ignored true academic research, and have allowed societal perceptions of crime to influence legislation.

Metaphor

A metaphor is a rhetorical figure in which a word is used to describe a thing or action to which the word doesn't normally apply, often to create a mental image in an audience. For example, if you were to describe the sun as a "big, yellow beach ball," you would be employing metaphor to create an image.

Essentially, all of these figures work by creating mental images for readers, often in ways that create an emotional impact—in rhetorical terms, a pathos response. Here is a series of metaphors from King's speech.

> The whirlwinds of revolt will continue to shake the foundations of our nation until the bright day of justice emerges.

In his conclusion, Terrence decided to try out a metaphor to create emotional impact.

First Draft

Our Children's Place shows great promise and has had nothing but great results. It is these types of ground-breaking initiatives that have really been able to grasp the true effects of incarceration on the parent and the child.

Revision

Our Children's Place shows great promise and has had nothing but great results; it is a ray of sunshine breaking through the cloudy firmament of prison policies. It is these types of ground-breaking initiatives that have really been able to grasp the true effects of incarceration on the parent and the child.

Simile

A simile is similar to a metaphor, only it makes the comparison more explicit, usually using "like" or "as." Many similes are common phrases, or clichés, that can lose their effectiveness over time. For example, it would be a cliché to write that someone is as skinny as a rail or as happy as a clam. Try to find fresh similes that will catch the reader's attention.

In his speech, King used simile often; in the example that follows, he used the word "as" to indicate a simile—comparing cross-racial friendship to siblinghood.

> [O]ne day right there in Alabama little black boys and black girls will be able to join hands with little white boys and white girls as sisters and brothers.

In his revision of his paper, Terrence used the word "like" to indicate a simile.

First Revision

Our Children's Place shows great promise and has had nothing but great results. It is these types of ground-breaking initiatives that have really been able to grasp the true effects of incarceration on the parent and the child.

Second Revision

Our Children's Place shows great promise and has had nothing but great results. Like sunlight, these types of initiatives have helped healthy relationships grow between incarcerated parents and children.

Alliteration

Alliteration occurs when you use several words in a sentence that start with the same letter or sound. You can use alliteration to create a memorable turn of phrase, or to convey certain emotions or attitudes. Here is a sentence from King's speech that employs alliteration upon the letter "s."

> We can never be satisfied as long as our children are stripped of their self-hood and robbed of their dignity by signs stating: "For Whites Only."

Here is how Terrence revised his draft to employ alliteration upon the letter "p."

First Draft

Our Children's Place shows great promise and has had nothing but great results.

Revision

Our Children's Place shows great promise and even greater potential as a

model for future initiatives.

Notice that introducing alliteration in the revised sentence led Terrence to employ parallelism and repetition, as well.

Antithesis

An antithesis is a pattern that expresses a contradiction or relation of opposites. You can use antithesis to emphasize two opposing points or ideas. Terrence used antithesis to show how scientific research has been ignored by policy-makers who shape prison visitation rules for children.

First Revision

Unfortunately, current policies have generally disregarded the subject, have

ignored true academic research, and have allowed societal perceptions of crime

to influence legislation.

Second Revision

Unfortunately, current policies have generally disregarded the subject, have

ignored true academic research, and have allowed societal perceptions of crime

> to influence legislation. While academic research suggests visitation can be
>
> positive, current legal policies have portrayed it as uniformly negative.

By emphasizing the antithesis between the current policies and the academic research, Terrence also put his sentence into more parallel form.

G. Tips for Developing Style

To improve your repertoire of style choices, try the following:

- Whatever you read, whether it is for work or pleasure, keep an eye out for effective style (vivid description, metaphor, etc.). The same goes for oral language—pay attention to effective political speeches, for example.
- Keep a computer file, blog, or notebook where you copy interesting passages from documents you read. Traditionally, rhetoricians suggested that their

Table 21.4 Matching Style to Genre, Audience, and Purpose

	Persona	**Tone**
What Is It?	What persona, or role, do writers take in this genre?	What tone, or attitude, do writers take in this genre?
Who Reads It?	What persona, or role, is most effective or expected by the audience for this genre?	What tone, or attitude, would appeal most to readers?
What Is It For?	What persona will best help me to accomplish my rhetorical goals?	What tone best matches my purpose?

students keep a commonplace book of quotations, poems, and so on. Your computer file could be a modern-day equivalent. Consider this an "inspiration file" that you can consult when you need ideas for an important document or oral statement.

- Pay close attention to examples of the genre you are producing. Even better, look for examples of that genre that are also in the target publication for your writing. If you are writing an op-ed for your student newspaper, get examples of op-eds from your student newspaper. Read your draft out loud, and then read one of the examples out loud. Do they sound about the same, in terms of style? If not, should you adopt more features of that genre?
- Picture the audience for your writing. What are they wearing? How do they act? And what would you wear if you were to speak to them directly? For instance, would you address a judge wearing jeans and a t-shirt? Or would you put on your best suit? Your language should reflect a similar level of formality, style, and tone as your dress.
- Create time in your writing process to revise your writing for style. Look for places where you can adjust your style to suit your genre, audience, and purpose. You can use Table 21.4 as a guide.

Vocabulary	Formality	Rhetorical Figures
What kinds of vocabulary do writers use in this genre? (e.g., academic jargon? Latinate words?)	What level of formality is typical for this genre?	What kinds of rhetorical figures do writers use in this genre? (metaphor? analogy?)
What kinds of vocabulary will readers find most effective or easiest to understand?	What level of formality is appropriate for my audience?	What kinds of rhetorical figures will be most persuasive to readers of this genre? What rhetorical figures will help them understand the argument or content?
What vocabulary choices will best suit my rhetorical goals?	What level of formality best suits my purpose?	What kinds of rhetorical figures could help to achieve my purpose?

Polishing It Up

After you have researched, drafted, and organized your paper, you need to revise and edit it. This chapter gives you strategies for revision, for editing by yourself, and for editing with the help of others. Let's take a look at how one student author, Terrence, revised and edited his paper.

A. Revising

Revision is the process of taking another look at your writing and thinking about what you can do better. During revision, your paper may change dramatically. Here are some strategies for revision that have worked well for other writers.

Reverse Outline

Once you have a draft of your document (in Terrence's case, an academic research paper), you may find it useful to write a reverse outline of your piece. To write a reverse outline, go paragraph-by-paragraph and write a short summary of what each paragraph is doing.

Then, consider whether you could rearrange your document for greater effect. Are there paragraphs that need to be combined or divided in two? Paragraphs that start out saying one thing but end up saying something else? Paragraphs that need to be rearranged?

Topic Sentence Outline

Another option is to write a topic sentence outline. With a topic sentence outline, you write down all of the topic sentences of your document as though they were a single paragraph. Try reading the paragraph. Does it make sense? Are some of your sentences (in other words, your paragraphs) out of order?

Terrence wrote a topic sentence outline of his paper (see Chapter 28 for his entire paper) to see if his paragraphs were in order. Here is the list of topic sentences from the beginning paragraphs of his paper:

- Today in America millions of children are being torn away from their mothers, and it is perfectly legal.
- The United States legal system prohibits these children from visiting their incarcerated parents, specifically mothers.

- The field of psychology has taken a different perspective on incarceration than that taken by the legal system.
- To conduct this study, I reviewed legal research describing the current barriers for incarcerated mothers to gain visitation of their children.

Examining these sentences, Terrence felt that his organization was strong, moving from an opening paragraph that catches the reader's attention, to a second paragraph that explains the challenging situation that his paper critiques, to a third paragraph that explains the interdisciplinary angle that his paper takes, to the fourth paragraph that describes his paper's methodology. He continued reviewing the topic sentences for the rest of his paper, ensuring that his paragraphs were in the proper order and rearranging them as necessary.

USE THE TOOLKIT

As you revise your writing, revisit the three genre toolkit questions (Chapter 1) to ensure that you have met the requirements of the genre that you are writing.

What Is It?
Have I used the expected conventions of the genre? If not, do I have a reason for deviating from the expected conventions?

Who Reads It?
Have I met the expectations of my audience? Will my audience find my document appropriate, easy to read, and useful?

What's It For?
Have I kept my document's purpose in mind? Does my document fulfill its purpose?

B. Self-Editing and Proofreading: Creating Fresh Eyes

Editing is the process of polishing your writing at the sentence level, including changing sentences to improve style, clarity, focus, and concision. Proofreading refers to the process of checking sentences for errors, such as typographical errors (typos), grammatical mistakes, or misspelled words. Many writers have trouble editing and proofreading their own work. They have trouble viewing their work with "fresh eyes."

All of the strategies described in this section will help you gain distance (sometimes called "critical distance") from your writing. Critical distance is the ability of a writer to view her own work critically and to discover problems.

Giving Yourself Time

When it comes to editing, the greatest gift you can give yourself is time. If you are able to finish a draft and let it "rest" for a few days before editing it, you are more likely to have critical distance, and therefore more likely to find errors or to spot places where you might edit the text to improve style (Chapter 21), accuracy, or concision.

Reading Out Loud

Reading your paper out loud can also help you spot stylistic flaws or errors in your writing. Take a piece of blank paper or a ruler, and hold it below the first line. Then, start reading. Blocking out the line below, combined with the slower pace that reading out loud forces you to take, helps create fresh eyes on your writing.

Recording Your Voice

In addition to reading out loud, you can record yourself reading your paper out loud and then listen to it. Use the voice recorder on your cell phone (most phones have them these days) or voice recording software on your computer. If you listen to your recording while silently reading your paper to yourself, you are likely to find errors that you might have missed or sentences whose style could be improved (Chapter 21).

C. Conducting Peer Review

An alternative to trying to edit and proofread your own work is to seek help from peers, such as your classmates or other friends. Giving (and receiving) peer feedback is a crucial process in successful writing.

Providing Useful Feedback

You might think that because you are not an expert writer that you don't have good feedback to give. This is not true. You can easily come up with plenty of suggestions for a fellow writer if you draw on your own experience as a reader and writer.

Revising at the idea level　Focus on the ideas of the document that you are reading. As you read, focus on how you respond as a reader.

First, try reading as someone who *supports* the ideas. When you read as a supporter, ask yourself the following:

- What is good about this idea?
- How could the writer make this idea clearer? Stronger?

Next, try reading as a naysayer, someone who *does not support* the ideas. Consider the following:

- How could you rebut this idea (Chapter 18)? What evidence is there against it?
- How could the writer address objections?

When you give feedback to the writer, provide both the supporter and the naysayer perspectives. Then, the writer can figure out how to make their writing even stronger.

Editing at the sentence level   If you are nervous about giving feedback for this first time, try this strategy:

For every sentence that you had to read twice or three times in order to understand it, put a question mark in the margin. Every time you spot a problem with the writing, such as a word or phrase that is unclear or clunky, put an "X" in the margin. And every time you read a sentence that you think is great, put a check mark in the margin.

Just this much feedback can really help another writer improve his or her writing. Of course, if you have further comments to make—and you will find yourself having more comments the more you critique others' work—write those down too.

Proofreading   As a peer reviewer, you will often catch small mistakes that the writer missed. Don't spend all of your time focused on these little mistakes; however, it is very useful for you to circle them so that the writer can fix them later. Your fresh eyes can often spot errors that the writer's eyes cannot.

Soliciting Good Feedback

Sometimes, students find that they do not get sufficient feedback from peer review sessions. Part of your responsibility as a group member is to actively seek out good feedback. That means that you should prompt your group members to help you with specific elements of your writing. You can do this by asking questions like these:

- How can I improve the organization of my document? Did you get lost or find the argument hard to follow?
- What do you think of my introduction? Did I capture your attention right away, or does it seem too dry?
- What are some places where I can improve the style to suit this genre?

By prompting your group members to answer specific questions, you can get better feedback than if you ask a general questions, like "What do you think of my document?" or "Does it flow?"

Critiquing with Respect

Giving useful critique is an excellent skill to have. But you must also temper your criticism with respect for the other writer. If your comments come across as mean-spirited, the recipient will either have his or her feelings hurt or just ignore your comments completely. Put yourself in the recipient's shoes and re-read all of your comments before you share them to ensure that you are critiquing with respect. Try using phrases such as these:

- "When I read this, I thought. . . . "
- "What I think you are saying is . . ."
- "As a reader, I felt . . .
- "The introduction seems to need work . . ."

Try to avoid phrases such as these:

- "You should . . ."
- "Don't. . . ."
- "This is stupid/silly/ridiculous."

Using Electronic Tools

There are many electronic tools that can make peer reviews easier. For example, simply emailing documents back and forth and making comments in the text on your computer is a fine way to collaborate without having to meet in person. Using Microsoft Word's track changes and commenting features are a great way to do this. Here is an excerpt from Terrence's draft with peer comments written using Microsoft Word's track changes and commenting features.

> ~~Using T~~the psychological research that is available~~, findings~~ consistently ~~conclude~~ shows that when a child is ~~withheld~~ prevented from visiting his or her mother, negative ~~side~~ effects occur. However, when visitation is allowed, there are numerous positive ~~implications~~ effects. Snyder, Carlo, & Mullins (2001) found that, when a parent is incarcerated, the child has an increased risk of suffering from anxiety, depression, sleeplessness, anger, and attention

deficiencies. However, these risks can be alleviated through visitation programs, and

parenting classes can improve the relationship between incarcerated mothers and

their children (Snyder, Carlo, & Mullins 2001). If visitation is allowed, then the problem

may be prevented earlier, and the child's future will be more promising as a result (Snyder,

Carlo, & Mullins 2001). Clearly, parenting classes must be utilized more; the classes

would be beneficial for parent, child, and other family members. And, since prison today is

a business, the parenting classes will ultimately be more economical. Although it appears

that adding a new program would be more expensive, the parenting programs may actually

reduce the overall costs related to the incarcerated parents' mental and physical health

treatments because of the motivation that parents will gain by having continued positive

contact with their children.

Comment [1]: Perhaps avoid words like "clearly." Whenever I read words like clearly (or "obviously"), it makes me wary that the argument the author is about to make is a weak one. Otherwise, why would the author need to *tell* me that the argument is clear?

Comment [2]: Do you mean parenting classes in prison? I'm confused by the connection between parenting classes and child visitation.

Comment [3]: Great to provide a counterargument to preempt the naysayers to your proposal! This really worked for me as a reader.

Your instructor may prefer that you use a course management system to conduct peer review, perhaps using a message board or forum. You can also use real-time collaboration software such as Google Docs, which allows two or more people to write on the same document at the same time. Another option is a file sharing system like Dropbox.com or Evernote, which allows writers to share files across the Internet.

PART 4

Research

Getting Started with Research

As a college student, much of the writing you will do will require research. Sometimes, your instructor will provide you with a clear topic and suggest research methods (Chapter 24) for you to use. In other cases, however, you may simply be assigned a research paper (Chapter 11) or report (Chapter 14), and it will be up to you to determine how to get going. In this chapter, you will learn how to find a topic, locate a gap in existing research, develop a research question, and create a research plan.

A. Considering Your Genre

As a college student, much of the writing you will do will require research. Sometimes, an assignment might clearly call for research, such as a "research paper." However, in other cases, you might be writing a genre that does not clearly advertise itself as research—such as a rhetorical analysis (Chapter 8), a recommendation report (Chapter 14), or an informative article (Chapter 6). These genres all use research, but they might use different kinds of research and in different ways.

Before you begin research for a project, you should first determine what genre you are writing and what kind of research it entails. Are you writing a research article (sometimes called a "research paper")? A literature review? A conference presentation? You can use the three genre toolkit questions (Chapter 1) to help you determine a good topic and research strategy for your assignment. Let's see how one student, Jay Zhang, began his research after being assigned to write a rhetorical analysis that could be published in the undergraduate journal *Young Scholars in Writing*. You can read Jay's completed rhetorical analysis in Chapter 28.

USE THE TOOLKIT

What Is It?

First, Jay looked for examples of rhetorical analysis articles in *Young Scholars in Writing* and examined the web page for the journal. He found the journal's mission statement on the website, which gave him several clues about his assignment by identifying his audience:

Young Scholars in Writing: Undergraduate Research in Writing and Rhetoric is a refereed journal dedicated to publishing research articles written by undergraduates in a wide variety of disciplines associated with rhetoric and writing. It is guided by these central beliefs: (1) that research can and should be a crucial component of rhetorical education and (2) that undergraduates engaged in research about writing and rhetoric should have opportunities to share their work with a broader audience of students, scholars, and teachers through national publication.

Young Scholars in Writing is intended to be a resource for students engaged in undergraduate research and for scholars who are interested in new advances or theories relating to language, composition, rhetoric, and related fields.

Jay determined that his article needed to represent "undergraduate research." He took this to mean that his article should employ either empirical or database research (Chapter 24), and that he needed to make a contribution to the field under study: rhetoric and composition.

From the submission guidelines on the website, Jay learned that his article should be between 10 and 25 pages, double spaced, and that he should use MLA format (Chapter 28).

Who Reads It?

The journal website also helped Jay to determine his audience. The website indicated that articles submitted to the journal would be read by the editor, who would then send the best essays on to be peer reviewed by other undergraduate students or students who had published in the journal previously. Jay determined that his audience would be other undergraduate students as well as the editors of the journals, who were professors of rhetoric and composition.

What's It For?

Jay reasoned that the undergraduate journal helped students to polish and publish their research and gave students a place to share their findings. The goal of each article, he determined, is to offer a persuasive case for a new set of findings.

By using the genre toolkit questions, Jay determined that he would need a compelling topic that would interest an audience of undergraduate students, that he should be able to do original research on that topic, and that he would need to be able to say something new and interesting about that topic.

B. Finding a Good Research Topic

If you are assigned to write on a topic of your choice, you should spend some time developing a topic (Chapter 15) before you settle on one. That way, you can choose the topic that best fits the genre you are writing and offers the best research avenues. You might try out one of the following strategies for developing a topic.

Your Class Notes and Readings

Your class notes and readings may be a good starting point for research topics. Jay was inspired by one of the class readings from his course, a rhetorical analysis of Subway's food marketing that was published in his target journal, *Young Scholars in Writing*. Since Jay was interested in health and planned to be a public health major, he decided to see if he could extend the analysis of Subway's marketing rhetoric by looking at other types of food marketing.

If you are reading scholarly sources (Chapter 25) in your classes, you can take a close look at the references cited for more ideas. You might find a book or article on a topic that interests you and use that as a starting point for your research.

Browsing for Recent Research

In addition to class readings, you can find research topics by browsing library sources, such as databases or journals (Chapter 24) in your subject area. For example, other students in Jay's class browsed the table of contents for other issues of *Young Scholars in Writing*. They found research topics such as the rhetoric of Hillary Clinton's human rights speeches, a series of student protests at Penn State University, and the website PostSecret (which posts anonymous postcards sent to the web developer sharing secret wishes and confessions). Some of Jay's classmates used this research to inspire their own studies.

You might also browse websites that report on recent research. For example, the latest research findings are often reported in newspapers or on specialized websites. Here are some good websites to try for recent research findings.

For sciences:

- The *New York Times* Science section, http://www.nytimes.com/pages/science/index.html
- ScienceDaily.com, http://www.sciencedaily.com
- Phys.org, http://phys.org

For humanities:

- Arts and Letters Daily, http://www.aldaily.com/
- National Endowment for the Arts and Humanities (NEH) Magazine, http://www.neh.gov/humanities

- The *New York Times* Books section, http://www.nytimes.com/pages/books/index.html

For social sciences:

- PhysOrg.com, http://www.physorg.com/science-news/social-sciences
- Social Science Space, http://socialsciencespace.com
- Social science sections of ScienceDaily.com, http://www.sciencedaily.com (Search under tabs for political science, sociology, etc.)

Note that these sites do not actually publish research papers or academic books—they publish news reports (Chapter 14) or book reviews (Chapter 9) about them. If you find an interesting topic on one of these sites, try to track down the original research source (the book or article discussed) using your library website. If you have trouble finding the source, ask your librarian for help.

Jay found a research study cited on ScienceDaily.com about the effects of food images on consumers. This inspired him to look at the images McDonald's used in their food marketing campaigns as part of his rhetorical analysis.

Ask an Expert

If you are having trouble finding a good research topic, try asking an expert. Your college or nearby colleges are stocked with experts who have conducted research in their areas of expertise. If you need a research topic related to psychology, for instance, ask your Psych 101 instructor what areas of research she thinks are cutting-edge. You can also search the websites for your college or a nearby research university to see what kinds of research projects professors and graduate students are conducting.

C. Identifying a Gap

Reading other research can not only help you to develop a topic, but also it can extend that research by offering a new perspective, taking the inquiry into a new direction, or addressing issues that researchers had not considered. Academic writers call this "identifying a gap."

Students often assume that the idea that they can contribute new research to an area seems pretty far-fetched. You are a student, after all. What could you possibly contribute that an important professor or researcher hasn't already written?

The answer is this: a lot. You bring a unique perspective to your topic, simply because you are *you*. Also, you are writing *now*, when all of what you are reading was written *then*. This means that you can respond to what other researchers have written, and modify their ideas with your own insights and interpretations.

When you are conducting your preliminary research on your topic, you should look for gaps to fill. Keep the following ideas in mind.

Gaps Can Be Small

A research gap can be very small. If you were writing about the rhetoric of food, as Jay was, you might find articles about the rhetoric of slow food, organic food, and health food, but surprisingly little on the rhetoric of junk or fast food. While this might seem like a small gap, it might actually add something important to the conversation.

After reading the article on Subway's nutritional rhetoric, Jay jotted down the following questions:

- *What about junk food or fast food advertising (vs. Subway, which focuses on health)? Do they use the same rhetorical strategies, or different ones?*
- *What about junk food advertising to particular ethnic groups? What rhetorical strategies are used?*
- *What about junk food advertising to children? What rhetorical strategies do they use?*

Jay searched databases that feature articles on rhetoric, such as Communication and Mass Media Complete, and found that while there were many articles on rhetoric and food, there were very few about the rhetoric of fast food or junk food. While this gap seemed small, Jay felt it was important to explore fast food rhetoric because it could offer new insights.

Gaps Can Be Continuing Conversations

You might feel great that you have narrowed your topic down to something both manageable and interesting. But then, disaster strikes. As you continue to research, you find an article that seems to discuss your very same topic.

Relax. This is a *good* thing. The fact that someone else has written on your topic means that your topic is relevant and important. You need to adjust your topic so that you are *responding* to the earlier article. Read the article carefully: are there any ideas that seem wrong or outdated? It is unlikely that you agree completely with what the other researcher has to say. Are there ideas that you can respond to?

Gaps Can Be Modifications or Syntheses

If you find other research that is similar to your topic, you can conduct new research and modify what the earlier researcher wrote. You can also find multiple articles and synthesize (or put together) their ideas to create a new idea for you to write about.

To determine how he might modify or synthesize what others had written, Jay searched several general research databases (such as *Academic Search Complete*, *Infotrac*, or *LexisNexis*) using his library's database tools (Chapter 24). From an initial search of these general databases, you can get a good sense of what kind of research is being done on a topic. If you do not find much research available on your topic, you might decide to switch topics.

D. Developing a Research Question

Once you have chosen a topic and identified a gap, you can generate a focused research question. Your research question should suit the genre you are writing, and it should be something you can answer (or at least begin to answer) with the type of research you have chosen to do. In Jay's case, his research question had to be something he could answer using rhetorical analysis (Chapter 8). This type of genre and approach could not answer the question "Does advertising lead to obesity?" for instance, since that would require empirical research (Chapter 24).

Asking Questions

To start developing your research question, try asking basic questions—who, what, where, when, why, and how? Here's how Jay used these questions to brainstorm his topic.

Topic: Fast food advertising

Questions:

- Who advertises specifically to children and minorities?

- What ethnic groups are singled out by food marketers?

- Where are people most likely to view these ads?

- When did these types of ads begin?

- Why do fast food companies target specific groups?

- How do fast food companies advertise? Using what rhetorical strategies?

In the case of this topic, not all of the preceding questions would make a good research question for an analysis of the *rhetoric* of fast food advertising. Jay realized that the "how" question best suited his rhetorical analysis genre (Chapter 8). But he also realized that he would need to answer other questions (the who, what, when, and why) in his analysis as well to establish the context for his analysis. While most research begins with one main question, answering that question can involve other questions as well.

Narrowing Your Topic and Question

Students often struggle with going beyond a very general topic or question to a more specific research question that is suitable for a research project. For example, if you are writing a research paper (Chapter 11) for a sociology course, you might have trouble going beyond a basic topic like "social media" or a basic question such as "How does social media affect teens?" These ideas are too broad for a research paper.

To find a good *research* topic, you might start by doing some preliminary research using databases (Chapter 24). In Jay's case, he located plenty of articles in these databases about the effects of marketing fast food to children and minorities. Jay decided to extend this research to consider the rhetorical techniques used to market fast food to those groups.

So, he revised his research question as follows:

> - How do fast food companies market to children and minorities? Using what rhetorical strategies?

To narrow your topic and research question, you should also consider the scope of the empirical research (Chapter 24) you will conduct. For example, if you are conducting interviews to generate data for a recommendation report, how many people will you interview? What kinds of people? By focusing on, say, female college students, you will have narrowed your research topic.

Because he was writing a rhetorical analysis, Jay needed to focus on a text or set of texts to analyze—in this case, advertisements from fast food companies. To narrow the scope of his research, he decided to confine his study to one fast food company: McDonald's.

E. Developing a Research Plan

Once you have developed your topic and research question, you can begin to develop a research plan. Your research plan includes the steps you will take to help you to answer your research question.

Your research will fall into two main types:

- **information you collect yourself** (through observations, experiments, interviews, surveys, or analysis), or empirical research
- **information collected and published by others (such as books, articles, and encyclopedias)**, or database research

For more on collecting empirical and database research, refer to Chapter 24. For Jay's rhetorical analysis article, both empirical and database research were needed.

Jay needed to analyze fast food advertisements targeting children and minorities (empirical research), but he also did database research to find out how successful the advertising campaigns had been, and what might have prompted the new campaign in the first place. In particular, Jay examined business databases to find information published in sources dedicated to marketing and advertising.

Other topics might require you to do empirical research. For example, if you wanted to know what college students think about fast food advertising, you might do empirical research in the form of interviews or surveys.

Consider Your Genre

The kind of research you conduct depends on the genre you are writing, as shown in Table 23.1. For instance, the genre of the field report in anthropology usually depends on empirical research—observations of individuals in a specific setting. The genre of the literature review depends on database research—an analysis of previously published research.

Table 23.1 Purposes of Empirical and Database Research by Genre

Genre	Purpose/Type of Empirical Research	Purpose/Type of Database Research
Profile article (Chapter 5)	Get information about a person, company, or organization directly from the source.	Find information about a person, company, or organization from published sources.
Informative article (Chapter 6)	Interview experts to get information about a topic.	Provide facts, data, or statistics.
Observation notes (Chapter 7)	Make observations in the field or at a particular site.	n/a
Rhetorical analysis (Chapter 8)	Rhetorical analysis of a text (your own observations and ideas)	Provide historical context for the text; indicate what other scholars have said about the text.
Film review (Chapter 9)	Qualitative evaluation of a film	Provide background or context; find out what other reviewers said about the film.
Op-ed (Chapter 10):	Provide testimony from individuals (from an interview, for instance).	Provide historical context; provide statistics or evidence to support a claim.
Literature review (Chapter 11)	n/a	Identify and evaluate previous research in a field.

continued

Table 23.1 Purposes of Empirical and Database Research by Genre *(continued)*

Genre	Purpose/Type of Empirical Research	Purpose/Type of Database Research
Research paper (Chapter 11)	Share experimental, observational, quantitative, qualitative, or archival evidence from an original study with other researchers.	Identify previous research in a field; indicate a gap in that research that the empirical research will fill.
Grant proposal (Chapter 13)	Include preliminary results from empirical research (such as an experiment).	Indicate what other scholars have researched in this area; demonstrate a gap in existing research.
Recommendation report (Chapter 14)	Include results from interviews, observations, etc. that support recommendations.	Provide cultural and historical background; support recommendations with published accounts by other researchers.

Consider Your Academic Discipline

Your choice of research method also depends on the academic discipline in which you are writing. In scientific fields, empirical research tends to be experimental (conducted in a laboratory) or observational (such as observing bird mating patterns in nature). In social scientific fields (sociology, psychology, etc.), research may be experimental, but also tends to include qualitative and quantitative research (surveys, interviews, case studies). In the humanities, empirical research may involve close analysis of original objects (texts, works of art, films, etc.), but also archival research using specialized documents housed in libraries and museums. In Jay's case, while his topic might be considered related to health or business, he was writing for readers in the discipline of rhetoric and composition. These readers tend to value careful analysis of texts, in this case advertisements.

Make a Timeline

Once you have identified your topic, question, genre, and discipline, you can begin to create a research plan.

For example, Jay listed the following tasks:

- *Research what scholars have said about the rhetoric of junk food/fast food advertising (database research).*
- *Research business/marketing side—strategies used and their effectiveness in terms of sales; Identify key events that brought about the McDonald's "I'm Lovin' It" campaign (database research).*
- *Find and analyze advertisements (database and empirical research).*
- *Analyze how advertisements use rhetorical strategies.*

Or, if you were writing a profile (Chapter 5) of a student running for president of the student council at your university, you might list the following tasks:

- *Interview the candidate (empirical research).*
- *Interview candidate's friends/colleagues from student organizations (empirical research).*
- *Look for student newspaper columns that mention the candidate and her platform (database research).*
- *Look online for other information about the candidate (database research).*

To help you stay organized, it can be useful to create a timetable, with clear goals and deadlines. Table 23.2 shows how Jay scheduled different types of research for his rhetorical analysis paper, leaving extra time for drafting, revising, and editing.

Table 23.2 Sample Research Timetable

Task	Deadline
Research what scholars have said about the rhetoric of food/junk food.	January 25
Research business/marketing side—why this campaign at this time?	February 1
Locate a set of advertisements (print and online).	February 4
Analyze rhetorical strategies used in ads.	February 5–6
Write first draft	February 7–10
First draft due	February 11
Revise and edit	February 12–13
Assignment due	February 14

To stay on task, you can use a range of tools, from a traditional student planner to online applications or mobile phone apps. For example, Google Calendar allows you to create task lists and send automatic due-date reminders to your email or cell phone.

F. Generating Search Terms

Before you begin to search for sources, you will need to develop a set of search terms. Search terms are the keywords you will use in databases and search engines to help you find sources. For example, if your research question is "How does the McDonald's 'I'm Lovin' It' campaign market to children and minorities?" you might brainstorm the following list of terms:

- junk food
- rhetoric
- fast food
- advertising
- children

- minorities
- kids
- African Americans
- Latinos
- Asian Americans

When you start to search for sources, you can try different combinations of those terms. Sometimes, you might find very few sources using one set of terms, but hundreds of sources using another.

As you find sources, you might also notice other search terms. Some research articles and databases even list keywords or subject terms, so you can try searching your library database (Chapter 24) for those. In Jay's case, he found more search items alongside the findings for one of his database searches, such as "fast food industry" and "marketing strategy," so he tried searching with those terms as well.

If you are having trouble finding good search terms, ask a librarian to help you.

Conducting Research

Once you have chosen a topic, identified your genre, and developed a research question, you can begin conducting research. You may have heard the terms "primary" and "secondary" research to refer to the different kinds of research you may conduct. However, we find these terms confusing, in part because they overlap with the terms "primary" and "secondary" sources—but not exactly. Instead, we use the terms "empirical" and "database" research. Empirical research refers to any research that involves observation and experience, such as interviews, experiments, or surveys. Database research refers to any research that relies primarily on published sources (most of which you now access through a database, such as a library catalog, online journal database, or even the Internet—which can be considered one big database).

A. Conducting Empirical Research

The goal of empirical research is to make a new contribution to a field through observation or experimentation. Empirical research allows you to ask original research questions and find new information, information that has not been published elsewhere. For this reason, researchers are unlikely to simply replicate what others have done (although they sometimes repeat experiments to verify results, or may repeat a survey year after year to see how responses change over time). Instead, they are always on the lookout for new problems to explore, new texts to analyze, or new ideas to examine.

There are many types of empirical research.

Experimental Research

Experimental research refers to any study in which the researcher seeks to test a hypothesis in a controlled setting. An experiment usually includes a control condition and an experimental condition. For example, you might ask half the students in your class to eat as many chips as they want (measuring the amount of chips each person consumes). Then, you might ask the other half to eat a grapefruit, and then eat as many chips as they want. The goal of this experiment would be to see whether eating the grapefruit affected the quantity of chips consumed.

When conducting experimental research, you might write lab notes (Chapter 7) to keep track of your results, and then write a research paper to share your results (Chapter 11).

Observational Research

Observational research refers to any study in which the researcher observes behavior in a given setting, but without intervening to change that behavior. Researchers might observe how people behave in different situations, or how animals and plants behave, or even how inert matter behaves under certain conditions (such as how sub-atomic particles behave at extremely low temperatures). Unlike in an experiment, in an observation you do not seek to change how your subjects behave, but instead observe them in a natural state.

One useful type of observation is a structured observation, in which you look for a set number of instances of specific events. For example, for a recommendation report (Chapter 14) on how to improve hygiene at your campus gym you might observe 50 people (25 male, 25 female) exercising at your campus gym, and note how many individuals wiped off the equipment after using it.

When conducting observational research, you might write observation notes to keep track of what you see (Chapter 7). For your observation, you might note quantitative information (the number of people who wiped off the machines) as well as other observations that you noticed (e.g., that men were more likely to wipe off the machines if a woman was using it after them). Then, you might write a research paper (Chapter 11) or even a recommendation report (Chatper 14) based on your results.

You can present your findings in a table called a "cross-tab," as shown in Table 24.1.

Table 24.1 Cross-Tab Table for Observational Research

	Did wipe	Did not wipe	Total	Notes
Males	3 30%	7 70%	10	Men were sweatier One guy went looking for spray bottle but didn't find it so he just wiped it with his shirt Men seemed more likely to wipe if a woman was using the machine next
Females	8 80%	2 20%	10	Women more likely to offer spray bottle and towel to others exiting machines One woman chastised a guy for not wiping the machine off One woman grimaced and left the line for a machine after sweaty guy did not wipe
Total	11	9	20	

Strategies for Observational and Experimental Research

To begin observational or experimental research, start by considering what research method is appropriate for your genre. For example, observational research might be useful for a research paper in sociology, but not for a literature review (Chapter 11), since literature reviews report on published research, not original studies.

You should also consider your discipline. Experimental research might be appropriate for a psychology course, but is less likely to be used for a history course.

Next, form a hypothesis. A hypothesis is a prediction or guess about what you think will happen in your observation or experiment. For example, for an observation, your hypothesis might be: "Men will be less likely to wipe down equipment after exercising than women." For an experiment, your hypothesis might be: "Participants will be more likely to wipe off equipment if there are signs posted about germs on equipment."

Once you have chosen a hypothesis, develop a study design to test that hypothesis. Your study design might include participants, locations, materials needed, and so on. For an observation, you need to determine who you will observe, where, and when. Sometimes, researchers use a structured observation, where they decide on a number of instances to observe—such as 50 instances of birds feeding at a backyard feeder, or 100 instances of patrons ordering coffee at a coffee shop.

For an experiment, you need to consider what will be your control condition, and what will be your experimental condition. Your experimental condition will differ from your control in one variable only. For example, you might decide to study whether students are more likely to wipe down exercise equipment at the gym if there are signs posted about the importance of cleanliness and the amount of germs on exercise equipment. In your control condition, you would observe a certain number of students (say, 50 or 100) before the signs are posted, and the same amount afterward. You would try to keep the other variables the same for each condition, such as time of day and day of the week.

Finally, take careful notes during your observation or experiment (Chapter 7). Record quantitative information (such as how many people wiped off the equipment) as well as other observations (time of day, unusual events, reactions, etc.).

Checklist for Observational and Experimental Research

☐ Consider your genre—Is observational or experimental research typically used in my genre?

☐ Consider your discipline—Is observational or experimental research typically used in my discipline? What kinds of observations or experiments are conducted?

☐ Form a hypothesis—What do you think will happen?

☐ Determine location/subjects (for observations) and participants/variables (for experiments).

☐ Take careful notes.

Qualitative and Quantitative Research

Another type of empirical research involves asking people questions about their attitudes, beliefs, behaviors, or opinions. This type of research is most often used in the social sciences. The information you collect by asking questions can be presented in quantitative form (statistics, graphs, charts, etc.) or in qualitative form (quotations or summaries of responses). You can collect this type of information using several different methods.

Surveys   A survey refers to a set of questions that the researcher asks of a large group of participants. Usually, participants are chosen to reflect a specific demographic (such as history majors at your college, or members of a political party, or American voters). The results of a survey may be tabulated in numerical terms, using statistical methods. However, surveys may also include open-ended questions that can provide more in-depth information about students' attitudes. For instance, for an op-ed (Chapter 10) on proposed tuition increases, you might survey students about their opinions. You might read those responses and tally how many students mentioned a specific idea when given the chance to elaborate on their opinion, such as the idea that higher tuition is "unfair" or "a burden on lower income students."

Interviews   An interview refers to a set of questions that the researcher asks of a smaller set of participants, usually one-on-one. Like survey participants, interview participants are chosen to reflect a specific demographic or group, but they may also be chosen because they are particularly prominent or interesting. For an op-ed (Chapter 10) on tuition increases, you could interview students about their opinions (as representatives of a group), or you could interview a college administrator (as a prominent campus individual) about how the increases would affect students.

An oral history interview is a type of interview in which the participant is asked to discuss their own life history and/or their involvement with an historical event. For a history class, you might interview your grandfather about growing up in your hometown. However, you could also use an oral history interview as the basis for a profile article about a prominent alumnus (Chapter 5) to be published in your college magazine.

Focus group   A focus group refers to a less formal type of interview in which many individuals participate at once. The goal of a focus group is to get a sense of people's attitudes or beliefs about a topic. The idea is that when individuals consider a topic together, they are likely to generate more ideas than if they are each surveyed or interviewed separately. Focus groups are commonly used in marketing and advertising, but also as research tools in the social sciences. For instance, an advertising company might ask a focus group to respond to three possible new ads for a product, using their opinions to modify the ad campaign. A researcher in city planning might use a focus group to determine how low-income individuals are affected by urban development. You might use a focus group for a recommendation report (Chapter 14) on how your college might prevent high-risk drinking among students.

Strategies for Quantitative and Qualitative Research

To begin qualitative or quantitative research, start by deciding on a research method. Different genres tend to rely on different kinds of research methods. For instance, you would be unlikely to conduct a focus group when writing an op-ed (Chapter 10), but you might use an interview. However, a focus group might be a useful research tool if you were writing a proposal (Chapter 13) or a recommendation report (Chapter 14).

You should also consider your discipline. Quantitative and qualitative research methods are most common in the social sciences and business. Some humanities fields use specialized versions of these approaches, such as an oral history interview in history.

Once you have determined your research method, choose an appropriate sample size. For an interview, you can choose a very small sample size—even a single person. For a focus group, you need a small number of people—somewhere between 5 and 12 could work—that represent the group you would like to know more about (say, students on your campus who live in dorms). For a survey, you will need a larger number of respondents. Keep in mind that many people will not respond to a survey request, so you should ask more people to respond than you would like.

Next, develop good questions. For surveys, you can choose from a variety of question types, including:

- Yes/no or true/false
- Multiple choice
- Likert scale. Example: How strongly do you agree with the proposal to increase tuition?
  - 1-strongly agree
  - 2-agree slightly
  - 3-neither agree nor disagree
  - 4-disagree slightly
  - 5-strongly disagree
- Open-ended (write-in responses)

For an interview or a focus group, you will do best with open-ended questions, not yes/no questions, since those will give people a chance to elaborate on their ideas. You can plan for follow-up questions that ask people to expand on a statement or idea—that way, you can be sure to get lots of detailed information.

Finally, take advantage of digital tools to help with your research. For surveys, you can use free online tools such as Survey Monkey to design and distribute your survey via email, and to view the results. You can also use free polling tools available through Facebook or your course management system. Digital tools can also help you to record interviews or focus groups. You can use your laptop or cell phone to record the conversation, or an app (such as Dragon Dictation) to automatically transcribe spoken text (always with the participants' permission).

Checklist for Quantitative and Qualitative Research

☐ Consider your genre: Is qualitative or quantitative research typical for this genre?

☐ Consider your discipline: Is qualitative or quantitative research typical for my discipline?

☐ Consider your sample size and goals:

   ☐ Do you want to know a little bit about what a lot of people think? Use a survey.

   ☐ Do you want to know a lot about what a few people think? Use an interview.

   ☐ Do you want to know a lot about what a group thinks? Use a focus group.

☐ Develop good questions.

☐ Take advantage of digital tools.

Here is an example of a survey used by a student writer. You can read the full article in which this research appears in Chapter 11, "Academic Research Genres."

EXAMPLE: Student Research Survey

Investigator: Kristine Thompson

Study: The Social and Psychological Motivations of UNC Sports Fans

This is a survey for my English 102 class and should take no more than a few minutes. The information you provide is strictly confidential and you will not be asked to provide your name, PID, or any other information. Your answers will be used in a study of sport fan motivation at UNC. Thank you for your time.

1. How often are you involved in sports at UNC (this includes attending games, playing club or intramural sports, reading sports articles in the *Daily Tar Heel*, etc.)? Please circle one.

Never   Rarely   Sometimes   Often   Very Often

2. Please rank the following reasons you have for your current level of sports involvement, with 1 being the most important and 5 being the least important.

   I enjoy the tension and anxiety when my team is involved in a close game and winning and losing comes down to one play. _____

I feel better about myself when I watch sports and I enjoy increased self-esteem after my team wins. _____

Going to games or playing sports relieves stress and helps me forget about reality for a moment. _____

Sports are a form of entertainment and I enjoy watching the game itself. _____

I am a sports fan because I like gambling or betting on games. _____

I enjoy the beauty and grace of athletics. _____

I enjoy watching sports with large groups of people and I like feeling like I am part of something bigger than myself. _____

Watching games gives me an opportunity to be with my family. _____

I like Carolina sports because of the rich sports history and tradition. _____

3. Please state any other specific reason you have for being involved in Carolina Athletics.

Archival Research

Archival research is sometimes considered a form of empirical research because it involves accessing unique documents that are not widely accessible. An archive is a specialized set of sources usually housed in a library or museum. These texts are usually not available elsewhere, because they are unique, old, rare, or unpublished (or all four). Examples include letters from the Civil War, or the diaries of a famous political figure, or the unpublished essays of a famous author. You might use those materials to find out something new about an historical event or person. For example, imagine you are writing a conference paper (Chapter 11) for a history class on the history of a civil rights memorial on your campus.

To locate archival materials, you can check to see whether your library, city hall, or a local museum or historical society, has original materials you can use.

Strategies for Archival Research

To begin your archival research, check the website for the archive to determine the protocol. Sometimes, you need to contact the archive ahead of time for an appointment to use the archives; in other cases, the archive will have regular business hours.

Also check to ensure that the archive you are interested in is open to the public—some archives are restricted and may require special permission to use.

Before your visit, check the finding aid for your source—these are often posted online. A finding aid is a guide to the archival collection, and it usually includes a short overview, a list of contents, and description of special conditions for use. Since some archives are very large, consisting of tens or even hundreds of boxes, you will need to specify which box and folder you would like to use. For example, imagine that you have identified an archive that might help you to write your conference paper on the Civil Rights Memorial. You might find the finding aid shown in Figure 24.1.

Figure 24.1 Finding Aid for a Physical Archive
① Look here for more information about this collection.
② Check to see if there are any restrictions for using these items.
③ Look here for an overview of the size of this collection.
④ Look here for detailed contents.

When you get to the archive, you may first need to fill out a form listing your name, status (such as undergraduate student), and research topic. You may need to show your student ID or driver's license, or you may even need to get a special researcher's card, which is the case at the Library of Congress in Washington, DC.

Next, you will need to request the boxes or folders you would like to see. Archival materials are not housed in open stacks as they are in a library. Instead, they are stored in a separate location that only library workers can access. Usually, you will go to a separate reading room to use the materials you request, and then return the materials before you leave the room. That way, the library can make sure the materials aren't damaged or stolen.

When you go to the reading room, you may need to check your belongings in a locker or storage room. Usually, you can only bring limited materials into the reading room—no pens, binders, or notebooks are allowed in most cases. Check to see if you can bring your laptop or digital camera—some collections permit them. At some archives, you are encouraged to use your digital camera to photograph documents you want to use in your research, since photocopying can damage delicate old materials.

In other cases, you will be allowed to bring nothing at all. Pencils and papers are often provided in the reading room.

When you receive your materials, be sure to carefully note the Collection Name and number, Box number, and Folder number that you are using. If you are allowed to take pictures with a digital camera, include the box and folder label in your shot. You will need this information for your works cited list (Chapter 28).

Some materials may be too delicate for digital photography or for photocopying. In that case, your only choice is to take careful notes about your findings. Be sure to double-check any information you plan to quote (Chapter 26).

Increasingly, libraries are scanning their archival materials and placing them online. An online archive can provide you with access to materials around the country (or even the world) that you would not otherwise be able to see. For example, for a project analyzing the visual rhetoric of the civil rights movement, you could look up archival images housed in special collections and digitized for public use. Figure 24.2 shows an example of a finding aid for a digital archive.

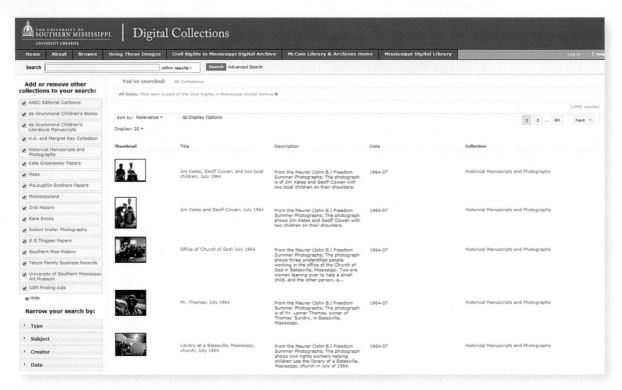

Figure 24.2 Finding Aid for a Digital Archive

Checklist for Archival Research

☐ Ask the librarian for a Finding Aid, which describes the archive and its contents.

☐ Identify what items or folders you'll need and request them from the library.

☐ Bring a digital camera (if allowed) to take pictures of relevant documents. Otherwise, use pencils and paper or a laptop, if permitted. Check with the librarian about materials allowed in the reading room.

☐ Take careful notes: List the Collection Name and number, Box number, and Folder number for each document you use.

☐ Look for items that have been scanned and made available online.

Empirical Research in the Humanities

In the humanities, you are more likely to encounter the term "primary sources" or "primary research" instead of empirical research. Primary research refers to the texts (or other objects of study) you examine or analyze. The kinds of sources you consult differ in different genres and disciplines. For example, for his rhetorical analysis of junk food advertising (Chapter 28), Jay's primary sources were advertisements and websites from McDonald's.

To determine what kinds of primary sources are most suitable, consider your genre and academic discipline. For instance, in a history class, your primary research may involve examining original documents from the time period under study—for a project on the March on Washington, an event from the civil rights movement, you might read newspaper accounts written around the time of the march, or original speeches read at the event. For a literature class, your primary research would involve reading and analyzing (Chapter 8) a text or set of texts, such as a series of poems written by a single author. The texts you use for your analysis are referred to as "primary sources," because they are the ones you are using to make your original research contribution.

B. Conducting Database Research

For some genres, you will rely on research conducted and published by others, such as journal articles, newspapers, magazines, and books. For instance, a literature review (Chapter 11) may require you to work only with published sources. You might also use database research in genres such as an op-ed (Chapter 10), a literary analysis (Chapter 8), or a recommendation report (Chapter 14). We are calling this type of research "database research," since it usually involves searching through collections of sources in a database or library catalog.

A database allows you to search many sources at once, rather than searching through individual journals, books, newspapers, and magazines. Your college library probably subscribes to many different databases. Databases might also include your library catalog (a database listing books and journals owned by your library) or even a search engine (a database of websites).

When you begin database research, first consider your genre and discipline. What kinds of database research are included in your genre? For example, a research paper (Chapter 11) might call primarily for research from books and journals, since these are considered the most authoritative scholarly sources (Chapter 25).

However, you should also consider your discipline. For instance, if you are writing a research paper in a science class, you might be less likely to use books, since scientists primarily share their results through journal articles and literature reviews.

To start your database research, ask a librarian what databases to consult for your topic, or try looking at the list of databases by subject on your library's website, which might look something like the one shown in Figure 24.3.

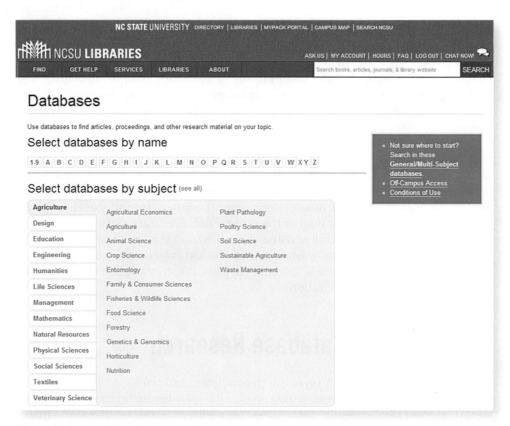

Figure 24.3 List of Databases by Subject
On this page, choose your general subject area first, then select a particular topic or sub-field.

Once you have selected a subject, you will see a list of databases that index research in that area, which might look something like the one shown in Figure 24. 4, a list of databases for research in nutrition.

Some general databases cover a wide range of subjects, while others include a narrower set of publications for a single discipline. You can look for a description of the database to identify what kinds of sources and topic are included, and for the date range. Some databases archive older items only, so they may not be useful if you are looking for recent research.

It is often a good idea to start with a general database when you are trying to narrow your topic (Chapter 23) or get an overview of a field. Some general databases include Academic Search Complete, Google Scholar, and CQ Researcher. In other cases, you will consult a discipline-specific database, one that only focuses on research from a particular field (Table 24.2). For example, if you are writing a research paper for an English class, you might consult the Modern Languages Association (MLA) Bibliography. Again, you can ask a librarian to help you select the best database to start your research.

Figure 24.4 List of Databases Relevant to a Single Discipline
Read the descriptions to get a sense of what each database includes.

Table 24.2 Discipline-Specific Databases

Discipline	Database
Literature and Languages	Modern Languages Association (MLA) Bibliography
Sciences	ScienceDirect
Medicine and Health	PubMed
Psychology	PsycInfo
Sociology	Sociological Abstracts
Political Science and Law	LexisNexis Academic
Business	Factiva
History	Historical Abstracts

There are several purposes for database research. You can use database research to provide historical background or context for an event or an idea. You might use database research to provide evidence for a claim, as in an op-ed (Chapter 10). Or, you might use database research to show that other scholars either support your claims, a way to build *ethos* (Chapter 18), or that they have not yet addressed your research question, a way to identify a gap (Chapter 23). For his rhetorical analysis, Jay used database research to help him identify the context for McDonald's advertising campaigns. He searched a general academic database, Academic Search Complete, as well as specialized databases in business and marketing.

Sources Found in Databases

A number of sources are available to you through database research. These sources vary in their level of detail, depth, and difficulty.

Journals

A journal is an academic publication that includes articles written by researchers for a specialized audience. Most academic fields have a set of journals in which researchers share new findings (usually in the form of research articles). Journals may also publish literature reviews (Chapter 11), book reviews (Chapter 9), and opinions or commentaries. They differ from magazines in that they tend to be written for a specialized academic audience.

For most research projects, you consult journal articles to see what other scholars have published on your topic. This can help you to provide evidence for your own claims, or to distinguish your research question from similar studies. For example, for his rhetorical analysis of fast food advertising, Jay consulted a journal article on the effects of fast food on obesity.

Many (but not all) journals require the articles they publish to be peer-reviewed, which means that other scholars in the field evaluate each article for its credibility and its contribution to the field.

To learn how to distinguish a scholarly journal from other sources, see Chapter 25.

To locate journals relevant to your field, begin with your library's reference desk—either in person or online. You can also use Google Scholar, which limits searches only to scholarly sources. Many scholarly journals are not accessible to the general public without a subscription, but you are very likely to have full access to many academic journals through your campus library.

If you know the name of a specific journal that might be relevant to your research, you can search for it through your library website.

In Jay's case, his project touched on two different areas of study: nutrition and advertising. Jay started by searching for nutrition journals that might have articles about the negative effects of fast food, because he wanted to establish that fact early on in his analysis. By searching for journals in the area of nutrition, he might have seen a list something like the one shown in Figure 24.5.

In most cases, though, your best bet is to search a number of journals at once using a database.

Figure 24.5 Partial List of Online Journals for One Subject Area

Newspapers and magazines   Newspapers and magazines can provide good sources of information for some subjects and genres (see Table 24.3). For example, if you were researching junk food advertising, you might use newspapers and magazines to establish the current context for your research question or to identify whether any new advertising campaigns were currently in progress. News reports about fast food campaigns were useful for Jay's rhetorical analysis of fast food advertising, because they provided background about McDonald's marketing strategy.

You can search for individual newspapers or magazines through your library website, or you can search many newspapers and magazines at a time through a database provided by your college library. This is usually preferable to accessing the publication's own website, because your college might provide special access to older editions or extra content.

Databases for Newspapers and Magazines

- *New York Times* Historical Database
- LexisNexis Academic
- America's News

Books   Books range widely in their scope and intended audience. Some books in your college library will be meant for a general audience and may be written by journalists or other kinds of writers. These books are called "popular books," and they tend to be easy to read and understand. However, the information provided may not be as detailed, and the credibility of that research may be lower since the writer is likely not a professional scholar, and his or her work was probably not submitted to peer review prior to publication. (See Chapter 25 for more on evaluating credibility of books.)

Other books are meant for a scholarly audience (students and researchers). These academic books will be written by researchers, and are likely to have been subject to peer review. Books published by researchers tend to provide detailed, in-depth information about a topic, but as they were written for scholarly audiences who already possess a great deal of knowledge about a subject, they can be harder to wade through than a book meant for a general audience. (See Chapter 25 for more on how to identify a scholarly book.)

Your library will also include textbooks—books written to introduce students to a topic.

The type of book that will best support your research depends on the assignment you are given and the genre you are writing. For a research assignment (such as a research article, conference paper, or literature review), chances are you will be expected to consult and cite scholarly books. Popular books and textbooks may be consulted, but check with your instructor before you cite information from those sources.

For instance, if you were studying fast food advertising, you might look for a book that provides a history of fast food in the United States. However, you might also refer to popular books to give readers a sense of how the issue of fast food is viewed by the public.

You can search for books using your library's online catalog, a type of database that lists only books available at your library. You may also be able to access catalogs that include books available at nearby colleges, or colleges affiliated with your school. Or, you can sometimes request books not available at your library using interlibrary loan—the book will be sent to you from another institution.

Government documents, legal tracts, and reports   Government documents, legal tracts, and reports share one thing in common: they are all official documents written by a governmental group, an organization, or a corporation. For example, a Supreme Court opinion carries the official stamp of the highest judicial authority in the country, while a report by the United States Environmental Protection Agency carries the authority and status of that administrative agency. These kinds of documents are useful when you want to refer to laws, court rulings, regulations, and the like.

For example, for his rhetorical analysis of fast food advertising, Jay might have looked up state or federal guidelines referring to marketing and sales of food to children.

You can often find these kinds of documents posted to government or agency websites. Look for websites ending in .gov, such as epa.gov for the Environmental Protection Agency or supremecourt.gov for the Supreme Court. You may also try databases such as LexisNexis or the United States Government Printing Office's Federal Digital System (www.gpo.gov/fdsys).

Note that organizations can vary widely in their credibility. Some organizations with official-sounding names may be heavily biased by political opinions. Look at the About section on a website to find out who funds an organization and what values they espouse. (See Chapter 25 for more on evaluating these sources.)

Encyclopedias, dictionaries, and other reference items Encyclopedias are comprehensive sources that offer a little information about a wide range of sources. You may be most familiar with general encyclopedias, such as *Encyclopedia Britannica*, which provides information about everything from particular animal species, to countries, to medical conditions, to famous people. However, your library may also include more specialized encyclopedias and reference material that can be a useful starting point for more in-depth research. For instance, if you are researching a particular author or person, you might look for biographical encyclopedias or databases, such as the Biographical and Genealogical Master Index or American National Biography.

Dictionaries can also be useful for research. In addition to general dictionaries, which can help you to define commonly used words, you can look for specialized dictionaries to help you with a particular research topic or area. For instance, you could use the *Oxford English Dictionary* to help you identify how a particular word was used in a given time period, or to see how the meaning of that word has changed over time. You might use the *Dictionary of Marketing* to help you understand terms you encounter while reading research about marketing or to define a term in your own writing.

Other reference sources can be good for finding statistics, such as *Historical Statistics of the United States*, which can tell you information about population, the workforce, and the like.

Online sources You might use another type of database—a search engine—to find other kinds of online or digital sources. Online sources range from blogs and personal websites, to websites belonging to specific organizations and companies, to online versions of magazines, newspapers, and journals. Online sources vary widely in their credibility, so be sure to evaluate them carefully (Chapter 25). In some cases, though, you might use online sources to provide context, or to show what key figures think about the issue. For instance, in his rhetorical analysis of fast food advertising, Jay found it appropriate to cite the website for a fast food company. He did not use these sources as authoritative evidence of the effects of fast food advertising, since scholarly studies (such as journal articles) would be more likely to examine that particular issue.

Strategies for Database Research

As you can see, your library likely offers a wide range of databases, each including different types of sources. Each source might be useful for a different purpose and genre. In Table 24.3, we have summarized each type of source: what it is, what it's good for, and how to find it. You can use this table to help you determine what kind of source to use, and when.

Table 24.3 Types of Database Research Sources

Type of Source	What It Is	What It's Good For	How to Find It
Journals	• Specialized publication for students and researchers • Written by scholars/researchers • Includes peer-reviewed articles	• Focused, specific findings from original research • Writing research genres (Chapter 11) and reports (Chapter 14), especially on scientific and social scientific topics	• Online databases through your library website
Newspapers and Magazines	• General publication for wide audience • Written by journalists • Information in credible publications is fact-checked (but not peer-reviewed)	• Finding information about current events • Finding information about an historical event, as it was described at the time	• Online databases through your library website (for powerful searching of archived editions) • Websites for the publication itself (for current content and some archives)
Academic Books	• Specialized publications written for students and scholars • Written by researchers • Evaluated by other researchers (usually) • Published by an academic press	• Overviews or surveys of scientific, social scientific, and humanities topics • In-depth, extended studies of humanities topics	• Your library's online catalog

Type of Source	What It Is	What It's Good For	How to Find It
Popular Books	• General publication for wide audience • Written by journalists • Information in credible publications is fact-checked (but not peer-reviewed)	• Getting a general overview of a topic before moving on to more scholarly sources • Studying how a topic is presented to general audiences	• Your library's online catalog
Textbooks	• Written for students as an introduction to a topic or field	• Getting an overview or background on a topic	• Your library's online catalog
Government Documents, Legal Tracts, and Reports	• Official documents by an organization or corporate author • Represent official regulations, recommendations, or laws	• Finding out about government laws and regulations • Determining how policy organizations attempt to influence public issues	• Library search engines • Web searches for .gov or .org sites
Encyclopedias, Dictionaries, and Other Reference Items	• Overviews of topics written by experts • Definitions of specialized terms • Statistics gathered by government or other organizations	• Getting background information on a research topic • Finding definitions for key terms • Finding statistics to support a claim or give background	• Online databases available through your library
Online Sources	• Blogs, websites, online versions of journals, magazines, and newspapers • May be written by journalists, or scholars, or amateurs (non-professionals) • Information may or may not be fact-checked or peer-reviewed	• Finding up-to-the-minute information about rapidly changing topics or events • Discovering informal, personal opinions and beliefs about issues	• Web search engines

Reading Database Sources

Finding research related to your topic is one thing. But what do you do with the research you find?

Your first goal should be to get a quick sense of what the source is about. Then you can decide if you need to read it more thoroughly.

For scholarly articles and books, you can usually locate key information by skimming the abstract, introduction, and conclusion (for an article or report) or the table of contents, introduction, and conclusion (for a book). As you skim, look for this information:

- What is the main research finding?
- What methods were used for this research?
- What limitations might there be for this study?
- Does this study support my thesis or hypothesis? Or, does it detract from my thesis or hypothesis?

Let's look at an article Jay may have encountered in his research for his rhetorical analysis of fast food marketing (Figure 24.6).

You should also consider the type of document you are writing, since different genres typically call for different kinds of research. Your analysis of the genre you are writing will help you to identify what kinds of information to gather from your database research. Then, as you read your sources, you can be on the lookout for those kinds of information. For example, if you are writing a profile article (Chapter 5), you might look for key biographical facts about your subject. If you are writing a research paper (Chapter 11), you might note how others have approached the topic or question, since your goal will be to argue that you are posing a new, original question or making an original claim. You might also look for evidence from research findings to support your claim.

C. Managing Database Research

Each database source works differently, so we cannot provide one-size-fits-all directions here. However, for most online sources of information, you can try the following strategies.

Locating Full Text

Some databases will include access to articles in full text format (usually as an HTML or PDF file). In that case, you can download and read or print the article right away. Look for a link that says "full text" or a logo (shown in Figure 24.7). In other cases, you may need to search your library catalog to see if the journal in question is available to you online, or if you need to find it in the print version.

Do health-promoting schools improve nutrition in China?

DONGXU WANG[1*], DONALD STEWART[1], YANFEI YUAN[2] and CHUN CHANG[2]

[1]School of Public Health, Griffith University, South Bank Campus, Grey St, South Brisbane, Brisbane, QLD, Australia and [2]Department of Social Medicine and Health Education, Peking University Health Science Center, No. 38 Xue Yuan Road, Hai Dian District, Beijing, P.R. China
*Corresponding author. E-mail: p06240401@163.com

② SUMMARY

To demonstrate the effectiveness of health-promoting school framework to promoting healthy eating behaviours and nutrition knowledge among Chinese middle school students, their parents and school staff. Three schools were randomly selected from 15 rural middle schools, then were randomly assigned to either (i) school using HPS framework (HPS school), (ii) school with improved health education only (HE school) or (iii) school received no intervention (control school). Nutrition knowledge and eating behaviours were measured at baseline and 3-month after interventions, using the same instrument. Students and parents in the HPS school had the largest improvement in nutrition knowledge, from 4.92 to 8.23 and 4.84 to 7.74, followed by those in the HE school, from 4.98 to 8.09 and 4.78 to 5.80. School staff in the HE school had the largest improvement in nutrition knowledge (from 4.40 to 8.45), followed by those in the HPS school (from 5.20 to 9.15). Students in the HPS school had the largest improvement in eating behaviours (from 3.16 to 4.13), followed by those in the HE school (from 2.78 to 3.54). There was a statistical difference in the improvement of nutrition knowledge of all target population and of eating behaviours of students after interventions across three schools ($p < 0.05$). Both HPS framework and health education can increase nutrition knowledge among Chinese middle school students, their parents and school staff. However, HPS framework was more effective than health education only. Noticeably, HPS framework had a positive impact on students' eating behaviours, which should be in the subject of further research.

① Key words: nutrition knowledge; eating behaviours; health-promoting school; China

Figure 24.6 First Page of a Nutrition Journal Article
① Look here for other search terms to try.
② Look here for an overview of what the study found.

Finding Additional Sources

Many databases offer helpful tools that suggest additional sources. Once you have found a useful source, you can:

- Look at its reference list for related articles on that topic.
- Check to see if the database or search tool suggests additional subject terms or links (shown in Figure 24.7).
- See if the database provides links to other articles that cite the source you have found, or to sources cited in your article.

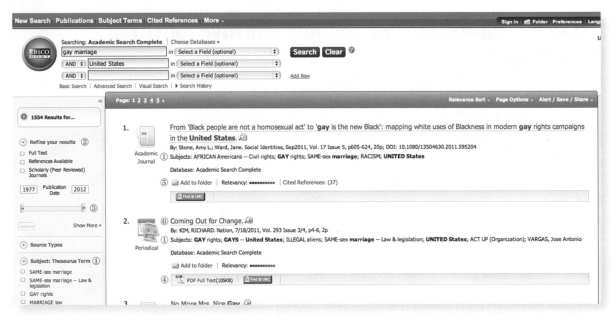

Figure 24.7 Online Database Search Page
① Look here for additional search terms, or click the link to search directly.
② Click these boxes to narrow your search to scholarly journals or to items available online.
③ Use this tool to narrow your results to more recent sources.
④ Click here for full text in PDF format.
⑤ Click here to save this source to print or email later.
⑥ Click here to see the abstract for an article.

Keeping Track of Your Findings

Most online databases will allow you to keep track of the sources you find in several different ways. You can usually mark sources and save them to a "folder" or "clipboard." Then, you can email yourself a list of sources, or print your list, or export it to a digital bibliography tool (such as Endnote, Refworks, or Zotero). A digital bibliography tool can help you to keep track of your research sources, search them using tags or keywords you add, and automatically generate a works cited page in a scholarly citation style, such as APA or MLA (Chapter 28).

Digital Documents

Most university libraries now provide online access to digital copies of books, articles, newspapers, periodicals, and other print resources. You may have several options for working with these files. In some cases, you can only view them through your web browser (as is often the case for electronic books that remain copyrighted),

1162   July 2010

Amer. J. Agr. Econ.

Table 7. Effect of Fast-food Availability on BMI from BRFSS 2004–2006 by Location, Gender, and Race/Ethnicity

	IV without Subway	IV with Subway
Medium Density		
Females	0.061 (0.025)[b]	0.044 (0.018)[b]
Males	0.032 (0.024)	0.023 (0.017)
Blacks	0.263 (0.138)	0.170 (0.089)
Hispanics	0.159 (0.119)	0.112 (0.084)
Blacks and Hispanics	0.195 (0.092)[b]	0.129 (0.061)[b]

Note: Entries are coefficient estimates on number of fast-food restaurants including Subway restaurants. All regressions include controls for county characteristics, age, sex, race, marital status, presence of children, education, income, employment status, a constant and state dummies. Medium density: density >90/sqm and <400/sqm and less than 25 exits. Robust standard errors clustered at the county level are in parentheses.
(a) denotes significant at 1% level
(b) de

> Results are "statistically significant" -- so that means I can cite them with some confidence... might look for other studies saying the same thing.

a m ... Mc ... from ... rest ... fast ...

remarkably similar to those in table 4. Mechanically, the coefficient estimate will be smaller, but the effect of a 1 *SD* increase in the number of restaurants is 0.78 BMI points, which is not statistically different from the 0.67 point increase when Subway was omitted.

Discussion and Conclusion

This paper adds to the existing literature on the effect of fast food on obesity by examining the question separately by geography, gender, and race/ethnic group. Once potential endogeneity is accounted for through the use of instrumental variables, a number of robust findings emerge.

First, interstate highway exits are close enough to being exogenous to be useful instruments. While the interstate system was originally planned to speed the movement of goods and war materiel between manufacturing centers, there are good reasons to suspect that individuals have responded to its presence in nonrandom ways. The findings of the current paper, as well as by Anderson and Matsa (2009), provide strong evidence that this is not the case with respect to behaviors that affect weight outcomes—like smoking, physical activity, and consumption of fruits and vegetables.

Second, consistent with Anderson and Matsa (2009) and Dunn (2009), greater fast-food availability has little impact on obesity outcomes among whites in rural areas. The effect on blacks is less clear, however, as coefficient estimates are sometimes large and negative but are never statistically significant and are relatively unstable. Greater data gathering efforts for this subpopulation are necessary, though potentially feasible, since rural blacks are highly concentrated in the southeastern portion of the

Third, grea ... increase the B ... counties, whi ... studies by Ka ... Harnack, an ...

> Use this section on ethnic marketing by fast food companies -- why it is a problem.

Eales, and Jekanowski (2000). Females may respond more than males to fast-food availability because of differences in household production tasks, particularly child care. Women who might otherwise not stop at a fast-food restaurant may do so at the less than subtle urging of a determined child in the backseat. Thus the positive association between fast-food availability and obesity for females may also signal a positive association for children. This cannot be tested using BRFSS data, but certainly deserves future research efforts.

Fourth, both blacks and Hispanics in medium-density counties exhibit a positive relationship between the availability of fast food and weight outcomes, and the result is statistically significant when both groups are pooled to increase precision. Like the result for females, this is a new finding that should be investigated further. It is possible that the availability elasticity of fast food is higher for minority groups either because of differences in preferences or because of differences in resources that affect household purchasing decisions. For example, previous work has found that neighborhoods with high proportions of minority residents face reduced access to supermarkets and that the availability or affordability of healthy food items at these types of stores may mediate the effect of fast-food availability (Morland, Wing, and Roux 2002; Morland et al. 2002; Inagami et al. 2006).

As the estimation results suggest that the effects of greater fast-food availability are concentrated in specific demographic groups (females and minority groups in medium-density areas), any policy interventions that imposed additional cost on fast-food consumption should also be suitably narrow. Broad restrictions on fast food—such as hefty taxes or zoning restrictions—will impose nontrivial costs on large segments of the population

Figure 24.8 Jay's Notes on a .PDF File

while in other cases you can download and read them at any time on an eBook reader, tablet, or computer. Articles from journals, newspapers, and magazines may come in a range of formats as well. Your task as a researcher is to figure out how best to read, take notes, and save information about each source. Jay used the annotation tools provided in his PDF reader to highlight key information and add notes using text bubbles (Figure 24.8).

For each digital document, ask yourself:

- Can I download this and save it on my computer (or eBook reader or tablet, etc.) for later?
- Can I bookmark this in my browser and come back to it later?
- Can I save the bibliographic information for this source so I can cite it properly (Chapter 28)?
- Can I open this in another program so that I can mark it up or take notes? (A number of digital tools exist that allow you to read, highlight, and mark up digital files. Some popular ones include GoodReader, Evernote, and Adobe Acrobat.)

Digital Bibliography Tools

You can use a variety of digital tools to help you track your sources and generate correct bibliographies and citations (Chapter 28). Some popular programs include Refworks, Endnote, Zotero, and Mendeley. Your library may also provide access to a citation tool, so ask your instructor or your librarian for help. Some of these are available for free!

If you decide to use a digital bibliography tool, learn how to use it to perform the following functions (Figure 24.9):

- Organize your sources, including full bibliographic information, notes, and links to online content.
- Automatically import bibliographic information from an online database.
- Generate bibliography or works cited lists in a variety of formats (such as MLA, APA, or CSE).

Troubleshooting Database Research

Students tend to run into some common roadblocks when they are new to database research.

I'm finding too many sources on my topic.   Refer back to Chapter 23 on developing your topic. Your topic may be too broad, or you may need to narrow your search terms.

> **Problem**: "fast food" yields 10,000 sources.
> **Solution**: Search for "fast food AND advertising."

Figure 24.9 Digital Bibliography Tool
① Use this tool to generate a bibliography using sources you've added to your database.
② Most tools allow you to add sources manually, or to import them from a database file.
③ Most bibliography tools give you an option to search sources you've collected.

I'm not finding enough sources on my topic.

- Try broadening your search terms.
  - Search for "fast food AND advertising" instead of "fast food AND McDonald's advertising."
- Try using synonyms for your search terms.
  - Search for "junk food" instead of "fast food."
- Try a different database or search engine.
- Ask a librarian for help.

I can't find research that supports my thesis or hypothesis. If you're having trouble finding sources that support your thesis, you should consider changing your thesis or hypothesis to reflect your research findings. Unlike an op-ed (Chapter 10) or personal essay (Chapter 4), a research genre (Chapter 11) should reflect what your research sources say. If you cannot find evidence to support your thesis, then you are probably trying to prove something that isn't true. Imagine a scientist trying to argue that smoking does not cause cancer—even though scientific studies clearly show that it does. In the 1990s, cigarette companies were sued (and lost millions) for trying to pay scientists to support the claim that cigarette smoking did not cause cancer. Scientists who agreed to write articles for the cigarette industry were acting dishonestly. For this reason, while you may begin with a tentative thesis or hypothesis, you should expect that it may change as you conduct more research.

In some cases, though, if you do not find adequate published research to support your thesis, that may mean that you have discovered a new angle on a research topic. This means you can make an original argument about your topic. For example, say you cannot find any studies that analyze the rhetorical strategies scientists used to argue that smoking did not cause cancer. In that case, you are not agreeing with the fraudulent scientists, but instead you would be offering an original claim about how those scientists tried to persuade readers of their claims.

Checklist for Database Research

☐ Consider your genre—what kinds of database research are usually included? (books, journals, newspapers, government documents, encyclopedias, online sources?)

☐ Consider your discipline—what kinds of database research are preferred in my field?

☐ Choose databases suitable for your discipline and topic.

☐ Search different databases for different types of sources.

☐ Read and annotate sources carefully.

☐ Manage your database research using digital tools.

Evaluating Sources

Once you have identified where to find sources for a research project, you must not simply grab the first sources you find that pertain to your topic. Instead, you must carefully weigh how credible the sources are. Doing so will help you to ensure that you present the most accurate and up-to-date findings in your own paper, thereby boosting your own *ethos*, or credibility (Chapter 18). In this chapter, you will learn how to identify credible sources, find authoritative (or scholarly) sources, and, most importantly, find sources that are suitable for the genre you are writing.

A. Identifying Credible Sources

For college writing assignments, you will often be asked to employ "credible" sources. Usually, when an instructor asks for credible sources, this means that they expect you to consult your library for well-researched books and articles that have been written by experts in a field.

Most often, these credible sources represent database or secondary sources (Chapter 24)—the sources you use to support the claims you make, establish the history or context for a topic, or show what research has been done in a field. These sources should be credible because you are using them to establish your own credibility, or *ethos*, as a writer (Chapter 18). It would be damaging to your *ethos* if you quoted an incorrect fact or statistic, for instance. To avoid making such a mistake, you should try to locate the best sources you can find: sources that have been evaluated, or vetted, by other experts who have vouched for their credibility.

Academic research is rapidly changing. While the Internet has given us a vast array of sources that we can use to learn about new ideas and current research in just about any field, most colleges still have a library filled with books and periodicals. These print tools can be just as useful to your research process as the Internet.

Most significantly, the print resources in your library and the digital resources that you find online often overlap and intersect. Understanding just what it means to be in "print" or "online" is an important part of learning how to research.

After you determine whether a source is a "print" source or an "online" source (whether it appears in digital form or not), you will need to figure out how *credible* that source is. A credible source is a source whose information can be relied on. This section discusses how to figure out whether a source is credible.

Credible Print Sources

Typically, a print source that you find in your school's library will be credible. You can divide these print sources into two types: books and periodicals (journals and magazines). Scholarly journals and books tend to be the most credible sources in your library.

Credible books   You can tell if a book is a credible source by looking at a variety of factors:

- **Who wrote it?** Is the book authored by a professor or researcher? Professors and researchers have the knowledge and training necessary to conduct good research.
- **Has it been vetted?** Is the book published by a university press or other scholarly press? University presses have reputations for publishing credible books, in part because they only publish work that has been evaluated by other experts for its accuracy.
- **How objective is it?** Does the book have an index, footnotes, and/or a list of references or a bibliography? These kinds of references and citations indicate that the writer has sought to maintain objectivity by referring to other sources, not just his or her own opinions or viewpoints.

Figure 25.1
Back Cover of a Scholarly Book

You can determine who wrote a book, of course, by looking at the author's name on the book cover or title page. Sometimes, a book will also feature a short biographical statement about the author on the back cover or back flap. In other cases, you may have to research the author online to determine what their credentials may be. You can start by looking at the cover of the book.

In the example shown in Figure 25.1, the author is identified as a professor at Harvard University, so you can conclude that the author is an expert. You'll notice that there are also quotations from other scholarly authors, such as Howard Gardner and Richard Dawkins, who attest to the value of this book.

You can figure out what press published the book by looking at the title page of the book. Some examples are shown in Figures 25.2 and 25.3.

Each of these images presents the title page of a book published on a scholarly topic by a professor. The title pages give the author's name, the book title, and the publisher. Sometimes title pages also provide the cities in which the publishers

Language, Cognition, and Human Nature

SELECTED ARTICLES

STEVEN PINKER

OXFORD
UNIVERSITY PRESS

Figure 25.2
Title Page of a Scholarly Book on Science

Law *and the* Limits *of* Reason

Adrian Vermeule

OXFORD
UNIVERSITY PRESS

Figure 25.3
Title Page of a Scholarly Book on Law

are located, the years in which books were published, and job titles and credentials of authors.

If you take a deeper look at either of these books, you'll see that each writer cites other sources using footnotes and a bibliography. Those citations show you that the researcher has drawn his information from other credible sources.

As you can see from this examination of books' title pages, spotting a credible book can be fairly simple. Sometimes, though, you won't be sure if a book is a credible source. In those situations, ask a reference librarian at your library for advice, or ask your professor.

Credible periodicals   The source may also be a scholarly journal published by a professional organization of researchers. Usually, the term *journal* refers to a scholarly periodical published by scholars, for scholars. Your library will most likely have magazines as well; magazines are typically written by journalists for a popular (rather than scholarly) audience.

One way to tell whether the periodical you are looking at is a journal is to examine it closely:

- Who writes it?
  - Are the articles written by credible authors, such as a scholars, researchers, or professors?
- Who vets it?
  - Is the journal published by a professional or scholarly organization?
  - Are articles published in the journal peer-reviewed?
- How objective is it?
  - Are there a lot of footnotes or citations? (Citations are markers of scholarly writing.)
  - Are there few, if any, advertisements?
  - Are there few, if any, photographs or other pictures—aside from technical diagrams, charts, or graphs (common in scientific journals)?

Journals derive their credibility, in part, from the fact that they are usually peer-reviewed, which means that other scholars in the field approved the articles for publication through a review process, one that is often blind. This means that the people evaluating an article for publication do not know who has written the article, so they will not be swayed by what they may know about an author's previous research or reputation.

A magazine, on the other hand, will often be full of images, such as photographs, and advertisements as well. The authors will be journalists, rather than professors or researchers. And there will be few, if any, citations or footnotes. Furthermore, magazines are rarely vetted, or "peer-reviewed," while most scholarly journals are. This vetting process helps ensure that the material published in journals is credible. Let's take a look at an article found in a scholarly journal (Figure 25.4). In this example from the first page of a journal article, you can learn a lot of information.

Journal of Public Health | Vol. 29, No. 4, pp. 358–367 | doi:10.1093/pubmed/fdm067 |

Advertising of food to children: is brand logo recognition related to their food knowledge, eating behaviours and food preferences?

C. A. Kopelman[1], L. M. Roberts[2], P. Adab[3]

[1]Birmingham University Medical School, University of Birmingham, Birmingham B15 2TT, UK
[2]Department of Primary Care and General Practice, University of Birmingham, Birmingham B15 2TT, UK
[3]Department of Public Health and Epidemiology, University of Birmingham, Birmingham B15 2TT, UK
Address correspondence to L. M. Roberts, E-mail: l.m.roberts@bham.ac.uk

ABSTRACT

Background There remains controversy about the contribution of food advertising targeted at children to the epidemic of childhood obesity in the UK. The aim of this study is to explore the relationship between the ability to recognize brand logos featured in promotional campaigns of the food industry and eating behaviours, food knowledge and preferences in children aged 9–11 attending six primary schools in Birmingham, West Midlands.

Methods A '20 flashcard' brand logo quiz assessed children's brand logo recognition ability; a self-completed questionnaire collected information on children's socio-demographic characteristics, eating behaviours, food knowledge and preferences ($n = 476$).

Results Children demonstrated both high brand logo recognition abilities with 88.4% (420/476) recognizing at least 16/20 brand logos in the quiz and high levels of poor diet. No strong correlation was found between higher brand logo recognition ability and poorer eating behaviours, food knowledge and preferences.

Conclusion Although many children are familiar with commonly presented logos of food products, brand awareness does not appear to be a major influence on the consumption of a poor diet amongst children. The regulation or restriction of food advertising to children is unlikely to have a significant impact on obesity rates among children unless combined with measures to address other detrimental influences.

Keywords advertising, children, obesity, diet, food preference

Figure 25.4
First Page of a Journal Article

First, the authors' names and titles are listed under the article title, and their affiliations are listed in a note below that. We learn that these authors are professors at the University of Birmingham in the United Kingdom.

For this article, we can also see an abstract (Chapter 11) and keywords, common features of a scholarly article.

By examining this first page, we can determine that this source is authored by an expert and is written using academic conventions. Therefore, this article is probably a credible source.

Credible Online Sources

Determining whether a source you discover online is credible can pose a much greater challenge than determining the credibility of print sources. Here are some steps that you can take to determine whether an online source is credible.

Is it a digital version of a print resource?   Many sources that you can read online or download to your computer are actually digital versions of print resources. For example, the *New York Times* and other newspapers often publish the same articles both in print and online. (They often have enhanced, online-only content as well.) Furthermore, scholarly journals often make their content available via electronic databases such as Lexis-Nexis or EBSCO. These databases usually require a paid subscription, and you access them through your library's website or an on-campus computer network.

If you download an article from EBSCO in PDF format, chances are that you are looking at a digital version of a print journal. In fact, the digital document that you are viewing is most likely *identical* to the print version in appearance and content.

Thus, discovering whether a digital version of a journal or book is credible simply involves going through the steps outlined previously for discovering credible print resources.

Some sources, however, exist only online. The world of online sources is vast and varied: online sources can be online-only scholarly journals; blogs published by anonymous bloggers; or websites maintained by think tanks or government entities. As a researcher, your first priority should be to determine who authored the online content and who hosts the website where the content is located. In your research, you need to weigh the reliability of both the author and the organization.

For example, a professor writing a blog hosted by a university is probably more reliable than an anonymous blogger writing on a free blogging platform. However, information published in an online journal will probably be more authoritative than the same information on a professor's blog, since the information will have been vetted by the journal editor (and possibly peer reviewers).

Who writes it? Research the author   When you encounter a web site, web article, blog post, or other text online that seems pertinent to your topic of research, you first need to figure out who the author is. Sometimes the author's name appears at the beginning or at the end of the text that you are reading, or at an "about this site" or "about this page" link on the page. Once you have discovered the author's name, see if you can discover any information about this author. Why is this person a credible author, or not? Is there a mini-biography of the person on the website? Can you find the author using a search engine, such as Google?

If you can't find anything about the author at all, tread carefully. It is possible that the person is not a reliable source. You can also ask a reference librarian or your professor for guidance in this situation.

Sometimes it seems that a website or web article has no author, because no single name is given. In this situation, a group or other organization may be the author of the material. You would say that the text has an institutional author.

Whether the text has an institutional author or an actual person as an author, you must next determine what organization sponsors the website and whether that organization is credible.

Who vets it? Research the sponsoring organization   The easiest way to figure out what organization sponsors the website is to read the domain name, or URL. For example, URLs for universities often have the university's name (or an abbreviation) followed by ".edu":

- **http://www.durhamtech.edu:** Home page for Durham Technical Community College
- **http://www.ucla.edu:** Home page for the University of California–Los Angeles
- **http://www.sru.edu:** Home page for Slippery Rock University

If a university sponsors the web page you a reading, and the author seems to be a credible researcher, chances are high that the web page is a credible source. Note, though, that sometimes works posted on a .edu website may be student papers, early drafts of research papers, or similar material that may not be as reliable as a published article.

Other credible sources are often hosted by the government; these domains end in ".gov":

- **http://www.loc.gov:** Home page for the Library of Congress
- **http://www.justice.gov:** Home page for the U.S. Department of Justice

Sometimes, there are sub-domains within one larger organization, like this:

- **http://www.justice.gov/ndic/index.htm:** Home page for the National Drug Intelligence Center, a sub-organization of the Department of Justice

If a government agency sponsors the web page you are reading, chances are also high that the web page is a credible source. In most cases, information posted on a .gov website represents the views or knowledge of that organization as a whole, so it has probably been vetted by a number of individuals associated with that organization. For example, dietary standards on the United States Department of Agriculture (USDA) website have been vetted by government and independent nutrition researchers.

You may also find information posted to the website for a non-profit or non-governmental association. These websites tend to have domains ending in ".org," such as:

- **http://www.npr.org:** Home page for National Public Radio
- **http://www.cato.org:** Home page for the Cato Institute

While the names of these websites may lead you to believe that they are somehow associated with the United States government, the .org domain tells us that these are independent organizations. While National Public Radio receives some government funding, it is not a government institution. Some information posted on the NPR website might be news reports, and NPR is generally considered a credible news source. However, other material on the website may reflect the individual opinions of reporters or radio hosts. It is your job to carefully consider whether an article from this type of website constitutes a credible source.

Let's examine the web page for one organization, the Cato Institute (Figure 25.5), more closely.

Figure 25.5
Web Page of an Organization

You can see from the ".org" at the end of the domain that this organization is probably a non-profit organization. The word "Institute" indicates that this is most likely an organization that exists to fund and conduct research. Their tagline, "Individual Liberty, Free Markets, and Peace," gives you an idea about what the organization's political ideology might be. The Cato Institute tends to support causes associated with libertarians, such as small government, privacy, and low taxes.

If a student were to use an article from this website for research, she would have to take into account the possible influence that the political ideology of the organization might have on the article. To learn more about the political ideology of an organization, click the "About" link on the website. Most organization websites have "About" pages. Often, these "About" pages have mission statements. When you read about the organization, see what you can learn about the organization's political ideology and think about how that ideology might influence the objectivity (and overall credibility) of their articles.

Perhaps the type of website you encounter most often in day-to-day websurfing are those sponsored by companies, which usually end in ".com":

- **http://www.washingtonpost.com:** The *Washington Post* newspaper
- **http://www.pocketliteracycoach.com/blog:** Blog about children's literacy

For .com websites, like .org websites, you have to be even more careful.

The *Washington Post* is a respected newspaper, and so you can expect that articles will be written according to the standards set by professional journalists. Articles will be vetted by the editors, and the newspaper will strive to set a standard for objective reporting in order to maintain its reputation.

The second website, *Pocket Literacy Coach* (Figure 25.6), offers blog posts about how best to encourage children to learn reading and writing. Some of this information could be useful if you were writing a paper on this topic, but the website in question markets a paid product, a text-messaging service for parents of young children. Although the writer of this blog post has a Ph.D. in literacy and composition, because this is a commercial website, it might be better to look up the original research the blogger refers to in his post, and cite that instead. The information posted on the blog may not be vetted directly by other researchers, and because the author is selling a product, he may be tempted to present only information that supports his product's effectiveness.

If there is no sponsoring organization for the article that you are reading—say, because it is an anonymous blog posted on a free blogging website (such as blogger .com or wordpress.com), then you have little information about the source. In fact, you probably have too little information to rely upon the source in your research, if you don't know the sponsoring organization or the author's name.

Figure 25.6
Blog Post from a Company

B. Finding Authoritative Sources for Your Field

Now that you know how to determine whether a source is credible generally—rather than one that is poorly researched or is driven by commercial interests or political ideology—you need to figure out whether a source is authoritative in your particular field of research. Jay's instructor specified that students were to use authoritative sources, so he evaluated each one carefully.

In most fields, sources are considered more authoritative if they are published under certain conditions:

- **Timeliness**: In most fields, researchers give more weight to sources that have been published recently. For example, if you are writing a paper on current trends in child psychology, a source that was published in the 1920s might not be useful or even accurate, because it is most likely outdated. The exception to this rule might be if you are using those sources to establish the history of a topic or field, or you are citing sources published by the founders or "heroes" in a field. (For example, Charles Darwin may still be cited by researchers in evolutionary biology, even though he wrote over 150 years ago; researchers in sociology may still cite research by Max Weber, one of the most influential figures in that field, who published his most important work in the early 20th century.)
- **Prestigious venues**: Most fields have an internal ranking system that they use to evaluate how authoritative a given work may be. In most fields, scholars consider some journals more influential and authoritative than others. For example, scientists consider the journals *Science* and *Nature* to be among the most authoritative journals, since they are highly selective and publish only the most groundbreaking, top-quality research. Similarly, some academic book presses are considered more authoritative than others. If a press has built a reputation for publishing excellent research in a field, it may be considered more authoritative than a newer press or one that is less selective. Oxford University Press, the publisher of this textbook, is usually considered one of the most prestigious presses in the world.
- **Reputation**: In addition to the publication venue (the journal or academic press), scholars tend to evaluate the reputation of the researcher who wrote the article. A senior scholar (a full professor with many years of experience) may carry more authority than a junior scholar or graduate student who is just starting out. In science, researchers may look at the lab sponsoring the research—a junior scholar who is working in the lab of a senior scientist with a strong reputation may benefit from his or her supervisor's credibility.

Finally, you may wish to consider the audience for the work you are evaluating. There are two main types of sources that you may want to use in your research: those published by scholars in a field, and those published by non-scholars. As a general rule, sources published by scholars in the field have more authority.

Scholarly Sources

Scholarly sources are sources published by scholars in a field of research, in venues read and vetted by other researchers. A cell biologist who has published a journal article on her research in the journal *Cell* has published in a scholarly source. But there are audience and purpose considerations that you must weigh in determining whether a source is scholarly, and just how scholarly a source might be.

Written for scholars   A source written by a scholar for an audience of other scholars possesses the highest level of scholarly authority. These sources appear in scholarly journals or in books published by scholarly presses. The article Jay found, shown in Figure 25.4, is a perfect example of a scholarly source written by scholars in a field for other scholars in that field to read.

Written for students   Many researchers write textbooks for use in undergraduate or graduate courses. In fact, you are reading one right now! These sources are generally authoritative, since they represent an expert's summary of a research field, but they do not usually go into as much detail about a topic or research area as you might find in a journal or scholarly book on the same topic. For example, if you wanted to study the concept of "genre" for a research project, you might start with this textbook, but then look for articles and books written about genre theory for other scholars in rhetoric and composition.

Written for non-scholars   Sometimes, scholars write books or articles for a non-scholarly or popular audience. For example, Stanley Fish, a prominent law and English professor, writes an online column for the *New York Times*. Sometimes he writes in his areas of expertise—for example, education policy, or rhetoric, or legal philosophy. In those columns, he is writing as a scholar for a non-scholarly audience. Many researchers also write books for popular audiences, especially if their research holds interest for general readers. For example, the book *The Tell-Tale Brain: A Neuroscientist's Quest for What Makes Us Human*, is written by the prominent neuroscientist V.S. Ramachandra, a researcher at the University of California, San Diego. But the goal of the book is to share interesting findings with non-scientists, not to advance cutting-edge arguments about scientific research among scientists. This source may still be considered scholarly, but it possesses a lower level of scholarly authority than the scholarly articles written for scholarly audiences.

Written outside a scholar's area of expertise   Sometimes scholars write texts on subjects that are outside of that scholar's area of expertise. Often, these texts are intended for a popular audience, not a scholarly one. For example, a famous physicist might write a memoir about her childhood: this memoir would not be a scholarly text because it does not deal with the scholarly subject that is the author's area of expertise (physics) nor is the memoir intended for a scholarly audience (other physicists); instead, it is intended for a broad audience—a popular audience. This text should be considered a non-scholarly source.

Non-Scholarly Sources

Non-scholarly sources comprise texts such as the following:

- Texts written by non-scholars (e.g., a journalist reporting a new discovery in genetics);
- Texts written by scholars on subjects that are outside their areas of expertise (e.g., a lawyer writing about gardening); and
- Any text written by an author whose identity you cannot verify or published in a forum whose sponsoring organization you cannot verify or that is unreliable.

C. Finding Authoritative Sources for Your Genre

Depending on the genre in which you are writing, you might need to use certain kinds of sources. Less formal genres, for example an editorial, might allow you to use less authoritative sources—such as newspaper reports.

However, highly formal genres, such as a research article, require highly authoritative sources—such as peer-reviewed articles by other scholars.

In order to discover which sources are authoritative for your genre, you need to look at examples of writing in your genre and discover what kinds of sources the authors use. Are anonymous sources permitted? Must sources be scholarly?

Here is an example of an entry in Wikipedia Jay consulted in the early stages of his research on fast food marketing (Figure 25.7). What kinds of sources do the authors use? What can you learn about the acceptable sources for the genre of Wikipedia entries from this example?

If you go to Wikipedia online and look at the full "References" section of this article, you will see that the sources that are acceptable in a Wikipedia entry are varied. The authors cite fast food companies, such as Subway and Burger King; articles from news sources such as the BBC and National Public Radio; data from the United States Bureau of Labor Statistics; and a popular book, *Fast Food Nation*. Only one of these sources is a scholarly source, the research article from the journal *Nutrition Research*. Although most of these sources are not scholarly, most, including the BBC, for example, are fairly credible. Thus, it appears that Wikipedia articles require sources to be credible, but not necessarily scholarly.

In comparison, take a look at the last page of a research article Jay encountered in his rhetorical analysis (Figure 25.8). You'll notice that this article refers primarily to scholarly sources, including statistics gathered from national studies, government and organizational reports, and recent articles by other scholars.

Before embarking on research, familiarize yourself with the kinds of sources that are acceptable in your genre. In general, though, the more scholarly your genre, the

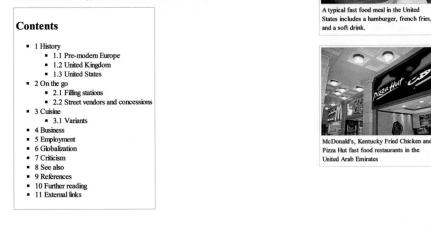

Fast food

From Wikipedia, the free encyclopedia

Fast food is the term given to food that can be prepared and served very quickly, first popularized in the 1950s in the United States. While any meal with low preparation time can be considered fast food, typically the term refers to food sold in a restaurant or store with preheated or precooked ingredients, and served to the customer in a packaged form for take-out/take-away. Fast food restaurants are traditionally separated by their ability to serve food via a drive-through. The term "fast food" was recognized in a dictionary by Merriam–Webster in 1951.

Outlets may be stands or kiosks, which may provide no shelter or seating,[1] or fast food restaurants (also known as *quick service restaurants*). Franchise operations that are part of restaurant chains have standardized foodstuffs shipped to each restaurant from central locations.[2]

Contents

- 1 History
    - 1.1 Pre-modern Europe
    - 1.2 United Kingdom
    - 1.3 United States
- 2 On the go
    - 2.1 Filling stations
    - 2.2 Street vendors and concessions
- 3 Cuisine
    - 3.1 Variants
- 4 Business
- 5 Employment
- 6 Globalization
- 7 Criticism
- 8 See also
- 9 References
- 10 Further reading
- 11 External links

A typical fast food meal in the United States includes a hamburger, french fries, and a soft drink.

McDonald's, Kentucky Fried Chicken and Pizza Hut fast food restaurants in the United Arab Emirates

References

1. ^ Jakle, John (1999). *Fast Food: Roadside Restaurants in the Automobile Age*. Johns Hopkins University Press. ISBN 0-8018-6920-X.; Brueggemann, Walter (1993). *Texts Under Negotiation: The Bible and Postmodern Imagination*. Fortress Press. ISBN 0-8006-2736-9.
2. ^ Talwar, Jennifer (2003). *Fast Food, Fast Track: Immigrants, Big Business, and the American Dream*. Westview Press. ISBN 0-8133-4155-8.
3. ^ Stambaugh, John E. (1988) *The Ancient Roman City* JHU Press ISBN 978-0-8018-3692-3 pp. 200, 209.

Figure 25.7
Wikipedia Entry

more scholarly your sources should be. Examples of scholarly genres would be research articles, conference presentations, and literature reviews (Chapter 11). The audiences for these genres tend to be other scholars or researchers, and they will expect you to cite scholarly information. The more popular your genre, the more popular sources you can typically use. Examples of popular genres might include profiles, book reviews, and editorials (Chapters 5, 9, and 10). The audiences for these genres tend to be readers of general interest magazines, news sources, or websites, and while they may expect you to use credible information, they will be less stringent about the kinds of sources you cite.

366   JOURNAL OF PUBLIC HEALTH

children from highly motivated schools, it is likely that the current study has underestimated the size of the overall problem.

Acknowledgments

The authors would like to thank Mr Daniel Alton, Medical Student, University of Birmingham for his assistance with data collection and also all the children, parents and school staff who supported the project through their involvement. C.A.K. was responsible for the design of the study, data collection and analysis and the drafting of the manuscript. L.M.R. supervised the design and conduct of the study and was involved in the critical revision of the manuscript. P.A. was involved in the conception of the study, supervision during conduct of study and fieldwork and critical revision of the manuscript.

Competing interests

All authors declare that there are no competing interests.

Funding

The study was conducted to fulfil the requirements of an intercalated BMedSc Public Health and Epidemiology degree. Claire Kopelman received financial support from the Medical School, University of Birmingham and the Arthur Thompson Trust. Funders did not contribute to the design, conduction or reporting of findings.

References

1   Anonymous. Selling to-and selling out-children. *Lancet* 2002;**360**:959.

2   McLellan F. Marketing and advertising: harmful to children's health. *Lancet* 2002;**360**:1001.

3   The Food Commission. The Children's Nutrition Action Plan (online). 2001 (cited 6 September 2005). http://www.foodcomm. org.uk/PDF%20files/childrens_Nutrition_Action_Plan.pdf

4   Huhman M, Potter LD, Wong FL *et al.* Effects of a mass media campaign to increase physical activity among children: year-1 results of the VERB campaign. *Pediatrics* 2005;**116(2)**:e277–84.

5   King R, Bickman L, Nurcombe B *et al.* The impact of a poster advertising campaign in buses on young people's awareness and knowledge of a telephone counselling service. *Health Promot J Austr* 2005;**16(1)**:74–7.

6   Lovato C, Linn G, Stead LF *et al.* Impact of tobacco advertising and promotion on increasing adolescent smoking behaviours. Cochrane Database Syst Rev 2003;Issue 3:Art No. CD003439.

7   Hastings G, Stead M, McDermott L *et al.* Review of research on the effects of food promotion to children (online). 22 September 2003 (cited 5 October 2005). http://www.food.gov.uk/multimedia/ pdfs/foodpromotiontochildren.pdf

8   Office of Communications. Childhood obesity—food advertising in context. London: Office of Communications, 2004.

9   Ashton D. Food advertising and childhood obesity. *J R Soc Med* 2005;**97(2)**:51–2.

10 ISBA. Food advertising and children: position report (online). January 2004 (cited 23 October 2004). http://www.isba.org.uk/ public_documents/food-advertsing.pdf

11 International Association of Consumer Food Organisations. Broadcasting bad health: why food marketing to children needs to be controlled. London: The Food Commission, 2003.

12 Office of Communications. Television advertising of food and drink products to children—statement and further consultation (online). 17 November 2006 (cited 24 May 2007). http://www. ofcom.org.uk/consult/condocs/foodads_new/summary/

13 Kennedy C. Examining television as an influence on children's health behaviours. *J Pediatr Nurs* 2000;**15(5)**:272–81.

14 Institute of Community Health Sciences. Health of young people in East London: the relachs study. London: Institute of Community Health Sciences, 2001.

15 Office of the Deputy Prime Minister. Indices of deprivation 2004—summary (revised) (online). 2004 (cited 10 March 2006). http://www.odpm.gov.uk/stellent/groups/odpm_urbanpolicy/ documents/page/odpm_urbpol_028470-01.hcsp

16 Calfas KJ, Sallis JF, Nader PR. The development of scales to measure knowledge and preferences of diet and physical activity behaviour in 4- to 8-year-old children. *J Dev Behav Pediatr* 1991;**12(3)**:185–90.

17 Birmingham City Council. Profile for Birmingham (online). 2003 (cited 24 September 2007). http://www.birmingham.gov.uk/Media? MEDIA_ID=84931

18 National Statistics. Ethnicity (online). 13 February 2003 (cited 24 September 2007). http://www.statistics.gov.uk/cci/nugget.asp?id= 273

19 Birmingham City Council. Index of Multiple Deprivation 2004 (online). 2004 (cited 24 September 2007). http://www.birmingham. gov.uk/Media?MEDIA_ID=97715

20 Gregory J. National Diet and Nutrition Survey: young people aged 4–18 years, Volume 1—findings. London: The Stationary Office, 2000.

21 Ludwig DS, Peterson KE, Gortmaker SL. Relation between consumption of sugar-sweetened drinks and childhood obesity: a prospective, observational analysis. *The Lancet* 2001;**357**: 505–8.

22 Berkey CS, Rockett HRH, Field AE *et al.* Activity, dietary intake, and weight changes in a longitudinal study of preadolescent and adolescent boys and girls (online). *Pediatrics* 2000;**105(4)**. http:// www.pediatrics.org/cgi/content/full/105/4/e56

23 Strauss RS, Knight J. Influence of home environment on the development of obesity in children (online). *Pediatrics* 1999;**103(6)**. http://www.pediatrics.org/cgi/content/full/103/6/e85

Figure 25.8
Research Article (excerpt)

Integrating Sources

Once you have located and evaluated sources, you need to figure out how you want to incorporate those sources into your research paper.

Here is an example paragraph from Jay Zhang's rhetorical analysis (Chapter 28) on McDonald's marketing (with citations in MLA style).

Jay's Example Paragraph

In 2007, McDonald's created the Moms' Quality Correspondents, a campaign that recorded the positive responses of a diverse group of mothers given access to McDonald's food supply system (McDonald's, "Moms' Quality Correspondents"). The unprecedented strategy established parents, especially mothers, as a new target audience. One product of the campaign is Tonia Welling's testimonial titled "What It Means to My Family." She starts off by admitting to her negative impressions of McDonald's but assures the reader her opinions have changed, saying, "I know I have options to feed my family a nutritious meal out, just as I am able to feed them a nutritious meal at home. It's all about my choices" (Welling). Her carefully chosen words invoke the audience of modern moms, and portray McDonald's as an integral part of the busy lifestyle. Speaking from her experience as a mother, Welling praises McDonald's offerings of unhealthy comfort foods. Her portrayal as a member of the target audience conveys trust while she repeats the keyword "choice" to highlight parental responsibility. The focus on choice is reminiscent of its famed obesity lawsuit *Bradley v. McDonald's* where the company argued "the dangers of its food are widely known" and insisted controlling overeating was purely the responsibility of consumers. Considering the numerous lawsuits that charge McDonald's irresponsibly markets unhealthy products towards children, the rhetoric downplaying corporate responsibility in Welling's testimonial, ostensibly written by an ordinary mother, corresponds suspiciously with the company's defensive legal rhetoric ("McDonald's Dismisses Fresh Lawsuit Attack on Obesity").

In this paragraph, Jay uses three sources to convey the idea that McDonald's "established parents, especially mothers, as a new target audience." First, let's examine this paragraph more closely to learn how Jay uses sources strategically, that is, to gain the most power for his argument. Second, let's learn how Jay integrates the sources into his text so that his words and the words of his sources flow together seamlessly. Last, let's look at the various ways he conveys the ideas of his sources: by quoting, by paraphrasing, and by summarizing.

A. Using Sources Strategically

In this paragraph, Jay uses his sources strategically to gain the most impact. For example, he introduces the testimonial of Tonia Welling in this fashion:

One product of the campaign is Tonia Welling's testimonial titled "What It Means to My Family." She starts off by admitting to her negative impressions of McDonald's but assures the reader her opinions have changed, saying, "I know I have options to feed my family a nutritious meal out, just as I am able to feed them a nutritious meal at home. It's all about my choices" (Welling). Her carefully chosen words invoke the audience of modern moms, and portray McDonald's as an integral part of the busy lifestyle.

In this passage, Jay explains who the source is (Tonia Welling, whose testimonial he calls "a product of the campaign"), and speaks to her lack of credibility as well, noting that her words are "carefully chosen" to "portray" McDonald's in a positive light.

Other Ways to Introduce Authors

In other fields, particularly the sciences, authors are rarely introduced in the text itself. Instead, authors are introduced in citations. In other words, the results of a study take precedence over who found those results.

Following is an example from a biology article, which includes the first couple of sentences from an article on genetics (including the first two footnotes).

EXAMPLE: Biology Article (excerpt)

Ray M. Marín and Jiří Vaníček

Optimal Use of Conservation and Accessibility Filters in MicroRNA Target Prediction

PLoS ONE

MicroRNAs (miRNAs) are endogenous small single stranded RNAs that modulate mRNA levels and/or translation in the cell. Recognition of the messenger by the miRNA is followed by either mRNA cleavage or translational repression, leading to a reduction in protein synthesis [1], [2].

. . .

1. Filipowicz W, Bhattacharyya SN, Sonenberg N (2008) Mechanisms of post-transcriptional regulation by microRNAs: are the answers in sight? Nat Rev Genet 9: 102–114.
2. Guo H, Ingolia NT, Weissman JS, Bartel DP (2010) Mammalian microRNAs predominantly act to decrease target mRNA levels. Nature 466: 835–840.

Note that the authors of the excerpted biology article do not introduce the sources in the text. Rather, they simply tell the information that the sources provide and then give the sources in footnotes.

In the social sciences, writers tend to introduce authors in a list, like in this example.

● ●

EXAMPLE: Social Science Article (excerpt)

Shulman, J. L., Gotta, G., & Green, R.

Will Marriage Matter? Effects of Marriage Anticipated by Same-Sex Couples

Journal of Family Issues

Research consistently suggests that marriage can serve as a protective factor in that people who are married demonstrate superior levels of mental health compared with unmarried individuals (Diener, Suh, Lucas, & Smith, 1999; Dush & Amato, 2005; Mathy, Kerr, & Lehmann, 2003; Mathy & Lehmann, 2004). Married people report fewer symptoms of depression and substance abuse (Brown, 2000; Horwitz, White, & Howell-White, 1996; Marcussen, 2005).

● ●

In the preceding example (which uses APA style), the authors do not introduce the sources into the text, but focus their writing on the findings from previous scholars and then introduce sources in parentheses.

The point is, before you write a research paper for a class, you need to do some research about what sorts of expectations your professor might have for how you use sources. You should also research how writers in the field use sources by looking at examples of the genre you are approximating—in most cases, a journal article.

B. Integrating Sources into Your Work

When you use sources in your work, you must give thought to how the source material and your own writing work together. Integrating sources into your work requires multiple steps: selecting the proper source material (quotations, paraphrases, or summaries); introducing the source material with an introductory verb; and then providing an explanatory sentence (if necessary) to help your reader understand the significance of the source material.

Let's discover how Jay integrates sources into his paragraph. Here is his paragraph on the targeting of mothers by McDonald's. Pay attention to the highlighted words.

In 2007, McDonald's created the Moms' Quality Correspondents, a campaign that recorded the positive responses of a diverse group of mothers given access to McDonald's food supply system (McDonald's, "Moms' Quality Correspondents"). The unprecedented strategy established parents, especially mothers, as a new target audience. One product of the campaign is Tonia Welling's testimonial titled "What It Means to My Family." She starts off by admitting to her negative impressions of McDonald's but assures the reader her opinions have changed, saying, "I know I have options to feed my family a nutritious meal out, just as I am able to feed them a nutritious meal at home. It's all about my choices" (Welling). Her carefully chosen words invoke the audience of modern moms, and portray McDonald's as an integral part of the busy lifestyle. Speaking from her experience as a mother, Welling praises McDonald's offerings of unhealthy comfort foods. Her portrayal as a member of the target audience conveys trust while she repeats the keyword "choice" to highlight parental responsibility. The focus on choice is reminiscent of its famed obesity lawsuit *Bradley v. McDonald's* where the company argued "the dangers of its food are widely known" and insisted controlling overeating was purely the responsibility of consumers. Considering the numerous lawsuits that charge McDonald's irresponsibly markets unhealthy products towards children, the rhetoric downplaying corporate responsibility in Welling's testimonial, ostensibly written by an ordinary mother, corresponds suspiciously with the company's defensive legal rhetoric ("McDonald's Dismisses Fresh Lawsuit Attack on Obesity").

Introductory Verbs

By using the words highlighted in the preceding excerpt, Jay takes special care to ensure that readers know when the information that he is conveying comes from his sources, rather from his own ideas. These words, called introductory verbs, let a reader know when an idea derives from source material rather than from the author's own writing. Introductory verbs are a crucial tool for integrating sources into your writing.

For example, Jay writes, "She [Welling] starts off by admitting to her negative impressions of McDonald's but assures the reader her opinions have changed, saying, 'I know I have options to feed my family a nutritious meal out, just as I am able to feed them a nutritious meal at home. It's all about my choices' (Welling)."

Jay uses introductory verbs like "admit," "assure," and "say" to indicate when Welling is "speaking" in his paper. Table 26.1 shows some common verbs and phrases you can use to introduce a source.

Table 26.1   Introductory Verbs and Phrases

Verbs
acknowledges, admits, advises, agrees, alleges, argues, asserts, assures, avows, believes, charges, claims, comments, concludes, concurs, confirms, contends, declares, denies, disagrees, disputes, emphasizes, grants, illustrates, implies, insists, maintains, notes, observes, points out, reasons, rejects, reports, responds, states, stresses, suggests, thinks, writes
Phrases
According to, As stated by, In the words of, As one scholar puts it, As one critic notes

Note: Verb tenses   Different citation styles require different verb tenses when you use introductory verbs in your writing. For example, MLA style usually requires that you write the verb in the present tense when discussing a text or quotation, in the fashion that Jay uses here: "She starts off by admitting. . . ."

In APA style, however, the verb tense depends on how the source is being used. If Jay were using APA, then he would use the past tense of the verb to introduce findings or results: "Welling has shown that. . . ." However, if he were introducing a quotation by discussing the implications of the results, he would use the present tense: "Welling's research suggests that. . . ."

Introductory verbs and phrases signal to your reader that the words that follow belong to your source, and not to you. This signaling is one strategy that you can employ in order to avoid plagiarism (Chapter 27).

Explanatory Sentences

After you introduce your source with an introductory verb, then provide your source material, you might need to provide some explanation of the source material in your own words to help your reader.

For example, Jay wrote the following explanation after a quotation in his paper:

> She [Welling] starts off by admitting to her negative impressions of McDonald's but assures the reader her opinions have changed, saying, "I know I have options to feed my family a nutritious meal out, just as I am able to feed them a nutritious meal at home. It's all about my choices" (Welling). Her carefully chosen words invoke the audience of modern moms, and portray McDonald's as an integral part of the busy lifestyle.

Jay's explanatory sentence after the quotation (highlighted) accomplishes three important tasks:

1. It explains Welling's quotation to the reader.
2. It helps integrate the quotation within Jay's paper by transitioning from Welling's voice back to Jay's voice.
3. It moves Jay's argument forward by explaining how Welling's words function rhetorically.

That's a lot of work for one sentence to accomplish. Integrating sources into your writing is hard work, but it is very important for your writing to be successful.

Jay uses three different strategies in his paragraph to convey the ideas of others. He summarizes others' ideas, he paraphrases others' words, and he quotes others' words directly. These three strategies give you a variety of tools to incorporate sources into your work.

C. Summarizing

Summarizing means putting the general idea of another author's work in your own words. Use a summary to convey in a brief fashion the general ideas of another. Often, a single sentence of summary can convey the ideas of an entire paragraph, or even an entire article, chapter, or book.

Halfway through his paragraph, Jay summarizes the testimony of one of the moms in McDonald's campaign using only one sentence: "Speaking from her experience as a mother, Welling praises McDonald's offerings of unhealthy comfort foods."

Jay uses the introductory verb "praises" to convey that the ideas that follow belong to another (the McDonald's mother, Welling), even though he conveys Welling's ideas in his own words, even modifying them somewhat (noting that the food she is praising is "unhealthy").

Summaries are very common in APA papers as well. For example, in his article on incarcerated parents, Terrence writes the following summary:

> Lewis (2004), a family lawyer, argues that although courts have indeed agreed
>
> that visitation is a fundamental right that incarcerated individuals should have,
>
> there are numerous legal barriers and prison regulations that prevent visitation
>
> from occurring as much as needed.

Terrence summarizes the entire argument of Lewis's journal article in one sentence and cites the article using APA style (the year in parentheses after Lewis's name).

D. Paraphrasing

A paraphrase is similar to a summary in that the writer uses her own words to convey the ideas of another. A paraphrase differs from a summary in that the paraphrase presents the ideas of another in roughly the same number of words as the original source material. Use a paraphrase when the ideas of the original source are important, but the way those ideas are originally conveyed is not important—or worse, confusing or difficult to understand.

Here is an example of a paraphrase from Jay's paragraph (note his MLA parenthetical citation at the end of the sentence):

> In 2007, McDonald's created the Moms' Quality Correspondents, a campaign
>
> that recorded the positive responses of a diverse group of mothers given access to
>
> McDonald's food supply system (McDonald's, "Moms' Quality Correspondents").

Here is an example of a paraphrase from Terrence's paper, which includes an APA citation at the end:

Numerous negative issues such as attachment disruption, disorganization, delinquency, risky behavior, and even risk for future incarceration are correlated with a child having an incarcerated mother (Dallaire, 2007).

In APA style, it is usually less important to convey who the source author is than it is to convey the source author's research. Here, Terrence quickly paraphrases the data from Dallaire's study, and he allows the parenthetical to convey to the reader where the source material can be found.

Students often struggle with writing good paraphrases. Sometimes, student writers end up plagiarizing the author's work by writing a paraphrase that tracks too closely to the source material.

Here is the source material that Jay paraphrased in his paper from a page on the McDonald's website, titled "Moms' Quality Correspondents."

A few years ago, we launched Moms' Quality Correspondents, an exciting project to address questions that moms—and dads—have been asking about what their kids are eating. Representing real families from across the country, a group of moms came with different backgrounds but a common concern: they care about what their kids eat.

Here are four common mistakes Jay might have made when paraphrasing this source:

1. Using the **same terms and phrases** that appear in the original source.
2. Using the **same sentence structure** that appears in the original source.
3. Using **substituted synonyms** rather than rephrasing the entire idea of the original source in a new way.
4. **Failing to cite** the original source material.

Here's how an incorrect paraphrase would look:

A few short years ago, McDonald's began Moms' Quality Correspondents, an enthralling project to answer questions that moms have asked about what their kids eat. Moms with different backgrounds came together because they all cared about what their children were eating.

The preceding paraphrase is plagiarism, for a variety of reasons (see Chapter 27). First, it is plagiarism because it fails to cite the original source (and that is pretty basic). It also is plagiarism because when you (1) keep the same terms and phrases (e.g., "a few short years ago"); (2) keep the same sentence structure (e.g., "we launched" and "McDonald's began"); and (3) substitute synonyms (e.g., "enthralling" for "exciting"), you have not paraphrased at all, but basically stolen the words of another. This is not a paraphrase; it is a modified quotation without quotation marks—and that is plagiarism. The author has two choices: craft a genuine paraphrase or use the original quotation properly.

Here is a correct version of the same paraphrase. Notice that it provides new information, in new words and using new sentence structure:

> In 2007, McDonald's created the Moms' Quality Correspondents, a campaign
>
> that recorded the positive responses of a diverse group of mothers given access
>
> to McDonald's food supply system (McDonald's, "Moms' Quality
>
> Correspondents").

Note: Do *not* use a paraphrase when the actual words of the source material are important or memorable. Instead, quote the source material to convey the strength of the source material's original words in your paper.

E. Quoting

A quotation involves using the exact words that the author uses in the source material. Use a quotation when the wording from the original sources is important. For example, you might quote the exact words from a poem in a literary analysis, or the exact wording of a law for a paper in political science.

Here is an example of a quotation from Jay's paper.

> [Welling] assures the reader her opinions have changed, saying, "I know I have
>
> options to feed my family a nutritious meal out, just as I am able to feed them a
>
> nutritious meal at home. It's all about my choices" (Welling).

Jay uses the introductory verbs "assures" and "says" to convey that the language that follows belongs to his source. He also places the quotation within quotation marks.

Here is a quotation from Terrence's paper. First, he summarizes the argument of the author, then highlights a point of the author's argument with a quotation:

> Lewis (2004)[5], a family lawyer, held that although courts have indeed agreed that visitation is a fundamental right that incarcerated individuals should have, numerous legal barriers and prison regulations prevent visitation from occurring as much as needed. She points out several legal factors that prohibit child visitation. First she cites the case *Alexander v. Alexander,* in which "the Kentucky Court of Appeals held that incarceration does not preclude or interfere with the parent's right to a hearing on the matter of visitation" (p. 105). This means that regardless of a parent's incarceration, she still has a right to petition the court for visitation.

Why did Terrence choose to quote the particular material that he quoted? Let's examine the words of the quotation more closely. Notice how powerful and descriptive the language is. The quotation contains many powerful phrases, including "intensely distressing," "suicidal thoughts or actions," and "loss of contact with children." Terrence included this quotation because he knew that this powerful language would help persuade his readers to agree with his position that children should be allowed to visit their imprisoned mothers.

Whichever way you choose to integrate a source into your writing—summarizing, paraphrasing, or quoting—be sure that you carefully cite your sources to ensure that you do not commit plagiarism (Chapter 27).

Note that different disciplines tend to rely on summary, paraphrase, and quotation differently. In the natural sciences, scholars rarely use direct quotes and tend to rely mostly on summaries of the findings from other research studies. They find the results of these studies more important than the words used to describe them. In the social sciences, quotations are used occasionally, especially if they are from interviews or survey responses from the authors' research, but researchers usually summarize or paraphrase findings from other research studies.

In contrast, many humanities fields, such as history and literature, rely heavily on quotations from the source texts, since scholars in these fields focus on the wording of those texts (such as poems, historical documents, etc.).

Avoiding Plagiarism

As a college student, you are expected to uphold the highest ethical standards for your research and writing. Most colleges have an official policy on academic honesty, and that includes a policy about plagiarism. In this chapter, you will learn about what, exactly, constitutes plagiarism, the different types of plagiarism you must avoid, and what you can do to avoid plagiarism in your own work.

A. What Is Plagiarism?

There are two ways that you can think about plagiarism: one is as a practical issue, the other is as a rhetorical issue.

Plagiarism as a Practical Issue

Plagiarism, strictly defined, is the use of the words or ideas of another without proper attribution (e.g., citation).

For many students, plagiarism is a practical issue. Students fear committing plagiarism, and rightly so. Most colleges and universities have severe punishments for students who do commit plagiarism. Students also fear plagiarism because they are not sure exactly what plagiarism entails. Because of this confusion, many students actually commit plagiarism by accident.

But what does that mean in practice? What steps can a writer take to avoid accidentally plagiarizing a source?

- You need to *give proper credit* whenever you quote, summarize, or paraphrase another author's words (Chapter 26).
- You also need to be sure that you give credit to the *proper author* and avoid mixing up your sources.
- Lastly, you need to be sure that you give proper credit whenever you use *someone else's ideas*, not just their exact words—whenever you summarize or paraphrase, not just when you quote directly (Chapter 26).

Plagiarism as a Rhetorical Issue

Plagiarism is also a rhetorical issue. Many students are concerned that their writing is not "original" enough. They are tempted to use the ideas of others in order to seem smarter. But, rhetorically speaking, using the ideas of others can make your writing *stronger*, not weaker. By properly citing, you have shown that others agree with your position.

Citing sources strengthens your writing in a variety of contexts. For example, academic research requires that you join an ongoing conversation on a topic (Chapter 11). You must cite sources in order to demonstrate what that conversation is and what your contribution to it is—even if your contribution is small. Journalism requires that your sources be credible. Even if you do not reveal the name of a source for material that you are reporting, you must at the least reveal that you used a source. In the business world, if you use the words or ideas of others in a speech or proposal, you are committing plagiarism at the least, and maybe even fraud or copyright infringement.

As you can see, in a wide variety of writing contexts, it is important to properly acknowledge sources.

B. Types of Plagiarism

Plagiarism comes in different varieties. Here are some descriptions of types of plagiarism that you need to avoid in order to steer clear of plagiarism violations.

Wholesale Plagiarism

Wholesale plagiarism occurs when a writer turns in a document produced by another, claiming that the work is original. This type of plagiarism is deliberate (as opposed to accidental), and has become easier and easier with the advent of "essay mills" on the Internet. Before essay mills, students paid others to write papers for them or "borrowed" a paper from a friend. (Of course, these practices still occur today.)

Students are often tempted to use an essay mill or to use someone else's paper when they save their writing assignment for the last minute. Be sure to plan ahead when you have a paper to write, and set intermediate deadlines for yourself so that you have plenty of time to research, write, and revise your paper.

Patchwork Plagiarism

Sometimes students accidentally plagiarize large chunks of text from a source. This is called "patchwork plagiarism," because the plagiarized text appears, in patchwork fashion, in between blocks of text written by the student. Patchwork plagiarism often occurs because a student cuts and pastes a paragraph from a source into her paper, and then forgets to cite the entire paragraph. Or, the student pastes the paragraph, changes a few words, and believes that the resulting paragraph is sufficiently original.

Unfortunately, both of these scenarios will lead to plagiarism. Your best bet is to *never* cut-and-paste an entire paragraph into your paper. Instead, be selective with your quotations, paraphrases, and summaries, and keep track of what words and ideas belong to another by using placeholder citations.

Here's how a paragraph from Jay Zhang's rhetorical analysis paper (Chapter 28) would look if he had committed patchwork plagiarism. Some of the words in the following paragraph are Zhang's own ideas and words, but much of the ideas and words belong to McDonald's. If Jay did a lot of cutting-and-pasting from the Internet, he might have lost track of his citations and committed plagiarism, ending up with a paragraph something like this:

> On McDonald's black-tailored 365Black website, the main appeal is community connection. McDonald's appeals to several specific target audiences in the black demographic but its main message is being deeply rooted in the community. Some pages of the 365Black connect with the concerns of the nuclear family and traditional African culture, announcing we believe African-American culture should be celebrated 365 days a year . . . Like the unique African Baobab tree, which nourishes its community, McDonald's has branched out to the African-American community. With imprecise language and suggestive imagery, the chain's rhetoric facilitates positive identification for African-Americans. Language promoting community welfare is supplemented with pictures of smiling families and professionally dressed young adults. McDonald's confronts its reputation as purveyor of inferior goods to historically disadvantaged demographics by providing visual and textual symbols of social and financial success.

Jay's actual paragraph correctly uses quotation marks as well as citation. As a result, it no longer includes plagiarism.

> On McDonald's black-tailored 365Black website, the main appeal is community connection. McDonald's appeals to several specific target audiences in the black demographic

but its main message is being "deeply rooted in the community" (McDonald's 365Black, "Home"). Some pages of the 365Black connect with the concerns of the nuclear family and traditional African culture, announcing "we believe African-American culture should be celebrated 365 days a year. . . . Like the unique African Baobab tree, which nourishes its community, McDonald's has branched out to the African-American community" (McDonald's 365Black, "What Is 365Black?"). With imprecise language and suggestive imagery, the chain's rhetoric facilitates positive identification for African-Americans. Language promoting community welfare is supplemented with pictures of smiling families and professionally dressed young adults (McDonald's 365Black, "Opportunities"). McDonald's confronts its reputation as purveyor of inferior goods to historically disadvantaged demographics by providing visual and textual symbols of social and financial success.

> Here, the words that Jay quoted are now properly placed inside quotation marks and followed with a parenthetical citation.

> Here, Jay properly provides a citation for a summary of a web page.

Paraphrasing Plagiarism

Some writers mistakenly believe that when they convey the ideas of another in their own words, then they do not need to cite the source from which the ideas came. Remember, you must give proper attribution when you use the *ideas* of another, not just the words (Chapter 26). Anytime you summarize or paraphrase a source, you should cite it.

Avoiding plagiarism might seem like a daunting task. This rest of this chapter will guide you through it. The first step is getting organized. You need to work hard to keep track of all of the sources that you use in a research paper.

C. Keeping Track of Sources

One major cause of accidental plagiarism is failing to stay organized while you conduct research. Let's examine how Jay organized his notes while he wrote his rhetorical analysis of McDonald's marketing.

Here's a paragraph from Jay's paper. We have used boldface to indicate the words and ideas drawn from his sources.

On McDonald's black-tailed 365Black website, the main appeal is community con-

nection. McDonald's appeals to several specific target audiences in the black demographic

but its main message is being **"deeply rooted in the community"** (McDonald's 365Black,

"Home"). Some pages of the 365Black connect with the concerns of the nuclear family and

traditional African culture, announcing **"we believe African-American culture should be**

celebrated 365 days a year. . . . Like the unique African Baobab tree, which nourishes its com-

munity, McDonald's has branched out to the African-American community" (McDonald's

365Black, "What Is 365Black?"). With imprecise language and suggestive imagery, the

chain's rhetoric facilitates positive identification for African-Americans. **Language promot-**

ing community welfare is supplemented with pictures of smiling families and professionally

dressed young adults (McDonald's 365Black, "Opportunities"). McDonald's confronts its

reputation as purveyor of inferior goods to historically disadvantaged demographics by

providing visual and textual symbols of social and financial success.

Keeping Good Notes

First, Jay kept good notes as he went along. For example, in MLA style (Chapter 28), the works cited entry for the sources Jay uses in the preceding paragraph are these:

365Black. Home page. 365Black. McDonald's, 2011. Web. 24 Feb. 2013.

---. "Opportunities." 365Black. McDonald's, 2011. Web. 24 Feb. 2013.

---. "What is 365Black?" 365Black. McDonald's, 2011. Web. 24 Feb. 2013.

But, while he was researching and writing, Jay didn't worry about getting his citations perfect. Instead, he kept notes with information about his sources.

Here's what Jay wrote for one of the websites he cites in his article:

Author: McDonald's 365Black.
Title: What is 365Black?
Publication: McDonald's 365Black web site
Volume, Issue, Year, Pages, URL: http://www.365black.com/365black/whatis.jsp

Notice that Jay kept track of all of the information that he would need in order to find the web page again. Some students print all sources and keep them in a binder, to ensure that they always have a copy of a source on hand. Others use a free cloud-based program, such as Endnote or Evernote, to organize articles, notes, and other resources for a writing project. These organization strategies will help you keep track of your sources during your research and writing process.

Using Placeholders to Cite While You Write

Once you have an efficient way to keep track of the sources that you will use in a research paper, you need an efficient way to cite those sources while you are writing your paper.

Unless you have a citation style memorized, don't worry about citing perfectly as you are composing. If you are too worried about citation style, you might distract yourself from your writing.

Instead, use placeholders to indicate sources. For example, when Jay was drafting this paragraph, he used placeholder parentheticals like this:

> With imprecise language and suggestive imagery, the chain's rhetoric facilitates positive identification for African-Americans. Language promoting community welfare is supplemented with pictures of smiling families and professionally dressed young adults (365Black "Opportunities" web page). McDonald's confronts its reputation as purveyor of inferior goods to historically disadvantaged demographics by providing visual and textual symbols of social and financial success.

He underlined the placeholders to remind himself to go back through and cite them properly later (Chapter 28). These placeholders ensured that Jay didn't forget to give proper attribution to his sources when he paraphrased ideas in his paper.

Using Digital Tools

There are many computer programs that can help you keep track of sources that you use in your paper. For example, Microsoft Word comes with a built-in citations feature. You type in the bibliographic data of a source, select a citation style, and then insert a citation into the text whenever you use a source in your paper.

There are also freestanding programs that integrate with word processors to help you keep track of sources. They function similarly to the citations feature in Word. Here is a list of programs that you might want to investigate:

- Endnote
- Mendeley
- Papers
- Refworks
- Sente (Mac only)
- Zotero

Your campus library system may provide a citation engine that works with its own catalog, databases, and journal subscriptions. Check out your library's home page or ask a reference librarian to see what free digital source management resources are available to you. Often, your library will provide training sessions free of charge to students who want to learn how to use these tools.

Citing Sources

When you use the words or ideas of another in your writing, you must cite the source material from where you found those words or ideas. By citing your sources, you make your writing more powerful because you demonstrate that you relied upon credible sources (Chapter 25). Citing sources properly also helps you avoid plagiarism (Chapter 27). In this chapter, you will learn some general principles about citation, and then we will present guidelines for two of the most common citation styles, MLA and APA. You will also see how two students (Jay and Terrence) used these citation styles for their own research papers, which we include here in full.

A. When to Cite

Knowing when to cite is the first step to citing properly.

Generally, determining when to cite means first determining whether you are reporting specialized knowledge. Citing sources is also genre-specific, since less formal genres have less formal citation requirements.

Common versus Specialized Knowledge

As a general rule, you must properly cite the words or ideas of another.

However, sometimes the ideas that you find in a source are actually common knowledge. For example, the date of the signing of the United States Declaration of Independence (July 4, 1776) is common knowledge—at least in the United States. You do not need to cite to a source when you mention that fact in your writing.

Specialized knowledge, however, should be cited. Specialized knowledge is (1) knowledge that other researchers have created or (2) knowledge that is not commonly known to your particular audience.

Determining Common Knowledge for Your Field

What is "common knowledge" depends on the field that you are writing in. For example, in Jay's rhetorical analysis on McDonald's marketing, he cites specialized knowledge, but he also allows for some common knowledge in the field of business and advertising. Here is an excerpt from his paper:

> **In late 2002, McDonald's posted its first quarterly loss since its founding over six decades ago.** The sluggish growth and plummeting sales were caused in part by McDonald's inability to adapt to its changing consumer base that developed a greater appetite for healthy foods.

The statement in bold, "In late 2002, McDonald's posted its first quarterly loss since its founding over six decades ago," is common knowledge in the field of business. This fact is easily found in a public resource such as *Yahoo! Finance* or any other aggregator of information about stocks traded on the New York Stock Exchange. It is a fact that wasn't discovered or created by a researcher and need not be cited.

After providing this common—or readily accessible—knowledge, Jay provides detailed information from researchers in the fields of health and nutrition, and he cites these sources:

> Despite menu revisions that have added healthier alternatives, the offering of burgers and fries that compose the bulk of McDonald's menu remain unchanged. Compared to Subway, another restaurant famous for health claims (Lundgren 110), McDonald's "overall product portfolio is more on the fatty side" (Joppen 49).

Here, Jay is citing information that is not necessarily common knowledge for his audience, information that was created by researchers in this subject area. Thus, Jay carefully treads the delicate line between specialized and common knowledge.

The most important rule is this: when in doubt about whether information constitutes common knowledge, you should cite a source.

Formal or Informal Citation?

Sometimes, the genre that you are writing dictates the type of citation that you need to provide. For example, a formal research paper requires strict adherence to a citation style such as APA or MLA.

However, some genres, such as a newspaper editorial, do not require such strict or formal citation. For these genres, a clear reference to a source is adequate. Here is an example from an excerpt from a newspaper editorial titled "A Campus Climate Change," which appeared in *New University,* a student newspaper from the University of California at Irvine.

> Pennsylvania State University professor Susan Rankin, who is the lead consultant on the UC Campus Climate Study Team and head of Rankin & Associates, defines campus climate as "the current attitudes, behaviors and standards of faculty, staff, administrators and students concerning the level of respect for individual needs, abilities and potential."

Although the editorial uses a quotation, it does not follow a strict citation style to indicate where the quotation comes from. Instead, it uses informal citation, mentioning the name of the source and her qualifications. This type of informal citation is acceptable in journalistic genres such as op-eds (Chapter 10), film reviews (Chapter 9), and profile articles (Chapter 5). However, if you are writing one of these genres as an assignment for a class, be sure to check with your instructor to see if he or she would like you to use a formal citation style.

B. Discovering Citation Styles: MLA and APA

Scholars use different citation styles, depending on the field in which they are writing and the journal in which they are publishing. Two common styles are the Modern Language Association (MLA) style and the American Psychological Association (APA) style, but you may be required to use other styles in your college career for different courses.

MLA and APA citation styles are indeed different, but they share some fundamental characteristics. For any citation style, you can figure out what you need to do by asking the following questions.

What's the In-Text Signal?

First, all citation styles provide an in-text signal alongside the quoted, paraphrased, or summarized text, to indicate that the words or ideas used belong to another. In MLA and APA, this signal is a parenthetical, or information provided within parentheses at the end of a sentence or clause.

Here's an example of MLA parentheticals from Jay's paper:

> Compared to Subway, another restaurant famous for health claims **(Lundgren 110),** McDonald's "overall product portfolio is more on the fatty side" **(Joppen 49).**

In the preceding example, the name "Lundgren" and the number "110" in the first parenthetical indicate the author and the page number where the information preceding the parenthetical can be found. Readers familiar with MLA style know that the full citation will appear at the end of the paper on the alphabetical Works Cited page under "Lundgren."

In the APA style, the citation would include only the author of the source and the year it was published. This type of signal is called the author-date style. If Jay had written his paper in APA style, the Lundgren parenthetical would appear like this:

> Compared to Subway, another restaurant famous for health claims **(Lundgren,**
>
> **2008), . . .**

Other citation styles, such as Chicago style, use superscript numbers (i.e., footnotes or endnotes) to indicate the use of a source (although Chicago style also allows for use of the author-date system).

Whatever style you are using, first figure out what sort of in-text signal the style employs.

Footnote or Reference List, or Both?

Both APA and MLA style use a list of references at the end of a paper to give the full citations of sources. In MLA, this list is called a Works Cited page. In APA, it is called a Reference list.

Here is the MLA Works Cited entry for Lundgren's article in Jay's rhetorical analysis:

> Lundgren, Jessica. "Eating Fresh in America: Subway Restaurant's Nutritional
>
> Rhetoric." *Young Scholars in Writing* 6 (2008): 110–117. Web. 13 Mar. 2013.

The Works Cited entry provides all the details that a reader would need to know in order to locate the source. In other words, the full entry allows the reader to follow in the tracks of a writer's research.

Other citation styles, such as Chicago, sometimes do not use a reference list and instead put the full citation in a footnote.

Whatever style you are using, you need to figure out whether the style uses a reference list, footnotes/endnotes, or both.

Reference List: Alphabetical or Numerical Order?

If your style does use a reference list, you need to determine how to order the references. MLA and APA both order references alphabetically by the first author's last name. However, other citation styles (especially in the sciences) may order sources numerically based on the order they appear in the article.

C. Discovering Citation Guides for Other Styles

Suppose you have to write a paper in a citation style that is neither APA nor MLA. How do you go about finding out the citation rules for the new style?

You can conduct an Internet search of the style to discover what publications exist to assist you. Suppose your professor has asked that you use "CSE style," but you have no idea what that is. If you conduct a search for "CSE Style" on the Internet, you will discover that rules for CSE style are published by the Council of Science Editors in *Scientific Style and Format: The CSE Manual for Authors, Editors, and Publishers.* You can then go to your library and check out the style manual, or look for an online guide on your library's website.

D. MLA Citation Guide

What follows is a short guide to MLA citation format. MLA style was developed by the Modern Language Association, a professional organization with members in the fields of literature and languages. MLA is a citation style commonly used in the humanities. For more information about MLA style, consult the most current edition of the *MLA Handbook for Writers of Research Papers.*

Principles of MLA Citation

MLA uses an author-page format for in-text citations: you provide a parenthetical with the author's name and the page number whenever you cite a source. Writers in the humanities often use direct quotations, because textual analysis is central to much of the work that humanities scholars do. They often use quotations from a text—such as a poem or a novel—as evidence for a point they are making in an analysis. You should include a parenthetical citation for each quotation you use, but also for any summary or paraphrase of a source (Chapter 26).

A paper formatted in MLA style should also include a Works Cited list, which gives the complete citation for each source mentioned in the text. At the end of this chapter, you can find a sample paper formatted in MLA style.

MLA In-Text Citations

The basic format for parentheticals in MLA style is to provide the author's last name— if you did not provide it in the text preceding the quotation (or paraphrase or summary)—and the page number where the quotation (or paraphrase or summary) is located. Titles of sources are included if you use multiple works by the same author.

Single author's name included in in-text signal   If you give the author's name in an in-text signal, you only need to include the page number in parentheses:

> Austen's most famous novel begins with a sentence that is nearly as famous as the novel itself: "It is a truth universally acknowledged, that a single man in possession of good fortune must be in want of a wife" (1).

Single author's name not included in in-text signal   If you do not include the author's name in a signal phrase, you need to include the author's last name and the page number in parentheses. Do not place a comma in between the author's name and the page number:

> Many readers are familiar with this famous maxim: "It is a truth universally acknowledged, that a single man in possession of good fortune must be in want of a wife" (Austen 1).

Citing a long quotation   If the quotation is longer than four lines (of prose, poetry, or drama), do not use quotation marks, but set off the quotation from the text by starting the quotation on a new line and indenting the entire quotation by one inch.

> Twain's *Huckleberry Finn* begins in a memorable fashion:
>
>> You don't know about me, without you have read a book by the name of "The Adventures of Tom Sawyer," but that ain't no matter. That book was made by Mr. Mark Twain, and he told the truth, mainly. There was things which he stretched, but mainly he told the truth. That is nothing. I never seen anybody but lied, one time or another, without it was Aunt Polly, or the widow, or maybe Mary. Aunt Polly—Tom's Aunt Polly, she is—and Mary, and the Widow Douglas, is all told about in that book—which is mostly a true book; with some stretchers, as I said before. (1)

Note that the parenthetical citation is placed *after* the end punctuation, and it is *not* followed by a period.

A source with two or three authors   In the humanities, articles and books sometimes have more than one author. Whether or not you mention all of these authors depends on the number of authors.

For a source with two or three authors, name all of the authors in your text (whether in an in-text signal or a parenthetical). Order them in the order they appear in the source:

Marx and Engels suggest that "[a] spectre is haunting Europe—the spectre of Communism" (1).

The authors of *The Communist Manifesto* suggest that "[a] spectre is haunting Europe—the spectre of Communism" (Marx and Engels 1).

A source with three or more authors   If a work has three or more authors, you may choose to list the last names of all of the authors:

In their study of consumers in Alabama, Alonso, O'Neill, and Zizza found, "[O]verall the findings point to a rather low degree of consumer interest in learning about foods they consume outside their homes" (296).

In a study of consumers in Alabama, researchers found, "[O]verall the findings point to a rather low degree of consumer interest in learning about foods they consume outside their homes" (Alonso, O'Neill, and Zizza 296).

Or you may choose to list only the first named author and use "et al." to indicate the rest of the authors (if there are three authors or more):

In their study of consumers in Alabama, Alonso et al. found, "[O]verall the findings point to a rather low degree of consumer interest in learning about foods they consume outside their homes" (296).

In a study of consumers in Alabama, researchers found, "[O]verall the findings point to a rather low degree of consumer interest in learning about foods they consume outside their homes" (Alonso et al. 296).

Citing multiple authors with the same last name   If you cite sources by authors with the same last name in your paper, then you must provide the first initial of an author's first name in your parenthetical.

Jo March had "the uncomfortable appearance of a girl who was rapidly shooting up into a woman and didn't like it" (L. Alcott 3).

Note: if two authors have the same first initial *and* last name, provide the full first name of each author.

Citing multiple sources by the same author   If you cite multiple sources by the same author, and you do not include the title of the work in the in-text signal, you must include the title in the parenthetical. Use a shortened title if appropriate. For example, you might shorten the title of a book called *Consuming Higher Education: Why Learning Can't Be Bought* to simply *Consuming Higher Education*. (Often, dropping the subtitles of books and articles, like in the preceding example, will create a strong short title.) Format book titles in italics or underlining (but be consistent in your document); place article titles inside quotation marks. Do not place a comma in between the title of the work and the page number. If you need to provide the author's name as well, do separate the author's name from the title with a comma.

Author's name included in in-text signal

Austen's most famous novel begins with a sentence that is nearly as famous as the novel itself:

"It is a truth universally acknowledged, that a single man in possession of good fortune must be in want of a wife" (*Pride and Prejudice* 1).

Author's name not included in in-text signal

One of the most famous novels in English begins with a sentence that is nearly as famous as the novel itself:

"It is a truth universally acknowledged, that a single man in possession of good fortune must be in want of a wife" (Austen, *Pride and Prejudice* 1).

Citing works with no page numbers   If you are citing a source that does not have page numbers, such as a web page, poster, or pamphlet, use "n. pag." to indicate "no page numbers."

According to the United States Food and Drug Administration, signs of heart disease include trouble breathing, trouble sleeping, an ache in the chest, and pain in the back, between the shoulders (n. pag.).

Citing works by an organization or company   If you are citing sources from a government website, an organization, or a company, you may not find an individual author's name. Instead, you can consider the organization or company to be the author, and cite its name the same way you would cite an author. Provide a page number if possible.

The "Spot the Block" program is meant to encourage "tweens" to make healthy food choices (U.S. Food and Drug Administration 16).

Citing works by an unknown author   If you cannot find the author of a work, look for the name of the organization, company, or institution that produced it. If you cannot find out who produced the source (an individual or a group), then you should be hesitant about citing it, since that source may carry little authority. However, if you must cite a source from an unknown author, use the title of the work instead of the author. Furthermore, it would be helpful to indicate in your text that the author is anonymous, so that your reader understands more about the source.

One anonymous blogger claims that the fast food industry is responsible for his excessive weight gain, since he was influenced by their misleading health claims ("Why McDonald's Made Me Fat").

Citing indirect sources   Sometimes you must use a source that is quoted by another writer. However, you should do this very rarely. Instead, locate the original source, and cite that. Citing the original source shows that you are a strong researcher; it also prevents the possibility that you are replicating an error of quotation (or understanding) made by another writer. If you must cite an indirect source, write "qtd. in" plus the author's name and page number, like this:

> Bitzer argues that a rhetorical situation is "a complex of persons, events, objects, and relations" (qtd. in Miller 152).

MLA Works Cited list   In MLA format, a Works Cited list is included to provide full information about each source included in the paper. Sources on the Works Cited list should appear in alphabetical order, by last name of the author. You should use a hanging indent, so that the first line of each reference is not indented, but every line after that is indented by half an inch. (Many word processors have a feature called "hanging indent," which can be found under paragraph formatting settings. Use this feature rather than spacing or tabbing over to indent the paragraph.)

A standard MLA Works Cited list includes the following features:

- **Authors' names**: List an author's last name, followed by a comma, then the author's first name.
  - If there are **multiple authors** of a work, list the first author with the last name first, then list the rest with the first name first.
  - If you cite **multiple works by the same author**, sort the works in alphabetical order by title, provide the author's name with the first work, then replace the author's name with three hyphens (---) with the rest of the author's works.
  - If the work has an **organization or corporation** as its author, put the organization in the author position in the Works Cited entry.
  - If the work has **no named author** (an unusual occurrence), list the work on the Works Cited list by the title of the work.
- **Titles**: Capitalize all major words in a title. You do not need to capitalize article words ("a" or "the"), coordinating conjunctions (e.g., "and" or "but"), or short prepositions (e.g., "of" or "on"). Place journal or magazine article titles inside quotation marks. Italicize or underline book titles or the name of the journal. (Either italicize or underline—be consistent.)
- **Source information**: For journal articles, give the name of the journal, the volume and issue numbers, the page numbers for the article, and the year of publication. For a book or longer work, provide the place of publication and the name of the publisher along with the year of publication. Indicate whether the source was found in print or on the Web.

In what follows, you will find a detailed guide to citing each type of source in your Works Cited list.

INDEX OF CITATIONS

Citing Books

A standard MLA citation form for a book includes the author's name (last name first), followed by a period; the title of the book (in italics or underlined, with the first letter of appropriate words capitalized), followed by a period; the city of publication, followed by a colon; the name of the publisher, followed by a comma; the year of publication, followed by a period; and the medium of publication (e.g., print or web), followed by a period.

1. A book by a single author

Wallace, David Foster. *A Supposedly Fun Thing I'll Never Do Again: Essays and Arguments.* New York: Little, Brown, 1997. Print.

2. A book by two or three authors

Roskelly, Hephzibah, and Kate Ronald. *Reason to Believe: Romanticism, Pragmatism, and the Teaching of Writing.* Albany: State U of New York P, 1998. Print.

Note the comma after the name of the first author. Note also that after the first author, additional authors are listed by first name, then last name.

3. A book by more than three authors

Dernbach, John C., et al. *A Practical Guide to Legal Writing and Legal Method.* 4th ed. New York: Aspen, 2010. Print.

Note the comma after the name of the first author. Also note the correct punctuation of "et al.": do not put a period after "et," but do put a period after "al."

4. An electronic book

Elbow, Peter. *Writing Without Teachers.* New York: Oxford UP, 1998. Kindle file.

5. A new edition of a book

Vaughn, Lewis. *Bioethics: Principles, Issues, and Cases.* 2nd ed. New York: Oxford UP, 2012. Print.

6. A book with an editor

James, William. *Pragmatism and Other Writings.* Ed. Giles Gunn. New York: Penguin, 2000. Print.

Citing Articles, Book Chapters, and Periodicals

A standard MLA citation form for a book chapter or article includes the following:

- the author's name (last name first), followed by a period;
- the title of the article (in quotation marks, with the first letter of every appropriate word capitalized)—with a period inside the quotation marks;
- the title of the periodical (in italics, with the first letter of every appropriate word capitalized), NOT followed by a period;
- the volume and issue numbers (if applicable);
- the year of publication, followed by a period;
- the medium of publication (e.g., print or web), followed by a period.

7. An article in a scholarly journal

Devitt, Amy J. "Integrating Rhetorical and Literary Theories of Genre." *College English* 62.6 (2000): 696–718. Print.

Note that the current MLA style (7th ed.) requires that writers always provide issue numbers in a journal article citation when possible.

8. An article in a magazine

Gladwell, Malcolm. "The Order of Things: What College Rankings Really Tell Us." *The New Yorker* 14 Feb. 2011: 68–75. Print.

Note the day-month-year format of the date. Note also that there is no period between the title of the magazine and the date.

9. An article in a print newspaper

Carter, Andrew. "Penn State Saga Hits Home with ACC: 'It's a Tragic Situation.'" *The News and Observer* [Raleigh, NC] 24 Jul. 2012: C1+. Print.

Note that for newspapers that are less well known, such as in this example, you should include the city and state in brackets after the paper's title. Cite the newspaper's section and page number. (Sections are usually numbered alphabetically, with the first section being A.) If the article continues on another page, add a plus sign, as in "A2+."

10. A review (of a book/film/television/play)

Acocella, Joan. "Cloud Nine: A New Translation of the *Paradiso*." Rev. of the *Paradiso*, by Dante Alighieri, trans. Robert and Jean Hollander. *The New Yorker* 3 Sept. 2007: 126–33. Print.

Note that the author and title of the review are included. Next there are the words "Review of" (shortened to "Rev. of"), followed by information about the work being reviewed.

Citing Online and Other Non-Print Sources

In its most recent edition, the MLA style manual no longer requires that writers provide the URLs (web addresses) of online sources. However, writers are still permitted to do so. Since one of the purposes of a Works Cited list is to enable a reader to follow in your research footsteps, it is often useful to provide the URLs of sources that *cannot be found in research databases* (such as *LexisNexis*).

Here is our advice: whenever you use online sources, be sure to jot down the URL right away so that you can refer back to the source when you create your Works Cited list. Try bookmarking online sources in your browser as you find them, printing online sources, or saving online sources using a program such as Evernote or Zotero.

The basic format for citing an online source in MLA is this:

- the name of the author (last name first), when available, followed by a period;
- the article name in quotation marks, if available, followed by a period;
- the title of the website (or book or periodical) in italics (or underlined), followed by a period;
- the version number or publication date of the web page (or "n.d." to indicate "no date"), followed by a period;
- publisher information, which can be the website sponsor (or "n.p." to indicate "no publisher"), followed by a comma;
- the word "Web," followed by a period;
- and the date you last accessed the site, followed by a period.

11. An article from an online database (such as LexisNexis or JSTOR) Citations for articles retrieved from online databases are similar to citations for print articles, only you should also include the title of the database in italics, followed by a period; the word "Web," followed by a period; and your access date, followed by a period.

Ramirez, Charles E. "Soldier: Judge Should Lift Ban on Service Dog in Courtroom." *The Detroit News*. Detroit Media Partnership, 30 Jan. 2013. *America's News*. Web. 31 Jan. 2015.
Koster, Jeremy. "Hunting Dogs in the Lowland Neotropics." *Journal of Anthropological Research* 65.4 (2009): 575–610. *JSTOR*. Web. 30 Jan. 2015.

12. An article from an online-only journal An online-only journal is one that does not have a print version. To determine whether you are using an article from an online-only journal, read the "About" information for that journal.

Carpenter, Rick. "Disability as Socio-Rhetorical Action: Towards a Genre-Based Approach." *Disability Studies Quarterly* 31.3 (2011): n. pag. Web. 24 July 2015.

Note: when citing an online journal *that also appears in print*, include the page numbers of the article as well. Some online-only journals do not include page numbers. In that case, put "n. pag." instead of the article's page numbers.

13. An article in an online-only newspaper or magazine   An online-only newspaper or magazine is one that does not have a print version. To determine whether you are using an article from an online-only newspaper or magazine, read the "About" information for that publication.

Goldstein, Katherine. "I'm with the Band: How I Fell in Love with a Computer Nerd and Ended up Marrying a Rock Star." *Slate*. The Slate Group, 24 July 2012. Web. 15 August 2015.

14. An article in an online newspaper or magazine that also appears in print   Some print newspapers or magazines also publish content online. To determine whether you are using an article from an online newspaper or magazine that also appears in print, read the "About" information for that publication.

Singer, Natasha. "Medical Papers by Ghostwriters Pushed Therapy." *New York Times*. The New York Times Company, 4 Aug. 2009: A1. Web. 24 July 2015.

15. A web page authored by an organization or company

Monsanto Company. "The Monsanto Pledge." *Monsanto.com*. Monsanto, 2012. Web. 24 July 2015. <http://www.monsanto.com/whoweare/Pages/monsanto-pledge.aspx>.

Note that, in this example, the writer chose to include the URL of the web page in order to make it easier for a reader to find this rather obscure source. When used, URLs should come at the end of the Works Cited entry and be enclosed in angle brackets, followed by a period.

16. A Web page with an unknown author   If you cannot find the author for a web page, look for the name of the organization, company, or institution that produced it. If you cannot find out who produced the page (an individual or a group), then you should be hesitant about citing it, since that source carries little authority. However, if you must cite a web page from an unknown author, use the title instead, placing it in inside quotation marks. It is a good idea to include the URL as well, since this kind of source is usually difficult to find again.

"Hotter, More Acidic Ocean Threatens Food Security." *Ecocentric*. N. pag., 28 Dec. 2012. Web. 31 Aug. 2015. <http://www.gracelinks.org/blog/>.

17. A podcast

Davies, Dave. "What's Driving College Costs Higher?" *Fresh Air. NPR.org.* WHYY, 26 Jun. 2012. Web. 2 Dec. 2015. <http://www.npr.org/programs/fresh-air/>.

Note that the writer included the URL here to make the source easier to locate.

18. A professional film or video recording

Bowling for Columbine. Dir. Michael Moore. MGM DVD, 2003. DVD.

Note the title is written first, followed by the director of the film (after the abbreviation "Dir."). Next, put the distributor (which is different for a film release and a DVD release). Lastly, put the medium (Film, DVD, VHS, or MP4 Video).

19. An online video

Carlson, Robert. "Breast Cancer: Risk Factors, Diagnosis and Treatment." *YouTube.* YouTube, 21 Feb. 2011. Web. 27 Nov. 2015.

Note that MLA does not specify a format for citing online videos. We suggest using this format, which is similar to other online sources. Include the date the video was posted, and the date you accessed the video.

20. A television or radio program

"Autism Now: Exploring the 'Phenomenal' Increase in U.S. Prevalence." *PBS News-Hour.* PBS. UNC-TV, Durham, NC. 18 April 2011. Television.

Note: provide the network name ("PBS") *and* the local affiliate channel and the city of that affiliate.

21. A song or audio recording

King, Carole. "You've Got a Friend." *Tapestry.* Sony, 1999. CD.

Note: to cite an entire album, just leave off the song title.

22. An online forum, discussion board, or blog post

Angelik. "Gay with Asperger's." 28 Feb. 2011. *WrongPlanet.net.* Wrong Planet, 5 Nov. 2015. Web. <http://www.wrongplanet.net/postt153364.html>.

Note: provide the URL if the post might be difficult for a reader to find.

23. An interview that you conduct

James, Louisa. Personal interview. 23 Nov. 2012.

24. A published interview

Johnson, Charles. "The Root Interview: Charles Johnson." Interview by Michael E. Ross. *The Root*. The Slate Group, 7 Jan. 2010. Web. 15 Aug. 2014.

25. An email

Donaldson, Joanne. "Some Thoughts about Metonymy." Message to Cordell Smith. 28 Dec. 2013. Email.

E. Formatting a Paper in MLA Style

When you are asked to submit a paper using MLA style, you should not only cite your sources according to MLA guidelines. You should also use MLA formatting guidelines, unless otherwise directed.

General Formatting Guidelines

Here are some general formatting guidelines for MLA-style papers:

- Type your paper using a 12-point font. Use a standard serif font such as Times New Roman, Cambria, or Garamond. As a general rule, fonts with serifs are easier to read than fonts without serifs (such as Arial or Calibri).
- Double-space your entire paper, including block quotations. But do not put extra spaces between paragraph text and text of block quotations. Do not put extra space between paragraphs.
- Print on white, 8.5-by-11-inch paper.
- Use 1-inch margins on all sides.
- Indent paragraphs .5 inch. Use your tab button to do so, rather than the space bar.
- Put your last name plus page numbers in the header in the top-right corner. Include this header on the first page.
- Put only *one* space after periods, not two.

First Page Format

MLA style does not require a title page, so you do not need to make one unless you are asked to by your instructor. For the first page:

- In the top-left corner of the first page, put your name on the first line, your instructor's name on the second line, your course name on the third line, and the date (in MLA style) on the fourth line. This header should be double-spaced just like the rest of the manuscript.
- On the next line, write your title. Capitalize all major words of your title. Center your title, but do not boldface it, italicize it, or put it inside quotation marks. The title should be double-spaced just like the rest of the manuscript—do not add extra spacing before or after the title.
- Begin the first paragraph of your paper after the title. Indent the first paragraph.

Body Pages Format

For the body of your MLA paper:

- Maintain double-spacing throughout.
- MLA style does not suggest a particular format for section headings. However, if you would like to use section headings to break up a long paper, be sure to use a consistent, simple format. For example, you could number sections using Arabic numerals and a period (e.g. "1. The Critical Response to *White Noise*").
- Insert any figures or tables within the text, being sure to introduce them in the text and label them properly (Chapter 29).

Works Cited Page Format

For the Works Cited list:

- Start a new page.
- Center the words "Works Cited" at the top (without the quotation marks)
- Include your references in alphabetical order, using a hanging indent (indent each line after the first one for each source by .5"). Note: In Word, go to Format → Paragraph and choose Special → Hanging. If you try to indent the paragraphs yourself, you will run into a layout mess.
- Double space all entries.

Insert your last name and page number aligned flush right on each page, beginning at 1.

EXAMPLE 28.1: A Student Research Paper in MLA Style

Zhang 1

Include your name, the professor's name, the course title, and the date at the top of the page, double-spaced and aligned left. Dates in MLA appear as follows: day, month, and year, with no commas or other punctuation.

Jay Zhang

Professor Jordynn Jack

English 102

15 March 2015

On the title page, include the full title of your paper, capitalizing all the main words.

McDonald's: A Limited Response to Increased Health Consciousness

In late 2002, McDonald's posted its first quarterly loss since its founding over six decades ago. The sluggish growth and plummeting sales were caused in part by McDonald's inability to adapt to its changing consumer base, a base that had developed a greater appetite for healthy foods. For months, reports detailing the severity of the global obesity epidemic flooded the public consciousness and took center stage in political debate. As McDonald's customers started seeking healthier alternatives from competitors such as Subway, pressure mounted. Faced with dismal profits and an obsolete growth plan, McDonald's adopted a health-conscious image that better reflected the attitudes of its customers. Over the next 12 months, McDonald's experienced record same-store sales growth while company profits increased, increasing their profit margin from 5.8 percent in 2002 to 20.38 percent in 2011 (fig. 1).

McDonald's incredibly successful rebranding focused on reconnecting with the minds of consumers who adopted a youthful health-conscious attitude. In 2003, it launched

Zhang 2

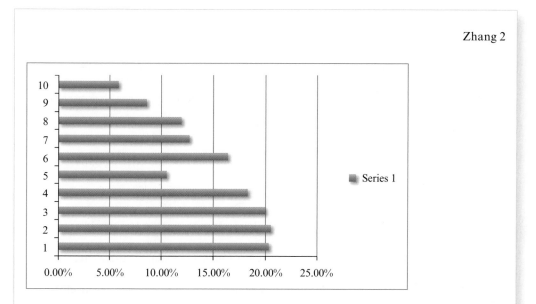

Fig. 1. McDonald's Profit Margins from 2002 to 2011 from Hoover's, "McDonald's Corpo-

ration"; Hoovers.com, 2012; Web; 13 Mar. 2013.

"i'm lovin' it," the chain's first tagline used on a global scale. According to the advertis-

ing agency Heye, the informal lowercase line was chosen because of its "hip, relevant

and powerful" message (qtd. in Datamonitor). McDonald's further connected with the

youth market by producing a series of advertisements featuring singer Justin Timberlake.

The youthful presence reflected the chain's focus on health issues reinforced by rhetoric

supporting active lifestyles and better nutritional choices. The campaign highlighted

the availability and quality of fruits and vegetables, improvements in image that were

realized by extensive menu changes (Macarthur, "Fast-Food Goes on Health Kick").

Although some professional critics of the campaign argued its unified message was too

Zhang 3

simplistic and did not effectively target local markets, its success is indisputable. Mc-Donald's regained profitability in 10 months and has maintained the health conscious image to this day.

Despite menu revisions that have added healthier alternatives, the offering of burgers and fries that compose the bulk of McDonald's menu remain unchanged. Compared to Subway, another restaurant famous for health claims (Lundgren 110), McDonald's product line tends to have more calories and saturated fat per meal (Joppen). Furthermore, the sudden rise of obesity in the American political consciousness has largely been an elite discourse espoused by the mainstream media. Contrary to the opinions of health experts, most Americans are not seriously concerned about obesity and are not likely to modify their personal behaviors (Oliver and Lee 925). Accordingly, McDonald's seeks a fine balance, pushing its healthier image without alienating its traditional consumer base. It is caught in the delicate position of fervently expressing a new commitment to health and nutrition while continuing to serve the same unhealthy foods. The new marketing strategy and image have been criticized as unrepresentative of a typical meal. Misleading the public in this way represents deception by omission, and thus McDonald's rhetoric of healthy fast food deserves further analysis.

McDonald's multimedia websites provide representative profiles of McDonald's marketing intentions by bringing text, images, and video together without the time or space restraints of other media. I have identified two interrelated marketing strategies that

If the author's name is not included in the sentence, put it in the parentheses along with the page number.

Zhang 4

McDonald's uses: (1) marketing towards children by emphasizing choice and (2) marketing in an ethnically targeted fashion. I will consider what external pressures encouraged McDonald's to adopt these rhetorical strategies and how each could contribute to the aforementioned deception by omission.

1. Defending Marketing Towards Children

McDonald's has recently tried to reshape consumer perception of its child-centered marketing. From Ronald McDonald's first appearance in 1963 to its 2006 partnering with Funky Friends, the chain maintains constant notoriety for its appeals to children. PR pundits have suggested this marketing in electronic media bypasses parents and "is effective at conditioning opinion" (Tiltman). Starting in 2004, several high profile documentaries, including *Super Size Me*, have condemned McDonald's as a major contributor to America's obesity problem, specifically citing the company's targeting of children and low socioeconomic strata (Macarthur, "McD's May Take Hit"). At the same time, the company was defending itself from a myriad of related lawsuits. McDonald's continued to use this time-tested marketing strategy, and has defended the practice by emphasizing consumer choice controlled by parental responsibility.

In 2007, McDonald's created the "Moms' Quality Correspondents," a campaign that recorded the positive responses of a diverse group of mothers given access to McDonald's food supply system (McDonald's, "Moms' Quality Correspondents"). The unprecedented strategy established parents, especially mothers, as a new target audience. One text of the campaign is

Jay used section headings because he felt this long paper needed them to indicate the main sub-topics. He numbered sub-headings consistently using an Arabic numeral and period, and kept the font simple.

Zhang 5

Tonia Welling's testimonial titled "What It Means to My Family." She begins her testimonial

by admitting to her negative impressions of McDonald's but assures the reader her opinions

have changed, writing, "I know I have options to feed my family a nutritious meal out, just

as I am able to feed them a nutritious meal at home. It's all about my choices" (Welling). Her

carefully chosen words invoke the audience of modern moms and portray McDonald's as

an integral part of the busy lifestyle. Speaking from her experience as a mother, Welling

praises McDonald's offerings of unhealthy comfort foods. Her identity as a member of the

target audience conveys trust, and her repetition of the keyword "choice" highlights parental

responsibility. The focus on choice is reminiscent of the famed obesity lawsuit *Pelman v.*

McDonald's. The plaintiffs, parents of obese children, argued that "McDonalds' products are

inherently dangerous because of the inclusion of high levels of cholesterol, fat, salt and sugar"

(531). In response, "McDonald's argue[d] that because the public is well aware that hamburg-

ers, fries and other fast food fare have such attributes, McDonald's cannot be held liable"

(531). McDonald's essentially insisted that controlling overeating was purely the responsibility

of consumers ("McDonald's Dismisses"). Considering the numerous lawsuits charging that

McDonald's irresponsibly markets unhealthy products towards children, the rhetoric down-

playing corporate responsibility in Welling's testimonial, ostensibly written by an ordinary

mother, corresponds suspiciously with company's defensive legal rhetoric.

McDonald's further defends consumer choice by suggesting it has broad commitment to

child nutrition using expert testimony. Under the Kids Nutrition section of the website,

When you have mentioned an author's name in the text, you include only the page number in the parentheses.

Zhang 6

McDonald's declares its product is "Food to Feel Good About." The page invites visitors to

meet their nutrition executives Dr. Cynthia Goody and Julia Braun. Congruous with the

motherly imagery plastered about the page, the two professional women are pictured to put

a trustworthy human face behind their titles. The strong ethos appeals are made by textual

blurbs which detail the experts' extensive educations, previous experience, and current roles

at the company. Julia Braun's profile exemplifies a direct response to the accusations of poor

nutritional fact accessibility by the famed documentary *Super Size Me*; it addresses Braun's

role in ensuring "the accuracy and accessibility of nutrition and ingredient information"

(McDonald's, "Food to Feel Good About"). With text wrapped around a picture of a crisp

green apple (see fig. 2), Dr. Cynthia Goody, Director of Nutrition, lists "options that can

help even [the] youngest customers make good, fun choices" (McDonald's, "Food to Feel

Good About"). Every option suggests options with increased fruits, vegetables and milk.

Wholesome Choices

A quick glance at our menu can help our customers of all ages make balanced choices and enjoy options that are recommended food groups from the U.S. Department of Agriculture's *MyPlate*.

- **Milk:** Our 1% Low-fat White Milk Jug and Fat-free Chocolate Milk Jug each provide 30% of the Daily Value for calcium, offering one of the three daily recommended servings of dairy.
- **Fruit:** Apple Slices provide about ¼ cup of fruit and the McCafé Smoothies are made with at least ½ serving of fruit. Minute Maid® 100% Apple Juice Box (6.75 fl.oz) counts as one serving of fruit (½ cup/4 fl. oz of 100% juice). These choices contribute to an individual's daily recommended intake for fruit.[1]

Fig. 2. Healthy Food Imagery on McDonald's Website from McDonald's; "Food to Feel Good About"; McDonalds.com, 14 Mar. 2011. Web. 24 Feb. 2015.

Introduce figures in the text before they appear. Include the caption and source information underneath the figure. Place the figure within the text (not at the end of your paper), as close as possible to the in-text reference.

Zhang 7

The rhetoric consistently reflects McDonald's contention that its only responsibility is to provide healthy choices.

By highlighting the role of parental choice, McDonald's downplays the importance of corporate responsibility. Since some of the company's positive claims about its food have been challenged in high-profile lawsuits, the chain continuously invokes the idea of choice instead of claiming its food is healthy. This direct response to popular condemnation of its child-targeted marketing was made in a timely manner to prevent the negative views from crystallizing in the public consciousness. McDonald's embellishes this transfer of responsibility with maternal imagery and expert testimony to portray itself as a viable, even integral, tool of the modern parent. On its child nutrition webpages, there are no direct references to the value and speed at which McDonald's delivers its products; the sole focus is health and nutrition. By emphasizing choice, the campaign omits the predominance of McDonald's unhealthy sales. Such marketing could be considered deceptive because the broad appeals overgeneralize McDonald's healthy image.

2. Ethnic Marketing

McDonald's routinely uses ethnic marketing to appeal to black and Hispanic audiences. Responding to professional critiques declaring "i'm lovin' it" did not effectively address its diverse consumer base, McDonald's tailored similar campaigns for these markets ("McDonald's Case Study"). In 2006, McDonald's launched web and television campaigns 365Black, MeEncanta, and MyInspirAsian, respectively aimed at black, Hispanic, and

Zhang 8

Asian markets. The marketing of inferior goods including fast food to historically disad-

vantaged demographics has been considered exploitative, but McDonald's maintains it

appeals to these communities responsibly, citing its support of stay-in-school programs and

black entrepreneurship (Elliott). McDonald's ethnic marketing remains questionable as

numerous studies show black and Hispanic Americans have suffered higher obesity rates,

possibly correlated to the increased availability of fast food (Dunn 1160). Although the

chain runs many advertisements with positive messages, the recent appeals to health found

in its mainstream ads are markedly absent in its ethnically targeted campaigns.

On McDonald's black-tailored 365Black website, the main appeal is community con-

nection. McDonald's appeals to several specific target audiences in the black demographic

but its main message is being "deeply rooted in the community" (McDonald's 365Black,

"Home"). Some pages of 365Black connect with the concerns of the nuclear family and tra-

ditional African culture, announcing

> [W]e believe African-American culture should be celebrated 365 days a
>
> year. . . . Like the unique African Baobab tree, which nourishes its community,
>
> McDonald's has branched out to the African-American community. (McDon-
>
> ald's 365Black, "Opportunities")

With imprecise language and suggestive imagery, the chain's rhetoric facilitates posi-

tive identification for African-Americans. Language promoting community welfare is

supplemented with pictures of smiling families and professionally dressed young adults

For quotations longer than 3 lines, indent one inch. Do not use quotation marks. Insert a period at the end of the quotation, followed by the citation information in parentheses. Do not include a period at the end of the citation information.

Zhang 9

(McDonald's 365Black, "What is 365Black?"). McDonald's confronts its reputation as pur-

veyor of inferior goods to historically disadvantaged demographics by providing visual and

textual symbols of social and financial success.

Contrary to McDonald's appeals to corporate advancement and domesticity, 365Black

also heavily embraces hip-hop imagery. The website's home page displays a cartoon art-

ist dressed in a McDonald's red and yellow jumpsuit while gold-embossed bubble letters

endorse the "HBCU classics." On another page, a video advertisement titled "MPS: Hype-

man" features a black rap artist promoting McDonald's with music (McDonald's 365Black,

"Home"). Despite its recent commercialization, the hip-hop movement retains many of the

counter-culture attitudes of its origins as the expression of disenfranchised urban youth.

Scholars Derrick P. Alrdige and James P. Stewart argue, "For many youth, Hip Hop reflects

the social, economic, political, and cultural realities and conditions of their lives, speaking

to them in a language and manner they understand" (190). Although the McDonald's web

image lacks the anti-corporate and anti-white sentiments of the early hip-hop movement,

the campaign similarly allows disadvantaged social groups to identify with an alternative

culture. By associating itself with hip-hop imagery, McDonald's appeals to an alternative

segment of the black community.

Consistent with this alternative image, McDonald's ethnic marketing includes signifi-

cant deviations from its mainstream campaign. As the absence of the fruit and vegetable

imagery indicates, the recent focus on health is often omitted from ethnic marketing.

Zhang 10

According to health researchers Dong-Chul Seo and Mohammad R. Torabi, attitudes

toward obesity vary by demographic, including ethnic groups (1305). McDonald's adjusts

the importance of health accordingly. When the company started McCafe and began

advertising gourmet coffee drinks under the McDonald's brand, "[A]ds emphasized the

indulgent aspects of sweeter drinks like mochas, a message that resonated with blacks"

(Helm). Neither the 365Black website nor the Hispanic-focused MeEncanta website fea-

tures sections dedicated to nutrition and health; instead, each emphasizes McDonald's

value. While banners on the company's main website link to the nutrition FAQ and the

healthier products such as Fruit & Maple Oatmeal, MeEncanta prominently advertises

the McRib sandwich. The burger is pictured with sauce-drenched ribs bulging out over a

side of fries while a banner below advertising the Dollar Menu suggests, "[S]tart your day

smart" (McDonald's MeEncanta). Both the Hispanic and black websites lack the health

focus and nutrition resources that the main website provides. The disparity is especially

pronounced for Spanish-speaking consumers as MeEncanta's default language is Spanish,

but the main McDonald's website has not been translated. Popular criticism has forced

McDonald's to adopt a more health-conscious image, but the rhetoric is mostly part of a

mainstream discourse. The lack of pressure specifically encouraging the company to ad-

dress health among minority demographics allows McDonald's to omit the health focus in

its ethnically targeted campaigns.

3. Conclusion

After dismal performance in the early 2000s, McDonald's revamped its image to better reflect the youthful health-conscious attitudes of the new generation. After the famed documentary *Super Size Me* criticized McDonald's for poor nutrition labeling, low quality of ingredients, and generally unhealthy food, the company swiftly responded to popular criticisms by launching "i'm lovin' it." The campaign addressed specific complaints that had reverberated throughout the mass media. Despite having made real menu additions including premium salads and apple slices, the health-conscious appeals of the new advertising, including the use of fruit and vegetable imagery, overemphasizes the healthiness of McDonald's products. As a remarkably successful marketing strategy, "i'm lovin' it" addressed the company's public relations problem but allowed the chain to serve unhealthy food unchallenged. Although some healthier menu items currently reflect this positive change in the attitude, the bulk of McDonald's business still relies on selling the unhealthy products that generated the original outcry. In its 2009 Annual Report, the company attributes its astounding growth to "a continued focus on classic menu favorites such as the Big Mac, Quarter Pounder, increased emphasis on everyday affordability . . . and the premium Angus Third Pounder" (McDonald's Investor Relations). The importance of classic menu items and the introduction of Angus Third Pounders comes contrary to McDonald's espoused health commitment but is, in the company's own words, very conducive to business.

Zhang 12

McDonald's health rhetoric represents a brilliant response to popular criticisms with respect to content and timing, but the success stems directly from the omission of basic statistics regarding the restaurant's actual business practices. McDonald's direct marketing towards children was heavily lambasted, but the company was unwilling to discontinue the time-tested practice. Instead, it defended the marketing with rhetoric reminiscent of its recent legal defenses, highlighting healthy choices that transferred responsibility from corporation to consumer. By appealing to mothers and adopting a healthy image, the campaign once more ignored the predominance of unhealthy sales.

Congruent with the scope of the new health discourse, McDonald's health rhetoric is limited to mainstream audiences. Because no pressures have encouraged the company to add the same nutrition focus to its ethnically targeted campaigns, McDonald's has not done so and, in a reversal of typical marketing strategy, has even used the minority image in ads targeting conventional audiences (York). The lack of health rhetoric invested in these campaigns suggests McDonald's is not truly committed to the image it has adopted for mainstream market. By its own count, 40 percent of current business comes from minority markets with 50 percent of consumers under the age of 13 coming from this segment (York). With higher child and adult obesity rates in these historically disadvantaged demographics, the chain's reluctance to adopt the same health focus afforded to mainstream audiences is especially concerning.

McDonald's implements its health-conscious image to the extent that it does not interfere with marketing strategies that have remained effective even through the recent rise in

Zhang 13

health consciousness. Contrary to the opinions of health experts, numerous studies suggest

Americans are not seriously worried about obesity issues (Oliver and Lee 932). The elite

nature of the recent health discourse allows McDonald's to meet public relation needs with

minimal interference to the sales of unhealthy foods that comprise the majority of its busi-

ness. The chain defends its extremely effective child-directed advertising and neglects its

ethnic markets which did not experience the same rise in health consciousness. Although

it has made healthy menu additions and expanded the availability of nutrition information,

McDonald's limits its goals in markets of high profitability.

Zhang 14

Works Cited

365Black. Home page. *365Black*. McDonald's, 2011. Web. 24 Feb. 2015.

---. "Opportunities." *365Black*. McDonald's, 2011. Web. 24 Feb. 2015.

---. "What is 365Black?" *365Black*. McDonald's, 2011. Web. 24 Feb. 2015.

Alridge, Derrick P., and James B. Stewart. "Hip Hop in History: Past, Present, and Future."

      Journal of African American History 90.3 (2005): 190–95. *JSTOR*. Web. 5 Mar. 2015.

Barnes, Rachel. "McDonald's Shakes Up Menu with Salad Range." *Marketing*. Haymarket,

      11 Mar. 2004. Web. 8 Mar. 2015.

Datamonitor. "McDonald's Case Study: Launching Food to Appeal to the Health Conscious

      Consumer." *Datamonitor*. MarketResearch.com, 29 June 2005. Web. 1 Mar. 2015.

Dunn, Richard A. "The Effect of Fast-Food Availability on Obesity: An Analysis by Gen-

      der, Race, and Residential Location." *American Journal of Agricultural Economics*

      92.3/4 (2010): 1149–64. *Business Source Complete*. Web. 5 Mar. 2015.

Elliott, Stuart. "McDonald's Promotes Image Among Blacks." *New York Times*. New York

      Times, 10 July 1993. Web. 3 Mar. 2015.

Helm, Burt. "Ethnic Marketing: McDonald's Is Lovin' It." *Bloomberg Businessweek*.

      Bloomberg, 8 July 2010. Web. 3 Mar. 2015.

Joppen, Lucien. "McDonald's Health Move Pays Off." *Food Engineering and Ingredients*

      30.1 (2005): 46–49. Web. 1 Mar. 2015.

Begin the Works Cited on a new page. Center the title "Works Cited." List sources alphabetically.

Zhang 15

Lundgren, Jessica. "Eating Fresh in America: Subway Restaurant's Nutritional Rhetoric."

Young Scholars in Writing 6 (2008): 110–17. Web. 28 Feb. 2015.

Macarthur, Kate. "Mcd's May Take Hit From 'Fast Food Nation' Film." *Advertising Age.*

Crain Communications, 10 Apr. 2006. Web. 28 Feb. 2015.

---. "Fast-Food Goes on Health Kick." *Advertising Age.* Crain Communications, 28 Apr.

2003. Web. 28 Feb. 2015.

McDonald's. "Food to Feel Good About." *McDonald's.* McDonald's, 2011. Web. 24 Feb. 2015.

---. Home page. *McDonald's.* McDonald's, 2011. Web. 24 Feb. 2015.

---. "Moms' Quality Correspondents." *McDonald's.* McDonald's, 2011. Web. 24 Feb. 2015.

---. "What We're Made Of." *McDonald's.* McDonald's, 2011. Web. 24 Feb. 2015.

---. "Your Questions Answered." *McDonald's.* McDonald's, 2011. Web. 24 Feb. 2015.

"McDonald's Dismisses Fresh Lawsuit Attack on Obesity." *Caterer and Hotelkeeper*

192.4261 (2003): 14. *EBSCOHost.* Web. 5 Mar. 2015.

McDonald's Investor Relations. *McDonald's Annual Report 2009.* 2009. Web. 3 Mar. 2015.

MeEncanta. Home page. *MeEncanta.* McDonald's, 2011. Web. 24 Feb. 2015.

MyInspirAsian. Home page. *MyInspirAsian.* McDonald's, 2012. Web. 25 Feb. 2015.

Oliver, J. Eric, and Taeku Lee. "Public Opinion and the Politics of Obesity in America."

Journal of Health Politics, Policy and Law 30.5 (2005): 923–54. *PubMed.* Web.

5 Mar. 2015.

Pelman v. McDonald's Corp., 237 F.Supp.2d 512 (S.D.N.Y. Jan 22, 2003).

Zhang 16

Seo, Dong-Chul, and Mohammad Torabi. "Racial/Ethnic Differences in Body Mass Index,

Morbidity, and Attitudes toward Obesity Among U.S. Adults." *Journal of the*

National Medical Association 98.8 (2006): 1300–08. *EBSCOHost.* Web. 5 Mar. 2015.

Super Size Me. Dir. Morgan Spurlock. Samuel Goldwyn Films 2004. Film.

Tiltman, David. "McDonald's Takes Online Gamble." *Marketing.* Haymarket, 26 Apr. 2006.

Web. 3 Mar. 2015.

Welling, Tonia. "What It Means to My Family." *McDonald's.* McDonald's, 2011. Web.

24 Feb. 2015.

York, Emily Bryson. "Ethnic Insights Form Foundations of McDonald's Marketing."

Advertising Age. Crain Communications, 6 Nov. 2009. Web. 28 Feb. 2015.

F. APA Citation Guide

The American Psychological Association (APA) developed the APA Style guide for researchers in psychology, but it has become one of the most commonly used style guides for the social sciences and health sciences. What follows is a short guide to citing sources using APA style. For more information about APA style, consult the most recent editions of the *Publication Manual of the American Psychological Society* and the *APA Style Guide to Electronic References*.

Principles of APA Citation

APA follows an author-date format for in-text citations: for each source mentioned, you provide a parenthetical that includes the author's last name and the year of publication.

If you include a direct quotation from a source, you should also include the page number for that quotation. In the social sciences, though, writers may not include direct quotations very often. They frequently refer to the overall finding or claim of an article or book, in which case providing the author and the year is sufficient.

A paper formatted in APA style should also include a reference list, which gives the complete citation for each source mentioned in the text.

APA In-Text Citations

The basic format for APA style is the author's last name and the date of publication for any source you mention. Page numbers are included only for direct quotations.

Citing a General Claim, Finding, or Main Idea

If you are referring to the main finding, idea, or claim from a study, you do not need to give a page number. In this case, you may either introduce the author's name in an in-text signal, or only include the author's name in the in-text citation, as follows.

Author's name included in in-text signal   If you give the author's name in an in-text signal, you only need to include the date in parentheses. Place the parentheses directly after the author's name in the sentence:

> Reis (2012) studied food insecurity in Brazil and found that children living in households with low food security had poor nutrition and health outcomes.

Author's name not included in in-text signal   If you do not include the author's name in a signal phrase, you need to include the author's last name and the date in parentheses. Place the parentheses at the end of the sentence, *before* the final punctuation.

> In Brazil, food insecurity is related to low nutrition and health outcomes (Reis, 2012).

Citing a General Claim, Finding, or Main Idea Made by Multiple Sources

Social science and science writers often provide several citations for a general idea in order to show that a claim or finding has been well established by researchers. The most common way to do this is to include the authors' names in parentheses, without an in-text signal. To do this, you separate each author-date pair with a semi-colon. Again, you only need to provide the last name of each author unless multiple authors have the same last name.

Author's names not included in in-text signal

> Food insecurity is related to poor nutrition (Reis, 2012; Case, 2008; Currie, 2007).

Author's names included in in-text signal   Or, you can include in-text signals, if you think it is important to mention the author's last names:

> Studies by Reis (2012), Case (2008), and Currie (2007) have shown that food insecurity is related to poor nutrition.

Citing a Direct Quotation

Writers in the social sciences do not often quote directly from sources, because they are usually more interested in providing the main findings or claims from a study than in the writer's particular words. However, if you do include a quotation, you should provide a page number in parentheses after the quote.

Author's name included in in-text signal   If you give the author's name in an in-text signal, you only include the date after the author's name, but the page number in parentheses after the quotation:

> Reis (2012) found that "Food insecurity seems to be related not only to nutritional outcomes, but also to some children's health indicators, in particular, the prevalence of diarrhea and cough" (p. 422).

Author's name not included in in-text signal   If you do not give the author's name in an in-text signal, you need to include the author, date, and page number after the quotation:

According to researchers, "Food insecurity seems to be related not only to nutritional outcomes, but also to some children's health indicators, in particular, the prevalence of diarrhea and cough" (Reis, 2012, p. 422).

Citing a Long Quotation

If the quotation is longer than 40 words, do not use quotation marks, but do start the quotation on a new line and indent it ½ inch from the left margin.

According to Reis,

> Food insecurity seems to be related not only to nutritional outcomes, but also to some children's health indicators, in particular, the prevalence of diarrhea and cough. So, according to the estimated results in this paper, it seems that the lack of financial resources for food may have negative consequences for children's well-being in Brazil, leading to worse nutritional outcomes and health indicators. (Reis, 2012, p. 422)

Note that with a long quotation, unlike a short quotation, the parenthetical is placed *after* the end punctuation, and it is *not* followed by a period.

Citing a Source with Multiple Authors

In the social sciences, an article or book often has several authors. Whether or not you mention all of these authors depends on (1) the number of authors and (2) whether it is your first mention of a study or a subsequent mention. For sources with more than three authors, you can shorten the reference by using the first author's last name followed by "et al." after the first mention.

Two authors, first mention and subsequent mentions

Bendayrel and Wong (2011) found that nutrition counseling for older adults works best when it involves active participation and collaboration.

Nutrition counseling for older adults works best when it involves active participation and collaboration (Bendayrel & Wong, 2011).

Three to five authors, first mention

In their study of consumers in Alabama, Alonso, O'Neill, and Zizza (2012) found that nutrition education strategies do not appear to be effective for groups that already tend to choose unhealthy foods.

Nutrition education strategies do not appear to be effective for groups that already tend to choose unhealthy foods (Alonso, O'Neill, & Zizza, 2012).

Three to five authors, subsequent mention

Alonso et al. (2012) also found "a rather low degree of consumer interest in learning about foods they consume outside their homes" (p. 296).

In general, consumers do not seem to be interested in learning about the foods they consume in restaurants (Alonso et al., 2012).

Six or more authors, all mentions

Roberto et al. (2012) found that nutrition labels on the front of cereal packages do not influence behavior.

Nutrition labels on the fronts of cereal packages do not seem to influence consumers' choices (Roberto et al., 2012).

Citing Multiple Authors with the Same Last Name

If you cite multiple authors with the same last name, you use the first initial of each author to distinguish them from one another.

Many have studied the positive consequences of early childhood education programs (B. Smith, 2011; C. Smith, 2009).

Citing Multiple Sources by the Same Author

If you cite the same author more than once, but the sources were published in different years, then you do not need to worry—readers can distinguish each source by the year.

If you cite the same author more than once, but the sources were published in the same year, then you need to add a lower case letter after the publication date to indicate which source you are referring to.

Author's name included in in-text signal

In one study, Roberto et al. (2010a) found that placing cartoon characters on food packages influenced young children's snack choices. In another study, they found that including calorie labels on menus led adults to choose lower-calorie meals (2010b).

Author's name not included in in-text signal

> Placing cartoon characters on food packages influences young children's snack choices (Roberto et al., 2010a). Including calorie labels on menus leads adults to choose lower-calorie meals (Roberto et al., 2010b), but the effects of calorie labels have not been studied in children.

You append the letters in the order that the sources appear in the list of references—that is, in alphabetical order by title. Also, you include the letter when you give the year in the list of references.

Citing Works by an Organization or Company

If you are citing sources from a government website, an organization, or a company, you may not find an individual author's name. Instead, you can consider the organization or company to be the author, and cite its name the same way you would cite an author.

> The "Spot the Block" program is meant to encourage "tweens" to make healthy food choices (United States Food and Drug Administration [FDA], 2011).

Note: You can use an acronym for references to organizations. After the first mention of the organization, include the acronym in square brackets. From then on, you can just use the acronym:

> Since "tweens" are at a critical age for developing good food habits, the FDA program teaches them key skills, such as identifying nutritional labels on foods (FDA, 2011).

Citing Works by an Unknown Author

If you cannot find the author of a work, look for the name of the organization, company, or institution that produced it. If you cannot find out who produced the source (an individual or a group), then you should be hesitant about citing it, since that source carries little authority. However, if you must cite a source from an unknown author, use the title instead, placing it in quotation marks:

> One anonymous blogger claims that the fast food industry is responsible for his excessive weight gain, since he was influenced by their misleading health claims ("Why McDonald's Made Me Fat," 2012).

Citing Indirect Sources

In rare cases, you may cite a source that is quoted by another writer. If possible, track down the original source yourself, and use that citation. This demonstrates that you are a careful researcher. If you must cite an indirect source, introduce the original source in your signal phrase, and include the source you consulted in the reference list and in the parenthetical citation, preceded by the words "as cited in," like this:

> Bitzer argues that a rhetorical situation is "a complex of persons, events, objects, and relations" (as cited in Miller, 1984, p. 152).

Citing E-mail, Interviews and Other Communications from Individuals

In APA format, cite e-mails, letters, interviews, and any other kind of correspondence you conducted with individuals as personal communication, like this:

> One expert indicated that she did not think the results would be borne out by future research (P.J. Grimes, personal communication, April 29, 2013).

In APA format, you do not need to include personal communication in your reference list, just in the text.

APA Reference List

In APA format, the list of works cited is called "References." The reference list is included to provide full information about each source included in the paper. The reference list should appear in alphabetical order, by last name of the author. You should use a hanging indent, so that the first line of each reference is not indented, but every line after that is indented by half an inch. (Many word processors have a feature called "hanging indent," which can be found under paragraph formatting settings.)

A standard APA reference includes the following features:

- **Authors' names**: Include only the author's first initials, not their first names. List all authors by last name, followed by first initials. (Initials should include periods and be separated by a space.)
- **Titles**: Capitalize the first word in the title and all proper nouns, but not every word. (This is called "sentence case.") You should also capitalize the first word of a subtitle.
- For articles, do not use quotation marks—just list the title. For books or longer works, use italics.
- **Source information**: For journal articles, give the year, the name of the journal, the volume, issue number, and the page numbers for the article. For a book or longer work, provide the year of publication, place of publication and the name of the publisher. In APA format, you may also include a unique identifier, called a Digital Object Identifier (or DOI) for any article you cite. The DOI is assigned by a registration agency to each article published, and it provides a permanent link to the article's location on the Internet.

INDEX OF CITATIONS

Citing Books

1. A book by a single author
2. A book by two authors
3. A book by up to seven authors
4. A book by eight or more authors
5. An electronic book
6. A new edition of a book
7. A book with an editor

Citing Articles, Book Chapters, & Periodicals

8. An article by a single author
9. An article by two authors
10. An article by up to seven authors
11. An article by eight or more authors
12. An article in a journal with continuous pagination
13. An article in a journal without continuous pagination
14. An article in a magazine
15. An article in a print newspaper
16. A review of a book, film, or video

Citing Online and Other Non-Print Sources

17. An article from an online database (such as *LexisNexis* or *JSTOR*)
18. An article from an online journal with a Digital Object Identifier (DOI)
19. An article from an online journal without a DOI
20. An article in an online newspaper or magazine
21. A Web page authored by an organization or company
22. A Web page with an unknown author
23. A podcast
24. A professional film or video recording
25. An online video
26. A television or radio program
27. A song or audio recording
28. An online forum or discussion board posting
29. A blog post
30. An interview that you conduct
31. A published interview
32. An email

Citing Books

A standard citation for a book includes the author's name, the year of publication, and the title of the book (in italics), the place of publication (city and state), and the publisher.

1. A book by a single author

Nestle, M. (2002). *Food politics: How the food industry influences nutrition and health.* Berkeley, CA: University of California Press.

2. A book by two authors

Stage, S., & Vincenti, V. B. (1997). *Rethinking home economics: Women and the history of a profession.* Ithaca, NY: Cornell University Press.

3. A book by up to seven authors

Nolen-Hoeksema, S., Fredrickson, B., Loftus, G. R., & Wagenaar, A. (2009). *Atkinson & Hilgard's introduction to psychology.* Belmont, CA: Wadsworth.

4. A book by eight or more authors   List the first six authors, then an ellipsis (...) and then the last author in the group.

Goldsmith, L. A., Lee, I., Lugo-Somolinos, A., McKinley-Grant, L., Papier, A., Adigun, C. G., . . . Fredeking, A. (2012). *VisualDx: Essential dermatology in pigmented skin.* Philadelphia, PA: Lippincott Williams & Wilkins.

5. An electronic book also available in print

Silverman, C. (2012). *Understanding autism: Parents, doctors, and the history of a disorder* [Kindle version]. Retrieved from http://www.amazon.com

6. An edition of a book

Breedlove, S. M., Watson, N. V., & Rosenzweig, M. R. (2010). *Biological psychology: An introduction to behavioral, cognitive, and clinical neuroscience* (6th ed.). Sunderland, MA: Sinauer Associates.

7. A book with an editor

Einstein, G. (Ed.). (2007). *Sex and the brain.* Cambridge, MA: MIT Press.

Citing Articles, Book Chapters, and Periodicals

The standard citation for an article from a journal or magazine includes the authors' names, the year of publication, the title of the article, the title of the journal or magazine, the volume, and page numbers. You may or may not need to include the specific issue number of the journal or magazine.

8. An article by a single author

Friedlander, S. F. (1998). Consultation with the specialist: Contact dermatitis. *Pediatrics in Review, 19*(5), 166–171.

9. An article by two authors

Wolf, R., & Wolf, D. (2000). Contact dermatitis. *Clinics in Dermatology, 18*, 661–666.

10. An article by up to seven authors

Ju, E., Adigun, C., Dunphy, C., Gold, S., & Morrell, D. S. (2012). Anaplastic large cell lymphoma: An unusual presentation in a 7-year-old girl. *Pediatric Dermatology, 29*(4), 498–503. doi: 10.1111/j.1525-1470.2011.01465.x

11. An article by eight or more authors   List the first six authors, then an ellipsis (. . .) and then the last author in the group.

Blaine, S. M., Cremin, C., Allanson, J., Dorman, H., Gibbons, C. A., Honeywell, C., . . . Carroll, J. C. (2009). Genetics: Hereditary colorectal cancer. *Canadian Family Physician*, 55: 379.

12. An article in a journal with continuous pagination   For an article in a journal with continuous pagination (the journal continues page numbering from issue to issue for each year), you do not need to include the issue number:

Roberto, C. A., Shivaram, M., Martinez, O., Boles, C., Harris, J. L., & Brownell, K. D. (2012). The Smart Choices front-of-package nutrition label: Influence on perceptions and intake of cereal. *Appetite, 58*, 651–657.

13. An article in a journal without continuous pagination   For an article in a journal without continuous pagination (the journal restarts page numbering for each issue), you do need to include the issue number:

Ahmed, F. E. (2004). The rise of the Bangladesh garment industry: Globalization, women workers, and voice. *NWSA Journal, 16*(2), 34–45.

14. An article in a magazine

Begley, S. (2001). How it all starts inside your brain. *Newsweek, 137*(7), 40.

15. An article in a print newspaper

Bronner, E. (2013, Jan. 31). Law schools' applications fall as costs rise and jobs are cut. *New York Times*, pp. A1+.

16. A review of a book, film, or video

Fuehrer, A. F. (2012). [Review of the book *The psychology of women*]. *Psychology of Women Quarterly, 36*, 116–117.

Citing Online and Other Non-Print Sources

The standard citation for an article from an online source includes the authors' names, the year of publication, the title, name of the source (such as an online journal or organization's website), volume and issue number (if applicable), and page numbers. This information is followed by either a URL or a different type of locator, called a Digital Object Identifier (DOI).

APA style prefers a Digital Object Identifier (DOI) whenever possible. Most major journals assign a DOI to each article that they publish, and the DOI is used to identify and locate articles. The DOI may appear as a long string of alphanumeric characters (e.g., 10.1111/j.1525-1470.2011.01465.x) or as a hyperlink (e.g., http://dx.doi.org/10.1007/s11207-012-0179-2).

If your source does not include a DOI or a DOI hyperlink, include the website address (URL) for the source, preceded by the words "Retrieved from."

Whenever you use online sources, be sure to write down the URL right away so that you can refer to it in your reference list. Try bookmarking online sources as you find them, printing them, or saving them using a program such as Evernote or Zotero.

17. An article from an online database (such as LexisNexis or JSTOR)   APA style does not require you to indicate the database you used to find a source, unless that source is not widely available. For example, you would not need to indicate the database you used to find an article published in a major journal. However, you might indicate the URL for a source you found in a specialized database that is not widely available, like this:

Weldon, G. (1879). How I escaped the mad doctors. *Counseling and Psychotherapy Transcripts, Client Narratives, and Reference Works.* Retrieved from http://asp6new.alexanderstreet.com.libproxy.lib.unc.edu/psyc/psyc.object.details.aspx?dorpid=1004340029

18. An online journal with a Digital Object Identifier (DOI)

Soulieres, I., Dawson, M., Gernsbacher, M. A., & Mottron, L. (2011). The level and nature of autistic intelligence II: What about Asperger syndrome? *PLoS ONE, 6*(9), e25372. doi: 10.1371/journal.pone.0025372

Note: The preceding article uses a DOI that is a string of alphanumeric characters.

Beckerman, A. (1989). Incarcerated mothers and their children in foster care: The dilemma of visitation. *Children and Youth Services Review, 11*(2), 175–183. http://dx.doi.org/10.1016/0190-7409(89)90032-7

Note: The preceding article uses a DOI that is a hyperlink.

19. An article from an online journal without a DOI

Carpenter, R. (2011). Disability as socio-rhetorical action: Towards a genre-based approach. *Disability Studies Quarterly, 31*(3). Retrieved from http://dsq-sds.org/article/view/1666/1605

20. An article in an online newspaper or magazine

Singer, N. (2009, August 4). Medical papers by ghostwriters pushed therapy. *The New York Times*. Retrieved from http://www.nytimes.com

21. A Web page authored by an organization or company

Monsanto Company. (2012). *The Monsanto Pledge*. Retrieved from http://www.monsanto.com/whoweare/Pages/monsanto-pledge.aspx

22. A Web page with an unknown author   If you cannot find the author for a web page, look for the name of the organization, company, or institution that produced it. If you cannot find out who produced the page (an individual or a group), then you should be hesitant about citing it, since that source carries little authority. However, if you must cite a web page from an unknown author, use the title instead, placing it in italics:

"Hotter, more acidic ocean threatens food security." *Ecocentric* (2012). Retrieved from http://www.gracelinks.org/blog/1787/hotter-more-acidic-ocean-threatens-food-security

23. A podcast

National Public Radio. (Producer). (2012, June 26). *What's Driving College Costs Higher?* Podcast retrieved from http://www.npr.org/2012/06/26/155766786/whats-driving-college-costs-higher

24. A professional film or video recording

Potash, S., & Potash, Y. (Producers and Directors). (2011). *Food stamped* [Motion picture]. United States: Summit Pictures.

25. An online video

Carlson, R. (Speaker). (2011, February 1). Breast cancer: Risk factors, diagnosis
and treatment [Video file]. Retrieved from http://www.youtube.com/
watch?v=hrCZanRppzA

26. A television or radio program

Darabont, F., Kirkman, R., Moore, T., Adlard, C., & Gimple, S. M., (Writers), & Nico-
tero, G. (Director). (2013). 30 days without an accident. [Television series episode].
In S. M. Gimple, R. Kirkman, T. Luse, and G. Nicotero (Executive producers), *The
Walking Dead*. New York, NY: American Movie Classics.

27. A song or audio recording

King, C. (1999). You've got a friend. On *Tapestry* [CD]. New York, NY: Sony.

28. An online forum or discussion board posting

Angelik. (2011, February 28). Gay with Asperger's [Online forum comment].
Retrieved from WrongPlanet website: http://www.wrongplanet.net/postt153364
.html

29. A blog post

Zimmer, C. (2012, June 24). We are viral from the beginning [Blog post]. Retrieved
from http://blogs.discovermagazine.com/loom/2012/06/14/we-are-viral-from
-the-beginning/

30. An interview that you conduct   In APA format, cite interviews in the text as personal communication, but do not include in the reference list.

31. A published interview   APA format does not specify how to cite published interviews. Instead, use the format appropriate for the source of the interview (such as a
book, article, etc.).

32. An email   In APA format, cite email and other personal correspondence in the
text only, not in the reference list.

G. Formatting a Paper in APA Style

When you are asked to submit a paper using APA format, use the following formatting guidelines, unless otherwise directed.

General Formatting Guidelines

Here are some general guidelines for formatting APA style papers:

- Use 12-point font
- Double space everything, including the list of references
- Use 1″ margins on all sides
- Use standard 8.5″ by 11″ paper
- Include a header on each page that includes an abbreviated version of your title in all capital letters and the page number. Note: Use your word processor's header feature for this. Do not type the running head individually onto each page, as this will cause layout problems (you will have to redo the running header whenever you add or subtract a line of text).
- Include four main sections: a title page, abstract, main body, and list of references.

First Page Format

On the title page, you should include:

- The title of your paper—a concise statement of the main topic and issues investigated
- Your name
- Your institutional affiliation (the name of your college or university)
- The running header, adding the words "Running Head:"

You may be asked to include your professor's name and the course title as well. Center all of these items on the page.

Abstract Page Format

For the abstract page, you should:

- Begin a new page
- Center the title "Abstract" at the top of the page.
- Write a short abstract (Chapter 11) of your paper. Your abstract should be between 150 and 250 words. For the abstract, APA recommends that you describe your main research problem, methods, findings, and conclusions.

Body Pages Format

For the body:

- Start a new page
- Center the title of your paper on the top of the page

- Maintain double-spacing throughout
- Introduce any figures or tables in the text, and label and caption them properly (Chapter 29)

Note: If you would like to use a section heading to indicate parts of your paper, APA specifies different formats for up to five levels of sub-headings. Use the following guidelines:

1-Level Heading: Centered and Bold, Using Upper and Lowercase
2-Level Heading: Flush Left and Bold, Using Upper and Lowercase
3-Level Heading: Indented and bold, using sentence case, ending with a period.
4-level heading: Indented, bold, italicized; using sentence case, ending with a period.
5-level heading: Indented, italicized, using sentence case, ending with a period.

To structure your paper, APA recommends that you include the following sections:

- **Introduction**: introduce the problem, describe its importance, review relevant scholarship, and state your own hypothesis or research question
- **Methods**: identify how you studied the problem, including what empirical or database research you conducted (Chapter 24), and, for empirical research, how you chose participants and designed your study tools (such as an interview or experiment)
- **Results**: summarize the data you collected, including your main findings
- **Discussion**: evaluate and interpret your results
- **References**

This format is commonly used in research genres in the sciences and social sciences (Chapter 11).

Format for the Reference List

For the Reference List:

- Start a new page
- Center the word "References" at the top (without the quotation marks)
- Include your references in alphabetical order, using a hanging indent (indent each line after the first one for each source by .5"). Note: In Word, go to Format → Paragraph and choose Special → Hanging. If you try to indent the paragraphs yourself, you will run into a layout mess.
- Double space throughout

EXAMPLE 28.2: A Student Research Paper in APA Style

BEING MOMMY BEHIND BARS   1

Being Mommy Behind Bars: The Psychological Benefits

of Child Visitation with Incarcerated Mothers

Terrence Bogans

University of North Carolina, Chapel Hill

On the title page, include the full title of your paper, your name, and the name of your college or university. Double-space this information and use center alignment.

BEING MOMMY BEHIND BARS   2

Abstract

Many legal statutes currently prohibit children from visiting their mothers in prison. While these policies are supported by "best interests of the child" arguments, they fail to consider psychological research supporting the benefits of prison visitation for children. This article reviews psychological research to show that withholding a child from his or her mother is more detrimental than any negative effects of a visit to a prison environment, and argues that legal scholars should take these psychological perspectives into account when considering visitation for children of incarcerated mothers.

Insert the page number aligned flush right on each page, beginning at 1.

On a separate page, include an abstract for your paper (Chapter 11). The abstract should be double-spaced, with the heading "Abstract" centered above it.

Insert a "running head," or a shortened version of your paper's title, on every page, aligned flush left. Use all caps. On the first page, insert the words "Running Head:". On the remaining pages, just include the actual running head, without the words "Running Head:".

Being Mommy Behind Bars: The Psychological Benefits
of Child Visitation with Incarcerated Mothers

Today in America millions of children are being torn away from their mothers, and it is perfectly legal. Over 1.5 million children in the United States have at least one incarcerated parent (Glaze & Maruschak, 2010). As shown in Figure 1, this number has risen by over fifty percent over the course of the last two decades, and is likely to continue to rise as the prison population grows.

> Introduce figures in the text before they appear. Include the caption and source information underneath the figure.

Figure 1: Number of parents in state and federal prisons, and their minor children. Adapted from Glaze, L. E. & Maruschak, L. M. (2008). *Parents in prison and their minor children.* Washington, D.C.: United States Department of Justice (p. 1).

BEING MOMMY BEHIND BARS   4

Mothers account for a smaller proportion of these totals than do fathers; however, be-

cause female prisoners tend to receive less attention than do male prisoners, in this essay I

focus on mothers.

As shown in Table 1, the number of mothers in prison has risen from 1991, when 29500

children had a mother in prison, to a total of 65600 in 2007.

Table 1 Number of Mothers in State and Federal Prisons

Number of Mothers	In State Prison	In Federal Prison	Total
2007	58200	7400	65600
2004	51800	6600	58400
1999	48500	5100	53600
1997	42900	4000	46900
1991	26600	2900	29500

Adapted from Glaze, L.E. & Maruschak, L.M. (2008). *Parents in prison and*

their minor children. Washington, D.C.: United States Department of Jus-

tice. Appendix table 1.

Most of these mothers have more than one child: in 2007, a total of 147,400 children had a

mother in prison, as shown in Table 2.

The United States legal system prohibits these children from visiting their incarcerated

parents, specifically mothers. Many argue that children should in no way be exposed to

Introduce tables in the text before they appear. Include the caption above the table. Include the source of data underneath the table.

Table 2 Number of Minor Children with a Mother in Prison

Number of Minor Children	Mother in State Prison	Mother in Federal Prison	Total
2007	131000	16400	147400
2004	116600	14600	131200
1999	115500	10600	126100
1997	102400	8300	110700
1991	58000	5900	63900

Adapted from Glaze, L.E. & Maruschak, L.M. (2008). *Parents in prison and their minor children*. Washington, D.C.: United States Department of Justice. Appendix table 1.

prison, and that any visitation of an incarcerated parent is both emotionally unhealthy and detrimental to a child (Armsden & Greenberg, 1987; Poehlmann, 2005b, Dallaire et al, 2009). It is true; prison is a cold and awful life situation for anyone to experience. But, regardless of what incarcerated parents may have done, they still have children who depend on them. The law has ignored this fact, stating that the courts have the ability to deny visitation if they find it would be detrimental to the child. But what factors exactly determine detriment? Often, the factors used to prove detriment are not based on any actual evidence; the stigma surrounding incarceration is all that is needed to establish "detriment."

The field of psychology has taken a different perspective on incarceration than that taken by the legal system. Psychological experts understand that withholding a child from her mother is often more detrimental than exposing her to the world of prison. A review of psychological literature on the effects of incarceration on children indicates that, by denying visitation, the legal field has simply been narrow-minded in its policies and perspectives on incarcerated parents.

Methods

To conduct this study, I reviewed legal research describing the current barriers for incarcerated mothers to gain visitation of their children. Next, I examined psychological research on how child visitation of incarcerated mothers affects the development of the child, parental strain, and the mother-child relationship. This review yielded five studies of the legal doctrines behind child visitation policies, and eight studies of the psychological effects of those policies.

Results

Barriers for Visitation

Incarcerated parents often long to maintain or mend their relationship with their children. Many mothers would want nothing more than to get the chance to see their child, and try to comfort them with love and an explanation. Yet, even if the family wants to participate in visitation, the process is not easy. Lewis (2004), a family lawyer, held that although courts have indeed agreed that visitation is a fundamental right that incarcerated individuals should have, numerous legal barriers and prison regulations prevent visitation from occurring as much as

When you have mentioned an author's name in the text, you include only the year of publication in the parentheses.

BEING MOMMY BEHIND BARS   7

needed. She points out several legal factors that prohibit child visitation. First she cites the

case *Alexander v. Alexander,* in which "the Kentucky Court of Appeals held that incarcera-

tion does not preclude or interfere with the parent's right to a hearing on the matter of visi-

tation" (p. 105). This means that regardless of a parent's incarceration, she still has a right to

petition the court for visitation. However, as Lewis describes, the hearing usually proves to be

problematic, as there is limited access to legal services involving domestic issues for incarcer-

ated parents. Many states only provide legal counsel to incarcerated parents when their rights

are being terminated. The courts have set up an impossible situation by expecting a mother

to win visitation without providing her the legal aid necessary to prove that visitation will be

beneficial to the child. These regulations are flawed because states are either outright denying

or making it extremely difficult to even fight for one's child.

Another legal factor that prevents child visitation for incarcerated mothers is the "best in-

terest of the child standard," the test used in most jurisdictions when deciding on issues of vis-

itation and custody (Lewis, 2004, p. 106). This test allows visitation to be determined solely by

the opinion of the court. For instance, a court might rule that a child should live with his adop-

tive parents, not his biological parents, based on the logic that the adoptive parents provided a

more stable home environment. That decision would rest on the doctrine of "best interests."

Lewis has claimed that the test is not a factor-specific one, meaning that individual cases

and circumstances are not taken into consideration. Ultimately, the decision often resides

If the author's
name is not in-
cluded in the sen-
tence, put it in the
parentheses along
with the year of
publication.

on personal bias rather than facts. This is a major defect: a legal system that supposedly

sets out to rely only on the facts and hard evidence is falling short of that promise.

When it comes to prison regulations, prison administrators can enforce visitation re-

strictions so long as they are "rationally related to a legitimate penological interest" (Lewis,

2004, p. 108). Cultural biases can occur, however, because it is extremely difficult to make

a rational decision with the vast amount of negative attention incarceration receives.

Through education, the media, employment, and even the law itself, "criminals" have had

their human qualities stripped away and are often portrayed as demonized creatures, lack-

ing any of the qualities that make for a good citizen. If those in power believe the stigma

that surrounds incarceration, their views can be slanted and an unjust assessment of visita-

tion can be made.

In regards to the visitation rights of incarcerated parents, especially mothers, there

has been a cold stance taken that avoids the true needs of the parent's rehabilitation and

the child's development. Many believe that visiting an inmate is detrimental to the child.

Costa (2003), a legal scholar, has described how prison is not a healthy environment for

children as "it epitomizes all that is unhealthy and dangerous" (p. 68). She asserts that

it is unfair for an innocent child to have to attempt to understand that her parent did

something "bad" and has to stay at that "very bad place" (p. 67). The constant tension of

visiting an incarcerated mother and the emotional trauma of having to say "goodbye" is

detrimental to the child's development, Costa argues: "Prison is not an atmosphere appropriate for the growth maturation of our youth. 'Ah what childhood memories these kids
will have'" (Costa, 2003, p. 97).

   Costa exemplifies the blanket bias that is present in our society, which in turn is reflected
in the laws; however, the "facts" Costa describes are simply not supported by research.
More attention must be given to psychological research, which takes a less biased stance on
incarceration. Stewart (2002), a legal scholar, has argued that more psychological research
needs to be done to continue assessing the positive effects on development of child visitation with incarcerated mothers. In his analysis of several studies and programs, including
Project H.I.P. ("Helping Incarcerated Parents"), Stewart concluded that: (1) there is no
reason to believe that visitation in prison is more harmful to children than other types of
visitation with a non-custodial parent and (2) there is no evidence that mere exposure to the
prison environment leads to long-term harm in children.

   As an individual who spent a large portion of my childhood visiting my incarcerated
father, I could not agree more with Stewart. When I was six years old, I visited my father
for the first time. As my mom and I pulled up to the gray, cement block of a building, my
heart was pounding in my throat, but it wasn't from fear—my heart pounded in anticipation. I couldn't wait to see my dad again—to gaze into his deep brown eyes and hear his
hearty chuckle. When the prison gate clanked opened, I practically skipped into the room,

ignoring the fetid smell of cigarettes, urine and bleach. That night, I fell asleep thinking

about my dad, the warm touch of his hand on my shoulder, the taste of the warm orange

drink we shared. Clearly, visiting my dad did not have negative effects for me—instead, it

was a positive experience. Although I understand that everyone has his or her own unique

experiences, I always looked forward to these visits rather than having any feeling of an-

guish or anxiety. If more research is conducted, maybe it would be discovered that I was

indeed the norm, and not the exception.

Psychological Outcomes of Visitation for Children

The psychological research that is available consistently shows that when a child is pre-

vented from visiting his or her mother, negative effects occur. However, when visitation is

allowed, there are numerous positive effects. Snyder, Carlo, and Mullins (2001) found that,

when a parent is incarcerated, the child has an increased risk of suffering from anxiety,

depression, sleeplessness, anger, and attention deficiencies. However, these risks can be

alleviated through visitation programs, and parenting classes can improve the relationship

between incarcerated mothers and their children (Snyder, Carlo, & Mullins 2001). If visi-

tation is allowed, then the problem may be prevented earlier, and the child's future will be

more promising as a result (Snyder, Carlo, & Mullins 2001). Parenting classes must also

be utilized more; the classes would be beneficial for parent, child, and other family mem-

bers. And, since prison today is a business, the parenting classes will ultimately be more economical. Although it appears that adding a new program would be more expensive, the

parenting programs may actually reduce the overall costs related to the incarcerated par-

ents' mental and physical health treatments because of the motivation that parents will gain

by having continued positive contact with their children.

Numerous negative issues such as attachment disruption, disorganization, delinquency,

risky behavior, and even risk for future incarceration are correlated with a child having an

incarcerated mother (Dallaire, 2007). However, "visitation with parents has been identified

as a protective factor in the population of children with incarcerated mothers" (Dallaire,

2007, p. 17). This research suggests that numerous psychological benefits in a child's de-

velopment occur when he or she is able to visit an incarcerated parent. The child will have

a better understanding of her parent's situation, have a possibility of a stable relationship,

and can reach a more mature mental state.

Psychological Outcomes of Visitation for Parents

Child visitation will help ease parental stress while incarcerated. Being arrested can be

one of the most tragic and confusing events that can occur in one's life, and having a child

will certainly complicate the experience for most. Many negative side-effects come with a

mother being incarcerated. Arditti, Lambert-Shute, and Joest (2003) found that economic

hardship is dramatically increased with the incarceration of a parent, along with parent-

ing strain, emotional stress, and concerns about children's loss of involvement with their

BEING MOMMY BEHIND BARS   12

incarcerated parent. Each of these issues can increase the amount of stress surrounding

the incarceration of a mother, and perhaps delay her release by slowing the rehabilitation

process. A mother's motivation can quickly evaporate while her child is being withheld.

Poehlmann (2005a) discusses how incarcerated mothers usually experience trauma and de-

pressive symptoms when separated from their child, sometimes leading to suicidal thoughts

or even actions. However, the negative side-effects are alleviated with increased contact,

providing a better mother-child relationship (Poehlmann, 2005a).

The mother-child relationship is especially threatened when an incarcerated mother is

forced to give her child up to foster care. Child visitation eases the strain and complications

of foster care. Mothers, often temporarily, lose their children to the foster care system when

incarcerated. It is very difficult for a mother to handle the emotional strain with losing a

child and balancing the legal means of regaining custody of that child. Beckerman (1989)

highlights several problems that arise during this process, including how the mother can

stay involved in the case planning while behind bars. Beckerman describes how "[c]ase-

workers' ability to arrange for visitation and maintain the mother's involvement may be

curtailed by time, cost, and logistical factors unique to the imprisoned population" (p. 176).

The mother can be overwhelmed with worrying about her child's welfare, their current re-

lationship while still incarcerated, and how their incarceration will ultimately affect their

relationship and the family upon release (Beckerman, 1989).

Discussion

A review of psychological research indicates that increasing visitation would allow the mother to maintain a relationship with her child, calm her down, and allow her to explain to the child their current situation. The child needs to know, from the mother herself, that she is fighting for the child, and that she has not abandoned the child.

Additionally, increased visitation will help the reunification process between mother and child. During the stressful and seemingly never-ending process of regaining custody of one's child, visitation can help motivate the incarcerated mother and encourage her not to give up in battle. Rosenberg (2000) cites the legal case *Precious J v. Contra Costa County Department of Social Services* in which the court ruled that if the prison had granted the mother more visitation rights, she would have had the motivation to complete her sentence and follow all the appropriate procedures to reclaim custody of her daughter. The court's decision points to a vital portion of my argument. Child visitation does, in fact, give mothers the motivation they need to make the appropriate changes in their lives and return to society, the very notion of rehabilitation. If child visitation is a determining factor in this process, then it needs to be approached more readily. The growth in the amount of rehabilitation successes of incarcerated mothers can reach levels higher than any other group of incarcerated individuals.

Increased visitation will also have a positive impact on the broader society by helping break the cycle of crime. Indeed, there are studies that find that a child's risk of one day being incarcerated is increased if that child had a parent who was at some point incarcerated. Conner (2008), for instance, discusses the relationship between visiting an incarcerated parent and future acts of domestic violence against women. However, if visitation is increased, children will better understand the consequences of committing crimes. Furthermore, the individuals who have actually committed crimes are the best teachers in informing children on how to avoid the same mistakes in their lives. This notion has been tested and proven in several pioneer programs across the United States, including an organization based in North Carolina called Our Children's Place (2010), which is a residential initiative allowing young children (babies and preschoolers) to live with their mothers while the women serve out their sentences for nonviolent offenses. It is designed to: (1) break the intergenerational cycle of crime, poverty, substance abuse, and family violence, and (2) empower the child with the help of his/her mother to enhance his/her cognitive, social, physical and emotional development (Our Children's Place, 2010).

Our Children's Place shows great promise and even greater potential as a model for future initiatives. Like sunlight, these types of initiatives have helped healthy relationships grow between incarcerated parents and children. It is these types of ground-breaking initiatives that have really been able to grasp the true effects of incarceration on the parent and the child. Unfortunately, current policies have generally disregarded the subject, have ignored true academic research, and have allowed societal perceptions of crime to influence legislation. While academic research suggests visitation can be positive, current legal policies have portrayed it as uniformly negative. In recent years, the field of psychology has made great strides in assessing the true effects of incarceration on children. Experts have proven that child visitation is positive for both the parent and the child. Better-informed visitation policies may even break the relentless cycle of crime, a cycle whose costs for society are much too high, a cycle that reduces children's potential, a cycle that must be broken. Child visitation must be increased in order to alleviate the psychological strains that take place during incarceration.

References

Arditti, J. A., Lambert-Shute, J., & Joest, K. (2003). Saturday morning at the jail: Implica-

   tions of incarceration for families and children. *Family Relations, 52*(3), 195–204.

   doi: 10.1111/j.1741–3729.2003.00195.x.

Armsden, G. C., & Greenberg, M. T. (1987). The inventory of parent and peer attachment:

   Relationships to well-being in adolescence. *Journal of Youth and Adolescence, 16,*

   427–454. doi:10.1007/BF02202939.

Beckerman, A. (1989). Incarcerated mothers and their children in foster care: The di-

   lemma of visitation. *Children and Youth Services Review, 11*(2), 175–183. http://

   dx.doi.org/10.1016/0190-7409(89)90032-7.

Conner, D. H. (2008). Do no harm: An analysis of the legal and social consequences of

   child visitation determinations for incarcerated perpetrators of extreme acts of

   violence against women. *Columbia Journal of Gender & Law, 17*(1), 163–243.

   Retrieved from http://papers.ssrn.com/sol3/papers.cfm?abstract_id=1334951.

Costa, R. D. (2003). Now I lay me down to sleep: A look at overnight visitation rights

   available to incarcerated mothers. *New England Journal on Criminal & Civil*

   Confinement, 29, 67–97.

Begin the references on a new page. Center the title "References." List sources alphabetically.

BEING MOMMY BEHIND BARS   17

Dallaire, D. (2007). Children with incarcerated mothers: Developmental outcomes, special

challenges and recommendations. *Journal of Applied Developmental Psychology,*

28(1), 15–24. doi:10.1016/j.appdev.2006.10.003.

Dallaire, D. H., Wilson, L. C., & Ciccone, A. (2009, April). Representations of attachment

relationships in family drawings of children with incarcerated parents. Paper pre-

sented at the biennial meeting of the Society for Research in Child Development,

Denver, CO.

Glaze, L. E. & Maruschak, L. M. (2008). Parents in prison and their minor children.

Bureau of Statistics Special Report. Washington, D.C.: United States Department

of Justice. Retrieved from http://bjs.ojp.usdoj.gov/content/pub/pdf/pptmc.pdf

Lewis, P. (2004). Behind the glass wall: Barriers that incarcerated parents face regarding

the care, custody and control of their children. *Journal of the American Academy*

of Matrimonial Lawyers, 19, 97–116. Retrieved from http://www.aaml.org/sites/

default/files/barriers%20that%20incarcerated-article.pdf

Our Children's Place. (2010). Home. Retrieved from http://ourchildrensplace.com

Poehlmann, J. (2005a). Incarcerated mothers' contact with children, perceived family rela-

tionships, and depressive symptoms. *Journal of Family Psychology, 19*(3), 350–357.

doi: 10.1037/0893-3200.19.3.350

Poehlmann, J. (2005b). Representations of attachment relationships in children of incarcer-

ated mothers. *Child Development, 76,* 679–696. doi:10.1111/j.1467-8624.2005.00871.x

Rosenberg, H. (2000). California's incarcerated mothers: Legal roadblocks to reunification.

Golden Gate University Law Review, 30(2), 285–330. Retrieved from http://

digitalcommons.law.ggu.edu/ggulrev/vol30/iss2/4/

Snyder, Z. K., Carlo, T. A., & Coats Mullins, M. M. (2001). Parenting from prison: An

examination of children's visitation program at a women's correctional facility.

Marriage & Family Review, 32(3-4), 33–61. doi: 10.1177/0032885510382087.

Stewart, B. G. (2002). When should a court order visitation between a child and an incar-

cerated parent? *University of Chicago Law School Roundtable, 9,* 165–178.

PART 5

Presentation

Choosing Visual Elements, Layout, and Design

In this chapter, you will learn how to employ visual elements, layout, and design effectively when you compose documents of all kinds. Visual elements refer to items such as photographs, drawings, charts, and graphs that you might include in a document. Layout refers to how those elements (along with text) are organized on the page or screen. Design refers to the visual qualities you apply to your documents. This may include colors, shapes, font types and sizes, and so on. You will learn how to choose these features based on the genre you are composing and the rhetorical situation for your document.

A. Matching Design to Genre

The first consideration when selecting visual elements, layout, and design features for a document should be the genre you are writing. Start by gathering examples of the genre.

Any genre includes some design features, even if it is a regular paper in MLA or APA format (Chapter 28). The design features for academic papers might include double spacing, headers, and a serif typeface (such as Times New Roman or Cambria). The design features for a research paper are dictated by the style guide, such as the *MLA Style Manual*. Similarly, if you submit a paper to an academic journal, the layout and design will be dictated by the journal.

In other cases, you will have a choice of design options. While résumés tend to have similar features, you can choose different options for fonts, headings, and layout (Chapter 12). Your analysis of your genre will give you a sense of the range of options open to you. While it might not be advisable to add colorful sub-headings to a research paper, you might be able to do so for a website, blog post, conference poster, or brochure.

While Terrence originally wrote his research paper (Chapter 11) on incarcerated mothers and visitation rights as a research article, for a later assignment he was asked to rework it into a one-page factsheet (Chapter 6) to summarize his findings. Unlike the article, the factsheet offered Terrence more visual choices.

Terrence started by researching examples of factsheets, and he located several to get a sense of what visual elements he could include (Figure 29.1 and Figure 29.2).

EXAMPLE 1: Factsheet on HIV/AIDS

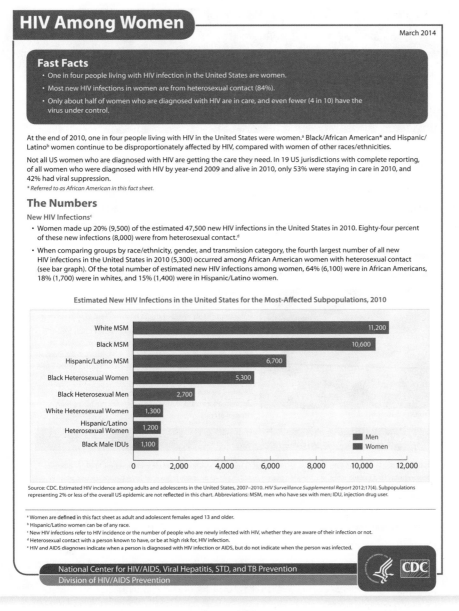

HIV Among Women

March 2014

Fast Facts
- One in four people living with HIV infection in the United States are women.
- Most new HIV infections in women are from heterosexual contact (84%).
- Only about half of women who are diagnosed with HIV are in care, and even fewer (4 in 10) have the virus under control.

At the end of 2010, one in four people living with HIV in the United States were women.[a] Black/African American* and Hispanic/Latino[b] women continue to be disproportionately affected by HIV, compared with women of other races/ethnicities.

Not all US women who are diagnosed with HIV are getting the care they need. In 19 US jurisdictions with complete reporting, of all women who were diagnosed with HIV by year-end 2009 and alive in 2010, only 53% were staying in care in 2010, and 42% had viral suppression.
Referred to as African American in this fact sheet.

The Numbers

New HIV Infections[c]
- Women made up 20% (9,500) of the estimated 47,500 new HIV infections in the United States in 2010. Eighty-four percent of these new infections (8,000) were from heterosexual contact.[d]
- When comparing groups by race/ethnicity, gender, and transmission category, the fourth largest number of all new HIV infections in the United States in 2010 (5,300) occurred among African American women with heterosexual contact (see bar graph). Of the total number of estimated new HIV infections among women, 64% (6,100) were in African Americans, 18% (1,700) were in whites, and 15% (1,400) were in Hispanic/Latino women.

Estimated New HIV Infections in the United States for the Most-Affected Subpopulations, 2010

Subpopulation	Value
White MSM	11,200
Black MSM	10,600
Hispanic/Latino MSM	6,700
Black Heterosexual Women	5,300
Black Heterosexual Men	2,700
White Heterosexual Women	1,300
Hispanic/Latino Heterosexual Women	1,200
Black Male IDUs	1,100

Men
Women

0   2,000   4,000   6,000   8,000   10,000   12,000

Source: CDC. Estimated HIV incidence among adults and adolescents in the United States, 2007–2010. *HIV Surveillance Supplemental Report* 2012;17(4). Subpopulations representing 2% or less of the overall US epidemic are not reflected in this chart. Abbreviations: MSM, men who have sex with men; IDU, injection drug user.

[a] Women are defined in this fact sheet as adult and adolescent females aged 13 and older.
[b] Hispanic/Latino women can be of any race.
[c] New HIV infections refer to HIV incidence or the number of people who are newly infected with HIV, whether they are aware of their infection or not.
[d] Heterosexual contact with a person known to have, or be at high risk for, HIV infection.
[e] HIV and AIDS diagnoses indicate when a person is diagnosed with HIV infection or AIDS, but do not indicate when the person was infected.

National Center for HIV/AIDS, Viral Hepatitis, STD, and TB Prevention
Division of HIV/AIDS Prevention

CDC

Figure 29.1
This factsheet uses bulleted lists, color, a graph, and photographs
to visually present information alongside text.

EXAMPLE 2: Factsheet on Tornado Preparation

How to get ready for tornadoes

Known as nature's most violent storms, tornadoes can strike with little or no warning, destroying entire neighborhoods in just a few minutes. But preparing ahead of time, knowing the signs of a coming tornado and familiarizing yourself with tornado warning systems can help keep you and your loved ones safe.

What's a tornado?

Photo courtesy iStockphoto–Sonja Foos

A tornado is a dangerous rotating column of air that is in contact with both the ground and a cumulonimbus cloud, which is the type of cloud involved in thunderstorms. Its violent winds can reach hundreds of miles per hour.

Tornadoes can happen anywhere in the world, but they mostly happen in the United States. Every state is susceptible to tornadoes, however they are most common in regions east of the Rocky Mountains in the spring and summer. According to the National Weather Service, the United States experiences 800 tornadoes in an average year.

Tornadoes are extremely powerful, capable of destroying even well-constructed homes and buildings, uprooting trees and hurling heavy pieces of debris.

Know the signs, be prepared

Tornado warning systems can differ from town to town, so get to know your community's tornado warning system. Know the difference between alerts for a tornado watch, which is when weather conditions mean a tornado is possible, and a tornado warning, which is when a tornado funnel has been sighted. Also, if you have children, get to know their school's tornado plan.

During thunderstorms, use a battery-operated radio to listen to weather updates and instructions from local officials. Also, be aware of tornado warning signs: dark, greenish skies; large hail; a large, dark, low-lying cloud; a visible, rotating funnel; or a loud roar.

Photo courtesy iStockphoto–Laura Young

aphagetready.org

Figure 29.2
This factsheet uses bold colors, high-contrast sub-headings,
and photographs to present information effectively.

From these two examples, Terrence learned that factsheets tend to combine text and images, often using color, contrast, visual elements, and bulleted lists to display information. Both of these examples arrange items into columns or sections, sometimes blocking off sections with borders or shading.

To come up with design ideas, you can also collect examples of other kinds of designs you like. Designers of all kinds, from web developers to fashion designers, collect materials for inspiration boards. You can keep a file of interesting designs, pin examples to a bulletin board, or you can create a digital one using online tools such as Pinterest. Terrence simply pinned flyers and magazine pages that he found interesting on the bulletin board in his room. He then came up with the following list of design features he wanted to include in his own factsheet:

Factsheet:
- *Use greys/black to convey cold/sadness of prison*
- *Contrast with a warm color (yellow/orange?) to convey hope/potential for change*
- *Use different fonts and/or colors? for headings/sub-headings*
- *Perhaps contrast risks of incarceration with benefits of visitation—use bulleted lists?*

B. Matching Design to Audience, Purpose, and Situation

In addition to genre, your layout and design choices should be guided by the audience, purpose, and context for your document.

Audience
Consider how your audience will view and use your document. For example, users of a website will expect a clear navigation scheme so that they can move from one area to another. On this website (Figure 29.3), the primary navigation scheme is a bar across the top, with tabs for articles, exhibits, and information about individual women.

EXAMPLE: Student Website Design

20TH CENTURY WOMEN AT UNC

| Home | Anne Queen | Dean of Women | Mary Mebane | Karen L Parker | | Subscribe |

20th Century Women at UNC

aemerson — Filed under Uncategorized

Apr 22 2010

"*The American South is a geographical entity, a historical fact, a place in the imagination, and the homeland for an array of Americans who consider thremeselves southerners. The region is often shrouded in romance and myth, but its realities are as intriguing, as intricate, as its legends.*" – Bill Ferris

It is common to think about the 1960's and 1970's and immediately reflect upon the time as one of great change. During this time, diversity was beginning to become something more than just a word, it was becoming an ideal and a way of life. The women on the campus of the University of North Carolina at Chapel Hill were embracing this and taking great strides to make this relevant both on and off campus.

Take a look around the site to learn more about several very influential women and their contributions.

Images Courtesy of:

Southern Historical Collection at the University of North Carolina at Chapel Hill

Southern Oral History Program at the University of North Carolina at Chapel Hill

The Carolina Story: A Virtual Museum of University History

University of North Carolina Housing and Residential Education

LATEST POSTS

:: 20th Century Women at UNC

SEARCH

[   ] Go

BLOGROLL

:: Southern Women's Activists
:: Southern Women's Rhetorics

ABOUT

CATEGORIES

:: Uncategorized (1)

TAGS

MONTHLY

:: April 2010 (1)

PAGES

:: Anne Queen
:: A True Model in the Fight for Civil Rights
:: Anne Queen: Majesty of Ethos
:: Dean of Women
:: Karen L Parker
:: Mary Mebane

Figure 29.3
A clear navigation scheme helps users locate content on a website.

As with a website, readers of a long print or online document might appreciate headings and sub-headings, a table of contents, and an index to help them locate information. In the following example, a United States Department of Agriculture report (Figure 29.4), you can see several design features to help readers locate information: a table of contents, bold headings, and color.

EXAMPLE: Government Report (excerpt)

Contents

Recommended citation format for this publication:

Dimitri, Carolyn, and Lydia Oberholtzer. *Marketing U.S. Organic Foods:
Recent Trends From Farms to Consumers*. Economic Information Bulletin No.
58. U.S. Dept. of Agriculture, Economic Research Service. September 2009.

Summary

Organic foods now occupy prominent shelf space in the produce and dairy aisles
of most mainstream U.S. food retailers, while offerings of organic meats, eggs,
breads, grains, and beverages have increased. The marketing boom has pushed
retail sales of organic foods up to $21.1 billion in 2008 from $3.6 billion in 1997.
Supermarkets, club stores, big-box stores, and other food retailers carry organic
products; many retailers have introduced lines of organic private-label products;
and manufacturers continue to introduce large numbers of new organic products.

What Is the Issue?

The rapid growth of the U.S. organic industry has caused a major shift in the types
and numbers of organic food retailers, manufacturers, and distributors and has
widened the retail customer base. In addition, organic farmland acreage more than
doubled from 1997 to 2005. With those changes has come an increased desire for
research and analysis of the U.S. organic marketing system. The 2008 Farm Act
allocated $5 million in initial spending for an expanded organic data collection
initiative, along with an additional $5 million per year of authorized funding for
researchers to:

- collect and distribute comprehensive reporting of prices relating to
  organically produced agricultural products

- conduct surveys and analysis and publish reports relating to organic production, handling, distribution, retail, and trend studies (including consumer
  purchasing patterns)

- develop surveys and report statistical analysis on organically produced
  agricultural products

While new data are being collected and analyzed, policymakers and other interested groups have expressed particular interest in: what types of consumers purchase organic food; how structural change has affected the retailing, distribution,
and manufacturing of organic food; and why increases in the supply of organic
products at the farm level lag behind growth in demand at the retail level. This
study analyzes the most recent data available to examine each level of the organic
supply chain.

What Did the Study Find?

The number and variety of consumers of organic products has increased, but those
consumers are not easily categorized. The one factor that consistently influences
the likelihood of a consumer's buying organic products is education. Consumers
of all ages, races, and ethic groups who have higher levels of education are more
likely to buy organic products than less-educated consumers. Other factors, such
as race, presence of children in the household, and income, do not have a consistent effect on the likelihood of buying organic products.

Retailing of organic products has evolved since 1997, when natural foods stores
were the main outlet. By 2008, nearly half of all organic foods were purchased
in conventional supermarkets, club stores, and big-box stores. Although produce
remained the top-selling organic category, sales of dairy products, beverages,

Figure 29.4
To help readers navigate a print document, use a table of contents, contrast,
and consistent headings and sub-headings.

Your analysis of your audience and genre can help you to pinpoint the right type of visual elements to use. Terrence noted that factsheets about public policy issues tended to use more photographs and fewer technical images, so he planned to include photographs of women and children.

Purpose

Visual elements can help you to achieve the purpose of your document. If your purpose is to inform, you might choose visual elements that help to illustrate key concepts, provide facts or statistics, or help people to perform a task. If your purpose is to persuade, then you might choose visual elements that support your argument or attract the reader's interest.

Terrence wanted his factsheet to persuade policy makers to change visitation policies for children of incarcerated parents, so he chose photographs that he thought would attract policy makers. He thought images of mothers and their children might create an emotional connection with readers. He located images from government websites, since those are usually free of copyright. He made sure to note the source for the images, though, so that he could include a credit line for them on his factsheet.

Situation

Consider how readers will actually interact with your document. In what setting will they be reading, and how can you add elements to make it easier for them?

As he was designing his factsheet, Terrence considered where it might appear, such as on a government or non-government organization's website. Audience members might be policymakers seeking to change policies about child visitation in prisons, in which case they would want to access information quickly and easily. Terrence decided that putting information into boxes with clear headings would help them to find what they need.

C. Putting Things in Place: Layout

As you begin working on the layout for your document, you might start with a rough sketch on paper. As you work on your sketch, consider the following design principles:

Proximity: Group similar items close together. For example, on a conference poster you would probably put your name, department, and school in one place so readers can find them easily.

Alignment: Create clean lines by making sure every item on a page connects to something else on the page. Left justification tends to create the strongest alignment, while centering creates a jagged alignment that is more difficult for the eye to follow. Right justification is unusual, and can therefore attract attention, but it is also harder to read than left justification, since we read from left to right.

Repetition: To create a consistent design, repeat key elements throughout. For example, you might choose a consistent color scheme and font for each heading, varying only the size to indicate the importance of the heading. For a website, you might include a logo on each page so readers know they are on the same website when they navigate from page to page.

Contrast: Use color, bold text, or size to make important elements stand out. For example, on a conference poster you might want to bold the main headings and sub-headings using a large, bold font. Be careful not to make everything big and bold, though—if everything stands out, nothing stands out!

Let's evaluate how this draft of Terrence's factsheet uses design principles (Figure 29.5).

EXAMPLE: Terrence's Factsheet Draft

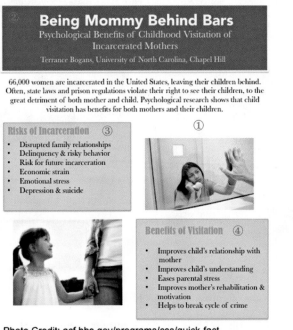

Figure 29.5

1. Proximity: Here, it is not clear which photograph goes with which block of text.
2. Alignment: Notice that the heading and first block of texts are centered, while the blocks of texts are not aligned with the photographs.
3. Repetition: The design uses different fonts for the main heading and the sub-headings, leading to a less cohesive look.
4. Contrast: Note that the large font sizes and colors distinguish them from the rest of the text.

After a draft workshop in class, Terrence realized that he needed to tweak his design to improve the proximity, repetition, and contrast. As shown in Figure 29.6, for his revised factsheet he chose a bold font for the headings and sub-headings, aligned everything flush left, and moved each block of text in the bottom half next to the photograph that went with it.

EXAMPLE: Terrence's Revised Factsheet

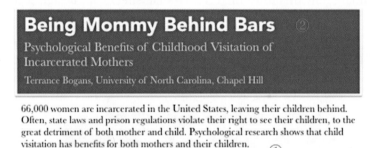

Being Mommy Behind Bars ②
Psychological Benefits of Childhood Visitation of Incarcerated Mothers

Terrance Bogans, University of North Carolina, Chapel Hill

66,000 women are incarcerated in the United States, leaving their children behind. Often, state laws and prison regulations violate their right to see their children, to the great detriment of both mother and child. Psychological research shows that child visitation has benefits for both mothers and their children. ①

Risks of Incarceration ③
- Disrupted family relationships
- Delinquency & risky behavior
- Risk for future incarceration
- Economic strain
- Emotional stress
- Depression & suicide

Benefits of Visitation ④
- Improves child's relationship with mother
- Improves child's understanding
- Eases parental stress
- Improves mother's rehabilitation & motivation
- Helps to break cycle of crime

Photo Credit: acf.hhs.gov/programs/css/quick-fact

Figure 29.6
1. Proximity: Here, it is clearer which photograph goes with which block of text.
2. Alignment: The left alignment makes everything connected in a straight line to something else on the page.
3. Repetition: The design uses only two different fonts, one for the main heading and the sub-headings, and one for the body text, leading to a more cohesive look.
4. Contrast: Note that the large font sizes and colors distinguish them from the rest of the text.

D. Types of Visual Elements

Visual elements refer to the types of images you might include in a design. Each type of image may work best for a particular purpose, audience, and genre. Use the three genre toolkit questions to help you determine what kinds of images to include.

What Is It?

Does your genre include images? What kinds? For example, in a profile article (Chapter 5) you might include a photograph of the person you are writing about, while a résumé (Chapter 12) would likely not include any images.

When choosing images for a project, you should also consider your audience's level of expertise and purpose for reading your document, as well as the genre you are writing. Some visual elements may be difficult for non-specialized audiences to interpret at a glance. For example, in his research paper (Chapter 28), Terrence chose a table to display numerical data because he thought it would appeal to an audience of policymakers and lawyers, and because he was writing for an academic audience. If this information were to appear in a popular magazine article, it might be simplified and displayed in a bar graph or even an infographic.

Who Reads It?

What kinds of images are best for your audience? Some images are best for technical readers, while others are more appropriate for a general audience. For example, a detailed architectural blueprint of a new house might be appropriate for the contractor who will build it, but a drawing of the house's façade might be more appropriate for potential buyers.

What's It For?

Does the image help to achieve your purpose? For example, if you would like to show readers a particular function in a computer program, you'd be better off with a screen capture of the actual program, rather than a pencil sketch. Table 29.1 can help you determine the most effective visual element for your purposes.

Table 29.1 Types of Visual Elements and Their Uses

Type of Visual Element	Purpose	Audience	Possible Genres

Graphs:
  Line
  Bar
  Pie
  Infographic
	Demonstrate trends or patterns in data	Usually technical or expert audiences, depending on type of graph	Research paper
			Conference poster
			Report
			Factsheet

Tables and Charts:
  Table
  Flow chart
  Organization chart
	Display information and data	Often used for more technical or expert audiences	Research paper
			Conference poster
			Report

Images:
  Diagram
  Drawing
  Photograph
  Map
  Screen capture
	Represent a real or imagined object (person, place, thing)	Often used for those who are learning how something works or how to do something; may be used to show readers how something will be constructed (e.g., in a proposal for a new bridge).
		Sometimes used simply for visual interest.
		May be for general or specialized audiences (as in a blueprint).
			Tutorials
			Reports
			Proposals
			Factsheet
			Websites
			Conference poster
			Blog

Graphs

Graphs are used to display trends or patterns in numerical data. You are probably already familiar with using and making graphs from your math or science courses. However, you may not have considered when to use them in writing assignments. Obviously, you might use a graph in a lab report for a science class, but a graph could also be used to display data in a recommendation report (Chapter 14) written for a business class or the results of a survey for a research paper (Chapter 11) in a sociology course.

There are many different types of graphs you might use in a document. Be sure to consider what types of graphs are appropriate for your genre, audience, and purpose.

Line Graphs   Line graphs are useful to indicate trends over time. In the following graph (Figure 29.7), prepared by the website WhiteHouse.gov, viewers can see that the average age at which Americans marry for the first time has increased since 1970, from around 23 for men and 20 for women, to 28 for men and 26 for women. The graph also shows that men tend to be older when they first get married than women.

EXAMPLE: Line Graph

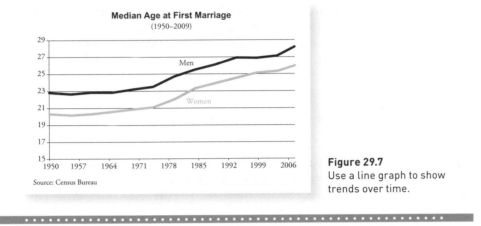

Figure 29.7
Use a line graph to show trends over time.

In his research paper (Chapter 28), Terrence used a line graph to show how the number of incarcerated parents was on the rise—and also that the number of children of incarcerated parents was on the rise. He was able to import the line graph directly from a PDF copy of the source he cites in the image caption. Here's how it looked in his finished paper:

As shown in Figure 1, this number has risen by over fifty percent over the course of

the last two decades, and is likely to continue to rise as the prison population grows.

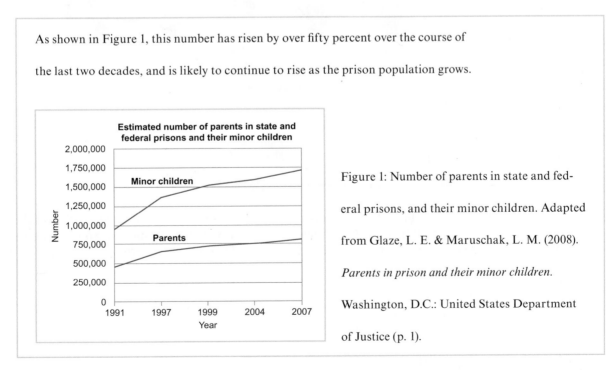

Figure 1: Number of parents in state and federal prisons, and their minor children. Adapted from Glaze, L. E. & Maruschak, L. M. (2008). *Parents in prison and their minor children.* Washington, D.C.: United States Department of Justice (p. 1).

Notice that Terrence introduced the graph in his text, referring to it as a "Figure," which is common in most citation styles. He then included a label and caption for the figure below it, and provided the source for the data he used.

Bar Graphs   Bar graphs are useful for displaying quantities of an item or measure. In the following bar graph (Figure 29.8), viewers can see how much money men and women earn, on average, according to the education they have achieved. It is easy to see that men and women earn more money each week, on average, if they have a bachelor's degree. Viewers also can see that men still tend to earn more money than women.

EXAMPLE: Bar Graph

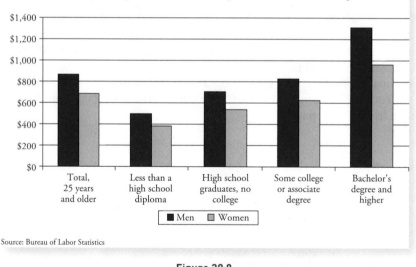

Earnings by Educational Attainment
(Median Weekly Earnings of Full-Time Workers Age 25 and Older, Annual Averages, 2009)

Source: Bureau of Labor Statistics

Figure 29.8
Use a bar graph to compare quantities.

Pie Graphs   Pie graphs are used to show the percentages that make up the whole. This pie graph (Figure 29.9) shows the proportion of federal spending on education that goes to instruction, support services, and other expenditures.

EXAMPLE: Pie Graph

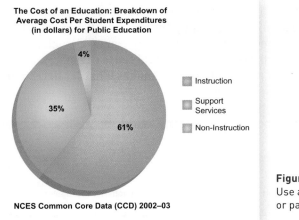

The Cost of an Education: Breakdown of
Average Cost Per Student Expenditures
(in dollars) for Public Education

4%

35%

61%

Instruction

Support
Services

Non-Instruction

NCES Common Core Data (CCD) 2002–03

Figure 29.9
Use a pie graph to show percentages
or parts of a whole.

Infographic   An infographic is a stylized graph used to display multiple data points in one frame. In this infographic (Figure 29.10), we can see information about the effects of the national Do Not Call registry as well as a timeline of key events in its history. The infographic uses another type of graph, a bubble graph, to visualize the data.

EXAMPLE: Infographic

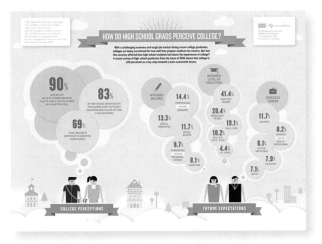

Figure 29.10
Use an infographic to display multiple data points in a single frame.

Tables and Charts

Tables and charts are used to display detailed information and data, or to illustrate concepts.

Tables   A table makes it easy for readers to compare numbers, especially those listed horizontally (since we read from left to right). In this table (Figure 29.11), readers can compare how much time people spend, on average, on tasks such as eating and sleeping. Unlike a graph, which would give a general sense of the trends or patterns in the data, here we get all of the numbers. This makes it harder to recognize patterns, but easier to find the exact numbers.

EXAMPLE: Table

Table 1. Time spent in primary activities [1] and percent of the civilian population engaging in each activity, averages per day by sex, 2012 annual averages

Activity	Average hours per day, civilian population			Average percent engaged in the activity per day			Average hours per day for persons who engaged in the activity		
	Total	Men	Women	Total	Men	Women	Total	Men	Women
Total, all activities [2]	24.00	24.00	24.00	–	–	–	–	–	–
Personal care activities	9.49	9.22	9.74	100.0	99.9	100.0	9.49	9.22	9.74
Sleeping	8.73	8.60	8.86	99.9	99.9	99.9	8.74	8.61	8.86
Eating and drinking	1.25	1.30	1.20	96.0	95.9	96.0	1.30	1.35	1.25
Household activities	1.74	1.29	2.17	73.7	64.5	82.3	2.36	1.99	2.63
Housework	.60	.28	.90	34.6	19.8	48.4	1.73	1.40	1.86
Food preparation and cleanup	.53	.28	.75	52.5	39.2	64.9	1.00	.72	1.16
Lawn and garden care	.18	.25	.12	9.8	11.7	8.0	1.87	2.11	1.53
Household management	.13	.10	.15	16.3	13.6	18.8	.78	.77	.79
Purchasing goods and services	.72	.60	.84	41.4	37.2	45.3	1.74	1.60	1.85
Consumer goods purchases	.35	.27	.43	37.5	34.0	40.8	.94	.80	1.05
Professional and personal care services	.08	.06	.10	7.4	5.6	9.0	1.10	1.05	1.13
Caring for and helping household members	.51	.35	.66	24.5	19.7	28.9	2.09	1.79	2.27
Caring for and helping household children	.40	.27	.53	20.4	15.6	24.8	1.98	1.71	2.14
Caring for and helping nonhousehold members	.18	.16	.20	11.2	9.9	12.3	1.62	1.59	1.64
Caring for and helping nonhousehold adults	.06	.06	.05	7.3	7.0	7.5	.80	.91	.70
Working and work-related activities	3.53	4.17	2.94	43.9	48.8	39.3	8.05	8.54	7.49
Working	3.19	3.74	2.67	41.8	46.5	37.4	7.63	8.05	7.13
Educational activities	.50	.53	.47	8.5	8.8	8.2	5.87	6.01	5.73
Attending class	.28	.30	.26	5.4	5.8	5.1	5.16	5.17	5.14
Homework and research	.17	.18	.16	6.2	6.1	6.2	2.75	2.89	2.63
Organizational, civic, and religious activities	.32	.26	.38	13.8	10.9	16.6	2.33	2.42	2.27
Religious and spiritual activities	.15	.12	.18	9.0	6.7	11.1	1.66	1.72	1.63
Volunteering (organizational and civic activities)	.13	.11	.15	6.0	5.0	7.0	2.13	2.21	2.08
Leisure and sports	5.37	5.79	4.97	96.2	96.9	95.6	5.58	5.98	5.20
Socializing and communicating	.74	.72	.76	37.2	35.4	38.9	2.00	2.04	1.96
Watching television	2.83	3.07	2.61	80.1	80.9	79.3	3.54	3.80	3.29
Participating in sports, exercise, and recreation	.32	.41	.24	19.3	21.7	17.0	1.67	1.90	1.39
Telephone calls, mail, and e-mail	.16	.11	.20	19.8	15.7	23.6	.78	.70	.84
Other activities, not elsewhere classified	.24	.23	.25	14.1	12.8	15.3	1.69	1.80	1.60

[1] A primary activity refers to an individual's main activity. Other activities done simultaneously are not included.
[2] All major activity categories include related travel time. See Technical Note for activity category definitions.
– Not applicable.
NOTE: Data refer to persons 15 years and over.

Figure 29.11
Use a table to help readers compare numerical data.

Terrence included a table in his research paper to show readers the actual numbers of incarcerated mothers and the number of children affected. Here is how it looked in his paper:

As shown in Table 1, the number of mothers in prison has risen from 1991,

when 29500 children had a mother in prison, to a total of 65600 in 2007.

Table 1 Number of Mothers in State and Federal Prisons

Number of Mothers	In State Prison	In Federal Prison	Total
2007	58200	7400	65600
2004	51800	6600	58400
1999	48500	5100	53600
1997	42900	4000	46900
1991	26600	2900	29500

Source: Glaze, L.E. & Maruschak, L.M. (2008). *Parents in Prison and Their*

Minor Children. Washington, D.C.: United States Department of Justice.

Appendix table 1.

Most of these mothers have more than one child: in 2007, a . . .

Notice that Terrence numbered the table separately from the other figures (graphs, pictures, etc.) in his research paper. He included a label and caption for the table before it appeared. He also introduced the table in the text beforehand, pointing readers to the most important information.

Charts   Use charts to show how things are organized or sequenced. Charts can be good for showing steps in a process, as in a flow chart, or how a company is organized into different departments. In this chart (Figure 29.12), viewers can see the organization of the National Oceanic and Atmospheric Association's Earth System Research Laboratory. The chart is organized hierarchically, so the person on top is the director of the whole laboratory—the boss of those below him on the chart.

EXAMPLE: Organization Chart

Figure 29.12
Use a chart to show how a system or organization is ordered.

Images

Images are visual representations of objects (persons, places, things). They may include images of real things, or of hypothetical things (such as a blueprint for a building that has not yet been built). Some images appeal to a wide audience, while others are used for more specialized audiences (as in a blueprint or diagram).

Diagrams   Diagrams are useful for showing parts of a system or machine and their functions. In this diagram (Figure 29.13), viewers can see the parts that make up the respiratory system, and they can see a cutaway view of a normal and diseased bronchial tube. Notice that these diagrams offer an idealized view of the system, one that you cannot see in real life. (If you've ever dissected a frog in biology class, you'll remember that the actual specimen looks a bit different, and messier, than the diagrams in your textbook.)

EXAMPLE: Diagram

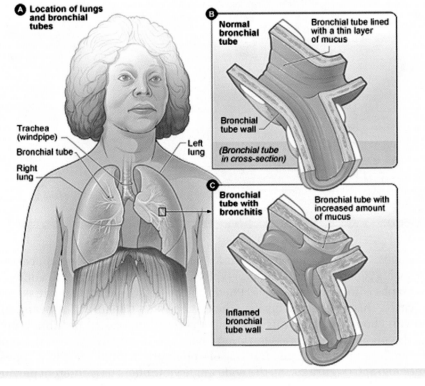

Figure 29.13
Use a diagram to show parts of a system and their functions.

Drawings Drawings are good for displaying details, or for displaying something that does not (yet) exist in real life, such as a drawing of a new house design. This drawing (Figure 29.14) shows an early vision for the United States Capitol Building, from around 1797, before it was fully constructed.

Drawings might also include specialized architectural drawings, the sketches fashion designers make for a new design, or the courtroom sketches made when photographers are not permitted in the courtroom. Drawings might also be idealized or informal images, as in a cartoon.

EXAMPLE: Drawing

Figure 29.14
Use a drawing to display details.

Photographs   Photographs are useful for showing how something appears in real life. Viewers generally assume photographs are realistic, although the ability to edit photographs with programs such as Photoshop has led viewers to be more skeptical in some cases. This photograph displays the United States Capitol as it appears today.

You can choose photographs to create a certain impression or fulfill a purpose. Here, the photograph impresses viewers with the impressive size of the building. Note that the angle, scope, and framing of a photograph influence how it appears. In this photograph (Figure 29.15), the wide angle view offers us a different perspective than we would get from a close-up. While the wide angle allows us to see the scale and imposing size of the building, a close up might provide more detail about some aspect of the building (such as the shape of the columns). The people in the photograph also give us a sense of the scale of the building.

EXAMPLE: Photograph

Figure 29.15
The angle, scale, and framing of this photograph provide a sense of the imposing stature of the United States Capitol Building.

Maps   Maps are used to show where things are located, or how they are situated with relation to other landmarks. Of course, sometimes readers will use maps to actually find a place, but in other cases they will use a map just to get a sense of how an area is laid out. In this map (Figure 29.16), viewers can see where the Capitol Building lies in relation to other buildings, such as the Supreme Court. Notice that maps usually include features to help readers interpret the map, such as a legend, numbers, or symbols. The scale and angle of a map, like a photograph, can influence how viewers see it. This map employs one-point perspective so that the Capitol Building lies in the center, and buildings further away seem to recede in the distance.

EXAMPLE: Map

Figure 29.16
This map employs one-point perspective so that the Capitol Building lies in the center, and buildings further away seem to recede in the distance.

Screen Captures   A screen capture is useful anytime you want to save an image of something on your computer screen. For instance, you might find a screen capture useful if you are writing instructions. Say you want to explain how to edit a photograph. You might include a screen capture of the program, possibly with callouts to illustrate specific functions. Or, you might use a screen capture to show how a website looks, as in Figure 29.17. (Most computers have a keyboard command to create screen captures—check your help manual or look up the proper command online.)

EXAMPLE: Screen Capture

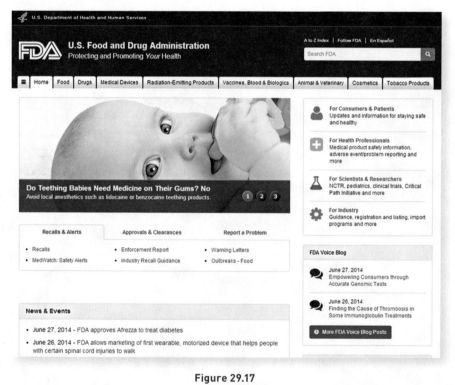

Figure 29.17
This is a screen capture of the U.S. Food and Drug Administration website.

E. Principles for Visual Elements

When selecting these types of images for your document, consider the following principles.

Follow Copyright Rules

Most images you find online are copyrighted, which means that you cannot just take them and stick them into your document. Here are a few options for finding copyright-free images:

- Make your own. Can you create your own graph in your word processing or spreadsheet program? (You will still need to cite the source for your data). Can you take your own photograph of a place? (Note that you will need permission from any people you include in a photograph, as long as their faces are identifiable.)
- Look for copyright-free images. Government images are almost always free, so try searching for images on government websites (such as archives.gov). You can also search websites such as Flickr or Wikimedia Commons for copyright-free images (look for language indicating that the content is covered by a Creative Commons license, which generally allows for free usage as long as the original source is credited). Be sure to read the terms of use for the site carefully.
- Ask. If you can contact the designer or photographer for an image, you can explain that you are using it for a class project and ask for permission to use it for free. In many cases, people are willing to grant an exception for students, as long as you are not publishing the image or making money from it.
- Investigate Fair Use. According to the United States Copyright Act, using images for non-profit educational purposes constitutes "fair use," or use for means of "criticism, comments, news reporting, teaching . . ., scholarship, or research" and is not a copyright infringement. Since Jay was commenting on the images in his rhetorical analysis (Chapter 28) and using them only for a class paper, he thought his use of the image constituted fair use. However, to publish the images in this textbook, we had to get permissions, since this textbook does not fall under the Fair Use policy. For class work, you may be able to claim Fair Use for images, as long as you do not plan on publishing them in print or online. However, check with your instructor to make sure this is okay.
- Attribute. Make sure you include a caption or footnote describing where you got the image.

Label and Caption Properly

Each image you include should have a label and caption, written according to the style guide you are using (such as MLA or APA). In most style guides, everything is labeled as a figure (Figure 1, Figure 2, etc.), except for tables, which are labeled separately (Table 1, Table 2, etc.). The labels for Figures appear below the visual, while the labels for tables appear above.

Here's an example from Terrence's research paper:

Today in America millions of children are being torn away from their mothers, and it is perfectly legal. Over 1.5 million children in the United States have at least one incarcerated parent (Glaze & Maruschak, 2010). As shown in Figure 1, this number has risen by over fifty percent over the course of the last two decades, and is likely to continue to rise as the prison population grows.

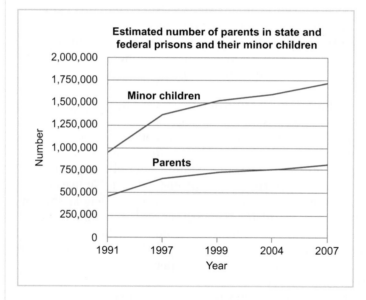

Figure 1: Number of parents in state and federal prisons, and their minor children. Adapted from Glaze, L. E. & Maruschak, L. M. (2008). *Parents in prison and their minor children.* Washington, D.C.: United States Department of Justice (p. 1).

Mothers account for a smaller proportion of these totals than do fathers; however, because female prisoners tend to receive less attention than do male prisoners, in this essay I focus on mothers.

As shown in Table 1, the number of mothers in prison has risen from 1991, when 29500 children had a mother in prison, to a total of 65600 in 2007. [8]

Table 1 Number of Mothers in State and Federal Prisons

Number of Mothers	In State Prison	In Federal Prison	Total
2007	58200	7400	65600
2004	51800	6600	58400
1999	48500	5100	53600
1997	42900	4000	46900
1991	26600	2900	29500

Source: Glaze, L.E. & Maruschak, L.M. (2008). *Parents in Prison and Their Minor Children*. Washington, D.C.: United States Department of Justice.

Appendix table 1.

Most of these mothers have more than one child: in 2007, a total of 147,400 children had a mother in prison, as shown. . . .

For graphs, you should also clearly label each axis and provide a legend to explain what colors or shading signify.

Introduce the Visual in the Text

In addition to a label and caption, each visual element should be introduced in the text itself before it appears. Then, if necessary, you can interpret each element after it appears. Your text signal should help readers to identify key patterns you want them to notice in the data. For example, Terrence wanted his readers to notice how the graph indicated a rise in the number of incarcerated parents in the United States. He signals the connection to the graph in the sentence beginning "As shown in Figure 1. . . ."

Acknowledge Sources

Below each table or visual element, list the source of information or the source of the visual. In the preceding example, Terrence generated his own tables and graphs, but he drew the information from a published, government source. If you use information from another study or source, you need to include that information. If you generated your own data (say, from a survey or your own calculations), you do not need to cite a source.

Use Consistent Fonts, Headings, and Colors

To create a unified design, try to employ the same fonts, colors, and headings in your images themselves. For example, for his paper, Terrence decided to use the same color scheme and fonts for all visual elements, in order to keep them consistent with the rest of the document.

Be Careful of Editing, Manipulation, and Distortion

Computer tools allow you to create and modify images in any number of ways. You may decide to modify an existing image to suit your rhetorical purpose. For example, Terrence might have used photo editing software to blur an image he included to illustrate the pain of an incarcerated mother, as in Figure 29.18.

Figure 29.18
Editing images using software can be effective, but be careful not to manipulate or distort images you are presenting as truthful representations.

In this case, the new image creates a certain effect, conveying more of the sadness and loneliness the woman pictured might feel. Since this was a government image, which carried no copyright, we felt it was appropriate to manipulate it for our own purposes. Manipulated images are often used on the web for humorous purposes as well, usually (not always) with no harm done.

However, altering photographs can also be unethical. It is unethical to take a copyrighted image and manipulate it, without seeking permission from the image's producer or owner.

It can also be unethical to alter images so as to scare or mislead readers, or to distort information. If you are using an image to demonstrate how things are, or what the facts are, be careful of distortions. For most genres and rhetorical situations for your writing, readers usually expect you to offer only truthful images. There are a few exceptions, though. For example, most readers now understand that the photographs of models used in fashion magazines have been retouched. Readers also expect to see manipulated images on humor websites, and are less likely to be misled. If you are using an image to evoke a feeling, mood, or idea, you may have more creative room.

Choose Fonts Carefully

For many genres, your choice of fonts is limited. Most academic style manuals specify a standard serif font (such as Times New Roman or Cambria). For other genres, you may have a wider range of choices open to you. Be sure to consider what font choices seem appropriate for your genre.

There are four main types of fonts:

- Serif (e.g., Times New Roman, Cambria, Garamond)
- Sans serif (e.g., Arial, Calibri, Franklin Gothic Book)
- *Italic or Script Fonts (e.g., Apple Chancery, Edwardian Script, Lucida Calligraphy)*
- Decorative (e.g., Curlz MT)

If you pay attention to the fonts used in documents you read, you'll start to notice how and when these fonts are used.

Most printed textbooks will use a serif font for the body text. That is because the extra embellishments, or feet, on each letter help readers to recognize the shapes of words. Serif fonts tend to be more readable for printed text.

However, for online documents, sans serif fonts tend to be more readable. This is because the screen resolution for most computers is still not as good as a printed page, so the extra embellishments on serif letters do not show up as easily.

Italic or calligraphic fonts are less likely to appear in academic or professional documents. They are difficult to read and tend to appear old-fashioned. For that reason, you might see a font of this type on a wedding invitation, on a menu at a fancy restaurant, or as part of a logo.

Like calligraphic fonts, decorative fonts are difficult to read in large quantities. They tend to appear informal, so they are less likely to appear in an academic or professional document. You may see decorative fonts used sparingly on a website, as part of a logo, or on a poster advertising a campus event.

As a general guideline, if you would like to use more than one font type in a document, you should choose one from each family. For example, a printed text might use a serif font for the body, and a sans serif font for the headers (Figure 29.19). The reverse might be best for a website: sans serif for the body, and serif for the headers (Figure 29.20).

Figure 29.19
A serif body text, such as Times New Roman, is easier to read on a printed page.

Figure 29.20
A sans serif body text, such as Arial, is easier to read on a screen.

F. Using Electronic Tools

When you are working on a design, determine what tools are available to you. Find out if your college has a multimedia laboratory where you can use specialized computer programs and equipment (such as scanners or digital cameras).

Use Layout Tools

Layout tools can help you to arrange items on a page (text, images, etc.) more efficiently than in a standard word processing program. Some popular layout and design programs include Adobe InDesign and Microsoft Publisher. Each program differs in its functions, but in general, you can see if your program allows you to do the following:

- Move text boxes, images, and other elements around easily
- Add design elements (boxes, shapes, etc.)
- Create a grid to align elements on the page
- Use or modify templates for your own purposes

Use Image Editing Tools

Image editing tools can help you to create and modify images. Some popular programs include Photoshop, iPhoto, and Picasa. These programs differ in functionality: some will allow you to create new images, while others are best for modifying existing images. See if your program allows you to do the following:

- Create a new image (such as a button or header for a website)
- Edit existing images for color, contrast, size, etc.
- Manipulate images using different filters (blur, posterize, etc.)
- Convert images to different file formats

Use Web Development Tools

Web development tools allow you to create websites. Some, such as Wordpress or Blogger, primarily use templates that you can easily apply yourself. These are sometimes referred to as platforms rather than web software.

Software programs, such as Dreamweaver or iWeb, allow you to create your own website from scratch, but they usually require more technical skill. To determine what type of program to use, ask the following questions:

- Does the program include templates to use/modify? Or will I need to create my own template from scratch?
- Will I need to learn some coding (e.g., HTML, JavaScript)? Or is the program a WYSIWYG editor (what you see is what you get) that requires little to no coding?
- How do I add images, text, links, and navigation elements?

Getting It Out There

In this chapter, you will learn how to get your work out into the world: how to give oral presentations, design multimedia presentations, create a portfolio of your work, submit your work for publication, or even self-publish your work (in print or online). For many college classes, you will be asked to present your work to classmates or even to outside audiences, such as at an undergraduate research conference or community event. Further, many colleges now make some kind of publication of your work, such as an electronic portfolio, a requirement for graduation. Of course, once you enter the workplace, presentations become even more common. This chapter will help you to develop strategies to use in all of these situations.

A. Delivering Oral Presentations

For many students, oral presentations represent one of the most nerve-wracking experiences of a college career. Yet, oral presentations are among the most common requirements for college courses. If you get nervous speaking in front of others (as many people do), take heart. Good preparation and practice can go a long way to alleviating nervousness.

Study the Genre

As is the case with written documents, oral presentations can also be understood as genres, in that they share common situations, purposes, and features (Table 30.1). For instance, the genre of the "opening statement" in a legal trial exists because lawyers regularly have to introduce the case for the defense or prosecution, outlining the key points they will prove. (You've probably seen examples of this genre on TV shows or in movies featuring a court case.) This type of oral presentation differs from the kind a political candidate gives while campaigning, which is known as a "stump speech." While a court case seeks to persuade an audience that has not already decided on an issue (a jury), political speeches are often targeted to the faithful "base" of a political party. The content, style, and delivery of these speeches differ accordingly.

Note that many of these oral genres have an immediate audience (those who are physically present) and a secondary audience (those who may be watching on television or the Internet). For example, presidential debates are often held at a community center or college, with audience members present from that community. However, many more audience members will watch the debate on a television broadcast or Internet feed.

Table 30.1 Genres of Oral Presentations

Genre	Audience	Purpose	Format
Spiel	Attendees on a tour or at an exhibit (e.g. at a tour of historical homes)	Provide information and background	Memorized or extemporaneous
Audio Tour	Visitors to a museum, heritage site, national park, etc.	Provide information and background	Memorized/recorded
Opening or Closing Argument	Judge, jury	Persuade the audience to acquit/convict the defendant	Extemporaneous
Conference Presentation	Conference attendees	Provide an overview of research findings; persuade audience of the importance and validity of those findings	Memorized (or read from a sheet) or extemporaneous
PowerPoint Presentation	Multiple—employees at a business meeting, students in a class, attendees at a conference	Support an oral presentation with visual elements, bulleted notes, etc.	Extemporaneous
Poster Presentation	Participants at a conference or fair	Provide information about a research project or initiative; persuade audience of the validity and importance of a project	Extemporaneous
Radio Broadcast	Radio listeners	Entertain and inform	Memorized (or read from a script), or extemporaneous, or impromptu (as in an interview)
Debate	People immediately present at a debate	Persuade the audience to accept an argument, show that one's argument is superior to the other debaters' (e.g., presidential debate)	Extemporaneous (debaters prepare with practice and notes)

continued

Table 30.1 Genres of Oral Presentations *(continued)*

Genre	Audience	Purpose	Format
Oral petition/ appeal	Members of a board or council (e.g. City Council)	Persuade audience to grant a request or appeal	Memorized, read, or extemporaneous
Eulogy	Mourners at a funeral or memorial service	Celebrate and honor the deceased	Memorized or read
Toast	Attendees at an award banquet, wedding, or other special event	Celebrate a guest of honor or award winner	Memorized, read, extemporaneous, or impromptu
Commencement Speech	Graduates, and their friends and families	Celebrate and honor the graduates' accomplishments	Memorized or read
Campaign Speech	Voters	Persuade voters to elect a candidate	Memorized or read from a teleprompter
Seminar	Students, employees	Inform audience about a topic	Extemporaneous
Roundtable or Panel Discussion	Attendees at a conference, members of a community	Provide multiple perspectives on an issue	Extemporaneous or impromptu
Interview	Public audiences (as on a tv show or radio show)	Inform audience about one's life, experiences, or expertise	Extemporaneous or impromptu (interviewees are sometimes given a list of questions to prepare)
Job Interview	Employers	Persuade audience to offer the job	Extemporaneous or impromptu

Choose a Format

Depending on the genre and assignment, you may choose from several different styles of speaking.

Impromptu Speaking

In an impromptu speech, you speak off the top of your head, without having rehearsed in advance. It takes a lot of practice at speaking, in general, in order to be a good impromptu speaker. Otherwise, you can easily lose track of what you meant to say and end up rambling or getting stuck with nothing to say.

Memorized Speaking   In a memorized speech, you write out a script and then learn it word for word. This approach tends to be used in formal occasions, such as a parent's speech at a child's wedding. A memorized speech tends to come across as more formal and polished than an impromptu speech, but can also seem too stiff for some occasions and genres.

Extemporaneous Speaking   Extemporaneous speaking lies halfway between impromptu and memorized speaking. In an extemporaneous speech, you use notes or talking points to keep you on track, but you do not memorize each word you will say. An extemporaneous speech can sound more natural than a memorized speech, but your talking points will help you to avoid rambling or getting lost.

If you choose an extemporaneous speech, be sure to keep your notes to a minimum, and practice giving your talk several times so that you do not end up simply reading your notes.

Plan Content and Organization

To get started, make sure you know the parameters for your presentation. How much time do you have? What type of presentation are you meant to give? Who is your audience? A five-minute memorized speech for city council members is very different from a ten-minute question and answer session with your classmates.

Select Key Points   Once you know the details of your speaking assignment, you can begin to plan the contents and organization for your presentation. Start by listing out the main point you want to get across to your audience. Then, sketch out an outline, such as this one:

> *Five-minute speech*
> *Min 1—introduce topic and main claim*
> *Min 2—supporting point 1*
> *Min 3—supporting point 2*
> *Min 4—example*
> *Min 5—conclude/recap*

You can see that a short speech does not give you much time. Rather than trying to cover too much ground, focus on a few key ideas that you can cover adequately in the time allotted.

Build In Signposts   Listeners can easily get lost in a long, rambling speech. To make it easier for them to focus on your key points, build in signposts. You might start by outlining the contents you plan to cover, and then use transitions (first, next, etc.) to signal each point or section.

Practice

The most important factor for a good oral presentation is practice. You should plan to rehearse your presentation several times. Try giving your presentation in front of your mirror, your roommate, or even your cat.

It can also be helpful to record yourself giving your presentation, if you have access to a webcam or digital camera. After recording your presentation, watch the video and take notes on what to improve.

Delivery

The difference between an engaging presentation and a boring one often comes down to delivery, not just to content. By delivery, we mean how you bring life to the presentation with your voice, body language, and gestures. As you practice, focus on the following:

Voice and Intonation   Practice using an authoritative, strong voice. If you normally speak quietly, imagine yourself addressing someone in the back of the room—can you make your voice reach that person? Try not to let your voice signal uncertainty. For instance, if every sentence sounds like a question, you might come across as less certain of your ideas. Try to focus on keeping your voice even, or even slightly lower than your regular speaking voice.

It might help to imagine yourself in a different persona (Chapter 21). If your assignment is to present the results of a research project, for instance, imagine yourself as a professor or scholar, not a student.

Gestures and Body Language   To convey authority with your body as well as your voice, pay attention to how you stand. You should try to look natural, not stiff. Let gestures happen naturally, if at all—if you force yourself to use certain hand gestures, you may come across as nervous or unnatural. The more you practice, the more natural you will feel.

If you videotape yourself practicing, you'll notice whether or not you have certain habits, such as brushing your hair from your eyes or putting your hands in your pockets.

Eye Contact   If you have practiced your speech enough, you will be able to look up from your notes (if you have them) and make eye contact with audience members. If you are doing a multimedia presentation or PowerPoint, try to avoid gazing at the screen or reading from the slides. Good eye contact helps to keep audience members focused and engaged.

B. Developing Multimedia Presentations

You may also choose to use multimedia to present your findings or ideas to an audience. Multimedia can accompany an oral presentation (as in a slideshow), or it can stand on its own (as in a podcast).

Choose a Format

If you are preparing a multimedia presentation, first, choose a format that suits your audience and purpose. For example, if you are presenting results from a research study, a slideshow presentation can help you to display your data visually. You might also consider how you might share your multimedia presentation online. For instance, a video can be posted to Vimeo or YouTube, where many viewers can see it.

Slideshow presentation (PowerPoint)   Speakers often use a slideshow presentation to accompany an oral presentation. You can use presentation software such as PowerPoint or Prezi to illustrate key points, or show visual elements (Chapter 29) to your audience as you speak. Slideshows are especially popular among business, scientific, and medical fields, where you may need to show graphs, charts, and diagrams to the audience.

When designing a slideshow presentation, keep the following tips in mind:

- Avoid cluttering each slide with too much information. Keep bullet lists short, and avoid adding too many design features.
- Include an overview slide to focus readers.
- Avoid reading from the slides as you present—practice your presentation so that you can move seamlessly through the slides as you speak.
- Arrive early to set up your presentation, and have a back-up plan (such as a handout) in case you have technical difficulties.

Podcasts   A podcast is a recorded presentation that you upload to a website or provide for listeners in some other way. (For example, some museums and art galleries now provide podcasts to visitors, who can listen to them on their cell phones or on a provided media player.)

Since listeners to a podcast will not necessarily have a visual aid, be sure to provide signposts to keep them focused—introduce the main points, and provide cues when you move from one point to another.

You might produce a scripted podcast, which you read as you go along, or you can create an extemporaneous podcast, such as an interview or debate. You should also consider what other kinds of sounds, if any, you would like to include. Can you use music or other recorded sounds to set the tone?

You can record your podcast on your computer, using audio software such as GarageBand or Audacity.

Videos   You might create a video to accompany an oral presentation, or you might create a standalone video that you upload to the web. A video might have a range of purposes or audiences. For instance, in a film class you might be asked to create a scene analysis in the form of a video you upload to YouTube (Chapter 8). Or, you might be asked to create a public service announcement (PSA) for a service learning class.

As is the case with oral presentations, there are genres of videos as well. As always, you can begin by finding examples of the type of video you wish to present. Looking at examples will give you ideas about what kinds of content to include, how to order your video, and what kinds of techniques to use.

Screencasts   A screencast is like a video that you take of your computer screen. You can use screencasting software, such as Camtasia, to record a set of actions you perform on your computer. A screencast can be useful as an instructional tool. For example, you could create a screencast to show new students how to use your online course enrolment system. Or, you can try something more creative, like a multimedia presentation with sound, video, text, and so on.

To create an effective screencast, keep the following tips in mind:

- Plan out your screencast in advance. Write down a sequence of actions and a script so that you know which action to perform and what to say, when.
- Do a practice run before you record, or plan to record a few times so that you can get it right.
- Pay close attention to pacing. When you revise, check to ensure that movements or transitions do not happen too quickly—this can make people dizzy.

Plan Content and Organization

As you plan the content for your multimedia presentation, keep in mind that you are not just writing a document users can read at their own pace—you are doing much of the pacing yourself. You will need to plan for sounds, movement, images, etc. to occur alongside a spoken text.

To make these plans, it might be useful to sketch out a storyboard: a visual and verbal description of each scene or stage in your production.

Create a Script

As you plan your script (text that will be spoken or possibly displayed on the screen), consider how you can make your text as easy for your audience to follow as possible. You should consider the following:

- Using signposts or forecasting to give readers a sense of what is coming next.
- Practicing your script out loud. Identify any stumbling points and revise the text if needed.

- If you are recording your voice, practicing and listening to the recording. Identify any quirks (such as saying "um" a lot or raising your voice at the end of sentences), then try again.
- Planning extra time to identify any technical difficulties or problems that need to be worked out.

C. Creating a Portfolio

A portfolio is a collection of your best work that you may submit in a class, as a requirement for your major or minor, or as a record of your achievements in college. The audience for a portfolio may be someone who is evaluating your work, such as your instructor or professor, or it could be something you put together for potential employers or as part of your application package to a post-college program.

Choose a Format: Print or Electronic
Take a look at some sample portfolios.

EXAMPLE 1: Digital Portfolio for a Nursing Major

Home | e-Portfolios Directory   Login

LAGUARDIA COMMUNITY COLLEGE REGISTERED NURSING PROGRAM CAPSTONE COURSE

Introduction | Nursing Philosophy Statement | Professional Goals | Nursing Competencies | Resume | Leadership and Community Service | Contact

Introduction

To view my student portfolio, please click here.

Welcome to my Capstone portfolio. My name is Shane de Gracia. I am a new graduate of LaGuardia Community College school of Nursing. The past 3 years of school have given me a higher level of respect for the field of nursing, and have made me even more determined to become a registered nurse. Being a nursing student and a mother at the same time has given me increasingly greater challenges everyday. Time management and task order has to be considered to fit what is best for me, my family, and my future career. The knowledge I have come to acquire through hands on learning, visual experience, textbook readings have equipped me in being a competent member of a medical workforce.

EXAMPLE 2: Digital Portfolio for an Art Major

Consider Potential Audiences

Portfolios may be written primarily for evaluation purposes, or for career advancement. On the one hand, you may be submitting a portfolio in order to earn a grade in a course or to complete your major or minor. Jorge's portfolio (Example 3, below) served this purpose, and, as the title page indicates, he included polished, revised examples of writing assignments he had completed. The portfolio served as an argument that he had met his course objectives.

On the other hand, your portfolio could serve as an argument that you should be hired. Each element you choose should help potential employers to understand that you have the skills needed to perform a job effectively. Both Shane and Darryle (Examples 1 and 2) aimed for an audience of professional employers and chose content to reflect that purpose.

Determine What to Include

If you are given the choice of what to include in your portfolio, think carefully about what kinds of items will be most effective for your audience and purpose. You might consider the following:

EXAMPLE 3: Print Portfolio for a Marketing Major

Jorge Sotelo

[Home address street number and name], [City], [St], [Zip code], [Phone number], [E-mail address]

[MONTH] [DAY], [YEAR]

[NAME]
[TITLE]
[COMPANY NAME]
[ADDRESS]

Dear Sales and Marketing Department Director:

I learned about the [JOB TITLE] open position with [COMPANY] through the [WEBSITE] on May 14, 2010. I am highly interested in this position and believe my experience with the California State Soccer Association (Cal South) and leadership with the Latino Business Student Association (LBSA) makes me a strong candidate for this position.

I recently obtained my Bachelor of Arts in Business Administration with an emphasis in Marketing from the Mihaylo College of Business and Economics at California State University, Fullerton. In my marketing degree coursework, I developed marketing plans for sports organizations, such as Major League Soccer and the United States Soccer Federation.

My professional career experience includes more than two years at Cal South with some of my responsibilities providing significant experience in:

- Game-related operations and logistics.
- Community outreach.
- Conduct and interpret market research for various projects.

In addition to the aforementioned skills, I have also proved success in this industry by:

- Reaching an overall growth of 21 percent of the Los Angeles Fútbol Circuit in 2009 year to date.
- Exceeding the 2010 Los Angeles Fútbol Circuit Spring League goals by 36 percent.

I look forward to speaking with you regarding this opportunity with [COMPANY NAME]. I will inquire within a week to follow up with you and answer any questions you may have. Should you require additional information, feel free to contact me via phone or via e-mail. Thank you for time and consideration.

Sincerely,

Jorge Sotelo

Enc. Resume

- Photographs
- A biographical statement
- A résumé (Chapter 12)
- Examples of a research genre (Chapter 11)
- Examples of informative writing (Chapter 6)
- Examples of other genres, such as a profile (Chapter 5), argumentative genre (Chapter 10), etc.
- Any writing you have published
- An example of a multimedia or visual document (Chapter 29 and this chapter)
- A statement of your professional or educational goals
- A statement about your philosophy toward your major or career
- A list of key skills
- A list of volunteer or work experiences

Provide an Overview

When you put together a portfolio, your goal is to highlight your best work and give examples of projects you have completed. However, you may also be asked to (or wish to) provide an overview that explains how each item fits with your goals, what you have learned, and what skills you can apply to other tasks.

Keep your audience in mind as you prepare the overview. If you are writing for instructors, then you are essentially trying to show that you have met the objectives for your course or program. If your audience may include potential employers, though, your goal is to show that you have learned skills relevant to your potential occupation. You can refer to specific examples from your work as evidence of your claims.

Develop a Design and User Navigation

Depending on the type of project, consider what design elements you can use to create a professional look and feel for your portfolio. For an e-portfolio, a portfolio that exists online, you will have several choices to make about colors, fonts, and styles. Remember to keep your audience and purpose in mind. If your audience includes potential employers, then you should consider what visual elements will strike the right tone.

Notice that Shane (Example 1) included a photograph of herself in her nursing uniform to convey her professional authority, along with the logo from the college she attended. Darryle chose a sleek, black and white color scheme because it fits with his goal of becoming a graphic designer. Refer to Chapter 29 for more on visual design.

Regardless of whether you are putting together a print or electronic portfolio, you can consider how to help readers find what they may need. For a print portfolio, you might include a table of contents, dividers with tabs, and headings to organize the contents, like Jorge did (Example 3). For an electronic portfolio, you might add an introductory page, a navigation bar, and/or a sitemap. Shane decided to include a simple bar across the top of the page for navigation. Darryle (Example 2) included links across the top as well as a box ("Check Out My Work") to point readers to different sections.

D. Submitting Your Work for Publication

As a college student, you may be encouraged to share your writing with an audience outside of your classroom. Increasingly, students are asked to present their work at conferences, submit it to newspapers or journals, or share it with professional audiences (such as a local organization). Publishing your work with outside audiences can help you to build your résumé, and it can also give you a chance to share your ideas with others.

Choose a Venue

First, consider where you might publish your work. Your college may host its own undergraduate research conference, publish its own newspaper or literary magazine, or put out an online research journal. You can also search online for conferences, newspapers, magazines, and journals that publish student research.

Make sure your venue matches the genre you would like to publish. For instance, you might submit a personal essay or poem to a literary magazine, but probably not to a research journal. If you look up the web page for your target venue, you can see what kinds of submissions they accept.

Follow Submission Guidelines

Once you have located a publication venue, check to see if there are submission guidelines available. Take careful note of any deadlines, formatting requirements, or other information. You may need to format your bibliography using a different style guide, for instance, or condense your document to meet their word limits. Doing everything exactly according to the guidelines will increase your chances of getting published.

In some cases, you may need special permissions to publish materials included in your work. For example:

- If you have used archival materials from a library's special collection (such as unpublished letters, manuscripts, photographs, etc.), you may need permission from your library and/or from the literary executor for the collection. **Check with your library.**
- If you are publishing research results that involved human subjects (such as interviews, surveys, focus groups, or experiments), you may need permission from your college's Institutional Review Board (IRB). You may need to show proof that you have complied with the IRB's guidelines. **Check with your college's Institutional Review Board.**
- If you are using photographs, images from films, or other visual material you did not create yourself, you may need copyright permissions to publish them. **Check with whoever owns copyright for those materials.**

Create a Checklist

Once you have checked the submission guidelines, create a checklist so you can keep track of everything you need to do. Here is one students' checklist:

- ☐ Consider your genre: Is qualitative
- ☐ Change bibliography to MLA format
- ☐ Double-check quotes and citations
- ☐ Cut 750 words from article (3500 max)
- ☐ Get permissions to publish archival photos and letters from library

☐ Sign and date copyright statement
☐ Get letter from faculty supervisor
☐ Write short abstract
☐ Choose 5 keywords
☐ Create cover page
☐ Write cover letter

You may need to include additional items that you have not already written, such as an abstract (Chapter 11), a list of keywords, or a cover page. Use the genre toolkit (Chapters 1–4) to help you. Look for examples of these items, preferably in your target publication or in the submission guidelines. Try to identify the common features, and then determine how you can create your own.

Write a Cover Letter

When you submit your work for publication, you may need to include a cover letter. This could take the form of an email, a professional letter (Chapter 12), or an online form. Check your submission guidelines to make sure. Cover letters typically include the title of the work you are submitting, a short summary of your work, and a short biographical note about yourself.

E. Self-Publishing Your Work

In addition to submitting your work for publication, you may wish to self-publish your work. This means that you do not need to seek approval from anyone else, but that you will be your own editor. That is, you will decide what standard to meet, how to format your work, and how it will be distributed.

Choose a Venue

The Internet provides many different options for self-publishing your work. Depending on the type of project, you might choose one of the following:

- A website
- A blog
- A post to an existing website, such as YouTube or Scribd
- A self-published book
- An entry on Wikipedia or another "crowdsourced" venue

Consider what audience you would like to reach for your work. Then, determine which type of venue would best help you to reach that audience. For instance, you might like a printed, bound copy of your poetry just for yourself and some close friends. You could self-publish and print that volume and order just enough copies from a website such as CreateSpace or Lulu.com. Or, you might want to create a website showcasing your research for a course, one that can be seen by a wide audience.

Determine Copyright Options

Even if you are self-publishing, you will still need to follow copyright regulations, especially if you are posting materials online. Check to see who owns the copyright for any images, videos, or other materials you have not created yourself. You can write to the owner and ask for permission, or search for materials that are copyright-free.

Check Publishing Guidelines

If you are creating a website or other document yourself, then your only restrictions will involve your technical skills and the affordances of the software or platform you are using. Of course, you will want to make choices about color, layout, and so on based on your audience and purpose. See Chapter 29 for more on visual elements and design.

If you would like to self-publish your material, then you may need to pay attention to layout concerns. For instance, you might need to build in margins of a certain size to accommodate the printing and binding specifications for a self-published book or pamphlet. Check with your online publisher or copy center for more information.

Style and Usage Guide

How Verbs Work

A. What Is a Verb?

What do you notice about the highlighted words in these sentences?

- The candidate attacked the opposition's proposal.
- The non-profit organization feeds children across the world.
- The program will create a culture of compassion on our campus.

In each of these sentences, the emphasized word or phrase carries the action of the sentence. These words are verbs, or "action words," and they can refer to an event, action, or state of being.

B. Common Problems

Be on the lookout for the following common verb problems.

Conjugation

A conjugation problem means that you have chosen the wrong ending for a verb in its conjugated form.

> **Problem:** He walk down the street.
> **Solution:** He walks down the street.

Subject–Verb Agreement

Each verb has a subject—a person, place, or thing—that performs the action.

- **The candidate** attacked the opposition's proposal.
- **Charity** is difficult to define.
- **The Bahamas** is an archipelago in the Caribbean.
- **The celebration** will occur in mid-July.

A subject-verb agreement problem occurs when the subject of your sentence does not match the verb. This is likely to happen when you are misled by a series of words in between the subject and the verb.

> **Problem:** **One** of the children **are** sleeping.
> **Solution:** **One** of the children **is** sleeping.
> **Problem:** The **president**, who is the proud owner of two cats, **are** going to speak at the cat convention.
> **Solution:** The **president**, who is the proud owner of two cats, **is** going to speak at the cat convention.

Overuse of Passive Voice

Verbs can appear in the passive or active form. In the active form, the subject is the same as the person or thing that performs the action:

- I kicked the ball.
- I wrote the documents.

In the passive form, the subject and object have switched places, so that the subject of the sentence is not the person or thing who actually performs the action:

- The ball was kicked [by Frank].
- The documents were written by Jane.

You can recognize the passive voice because it always uses a conjugation of the verb "to be" plus the past participle of a verb. The passive sentence may or may not tack on "by" to show who or what performed the action.

The passive voice is not incorrect—in fact, some genres, especially types of scientific writing, may use it frequently. However, if you use the passive voice too often you make your writing more difficult for the reader to easily understand. Try to revise your sentences so that they use the active voice more frequently:

> **Problem:** By the end of the year, the amendment **had been ratified**. Prohibition **was** still **opposed**, and bootleg operations **were initiated** to provide liquor to thirsty customers.
> **Solution:** By the end of the year, Congress **ratified** the amendment. Many still **opposed** the amendment, yet a happy cast of gangsters and bootleggers **began** to provide liquor to thirsty customers.

Overuse of Nominalizations

A nominalization is a verb that has been turned into a noun. Nominalizations are not grammatically incorrect. In fact, they are necessary in some academic writing because nominalizations often express key concepts (such as "evolution," "gentrification," or "colonialism"). However, they tend to make your writing more difficult to read and understand. To revise, try to turn some of your nominalizations back into verbs.

> **Problem:**   The **colonization** of Africa led to the **destabilization** of family structures and the **delegitimization** of existing political systems.
>
> **Solution:**   By **colonizing** Africa, Europeans **destabilized** family structures and **delegitimized** existing political systems.

Wrong Tense

Verbs may be used in different tenses to indicate whether the action happened in the past, is happening in the present, or will happen in the future.

- I **write** the policy. [present]
- I **wrote** the policy yesterday. [past]
- I **have written** the policy. [present perfect]
- I **had written** the policy. [past perfect]
- I **will write** the policy tomorrow. [future]
- I **am going to write** the policy tomorrow. [future]

In English, you indicate the tense of a verb either by adding an ending (such as -ed for past) or by using a helping verb (such as "will" or "am going" for future, and "have" or "had" for the past).

"Wrong tense" means that you have chosen the wrong form of a verb (past, present, or future) for the idea you are trying to express.

> **Problem:**   Yesterday, I **interview** Professor Steinberg about her research.
>
> **Solution:**   Yesterday, I **interviewed** Professor Steinberg about her research.

Watch out for the following expressions, which are sometimes misused in the past tense.

"Used to" and "Supposed to"

> **Problem**:   He **use to** work out a lot, but he doesn't any more.
>
> **Solution**:   He **used to** work out a lot, but he doesn't any more.
>
> **Problem**:   We are **suppose** to finish this assignment by tomorrow.
>
> **Solution**:   We are **supposed** to finish this assignment by tomorrow.

"Seen" and "Been"

> **Problem**:   I **seen** that movie already.
>
> **Solution 1**: I **saw** that movie already.
>
> **Solution 2**: I **have seen** that movie already.

Problem: I **been** in the library.
Solution 1: I **was** in the library.
Solution 2: I **have been** in the library.

Tense Shifts

A tense shift occurs when a writer has gone from using one form of a verb (past, present, or future) to another while writing about the same event. Try to keep the tense you are using consistent as long as you are talking about the same event or idea.

Problem: The Civil War **opened** with the Battle of Fort Sumter, when the Federal Government **attacked** the fortress outside of Charleston, South Carolina. In response, South Carolina authorities **seize** all federal property in Charleston. The situation in South Carolina soon **begins** to resemble a siege.

Solution: The Civil War **opened** with the Battle of Fort Sumter, when the Federal Government **attacked** the fortress outside of Charleston, South Carolina. In response, South Carolina authorities **seized** all federal property in Charleston. The situation in South Carolina soon **began** to resemble a siege.

Wrong Preposition

Some verbs have words that tend to follow after them, called prepositions. These kinds of verbs are called phrasal verbs. Some verbs use different prepositions in different circumstances. If you are unsure which preposition to use, use a dictionary.

Problem: I should **of** written to the professor ahead of time.
Solution: I should **have** written to the professor ahead of time.
Problem: I believe **in** it is important to keep student fees as low as possible.
Solution: I believe **that** it is important to keep student fees as low as possible.

Some verbs can go with a few different prepositions, depending on the sentence. Here are a few examples:

• Believe in (someone or something)
• Believe that (an event or occurrence)
• Try to (do something)
• Try on (an article of clothing)
• Apologize for (an act)
• Apologize to (a person)
• Hear of (a person, place, or thing)
• Hear that (an act or event)
• Argue with (a person or position)

- Argue about (an idea or theory)
- Argue that (a statement or claim is true)

Common confusions:

- Should (would, could) **of** → should (would, could) **have**
- Wanna, gonna (informal or oral form) → want to, going to (formal or written form)

Wrong Past Form

Many verbs in English do not follow the usual pattern of adding -ed to change to the past tense. For these verbs, called "irregular verbs," you use a different form to indicate the simple past tense.

Problem: She **creeped** through the house.
Solution: She **crept** through the house.
Problem: The war **becomed** more bloody and violent.
Solution: The war **became** more bloody and violent.

Here are some more examples of irregular verbs in the past tense:

- choose → chose
- cling → clung
- eat → ate
- build → built
- buy → bought
- burst → burst

To make things even more complicated, some irregular verbs use yet another form as their past participle (the form you use to write the present perfect or past perfect tenses).

Problem: He **has chose** to attend college.
Solution: He **has chosen** to attend college.

Here are some more examples:

- arise → arose (simple past) → arisen (past participle)
- eat → ate → eaten
- choose → chose → chosen
- give → gave → given
- begin → began → begun

If you have been told that your verb form is wrong, look in a dictionary to find the correct way to write the past participle.

How Nouns and Pronouns Work

A. What Is a Noun?

A noun is a word that identifies a person, place, or thing (e.g., professor, city, computer). If a noun *names* the person, place, or thing, then it is a *proper* noun (e.g., Professor Brown, New York City, MacBook).

B. What Is a Pronoun?

A pronoun can function like a noun in a sentence, but a pronoun *refers* to a noun that appears elsewhere in a written passage. Some common pronouns are he, they, it, you, him, mine, yours, etc. These pronouns refer to another noun; for example, "he" might refer to "Joseph" while "it" might refer to "the notebook."

C. Common Problems

Be on the lookout for the following common problems that arise with nouns and pronouns.

Capitalization of Nouns

If a noun *names* a person, place, or thing, then it should be capitalized, because the noun is a *proper* noun. All other nouns are *common* nouns.

   Do not capitalize common nouns.

> **Problem:** I went to the **Store** to buy towels.
> **Solution:** I went to the **store** to buy towels.

But do capitalize proper nouns.

> **Problem:**   I went to **target** to buy towels.
> **Solution:**   I went to **Target** to buy towels.

Other proper nouns include the names of the following:

- languages (French, Chinese)
- religions (Islam, Buddhism)
- cities (Paris, Moscow)
- states (Nebraska, Oregon)
- countries (Japan, Indonesia)

Vague Pronoun Referents

Pronouns must refer to nouns (called "referents" or "antecedents") in order to make sense. If it is unclear from your writing what a pronoun refers to, then you have written a vague referent.

Who does the pronoun "she" refer to in the following problem sentence?

> **Problem:**   Heather, Mary, and Jacinta are studying hard for the test. **She** hopes **she'll** get an A.
> **Solution:**   Heather, Mary, and Jacinta are studying hard for the test. **Jacinta** hopes **she'll** get an A.

What does the pronoun "it" refer to in the following problem sentence?

> **Problem:**   For the test tomorrow, I'll need my laptop, laptop charger, and textbook. I hope I don't forget **it**.
> **Solution:**   For the test tomorrow, I'll need my laptop, laptop charger, and textbook. I hope I don't forget my **laptop charger**.

Pronoun Shifts

Use a singular pronoun to refer to a singular antecedent and a plural pronoun to refer to a plural antecedent.

> **Problem:**   If a **student** has a problem with this course, **they** should talk to the professor.

This problem sentence has a singular antecedent ("student") paired with a plural pronoun ("they").

> **Solution 1:** If a **student** has a problem with this course, **he or she** should talk to the professor.

Solution 1 changes the plural pronoun to singular pronouns.

> **Solution 2:** If **students** have a problem with this course, **they** should talk to the professor.

Solution 2 changes the singular antecedent to a plural antecedent.

One note: using "they" as a singular, gender-neutral pronoun has become a popular usage. However, for academic writing, using "they" in this fashion is not the best choice. Use one of the preceding solutions instead, or check a style guide for your discipline for help (such as the *Publication Manual of the American Psychological Association* or the *MLA Handbook for Writers of Research Papers*).

Pronoun Confusion

Pronouns come in a variety of types:

- Subject pronouns: I, you, he, she, it, we, you, they
- Object pronouns: me, you, him, her, it, us, you, them
- Possessive pronouns: mine, yours, his, hers, its, ours, yours, theirs

When you write, you need to be sure that you are using subject pronouns as subjects of your sentences, object pronouns as objects, and possessive pronouns to indicate ownership.

In the problem sentence that follows, the writer incorrectly used an object pronoun where a subject pronoun should be used.

> **Problem:** **Them** were working on a group project.
> **Solution:** **They** were working on a group project.

They're, Their, and There

A common word confusion arises when writers mix up the contraction "they're" (which means "they are"), the possessive word "their," and the word "there."

Use "there" to indicate a location:

> **Problem:** Put the graded quizzes over **their**.
> **Solution:** Put the graded quizzes over **there**.

Use "they're" as the subject and verb ("they are") of a sentence:

> **Problem:** **Their** hoping to find out the election results today.
> **Solution:** **They're** hoping to find out the election results today.

Use "their" to indicate possession:

> **Problem:** That is **there** new apartment building.
> **Solution:** That is **their** new apartment building.

Who and Whom

Another common word confusion arises with the pronouns who (a subject pronoun) and whom (an object pronoun).

Use "who" as the subject of a sentence:

Problem: **Whom** was the fortieth president of the United States?
Solution: **Who** was the fortieth president of the United States?

Use "whom" as an object in a sentence:

Problem: **Who** does this computer belong to?
Solution: **Whom** does this computer belong to?

Your and You're

This type of pronoun confusion mixes up the possessive pronoun "your" with the contraction "you're" (which means "you are").

Problem: **Your** such a wonderful cook.
Solution: **You're** such a wonderful cook.
Problem: **You're** kitchen is amazing.
Solution: **Your** kitchen is amazing.

If you are unsure which one to use, just switch the contraction "you're" to its full form, "you are." If it does not make sense to say "you are" in the sentence, you should use "your." For example, you would not say, "You are kitchen is amazing."

Its and It's

This type of pronoun confusion mixes up the possessive pronoun "its" with the contraction "it's" (which means "it is").

Problem: **Its** a beautiful day.
Solution: **It's** a beautiful day.
Problem: That puppy keeps wagging **it's** tail.
Solution: That puppy keeps wagging **its** tail.

If you are unsure which one to use, just switch the contraction "it's" to the full form, "it is." If it does not make sense to say "it is" in the sentence, you should use "its." For example, you would not say "That puppy keeps wagging it is tail."

How Modifiers Work

A. What Is a Modifier?

A modifier is a word or phrase that gives more information about another word or phrase in a sentence. A modifier may be an adjective, adverb, or a prepositional phrase.

Adjective

Adjectives are words that modify nouns. Writers use adjectives to tell more about a noun (a person, place, or thing), such as color (a **red** balloon), size (a **small** apartment), or any other quality that a noun may possess.

Adverb

Adverbs are words that modify verbs (run **quickly**), adjectives (**brightly** colored), or other adverbs (**totally** differently, **really** well). Adverbs often end in -ly, but not all adverbs do so (such as soon, today, away, here, etc.).

Prepositional Phrase

A prepositional phrase is a modifying phrase that consists of a preposition and its object (a noun) and any words that modify the noun (such as adjectives).
   Here are some examples of sentences with prepositional phrases.

- Please leave your test booklets **by the door**.
- While you are **at the store**, could you buy some milk?

Common Prepositions

above	by	over
across	during	through
after	from	to
at	in	toward
before	inside	under
behind	into	until
below	near	upon
beside	of	with
between	on	without

B. Common Problems

Watch out for these common modifier problems.

Punctuating Multiple Adjectives

When you use more than one adjective to modify a noun, you must separate the adjectives from one another with commas.

> **Problem:** The **happy mellow** cat slept on the windowsill.
> **Solution:** The **happy, mellow** cat slept on the windowsill.

You should *not* put a comma between the final adjective and the noun.

> **Problem:** The **happy, mellow, cat** slept on the windowsill.
> **Solution:** The **happy, mellow cat** slept on the windowsill.

Punctuating Adverbs and Adjectives

Sometimes writers use an adverb-adjective pair to modify a noun. The adverb should *not* be separated from the adjective it modifies with a comma.

> **Problem:** My **superbly, crafted** fountain pen never leaks.
> **Solution:** My **superbly crafted** fountain pen never leaks.

Also, you should not attach any adverb that ends in -ly to an adjective with a hyphen.

> **Problem:** My **superbly-crafted** fountain pen never leaks.
> **Solution:** My **superbly crafted** fountain pen never leaks.

You should use a hyphen to attach an adverb that does *not* end in -ly to an adjective (so long as the adverb-adjective pair appears *before* the noun it modifies):

> **Problem:** They are going to take a **much needed** vacation.
> **Solution:** They are going to take a **much-needed** vacation.

However, an adverb-adjective pair should be separated from other adjectives (or adverb-adjective pairs) with commas.

> **Problem:** Following the **old carelessly drawn** map, we quickly got lost.
> **Solution:** Following the **old, carelessly drawn** map, we quickly got lost.

Misplaced Modifiers

Generally speaking, you should place a modifier close to the word or phrase it modifies. For example, adjectives appear adjacent to the nouns they modify.

To avoid confusion, an adverb that modifies a verb should be placed next to—or at least near—the verb it modifies.

> **Problem:** He realized that he forgot to put his name on the test **slowly**.
> **Solution:** He **slowly** realized that he forgot to put his name on the test.

To avoid confusion, a prepositional phrase should be placed near the word or phrase it modifies.

> **Problem:** We had a barbecue and cleaned up quickly afterwards **in our backyard**.
> **Solution:** We had a barbecue **in our backyard** and cleaned up quickly afterwards.

Dangling Participles

A participial phrase is a phrase that begins most commonly with an -ing verb (a present participle) and sometimes with an -ed verb (a past participle). When a sentence begins with a participial phrase, the phrase should modify the subject of the sentence (which follows the phrase). When the phrase does not modify the subject, then you have a dangling participle.

When reading the following sentences, ask yourself, "Who is walking?"

> **Problem:** Walking home after dark, the shadows were frightening.
> **Solution:** Walking home after dark, Sam felt frightened by the shadows.

When reading the following sentences, ask yourself, "Who is studying?"

Problem: Studying hard in the library, the chair grew uncomfortable.

Solution: Studying hard in the library, Molly grew uncomfortable in her chair.

When reading the following sentences, ask yourself, "What is dangling?"

Problem: Dangling loosely from the ceiling, Mark was afraid the light fixture might fall.

Solution: Dangling loosely from the ceiling, the light fixture looked like it might fall.

How Sentences Work

A. What Is a Sentence?

A sentence is a group of words that consists of, at minimum, a subject and a verb. A subject and verb unit can also be called a clause.

If a clause can stand on its own, it is called an independent clause.

> **Example:** George was walking down the street.

If a clause cannot stand on its own, it is called a dependent clause.

> **Example: While George was walking down the street,** he ran into his friend Julie.

If a group of words does not include both a subject and a verb, it is called a phrase.

> **Example: Walking down the street,** George ran into his friend Julie.

B. Common Problems

As a writer, be on the lookout for the following kinds of errors related to sentences.

Fused Sentence, Run-on Sentence, or Comma Splice

If you join two or more independent clauses into one sentence, you must punctuate the sentence properly. To properly join independent clauses, you can do any of the following:

- use a comma plus a coordinating conjunction (for, and, nor, but, or, yet, and so). Use the acronym "FANBOYS" to remember this list;
- use a semi-colon (or sometimes a colon);
- separate the clauses into separate sentences, ending each with a period;
- link one clause to the other, making one a dependent clause.

Often, though, beginning writers make the following kinds of errors when joining independent clauses.

Problem 1. Fused Sentence (no coordinating conjunction and no comma): The professor has not returned our **essays we** do not know our grades.

Problem 2. Run-on Sentence (no comma): The professor has not returned our essays **so we** do not know our grades.

Problem 3. Comma Splice (no coordinating conjunction): The professor has not returned our **essays, we** do not know our grades.

Each of these problems can be corrected in one of four ways:

Solution 1. Comma plus coordinating conjunction: The professor has not returned our **essays, so** we do not know our grades.

Solution 2. Semicolon (or sometimes a colon): The professor has not returned our **essays; we** do not know our grades.

Solution 3. Two sentences: The professor has not returned our **essays. We** do not know our grades.

Solution 4. Create a dependent clause: Because the professor has not returned our **essays, we** do not know our grades.

Sentence Fragment

A sentence fragment is a group of words that is missing one of the key components of a sentence (a subject or a verb) but is punctuated as a sentence. Usually, a sentence fragment is a dependent clause or series of phrases that needs to be joined to an independent clause. Or, the fragment can be turned into its own sentence or independent clause.

Here is a sentence fragment that is a dependent clause:

Problem: Over two million troops were deployed during the Iraq and Afghanistan war. **Although this number pales in comparison to the sixteen million deployed in World War II**.

Solution 1: Over two million troops were deployed during the Iraq and Afghanistan wars, although this number pales in comparison to the sixteen million deployed in World War II.

Solution 2: Over two million troops were deployed during the Iraq and Afghanistan wars. This number pales in comparison to the sixteen million deployed in World War II.

Here is a sentence fragment that is a phrase:

Problem: Over two million troops were deployed during the Iraq and Afghanistan wars. **Leaving their partners behind to cope with the emotional and economic difficulties**.

Solution 1: Over two million troops were deployed during the Iraq and Afghanistan wars, leaving their partners behind to cope with the emotional and economic difficulties.

Solution 2: Over two million troops were deployed during the Iraq and Afghanistan wars. Their partners were left behind to cope with the emotional and economic difficulties.

Lack of Variety

Lack of sentence variety occurs when a writer uses the same type of sentence too often. Lack of variety may refer to the length of your sentences as well as to their construction.

Short, simple sentences can be useful for providing emphasis, or for clarity, as when you are writing a tutorial or factsheet. However, too many short sentences may make your writing seem choppy:

Problem: Students have had enough. Our campus policies are ineffective. Our instructors are poor. Our leaders are inefficient. Our student fees are increasing. Our debts are piling up. Class sizes are growing. Administrators are enjoying fancy retreats. They are spending money on unnecessary consultants. They are raising their own salaries. It is time for a change. It is time to elect Holly Simpson for Class President.

Long, compound or complex sentences can provide detail and complexity, and are often used in narratives or research genres. However, they can easily overwhelm your reader when overused:

Problem: Students have had enough of ineffective campus policies, such as the ineffective policies, instructors, and leaders who have allowed our student fees to increase, our debts to pile up, and our class sizes to increase while administrators are enjoying fancy retreats, spending money on unnecessary consultants and raising their own salaries. It is time for a change, and it is time to elect Holly Simpson for Class President.

To revise, try to use different kinds of sentence constructions and lengths. You might combine some short sentences, or break up some longer ones.

Solution: Students have had enough. We have had enough of ineffective policies, ineffective instructors, and ineffective leaders. While we watch our student fees increase, our debts pile up, and our class sizes increase, administrators are enjoying fancy retreats, spending money on unnecessary consultants, and raising their own salaries. It is time for a change. It is time to elect Holly Simpson for Class President.

How Punctuation Works

A. What Is Punctuation?

Punctuation refers to the use of marks to separate words and sentences and to clarify meaning. Punctuation includes many types of marks.

End Punctuation

End punctuation consists of marks used to end sentences.

Period . A period is the most common mark used to end a sentence.

Exclamation mark ! Exclamation marks end sentences that express strong emotion. They should typically be avoided in academic writing unless you are quoting a strong statement made by someone else.

Question mark ? A question mark ends any sentence that poses a question.

Punctuation for Sentences

These marks are used to punctuate phrases and clauses in sentences.

Comma , A comma is used to separate parts of a sentence or to separate items in a list or series.

Semicolon ; A semicolon is used to link two independent clauses or to separate complex items in a list or series.

Colon : A colon is used to introduce a list or a quotation and to connect two independent clauses when the second clause builds upon or expands the first clause.

Dash — A dash can be used to separate out text that interrupts the main thought of a sentence and—in typically less formal occasions—to connect two independent clauses.

Parentheses ( )   Parentheses are used to separate less-important material from the main part of a sentence or to indicate citations in certain citation styles, such as MLA and APA.

Other Marks

The following punctuation marks typically change the meaning of individual words, rather than the meaning of whole sentences.

Apostrophe '   An apostrophe is used to indicate possession or to form a contraction. Contractions tend to make writing less formal, so they are not suitable for every genre. Your analysis of the genre you are writing can help you to decide whether a contraction is appropriate.

Brackets [ ]   Brackets are most commonly used to alter quotations.

Hyphen –   A hyphen is commonly used to join a compound word, such as a compound number ("twenty-one") or a compound modifier ("well-made").

Quotation marks " "   Quotation marks indicate when a writer is using the words of another, when a word is slang or its usage is uncommon, and sometimes to indicate sarcasm. In academic writing, you should avoid using quotation marks to indicate sarcasm.

B. Common Problems

Punctuating a List or Series

When you write a list of items in a sentence, you should separate the items in the list with commas:

> **Problem:** Michael went to the store and bought **pita hummus cucumbers and lettuce**.
>
> **Solution:** Michael went to the store and bought **pita, hummus, cucumbers, and lettuce**.

The comma before the "and" in the preceding sentence is called the "final comma." Some fields, such as journalism, prefer that the final comma be left off. Although the final comma is not required for your series to be punctuated properly, if your discipline allows its use, then you can always use the final comma to ensure clarity.

Sometimes, you should use semicolons instead of commas to punctuate a series, especially if the items in your list contain internal punctuation or complex items:

Problem: Michael went to the store and bought hand-made pita, hummus imported from Lebanon, organic, hydroponic cucumbers, and bibb lettuce.

Solution: Michael went to the store and bought hand-made pita; hummus imported from Lebanon; organic, hydroponic cucumbers; and bibb lettuce.

Punctuating a Quotation

Punctuating quotations can be tricky. You have to figure out (1) where to place your quotation marks, (2) how to separate the quotation from the rest of the sentence, and (3) how to punctuate the end of the quotation.

In general, you place quotation marks around the words of another. In the U.S., we use double quotation marks (not single).

Problem 1: Martin Luther King, Jr., once said, **I have a dream**.
Problem 2: Martin Luther King, Jr., once said, '**I have a dream**.'
Solution: Martin Luther King, Jr., once said, "**I have a dream.**"

In general, you should separate the quotation from the rest of the sentence with a comma (or sometimes a colon).

Problem: Martin Luther King, Jr., once **said** "I have a dream."
Solution: Martin Luther King, Jr., once **said,** "I have a dream."

But do not separate the quotation from the rest of the sentence with a comma if the quotation "goes with the flow" of the sentence.

Problem: Abraham Lincoln said **that,** "**our** fathers brought forth on this continent a new nation."
Solution: Abraham Lincoln said **that** "**our** fathers brought forth on this continent a new nation."

You can test whether a quotation "goes with the flow" by removing the quotation marks and seeing if you would use a comma. Since you wouldn't put a comma between "that" and "our" in the preceding sentence, you should not use one with the quotation.

In writing U.S. English (as opposed to British English, which you might encounter in texts you read in college), the final comma or period of a quotation always appears inside the quotation marks.

Problem: Abraham Lincoln said that "our fathers brought forth on this continent a new **nation**".

Solution: Abraham Lincoln said that "our fathers brought forth on this continent a new **nation.**"

Problem: Some believe that the Cold War was just a war of "ignorant **armies",** but others disagree.

Solution: Some believe that the Cold War was just a war of "ignorant **armies,"** but others disagree.

If you are using in-text citations (Chapter 28), the period may appear after the citation information in parentheses, depending on the citation style you are using:

Problem: Abraham Lincoln said that "our fathers brought forth on this continent a new **nation."** (22)

Solution: Abraham Lincoln said that "our fathers brought forth on this
(MLA Style) continent a new **nation"** (22).

Solution: Abraham Lincoln (1863) said that "our fathers brought forth
(APA Style) on this continent a **new nation."**

Be sure to check the guidelines for the citation style you are using so that you punctuate cited quotations correctly.

If your quotation is a question, then the question mark should be placed inside the quotation marks (just like a period). However, if the sentence containing the quotation itself is a question, and the quotation is *not* a question, then you should place the question mark outside the quotation marks. Do not use two end punctuation marks, such as a period and a question mark.

Problem 1: Did the professor really say, "No class **tomorrow?"**

Problem 2: Did the professor really say, "No class **tomorrow."?**

Solution: Did the professor really say, "No class **tomorrow"?**

Question Marks and Indirect Questions

Generally speaking, you should end a sentence that is a question with a question mark.

Problem: Are you going to the performance **tonight.**

Solution: Are you going to the performance **tonight?**

However, if the sentence contains an indirect question, then you do not end the sentence with a question mark. An indirect question is a question that is merely reported in a sentence that is not, itself, a question.

Problem: You should ask our professor whether we need to bring a pencil for the exam **tomorrow?**

Solution: You should ask our professor whether we need to bring a pencil for the exam **tomorrow.**

Apostrophes and Possession

In English, we use apostrophes to create contractions (such as "can't" or "won't") and to show possession.

When using an apostrophe to create a possessive noun, you should usually place an apostrophe plus -s at the end of a noun.

>   **Problem:**   Did you listen to the **senators** speech?
>   **Solution:** Did you listen to the **senator's** speech?

If the noun is a plural noun ending in -s, you should only add an apostrophe—no -s.

>   **Problem:**   Did you listen to the **senators** speeches?
>   **Solution:** Did you listen to the **senators'** speeches?

If the noun is a singular noun ending in -s, you can add *either* an apostrophe plus -s *or* just an apostrophe. You should follow the style guide for the discipline in which you are writing to determine how to pluralize nouns ending in s.

>   **Problem:**   Did you listen to our **boss** speech?
>   **Solution 1:** Did you listen to our **boss's** speech?
>   **Solution 2:** Did you listen to our **boss'** speech?

Placing Dashes Properly

A dash can be used to separate out text that you wish to emphasize or to connect parts of a sentence. However you use the dash, you must place it properly in your text—and ensure that you are using the correct punctuation mark in the first place. Most word processing programs will automatically create a dash when you type two hyphens between two words.

Do not confuse a dash (which is long) with a hyphen (which is short).

>   **Problem:**   My favorite dog-the poodle-is a highly intelligent breed.
>   **Solution:** My favorite dog—the poodle—is a highly intelligent breed.

Be sure to place the dash directly adjacent to the words that surround it; do not surround the dash with spaces.

>   **Problem:**   My favorite dog — the poodle — is a highly intelligent breed.
>   **Solution:** My favorite dog—the poodle—is a highly intelligent breed.

Selecting Brackets or Parentheses

Many students confuse brackets [ ] with parentheses ( ). These two sets of punctuation marks are not interchangeable in academic writing.

Use parentheses, not brackets, to set off less-important (parenthetical) material from the main part of a sentence.

Problem: This video [one of the first to appear on YouTube] demonstrates the power of online communication.

Solution: This video (one of the first to appear on YouTube) demonstrates the power of online communication.

Use brackets, not parentheses, to do minor alterations to quotations. (You should not do major alterations to quotations—paraphrase instead).

Problem: Lincoln said at Gettysburg, "(Eighty-seven) years ago our fathers brought forth on this continent a new nation."

Solution: Lincoln said at Gettysburg, "[Eighty-seven] years ago our fathers brought forth on this continent a new nation."

How Usage Conventions Work

A. What Are Usage Conventions?

Usage conventions are patterns of word choice and sentence structure that are dictated by custom or tradition. Sometimes, these patterns differ between disciplines or fields, and often they are described in a style guide (such as the *MLA Handbook*). These style guides describe conventions for punctuation, word choice, verbs (such as when to use present or past tense), and more. If you are unsure if you are using the right word or sentence structure, check the style guide for your field, such as the *MLA Handbook for Writers of Research Papers*, the *Publication Manual of the American Psychological Association*, or the *Chicago Manual of Style*.

B. Common Problems

Beware these common usage problems that arise in academic writing.

Inclusive Language

Most style guides recommend that you use words that do not exclude individuals on the basis of race, sex, gender, sexuality, age, or ability.

Avoid using masculine words (he, him, fireman, policeman) as defaults.

> **Problem:** Every **man** should thank **his** local **fireman** for **his** dedication.
> **Solution:** **Citizens** should thank **their** local **fire fighters** for **their** dedication.

Be sure to refer to disabilities only when relevant. Do not define people by their disability, but rather as people, first:

> **Problem:** The film will be shown with closed captioning so that **deaf people** can watch.

Solution 1 (no disability mentioned): The film will be shown with subtitles.

Solution 2 (people first): The film will be shown with closed captioning so that **people with hearing loss** can enjoy it.

Avoid singling out individuals for their gender, race, ability, sexuality, or age when it is not necessary or relevant:

Problem: Both James, **a gay psychology professor**, and Stewart, **a Black historian**, commented on the proposal.

Solution: Both James, **a psychology professor**, and Stewart, **a historian**, commented on the proposal.

Avoid making assumptions about sexuality:

Problem: Sorority members are welcome to bring their **boyfriends** to the event.

Solution: Sorority members are welcome to bring **dates** to the event.

Avoid making assumptions about competence based on gender, race, ability, sexuality, or age:

Problem: Mr. Jones is remarkably sharp **for a senior employee**.

Solution: Mr. Jones is one of our sharpest employees.

Weak Nouns and Verbs

To make your writing more powerful, look for places where you can replace weak, vague nouns with more specific ones, and weak verbs with stronger ones.

Look for nouns that refer to vague ideas ("thing," "notion," "person," "idea," etc.) rather than concrete nouns:

Problem: Poor nutrition **is one of the things** that causes tooth decay.

Solution #1 (stronger noun): Poor nutrition **is one cause of** tooth decay.

Solution #2 (stronger verb): Poor nutrition **can cause** tooth decay.

Look for the verbs "to be" ("is," "are," etc.) and "to have" ("has," "have," etc.) and see if you can replace them with verbs that carry more impact. Changing the passive voice to active voice (Chapter S1) can also create more impact:

Problem: Costa's work **is an example** of the blanket bias **that is present** in our society, which in turn **is reflected in** the laws.

Solution: Costa's work **exemplifies** the blanket bias **present** in our society, which the law **reflects** in turn.

You can also look for noun and verb clusters that can be condensed with a single, strong verb or noun:

> **Problem:** Increased visitation **will also have a positive impact on** the broader society by helping break the cycle of crime.
>
> **Solution:** Increased visitation **will benefit** the broader society by helping break the cycle of crime.
>
> **Problem:** Child visitation is also impeded by the "best interest of the child standard," the test used in most jurisdictions when deciding on **issues of visitation**.
>
> **Solution:** Child visitation is also impeded by the "best interest of the child standard," the test used in most jurisdictions when deciding on **visitation**.

Long Lead-ins

Sentences are more difficult to read if the subject and the verb appear later in the sentences. To make your sentences easier to read, try to put the subject and verb together, early in the sentence.

> **Problem:** Once we determine the factors involved, test each one experimentally, and distinguish key trends in the data, **we can** identify potential causes of bus delays on campus.
>
> **Solution:** **We can** identify potential causes of bus delays on campus once we determine the factors involved, test each one experimentally, and distinguish key trends in the data.

To get rid of long lead-ins, go through your draft and circle the main verb for each sentence. If the subject and verb appear toward the end of the sentence, try to rearrange the sentence so the verb and its subject come sooner.

You can also look for "dummy" or impersonal clauses, which tend to create long lead-ins and make readers wait for the main point of the sentence:

> **Problem:** **It is important to note that** not all politicians are corrupt.
>
> **Solution:** Not all politicians are corrupt.
>
> **Problem:** **Another interesting factor involved in** the Vietnam War protests was music.
>
> **Solution:** Music **catalyzed** the Vietnam War protests.

Separating Subject and Verb

A sentence may be more difficult to read if the subject and verb are separated.

Problem: **Another legal factor** that prevents child visitation for incarcerated mothers **is** the "best interest of the child standard," the test used in most jurisdictions when deciding on issues of visitation and custody.

Solution 1: **Child visitation is** also impeded by the "best interest of the child standard," the test used in most jurisdictions when deciding on issues of visitation and custody.

Solution 2: **The law also impedes** child visitation through the "best interest of the child standard," the test used in most jurisdictions when deciding on issues of visitation and custody.

Weak Openers

When we read a sentence, we tend to focus on the first part for key information. If you start sentences with "This is," "It is," "There are," and so on, you are not taking advantage of the reader's focus.

You can either revise the weak opener itself, or connect the sentence to a previous one:

Problem: Increased visitation will also have a positive impact on the broader society by helping break the cycle of crime. **There are** studies that find that a child's risk of one day being incarcerated is increased if that child had a parent who was at some point incarcerated.

Solution: Increased visitation will also have a positive impact on the broader society by helping break the cycle of crime. **Many** studies find that a child's risk of one day being incarcerated is increased if that child had a parent who was at some point incarcerated.

Clutter

Try to revise sentences that use lots of prepositions: to, of, that, so, by, at, etc. Go through your draft, and circle any preposition you see. Then, see if you can revise sentences that have more than two or three prepositions.

Problem: In recent years, the field **of** psychology has made great strides **in** assessing the true effects **of** incarceration **on** children.

Revision: In recent years, **psychologists** have demonstrated **how** incarceration **affects** children.

Doublings

Look for places in your writing where you say the same thing twice, or provide two words where one would do.

Problem: The child will have a better **understanding and concept** of her parent's situation, have a possibility of **a stable and steady** relationship, and can reach a **more mature and grownup** mental state.

Revision: The child will have a better **understanding** of her parent's situation, have a possibility of a **stable** relationship, and can reach a **more mature** mental state.

Readings

Reading Personal Essays

CHAPTER OUTLINE

JUAN GARCIA   SPRING BROKEN

This personal essay was published in 2012 by The Daily Californian, *the student newspaper of the University of California at Berkeley. At the time this was published, Garcia was an undergraduate at Berkeley.*

Read About It

Garcia's essay describes the apathy a student might feel after a break from school. The author uses this piece to reach out to other students who might feel as he does. As you read, note all of the strategies that the author uses to relate to his readers.

You know that feeling you get when you've only been back from spring break for a couple of days and already you're tired of school? That's exactly how I felt last week, as I'm sure so do many of you. All week long I've been bitching about how I desperately wish this semester would end and how one more day of being here might push me over the edge into insanity.

Everyone who happens to hear me says the same thing, "What are you talking about? You've only been back for a few days." Yes, I understand that we just came back from a glorious week of no school, meant to revitalize and re-energize the mind and soul. That, however, is the where the problem lies. You see, once you get a little taste of the outside, it's all you can think about. Just like the whale from 1993's smash hit *Free Willy*, I too want to leap over that impossible curtain of rocks (finals?) into freedom.

A week and a half ago I was on a beach in sunny Santa Barbara doing absolutely nothing. Life was great, life was grand, life was wonderful. Fast-forward to a week later and here I am in Doe's North Reading Room[1] trying to get back into academic mode. I have a few papers to write, a research project to finish and a fat stack of books to read by the end of this month. Instead of even pretending to care I just sit here and daydream about the splendor of May 9 (my last final). As it turns out, the weeklong break that we just recently enjoyed has in no way replenished my will to continue being studious. It actually completely demolished it.

It's natural for any student to not want to do assignments and put them off until the last possible second. As a fellow opinion writer wrote in a previous column, procrastination is in fact what makes us human. The result of spring break, however, is that it completely takes away any sense of responsibility. At least in procrastinating you know deep down that you will at some point succumb and try to accomplish a given task.

Since coming back from the break I haven't even cared to tell myself that I will do things at a later time. I have become afflicted with a disease that forces me to just refuse to acknowledge that school even exists. It's an unhealthy thing, but it's something most of us have experienced.

It's been about an hour since I sat down to write with the intention of finally shaking off this apathy that has so viciously taken over my spirits. I tried to unzip my rucksack to get a sheet of paper so I can finally get some homework done, but it just isn't happening. Across from me sits this guy who is so focused on his studies he is starting to make me look like an ass. Maybe I should move somewhere else. Perhaps, by grouping myself with all the other people using their laptops, I can blend in and not look so conspicuous. I'm sure I'm not the only one at Berkeley who is having trouble zoning in. But then again, this is Berkeley, so maybe I am the only one! Oh, the horror.

I've decided not to move from my current location. Spring break has caused within me such a rupture that I no longer even care how un-studious I may appear. See what I mean. This is exactly the thing I've been talking about all along. If any of you reading this are going through the same thing, hang in there. Maybe it will pass. Maybe.

---

[1] A study room in Berkeley's library.

Think About It

(1)   Garcia opens his essay with the word "you," asking a question of the reader. Why do you think Garcia chose to open in this fashion? What effect does reading that question have on you as a reader?

(2)   In this essay, Garcia draws from his own experience to make a claim about all students, indeed all people: "It's natural for any student to not want to do assignments and put them off until the last possible second. . . . [P]rocrastination is in fact what makes us human." Do you agree with his claim? Why or why not?

(3)   One of the rhetorical strategies Garcia employs is self-deprecation, that is, writing about himself in a critical or humble fashion. He even calls himself an "ass." Does his self-deprecating style make you feel more sympathetic towards him? Why or why not?

Write About It

Select a time during the school year that you find particularly difficult. Write a personal essay that tells the story about your experiences during this time.

JACQUE WEBER   LOVE AND LOSS

Weber published the following personal essay in the University Daily Kansan, *the student newspaper of the University of Kansas in Lawrence, Kansas, in 2010. At the time, she was an undergraduate at the University of Kansas.*

Read About It

There are many characters in this short essay. As you read, keep track of all of the characters by making a list. In what ways does the author help you remember who the characters are?

He sat there, not moving much, smiling faintly through looks of exhaustion and embarrassment. His once strong, defined arms now hung limply by his side, his bony hands rested on his lap. The arms that used to scoop me up and toss me in the air could now barely lift his small glass of water. The only familiar thing now were his caramel-colored eyes. That was the last day I saw my grandpa, about a month before he died of small cell carcinoma, a type of esophageal cancer associated with the lungs.

That Saturday afternoon in June at my grandparents' house in Gate, Okla., was just like any other. My aunt's family showed up an hour late, something we had all grown accustomed to. It seemed like my family and her family took turns showing up "fashionably late" to every forced family get-together we had.

My mom, like usual, kept herself busy by treating me like a child, persistently asking me if I'd like something to eat or drink as if I didn't know where the kitchen was. "No, Mom. If I want something I'll get it, okay?" It was a family joke that my mom babied me at every family dinner we had—one that my older cousins loved to point out every chance they got.

My older brother, Alex, sat next to me on the couch, doing his best to avoid conversation. I admired this task. Somehow, I couldn't seem to master it. His only words were triggered by my grandma's cat Fluffy, who is rightly nicknamed "The Crazy Cat" by every other member in the family because of her tendency to run up to anyone at any time and attack them. "She doesn't do it to me so you guys must be doing something to antagonize her," my grandma routinely says in Fluffy's defense.

The rest of the family stood around in the kitchen and the living room trying their best to make small talk. Every so often my younger cousins would bring in baskets full of giant, red tomatoes and bright green cucumbers as long as my arm for everyone to see. My grandpa started gardening when my grandparents moved to Oklahoma, but once he lost all his strength he couldn't keep up with it anymore. His once neat and manicured garden was now running wild with overgrown vegetables and weeds.

Everybody's objective, especially mine, was to avoid the reason we were all there. My family does not like family get-togethers. We aren't one of those families who gather at someone's house, break out the board games and have a good time. When we do get together, it's always for a cause: Thanksgiving, Christmas or someone's graduation. That particular Saturday's cause was my grandpa. Everyone knew he wasn't doing well and what better way to acknowledge that than to have a family dinner.

I watched my grandpa closely as everyone made their plates. He would have never admitted it, but I could see the sadness in his eyes. He had a look of defeat. I knew this look well. I'd seen it many times during the year and a half he was sick.

Before my grandparents moved to Gate, Okla., they lived in Garden City, Kan. I was attending Garden City Community College at the time. Because I still lived at home in Deerfield, Kan., which was 25 minutes from school, my grandma insisted I come over and eat lunch with my grandpa during the week while she picked up my cousin from school. At first, I loved it. I got to avoid the long drive-thru lines and save money at the same time. I also got to spend time with my grandpa. He knew I had quizzes on current events at school, so each day when I walked through the door he would be propped up in his recliner, remote in hand, listening closely to every word the newscaster said. "Did you see what happened today? I bet that will be on your quiz," he said.

I watched my grandpa get sicker during that time. At first, we ate lunch together, usually leftovers from the night before. Eventually, he stopped eating with me. I could see his body changing. He was getting thinner, weaker and even seemed to be getting shorter. He blamed it on the chemotherapy and radiation treatments. "I'm just not feeling too good today, but I bet tomorrow will be better," he would often say. Tomorrow didn't get better. In fact, it only got worse. He eventually stopped eating solid food altogether. His doctor advised him to drink special shakes with a fat supplement added to them to make him gain weight. They didn't help. I think he spent more time throwing them up than actually drinking them. The house took on a permanent sick smell, but I wanted to see my grandpa so I ignored it.

I couldn't, however, ignore the sadness I felt seeing my grandpa so sick. I eventually stopped going to my grandparents' house for lunch. I found myself making excuse after excuse for not going: I was too busy with school, I had to work on the magazine over my lunch break or I had to take one test or another. I will always regret not going because I can't have those days back.

I was on a camping trip in Colorado last July with friends when my mother called with the news of my grandpa's death. I didn't know what to say or how to act. All I could do was cry. I knew it would happen eventually, but I still wasn't prepared for it.

It's been more than a year since my grandpa passed away and not a day goes by that I don't think about him. I will forever cherish the moments we spent together, but I regret not getting to spend more time with him. There is never enough time you can spend with someone you love. Because of my grandpa, I don't take for granted the time I get to spend with my family now. I even look forward to our family get-togethers.

Think About It

(1)   Weber opens her personal essay by discussing a person—a "he"—that the reader knows nothing about: "He sat there, not moving much, smiling faintly. . . ." The reader does not learn who the person is until the end of the first paragraph. Did the mystery of the person's identity help draw you into the essay? Why or why not?

(2)   This story skips around in time. Can you identify the three main time periods in which it is set? Are the time periods chronological? How does the author help you identify when certain events happened? How does the author's use of time affect the essay?

(3)   This essay ends with the author undergoing an emotional transformation. Can you identify it? Do you believe that the events of the story could have created such a strong transformation?

Write About It

Think of a family event in your life that affected you deeply and caused you to view the world in a different way—similar to the transformation Weber describes in her essay. Tell the story of these events and the transformation in the form of a personal essay.

ANDREA VIEJO   MEXICAN IN NEW YORK

Viejo published this personal essay in the student newspaper of Columbia University, The Columbia Spectator, *in 2012. When she wrote this essay, Viejo was a first-year undergraduate student at Columbia, which is located on the island of Manhattan in New York City.*

Read About It

As you read this essay, take note of all of the specific details that the author uses to evoke Mexican and Latin American culture—food, music, language, etc. Think about how these specific details help the story come alive.

"You're Latin! Where are you from?" is something I often hear as soon as people notice my thick Spanish accent.

"I'm Mexican," I respond.

Upon which they ask, "Mexican-American?"

"No, I'm international. Born and raised in Mexico and on a Mexican passport."

Being Mexican in New York comes with a lot of baggage. This is true coming from any Hispanic country. You are instantly associated with the immigrant discourse, the last subway stops of Spanish-speaking boroughs, and the underground restaurant scene. They tell you, "I know a lot of Mexicans," but you will never know those Mexicans or what they are like because you do not eat, hear, speak, or feel the same thing that they do. The same is true of Dominicans, Puerto Ricans, Panameños, etc. We foreign Latin American students will be constantly classified as second-, third-, or fourth-generation immigrants who have settled in New York while being aware that we belong to different worlds. Unable truly to relate to such an association, I initially felt obliged to distance myself from "them." I clarified that I was a visiting student with a temporary visa. However, with time, I've learned to reconsider the immigrant discourse and emotionally attach myself to it.

When I feel homesick, it is the Latino immigrant diversity on campus and in this city that comforts me. I still remember the day I arrived alone at Columbia for International Student Orientation. I was lost, confused, and in desperate need of directions. Upon walking into Hartley Hospitality, I met a few Dominican and Mexican guards willing to lead me to my dorm. The warmth of their Spanish welcome resonated with familiarity. It offered a sense of home away from home and evoked a feeling of protection. Looking back, I must confess it was one of my favorite moments at Columbia, being introduced into a life for the first time through the lens of someone who was familiar with where I came from. I must confess that despite many reasons to complain about it, dinner at John Jay[1] is delightful because I am always greeted by a series of "hola joven" and "buenas noches" from the staff. Similarly, I love [sweeping] into my dorm building to the lyrics and music of Mexican pop singer Luis Miguel that the guard plays, and enjoy discussing enchiladas with classmates who have Mexican heritage.

With time, I have realized that the immigrants in New York keep me from losing a sense of home. They are always so eager to speak to me because they are afraid of losing a heritage that they have been away from for years, decades, or even a lifetime, and are only able to trace it through a distant blood line.

---

[1] A campus dining hall.

We live in an interconnected multicultural world. However, we are often unwilling to embrace, expose, and discuss the heritage that we share with others. When I finally opened myself to this heritage, I learned a lot more about my own culture and background than I could have ever imagined. The way I see it, the Mexicans I have talked to—whether in the subway or in a Latino Studies class—are so concerned with losing their Aztec heritage that they bring up aspects of Mexican culture that I have almost taken for granted. Through these interactions, I have discovered a new perspective on Diego Rivera's mural exposition at the Museum of Modern Art, the taste of Jamaica juice, and the struggle of Emiliano Zapata.

Above all, the immigrants in New York have taught me to reconsider the responsibility I have when it comes to immigration discourse. It is because "we"—foreign students pursuing an education abroad—do not work to improve the unemployment rates in our own countries that "they" come to live to the United States. Distancing myself from the immigration issue does nothing to solve the issue. Instead, I find it better to understand their perspective and advocate for immigration issues both in New York and back home.

I do not know if I will eventually try to settle in this country and undergo the same exhausting process of obtaining a green card. If I do, I will become one of "them." My children will probably grow up as Mexican-Americans, and I will be glad that I sought to open myself and understand the implications of the immigration discourse.

Think About It

(1)   At the beginning of this essay, Viejo describes feeling alienated from immigrants in New York. Why? Why does she change her feeling toward immigrant communities in New York?

(2)   Halfway through this essay, Viejo identifies what she sees as the reason why she is able to identify with Mexican immigrants in New York: "[I]mmigrants in New York keep me from losing a sense of home. . . . [T]hey are afraid of losing a heritage that they have been away from for years, decades, or even a lifetime, and are only able to trace it through a distant blood line." Try to describe the feeling that Viejo believes she shares with Mexican immigrants.

(3)   Viejo writes, "We live in an interconnected multicultural world. However, we are often unwilling to embrace, expose, and discuss the heritage that we share with others." Do you agree with her assessment? Why or why not?

Write About It

Think about a cross-cultural experience that you have had in your life. This experience can be as simple as meeting someone from another state, or from an urban area if you are from a rural area. In a personal essay, tell the story of this cross-cultural experience and reflect on how the experience affected you.

··

JANE KRAMER   THE FOOD AT OUR FEET: WHY IS FORAGING ALL THE RAGE? (EXCERPT)

Kramer published this article in The New Yorker *magazine in 2011. Kramer, an American born in 1938, lives primarily in Europe. She has published many books and pieces of journalism, and she is a regular writer for* The New Yorker.

Read About It

In her story, Kramer uses many specific details about the plants she finds, using foreign or scientific names, names that many readers might not be familiar with. Note the places where she uses food words that you are unfamiliar with. Think about how reading those words makes you feel as a reader: do you feel alienated by the language or eager to learn more?

I spent the summer foraging, like an early hominid with clothes. It didn't matter that the first thing I learned about that daunting pastime of hunter-gatherers and visionary chefs was that nature's bounty is a thorny gift. Thorny, or, if you prefer, spiny, prickly, buggy, sticky, slimy, muddy, and, occasionally, so toxic that one of the books I consulted for my summer forays carried a disclaimer absolving the publisher of responsibility should I happen to end up in the hospital or, worse, in the ground, moldering next to the Amanita phalloides that I'd mistaken for a porcini. I was not deterred. I had foraged as a child, although it has to be said that children don't think "forage" when they are out stripping raspberry bushes and blackberry brambles; they think about getting away before the ogre whose land they're plundering catches them and turns them into toads. I could even claim to have foraged as an adult, if you count a mild interest in plucking berries from the caper bushes that cling to the walls of an old hill town near the farmhouse in Umbria where my husband and I go, in the summertime, to write. Caper berries are like blackberries; they amount to forage only in that they are not *your* berries. . . .

June

. . . I arrived in Italy. I unpacked a carton of books with titles like "Nature's Garden" and "The Wild Table." I bought new mud boots—six euros at my local hardware store—and enlisted a mentor in the person of John Paterson, an exuberant Cumbria-to-Umbria transplant of forty-seven, who looked at my boots and said, "What's wrong with sneakers?" Paterson is a countryman, or, as he says, "not a reader." He is the kind of spontaneous forager who carries knives and old shopping bags and plastic buckets in the trunk of his car. (I carry epinephrine and bug repellent.) Being lanky and very tall, he can also leap over scraggly brush, which I, being small, cannot. Cumbrians are passionate about foraging—perhaps because, like their Scottish neighbors, they have learned to plumb the surface of a northern landscape not normally known for its largesse. What's more, they share their enthusiasm and their secret places, something the old farmers in my neighborhood, most of them crafty foragers, rarely do. The peasants of Southern Europe do not easily admit to foraging—at least not to strangers. For centuries, foraged food was a sign of poverty, and they called it "famine food," or "animal food." The exception was truffles and porcini, which today command enough money for a good forager to be able to wait in line at the supermarket, buying stale food with the bourgeoisie. Some of my neighbors have truffle hounds penned in front of their chicken coops, ostensibly keeping foxes at bay. But they never ask to truffle in the woods by my pond when I'm around and, by local etiquette, they would have to offer some of the precious tubers they unearth to me. They wait until September, when I'm back in New York, and keep all my truffles for themselves.

Paterson got his start foraging—"Well, not actually foraging, more like scrumping"—as a schoolboy, combing the farms near his uncle's Cockermouth[1] sawmill for the giant rutabagas, or swedes, as the English call them, that children in Northern Europe carve into jack-o'-lanterns at Halloween. He worked in his first kitchen at the age of twelve ("I washed the plates," he says. "I was too shy to wait on tables") and twenty-five years later arrived in Umbria, a chef. Today, he has a Romanian wife, two children, and a thriving restaurant of his own—the Antica Osteria della Valle—in Todi, a town where people used to reserve their accolades for the meals that Grandmother made and, until they tasted his, had already driven away two "foreign" chefs, a Neapolitan and a Sicilian. In early June, I was finishing a plate of Paterson's excellent tagliarini with porcini when he emerged from the kitchen, pulled up a chair, and started talking about the mushrooms he had discovered, foraging as a boy, in a patch of woods near a bridge over the River Cocker. "All those beautiful mushrooms!" he kept saying. He told me about green, orange, and red parrot mushrooms and parasol mushrooms and big cèpes called penny buns and bright, polka-dotted fly agarics "so huge they could fill a room" and mushrooms "like white fennels that grow from the shape of saucers into gilled cups." He ate judiciously, but admired them all. In Italy, he started foraging for porcini to cook at home. At the Osteria, where he has to use farmed porcini, he roasts the mushrooms in pigeon juice, fills them with spinach, and wraps them in pancetta. He said that foraging had inspired his "bacon-and-eggs philosophy of little things that work together."

A week later, we set out for some of his favorite foraging spots. We stopped at the best roadside for gathering the tiny leaves of wild mint known in Italy as *mentuccia* ("Fantastic with lamb") and passed the supermarket at the edge of town, where only the day before he'd been cutting wild asparagus from a jumble of weeds and bushes behind the parking lot ("Great in risotto, but it looks like I took it all"). Then we headed for the country. We tried the field where he usually gets his wild fennel ("The flowers are lovely with ham and pork") and found so much of that delicious weed that the fronds, rippling across the field in a warm breeze, looked like nature's copy of Christo's "Running Fence." I was hoping to find *strioli*, too. *Strioli* is a spicy wild herb that looks like long leaves of tarragon. It grows in fields and pastures in late spring and early summer and makes a delicious spaghetti sauce—you take a few big

---

[1] A city in northern England.

handfuls of the herb, toss it into a sauté pan with olive oil, garlic, and *peperoncini*, and in a minute it's ready. But there was none in sight, so we turned onto a quiet road that wound through fields of alfalfa and wheat and soon-to-be-blooming sunflowers, and parked next to a shuttered and, by all evidence, long-abandoned farmhouse that I had passed so often over the years that I thought of it as *my* house and dreamed of rescuing it.

Foraging places are like houses. Some speak to you, others you ignore. I wasn't surprised that the land around that tumbledown house spoke to Paterson. He jumped out of the car, peered over a thicket of roadside bush and sloe trees, and disappeared down a steep, very wet slope before I had even unbuckled my seat belt—after which he emerged, upright and waving, in an overgrown copse enclosed by a circle of trees. Cleared, the copse would have provided a shady garden for a farmer's family. To a forager, it was perfect: a natural rain trap, sheltered against the harsh sun, and virtually hidden from the road. Everywhere we turned, there were plants to gather. Even the wild asparagus, which usually hides from the sun in a profusion of other plants' leaves and stalks, was so plentiful that you couldn't miss it. We filled a shopping bag.

Wild asparagus has a tart, ravishing taste—what foragers call a wilderness taste—and a season so short as to be practically nonexistent. It's as different from farmed asparagus as a morel is from the boxed mushrooms at your corner store. I was ready to head back and start planning my risotto, but Paterson had spotted a patch of leafy scrub and pulled me toward it. He called it *crespina*. I had never heard of *crespina*, nor, after months of searching, have I found it in any Italian dictionary. It's the local word for spiny sow thistle—a peppery wild vegetable whose leaves taste a little like spinach and a lot like sorrel and, as I soon discovered, come with a spiky center rib sharp enough to etch a fine line down the palm of your hand if you've never handled them before. (I regard the small scar that I got that day as a forager's mark of initiation.) We added a respectable bunch of leaves to the shopping bag, and carried the overflow up to the car in our arms. An hour later, we were separating and trimming the morning's spoils in the tiny restaurant kitchen where, six days a week, Paterson cooks alone for fifty people ("Where would I put a sous-chef?" he said, stepping on my foot) and comparing recipes for wild-asparagus risotto. Here is his "most beautiful way" to make it: Snap off the fibrous ends of the asparagus spears and crush them with the blade of a knife. Simmer them in water or a mild stock until the stock takes flavor. Strain the stock. Pour a cupful of white wine into rice that's been turned for a minute or two in hot olive oil and some minced onion. As soon as the wine boils down, start ladling in the stock. Keep ladling and stirring until the rice is practically al dente and the last ladle of stock is in the pan. Now fold in the asparagus heads. In no time, all you will need to do is grate the Parmesan and serve.

I made Paterson's risotto for dinner that night, along with a roast chicken and the *crespina* leaves, sautéed for a minute, like baby spinach, in olive oil and a sprinkling of red-pepper flakes; the spines wilted into a tasty crunch. The next night, I chopped my fronds of wild fennel and used them to stuff a pork roast. When I called Paterson to say how good everything was, he told me, "Free food! There's nothing like it. It always tastes better." . . .

Think About It

(1)   Along with Kramer, John Paterson is a primary character in this essay. The author uses a few different rhetorical strategies to describe him. What are some of the strategies that she uses? How do these strategies help a reader get a full picture of Paterson's character?

(2)   Kramer uses a lot of parenthetical interjections in this story. Often, the interjections are the voice of Paterson, but sometimes they are her own voice. What effect do these parentheticals have on the story? Do they slow it down? Do they provide necessary information? Do you enjoy reading what is inside them?

(3)   There are class implications to Kramer's story. She touches on them lightly when she writes, "The peasants of Southern Europe do not easily admit to foraging—at least not to strangers. For centuries, foraged food was a sign of poverty. . . ." Kramer's story is about a successful journalist and a successful restaurateur foraging for food as a hobby—not because they are starving and cannot afford to buy it. How do you think that someone who needs to forage for food in order to survive would feel about this story?

Write About It

Think about a memorable experience that you have had with food, whether it was trying something new at a restaurant, or cooking something special with a family member. Tell the story of this food experience, providing as many vivid details about the food as you can. As you write your personal essay, think about what effect these details will have on your reader.

....

TAMARA WINFREY HARRIS   NAPPY LOVE: OR HOW I LEARNED TO STOP WORRYING AND EMBRACE THE KINKS

Tamara Winfrey Harris wrote this post for her blog, What Tami Said, *in 2007. An updated version appeared on the website* Racialicious *in 2008, where it generated a lively discussion in the comments. On her blog, Harris describes herself as "a writer, black woman, bibliophile, music lover, nappy head, geek, eccentric, Midwesterner, wife, stepmother, sister, aunt and daughter."*

Read About It

Harris uses a wide variety of terms to describe her hair, both in its natural state and when she used to treat it with relaxers. As you read, make note of these different terms, and consider how they contribute to the overall effect of the essay.

My hair is nappy. It is coarse and thick. It grows in pencil-sized spirals and tiny crinkles. My hair grows out, not down. It springs from my head like a corona. My hair is like wool. You can't run your fingers through it, nor a comb. It is impenetrable. My hair is rebellious. It resists being smoothed into a neat bun or pony tail. It puffs. Strands escape; they won't be tamed. My hair is nappy. And I love it.

Growing up, I learned to covet silky, straight hair; "bouncing and behaving" hair; Cheryl Tiegs and Christie Brinkley hair. But as a young black girl, my appearance was far from the American ideal. Making my hair behave meant hours wriggling between my grandmother's knees as she manipulated a hot comb through my thick, kinky mane. The process stretched my tight curls into hair I could toss and run my fingers through, something closer to the "white girl hair" that so many black girls admired and longed to possess.

My beautiful, straightened hair came at a price. It meant ears burned by slipped hot combs and scars from harsh chemicals. It meant avoiding active play and swimming pools, lest dreaded moisture make my hair "go back." It meant having a relaxer eat away at the back of my long hair until barely an inch was left. It meant subtly learning that my natural physical attributes were unacceptable.

I was not alone in my pathology. Pressing combs, relaxers, weaves and the quest to hide the naps are part of the fabric of black beauty culture. It is estimated that more than 75 percent of black women straighten their hair. In the book "Hair Story: Untangling the Roots of Black Hair in America," Ayanna Byrd and Lori Tharps write: "Before a black child is even born, relatives speculate over the texture of hair that will cover the baby's head, and the loaded adjectives 'good' and 'bad' are already in the air." In the same book, a New York City dancer named Joicelyn explains: "Good hair is that silky black shit that them Indian girls be havin' . . . Good hair is anything that's not crazy-ass woolly, lookin' like some pickaninny out the bush." Too often, black women find their hair hatred supported by media, men and the rest of the mainstream.

Cultural and professional pressures kept me relaxing my curls for 20 years. In the late 90s, the neo-soul movement caught fire in R&B. Young, bohemian singers like Jill Scott, Erykah Badu and India Arie were rocking stylish natural looks, and I began seeing more natural heads strutting down Michigan Ave. in Chicago, where I lived. Two of my close friends took the plunge, shearing their permed hair to start anew. Suddenly natural black hair was fashionable—at least for a small group of people.

Seeing more women, however few, freed from the tyranny of constant straightening, inspired me. I began poring over books about the care and politics of black hair. I became a member of a popular Web site devoted to championing natural hair. I learned about the toxic ingredients in chemical relaxers and the lasting damage they do. I discovered the origins of negative myths about black hair. I learned how to properly care for natural locks and discovered the myriad styles that can be achieved. I met women of all ages who embraced "nappy" as a positive description. And I slowly came to realize the inherent foolishness of believing black women's hair, apart from that of all other races, needs to be fixed—pressed, weaved and manipulated into something it isn't.

In August 2006, after years spent admiring the growing number of nappy heads around me; fretting whether my husband would still find me attractive; worrying whether my unruly 'fro would frighten my co-workers; I chopped my near shoulder-length hair off, leaving barely an inch of kinky curls. I was free!

My hair is nappy. It is soft and cottony, a mass of varying textures. My hair is fun to play with. I like to pull at the spiral curls and feel them snap back into place. My hair defies the laws of gravity. It reaches energetically toward the sky. My hair is unique. In a fashion culture that genuflects to relaxed, flat-ironed tresses and stick-straight weaves, my fluffy, puffy, kinky mane stands out. It is revolutionary. My hair is natural. It is the way God made it. My hair is nappy. And it is beautiful.

Read About It

(1)   Harris begins the first and last paragraphs of her essay with the same sentence: "My hair is nappy." Compare the structure and content of these two paragraphs. What effect do these paragraphs have on the overall message or story Harris tells? Do you find this repetition effective? Why or why not?

(2)   Harris includes several references to celebrities in her piece, from Christie Brinkley and Cheryl Tiegs (models popular in the 1980s) to India Arie and Jill Scott (musicians popular in the 1990s and 2000s). By including these references, what assumptions does Harris make about her audience? Did you recognize these names? If not, how did that affect your reading of the essay?

(3)   Harris writes that embracing her natural hair came about in part because of societal changes—she began to see more and more African American women, including celebrities and acquaintances, begin to go natural. Do you see similar changes happening currently? More broadly, do we see more examples of natural body shapes, sizes, and colors being celebrated? Or do you think a single beauty standard still prevails? Draw on examples from television, film, popular culture, and the like to support your answer.

Write About It

Using Harris' essay as inspiration, write a personal essay about a feature of your own appearance that has become part of your identity. Have you always accepted this feature? If so, how has it contributed to your self-confidence or identity? If not, how did you learn to accept this feature or even embrace it? Harris writes about her hair, but you might consider anything from your freckles to the gap in your teeth to the shape of your ears. In your essay, consider how you can use multiple, descriptive terms like Harris does to enliven your writing.

Reading Profiles

AUDREY WATTERS   A COLLEGE STUDENT AND A CEO: A PROFILE OF 21-YEAR-OLD ENTREPRENEUR JAY RODRIGUES

Audrey Watters wrote this profile in 2010 for ReadWriteStart, *a business website for individuals who are interested in starting their own businesses. Watters is a technology journalist and freelance writer whose pieces have also appeared in* Inside Higher Ed *and the* School Library Journal.

Read About It

Watters draws on an interview with Jay Rodrigues to create this profile. As you read, focus on how Watters uses material from the interview. When does she use an exact quotation, a paraphrase, and/or a summary? Jot down or highlight each quotation, paraphrase, and summary, and then make a note of why Watters uses each strategy in particular. Try using different colors of highlighter for each strategy if that helps.

In April, Flickr and Hunch co-founder Caterina Fake wrote a provocatively titled blog post: "Want to be an entrepreneur? Drop out of college." Her arguments were on my mind when I met Jay Rodrigues in early May. The 21-year-old University of Pennsylvania junior had just secured Series A funding for his startup DormNoise [a calendaring system for students]. And while that conversation was primarily about the college-calendaring system he has developed, he promised me a follow-up conversation about life as a CEO and college student—once finals were done.

And although he's now in the midst of summer school, we had a chance to speak again today.

The Importance of a College Education

Contrary to Fake's contention, Rodrigues believes "You need an education." Rodrigues admits that entrepreneurs should gain experience "in the trenches," but thinks that the education he's receiving at Wharton School gives him particular strengths and understandings that serve him well in those very trenches. A finance major, Rodrigues feels he can speak knowledgeably in business dealing with investors and clients thanks to some of his coursework. He admits, however, that certain classes, including marketing and management, are frustrating, in part because his own practical experiences on the subject seem to outstrip the textbook case studies.

Rodrigues points to the learning that happens outside the college classroom as well. College helps you meet people, learn to work with people, and, Rodrigues adds, "learn about yourself."

Time Management: Juggling Work, College, and Social Life

But balancing being a full-time college student with being a CEO is grueling. There's no escaping from the cellphone or email, Rodrigues notes, detailing a schedule that, on a typical day, alternates between dealing with school and work, from first thing in the morning till the wee hours of the next morning: email, phone, class, email, phone, class, email, phone, dinner, gym, homework. Rodrigues works about sixteen hours a day, adding jokingly "You can sleep when you die."

He does give his company a warning when it's exam time, asking to be disturbed only in case of emergencies.

Rodrigues insists that despite this hectic schedule, he carves out time for a good social life, including involvement in his fraternity.

Age: Help or Hindrance?

Rodrigues says he has benefited from good support, not just from his family, but from DormNoise's Advisory Board and now Board of Directors. He also says he's got a strong team with him at DormNoise. But he admits that despite having good business mentors, the missing piece might be a community of other college student entrepreneurs, colleagues who understand the unique demands of being 21 and of having both a college education and a corporation's success riding on your shoulders.

Rodrigues describes himself as a "kid with an idea that doesn't like to hear 'No,'" but admits that it's often difficult—as an entrepreneur in general, but as a 21-year-old one to boot—to be taken seriously. He feels he's had to work even harder to earn respect from potential investors and clients.

But Rodrigues also points to the benefits of being a college student, namely "energy, passion, fresh viewpoints." And as DormNoise targets the college market, he undoubtedly brings particular insights to bear on the development, implementation, and marketing of his product.

Jay's Advice to College Student Entrepreneurs: Stay in School

When I asked Jay what advice he'd give to other aspiring college student entrepreneurs, he praised the optimism, energy, and even naivete of youth, encouraging others his age to make the most of that. But be ready to work hard every single day. "Be 150 million percent sure this is what you want," says Rodrigues. "You'll need passion and confidence." And don't drop out of school, he adds, because for every Bill Gates and Mark Zuckerberg, there are hundreds of entrepreneurs who drop out and go nowhere. At least if you stay in school, you'll have an education.

You don't have to be a Zuckerberg or a Gates, says Rodrigues. You just have to be good at what you do. "You don't have to try to be the next Microsoft or Facebook," advises Rodrigues to other college student entrepreneurs, "but I hope you are."

Think About It

(1)   How does Watters organize this profile? Do you find the organization effective? Why or why not? What other kind of organization might Watters have used?

(2)   Do you agree with Rodrigues' suggestion that college students with entrepreneurial ambitions should stay in school? What reasons does Rodrigues give to support this idea, and how might you respond to them?

(3)   After reading the profile, how would you describe Rodrigues, in your own words? Does Watters give you a clear sense of him as a person? Why or why not?

Write About It

Based on this reading, write a social networking profile (Chapter 5) for Rodrigues. Use the format of a popular platform, such as Facebook or LinkedIn, to get you started.

LINDA WASMER ANDREWS   ADOPTIVE MOTHERS SHARE STORIES

Andrews wrote this article for American Profile, *an online magazine, in 2011. Andrews is a journalist who focuses on health and psychology topics, and her articles have also appeared in magazines such as* Parenting, Psychology Today, *and* Self.

Read About It

This article profiles three different families. As you read, write down what basic information or facts Andrews gives for each family. Do you think this information adds to the effectiveness of the profile? Why or why not?

"Typically, in order to adopt, a prospective parent must reach out for help. Touched by the kindness of strangers, she may want to give back by lending a hand to others," says adoption expert Deborah Siegel, a social work professor at Rhode Island College in Providence.

Here are more inspiring stories of adoptive moms who are sowing the seeds of love:

An Education in Adoption

For Joan Lefler Clark, 66, of Holliston, Mass. (pop. 13,801), attending an adoption conference in 1980 changed not only her personal life, but also her professional goals. After the conference, Joan and husband Donald, now 67, began the process to adopt their son Nicolas, now 28, from El Salvador. In 1984, two years after they brought Nicolas home, they adopted their daughter Cristina, now 27, from Colombia.

While waiting for the first adoption to go through, Joan, then a public-school teacher, volunteered for the organization that sponsored the conference. Although she had planned to return to teaching, in 1992 she began a 15-year run as executive director of the nonprofit group, which later was renamed the Adoption Community of New England (ACON; adoptioncommunityofne.org). Among other duties, she presented a pre-adoption introductory seminar every month. She estimates that more than 5,000 people attended her seminar over the years, including Patti Hyland, who heard Joan in 1998 and later worked with her organization as a volunteer.

"I got to see Joan in action," Hyland says. "She's an inspiration. She creates hope and instills belief in a happy ending."

Although retired since 2007, Joan still speaks at conferences and leads trainings for teachers on adoption-related issues. "Adoption, foster care, divorce, death, even having a family member who's away serving in the military—these are all things that impact kids not only at home, but also in the classroom," she says.

Her mission is to give teachers and parents the tools to help kids from all kinds of families feel good about where they come from. Looking back, Joan says the past three decades "just kind of happened. People needed to learn about adoption—and I was able to share the positive aspects of adoption."

A Tale of Two Countries

As a teenager in the early 1970s, Chris Futia, of Morton Grove, Ill. (pop. 21,934), spent a year as an exchange student in India. The experience left an indelible impression. Years later, when she and her husband, Carl, 63, decided to adopt, adopting from India seemed like a natural choice. In 1987 they adopted three tiny-at-birth babies from Kolkata, India: Leo, now 23, Annie, 21, and Peter, 16.

From the beginning, Chris, 54, wanted her children to know about their country of birth. When you adopt children from overseas, "you have a sacred responsibility to make their heritage real to them so they can know it and love it," she says. She and her family are actively involved in SPICE Indian Heritage Camp (spicecamp .blogspot.com), an annual get-together for families with children adopted from India, which attracts 40 to 50 families from around the nation each year. Last summer, the Futias attended the parent-run camp for the 21st consecutive year.

Chris also has led five biennial heritage tours to India. The group visits several sites together, and Chris arranges for each family to travel to the child's place of birth and, if possible, visit the orphanage where that child once lived.

Susan Rogers, of Wake Forest, N.C. (pop. 12,588), was there for the 2006 trip; it was a high school graduation gift for her daughter Kamila, now 22. The orphanage where Kamila began life had since closed, but she was able to meet some caregivers and nurses who had worked there. Susan remembers that one of the nurses suddenly pulled Kamila's ear forward and asked what had happened to the strawberry birthmark. In fact, Kamila did have a birthmark there as a baby that later faded away. "Kamila's dream that she had kept in her heart—that someone in India remembered her—had come true," Susan says. "It was definitely the high point of the trip."

The most recent tour, which left last November, was the smallest to date. With many people still in belt-tightening mode, only one other family signed up to accompany Chris and her teenage son, Peter, to India. Because Peter has cognitive and emotional disabilities, it was his first time on one of the tours. Three weeks before they were set to leave, "we got some shocking news," Chris says. During routine medical testing, doctors discovered that Peter has an incurable, and rapidly progressing, bone marrow disorder. "He didn't have symptoms yet, so we went ahead with the trip," Chris says. Although the news was devastating, she says, "the trip was a joyful experience."

In Kolkata, Peter got to visit the orphanage where he spent his first six months of life. Workers there took the unusual step of letting Peter see the document with which his birth mother had given him up for adoption. Because she was illiterate, she had signed with a thumbprint. "Peter got very quiet and put his thumb on the thumbprint," says Chris. "Then he looked up at me and said, 'Mom, it fits.' It's a memory I'll keep with me forever."

Think About It

(1)   What prompted each of the parents profiled here to consider adoption, in the first place, and then to become more involved in education about adoption? How do their stories compare?

(2)   Do the people featured in this profile come to life for you as a reader? Why or why not? What additional information or details would you like to know?

(3)   The profile ends with a particular anecdote about one child, Peter. What message do you think Andrews wanted readers to draw from this anecdote?

Write About It

What questions would you ask of someone you would profile for a profile article about modern families? Choose a person you would interview, and then write a list of at least six questions. To start, you might think about what questions Andrews would have asked the people she profiled.

WBAL-TV11 BALTIMORE   ILLEGAL IMMIGRANT BECOMES WORLD-RENOWNED BRAIN SURGEON

This profile, written by staff writers of WBAL-TV11 in Baltimore, aired in 2007 and remains available on the station's website.

Read About It

As you read, highlight the subject's quotations included in this profile of Dr. Alfredo Quinones-Hinojosa. Why do you think the report uses so many quotations? How do they contribute to the profile? Do they give you a better sense of the person profiled, or would you have rather read more descriptions or text from the authors themselves?

Currently, a wall is being built between Mexico and the United States because many Americans remain concerned illegal immigrants are draining our nation's resources without giving enough back.

But one illegal immigrant shared his remarkable journey with WBAL TV 11 News reporter John Sherman—a journey proving that potential can be hard to judge from across the border.

"I just take off, just like a sprint—all this adrenaline going through my body. I just go over the fence, jump about 16 feet to the floor and run towards the United States," Dr. Alfredo Quinones-Hinojosa said, remembering the day he fled to the U.S.

He was one of many Mexicans who flee to the U.S. out of desperation. He said poverty and the hope of a better life drove him to make the leap.

"We had no food. We had no place to live," he said. "I went from pulling weeds to pulling tomatoes, to picking cotton loops to picking grapes."

Quinones-Hinojosa said at first, he wasn't sure why he did it.

" (I thought) 'What am I doing here. Why did I do this.' I didn't have much in Mexico, but at least I had my family, my friends," he said.

But Quinones-Hinojosa doesn't work on a farm anymore. Nineteen years after he jumped a fence into San Diego with a few dollars and no English skills, he is now one of the best brain surgeons at the world-renowned Johns Hopkins Hospital in Baltimore.

"Every day, everything I do—it doesn't matter if when I was a welder or when I was a tomato picker—I gave it my best," he said. "I have been so lucky and I often wonder what set me apart from the rest. The same year that I came, there were thousands of other illegal aliens who also crossed the border."

Quinones-Hinojosa, known as Dr. Q at work, now uses his hands on patients where the slightest movement can separate life from death—the same hands that separated weeds from dirt not long ago.

"I do look at them sometimes, and I realize these are the same hands who now touch people's lives and brains. Nothing has really changed," he said.

Dr. Q's story bends the definition of possible. It's one that took him from the fence to the fields, from community college to the University of California at Berkeley and from Harvard medical school to Johns Hopkins Hospital.

"I had hopes. I had dreams," he said.

As a child in Mexico, cruel poverty was his family's reward for hard work. As a teenager, he said he found his father in tears.

"I found him crying because he just couldn't provide. And I promised myself that I would do everything within my power to make sure that I provided for not just my parents and my siblings, but for my future family," he said.

That commitment led Dr. Q to the fields of California's San Joachin Valley.

"I just knew that if you keep working hard, things are going to turn around. I just had no doubt in myself," he said.

Dr. Q said he slept in a trailer at night, but by day he kept pushing at every opportunity.

"Someone gave me an opportunity to drive a tractor. It just took me minutes to pick it up. Then (there was) an opportunity to drive the cotton picker and it took me minutes to pick it up," he said.

Now, Dr. Q splits his time between surgery and his research lab. He said he believes he can find the cure for brain cancer—a challenge the medical establishment has all but given up on.

"My heart just palpitates, and I wonder, 'How did I change this person's life today? How did I affect his or her memories? How did I change how this person will interact with his or her loved ones?'" he said.

One patient Dr. Q helped save was Rodney Banks, a 45-year-old construction worker with five grandchildren. Dr. Q successfully removed a benign tumor from Banks' brain.

"That's the thing about Alfredo. You take away his entire background and he's still a superstar in neurosurgery," said Dr. Matt McGirt, who works side by side in the operating room with Dr. Q for dozens of hours every week.

"That's truly amazing. And to do what he does now—he's been blessed," Banks said after finding out about Dr. Q's background.

"One thing that this country absolutely values is hard work," Dr. Q often says when he tells his story to student groups at least once a month. "If you don't have high dreams, it becomes a self-fulfilling prophecy."

If Dr. Q has a secret to success, it may be his unshakeable confidence that you don't always have to know exactly where you're going in life. You just take a leap of faith, knowing there's no safer bet than one on yourself.

"I may never find a cure for brain cancer. But I don't care about that right now. I care about trying," he said. "The potential is in everybody. The question is, 'How do we harvest that potential?'"

Dr. Q became an American citizen in 1997. He lives in Bel Air with his wife and three children.

Think About It

(1)   Take a look at the paragraphs in this piece. What do you notice about them? Why do you think they tend to be so short? How does this paragraph style differ from other genres and contexts?

(2)   This profile opens by evoking the context: "Currently, a wall is being built between Mexico and the United States because many Americans remain concerned illegal immigrants are draining our nation's resources without giving enough back." Why do you think profiles like this one tend to be published when there is a national debate about immigration? What message does this profile have, beyond its description of Dr. Q?

(3)   This profile suggests that those who simply work hard and believe in themselves will succeed in America. Where have you heard this message before? Do you find it true, or are there other factors involved?

Write About It

Choose an issue that is currently being debated in your college or community. Then, think of a person you might profile to address that issue indirectly, like this one does. Write a profile of that person, keeping in mind how your profile might contribute to the debate or add a new perspective on the issue in question.

YALE SUSTAINABLE FOOD PROJECT   HISTORY

This program profile appears on the website for the Yale Sustainable Food Project, a student organization at Yale University.

Read About It

What kinds of details does this profile give about the organization? As you read, jot down or highlight key pieces of information given, and then see if you can categorize your list according to types of details or facts.

The seeds of the Project were sown in 2000, when a group of Yale students enrolled in a class about environmental health and policy taught by Professor John Wargo in the School of Forestry and Environmental Studies. As these students learned about the harmful impacts of pesticides on human health and the environment, they became concerned about the food in Yale's dining halls, and began meeting with Yale's dining services to discuss increasing the amount of organic food in dining halls. These meetings led to Yale University Dining's decision to change procurement of several food items from conventional to organic, where this change was cost-neutral. The group of students also formed an organization, "Food From the Earth," and continued to raise awareness and support for organic food in dining halls. Food from the Earth held meetings and wrote petitions, and their efforts culminated in a 2002 conference called "Farming and Eating in New England."

The work of these students was supplemented early on by the interest of Alice Waters, owner of the world famous restaurant Chez Panisse. In 2001 Waters became interested in the culture of food at Yale when her daughter, Fanny Singer, enrolled in the college. A conversation between Waters and Yale President Richard Levin sparked the idea for an ambitious University undertaking: a project encompassing a sustainable dining program, a college farm, university composting, and increased education around food and agriculture. At the urging of Waters and of the students involved with Food from the Earth, the University hired Joshua Viertel, a Harvard graduate who had worked as a teacher, farmer, and shepherd. Viertel would report to the Assistant VP for Student Financial and Administrative Services.

Next, a steering committee was formed in early 2003; it consisted of the Assistant VP for Student Financial and Administrative Services, the Director of Yale Dining, an executive chef, a purchaser, students, and faculty. Together, Viertel and the steering committee created a scope and vision for the initiative and named it the Yale Sustainable Food Project. The Project would include a garden on campus, educational programming around food and agriculture, and a sustainable dining program.

With this ambitious vision before them, the committee tackled the dining program first, inaugurating a pilot project in Berkeley College's (one of Yale's twelve residential colleges) dining hall to serve all local, seasonal, and sustainable food. While planning for the change to sustainable food, Viertel and a group of students wrote a proposal for a Yale Farm, and over the course of a semester generated broad-based support for the idea from a wide range of faculty and administration. Viertel and students submitted the Farm proposal to President Levin, and with the approval from the VP of Finance and Administration hired the Yale Farm's first interns. In the summer of 2003, the interns broke ground at the Yale Farm, and ran a composting pilot to recycle waste from Yale's dining halls.

As the farm and the dining program were underway, the steering committee was also working to generate broad-based support for this program, and to solidify the strong relationship between the University's academic work and sustainable food. With these goals to guide them, they conceived of a conference on Yale's campus, and hired Melina Shannon-DiPietro, a Harvard graduate, teacher, and former consultant, to develop and oversee this project. More than 170 people from 19 schools attended "Tilling the Soil; Turning the Tables" on Yale's campus. Shannon-DiPietro then came on as co-director with Viertel.

After one year of planning and a summer of staff training, Berkeley's doors opened in the fall of 2003 with a full seasonal and sustainable menu. Seasonal menus and recipes were written to reflect local availability of different foods throughout the year. Initially, a limited number of local farmers delivered food directly to Berkeley College; over time, better distribution networks and relationships with cooperatives were set up to facilitate supply on a greater scale. Berkeley dining hall staff were trained to successfully execute recipes involving raw ingredients—a radical shift from the type of food preparation to which they were accustomed. The pilot was a huge success: it demonstrated both that sustainable food was wildly popular with students, and that serving a sustainable menu was operationally possible in all of Yale's dining halls. With this knowledge, and because of the program's overwhelming popularity, the Project expanded in 2004 to incorporate some sustainable food in the menus of all college dining halls.

As staff in the Berkeley College dining hall were training and preparing for the transition to sustainable food, student interns were working to transform a brambly acre of sod on the northern edge of campus into a productive market garden. In the summer of 2003, students harvested the Farm's first vegetable crop and began selling their produce at the New Haven farmers' market. Over the past five years, the farm has become a place where students, staff, and area residents gather to eat, work, and learn. Each summer, six undergraduates spend their summer as Yale Farm interns, learning the theory and practice of sustainable agriculture through work, classes, and field trips.

In 2005, summer interns helped a team of artisan masons build a wood-fired hearth oven at the farm, made with reclaimed wood and stone. When the weather permits, the oven is used regularly for cooking and baking. The Yale Farm is a four-season market garden; cultivation continues through the winter in an unheated hoophouse. Weekly workdays throughout the year are run by student farm managers, who teach and direct volunteer farm work. Workshops are held regularly at the farm, on topics ranging from bread-baking and fruit preserving to winter growing and pruning. The farm also hosts seasonal festivals, like a fall Harvest festival and a spring pig roast.

As the Farm grew, so did the dining program. In 2004, twenty percent of the food in each dining hall was sustainable. In 2006, Berkeley's role as a pilot was ended, and the percentage of sustainable food was increased in each of the colleges. All Yale's college dining halls now serve the same menu, and sustainable food is available in each of them, at every meal. In 2007 Rafi Taherian took over as the director of Yale Dining, at which point the Project shifted its focus from sourcing and meal planning to running educational programs for Yale students on issues surrounding food and agriculture. The Project now works with Dining on educational events but does not participate in sourcing ingredients for the dining halls.

In 2006, the Project began running a series of educational events, known on campus as the Chewing the Fat speaker series, in an effort to increase the portion of Yale's academic and extracurricular landscape devoted to food and sustainable agriculture. These events comprise speakers, films, workshops, and field trips. Also in 2006, the Project began administering the pre-orientation program Harvest, formerly an offshoot of FOOT, Yale's backpacking pre-orientation program. On Harvest, upperclassmen lead trips of 8–10 freshmen on family-owned, organic farms in Connecticut for five days before the start of on-campus orientation.

In its first few years, the Sustainable Food Project supported the student organization Food From the Earth, which played an important role in organizing events which created a culture of food and agriculture on campus. In the last several years, the Sustainable Food Project's educational programs have grown, as funding and staff have as well. In 2005, Lucas Dreier, a Yale graduate who had been involved in the original proposal for the Project, joined Viertel and Shannon-DiPietro as a full-time staff member. In 2006, with the generous support of the Lazarus Family, the Project created the Lazarus Fellowship, a two-year position for a recent Yale graduate who serves as the Project's Program Coordinator. The Project also employs roughly 20 paid student interns during the school year, who create and run programs and events, working on everything from running farm workdays to managing the office to writing copy for printed materials.

In 2008, Josh Viertel left the Project to become President of Slow Food USA. Melina Shannon-DiPietro assumed full responsibilities of directorship. In late 2010 Melina moved to New York to work as the Director of Food Programs at Friends of the High Line; Mark Bomford took over as Director of the program in the fall of 2011.

Since its founding, the Sustainable Food Project has also actively encouraged and supported the development of Yale courses related to food, agriculture, and sustainability, in departments as diverse as Psychology, Biology, and History. The Project's directors taught a college seminar in 2005 on "The Practice of Farming Well," and have served as guest lecturers and co-instructors in other courses. In 2007, due to student demand, the program in Environmental Studies formalized a concentration in food and agriculture within its major. One of the Project's major areas of focus in the coming years is to continue to collaborate with the administration to increase education at Yale related to food and agriculture, bolstering the number of faculty teaching these subjects and the number of courses taught on them.

Think About It

(1) One goal of a program profile is to create a positive impression of the organization in question. Does this profile create a good impression for the Yale Sustainable Food Project? If so, how do the writers accomplish this? If not, how could the writers create a better impression?

(2)   How do you think the writer(s) compiled information for this program profile? If you had to write a profile of an organization for a website, how would you go about doing research?

(3)   Who might be the audience for this profile? Write a list of the possible readers of this profile, and then describe how the profile might appeal to each type of reader.

Write About It

Gather some information about an organization on your campus or in your commu-nity: find out what key accomplishments, events, or individuals have contributed to the organization's history. Then, write a program profile that conveys a positive im-pression of that organization.

JULIE SLAYMAKER   DOOR OPENER

Julie Slaymaker wrote this profile essay for Indiana State University's alumni maga-zine in 2010. Slaymaker is a writer from Indianapolis and, like the woman she profiles here, she has been a pioneer in journalism. She has served as president of the Woman's Press Club of Indiana and the Professional Chapter of the Society of Professional Journalists.

Read About It

As you read, make a timeline of major events in Wanda Ramey's life. Then, compare your timeline to the organization of the article. Does the article follow a chronological organization (Chapter 20)? If not, how is it organized? Why do you think the profile writer uses this organization scheme?

In the KPIX-TV studios, the lipstick red sign flashed: "On Air." Earlier, Wanda Ra-mey, '45, had taken her seat as co-anchor of San Francisco's Noon News and pre-pared to make history.

On that day's broadcast in 1959, she would become the first woman news anchor in the western United States and only the second female anchor in the country.

At the time, women in broadcast journalism weren't considered for positions in hard news or news gathering, let alone anchoring or co-anchoring a newscast. In-stead, they were relegated to working the society beat or reporting on things such as food and recipes. Ramey's achievement represented a major step forward.

Typically, Ramey, who died in 2009, took her history-making accomplishment in stride. "I didn't consider myself a pioneer. We were all pioneers," said Ramey, who will be inducted into the Indiana Journalism Hall of Fame in April of this year, in a 1990 interview. "I was just doing my job."

She saw that job as doing more than reporting on "home hints and recipes," according to an interview she gave at the University of San Francisco in 2000. With that attitude, working in "hard" news seemed a natural career progression to her.

She had worked in broadcasting for more than a decade before she became the noon news co-anchor, making her reputation for her on-the-scene reporting as "The Girl on the Beat" at KPIX. By spending time riding in police cruisers to cover crime stories, peering into beatnik haunts and talking about construction from inside a building's steel skeleton, she added a new dimension to television journalism at a time when newscasts were conducted mostly from the studio. Her work soon earned her respect and the new moniker of "Woman on the Beat."

The "Woman on the Beat" was born Feb. 18, 1924, in Terre Haute to Hiram and May Stuart Ramey. She was the eldest of five children. Her sister, Dr. Vanita Gibbs, an ISU professor emerita of education, recalls: "Recognizing her speaking talents, our parents provided elocution lessons for her in her early teens. That training served her well. She was in several plays in high school and at Indiana State. While in college, she further developed her talents by writing for the *Indiana Statesman* and working in radio on campus."

Before receiving her bachelor's degree from ISU, where she majored in radio journalism, in 1945, Ramey hosted a children's show called "The Story Princess of the Music Box."

Her leadership skills surfaced early. She was junior class secretary, president of Kappa Kappa sorority and a member of Alpha Phi Gamma journalism honorary and Theta Alpha Phi theater honorary.

Before graduation, her father's employer, The Railway Express Agency, transferred him to San Francisco. Knowing she wanted to work in radio, she applied to be a contestant on a local radio amateur hour after rejoining her family.

"I went with her to the studio for the broadcast," Gibbs remembers. "She read poetry because she wanted her voice to be heard more than she wanted to win an amateur show."

She landed her first job at radio station KPIK in San Luis Obispo, Calif. She returned to the Bay Area in 1947 and worked at several radio stations, including KSFO, where she interviewed celebrities at the Hearst Ranch near Pleasanton, Calif.

In 1948, she was hired as the secretary to the program director for Oakland's KWBR radio. She soon assumed his duties when the post became vacant—at no extra pay. A year later, she jumped at the chance to be an on-the-air interviewer at KROW radio.

During her time at KROW, she was part of a star-studded broadcasting team that included Art Linkletter, "This Is Your Life's" Ralph Edwards and poet/composer/singer Rod McKuen. Always striving for bigger and better things, Ramey moved to San Francisco's KGO-TV in 1952, where she briefly hosted a news and interview show, "Midday With Wanda," aimed at housewives. Later, using her down-home warmth and wit, she interviewed the wives of famous men on her KGO show "The Woman Behind the Man."

According to her daughter, Kristi Queirolo Steadman of Novato, Calif., by the end of her mother's career, Ramey had interviewed more than 1,200 celebrities, including such figures as John F. Kennedy, Ronald Reagan and Eleanor Roosevelt, whom she cited as her most treasured interview.

At KGO-TV, Ramey also became life-long friends with comedienne Phyllis Diller. "I met Wanda in 1953 and we stayed close friends for 56 years until her death last August," the 92-year-old Diller said.

"I was a writer at the station, and Wanda and I shared an office," she continued. "We were two little girls from the Midwest. She was from Terre Haute and I was from Lima, Ohio, so we gravitated together and became bosom buddies. Because she was already a big celebrity in the Bay Area, she got free tickets to every event and took me along."

San Francisco's hilly streets soon became the stage for a comedic routine starring the comedienne and the newscaster. "We drove in Wanda's little black MG sports car. She was a great driver, but she couldn't park. On the other hand, I was a great parker. So she drove and I parked! We were like Abbott and Costello," Diller said, laughing.

The two were so close Ramey bought Diller a dress to wear for her opening night at The Purple Onion, San Francisco's legendary nightclub, in 1955, where she perfected her act. Diller told the *Wall Street Journal* about Ramey's unique way of promoting that event.

"She went on her Sunday TV interview show and told viewers there was a new comic in town who would break all the records," Diller said. "She took a stack of records in her hand and broke them right there on the set."

While Diller's career was growing, Wanda's suffered a setback. KGO General Manager Vince Francis fired her, citing the prevailing view at the time: women weren't credible as newscasters.

After leaving KGO, she worked at KCBS-AM radio, hosting "Meet Me at Manning's," featuring interviews with women. Following that she landed a job at KPIX.

One story Ramey and her cameraman husband worked on at KPIX led them to a larger commitment as volunteers. On New Year's Eve of 1960, the couple went to San Quentin State Prison for a story on inmate activities. That story led to their teaching an annual film and television production workshop that trained inmates in production skills. They also created SQTV, a prisoner-run, closed-circuit television station that still exists.

For her efforts, the prisoners named Ramey, the first woman reporter and female volunteer allowed inside San Quentin's walls, an "Honorary Inmate" in 1965.

Ultimately, family was to take precedence over career after Kristi was born Aug. 14, 1962. "She stayed at KPIX until I started school," Kristi noted. "She was one of the first broadcasters to be pregnant in public. The viewers followed her along, and she had an 'on air' baby shower.

"Her co-anchor, John Weston, and his wife, Leslie, had a baby named John, Jr., the same month. So, Mom and John brought both babies on TV to show us off to the viewers," she added.

By 1967, Ramey wanted more family time. She left her anchor's post to work for National Educational Television, the precursor to PBS. She also served as the Bay Area correspondent for the Voice of America during the 1970s. The 85-year-old broadcast journalism pioneer died of cancer on Aug. 15, 2009.

The respect Ramey earned during her career manifested itself in a number of awards and offices. Ramey's legacy will be further honored when she is inducted into the Indiana Journalism Hall of Fame on April 17 in Bloomington

In recognition of the role ISU played in her life, Ramey's family established the Wanda Ramey Scholarship in Communications through the ISU Foundation. "ISU has always been proud of Ms. Ramey," said Anna Christensen, ISU Foundation director of development. "This scholarship will honor her memory and legacy."

Think About It

(1) The author is herself a journalist. Is her own expertise reflected in the article? In what ways?

(2) Why do you think universities publish profiles like this one in magazines for alumni? What purpose do magazines like this one serve, and how do profiles help to accomplish that purpose?

(3) What do you think of Ramey's claim that she did not consider herself a pioneer, but that was just doing her job? Do you think other pioneers think about themselves in a similar way? Why might Ramey be compelled not to call herself a pioneer? How would she feel about this article, if she were still alive?

Write About It

Choose a person who excels at an activity you participate in or know a lot about, such as a hobby, sport, profession, or area of academic study. Write a profile article about that person, drawing on your own expertise in that area.

Reading Informative Genres

NATIONAL INSTITUTES OF HEALTH   FALL SEMESTER: A TIME FOR PARENTS TO REVISIT DISCUSSIONS ABOUT COLLEGE DRINKING

The National Institutes of Health, a federally funded medical research agency, released this factsheet on college drinking in August of 2010.

Read About It

The audience of this factsheet is parents of college-bound students. As you read, try to place yourself in the shoes of a parent. How does this factsheet affect you as a reader?

As college students arrive on campus this fall, it's a time of new experiences, new friendships, and making memories that will last a lifetime. Unfortunately for many, it is also a time of excessive drinking and dealing with its aftermath—vandalism, violence, sexual aggression, and even death.

According to research summarized in a College Task Force report to the National Institute on Alcohol Abuse and Alcoholism (NIAAA), the consequences of excessive drinking by college students are more significant, more destructive, and more costly than many parents realize. And these consequences affect students whether or not they drink.

Statistics from this report, which were updated recently, indicate that drinking by college students aged 18 to 24 contributes to an estimated 1,825 student deaths, 599,000 injuries, and 97,000 cases of sexual assault or date rape each year.

Early Weeks Are Critical

As the fall semester begins, parents can use this important time to help prepare their college-age sons and daughters by talking with them about the consequences of excessive drinking.

Some first-year students who live on campus may be at particular risk for alcohol misuse. During their high school years, those who go on to college tend to drink less than their non-college-bound classmates. However, during subsequent years, the heavy drinking rates of college students surpass those of their non-college peers.

This rapid increase in heavy drinking over a relatively short period of time can contribute to serious difficulties with the transition to college. Anecdotal evidence suggests that the first 6 weeks of the first semester are critical to a first-year student's academic success. Because many students initiate heavy drinking during these early days of college, the potential exists for excessive alcohol consumption to interfere with successful adaptation to campus life. The transition to college is often difficult, and about one-third of first-year students fail to enroll for their second year.

Parents Can Help

During these crucial early weeks, parents can do a variety of things to stay involved. They can inquire about campus alcohol policies, call their sons and daughters frequently, and ask about roommates and living arrangements.

They should also discuss the penalties for underage drinking as well as how alcohol use can lead to date rape, violence, and academic failure.

Resources Are Available

For parents who want to talk to their college-age sons and daughters about the consequences of college drinking, a variety of helpful resources are available from NIAAA.

A special guide for parents offers research-based information, including the need to stay involved during freshman year and how to get assistance if faced with an alcohol-related crisis.

Think About It

(1)   At the beginning, this factsheet tries to convince readers that the information it contains is important, or urgent. What rhetorical strategies do the authors employ to convince readers of the factsheet's importance? Are *you* convinced? Why or why not?

(2)   What are the primary emotions that the factsheet would evoke in readers who are parents? Can you pinpoint the words or passages that evoke these emotions?

(3)   The title of the factsheet indicates that the factsheet will be about parents discussing drinking with their children. How much of the factsheet is actually devoted to these discussions? Does the factsheet deliver what the title seems to promise?

Write About It

Identify a health problem on your campus that you think parents can help students cope with. From a student's perspective (yours), write a factsheet that identifies the problem, establishes urgency, and provides parents with advice for how to help students.

NATIONAL CONFERENCE OF STATE LEGISLATURES   HOW THE CHILD SUPPORT SYSTEM AFFECTS LOW-INCOME FATHERS

This factsheet on child support and low-income fathers was published by the National Conference of State Legislatures (NCSL) in 2000. The NCSL is a bipartisan group composed of all members of state legislatures, along with researchers and others who support legislative work. (The NCSL is not a government agency.) The NCSL uses factsheets such as this one to help legislators make policy decisions.

Read About It

As you read this factsheet, note the places where the factsheet seems to be trying to counter presumptions about fathers and child support that legislators might hold. Can you think of what these presumptions might be?

What Policymakers Need to Know

- Guideline formulas that determine child support orders are a matter of state discretion and these guidelines can be formulated in statute.

- Not all dads who do not pay child support are deadbeat dads; some fathers lack the financial resources to pay mandated child support amounts.
- Low-income fathers face many of the same barriers that welfare mothers face—low literacy, few job skills and poor employment history.
- Child support enforcement agencies are traditionally a cost-recovery agency set up to reimburse the state for welfare payments, although fewer than 15 percent of welfare families actually receive support.
- Child support agencies were not designed to deal with low-income parents who were never married.
- Most enforcement tools are targeted toward parents with assets and those who have means to provide support but actively evade paying support.
- Current child support policy does not have effective mechanisms to distinguish fathers who evade paying support from those who would pay support if they had the resources. No longer is enforcement "one size fits all."
- Granting a downward modification to low-income fathers may make it easier for them to make continuous child support payments.
- Many fathers do not know they can ask for a modification, or what circumstances warrant a modification.
- Many child support orders for low-income men are set as a result of a default order that may not take into consideration the actual wage earnings of a father, resulting in an order that is set too high.
- Fathers often receive default orders if they do not attend their court hearing. Fathers avoid these hearings because they are fearful that the child support system's only interest is in punishing them.
- Most families who receive welfare do not receive any collected support because the state retains this money to reimburse itself for money spent on welfare. Fathers view this as a disincentive to pay through the system.
- One of the barriers that low-income men face in paying child support orders is the massive arrearages that accumulate once a mother receives welfare.

What Policymakers Can Do

- Insist that child support workers establish proactive procedures that encourage fathers to come forward before default orders are entered.
- Provide easy access to information about the child support system that helps both mothers and fathers navigate the court system.
- Inform fathers about their rights and the child support proceeding before their court date to eliminate any misperceptions that could discourage fathers from attending.
- Pass through collected support to families—states can count these expenditures in their maintenance of effort.
- Develop procedures that ensure welfare caseworkers adequately communicate the implications of assigning child support rights to the state in exchange for receiving welfare benefits.
- Compromise arrearages for fathers who demonstrate a compliance with payment plans or employment requirements.

- Develop flexible policies regarding the accumulation of interest on past arrearages.
- Require that state agencies set welfare debt equal to the amount of a father's support order.
- Analyze how arrearages are set—retroactive to birth or to the date of a court proceeding—and craft policy that insures a father's debt will be set at an amount he is likely to pay.
- Conduct paternity establishment as early as possible. Suspend enforcement of an order if parents are cohabitating.
- Connect families with services to assist them to develop parenting and relationship skills.
- Conduct outreach to connect fragile families with services before they apply for welfare.
- Connect families with services to assist them to become and stay employed to minimize the use of welfare.

Think About It

(1)   The factsheet states, "Most enforcement tools are targeted toward parents with assets and those who have means to provide support but actively evade paying support." From what you have learned from this factsheet, does this description of a deadbeat parent describe low-income fathers who do not pay support? Why or why not?

(2)   The purpose of the first part of this factsheet, "What Policymakers Need to Know," is to convince lawmakers to change their opinions about dads who do not pay child support. Based on the arguments made here, what do you think those opinions might be?

(3)   In the second part of the factsheet, "What Policymakers Can Do," the factsheet provides suggestions for how to rewrite laws. Based on these suggestions, what sorts of presumptions can you draw about how the authors believe the system is structured now? For example, if the factsheet suggests creating "proactive procedures," the authors might believe that the current procedures are too passive and ineffective.

Write About It

Think of an issue that you believe is misunderstood on your campus. For example, "What do student government representatives really do?" or "How much are dining services employees really paid?" Research your topic and then produce a factsheet that shares this information with readers.

FUTURES WITHOUT VIOLENCE   THE FACTS ON IMMIGRANT WOMEN AND DOMESTIC VIOLENCE

Futures Without Violence (formerly called the Family Violence Prevention Fund) is a nonprofit organization that works to eradicate family and relationship violence around the world. The organization published this factsheet on immigrants and relationship violence in the mid-2000s. They make the document available through their website, endabuse.org.

Read About It

As you read this factsheet, think about who the audiences of this factsheet might be. Who would find this information relevant to their work? Who do the authors hope to influence?

Like all women, immigrant women are at high risk for domestic violence, but due to their immigration status, they may face a more difficult time escaping abuse. Immigrant women often feel trapped in abusive relationships because of immigration laws, language barriers, social isolation, and lack of financial resources.[i] Despite recent federal legislation that has opened new and safe routes to immigration status for some immigrant women who are victims of domestic violence, abuse is still a significant problem for immigrant women, as it is for all women in the United States.

- A recent study in New York City found that 51 percent of intimate partner homicide victims were foreign-born, while 45 percent were born in the United States.[ii]
- Forty-eight percent of Latinas in one study reported that their partner's violence against them had increased since they immigrated to the United States.[iii]
- A survey of immigrant Korean women found that 60 percent had been battered by their husbands.[iv]
- Married immigrant women experience higher levels of physical and sexual abuse than unmarried immigrant women, 59.5 percent compared to 49.8 percent, respectively.[v]
- Abusers often use their partners' immigration status as a tool of control.[vi] In such situations, it is common for a batterer to exert control over his partner's immigration status in order to force her to remain in the relationship.[vii]
- Immigrant women often suffer higher rates of battering than U.S. citizens because they may come from cultures that accept domestic violence or because they have less access to legal and social services than U.S. citizens. Additionally, immigrant batterers and victims may believe that the penalties and protections of the U.S. legal system do not apply to them.[viii]

- Battered immigrant women who attempt to flee may not have access to bilingual shelters, financial assistance, or food. It is also unlikely that they will have the assistance of a certified interpreter in court, when reporting complaints to the police or a 911 operator, or even in acquiring information about their rights and the legal system.[ix]

---

[i]   Orloff, Leslye, and Rachael Little. 1999. "Somewhere to Turn: Making Domestic Violence Services Accessible to Battered Immigrant Women." *A 'How To' Manual for Battered Women's Advocates and Service Providers.* Ayuda Inc.

[ii]   *Femicide in New York City: 1995–2002.* New York City Department of Health and Mental Hygiene, October 2004. http://www.ci.nyc.ny.us/html/doh/html/public/press04/pr145-1022.html

[iii]   Dutton, Mary, Leslye Orloff, and Giselle Aguilar Hass. 2000. "Characteristics of Help-Seeking Behaviors, Resources, and Services Needs of Battered Immigrant Latinas: Legal and Policy Implications." *Georgetown Journal on Poverty Law and Policy.* 7(2).

[iv]   Tjaden, Patricia, and Nancy Thoennes. 2000. *Extent, Nature and Consequences of Violence Against Women: Findings from the National Violence Against Women Survey.* The National Institute of Justice and the Centers for Disease Control and Prevention. Retrieved January 9, 2004. http://www.ncjrs.org/pdffiles1/nij/183781.pdf.

[v]   Dutton, Mary, Leslye Orloff, and Giselle Aguilar Hass. 2000. "Characteristics of Help-Seeking Behaviors, Resources, and Services Needs of Battered Immigrant Latinas: Legal and Policy Implications." *Georgetown Journal on Poverty Law and Policy.* 7(2).

[vi]   Dutton, Mary, Leslye Orloff, and Giselle Aguilar Hass. 2000. "Characteristics of Help-Seeking Behaviors, Resources, and Services Needs of Battered Immigrant Latinas: Legal and Policy Implications." *Georgetown Journal on Poverty Law and Policy.* 7(2).

[vii]   Orloff, Leslye, and Janice V. Kaguyutan. 2002. "Offering a Helping Hand: Legal Protections for Battered Immigrant Women: A History of Legislative Responses." *Journal of Gender, Social Policy, and the Law.* 10(1): 95–183.

[viii] Orloff et al., 1995. "With No Place to Turn: Improving Advocacy for Battered Immigrant Women." *Family Law Quarterly.* 29(2): 313.

[ix]   Orloff et al., 1995. "With No Place to Turn: Improving Advocacy for Battered Immigrant Women." *Family Law Quarterly.* 29(2): 313.

Think About It

(1)   This factsheet presents an argument and supports it with evidence. How is the evidence presented? Is this presentation effective?

(2)   How does this document differ from other genres such as a research paper or a report? Is there any information that you wish had been included to supplement what is already provided?

(3)   The authors refer to "immigrant women" as a group. However, they provide specific data on particular ethnic groups and nationalities in their list of statistics. How is this data about specific groups helpful (or hurtful) to their argument?

Write About It

In order to write the preceding factsheet, the authors drew from research (such as surveys) conducted by other researchers and published in research journals. Think of a public health issue (obesity, vaccination, etc.) that you and your fellow students know little about. Conduct research in scholarly journals (Chapter 24) about the issue you have selected. Compile a factsheet sharing your research results. Include citations to the sources that you used.

· ·

SARAH STARKEY   HOW TO MAKE YOUR OWN INDOOR COMPOST BIN

Sarah Starkey published this tutorial on the website Apartment Therapy *in 2011.* Apartment Therapy *and Sarah Starkey specialize in providing advice for living in small spaces (such as apartments).*

Read About It

As you read this tutorial, notice how the author uses subheadings to organize the information. Did you find the organization useful to you as a reader? Would you organize the tutorial differently?

There are a lot of options out there for apartment dwellers who want to compost, and like most things it's not as simple as one style fits all. It's about finding what works best for you. Try something! And if it doesn't work for you, try something else! This is an easy indoor compost option for people who need something cheap, customizable, and space friendly.

What You Need
Materials
- A container to house your compost. It can be as big or small as you like.
- A tray that fits under your container and allows room for spills, hopefully just dirt.
- A small bag of soil.
- Some old newspaper for shredding.

Tools
- Depending on what container you use you will need a drill or hammer and nail or scissors.

Instructions

1. Choose a location for your indoor compost bin. We used the space under the sink because it was in the kitchen, locked to protect tiny hands and large enough to keep a decent family sized compost.

2. Think about what you'd like to keep your compost in. You can use plastic boxes, metal containers, garbage bins or buckets . . . get creative and customize it to your use taste and your space, but consider: it will need to be covered. You might need to swap it out for a new one while it composts and you'll need to store it somewhere!

3. Once you have your container you'll need to punch holes in it. What you're using will determine what tools you need. We chose a metal garbage bin so we used a drill. Note: when we took the photos we only put holes in the bottom but later found that we needed a few holes around the rim as well.

4. Cover your tray with newspaper and put the compost bin onto the tray.

5. Now add dirt! Again it's about the size of the container and how much use it's going to get. We added a layer of soil about four inches deep.

6. Next step. Add a layer of dry stuff, in this case newspaper, and you're ready to go!

How to Use Your Compost Bin

1. Add your food scraps as you get them. It's an indoor bin so making them as small as possible will benefit you in the long run.

2. You want to keep the wet/dry balance so add a small handful of shredded newspaper when you add scraps.

3. Once a week you'll need to mix the compost and add a half scoop of new soil.

Tips

1. We found that having a small scoop next to the bin makes mixing and adding a lot easier.

2. If you have the space it would be handy to have a box of shredded paper and a small container of soil beside the bin.

3. Investigate what foods can and can't be composted indoors. It saves a lot of stress.

4. If the bin starts to smell it means the balance is off—you may need to add more newspaper or add extra holes.

5. You might want to have an extra bin on standby for when your old one gets full and hasn't completely broken down.

6. Give some thought to what you're going to do with your compost when it's done.

Think About It

(1) Do you think you could actually make a compost bin after reading this, or were there parts that confused you? How would you revise this tutorial to make it more user-friendly?

(2) What assumptions does the author make about readers, about what they do or want to do? Do you think that *you* would make a compost bin? Why or why not?

(3)   Why do you think that the tutorial uses the second person "you" to address
the reader? Do you find the use of "you" inviting? Why or why not?

Write About It

*Think of a particular handy skill that you have—everybody knows how to do some-
thing, whether it is repairing a broken lamp or crocheting a coaster. Using the preceding example for guidance, write a tutorial. As you plan your tutorial, think about who
your audience might be—other college students? People from you hometown? Your
circle of friends? Then, draft your tutorial, keeping your audience in mind: their skill
level, existing knowledge, and needs.*

WIKIHOW.COM   HOW TO FIGHT RACISM IN YOUR SCHOOL

This tutorial is published on the website WikiHow.com. *The website and its tutorials
are continually updated by a variety of authors. Like other wiki-based sites, such as*
Wikipedia, WikiHow *allows collaborative authorship—anyone can contribute an article or revise an existing article, following certain guidelines.*

Read About It

*As you read this tutorial, think about whether it would actually help someone to per-
form the task that the title promises it will perform. Note any part you found confusing
or unclear.*

Racism can become a major problem in a school. As a student, you may have to
deal with people who make hurtful remarks about your race. Just keep in mind that
these are about as meaningful as "You have cooties!" In scientific contexts, race is
considered nothing more than a social construct.

Steps

1. Stand up for yourself. If someone makes a racist comment, point out that race
   does not determine what kind of person one will become and what kind of life
   one will lead. You might remind the person about your good grades, abilities,
   or talents, despite your race "limitation."
2. Talk to your teacher, a principal, a head, or anyone like that. In some cases,
   discrimination of race is illegal. This would be an example of illegal discrimination: The cafeteria does not serve you lunch, even though you gave enough
   money, and they do this because of race.

3. Think about why the people are making these remarks to you. Do they appear to be jealous of you? Have they made racist comments to other students in your school as well? People who talk about race are often small-minded. They judge people before they get to even know them. Some people might be racist towards you simply because they do not like you or want you in their clique. There are mean people in the world who will have no particular reason for not liking you and will try to find something unkind to say to you.

4. Do not show your weakness. Try not to become emotional. Being emotional will make the people more likely to continue; they can see that your feelings are being hurt.

5. Ignore the hurtful remarks. This is the common target for antibullying. When the people see you ignoring them, they become bored of it and stop.

Tips

- Be tough. Hearing these remarks from other students may be upsetting, but try to dismiss them. They are unscientific and superficial.
- Go to another person who is being bullied. It is much more difficult to pick on more than one person.
- Tell someone whom you trust, such as a family member. He or she will probably be able to offer more advice.
- Do you believe these people? That hurts even more! Your personality isn't [determined] by the color of your skin, or a stereotype that has developed against your ethnicity!
- Talk to your school counselor—they will be able to help.
- Ignore them.
- Know who your real friends are and stick by them.

Warnings

- Do not harass the bully back. Doing so could get you in trouble and you would be in the wrong for bullying too.
- Think carefully before responding. Don't fight fire with fire. Be the better person! It is bad enough that the bully is being mean, but don't stoop to their level!

Think About It

(1)   You do not know who authored this tutorial—most likely it was written by multiple authors. How does this unknown authorship affect your opinion of the piece?

(2)   Do you find that the tutorial provides helpful advice? Why or why not? How would you revise it? What would you add or remove?

(3)   Who do you think the target audience of this tutorial is? Why?

Write About It

Go online and navigate to WikiHow.com. *Follow the directions for contributing a tutorial. You might write a new one, or revise an existing one. As always, keep your audience in mind when writing or revising your online tutorial.*

Reading Inquiries

MARK MONTGOMERY   VISITING COLLEGE CAMPUSES: OBSERVATIONS BY A PROFESSIONAL TOUR TAKER

Mark Montgomery is an educational consultant who helps students with college admissions. He wrote this blog post for his website, Montgomery Educational Consulting.

Read About It

In this blog post, Montgomery describes his observations while touring several college campuses in Minnesota. As you read, consider how the author uses specific, descriptive examples to bring his observations to life.

I spent a few days in Minnesota last week visiting colleges. My itinerary included (in alphabetical order) Augsburg College, Carleton College, Macalester College, University of Minnesota, and St. Olaf College.

Why do I spend so much time and money investing in college visits? So I can help you find the best college for you. I'm a matchmaker. I spend time to learn about you. I spend time learning about colleges. Then I can match you to the right place. But the subject of today's post is not about me. It's a list of observations that can help you get more out of your college visit.

ASK QUESTIONS. When I was at Macalester, it was preview day for admitted students. Scads of families wandering around campus in groups of three (one student, two parents). And tours left from the admissions office constantly all morning. So at any one time I could run between this tour and that one, listening in on the tour guides' patter and make some comparisons. I must have followed six different tours. Despite the constant refrain from the tour guides ("Do you have any questions?") virtually nobody asked any. If you don't know what questions to ask on a campus tour, look at this post of things you might consider asking.

DON'T LET THE PARENTS DO ALL THE TALKING. A word to the wise, folks. It's not a good idea for parents to ask all the questions. It makes the students look dorky and shy. It makes it seem that your parents are making this decision for you. I know it may feel uncomfortable in a group environment, but show some curiosity! You are considering investing four years of your life in a college, and to just follow a tour passively without engaging yourself is really a waste of time.

TAKE NOTES. I am constantly amazed that virtually no one on a college tour (except me) takes notes. This is a perfect job for a parent (let the student ask the questions, and the parents can be the silent scribes). Often I ask parents how many colleges they are visiting, and many cite double digit numbers. How can they keep it all straight? How can they make meaningful comparisons if they don't write down their impressions and discuss them afterwards? No one can possibly retain all the information divulged in a tour. While I do know that picking a college can have a "gut level" aspect to it, it's important to take notes to give yourself a "gut check" after the tour is over.

IGNORE THE WEATHER. It was raining in St. Paul the day I visited Macalester. Dreary. Cold. The weather can affect our moods, and it's important to keep that fact in mind when visiting a campus. Of course, you will want to consider climate when picking a college. For example, Minnesota's winters are not the same as Florida's. And you will want to take into account how the college is integrated into the environment (for example, St. Olaf has lots of skylights and enormous windows that let in tons of natural light—even on a frigid, winter morning, while Carleton—two miles away—has fewer windows, more classic "collegiate" architecture, and a less airy feel). But don't let the weather on a single day dampen your enthusiasm for a college that seems perfect in all other respects.

DON'T KILL (or HUG) the MESSENGER. Tour guides can be wonderful. Or awful. I really enjoyed my tour guide at St. Olaf. He was a funny, intelligent young man who showed his pride for St. Olaf without showing off. A few hours later, at Carleton, my tour guide was equally enthusiastic, but spent a good portion of the tour talking about herself. She came off as a smarty pants, and was much less helpful in communicating interest in her college. For example, when one prospective student declared her interest in art, the tour guide just pointed to the building. When the prospective student asked if we could take a short detour inside, the initial response was "it's not on the tour." But since she was the only student and I was also interested, I convinced the tour guide it was worth a quick look. It turned out that the tour guide had never been in that building before, and had never even looked into any of the art studios. The point is, some tour guides are great, and others are lousy. Don't judge the college by the quality of the tour guide.

TOURS ARE CAREFULLY CHOREOGRAPHED. It was fun to compare tours at Macalester. I could just hang out in the foyer of the library and wait for new tour groups to shuffle through. And for each tour, the guide's patter was virtually identical. Maybe the order in which the information was presented was different. But each guide used the same phrases. The same script. Keep in mind that every building, every stop on the tour has been carefully chosen by the director of admission to pique your interest and to show off all the positive aspects of the college. At all times you should be asking yourself, "what are they NOT showing me?" and "why did they pick this building and not that one over there?" The point is not to trip up the tour guide and hijack the tour. But once the tour is over, spend the time to investigate the corners of the campus you did NOT visit on the tour. For example, it's always a red flag for me when a tour does not stop at the library. Ordinarily, it should be the centerpiece of the intellectual life of the college. If the tour does not stop there, I know something is up. Perhaps it's ugly. Perhaps it's never used. Perhaps there is not enough study space. The point is that you have to look beyond the script and the choreography if you're really going to get the most out of your college visit.

I love visiting colleges. I learn a ton, and get a good feel for the campus geography, the "vibe" of the student body, and a sense of what it might be like to attend. But visiting is work, folks. Don't be a passive recipient of the college's party line. Investigate! Inquire!

Think About It

(1)   Did you tour campuses when you were deciding on a college? If so, do these notes resonate with your experience? What other notes would you add to the list? If you did not tour college campuses in person, what other tools did you use to help you decide on a college (such as the college website)? How would you add to this set of notes to reflect other ways of "touring" a college?

(2)   How would you describe the style of these observations? Are they informal or formal? What kind of vocabulary is used?

(3)   Do you think readers set to visit other types of colleges would find these observations interesting, or do they work best for readers visiting these particular colleges? Why?

Write About It

For a week, write down anything that strikes you as interesting, funny, or unique about your college. Then, pool your observation notes with your group. Select the best observations to publish as a blog post for an audience of potential students. What places should they be sure to visit if they come to your campus? How can they get the best sense of what college life is like at your campus—even if those are places that might not usually be featured on a tour?

VICTORIA SIMMONS   DEALING WITH DEPLOYMENT

Victoria Simmons is a homemaker whose husband serves in the United States Army. She published this entry on her blog, Mommy, Wife, & Everything Life, *in 2012, during her husband's first deployment.*

Read About It

As you read this blog entry, consider how it compares to a status update (Chapter 14). What elements of this blog entry make it seem like an informal report on the author's experience with deployment? What can other readers learn from this blog entry?

It's been a few weeks since my husband left. Honestly, I'm doing far better than I expected. Life goes on, even without constant communication with my hubby. The picture to the left was our last family picture for a while. It was such a bittersweet day.

I know that my husband enlisted to deploy. He hates sitting in garrison doing nothing. He compares it to being on the football team, but sitting the bench for every game. It just sucks (for him). I don't mind the view from the bench. Granted, I would hate to be the one sitting there, but I don't mind when he is. Of course, I'd rather have him be here with Adalin and me, but this is all part of the Army life. I had quite a bit of notice for this deployment, so I was much more mentally prepared than I expected. I definitely cried like a baby for a few days before he left, and for the first few days that he was gone. That was to be expected. The worst part was watching Jimmy say goodbye to Adalin. Knowing that he's missing so much doesn't make this any easier. Thankfully, she was sleeping when we said our last goodbyes so he just kissed her on the forehead, said his "I love you, Pumpkin," and walked away. Gosh, thinking about that moment is going to make me tear up. Moving on!

Much progress has been made already. I haven't cried in a few weeks. I am now visiting home, because I haven't been back here since last Christmas. I'm leaving to go back to Georgia next weekend, but I'll be back up here in Michigan again in December as long as Adalin doesn't have to have surgery then. I've been using my deployment countdown (I'll post a tutorial and pictures when I get back to GA) religiously. It has helped a ton. I'm such a visual person. I have about a million countdowns on my phone. I am doing a bunch for different holidays, the 25% mark, the half way mark, and days since he left/til he comes home. They are nice for me. I also use the "Donut of Misery" app on my phone (Android) that shows what percent you have completed, as well as a bunch of other statistics. I love numbers so it's great for me. I know that a lot of people struggle with that because they don't like seeing the "97% to go" (that's not how much I have left, following OPSEC), or the "286 days left." Even seeing "13 days done" (again not what we have done, OPSEC), can be overwhelming because we have a tendency to think, "That's it?! That's all we've got?! Ugh." I understand both sides, but I choose to think, "We've already got 13 days down! Woo hoo!"

We get to talk almost every day. We Skype a few times every week, and alternate between phone calls and just chatting on Facebook. We are so blessed with how amazing communication has been so far. I'm praying that it will continue to be this great throughout the whole deployment. I can't believe how fast the past few weeks have flown by. It just amazes me.

Overall, I try to keep positive as often as possible. I figure, there's no sense being upset over something you can't change. I'm hoping to keep this positive attitude going as long as possible. I've been doing great so far, it's definitely helping time fly by. God Bless ♥ Vi

Think About It

(1)   What different techniques does the writer use to describe her emotions? How does she try to bring them to life? Consider how she uses vivid language to describe her physical sensations, actions, and so on. Does she help you to picture the events as you read?

(2)   Who might be the main readers of this kind of blog? Why would those readers find this blog entry interesting or helpful?

(3)   Why do Internet media, like blogs, tend to encourage such personal reflections, on the one hand, yet also encourage writers to avoid giving out personal details, like names?

Write About It

Write a blog entry about a traumatic or emotional event in your own life. It could be a happy event, such as an important milestone or celebration, or a sad event, such as a funeral or separation. Try to use vivid language, like the writer does in this blog entry, to evoke the emotions you felt and to help readers picture the event.

RUTH BROWN   DIARY OF AN IMMIGRANT

In 2010, Ruth Brown wrote this blog entry for the Willamette Week, *a publication devoted to local news and events in the region of the Willamette Valley, home to Salem, Portland, and Eugene, Oregon. Brown is a journalist and writer from Melbourne, Australia, who moved to Portland, Oregon, in 2010.*

Read About It

Brown, an Australian, uses some words that might be less familiar to American readers than to Australians. As you read, highlight or jot down any words that seem to be more common to Australian English. Then, consider how those word choices contribute to the message of this piece.

I'm Ruth, the new *WW* music intern. For the last 24-odd years, I've lived in Melbourne, Australia. A little over a week ago, I chucked everything in to move halfway across the world to Portland.

I arrived in the country with little more than a backpack, a laptop and an "alien registration number," and have spent the last week trying to navigate my way through a new life in a new city in a new country.

It's more difficult because I don't *look* like an outsider (maybe fewer tattoos and piercing than the average Portlander, but give me time): I'm young, white, wearing Levis and Chucks and a messenger bag, with a coffee in one hand and an iPhone in the other. So I just seem a little bit "special" slowly holding up each individual coin to see what its value is when going to the grocery store, asking waiters things like "Uhm, what exactly is 'ranch dressing'?", and drawling out an incomprehensible "G'dayhowsitgoin'?" every time someone says hello.

And just about everyone in this country *does* say hello. The bus drivers, people in elevators, supermarket checkout chicks, military recruiters, security guards, the drifters who sleep under my building, buskers, maids. They all want to know how I am, and what I think of the weather, and where I'm going, and where I've been, and what I'm looking for, and if they can help me with anything.

Jan from New Seasons is very, very interested in how my first online grocery delivery went (two emails and three phone calls later, I'm not sure how much more I can tell her. The food arrived; I ate it; I didn't die). Derek from T-Mobile is desperate to know how I'm finding their mobile phone service (I am able to both make and receive calls. WHAT MORE DO YOU WANT TO KNOW, DEREK?). And the staff at Fred Meyers seemed genuinely sorry they didn't stock any of the items I required but were still *super keen* to know if I'd found everything OK. Some stores here actually seem to employ people just to stand at the door and say "hello." (Isn't there a recession on? Dear American businesses: I have discovered a simple yet effective way you can save yourselves some money. . . .)

Sunday I went to a pub to watch Australia get thrashed by Germany in the World Cup. I made my way through the sea of large blonde men (and even larger blonde women) holding pretzels and giant bier steins (no really) to the corner where a handful of gloomy-looking figures in green and gold were huddled over their stubbies (language lesson of the week: that's Aussie for "beer bottle"). We grunted "G'Day" then completely ignored each other for the following 93 minutes, after which we all grunted again and went on our merry ways.

I haven't felt so at home all week.

Think About It

(1)   Do you think readers of this publication would find these observations interesting? Who reads this publication, and would they find Brown's observations surprising? Why or why not?

(2)   How does Brown make her entry come alive? What kinds of details does she provide to do so?

(3)   Do you think Americans are really more likely to say hello? If so, what does this say about American culture more broadly? Do you think this holds true across the country, or just in certain regions?

Write About It

Think about a time you felt out of place somewhere (whether it was your first time at a new school, new job, or a different country). What did you notice about the people in this place and its habits or customs? Write a blog entry that points out a unique feature that people familiar with this place might not notice. Try to make your entry come alive with concrete details, as Brown does.

STEFANIE HOLLMICHEL   EATING ANIMALS

Stefanie Hollmichel posted these reading notes to her blog, So Many Books, *in 2010. Hollmichel is a librarian from Minneapolis, Minnesota, who began blogging about books in 2003.*

Read About It

These reading notes include several different types of observations about the book: facts from the book itself, the author's own reflections, and comments about the quality of the book. As you read, highlight or jot down each type of observation, and note your own opinion of how well they work together.

Jonathan Safran Foer's book *Eating Animals* is a carefully researched, well-balanced, and well-written book. I do, however, have to admit my bias. As a vegan who hasn't eaten meat or any animal product knowingly for 18 years (or is it 17? Without actually counting back and checking I can never remember so let's just say a very long time) Foer is admittedly preaching to the choir in my case. I wanted to read the book though because I wanted to know what he had to say, what his take on the matter was and how he approached the conveying of the terrible facts. I had to find out what he was saying so I could tell people to read his book or say how disappointing the book is in representing the cause. Read this book, especially if you eat animals.

Foer does not shy away from asking the big questions. Why do people eat animals? Why are some animals okay to eat and others not? For instance, what are your thoughts about eating dogs? If you cringe at the thought, why? What makes eating a dog different than eating a cow, pig, fish, chicken? All of them are animals, all of them feel pain and all of them have a sometimes surprising intelligence (did you know that fish pass on knowledge to younger generations?). Why do people who say they care about the environment and about animals continue to say it is okay to eat animals when, in the United States, about 99% of all meat comes from a factory farm (even the organic and free range varieties) where animals are kept in horrible conditions, regularly abused, pumped up with antibiotics and other drugs, and then slaughtered under conditions so inhumane that they are regularly still alive as they are being skinned or tossed into scalding vats of water.

The environmental toll of factory farming is tremendous. People who live near pig farms are constantly ill. If a person falls into a waste lagoon, they die within a few minutes. Animal waste from factory farms is not required by law to be treated like human waste is and it very often seeps into the ground and contaminates water and the surrounding area. Most, if not all the meat that comes from a factory farm is covered in fecal matter even if you can't see it. And people who have a 24-hour stomach bug/flu are actually suffering from food poisoning.

If that isn't threatening enough for a person's health, there is a global disease threat because of intensive animal farming. Not only are there antibiotic resistant diseases springing up because of the drug's use in animal farming, there is the influenza to worry about. Remember the swine flu? The virus didn't first appear in Mexico. It first appeared in the United States on a factory pig farm. Pig flu and bird flu can and do jump species and the swine flu, if I am remembering this from the book correctly, began as a bird flu that probably jumped to a person then recombined before jumping to pigs where it recombined again and jumped back to humans. This version of the swine flu was bad, but it wasn't as bad as it could have been. It will happen again with a different recombined flu virus and next time we might not be so lucky.

Of course Foer also takes us inside animal farms and slaughterhouses. There were times while I was reading that I had a hard time holding back the tears. I wanted to skip ahead, I didn't need to read this, I didn't need to "see." But I forced myself to keep reading because I wanted to know and I wanted to be able to talk about it with people who eat animals because everyone needs to know.

Foer became a dedicated vegetarian because of his research for this book and his wife and young son are also vegetarian. I'd be curious to know why he didn't go vegan. Even though I am already on Foer's side, he did challenge me by asking how, as somehow who does not eat meat can I sit down at a table with others who do? He suggests that even if you are vegetarian/vegan that remaining silent about the facts of eating animals implicates you in their suffering even if you don't eat them. In a way this is true. Ever since I became vegan I have been concerned about not being one of those in-your-face people. I was, and am, uncomfortable with it but I also didn't want to make people who eat animals uncomfortable. I have thought that being an example and politely answering questions was enough. But considering the global environmental and health impact, being silent is not enough. It's kind of like being a nonsmoker in a room with a bunch of smokers. I may not be smoking but I am breathing in the smoke secondhand. I may not eat animals but I am affected by the conditions created by those who do.

One of my coworkers, a vegetarian, is also reading this book and we had a conversation recently about how to talk with people who eat animals about their choices. Since Foer concludes his book talking about Thanksgiving and since Thanksgiving is next week, we asked, what would happen if we sat down to a dinner that had a big turkey in the middle of the table and we started talking about the horrible life of sickness and suffering that turkey had. I don't think we'd win any converts. In fact I think there would be a lot of resentment and anger at the dinner table. I don't know what Foer does in his personal life with the people he knows, but writing the book was one way he says he could not be that silent vegetarian. Well, I'm not going to write a book. This post is one way to not be silent but I doubt you would keep coming back if all I ever blogged about was how horrible eating animals is. I will have to find some other way and stop worrying about making my animal eating friends uncomfortable.

Think About It

(1)   The writer remarks upon how this book fits into her life—why she wanted to read it, how it relates to conversations she has had with friends, and how this book might help her to persuade others not to eat meat. Have you read any books that have fit into your life in that way?

(2)   Unlike the more formal genres you might write in school, these reading notes do not include specific quotations from the book or references to page numbers. Do you think those elements would have been helpful to you as a reader? Why? Or does this type of genre do something different that does not require specific references?

(3)   How would you describe the writer's ethos? Does the fact that she is herself a vegan (as she admits early on) make her seem more or less credible to you? Why?

Write About It

Write some informal reading notes about a book or article that your have read recently. Following Hollmichel's example, consider including information about the book as well as your own opinions or thoughts.

<hr>

STEVE BLANK   ELEVEN OBSERVATIONS ON WORKPLACE GENDER ROLES

Steve Blank originally posted these observations on his blog, and they were republished to Venurebeat.com, *a website dedicated to news about the technology industry. Blank is a retired entrepreneur who ran several companies in the high-tech industry, and he now teaches entrepreneurship at the college level.*

Read About It

As you read, think about how you might describe the persona (Chapter 21) the author takes in this article, with relation to his audience. How does the language he uses help to craft his persona? How do you react to this persona?

My two daughters are now in college and have put their toes in the working world with summer jobs. As they've grown older, they've heard their parents' advice about women in the workforce.

This post is not advice. Nor is it a recommendation of what you should do. It's simply my interpretation of what I have observed. Our circumstances were unique, times have changed, and your conclusions and opinions will most certainly differ.

When my girls were younger and started to play soccer, I used to remind them, "Make sure the people on the field aren't carrying sticks—because if they're playing field hockey while you're playing soccer, you're going to get hurt."

As they got older, they understood I wasn't only talking about sports but that I was trying to teach them how to figure out the rules of any game they were about to play— and that included the workplace.

My advice to our daughters about women in the workplace has been pretty simple:

- The language of business is about winners and losers. Bosses who read Sun Tzu's "The Art of War" as a guide to business strategy or "Leadership Secrets of Attila the Hun" are unlikely to create a culture of collaboration.
- There are implicit rules of competition and collaboration in companies. It's not that anyone is hiding a secret rulebook; it's just that no one has articulated the rules.

- In most companies, men set these rules. Again, nothing secret here, but men don't realize that they behave and think differently. They don't have to explain the rules to other men, so it never occurs to them to explain the rules to women.
- As women, they will be expected to perform to boy's rules as defined in their workplace: This means they need to spend the time understanding what the rules are in their company and industry. If they don't, they will find others who are less competent but more adept at playing the game getting promoted instead of them.
- Women can be equally competitive if they desire. It's not a question of competency, or a skill only boys have. If they want to succeed by competing, they can. They just have to learn the rules and practice them.
- Find mentors then become one. In every organization or industry there's someone who's figured out the rules. Seek them out and know what they know. By the time you do, it's your turn to mentor someone else.
- Collaboration can make you a stronger competitor. The irony is that organizations that collaborate are more effective competitors. When they reach a position of authority, use their instincts to build a fearsome organization/company.
- If they prefer to collaborate and don't want to play by boy's rules, they need to understand what their career choices are. There are plenty of other ways to be a productive member of society other than a position on a corporate org chart.
- Understanding the rules and career options doesn't mean the rules are right or they have to accept them as the only career choices. They can make change happen if they so desire. But they need to understand the personal costs of doing so.
- Some find the idea of gender differences uncomfortable. [. . .] Some simply won't accept that there are workplace gender differences.
- I may be wrong. Perhaps I misunderstood what I've seen or that time has changed the workplace significantly. Take this advice as a working hypothesis and see if it matches your experience.

Time will tell whether we gave our daughters good advice.

Think About It

(1) Early on, Blank says that he is only offering observations, not advice. Yet, he says he did give this advice to his own daughters. Do you think Blank is actually giving advice to readers—despite his warning? Why do you think he frames his piece as a set of observations, not advice?

(2) Do you agree with Blank's assessment of the workplace, and the ways his daughters (or presumably, female readers) should accommodate a workplace

run by men? Should women simply learn the rules and follow them, or else join a different profession? Or are there other possible courses of action?

(3)   Do you think there are "rules of the game" in the workplace, or in school, that women or men might be less likely to understand? Consider your own experiences in a workplace or school setting. Does your experience support Blank's observations? Can you think of any settings where males might be at a disadvantage if they do not recognize "the rules"?

Write About It

Think about a workplace or school setting with which you are familiar. Was there an unspoken set of rules that people were expected to follow? Write a set of observations that you might share with someone who does not know that place well.

Reading Analyses

MAX ABRAMS   IMMIGRANTS AND GALACTUS: JUNOT DIAZ'S WORLD IN *THE BRIEF WONDROUS LIFE OF OSCAR WAO* (EXCERPT)

Abrams authored this literary analysis on Junot Diaz's novel when he was student at Occidental College (in Los Angeles, CA). Occidental College publishes certain student research through an online database. This analysis was published in 2009 as part of a series of student research written for the Department of English and Comparative Literary Studies.

Read About It

In the following excerpt, from the beginning of Abrams's literary analysis, Abrams focuses on the language Diaz uses to compose his novel, what Abrams calls "a globalized discourse." As you read, note all the places where Abrams contrasts Diaz's use of language with "standard English" and the strategies that Abrams uses to do so.

Junot Diaz's *The Brief Wondrous Life of Oscar Wao* represents the new aesthetic of a globalized discourse. It is the story of a Dominican immigrant family and their trials throughout the decades. Oscar de Leon lives in New Jersey with his mother Beli and his older sister Lola. He is obsessed with comics and science fiction and as a result is not popular and has no luck with women. Diaz says at the opening of the book, "Our hero was not one of those Dominican cats everybody's always going on about" (p. 12). In a culture where he is expected to be highly masculine and [a] sexual dynamo, Oscar chooses to live his life with his comics and *Dungeons and Dragons.*

One might expect a typical immigrant story written in standard American English. However instead of adapting the dominant conventions of the western narrative, Diaz's novel is a mix of high and low culture, academia and pop, Spanish slang and standard English and everything in between. He does not privilege any one of these discourses over another. Diaz expresses the reality of the modern immigrant through a mix of images from all over the social spectrum. This collage breaks down the hierarchical structures implicit in the privileging of certain languages and cultural references. The narrative is disjointed, full of events with many interpretations, sometimes using language very few readers will understand. This creates a new reality, aware of itself as a result of history.

Oscar Wao is also the story of Trujillo's dictatorship in the Dominican Republic and the atrocities he committed. Diaz internalizes the mayhem done to the Dominican people so that he can joke and play with the facts. This creates a natural narrative that reflects the dialect and discussions of the time, while still educating the reader on the history of Trujillo. The fragmented history lesson, which is full of more hearsay than historical dates, better reflects the tragedy than past immigrant narratives. While many immigrant authors have adopted the dominant discourse of the official culture, which insists on a value judgment of language and information, Diaz brings all the references and stories he can to create a collage that more accurately reflects the modern multicultural world. This is no longer the self-contained, hierarchical pure first world narrative, but a new mixed up, disjointed aesthetic.

Marginalized communities deploy vernacular and slang to simultaneously express their unique reality and create a new one. Their world cannot be captured in "standard" English. Every marginalized community has invented new words or new uses for older words. Communities form a second language separate from the dominant primary one. The dominant society often appropriates the marginalized community's language for entertainment. This utilization can be seen in early 20th century Vaudeville Theater featuring the humor and language of the Jewish community or in the use of African-American slang in popular media today. However the validators of official culture usually do not encourage the use of slang, ranking people according to the way they speak. Those who use the vernacular of a supposed "lower" culture are separated out and often seen as outcasts. Classifying people according to their use of vernacular helps the dominant society retain power. Those who can reproduce the dominant discourse are seen as intelligent and worthy, while those who use a different vernacular are alienated. Society loses the benefit of multiple perspectives when those who do not conform to the standard language are ignored. Language becomes an organizing tool for the oppression of minority communities. The struggle for power is played out through the language practices of the society.

The language in literature has always been used to define "high and low" forms of art. Often the language of the immigrant is seen as a lower form of communication. This is true for the actual language of the country the immigrant is coming from (e.g., Spanish from the Dominican Republic) as well as the language developed by the immigrants in their communities (e.g., Spanglish slang used in Dominican areas of New Jersey and New York). These immigrant cultures have often been the victims of colonization and have to struggle to forge a new identity. While some try to maintain their previous traditions, others choose to adapt the language of their colonizers. Often the story of the immigrant turns into the plot theme of the victim. Books such as Amy Tan's *The Joy Luck Club* paint the picture of immigrants who are unable to fend for themselves. They are the victims and the world is responsible for their suffering. These books are written in standard American English and do not adapt the language and story arcs of their own culture. Instead of getting a multinational narrative, the reader receives a story that is written like a classic American tale, with characters from another culture.

Diaz does not adjust to accommodate the reader, but instead forces the reader to make meaning from all these discourses at the same time and see into his reality. The result is the subversion of the power hierarchy of knowledge. Cicero, Stan Lee, *The Sound of Music*, and Spanish slang are all written into the same sections, without privileging one over another. Instead of being preoccupied with Oscar's outsider status, the victim story of the immigrant, Diaz has demanded that his truth, his reality, is the central story. In the end, his use of multiple languages makes the novel a story of redemption and re-appropriation of power and agency for the Dominicans.

The narrator for the majority of *Oscar Wao* is Oscar's college roommate, Junior. His name is spelled Yunior in order to force the reader to pronounce his name the way the people in his community would. The reader must go into Diaz's world or not experience the book at all. Yunior serves as interpreter of what is going on. Through him, Diaz deploys a varied group of references and languages. These references often invoke the science fiction and fantasy worlds Oscar is interested in. When describing how physically weak Oscar is, Diaz will say he "had like a zero combat rating" (p. 15). This refers to the ratings a character may have in a role playing game, combat referring to their fighting skills. Although it is not imperative for the reader to know this to fully understand Oscar's life, these touches give dimension to Oscar's world. . . .

Think About It

(1)   What do you think is the main argument of the preceding analysis?

(2)   Abrams writes, "Marginalized communities deploy vernacular and slang to simultaneously express their unique reality and create a new one. Their world cannot be captured in 'standard' English. Every marginalized community has invented new words or new uses for older words. Communities form a second language separate from the dominant primary one." Where do you think that Abrams came by this information? Do you think that citations to sources or quotations from experts on language use would make this passage stronger? Why or why not?

(3)   Although Abrams discusses particular aspects of Diaz's novel throughout this excerpt, he only quotes the novel twice, in the first paragraph and the final paragraph. Do you think that more examples (quotations) from the novel would make this passage stronger? Why or why not?

Write About It

Select a short story to write a literary analysis about. Read the story carefully. Then, conduct database research (Chapter 24) and see if you can find any sources that discuss the author, the story, and/or any themes that arise in the story or techniques the author uses. Using these sources, write an analysis that contributes to an ongoing discussion about the author, the story, or the themes/techniques. Be sure to cite all of your sources accurately and to provide plenty of examples from the story itself.

CHRISTINA M. LAVECCHIA   OF PEERENTING, TROPHY WIVES, AND EFFEMINATE MEN: *MODERN FAMILY*'S SURPRISINGLY CONSERVATIVE REMEDIATION OF THE FAMILY SITCOM GENRE (EXCERPT)

LaVecchia's rhetorical analysis was published in the online magazine Harlot *in 2011. When this article was published, LaVecchia was a doctoral student in English at the University of Cincinnati.* Harlot, *whose subtitle reads "a revealing look at the arts of persuasion," publishes articles that study the rhetorics of everyday contexts, such as television.*

Read About It

As you read the well-organized rhetorical analysis that follows, write a brief reverse-outline in the margin (Chapter 20) to help you understand what each section of the analysis is doing. Once you have finished, see if the reverse-outline you wrote helps you answer the reading questions.

Toward the end of the aughts, network studio executives and producers began to fear that the family sitcom was dead. In 2009, *Los Angeles Times* entertainment staffer Scott Collins described the trend by writing, "Family comedy? Come on. Those things went out with 'Malcolm in the Middle.' Thanks to cable and the Internet, families today just don't watch TV together anymore." Instead, network producers decided that, "for the affluent viewers they sought, the workplace had become the new household, the cubicle the new bedroom and young careerist upstarts the precocious toddlers of the urban nursery" (Bellafante). It may be because of these popular and prevailing notions that, after the demise of *Arrested Development* in 2006, the only network sitcoms that found success were those that took place outside of the home: shows like *30 Rock*, *The Office*, and *Parks and Recreation* (Havrilesky).

Network producers have been left scratching their heads this past decade when trying to develop family programming. The vogue of the family sitcom genre was uncertain: not only did family sitcoms seem outdated and stale, but reality TV had (perplexingly) dominated ratings far longer than most had ever expected it to. *New York Times* reviewer Ginia Bellafante comments on this uncertainty:

> In recent years reality television has exerted an even more powerful force in displacing the genre, not simply because of its prevalence but also because its commitments to unchecked domestic lunacy render the entertainment value of mere dysfunction, the family sitcom's life-blood, obsolete.

Dramatized "reality" on TV was, in essence, out-crazying the family sitcom and normalizing the dysfunctional conflicts that drive the humor of shows like *Everybody Loves Raymond*, *Roseanne*, or *Malcolm in the Middle*. To many, it looked like the age of finding humor in the everyday, internal workings of the family was gone.

And yet, today the family sitcom endures. In 2009, Steve Levitan and Christopher Lloyd's *Modern Family* exploded onto the network scene and challenged notions that the sitcom was no longer a genre ripe for comedic insight and entertainment gold. In fact, says Collins, "the pilot tested so highly among focus groups that, in May [2009], ABC executives took the unusual step of screening the entire episode to a crowd of advertisers in New York, where it drew favorable reactions." The show and its popular characters were a surprise hit at the Emmys after the show's debut season, garnering wins for supporting actor Eric Stonestreet and outstanding writing while also upsetting *30 Rock*'s three-year winning streak for best comedy of the year. Its popular success and enviable ratings, declared Brian Stelter of the *New York Times*, are why the 2010 "sitcom blocks on CBS, ABC and NBC are looking more stable than they have in years" (" [In Bear Times]"). According to Tanner Stransky at *Entertainment Weekly*, the show has also inspired networks to develop a whole set of family sitcoms with non-normative families (that is, "Dad-driven family comedies") to follow in the successful footsteps of *Modern Family*'s first season.

***

As a product of the ambivalent media landscape that I've attempted to describe (which simultaneously declares the death of the family sitcom and yet finds it a still-bankable genre), *Modern Family* carries the promise to rebrand, revitalize, renew, and rethink the sitcom and bills itself as a show that depicts the unique situations encountered by a, well, modern family. The show follows three family units that make up one extended family.

At the head is no-nonsense patriarch Jay Pritchett, who re-married a much-younger Colombian bombshell named Gloria (also divorced) and became a stepfather to her son, Manny. Jay's daughter, Claire Dunphy, is a homemaker who wears the proverbial pants in her nuclear family, which also includes her goofball husband Phil and three children: ditzy Haley, brainy Alex, and dunce-like Luke. Jay's other son, Mitchell Pritchett, is an uptight lawyer who, along with his gay partner Cameron Tucker, adopts a Vietnamese baby girl (Lily) in the series pilot.

At first glance, *Modern Family* look like it delivers a new and different kind of family sitcom, as implied by its title. In a network TV milieu largely dominated by heteronormative nuclear families, *Modern Family*'s portrayal of a May-December romance and an adoptive gay couple seems downright revolutionary.

However, the all-out genre transformation touted by *Modern Family* seems more like a mild genre remediation in actual execution. That is, although *Modern Family* promises to deliver a new, more provocative kind of family program, the show falls short of actually challenging our expectations for how families work. In the end, *Modern Family* delivers a non-normative family that still functions with normative family dynamics. While its conservative play on the family sitcom genre has led to the show's commercial and critical success, it has hindered *Modern Family*'s ability to say, "Sayonara!" to conventional gender and familial roles: the show works because, in actuality, its "modern" families largely function in ways that ultimately reinforce the status quo.

***

The term remediation, as I see it in this context, means representing key components from an old form in a new one: the old and new are different in form, yet they are closely linked. Because I see the show as reinforcing familial and gender roles (not subverting them), I argue that *Modern Family* is a prime example of remediation. That is, while its format and style deviate from many earlier family shows—its families look "different" and it recasts traditional family sitcom tropes with a new twist—*Modern Family* still bears a strong resemblance to these earlier shows because its families function in ways that strongly resonate with more conservative ones.

The concept of remediation has long been applied to new media discussions. In *Writing Space*, Jay David Bolter describes the theory of remediation he developed in collaboration with Richard Grusin and, he examines the ways in which new media "define themselves by borrowing from, paying homage to, critiquing, and refashioning their predecessors" (24). In other words, remediation means that new media, genres, and modes are closely linked to—indeed, even still entwined with—their predecessors. When considering invention and beginnings in his book *Genre & the Invention of the Writer: Reconsidering the Place of Invention in Composition*, Anis Bawarshi writes that texts have no "stable origin": writers and texts are "always building on, always adding to other writers and texts" (ix). This intertextuality, I think, is also applicable to remediating genres: the new form and the old form are always in dialogue with each other and responding to other texts, whether consciously or not.

***

One feature of the show that makes it obviously different from its predecessors in the genre is the format. There is no laugh track or studio audience, and punch lines are often delivered with a deadpan understatement. Taking cues from other mockumentary-style comedies like *The Office*, *Modern Family* uses documentary camera angles and reality-TV style confessionals in place of traditional close cuts and pans. Indeed, the characters are obviously aware of a camera or cameraman's presence during episodes, and they even look directly into the camera on occasion. This creates "a disconcerting aside that has the effect of making the viewer feel both like a part of the family and an observer" (Feiler). According to Bruce Feiler at the *New York Times*, this mockumentary style is a first for a family program. Last, the show is also unique in its embracement of technology, which has such a pronounced presence

> that nearly every scene is refracted through a digital funhouse: an iPad screen, a cellphone camera, a baby monitor, a YouTube video. Characters spend half their time glancing past one another rather than communicating directly.
>
> "We used to talk about how cellphones killed the sitcom because no one ever goes to anyone's house anymore," said Abraham Higginbotham, a writer on the show. "You don't have to walk into Rachel and Ross's house, because you can call and say, 'Hey, what's up?' We embrace technology so it's part of the story." (Feiler)

These developments certainly demonstrate a break from the genre, and do signify that *Modern Family* is doing something different in an attempt to reflect contemporary culture. However, other aspects of the show's format, like its story arc, seem to more closely align it with earlier shows. For instance, "in nearly every 22-minute episode, the music swells in the 19th minute, any conflict gets resolved, and a tidy embrace ensues" (Feiler). While these resolutions are often less tidy than those on earlier shows like *Full House*, *Family Matters*, and *Home Improvement*—staples of my childhood, where characters always had honest conversations and children received heart-warming lectures from their parents or siblings in the last two minutes of the show—because sometimes things go unsaid or full truths are not revealed, there is always such a moment at the end of each episode. And often, these resolutions take place at family meetings or gatherings.

Feiler sees the nineteenth-minute resolution as a measure of the show's resonance with contemporary culture, but I see it as evidence of *Modern Family*'s strong resemblance to those nineties sitcoms of yore. The show resists breaking from a narrative structure that gives the audience a satisfying resolution and reinforces the centrality of the family unit. Further, the use of these end resolutions in each episode (usually accompanied by a character confessional voiceover) also give the show a platform for working with internal dynamics, reinforcing traditional family values like the importance of communication, understanding, support, or family togetherness.

***

The clearest links between the old and new—traditional sitcoms and *Modern Family*—can be seen in familial roles and relationships on the show. What seems to have earned the show most of its critical acclaim and cultural currency is its reflection of our own experiences of "assigned roles, inherited patterns of relating and invisible rules" within families (Clyman). This can be seen in the passive-aggressive behaviors, marital mis-communications, sibling bickering, and goofy dad buffoonery that fill episodes of *Modern Family*. Gloria, for instance, is a master of the art of passive-aggressive behavior. In Season 2, Episode 2, a frustrated Gloria retaliates at Jay for teasing her about her beliefs about the dead.

Pretending that ridiculous behaviors are part of her "culture," Gloria successfully embarrasses Jay by convincing him to slap the chicken she is preparing for their meal. Though the scene's premise relies on edgier ethnic jokes than many other shows might attempt, the behaviors that constitute the real substance of the scene could be straight out of any other family sitcom.

Although *Modern Family* might seem poised to redefine the assigned relationship roles in, expectations for, and communication within the heteronormative family—and does occasionally succeed at this—the relationships portrayed in the show feel remarkably familiar.

Take also, for instance, the strikingly heteronormative dynamics at play in the Pritchett-Tucker family composed of Mitchell, his partner Cameron, and their adopted daughter Lily. Although on the surface they represent the so-called "twenty-first century gay family," Cam and Mitch actually play two extremely gender-normative roles—roles it seems that the show has taken pains to concretely define.

Though [Mitch is] also an affectionate father, his identity is so closely tied to his career that the briefest of hiatuses from his job (which he quit in Season 1, Episode 17 because it was interfering with his family time) is enough to make him frantic to return just three episodes later (Season 1, Episode 20). The flamboyant Cam describes himself as the "stay-at-home Dad/trophy wife" and embraces the role of overprotective mother to their daughter Lily. Cam is Lily's primary caregiver, and the show makes it clear that he represents the mother figure in the Pritchett-Tucker household. For instance, he spends much of the episode in a hypervigilant watch over Lily's baby monitor, saying, "I'm like a mother bear. When I hear my cub crying, I have to run to her" (Season 1, Episode 11).

Through such portrayals, the show implies that a "modern" gay family must still identify with and embrace gender-normative roles of breadwinner and caregiver. More ambiguous roles of shared responsibility, either for earning the family's income or raising their child, are not seen in the Pritchett-Tucker household—nor, it should be said, in the heterosexual Pritchett or Dunphy households. All three households are structured around heterosexual arrangements. It seems that perhaps the show only remediates our idealized, heteronormative vision of what families look like, and not their actual function. That is, although *Modern Family* challenges our traditional notions of what constitutes a family with immigrant trophy wives and gay partners, the families in *Modern Family* still seem to fill familial and gender roles in much the same way as they did in more "conservative" predecessors. . . .

References

Bawarshi, Anis. *Genre and the Invention of the Writer: Reconsidering the Place of Invention in Composition*. Logan: Utah State UP, 2003. Print.

Bellafante, Ginia. " 'I'm the Cool Dad' and Other Debatable Dispatches from the Home Front." *NYTimes.com*. New York Times Company. 23 Sept 2009. Web. 6 Dec 2010.

Bolter, Jay David. *Writing Space: Computers, Hypertext, and the Remediation of Print*. 2nd ed. Mahwah, NJ: Lawrence Erlbaum, 2001. Print.

Clyman, Jeremy. "The Dynamics of a 'Modern Family'." *Reel Therapy Blog, Psychology Today*. Sussex. 11 Apr 2010. Web. 15 Nov 2010.

Collins, Scott. "A Reunion with the Family Sitcom." *LATimes.com*. Los Angeles Times. 20 September 2009. Web. 26 Mar 2011.

Feiler, Bruce. "What 'Modern Family' Says About Modern Families." *NYTimes.com*. New York Times Company. 21 Jan 2011. Web. 27 March 2010.

Havrilesky, Heather. " 'Parenthood' Fumbles, 'Modern Family' Triumphs." *Salon.com*. Salon Media Group. 13 Mar 2010. Web. 15 Nov 2010.

"In Bear Times, a Bull Market for Sitcoms." *NYTimes.com*. New York Times Company. 16 Apr 2010. Web. 4 Dec 2010.

Stelter, Brian. "A 'Family' Celebration at the Emmys." *NYTimes.com*. New York Times Company. 30 Aug 2010. Web. 6 Dec 2010.

Stransky, Tanner. "The 'Modern Family' Effect." *EW.com*. Entertainment Weekly. 15 Oct 2010. Web. 4 Dec 2010.

Think About It

(1)   Track down the main argument of LaVecchia's analysis; she states it plainly. Now that you have a grasp of her argument, do you believe that she has proven her argument with the evidence that she has provided? Why or why not?

(2)   How does LaVecchia use an analysis of the technical aspects of television filming to prove her point?

(3)   How does LaVecchia use specific examples from the show to prove her point? Does she provide adequate examples as evidence?

Write About It

What other shows on television today reinforce family stereotypes? Select one of these shows and perform a rhetorical analysis of the aspects of the show that maintain existing family structures (such as those described by LaVecchia).

DEBARATI BANDYOPADHYAY   NEGOTIATING BORDERS OF CULTURE: JHUMPA LAHIRI'S FICTION (EXCERPT)

This literary analysis appeared in the Journal of Literature, Culture and Media Studies *in 2009. Debarati Bandyopadhyay earned her Ph.D. in English from Calcutta University (in India) in 2004. Jhumpa Lahiri, the author whose work is the subject of this article, is an Indian American author (born in 1967) who won the Pulitzer Prize in 2000.*

Read About It

In the first paragraph that follows, the author sets forth the purpose of her literary analysis: "It is this movement [in Lahiri's fiction] across continents and cultures that I intend to map here." As you read this analysis, note places where the author points out movement, travel, and borders, both actual (such as borders of nations) and metaphorical (such as borders of cultures).

In *Indian English Literature : A Critical Survey 1980–2000*, M. K. Naik and Shyamala A. Narain praise Jhumpa Lahiri for creating "history in becoming the first Indian author to win [the] prestigious Pulitzer Prize in the USA for her collection of short stories, *Interpreter of Maladies.*" (1999: 36) Though Jhumpa Lahiri belongs to the second generation of an Indian family abroad, she retains her links with India even today, as amply proved by her subsequent work in the form of a critically-acclaimed novel, *The Namesake* (2003). In her work, Indians going abroad negotiate the borders and fringes of a foreign society in various ways and seek to establish their identity on alien shores. It is this movement across continents and cultures that I intend to map here.

Negotiating borders, moving across continents and the seven seas, when an individual in search of a better life reaches the First World, how does he assimilate himself with the citizens of the host nation? Is the process of such assimilation or its opposite—dissension—different in the case of men, women and children? This question arises because the response of Ashima in *The Namesake* is different from that of her children Gogol and Sonali, to the socio-cultural conditions of life in the USA, born as she is in Calcutta. Similarly there [are] different responses to life in the USA in the case of various characters in the collection of stories [. . .] *Interpreter of Maladies* reveals. Conflict between distinct cultural backgrounds and regular encounters between different worldviews shape the emotional life of the diaspora even in multi-ethnic, multicultural societies like India and the USA.

Culture suggests the arts, customs and institutions of a certain people or nation, thereby helping us to distinguish a certain group of people from others and one nation from another. It also helps in the burgeoning of a distinct national identity among its citizens. Multiculturalism in the context of one nation's experience of vicissitudes appears to institutionalize another way of expressing that nation's cultural identity. In Jhumpa Lahiri's fiction, Indian roots and American life, or, to be more precise, at least in the case of *The Namesake*, Calcutta on the one hand, and Cambridge and New York on the other, provide readers with different paradigms of life among people representing distinct cultures and worldviews. It is in this context, however, that we ought to remember Edward Said's scepticism with the concept of culture as something distinctive, representative of and exclusive to a certain group or nation in *Culture and Imperialism* (1993) so as to understand the basic problem with such terms. Said writes:

> Culture is a concept that includes a refining and elevating element, each society's reservoir of the best that has been known and thought, as Matthew Arnold put it in the 1860s. Arnold believed that culture palliates, if it does not altogether neutralize, the ravages of a modern, aggressive, mercantile and brutalizing urban experience . . . . In time culture comes to be associated, often aggressively, with the nation or the state; this differentiates "us" from "them," almost always with some degree of xenophobia. Culture in this sense is a source of identity, and a rather combative one at that. . . . (xiii)

Against this concept of culture as a homogenization of the good, patriotic attributes of a nation for the sake of exclusiveness, and creation and preservation of an identity, Said mentions "multiculturalism" and "hybridity" next, in order to praise their "permissiveness" and "relatively liberal philosophies" (xiv). In the case of Jhumpa Lahiri's characters, a search for their origin, finding a place or a nation that may be called one's own and belonging to either the Indian subcontinent or the USA, or, in other words, making a choice between the concepts of cultural identity and multiculturalism seem to remain juxtaposed always.

"Multiculturalism" suggests the coexistence of a number of different cultures. It does not prescribe homogenization and conformity directly, nor does it encourage overtly different ethnic, religious, lingual or racial constituents of a particular society to denigrate and alienate each other to such an extent that the fragile balance of such a society is damaged or destroyed permanently. It is at a transitional point between two hemispheres—East and West—and two segments of the world hierarchy—Third and First—or, the Indian subcontinent and the USA, that we may locate most of Jhumpa Lahiri's fictional world. India with her concept of "unity in diversity" and the USA as the melting pot of cultures and races, coexist in her fiction.

[. . .]

Though Jhumpa Lahiri has been living away from Bengal for the largest part of her life, in "When Mr. Pirzada Came to Dine," it is [. . .] yearning for one's homeland that finds expression. Mr. Pirzada, in the crucial days of 1971, comes to the [. . .] US home [of Lilia's] Bengali parents to dine and gradually, more important[ly], to listen to the news of the birth pangs of Bangladesh: "At six-thirty, which was when the national news began, my father raised the volume and adjusted the antennas." (31) Lilia's Indian parents and Mr. Pirzada [. . .] watch their "national news" of mass destruction avidly. In contrast, Lilia, born in the USA (in her mother's "estimation," unlike herself, and also her husband) is assured of an easy life during which she would never be compelled to eat "rationed food, or obey curfews, or watch riots from . . . rooftop, or hide neighbors in water tanks to prevent them from being shot." (26–27) And the price paid for this in the US is the limits imposed upon young Lilia's aware-ness of the non-US parts of the world:

> No one at school talked about the war followed so faithfully in my living room. We continued to study the American Revolution, and learned about the injustices of taxation without representation, and memorized passages from the Declaration of Independence. During recess the boys would divide in two groups . . . Redcoats against the colonies. (32–33)

While Lilia learns about [the] U.S. Declaration of Independence, East Pakistan's struggle to become independent as a nation is, ironically, neglected completely. Mr. Pirzada, the newcomer, separated from his wife and seven daughters, for whom he remained anxious throughout this period, must have yearned to return to his own country. Yet, like Lilia's parents, he graciously accommodates US celebrations into his life by helping Lilia celebrate Halloween like a typical American child. In contrast, when in the school library, Lilia finds and begins to read a book contain-ing a few pages on Dacca [the capital of Bangladesh], her teacher acts decisively:

> Mrs. Kenyon emerged . . . and lifted the book by the tip of its spine as if it were a hair clinging to my sweater. She glanced at the cover, then at me.
> "Is this book a part of your report, Lilia?"
> "No, Mrs. Kenyon."
> "Then I see no reason to consult," she said, replacing it in the slim gap on the shelf. "Do you?" (33)

This reading of Lahiri's short story reveals that though the author herself was born in London and grew up in Rhode Island, USA, yet she has Bengali parents and even celebrated her marriage in the Bengali manner and continues to write about both the countries, both the continents, thereby expressing the emotions that dis-turb all expatriate artists. Brati Biswas quotes Lahiri's words from an internet con-versation: "I began writing fiction seriously, my first attempts . . . were always set in Calcutta. . . . I learned to observe things as an outsider, and yet I also knew that as different as Calcutta is from Rhode Island, I belonged there in some fundamental way . . . " (187). Lahiri points out clearly in this conversation that though she lives in the USA and visits Calcutta as well as India from time to time she feels a sense of belonging here "in the ways I did not seem to belong in the United States" (187). It is in this sense that Suman Bala chooses to consider her as "an expatriate Indian writer . . . [who] stands in the same category as that of V.S. Naipaul, whom Bharati Mukherjee calls an Indian expatriate writer" (11).

However, in Lahiri's fiction the readers are constantly being invited to cross over from India to the USA along with the characters. Against a panoramic background of journeys—not merely in terms of physical and career relocation as in the case of Mrs. Sen in a short story and Ashoke in *The Namesake*, but also emotional, leaving behind permanent fault-lines marking rupture and patching up. The minute details representing socio-cultural parameters for acceptance and rejection stand out conspicuously. Amalgamation of typically Indian incidents and their American counterparts in detail help us to compare and contrast two different cultural patterns. In the first story in her collection, "A Temporary Matter," Lahiri begins by creating a typically Indian situation at the very centre of the USA, namely, that of power-cut [a power blackout]. Of course, where in the USA it is only a temporary matter and the local consumers receive notice and ample time for preparing for the situation, in India it is not so, as Shoba points out in the darkness lit up with candles: "It's like India. . . . Sometimes the current disappears for hours at a stretch. I once had to attend an entire rice ceremony in the dark. The baby just cried and cried. It must have been so hot" (11).

In this case, Lahiri makes the distinction quite vivid, but a mere hint can sometimes alert the readers to these situations that mark India and the USA as so far apart. For instance, in the same story, when Shoba used to go shopping [in the U.S.], she could be found "arguing under the morning sun with boys too young to shave but already missing teeth. . . . During the drive back home, as the car curved along the Charles [River, in Boston], they invariably marveled at how much food they'd bought" (7).

It is not the hint of violence in lower class life in the USA in the pre-adolescen[t] group but the other suggestion that links India with the American way of life by means of contrast. In the case of Boorima in "A Real Durwan," a refugee in Calcutta from East Pakistan, who had to work throughout the day in an apartment building full of middle to lower-middle class families in her old age, a time comes when her old bedding gets wet and turns into useless pulp. [Boorima must] sleep on discarded newspapers spread over a hard floor, and she does not even get a glass of tea or any food from the apartment owners. Suffering from pangs of hunger,

> Reed broom in [hand], sari smeared with newspaper ink, she wandered through markets and began spending her life savings on small treats: today a packet of puffed rice. . . . The next day she walked . . . to the produce markets in Bow Bazar. It was there . . . that she felt something tugging on the free end of her sari. When she looked . . . the rest of her life savings . . . were gone. (81)

Boorima had already lost not only her country of origin but her family and all her possessions. Now she loses all means of survival. The subtle hints localizing Shoba along the Charles and Boorima at Bowbazar suggest the yawning gap that exists between the old woman's starvation and Shoba's ability to purchase astonishingly rich food, both in quality and quantity, thereby indicating the nature of Lahiri's awareness of the socio-economic divide between First and Third World countries. . . .

References

Bala, Suman. 2002. "Jhumpa Lahiri: The Master Storyteller," *Jhumpa Lahiri: The Master. Storyteller: A Critical Response to* Interpreter of Maladies, ed. Suman Bala. New Delhi: Khosla.

Biswas, Brati. 2002. " 'Beyond' Ethnicity: A Study of *Interpreter of Maladies*," *Jhumpa Lahiri: The Master Storyteller: A Critical Response to* Interpreter of Maladies, ed. Suman Bala. New Delhi: Khosla.

Lahiri, Jhumpa. 1999. *Interpreter of Maladies*. New Delhi: Harper Collins.
——2003. *The Namesake*. London: Flamingo-Harper Collins.
Naik, M. K., and Shyamala A. Narayan. 2001. *Indian English Literature 1980–2000: A Critical Survey*. Delhi: Pencraft.
Said, Edward W. 1993. *Culture and Imperialism*. London: Vintage.

Think About It

(1)   The author describes "culture" as "the arts, customs and institutions of a certain people or nation, thereby helping us to distinguish a certain group of people from others and one nation from another." How does the author use this concept of culture to interpret the work of Lahiri?

(2)   The author writes, "[I]n Lahiri's fiction the readers are constantly being invited to cross over from India to the USA along with the characters." What are some examples of this cross-over that the author provides?

(3)   What does the author hope to prove with the story of Boorima (toward the end of the analysis)?

Write About It

Select one of Jhumpa Lahiri's short stories and read it carefully. You can find several of Lahiri's short stories, such as "Brotherly Love" and "Hell-Heaven," at the New Yorker *website (http://www.newyorker.com). Using Bandyopadhyay's analysis as a source, write a short literary analysis of the story. Be sure to properly cite (Chapter 28) both Lahiri and Bandyopadhyay.*

GREG BOONE   GLOBALIZING KOREA: A RHETORIC OF FOOD

This rhetorical analysis was published on the website and blog Harms-Boone Productions (harmesboone.org). At the time this piece was published, the blog was maintained by two teachers, Greg Boone (the author of the analysis) and Danielle Harms.

Read About It

This piece analyzes the persuasive strategies of the Korean food industry. As you read, note the different types of persuasive strategies that the author, Boone, examines.

Daniel Gray, a *Seoul Eats* food blogger, recently published an op-ed in the *Korea Herald* regarding the public and private efforts to export Korean culture to the West—particularly to the United States. With coverage from the *New York Times*, *CNN*, and other high profile news organizations in the US, the government seems to be doing a fair job of gaining the attention of Western eyes, and now is focusing on making Korean food America's Next Top Asian Cuisine.

Gray argues that Seoul should focus on which specific foods to export to different parts of the world, and how to market those foods abroad. He writes:

> Take the full page "Bibimbap" advertisement that was in the *New York Times* on Dec. 21. First of all, I applaud the Korean show "Infinite Challenge" for the initiative. The ad had a great headline: "How about Bibimbap for lunch today?" There was a gorgeous picture and they gave the phone numbers of several Korean restaurants in New York.
>
> The text is what I have a problem with: "It is said that this dish came from the customers of memorial service and rural villages. This dish is very convenient to provide, just mixing of cooked rice with various vegetables, namul, and red pepper paste together."
>
> First of all, death (customers of memorial service) doesn't arouse my appetite and non-Korean speakers will not know what "namul" is. It was a great idea, just poor execution.
>
> The way that Koreans market Korean food for Koreans will not work overseas. Korea's "four seasons," "well-being," "good-for-health," "kimchi," and the "5 colors" will not convince the average person to try Korean food.

Awkward language aside, this ad is problematic for more reasons than Gray's analysis reveals. Gray claims that the primary reason certain Korean foods will not catch on in the states and elsewhere is the taste and textures of the foods. It is true that some cultures are naturally more open to certain foods than others. For example, Gray writes about a series of interviews his company, O'ngo Food Communications, did with foreigners regarding their favorite Korean foods. His research, apparently, "found that many French people liked chicken and ginseng soup." They said it reminded them of a popular French dish: *poule au pot*. Gray believes that these results lead to the obvious conclusion that certain foods export across cultures better than others. While that may certainly be true, it is a myopic analysis that isolates food from the larger context of the food's cultural origin. The problem is not exclusively a taste issue, though that is certainly part, and cultural differences do determine what tastes "good" to people. So far, Korea has failed to recognize how their culture fits within another culture. That is, more than anything else, Korean companies have a rhetorical problem, not an attracting people into restaurants problem.

[. . .]

Think Global, Act Local

Salmon is right when he argues that the so-called "international" market research done by many food companies and the Korean government is insufficient and ignores the fact that not all foreigners are created equal. He writes,

> When testing perceptions of the international community, it needs to be done—as a general rule—on subjects outside Korea, rather than those

who are already here, who have in-built knowledge that the wider world will not. The latter approach results in misleading findings, and sets marketing strategies off on the wrong foot from day one.

If the Korean government and the Korean people are serious about exporting their food, they need to remove the blinders and think beyond their own borders. Gray is likewise correct when he writes about how terrible the Bibimbap advertisement in the *New York Times* was, but it is not just because death does not arouse an appetite in, at least, Americans. It is because death, dying, and funerals are not thought of in the same way in American culture as they are in Korean culture.

In the US there is a funeral ritual, and the deceased are respected and honored, but Korean culture has a totally different set of cultural properties associated with death and the dead. Americans do not, for example, have a three day holiday dedicated to paying homage to ancestors as Koreans do—Chuseok. There are no rules about serving food to dead people, nor are there colors in which we may not write someone's name without casting a death wish upon them. It may be the case that Bibimbap has a history of being food served to "customers of memorial services," but in the U.S. funeral food is not exactly a culinary delicacy. In addition, in modern Korea the rice and veggie "casserole" is everywhere, and there are plenty of ways to market it to Americans. It's a hearty bowl of rice, whatever vegetables are around, and a special sauce that makes it just spicy enough to give it some kick. It's a meal that's perfect for "carbing up" before a run or hike.

This is not to say that Seoul should surrender Korean values and tradition in order for its products to cross the Pacific. If Seoul is serious about selling Bibimbap—or any other Korean food—to Americans, however, it must meet Americans on their turf. Seoul needs to show Americans what they've been missing; how Korean food fits into the existing culture in the United States. This is hardly a new idea. When American companies export their products overseas, it comes with adjustments for the local culture. McDonald's for example, (it's worth noting here that a commentator on *Seoul Eats* made a similar argument) sells products in nearly every country in which it exists that are simply unavailable in the US—Curry Chicken McNuggets in China, bulgogi burgers in Korea, and beer in parts of Europe. It is no surprise, then, that McDonald's is wildly successful in Korea and other countries around the world. If Seoul does not account for other local traditions and culture when attempting to globalize their food, it simply will not work.

A Rhetoric of Food

It is obvious to many foreigners living in Korea that Koreans have a great deal of pride in their language, culture, and country. To see a country the size of Indiana set such an ambitious goal as to export their food all over the world is truly admirable. Seoul must change its strategy to realize this goal, however. The Korean government and private companies must target specific groups of Americans and determine what will cause them to add their neighborhood Korean restaurant to the list of places they frequent. Korean food already fits into the melting pot of the United States.

While some foods are totally foreign to American tongues, a lot of Korean food is similar to other Asian cuisines. Mandoo is nearly the same as Chinese dumplings, or wontons, and the noodle soups are similar to Chinese noodle soups that are already popular. A staple of Korean dining, the banchan are essentially side dishes, something Americans already know, love, and will even pay a premium to eat. Americans love grilling, and they love drinking while doing it—give them a restaurant in which they can do both, in a foreign and exotic environment, and you can play to American ideas of being worldly and cultured while engaging them in something familiar, something with which they can already identify. There is definitely a place for Korean barbecue in the United States, there is a place for tteokbokki, bibimbap, kalguksu, and there is a huge place for banchan and makgeolli, but Americans do not know it yet.

One of the best ways to promote Korean food in American culture might be to use the million or so foreigners in Korea to promote Korean food in their homelands. Maybe Seoul could set up a system offering grants, loans, or support to teachers who want to start up a Korean restaurant once they return home. As evidenced by the quantity and content of food blogs in Korea, there are many foreigners with strong opinions about Korean food. They are already semi-experts on Korean food—or at least more so than anyone else in the US—and they are also experts on the culture of their homeland, thus making them perfect candidates for promoting and selling Korean food and culture to the masses.

There are foreigners living in Korea who love Korean food. Some avoid it, but the majority are likely somewhere in the middle, with a few favorite dishes, and a few dishes they rarely touch. The best thing Seoul could do to promote Korean food is to get the foreigners into Korean restaurants upon repatriation, and to bring their friends and money with them. The bottom line is that food, like other parts of culture, is an idea unique to that culture. When it comes down to it, Seoul's goal is rhetorical. It is about finding a way for Americans to identify with Korean food.

In *A Rhetoric of Motives*, Kenneth Burke introduced the idea of identification as a significant part of rhetoric. He argued it is not enough to think about rhetoric as the ways someone might persuade an audience. Because we are born divided people (or cultures, for the purpose of this article), we strive to mitigate that division by joining with others that share our interests and values. Persuasion is driven by this intrinsic need to join with others, or have others join with us so that we may find some cohesion within the social order or hierarchy in which we find ourselves as individuals. In order to successfully export Korean food, Seoul needs to persuade Americans to accept Korean food into their existing social order, and it must do that by playing to the motives and ideas that Americans already share with each other, and with Koreans. As Burke might say, Seoul's rhetorical problem is persuading Americans that the two cultures are both "joined and separate."

Sources:

Burke, Kenneth. *A Rhetoric of Motives*. Berkeley: University of California Press, 1969.

Gray, Daniel. "How Not to Globalize Korean Food," *Seoul Eats*. 02 February 2010. http://www.seouleats.com/2010/02/how-not-to-globalize-korean-food.html accessed 5 May 2010.

Gray, Daniel. "Food for Thought, Misconceptions about Food Bloggers and About *Seoul Eats.*" *Seoul Eats.* 21 February 2010. http://www.seouleats.com/2010/02/food-for-thought-misconceptions-about.html accessed 5 May 2010.

Quigley, Brooke L., " 'Identification' as a Key Term in Burke's Rhetorical Theory," *American Communication Journal.* Vol. 1, Issue 3, May 1998. Accessed online: http://www.acjournal.org/holdings/vol1/iss3/burke/quigley.html 5 May 2010.

Think About It

(1)   Boone presents his main argument this way: "[M]ore than anything else, Korean companies have a rhetorical problem, not an attracting people into restaurants problem." In what ways is the problem "rhetorical," according to Boone?

(2)   How would you describe the "rhetoric of food"? In what ways can food be "rhetorical"? Think about the audiences of food, and the ways that food can "make a statement."

(3)   Toward the end, Boone writes, "When it comes down to it, Seoul's goal is rhetorical. It is about finding a way for Americans to identify with Korean food." What does Boone mean by "identify with"? How can a person "identify with" food?

Write About It

Select an American fast food chain restaurant that you are familiar with. Look at the restaurant's menu, advertising campaigns, and even the architecture and locations of its restaurants. Write a rhetorical analysis in which you identify the targeted audience(s) of the restaurant and the ways that the restaurant creates "identification" with that audience.

ROY PETER CLARK   WHY IT WORKED: A RHETORICAL ANALYSIS OF OBAMA'S SPEECH ON RACE

Clark published this rhetorical analysis on Poynter.org in 2008, a few weeks after then-candidate Barack Obama delivered his speech on race on March 18, 2008. Clark is a writing teacher; Poynter.org is the web site of the Poynter Institute, a journalism school.

Read About It

Before reading this rhetorical analysis, download a transcript of Obama's speech on race, "A More Perfect Union," and read it. Or listen to the speech or watch a video of it (it can be easily found online at websites such as YouTube.com*). As you read the following analysis, ask yourself whether you agree with Clark's assessment of the speech.*

More than a century ago, scholar and journalist W.E.B. DuBois wrote a single paragraph about how race is experienced in America. I have learned more from those 112 words than from most book-length studies of the subject:

> After the Egyptian and Indian, the Greek and Roman, the Teuton and Mongolian, the Negro is a sort of seventh son, born with a veil, and gifted with second-sight in this American world, a world which yields him no true self-consciousness, but only lets him see himself through the revelation of the other world. It is a peculiar sensation, this double-consciousness, this sense of always looking at one's self through the eyes of others, of measuring one's soul by the tape of a world that looks on in amused contempt and pity. One ever feels his two-ness,—an American, a Negro; two souls, two thoughts, two unreconciled strivings; two warring ideals in one dark body, whose dogged strength alone keeps it from being torn asunder.

Much has been said about the power and brilliance of Barack Obama's March 18 speech on race, even by some of his detractors. The focus has been on the orator's willingness to say things in public about race that are rarely spoken at all, even in private, and his expressed desire to move the country to a new and better place. There has also been attention to the immediate purpose of the speech, which was to reassure white voters that they had nothing to fear from the congregant of a fiery African-American pastor, the Rev. Jeremiah Wright.

Amid all the commentary, I have yet to see an X-Ray reading of the text that would make visible the rhetorical strategies that the orator and authors used so effectively. When received in the ear, these effects breeze through us like a harmonious song. When inspected with the eye, these moves become more apparent, like reading a piece of sheet music for a difficult song and finally recognizing the chord changes.

Such analysis, while interesting in itself, might be little more than a scholarly curiosity if we were not so concerned with the language issues of political discourse. The popular opinion is that our current president [George W. Bush], though plain spoken, is clumsy with language. Fair or not, this perception has produced a hope that our next president will be a more powerful communicator, a Kennedy or Reagan, perhaps, who can use language less as a way to signal ideology and more as a means to bring the disparate parts of the nation together. Journalists need to pay closer attention to political language than ever before.

Like most memorable pieces of oratory, Obama's speech sounds better than it reads. We have no way of knowing if that was true of Lincoln's Gettysburg Address, but it is certainly true of Dr. King's "I Have a Dream" speech. If you doubt this assertion, test it out. Read the speech and then experience it in its original setting recited by his soulful voice.

The effectiveness of Obama's speech rests upon four related rhetorical strategies:

1. The power of allusion and its patriotic associations.
2. The oratorical resonance of parallel constructions.
3. The "two-ness" of the texture, to use DuBois's useful term.
4. His ability to include himself as a character in a narrative about race.

Allusion

Part of what made Dr. King's speech resonate, not just for black people, but for some whites, was its framing of racial equality in familiar patriotic terms: "This will be the day when all of God's children will be able to sing with new meaning, 'My country 'tis of thee, sweet land of liberty of thee I sing. Land where my fathers died, land of the pilgrim's pride, from every mountainside, let freedom ring.'" What follows, of course, is King's great litany of iconic topography that carries listeners across the American landscape: "Let freedom ring from the snowcapped Rockies of Colorado! . . ."

In this tradition, Obama begins with "We the people, in order to form a more perfect union," a quote from the Constitution that becomes a recurring refrain linking the parts of the speech. What comes next is "Two hundred and twenty-one years ago," an opening that places him in the tradition of Lincoln at Gettysburg and Dr. King at the Lincoln Memorial: "Five score years ago."

On the first page, Obama mentions the words democracy, Declaration of Independence, Philadelphia convention, 1787, the colonies, the founders, the Constitution, liberty, justice, citizenship under the law, parchment, equal, free, prosperous, and the presidency. It is not as well known as it should be that many black leaders, including Dr. King, use two different modes of discourse when addressing white vs. black audiences, an ignorance that has led to some of the hysteria over some of Rev. Wright's comments.

Obama's patriotic lexicon is meant to comfort white ears and soothe white fears. What keeps the speech from falling into a pandering sea of slogans is language that reveals, not the ideals, but the failures of the American experiment: "It was stained by this nation's original sin of slavery, a question that divided the colonies and brought the convention to a stalemate until the founders chose to allow the slave trade to continue for at least twenty more years, and to leave any final resolution to future generations." And "what would be needed were Americans in successive generations who were willing to do their part . . . to narrow that gap between the promise of our ideals and the reality of their time."

Lest a dark vision of America disillusion potential voters, Obama returns to familiar evocations of national history, ideals, and language:

"Out of many, we are truly one."
"survived a Depression."
"a man who served his country"
"on a path of a more perfect union"
"a full measure of justice"

"the immigrant trying to feed his family"
"where our union grows stronger"
"a band of patriots signed that document."

Parallelism

At the risk of calling to mind the worst memories of grammar class, I invoke the wisdom that parallel constructions help authors and orators make meaning memorable. To remember how parallelism works, think of equal terms to express equal ideas. So Dr. King dreamed that one day his four children "will not be judged by the color of their skin but by the content of their character." (By the content of their character is parallel to by the color of their skin.)

Back to Obama: "This was one of the tasks we set forth at the beginning of this campaign—to continue the long march of those who came before us, a march for a more just, more equal, more free, more caring and more prosperous America." If you are counting, that's five parallel phrases among 43 words.

And there are many more:

". . . we may not have come from the same place, but we all want to move in the same direction."

"So when they are told to bus their children to a school across town; when they hear that an African America is getting an advantage in landing a good job or a spot in a good college because of an injustice that they themselves never committed; when they're told that their fears about crime in urban neighborhoods are somehow prejudiced, resentment builds over time."

". . . embracing the burdens of our past without becoming victims of our past."

Two-ness

I could argue that Obama's speech is a meditation upon DuBois' theory of a dual experience of race in America. There is no mention of DuBois or two-ness, but it is all there in the texture. In fact, once you begin the search, it is remarkable how many examples of two-ness shine through:

"through protests and struggles"
"on the streets and in the courts"
"through civil war and civil disobedience"
"I am the son of a black man from Kenya and a white woman from Kansas."
"white and black"
"black and brown"
"best schools . . . poorest nations"
"too black or not black enough"
"the doctor and the welfare mom"
"the model student and the former gang-banger..."
"raucous laughter and sometimes bawdy humor"
"political correctness or reverse racism"
"your dreams do not have to come at the expense of my dreams"

Such language manages to create both tension and balance and, without being excessively messianic, permits Obama to present himself as the bridge builder, the reconciler of America's racial divide.

Autobiography

There is an obnoxious tendency among political candidates to frame their life story as a struggle against poverty or hard circumstances. As satirist Stephen Colbert once noted of presidential candidates, it is not enough to be an average millionaire. To appeal to populist instincts it becomes de rigueur to be descended from "goat turd farmers" in France.

Without dwelling on it, Obama reminds us that his father was black and his mother white, that he came from Kenya, but she came from Kansas: "I am married to a black American who carries within her the blood of slave and slave owners—an inheritance we pass on to our two precious daughters. I have brothers, sisters, nieces, nephews, uncles, and cousins, of every race and every hue, scattered across three continents, and for as long as I live, I will never forget that in no other country on Earth is my story even possible."

The word "story" is [a] revealing one, for it is always the candidate's job (as both responsibility and ploy) to describe himself or herself as a character in a story of his or her own making. In speeches, as in homilies, stories almost always carry the weight of parable, with moral lessons to be drawn.

Most memorable, of course, is the story at the end of the speech—which is why it appears at the end. It is the story of Ashley Baia, a young, white, Obama volunteer from South Carolina, whose family was so poor she convinced her mother that her favorite meal was a mustard and relish sandwich.

"Anyway, Ashley finishes her story and then goes around the room and asks everyone else why they're supporting the campaign. They all have different stories and reasons. Many bring up a specific issue. And finally they come to this elderly black man who's been sitting there quietly the entire time. . . . He simply says to everyone in the room, 'I am here because of Ashley.'"

During most of the 20th century, demagogues, especially in the South, gained political traction by pitting working class whites and blacks against each other. How fitting, then, that Obama's story points in the opposite direction through an old black man who feels a young white woman's pain.

Think About It

(1) Clark argues that "Obama's patriotic lexicon is meant to comfort white ears and soothe white fears." Do you agree with this assessment? Why or why not? Do you think that Obama's tactic worked?

(2) Based on this rhetorical analysis, do you believe that Clark feels favorably toward Obama? Why or why not? What parts of the text lead you to this conclusion?

(3)   Clark compares Obama's speech to three famous figures from history: W.E.B. Du Bois, Abraham Lincoln, and Martin Luther King, Jr. What effect do you think this comparison is meant to have on readers?

Write About It

Clark writes that, for political candidates, "The word 'story' is [a] revealing one, for it is always the candidate's job (as both responsibility and ploy) to describe himself or herself as a character in a story of his or her own making." Select three speeches delivered by a political candidate during a recent campaign. Using those three speeches, write a rhetorical analysis of the "story" that the candidate is attempting to tell about himself or herself.

Reading Reviews

LAUREN HONEYCUTT   *A MIDSUMMER NIGHT'S DREAM* AT HOWARD COMMUNITY COLLEGE'S THEATRE PROGRAM AND STUDENT ARTS COLLECTIVE

Lauren Honeycutt wrote this performance review in 2011 for the Maryland Theatre Guide, *a website that highlights upcoming plays, profiles local actors, and provides news about theater events in the region. Honeycutt is a regular contributor to the* Maryland Theatre Guide.

Read About It

This review is about a well-known play, William Shakespeare's A Midsummer Night's Dream. *Some readers of the review will know the play well, but others will not have read or seen it. As you read, think about how the author addresses these different readers' needs. Does the author provide sufficient information about the plot, without overwhelming those who are familiar with the play?*

"Love looks not with the eyes but with the mind. . . ." While this quote from *A Midsummer Night's Dream* may apply to the play's characters, the Arts Collective at Howard Community College's production of this Shakespearean classic is a treat to both the eyes and the mind, and I certainly walked out of the theatre exclaiming, "I loved it!"

Expertly directed by Grace Anastasiadis, *A Midsummer Night's Dream* tells the stories of four couples, some of whom are already in love and some who have not realized that they should be in love. As the Duke of Athens Theseus (Keilyn Durrel Jones) and his beloved Hippolyta (Jillianne Grabau) prepare for their upcoming wedding, they are approached by a distraught Hermia (Rachael Sinnott), who wishes to marry her true love Lysander (Chris Sisson) and not her mother's choice Demetrius (John Sisson). Hermia's good friend Helena (Katie Tyler) would gladly take Demetrius off of Hermia's hands, but he will have nothing to do with Helena. Lysander, Demetrius, Hermia and Helena find themselves in the woods just at the same time as the Fairy King Oberon (also played by Jones) is feuding with his wife Titania (Grabau). Since Oberon has already assigned his servant Puck (Matt Winer) to use a love potion to play a trick on Titania, he suggests that Puck also use some of the potion to bring happiness to the unhappy Athenian couples. But, as with every Shakespeare play, things do not go as swimmingly as Oberon has planned.

Jones and Grabau are beautifully regal as the royal couples of both Athens and the Fairy Realm. There is a clear chemistry between the two that is apparent with every look and movement. Sinnott encaptures the dreamy Hermia, but what is even more impressive is her feisty side that comes out during an argument with Helena later in the show, as Hermia hurls herself at her enemy and must be held back by Demetrius and Lysander. In their roles as Demetrius and Lysander, John Sisson and Chris Sisson do well with their lines and blocking, but they lack the passion needed for such gallant noblemen. As the Rude Mechanicals, a traveling theatre troupe, Thomas Matera, Ashanti Cooper, Brendan O'Donnell, Melissa Paper, Jessica Welch and Keri Eastridge bring many laughs from the audience, and their performance at Theseus and Hippolyta's wedding is truly a "comedy of errors."

The two actors that steal the show are Katie Tyler and Matt Winer. Tyler's fiery Helena literally throws herself at Demetrius (even to the point of clinging to his back and leg), and she perfectly delivers every comical line. Winer's Puck is truly the "shrewd and knavish sprite" who lithely hops from toe to toe as he sprinkles love potion in the eyes of Titania and the Athenians. His facial expressions let the audience know that his character is constantly up to something mischievous, and his laugh is of one that is truly mad.

When walking into the theatre, I gasped at the beauty of the set and lighting. Set Designer Ryan Haase and Lighting Designer Terry Cobb's teamwork allows a set composed of a simple rotating centerpiece to be easily transformed from the palace in Athens to the Realm of the Fairies. When in Athens, Cobb's lights create the outline of buildings and fences in shadows on the back wall, but the shadows turn to those of tree branches when the characters enter the forest. Columns on either side of the stage are appropriate for Athens but double as trees in the forest. One of the most enchanting parts of the set is the strands of crystal beads that hang from above, showing both the elegance of Athens and the whimsy of the Fairy Realm. Erin Drum's sound also helps to create the scene with the addition of tinkling music and insect sound effects whenever the characters enter the forest.

Designed by Nicole McClam and Jessica Welch, the costumes are perfectly suited to the settings, both in color and style. Most of the Athenians wear white robes and togas trimmed with delicate embroidery. In the forest, the fairies are indeed magical in their pink, blue and green costumes, each one created with a gauzy or satin sparkly fabric.

Puck declares, "Lord, what fools these mortals be!" Do not be a foolish mortal—get thee to Howard Community College and see this show!

Running time: 90 minutes with no intermission.

A Midsummer Night's Dream plays through August 14th in the Smith Theatre in The Peter and Elizabeth Horowitz Visual and Performing Arts Center—at Howard Community College—10901 Little Patuxent Parkway, in Columbia, MD. To order tickets, call (555) 518-1500 or order them online.

Think About It

(1)   How is this review organized? What are the main elements of the play that the reviewer addresses in her review?

(2)   In addition to describing the play itself, Honeycutt offers some of her own impressions. Can you point to these in the review? Do you find these personal reflections effective? Did you expect to find them in this genre?

(3)   As you read this review, can you picture the actors and scenes on the stage? If so, what strategies does Honeycutt use to accomplish this? What elements of the play does she describe?

Write About It

Honeycutt writes a glowing review of this play. It is clear from this review that she liked the play very much. Think about a play or movie you have seen recently that you strongly disliked. Write a review of the play or movie, considering how you might modify elements of Honeycutt's review to suit your own purposes.

CHRIS BENDEREV   IN CHILDHOOD, WHEN "I WISH" EQUALS AN ACTION PLAN

Chris Benderev wrote this film review for National Public Radio (NPR) in 2012. Benderev is a production assistant at NPR. Benderev studied Japanese in high school and college, and he also visited Japan when he was a teenager.

Read About It

This film review is written for (mostly) American readers, but it deals with a film that was shot in Japan. As you read, consider how Benderev tries to connect his audience to a film that deals with a different culture and language. How does he make the film relevant to American readers?

When you're young, there's just so much to misunderstand about the world. And isn't that kind of what makes it such fun?

Hirokazu Kore-eda's film *I Wish* is designed to make us long for the misadventures of childhood by giving us another set of ups and downs to follow: the tribulations of Koichi Osako, a 12-year-old Japanese boy with a plan to reunite his family.

Things begin with Koichi (Koki Maeda) casting a sullen gaze at the active volcano that touches—quite literally—everything in his new hometown. The ash it spews 24-7 coats houses inside and out with a constant reminder of the possibility of a molten doom. You begin to wonder if the director is giving us a line into the Japanese psyche, battered by centuries of natural disasters.

But for Koichi, the volcanic dust doesn't tap into ancient history. It simply reminds him of the past six months, which have been miserable. His parents' divorce split the family in half, and he pines day and night to somehow undo what's already done. For now, though, Koichi lives with his mother in Kagoshima, an unfamiliar city he can't stand. His younger brother Ryu (Oshiro Maeda, Koki's real-life younger brother) is under the care of their father in Fukuoka, a couple of hours north by train.

As it happens, trains will figure heavily into Koichi's plan for family unity, which he only hatches in full one day at school upon overhearing a secret about *kiseki*, or miracles. Any wish you have will come true, his classmate explains with scientific certainty, if you wish it closely enough to the spot where two bullet trains pass each other for the first time. Koichi remembers that a new rail line is set to debut nearby, and suddenly he has his mission.

The narrative centers mostly on Koichi's trip to this miraculous train-passing zone, which will require backup (his brother and their friends), along with means (there are more loose coins than you'd think under Japan's vending machines) and a strong alibi for skipping class (it helps to get the school nurse on your side).

Kore-eda wants us to remember the way in which children desire the outlandish and impossible, so he gives them the majority of the screen time here. It's a decision that pays great dividends. The Maedas—a comedic duo by trade—pair well as the straight man and the jokester; Koki's Koichi is businesslike in every pursuit, while Oshiro's Ryu, who wears a constant grin and is prone to chasing dragonflies, tends to live so blissfully in the present that he can't be bothered with intricate schemes.

When Koichi and Ryu don't see eye to eye, the tension percolates believably beneath their dialogue. They're honest while navigating around their conflicts, just like real brothers might be. Of course maybe that's because they are, but it takes talented performers to make casting brothers as brothers come off as a smart—not simplistic—choice.

Kore-eda got his start in documentaries, and he treats the children in this film more like autonomous subjects than like actors. They weren't given scripts; instead, he fed them their lines on filming days. Do that, and you're bound to wind up with glitches of bad timing and jokes that fall flat. *I Wish* is no exception, but more often than not Kore-eda's technique creates space for something truly special in a film: kids talking like kids.

The film invites us into the world of a child in more ways than one, though. The director scores life in suburban Japan mostly with bouncy, playful tones and quirky instrumentation. The lighting feels true to life; no one's manufacturing ominous auras.

Kore-eda has a true talent for the "show, don't tell" method, letting the story unspool over long periods with minimal dialogue. Applied to subplots like Koichi's grandfather's burgeoning cake business, that can grow tiresome. But when the action picks up, his documentarian sensibilities engage. Then it's terrific fun as his wobbly camera rushes to keep up with our young band of adventurers.

Each of the seven children (Koichi, Ryu and their trusty sidekick friends) brings his or her own wish for the train-passing. Maybe that's one or two too many; it's hard to root equally for some of the peripheral characters. Still, it's the scenes where the kids gather into a circle and share their aspirations—competing with a cartoon superhero, marrying the fetching school nurse—in which Kore-eda succeeds in bottling the energy of that cusp between magical possibility and adulthood. It's a tiny miracle that we're allowed to revisit it here.

Think About It

(1)   Benderev focuses much of his review on the choices the director, Kore-eda, made. Which of the director's choices does Benderev find effective, and which ones does he find ineffective? Do you find Benderev's focus on the director's decisions to be helpful to you as a reader?

(2)   What elements of the film does Benderev choose to highlight in his review? Are there any elements he leaves out that you would like to know about?

(3)   Does this review make you want to see the film? Why or why not? What did the author of the review do, or what could he have done, to make you interested in the film?

Write About It

Benderev writes that this film deals with "the way in which children desire the outlandish and impossible." Write a review of a recent book or film that deals with the subject of childhood. Use Benderev's review and the film reviews in Chapter 9 as examples.

ANDY WEBSTER   **LIVING ALONG A CONTENTIOUS BORDER**

Andy Webster wrote this film review in 2011 for the New York Times. *Webster is a film critic who writes regularly for the* Times.

Read About It

In 2011, a number of U.S. states passed controversial immigration reform laws limiting rights for illegal immigrants, while others were arguing for reforms to make it easier for illegal immigrants to work and attend school legally. How does this film review reflect or participate in that debate?

A rich opportunity is squandered with "Laredoans Speak," a documentary of laudable aspirations suffering from its pronounced sympathies. There is a great, balanced report waiting to be assembled that gathers opinions in an American border city with Mexico and presents a range of political perspectives. Such a cross-section is not seen in this film, an unabashed appeal for immigration policy reform.

That point of view—articulated by its interview subjects, including Raul G. Salinas, Laredo's mayor; Congressman Henry Cuellar, a Democrat from Texas; Juan Garza, a former sheriff for Webb County, Tex.; and most eloquently, Robbie Greenblum, an immigration lawyer (now chief of staff to the mayor of San Antonio)—is entirely understandable. There are many reasons to revise United States immigration policy: the willingness of Mexicans to perform back-breaking farm labor that many Americans won't touch for the same pay; the length of time it takes to process citizenship applications; the imposing barrier arising from the Secure Fence Act of 2006.

But thorny issues like the Mexican crime cartels and America's voracious appetite for drugs are only briefly addressed; a spokesman for United States Customs and Border Protection offers the one remotely conservative opinion. The disgust toward the United States expressed by an anonymous coyote (a trafficker of illegal immigrants) doesn't help. Nor do the sanctimonious intonations of the credited host, the actor and motivational speaker Pepe Serna. Yes, immigrants made the United States great, as most New Yorkers know. And sound reform is urgently needed. But not another shot of the Statue of Liberty and pious recitation of Emma Lazarus's "New Colossus."

Think About It

(1)   Webster's review is largely critical of the film. What is his overall claim about the film, and when does he introduce it? Did you find this placement of his claim to be effective or ineffective?

(2)   What details does Webster provide about the documentary itself? As a reader, did you want to know more about the documentary? What else might Webster have addressed?

(3)   While this item appeared in the film review section of the *Times*, it might also be read as an argument regarding immigration reform. What argument do you think the author is making?

Write About It

Write a short review that is critical of a film, book, or performance. Then, write a positive review of the same film or book. See whether you draw on the same criteria for each review, or whether you need to change your criteria to evaluate the film differently.

· ·

ANDY FRANCIS   BOOK REVIEW: *THE OMNIVORE'S DILEMMA*

Andy Francis wrote this book review about The Omnivore's Dilemma, *a popular book by Michael Pollan, for his blog* The Francis Blog. *Here, Francis regularly shares his reviews of books, television shows, and music, along with other posts about current events.*

Read About It

Book reviews are typically written for readers who have not yet read the book in question. As you read, consider whether Francis' description of the book addresses your needs and interests. Does the review provide too much information—so much that you do not feel like you need to read the book itself? Or does it make you want to read the book itself so that you can learn more?

Michael Pollan's *The Omnivore's Dilemma* is a fascinating journey through the American food system, one that manages to tell a story and ask Big Questions about why we eat what we do, while simultaneously providing a wealth of information about the sources, costs, ethics, and politics that drive our decisions on what to have for dinner every night.

Pollan divides the book into three sections, each about a different sector of our food supply (Industrial, Organic, Hunter/Gatherer), concluding each with a meal representing his adventures within that particular food chain (two in the case of Organic). It's a clever way to structure the book, one that allows him to put such a far-ranging topic ("Food") under one roof and draw parallels and contrasts as he goes.

First up is Industrial, certainly the most enlightening and unnerving section of the book. I suspect that anyone who reads this portion of *The Omnivore's Dilemma* will take a serious look at where their own food supply comes from, because the hidden nutritional and environmental costs of processed food are so great. As Pollan writes, you either change your mind because you know the dark nature of the system, or you choose to ignore it. Most Americans choose the latter, of course, and what they're choosing in Pollan's telling is a system of poor health, driven by our increasing reliance on petroleum and corn to produce food that appears inexpensive on the surface but actually comes with a wide variety of unadvertised externalities. Among the characters he follows in this section is 534, a corn-fed steer he purchases and follows from birth through fattening and eventually death (though he's obviously not allowed in the slaughterhouse). If I wasn't already a vegetarian, this part of the book would have me leaning that way. Pollan concludes the section with a fast-food drive through McDonald's, which he somewhat predictably disdains. I agree with him totally on the drawbacks of the Industrial food chain epitomized by McDonald's, but he could have at least acknowledged that McDonald's actually tastes pretty good at times.

Even if you don't read this entire book, this section is well worth your time—Pollan's command of facts and ability to marshal them into a narrative is remarkable, and this is a subject about which people should be far better educated. In his follow-up book, *In Defense of Food*, he adopts the mantra: "Eat food. Mostly plants. Not a lot."—this work lays the foundation for that view quite nicely.

Second is Organic, which actually consists of two segments: Big Organic and Local Organic. Pollan talks about the origins of the organic food movement as a counterculture hippie thing and how today a lot of it has adopted the economic logic of conventional Industrial farming while there are still those who practice it in its more idealized, local, environment-friendly state. It's a distinction worth drawing, though I think he's a bit too dismissive of the positives that even Big Organic brings to the table. In some sense, it reminded me a bit of Saturn, a company that was supposed to change the mentality and culture of GM but instead the reverse happened. Yes, the major Organic companies can be loose with their definitions of "free-range" (with the USDA's complicity), and have indeed strayed from the original spirit of organic, but they've also taken a shitload of pesticides and chemicals out of the food supply, which seems to me an unalloyed positive.

Pollan spends considerable time at Polyface Farms, a remarkable self-sufficient organic farm in Virginia led by a feisty "christian libertarian" fellow named Joel Salatin. The chief difference Pollan outlines here, and something I hadn't really thought about before, is what the real driving forces are (and should be) in a food production system. In our modern Industrial farming supply, it's largely petroleum energy (through both fertilizer production and transportation) growing mountains of federally-subsidized surplus corn that basically supports everything else we eat.

In the organic model, as practiced by Polyface, it's solar energy harnessed by grass and other vegetables, turned into protein by animals. It's certainly a more logical way to produce food, but the question Pollan doesn't spend enough time on is: on how large of a scale it can be done? There are seven billion people on Earth, and as fascinating and innovative as Salatin and Polyface Farms are, one has to wonder how practical it is for everybody.

Salatin himself gets a bit tiresome with his anti-government haranguing and god-loving, and even Pollan seems exhausted with him at times (even though he keeps quoting Salatin), but his farm seems really neat and inventive. Pollan clearly sees Salatin's products as a terrific answer to his question "what should we eat for dinner?," perhaps one of the reasons he isn't more on the Big Organic bandwagon. You can tell as you're reading where he's going to fall on the organic debate, but I suppose that's OK. Either way, his presentation of the biological science (he keeps trying to contrast "science" and "biology" as if they were opposites) is really interesting, particularly his treatment of the easily-overlooked natural staple that is Grass.

The author spends a couple of chapters here experimenting with vegetarianism, though this venture is clouded by his openly stated desire not to be a vegetarian. In scientific terms, he's biasing the experiment, working backwards from conclusions, and instead of highlighting the positives of the lifestyle, he seems more interested in evaluating it vis-a-vis the ethical arguments of Peter Singer. I think this section would have been more interesting had Pollan actually approached it with an open mind.

Pollan closes the Organic section with meals from store-bought Organic and from (at, in fact) Polyface Farms, giving the former much higher marks than Industrial and the latter higher still. Predictable, though undoubtedly well-argued.

The final section finds Pollan preparing a meal consisting entirely of food he grew, found, or hunted. Here I must make an admission: I skimmed this section rather quickly because I had to get the book back to the library. I think I still owe the CPL $0.10. I did read his conclusions and the chapter about the meal he prepared at the end with mushrooms he picked, veggies he grew (and sometimes grabbed off of neighbors' trees), and some animal (a lamb?) he killed. He calls this "The Perfect Meal," and I just can't go there. He admits himself that it's wholly impractical and that it wasn't even necessarily the best food, so why still call it that? He sees it as perfect in the connection he makes with nature and his fellow man through this most direct of food production systems, and I guess I just didn't identify with that.

The most revealing thing that Pollan presents in this book is that the three food systems he outlines can be characterized best by the length of the food chain supporting each one. The Industrial food chain is comically (tragically?) long and complex, with numerous "value-added" steps and inputs, leading to disastrous consequences everywhere. It kind of makes me annoyed that Fritos are as good as they are.

The Organic chain, particularly the one epitomized by Polyface's intensively farmed model, is far shorter and logical. Sun powers vegetables and particularly grass, which powers ruminant animals like cows, and . . . that's it. Sun, grass, cow, food. I'll be the first to admit that my advocacy of vegetarianism rests considerably (though not entirely) on the environmental unsustainability of meat production and that this abbreviated food chain removes quite a bit of that motivation. A grass-fed arrangement also alleviates some of the herbivore's concern over the health aspects of carnivorosity, a word I just made up, and animal rights as well, given the considerably better treatment a cow gets at Polyface than at a "confined animal feeding operation," which is an actual thing.

The Hunter/Gatherer chain is less a chain than a link: you pick something up and eat it. Sadly, I don't see much food lying around the streets of Cleveland.

Overall, I highly recommend *The Omnivore's Dilemma*. Pollan is a masterful writer, and the subject matter is something that should be of deep importance and interest for all of us. I might question his advocacy and angles on certain topics a bit, but that doesn't change the fact that this book is painstakingly researched, expertly written, and comprises numerous examples of nonfiction storytelling at its finest.

Think About It

(1) This text performs the purpose of a book review but appears as a blog entry (Chapter 7). Which elements of this text do you think reflect the genre of a book review, and which reflect the format of a blog? Make a list of elements or features that might reflect each genre. Would you consider this a mixed genre (part blog, part review)? Or does it seem more like one of those genres?

(2) The author not only provides his personal opinions about the book, but connects the book's theme and contents to his own shopping and eating habits. Do you find this effective? Why or why not?

(3) Write a reverse outline of the review (Chapter 22). How would you describe the organization of the review?

Write About It

In this review, Francis provides both positive and negative comments about Pollan's book. Write a review of a book, film, or performance in which you take a similar approach, describing your reactions (both positive and negative) for interested readers.

SUSAN YUDT   SMART GIRLS AT THE PARTY

Susan Yudt, an editorial consultant from Portland, Oregon, has managed several nonprofit websites and worked with web companies such as Netflix and Rolling Stone .com. She also serves as a board member for the Girls Rock Institute, which organizes camps and other programs that help girls learn about and practice music in all genres.

Read About It

This review appears on a website called Common Sense Media, *which regularly publishes website reviews. As you read through this review, see if you can identify the audience and purpose for the review and guess at the audience and purpose for* Common Sense Media *as a whole. Is this review meant for a general audience or a more specific one?*

Smart Girls at the Party
http://www.smartgirlsattheparty.com/
Common Sense Media says: Amy Poehler's video site inspires.

What Parents Need to Know

Parents need to know that girls will find inspiring role models of all ages on this video site that features comedian Amy Poehler. The tone is upbeat, and there's an overarching theme of discovering your true self and following your dreams. Viewers have to go to YouTube to watch many of the videos, so kids could encounter inappropriate content if they linger there. Smart Girls itself doesn't collect any information.

What Kids Can Learn

Kids can learn about how to make their mark on the world by passionately pursuing the things they love to do. The cornerstone of Smart Girls at the Party is a series of interviews conducted by Amy Poehler, who talks to women and girls about their interests and achievements, from art to activism. Poehler also answers questions in "Ask Amy," dishing out sound advice on navigating friendships, feeling good about yourself, and other concerns common to teens. Video interviews and Q&A with Poehler drive home the site's motto: "Change the world by being yourself."

What's It About?

Created by a trio of friends—comedian Amy Poehler, TV producer Meredith Walker, and musician Amy Miles—SMART GIRLS AT THE PARTY is a collection of videos organized into different channels. The site's cornerstone is its eponymous web series, which features Poehler interviewing girls and women who do cool things, from skateboarding to storytelling. Poehler's also the star of "Ask Amy," answering viewers' questions on topics like courage, body image, and friendship. Other series spotlight girls who live in different countries and quirky musical guests.

Is It Any Good?

Smart Girls has a wonderful motto—"change the world by being yourself"—and a tone that's lively and fun, with cute theme songs and a dance party at the end of each episode. Although Poehler lacks polish as an interviewer, her off-the-cuff style makes her endearing and relatable, and her interviewees are a diverse bunch. It's inspiring watching a 79-year-old woman who decided it was never too late to learn to play drums, or a trio of skateboarding sisters who shine in a male-dominated sport. Girls (and women) of all ages will find something to smile about here.

Think About It

(1)   What criteria does Yudt employ for her review? Are they simply reflected in the subject headings (which are used for all the reviews on Common Sense Media), or are there other criteria listed? How do these criteria reflect the audience and purpose for Common Sense Media?

(2)   Do you think the actual users of the website (young girls) would agree with Yudt's review? Why or why not? What criteria would they be likely to privilege if they could evaluate the website?

(3)   In what ways does the gender of visitors to Smart Girls at the Party matter for Yudt? Does Yudt seem to have criteria in mind related to the kind of message the website is sending to girls, in particular? Do you think this is appropriate for this review? Why or why not?

Write About It

Using this review as a model, write a review of a website that might be featured on Common Sense Media. *First, choose a website that might target or attract children. Then, use the criteria just discussed to conduct and write your review.*

Reading Argumentative Genres

CHAPTER OUTLINE

RUI DAI   AMERICANESE: IN BETWEEN THE GAPS

When she wrote this opinion piece in 2012, Rui Dai was an undergraduate at Duke University studying neuroscience. This piece appeared in the online newspaper The Huffington Post, *in the newspaper's College section.*

Read About It

Rui Dai is a second-language writer of English, writing about her experiences as an immigrant in the U.S. You may notice some non-standard English usage in her writing. Highlight (or write down) examples you encounter. How does this non-standard usage contribute to the message of her piece?

At the turn of twentieth century's last decade, large numbers of Chinese students immigrated to study in Europe and the United States. The dust of Tiananmen Square had just settled. Surprisingly in response, both Chinese and Western governments dramatically loosened restrictions on educational exchange. The Chinese government wanted to send hormonal-driven students overseas in order to reduce political discontent. The western governments were in the early stages of testing ideas that would later crystallize into a theory known as "Brain Gain."

In 1991, there were less than ten thousand international Chinese students in the US. A year later, the number nearly doubled to twenty thousand. Since then, the number of international students in the U.S. has only multiplied. There are currently over 160,000 international Chinese students seeking some kind of educational degree in the United States. That's over sixteen times what it was twenty years ago. The number doesn't even include Chinese students who are U.S. permanent residents or green card holders.

My mother was part of the earlier waves emigrating out of China in 1993. We went to Germany in the search of an overseas education. In 1999, our family of three immigrated to the United States and has since then proudly called Cleveland home.

Over the past decade, I have settled comfortably into my identity as a Chinese-American. I have always thought that it meant I could be both Chinese and American. I have since found that is not completely true. Chinese-American is a separate identity by itself. It indicates someone who is American with physical Chinese features. It is neither completely American, and nor is it purely Chinese.

My parents and I have tried desperately to retain our Chinese roots. At home, we speak Chinglish (Chinese + English) and eat home-cooked traditional Chinese meals. We once even bought a three-foot satellite in an attempt to watch Chinese television directly broadcasted from CCTV.

As a result, I am able to speak Mandarin with barely a detectable accent and for all intents and purposes sound like a native Chinese person. But unless it is on a resume or I am trying to impress someone, I wouldn't call it fluent. My abilities to navigate Chinese society are quite literally at the level of a Chinese third-grade elementary student. I can read and understand the gist of a newspaper article without recognizing every character. I can also write a simple correspondence given that I can look up every other word on a dictionary. If someone were to ask me to name the ancient Chinese dynasties chronologically, I'll be sure to mix up the order and leave a few out.

Despite this I have always thought that if I were to move back to China, I will be able to survive and eventually become accustomed to the lifestyle. I have never been concerned with the seemingly small blemishes in my Chinese education. They really didn't matter in day-to-day experiences. I have always blended in every time that I visited my grandparents in China.

I soon realized that just blending-in was not enough.

Recently, I had the opportunity to attend a week-long academic exchange fully sponsored by Duke and Peking University concerning the challenges to higher education in the U.S. and China. I was one of nine Duke students who presented an original thesis concerning a specific challenge that is facing U.S. higher education.

One of the things that I noticed on the trip is that whenever I wear a tank top and shorts, people walking pass would look at me suspiciously. Men would look at me with lurid expressions, and women with disdain. At first, I thought it was just my imagination. Then a fellow Chinese-American student informed me that it was because tank tops and shorts are what prostitutes wear on the streets at night.

Why didn't I think of that?

The students from Peking University would never characterize me as truly Chinese. At most, I am just an American-wannabe who has lost my Chinese roots. I am not Chinese enough, but neither am I truly foreign.

And so wouldn't my fellow Duke classmates consider me as American. I can speak Mandarin and have no trouble eating the various strange delicacies that is presented during dinner. Chinese-Americans are usually considered by many as those born in American and can no longer speak Mandarin fluently. Since I was born in China and can at least pretend fluency in Mandarin, I am not really Chinese-American either.

In modern American society, there are two mainstream terms available to describe people of Chinese ancestry. You can either be Chinese-American or international Chinese. Chinese-American means that you're American in every sense of the word, but just has Chinese physical appearance. International Chinese means that you're Chinese, but just happens to live or study in America for a limited amount of time.

I am stuck in the middle and do not belong completely to either.

When my parents first moved to Germany, the concept of Chinese-Germans didn't exist. The term is only slowly starting to emerge in the past decade as more and more Chinese nationals obtain German citizenship.

As more and more international students from all over the world come to the U.S. and become immersed in American culture, perhaps a term like Americanized Chinese or Americanese can also emerge to indicate an identity that is not completely Chinese or quite Chinese-American.

Until that day, I would like to ask for your honest opinion: if you were in a similar position, had to choose between a nationality and Something-American, which one would you choose and why?

Think About It

(1)   At the beginning of her piece, Dai describes historical political unrest in China (Tiananmen Square) and politics on an international scale (the "Brain Gain"). By the end of the piece, she describes her personal experiences. How does Dai transition from large-scale historical topics to the very personal topics at the end?

(2)   Do you agree with Dai's characterization of the two options available to immigrants in the U.S.— what she calls "International Chinese" and "Chinese-American"? Do you think there may be other options besides these two? Do you think her notion of "Americanese" is a good idea?

(3)   Does the author's story make you feel sympathetic to her? Why or why not?

Write About It

At the end of her piece, Dai poses a question: "I would like to ask for your honest opinion: if you were in a similar position, had to choose between a nationality and Something-American, which one would you choose and why?" Write a letter to the editor (Chapter 10) of this newspaper in which you respond to Dai's article and answer the question she poses.

● ●

KELLY HUSTON   DID I VOTE ON YOUR MARRIAGE?

In 2008, photographer Kelly Huston took this photograph of a poster held by a protester in Sacramento, California. The caption to the photographic series of which this photograph is a part reads as follows: "People upset by the passage of Proposition 8, the anti-gay marriage initiative, protest at the California State Capitol in Sacramento on Sunday, November 9, 2008."

Read About It

You are probably familiar with other protest slogans from history, such as "Make Love, Not War" from Vietnam War-era protests, or "I Am a Man" from the Civil Rights protests of the 1960s. As you read the following poster and absorb the other visual elements of the photographs, try placing this poster within the context of other protests in U.S. history.

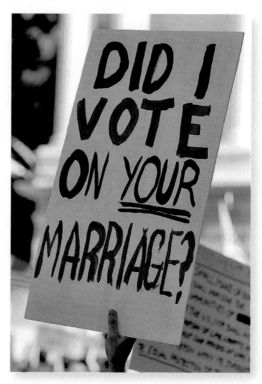

Figure R7.1
This photograph was taken by Kelly Huston at a protest in Sacramento, California.

Think About It

(1)   What does the sign's creator mean to imply by posing the question, "Did I vote on *your* marriage?"

(2)   How did the creator of this sign use color—alongside text—to get her point across? How does that color work with the other colors of the photograph?

(3)   For a moment, look around the poster that is the focal point of the image and see what you can see of the background. What objects or geographical features did you notice that you might not have noticed at first glance? How do they contribute to the meaning of the photograph?

Write About It

Choose a photograph from the front cover (or homepage) of a newspaper in your town. Write a rhetorical analysis of the photograph (Chapter 8). Consider how the audience of the newspaper might react to the photograph, as well as what message newspaper readers might take from it.

KRISTIAN DOUGHERTY   ALIENS, GET OUT!

This political satire was published in the Outlook Student Press, *the student newspaper of the State University of New York–Rockland, in 2010. At the time, Kristian Dougherty was a staff writer for the newspaper and a student at the university.*

Read About It

The following satire piece uses humor to approach a touchy political subject: illegal immigration. As you read, make a list of the many different people and groups that the piece satirizes.

The subject of illegal aliens is a sensitive one. It is an issue that has many differing viewpoints that can inspire passions in some, and incite fear in others. But to ignore the problem that exists right in front of our faces, or to even deny that such a problem exists in the first place, would be a huge mistake—on all of our parts.

For too long, many decent, hard-working people have been forced to deal with the problems brought by these "aliens," and they are often left helpless against them. Not only have these people had their livelihoods stripped away, but in some cases, the skin off their backs as well.

These aliens come from the stars, sometimes under the guise of friendship, and they look to destroy us from within. They vaporize our cities with their giant, blue death-rays; or in an effort to "better understand us," they snatch up poor, hard-working Midwesterners by the hundreds, continuously probing their bodies.

Sometimes, they come here bent on the conquest of the human race and the destruction of our way of life. Other times, they simply want to annihilate us, usually for no particular reason other than the fact that we exist. And no matter how many times we run them off with their tails between their legs, they just keep showing up—illegally, and without permission.

First off, let me say that I am not a xenophobe. I wasn't raised that way. I like aliens just fine. But what I don't like is when they come here illegally. They crash-land on some remote part of the globe, and when they wake up, they start shooting up and causing trouble. I have absolutely no tolerance for that.

They skulk around up in the trees like some merciless predator, hunting good old American folks, who are just trying to "have them some fun." This is unacceptable. Just because someone is carrying a gun around the jungle, it doesn't mean they should be targeted by some off-worlder who's looking to have a good time on safari. Last I checked we still had the right to bear arms without having to worry about having the back of our skulls blown out by some seven-foot tall alien with dreadlocks. If they want to skin people alive and collect skulls for their trophy collections, they should do it someplace else, because we don't want them here.

While I'm on the subject of their trophy collections . . . what the hell is up with that?

I don't know what they do where you come from, but here, on planet Earth, we don't participate in that sort of behavior. Alright, well some of us do, but those folks are not what I would consider normal. Sure, it might have been a ritual that was practiced a long time ago by our ancestors, but we've evolved. We're civilized now. You'd think a species that has mastered interstellar travel and created a portable thermonuclear device would be well beyond the barbaric practice of cutting off some poor, defenseless creature's head, and mounting it on the wall of their spaceship as a status symbol.

What gives them the right to come down here, and destroy a perfectly good patch of South American rain forest with one of their aforementioned portable nuclear devices? This is our planet, and they should have respect for it. Running around blowing up things for no reason, and engaging in foolhardy practices that destroy the environment might be acceptable where you come from, but here, we don't do that sort of thing. OK, maybe we do, but we live here—we can do what we want with it.

They come down here from a galaxy far, far, away, with their fancy technologies, and they think they can push us around and tell us what to do. If these aliens know what's good for them, they'll pack up their light-refracting stealth suits and their laser-guided rockets, and get back on their spaceships, and get the hell outta Dodge. If not, we may just have to take our case to the Governor of California. He might have something to say about that.

Think About It

(1)   At what point in this piece does the fact that it is a satire become apparent? What are the cues that the author uses to let a reader know that the piece is satirical?

(2)   At one point in the piece, the author declares, "I like aliens just fine. But what I don't like is when they come here illegally. They crash-land on some remote part of the globe, and when they wake up, they start shooting up and causing trouble." What sorts of arguments made by parties to the immigration debate does this passage satirize?

(3)   When the author notes that aliens are "[r]unning around blowing up things for no reason, and engaging in foolhardy practices that destroy the environment," who do you think he is actually criticizing? What gives you that impression?

Write About It

Write a satirical response to Dougherty's op-ed as a letter to the editor (Chapter 10). You might take an opposing stance on immigration, or write a letter supporting Dougherty's position.

WILL LEVITT   FOOD 101: WHY COLLEGE STUDENTS SHOULD LEARN TO COOK

When the Huffington Post *published this opinion piece in 2012, Will Levitt was a senior at Wesleyan University. He is the founder and editor of the blog* Dorm Room Dinner (http://www.dormroomdinner.com).

Read About It

As you read this opinion piece, think about whether Levitt convinces you to add "learning to cook" to the list of skills that you would gain in college. Write down your own reactions as you read.

We promise our college students a lot these days. We promise them a quality education, access to top professors and an intellectually active campus. We promise them the opportunity to think critically, build their leadership skills and express their creativity. We want them to have a solid foundation for the road ahead. And yet we have overlooked one of the most basic, fundamental skills anyone can have for leading a healthy and successful life.

We forgot to teach them how to cook.

In a nation where diet-related deaths have increased dramatically and eating has become not only a personal issue but a social and political one, we are not teaching students one of the easiest ways to improve the quality of their life and the vitality of their communities. We have to start eating well. And the only way to eat well is to know how to cook.

When I became interested in cooking during middle school, I had no idea what a difference it would make in my life. Cooking allowed me to take control of a large part of my life. In my case, it gave me the skills to start a catering business with a friend during high school, has been a large part of my social and extracurricular life at college, and has allowed me to eat well, whenever I want and with whatever resources might be available to me.

Many colleges throughout the country are already doing great work that allows their students to eat better. At Wesleyan University, where I attend, the dining service (we use Bon Appétit Management Company) is working with student groups to ensure twenty percent of the food used in campus dining halls is sourced from local vendors. Half an hour away, the Yale Sustainable Food Project runs an organic farm, looks into academic issues related to food and works with the sustainable dining program for their university. Additionally, projects like Alice Waters' Edible Schoolyard bring middle-school students into the garden and the kitchen for lessons in cooking and healthy eating. These and other programs are real steps in the right direction towards getting us to eat better and improve our relationship with food and with our communities.

But even at these universities, too many students leave college without any knowledge of how to cook for themselves. Learning how to microwave instant ramen is not a cooking skill. When we enter the real world, we need to be able to provide for ourselves. We aren't cooking or feeding ourselves in a way that is sustainable for our own lives, our communities or our country. When frozen dinners and fast food drive-by windows have become a norm in many households, we need to make a change. We need to teach people how to cook.

These skills, of course, should not only be provided to those fortunate enough to attend college. But college is a particularly appropriate place to educate our youth about food and cooking for a variety of reasons. For one, colleges have a concentration of individuals about to enter the real world with the time and interest to partake in activities that improve the quality of their lives. Otherwise they wouldn't be at college. Many colleges already have programs in place to improve the quality of students' relationship with food. Why should a skill as basic as cooking not be included in these initiatives? Colleges should offer cooking lessons and activities that teach students how to cook. Additionally, colleges are often a catalyst for social change. If we are going to change the way America eats, we should empower our college youth to take part in that change.

The food movement today is alive as ever and is improving the way we eat in real and significant ways. Much of the focus so far has been on greater availability of fresh, healthy food and on encouraging everyone to eat better, whether through making better choices at the grocery store or improving lunches at public schools. These are all vitally important steps in the process. But we must focus on teaching people how to cook food. The food movement cannot exist without everyone being able to take home fresh, local produce and make a delicious meal from it. The process of actually cooking is the most personal way we can connect with the food movement. We have a nation of college students waiting to learn how. Let's teach them.

Think About It

(1)   Levitt states, regarding college students, "We forgot to teach them how to cook." What arguments does the author make to convince his readers that learning to cook is a vital skill?

(2)   Levitt argues that college is an ideal locale for a youth-cooking revolution. How does he make this argument? What evidence or reasons does he provide for his argument?

(3)   Who is the audience of this piece? College students? Or others? Who has the power to make his arguments a reality?

Write About It

Think of a skill that you believe is vital for survival or success in our society, a skill that could be taught in college. Using similar rhetorical strategies to those employed by Levitt, write an opinion piece explaining why your skill should be taught to college students.

. . . .

KAITLYN VALOR BOURQUE   FEMINISM: HOW OUR IDEAS HAVE EVOLVED WITH US

This opinion piece was published in The South End, *the student-run newspaper of Wayne State University in Detroit, Michigan, in 2012. The author, Bourque, was a member of the newspaper staff.*

Read About It

Before you read this opinion piece, think about whether you have ever or would ever call yourself a "feminist." Write a list of your reasons for this, and then, as you read, check off which ones Bourque addresses in her piece.

Unless you live under a rock or slept through every single history class you've ever taken you're probably at least somewhat familiar with the concept of feminism.

Most likely, the word, itself, conjures up a plethora of images ranging from early 20th century suffragettes in long skirts and extravagant hats chaining themselves to the White House gates, to radical protests made by flannel-wearing "bra burners" of the 1960s, to the increasingly visible activism of modern-day feminists in response to the discriminatory attacks on women's reproductive rights.

The word might make you uncomfortable. You may even be supportive of women's equality—one can only hope in the 21st century—but refuse to refer to yourself as a feminist, whether you are male or female.

Why?

Feminism, unfortunately, has been excessively stigmatized in today's society to connote bitter, men-hating, loud-mouthed, hairy-legged, whining females (who are probably lesbians—gasp!) . . . and an assortment of other adjectives much less appropriate for print.

This indiscriminate stigmatization is a shame, considering the fact that the accurate definition of a feminist is simply an individual who supports the notion that all human beings are inherently equal, regardless of gender.

Another good, albeit sassy, description is the popular quote, "feminism is the radical notion that women are people."

Feminism has evolved out of the necessity for a cause that advocates for the rights of women based on the understanding that in spite of representing half of the human population, women have been subjected to severe social and political oppression on a global scale for centuries.

Such oppression has occurred in virtually every arena in the public sphere: voting and other legal rights, education and work opportunities, reproductive autonomy, health care, physical and sexual abuse, marriage and divorce, body image, leadership representation and the list goes on.

And yet, isn't feminism irrelevant in this day and age? Haven't we gotten what we wanted already? I do not venture to argue the fact that remarkable strides have been made in the arena of women's rights.

Legislatively, women have achieved most of what feminists have been striving for since Mary Wollstonecraft's publication of "Vindication of the Rights of Women" in 1792. Women have the right to vote in most industrialized societies worldwide. They are legally permitted to obtain all levels of education and professions. They are increasingly becoming more visible and influential as activists.

There truly has been no better time in human history to be a woman than right now.

But this is not because we are done. It is not because we have accomplished all the goals that first-, second-, and third-wave feminists have held for over a century.

In spite of the great legal strides we have made toward women's equality, power is still predominately held by white, middle aged men whose perspective is deemed a universal reflection on the thoughts, opinions and needs of all members of our society.

Inevitably, women's issues are swept under the rug, regarded as having no relevant role in decision-making that directly affect us, perpetuating our stigma as second class citizens.

Herein [lies] the principle reason why modern-day feminism not only exists, but is needed: representation.

On average, a pitiful 18 percent of American leadership positions are held by women, according to missrepresentation.org. This means that the most important venues of our society—politics, the military, business, law, non-profits, film and television, sports and academia—are disproportionately representing the perspectives and needs of American women.

It's no wonder that women continue to face such significant obstacles as a result of our gender. We cannot expect absolute equality under today's given circumstances. It's just not realistic.

In the words of Marian Wright Edelman, founder and president of the Children's Defense fund, "you can't be what you can't see."

Women represent what is now technically a majority—51 percent, according to the 2010 U.S. Census—of the American population. It's about time the American population started acting like it.

Think About It

(1)   Why do you think Bourque decided to write an opinion piece on feminism in 2012? What reasons does she give for deciding to write this piece?
(2)   How does Bourque argue that feminism should be defined or thought about? How does she make this argument?
(3)   Does Bourque argue that feminism still has work to do? What proof does she provide for her arguments?

Write About It

Suppose Bourque's opinion piece appeared in your college or local newspaper. Write a letter to the editor in which you respond to this piece. You can be supportive of the piece or not—but be sure you respond to her arguments in a rhetorically sound fashion (Chapter 18).

Reading Academic Research Genres

GEORGE W. DOWDALL AND HENRY WECHSLER   STUDYING COLLEGE ALCOHOL USE: WIDENING THE LENS, SHARPENING THE FOCUS

This literature review was published in The Journal of Studies of Alcohol *in 2002. Dowdall is a professor of sociology at St. Joseph's University in Philadelphia, Pennsylvania. Dowdall is author of a book,* College Drinking: Reframing a Social Problem, *which explores this topic in more detail. Wechsler is a lecturer at the School of Public Health at Harvard University, and was principal investigator for the College Alcohol Study, a major national study of college students' drinking practices.*

Read About It

Before you read this literature review, read the abstract as a preview to find the main claim. Then, as you read, list the different factors the authors address that relate to that claim.

Abstract

Objective: The study was designed to assess current trends in studying, and emerging approaches to furthering understanding of, college drinking. Method: A literature review was conducted of findings and methods highlighting conceptual and methodological issues that need to be addressed. Results: Most studies address clinical, developmental and psychological variables and are conducted at single points in time on single campuses. Factors affecting college alcohol use and methods of studying them are discussed. Conclusions: Most current studies of college drinking do not address the influence of the college and its alcohol environment. Our understanding of college drinking can be improved by expanding the scope of issues studied and choosing appropriate research designs.

Perhaps no topic in alcohol research has been more intensively studied and widely discussed in the past decade as college student alcohol use and associated problems. A bibliographical search using the term college turned up more than 2,200 references in the National Institute on Alcohol Abuse and Alcoholism ETOH database. The hundreds of studies share more than a common topic. Most share a common point of view and general approach. The methods used by researchers very powerfully shape the messages that come from the research literature. Much of the literature has been shaped by assumptions drawn from the study of individual alcohol dependence and individual alcohol-related problems, usually at a single point in time and often just at one institution. Although the literature has succeeded in improving the understanding of some of the microdynamics of college drinking, it largely neglects the broader economic, political and organizational factors. This article calls attention to issues that will shape research about college drinking in the coming years. It is our belief that the literature needs to move away from single campus studies of individuals with alcohol-related problems toward multiple campus studies of the broader factors that shape college student drinking behavior. Questions about complex sampling designs, measurement of broader environments and issues, longitudinal designs and those done at multiple points in time and statistical analyses of causal processes will all come to the fore, and so are given special attention here. To view college drinking more clearly, we argue for widening the lens and sharpening the focus of research. . . .

We need to examine those factors unique to college populations so that we can better understand why college students seem to be at higher risk of heavy episodic drinking than their peers who do not attend college.

Issues in Research about College Drinking

. . . Ecology of alcohol use. Empirical research has been conducted about alcohol outlet availability and various indicators of crime and violence in several U.S.

settings, with most research suggesting a substantial relationship. One national study (Wechsler et al., 1994) reported that colleges located more than a mile from the nearest alcohol outlet had lower rates of heavy episodic drinking than colleges with outlets within a mile. Clearly more structured research is needed on where and when students use alcohol. Developments in evaluating community initiatives (Fulbright-Anderson et al., 1998) should help in understanding these issues.

In part because of the dramatically lower cost and greater analytic power of geographic information systems (GIS) software and in part because of greater interest in how access to alcohol and other substances shapes behavior, GIS and mapping have become of much greater interest in research. In alcohol studies, the relationship between alcohol outlets and several outcomes such as violence and car crashes has been researched, yielding insight into the role of supply in shaping alcohol-related problems (e.g., Gruenewald et al., 1996; Rich, 1999). Mapping has become an active area of research about crime and justice issues more generally. Much will be learned about the occurrence of college alcohol-related problems by examining its spatial patterning (Croner et al., 1996), both for communities (Gruenewald et al., 1996; Scribner et al., 1999) and for campuses. . . .

Supply-side factors. Among the most understudied areas in college drinking are the supply-side factors. Most traditional-age college students are under 21, so consumption of alcohol often involves the violation of state and local laws by students and alcohol providers. The role of availability and context shapes behavior, but little is known about the issue, and even less about local alcohol markets, legal or otherwise. Evidence (e.g., Chaloupka and Wechsler, 1996, 1997) suggests that the cost of alcohol is an important factor. Wechsler et al. (2000a) found that availability, price and the use of beer were the strongest predictors of heavy episodic alcohol use in underage students.

Student residence and social context. Extensive research about the lives of college students (Astin, 1993; Pascarella and Terenzini, 1991) suggests that the formal structures of college life are of relatively less importance than the ways in which peer groups influence behavior. Gfroerer et al. (1997) examined data from the National Household Survey on Drug Abuse, finding that educational status and living arrangements were significant in predicting substance use among those of traditional college age. During the past decade there has been extensive growth in student living arrangements beyond the traditional dichotomy of dormitory or home. The rise of "resimuters," students who live near their institutions but are unsupervised by parents or colleges, needs to be more adequately studied.

Whether alcohol is permitted in the dormitory or the entire campus is related to the level of drinking, alcohol-related problems and secondhand effects experienced by nondrinking students. Wechsler et al. (2001a,b) examined substance-free dorms and campuses that ban alcohol, controlling for previous drinking behavior of these students in substance-free environments.

Social norms. Considerable attention has been given to the question of the prevailing norms that surround college drinking. One school of thought (Haines, 1996; Haines and Spear, 1996) suggests that students misperceive the actual behavior of their peers, assuming much higher rates of substance use than in fact prevails. This has led some to suggest that correcting the misperception of norms might lower alcohol use, although empirical evidence seems to be conflicting, with some universities reporting decreases and others reporting no change (Haines, 1996; Keeling, 2000). In addition, Wechsler and Kuo (2000) concluded that the potential role of social norms in influencing college students' drinking may have been overstated. Research is needed on other types of student norms, such as supplying alcohol to underage drinkers and tolerating disruptive secondhand effects, as well as on local community norms. . . .

Conclusions

Since Straus and Bacon (1953) published their pioneering work about drinking in college, there has been much progress in understanding the issue. Much more, however, remains to be learned. We have argued for widening the lens; incorporating new perspective, variables and methodologies; and sharpening the focus through better conceptualization, measurement and sampling. Substance misuse is arguably the nation's number one health problem, as much for college students as for other Americans (Robert Wood Johnson Foundation, 2001). A view of college drinking that is both expanded and clarified holds promise for advancing understanding and enhancing prevention.

References

ASTIN, A. What Matters in College? Four Critical Years Revisited. San Francisco, CA: Jossey-Bass, 1993.

CHALOUPKA, F.J. AND WECHSLER, H. Binge drinking in college: The impact of price, availability, and alcohol control policies. Contemp. Econ. Policy 14: 112–124, 1996.

CHALOUPKA, F.J. AND WECHSLER, H. Price, tobacco control policies and smoking among young adults. J. Hlth Econ. 16: 359–373, 1997.

CRONER, C.M., SPERLING, J. AND BROOME, F.R. Geographic Information Systems (GIS): New perspectives in understanding human health and environmental relationships. Stat. Med. 15: 1961–1977, 1996.

FULBRIGHT-ANDERSON, K., KUBISCH, A.C. AND CONNELL, J.P. New Approaches to Evaluating Community Initiatives, Vol. 2: Theory, Measurement, and Analysis. Washington, DC: Aspen Institute, 1998.

GELLER, E.S., RUSS, N.W. AND ALTOMARI, M.G. Naturalistic observations of beer drinking among college students. J. Appl. Behav. Anal. 19: 391–396, 1986.

GFROERER, J.C., GREENBLATT, J.C. AND WRIGHT, D.A. Substance use in the US college-age population: Differences according to educational status and living arrangement. Amer. J. Publ. Hlth 87: 62–65, 1997.

GRUENEWALD, P.J., MILLAR, A.B. AND ROEPER, P. Access to alcohol: Geography and prevention for local communities. Alcohol Hlth Res. World 20: 244–251, 1996.

HAINES, M.P. A Social Norms Approach to Preventing Binge Drinking at Colleges and Universities. Newton, MA: Higher Education Center for Alcohol and Other Drug Prevention, Department of Education, 1996.

HAINES, M. AND SPEAR, S.F. Changing the perception of the norm: A strategy to decrease binge drinking among college students. J. Amer. Coll. Hlth 45: 134–140, 1996.

KEELING, R.P. Social norms research in college health. J. Amer. Coll. Hlth 49 (2): 53–56, 2000.

PASCARELLA, E.T. AND TERENZINI, P.T. HOW College Affects Students: Findings and Insights from Twenty Years of Research. San Francisco, CA: Jossey-Bass, 1991.

RICH, T. Mapping the path to problem solving. Nat. Inst. Justice J. 10: 2–9, 1999.

ROBERT WOOD JOHNSON FOUNDATION. Substance Abuse: The Nation's Number One Health Problem. Key Indicators for Policy: Update. Princeton, NJ: Robert Wood Johnson Foundation, 2001.

SCRIBNER, R., COHEN, D., KAPLAN, S. AND ALLEN, S.H. Alcohol availability and homicide in New Orleans: Conceptual considerations for small area analysis of the effect of alcohol outlet density. J. Stud. Alcohol 60: 310–316, 1999.

STRAUS, R. AND BACON, S.D. Drinking in College. New Haven, CT: Yale Univ. Press, 1953.

WECHSLER, H. Binge Drinking on America's College Campuses: Findings from the Harvard School of Public Health College Alcohol Study (monograph), Boston, MA: Harvard School of Public Health, 2001.

WECHSLER, H., DAVENPORT, A., DOWDALL, G., MOEYKENS, B. AND CASTILLO, S. Health and behavioral consequences of binge drinking in college: A national survey of students at 140 campuses. JAMA 272: 1672–1677, 1994.

WECHSLER, H. AND KUO, M. College students define binge drinking and estimate its prevalence: Results of a national survey. J. Amer. Coll. Hlth 49 (2): 57–64, 2000.

WECHSLER, H., KUO, M., LEE, H. AND DOWDALL, G.W. Environmental correlates of underage alcohol use and related problems of college students. Amer. J. Prev. Med. 19: 24–29, 2000a.

WECHSLER, H., LEE, J.E., GLEDHILL-HOYT, J. AND NELSON, T.F. Alcohol use and problems at colleges banning alcohol: Results of a national survey. J. Stud. Alcohol 62: 133–141, 2001a.

WECHSLER, H., LEE, J.E., NELSON, T.F. AND LEE, H. Drinking levels, alcohol problems and secondhand effects in substance-free college residences: Results of a national study. J. Stud. Alcohol 62: 23–31, 2001b.

Think About It

(1)   A literature review does more than just list previous research on a topic. Instead, it makes a claim and supports it by referring to previous studies. What is the main claim of this review?

(2)   How do the authors employ previous research? Take a look at a few citations in the text. How much do the writers say about each source? How many sources do they typically mention in a paragraph? Why do you think this is the case?

(3)   How is the review organized? Do you think this organization is effective?

Write About It

Choose one subsection from the body of this review (e.g., "Student residence and social context" or "social norms"). Using the sources the authors cite as a starting point, try to find at least five more recent sources on that topic. (Try searching your library databases for "college drinking AND social norms," for instance.) Then, write a short literature review that takes up that topic, in particular, and offers a claim that responds to Dowdell and Wechsler. Does your review of the literature lead you to the same conclusions as Dowdell and Wechsler? Or does more recent scholarship address the gaps that they found in 2002?

NANSOOK PARK   MILITARY CHILDREN AND FAMILIES (EXCERPT)

Park published this literature review in American Psychologist *in 2011. A professor of psychology at the University of Michigan, Park's research often focuses on well-being, quality of life, and character strengths in children and adults.*

Read About It

This literature review relies on a variety of sources, including research articles, government reports, and newspaper articles. As you read, highlight each source mentioned, and then jot down how it is used. Do you see any difference in how different types of sources contribute to the main claim of the review?

Abstract: Throughout history, military children and families have shown great capacity for adaptation and resilience. However, in recent years, unprecedented lengthy and multiple combat deployments of service members have posed multiple challenges for U.S. military children and families. Despite needs to better understand the impact of deployment on military children and families and to provide proper support for them, rigorous research is lacking. Programs exist that are intended to help, but their effectiveness is largely unknown. They need to be better coordinated and delivered at the level of individuals, families, and communities. Research and programs need to take a comprehensive approach that is strengths based and problem focused. Programs for military children and families often focus on the prevention or reduction of problems. It is just as important to recognize their assets and to promote them. This article reviews existing research on military children and families, with attention to their strengths as well as their challenges. Issues in need of further research are identified, especially research into programs that assist military children and families. Military children and families deserve greater attention from psychology.

A common saying in the military is that when one person joins, the whole family serves. Military families may often be in the background of public discourse on the military, but they are critical to its success. Although aspects of military life can be difficult for families, positive family functioning boosts a service member's morale, retention, and ability to carry out missions (Shinseki, 2003). According to a recent report, service members reported positive family relationships as a source of resilience and problems at home as a source of stress and interference (Mental Health Advisory Team 6, 2009). Any efforts to build a strong, effective, and sustainable military force must also consider military families, improving the relationships of the soldier with his or her family members and strengthening the family itself (cf. Gottman, Gottman, & Atkins, 2011). . . .

Programs that try to assist military children and families often focus only on the prevention or reduction of problems. As important as it is to address problems, it is just as important to recognize the strengths and assets of military children and families and to promote and bolster them. A full and accurate picture of military children and families is needed upon which to base interventions. One of the best ways to prevent or solve problems is to identify what goes well and to use this as the basis of intervention (Park, 2004, 2009; Park & Peterson, 2008; Park, Peterson, & Brunwasser, 2009; Peterson & Park, 2003). . . .

This article describes what is known about military children and families: their demographics, their challenges, and their strengths, during both peace and war times. Also addressed are issues and gaps in the existing research and practice. The thesis is that greater attention to the strengths and assets of military children and families is needed in order to design and implement effective programs to support them. . . .

Strengths and Challenges among Military Children and Families

. . . The major challenge for military children and families during war is a lengthy deployment of the uniformed family member to a combat zone. Children not only miss the deployed parent, but they also experience obvious uncertainty surrounding his or her safety, especially in single-parent or dual-career families. There are other issues as well. Children may be asked to take on greater responsibilities, and daily routines may change (Pincus, House, Christenson, & Adler, 2001). Families may move to be closer to other relatives. Unlike relocation during times of peace, war-time relocation of families may require them to move off base into the civilian community where they lose the existing military support system (MacDermid, 2006).

Nearly 900,000 U.S. children have had at least one of their parents deployed since 2001, and currently 234,000 children have one or both parents at war (Zoroya, 2009). Long and frequent deployments of service members put military children and families at risk for psychosocial problems (American Psychological Association, Presidential Task Force on Military Deployment Services for Youth, Families, and Service Members, 2007). According to U.S. Department of Defense data, between 2003 and 2008 the number of military children receiving outpatient mental health care doubled, and during that period inpatient visits by military children increased by 50%, with a 20% jump from 2007 to 2008 ("Department of Defense Reaches Out to Children of Soldiers," 2009). This indicates potentially a cumulative toll of parental deployments on military children and urgent needs for proper mental health services for this population.

Although scarce, several studies have looked at the impact of parental deployment on children during current wars. Although military children and families cope relatively well with shorter separations (less than six months), longer and multiple deployments create measurable distress (Chandra et al., 2010; Flake et al., 2009). Parental deployment can affect physical health, academic performance, behavior problems, depression, and anxiety of military children. Adolescent children of deployed parents show significantly higher levels of stress, systolic blood pressure, and heart rate than their civilian counterparts (Barnes, Davis, & Treiber, 2007). Children of deployed service members also show decreases in their academic performance, school engagement, and overall school adjustment (Engel, Gallagher, & Lyle, 2010). More than one third of school-age children showed high risk for psychosocial difficulties during parental deployment, 2.5 times the national norm (Flake et al., 2009). Children of deployed parents, especially older youth and girls, reported more problems with school, family, and mental health. The longer the parental deployment is, the greater these problems are, during and after deployment (Chandra et al., 2010). . . .

Although military deployment poses risks, especially for some families, it is equally important to remember that many military children and families show resilience and growth. During the deployment of a family member, parents report that their children are closer to family and friends, and that they are more responsible, independent, and proud. Seventy-four percent of the spouses of service members report personal growth, despite also reporting increased loneliness, stress, and anxiety (U.S. Department of Defense, Defense Manpower Data Center, 2009b).

Resilience plays an important role in all phases of deployment. Resilience mitigates stress and improves adjustment to deployment by children and families. Families that function most effectively are active, optimistic, self-reliant, and flexible (Jensen & Shaw, 1996; Wiens & Boss, 2006). Families that function well find meaning in military life and identify with the work of their uniformed family member (Hammer, Cullen, Marchand, & Dezsofi, 2006; Marchant & Medway, 1987). Family preparedness for deployment as well as community and social support lead to better adjustment (Wiens & Boss, 2006). . . .

All things considered, military families on average have done well and show resilience during peace and even war. Problems of course exist for some military families, but rarely to a greater extent than among civilian families. Contrast this conclusion with the notion of the *military family syndrome*, which refers to a constellation of out-of-control offspring, authoritarian fathers, and depressed mothers (Lagrone, 1978). This alleged syndrome has been refuted repeatedly by relevant evidence (e.g., Jensen, Gordon, Lewis, & Xenakis, 1986; Jensen et al., 1991; Morrison, 1981), but it seems to be as resilient as the healthy military family that it fails to acknowledge. The fact that military families overall have done well in the past deserves greater dissemination in the present than seems to occur in today's popular media.

If nothing else, the historical strength of the military family can serve as a source of pride and inspiration. . . .

Issues and Recommendations

. . . the research literature on military children and families is too scant, especially in light of contemporary concerns with their well-being while the United States is at war. Several observations about this literature are offered, followed by recommendations for further research and interventions. . . .

Research on the effects of deployment on military children and families usually focuses only on the period of actual deployment. Redeployment and postdeployment are poorly understood and in need of greater explication. Although reunion can be joyous, it also requires changes and adjustments in roles and routines for all family members, and these can be stressful and confusing (American Psychological Association, Presidential Task Force, 2007). Furthermore, many families have to start preparing for the next deployment again. For both families and service members alike, the postdeployment stage is particularly long and complex (MacDermid, 2006). Many returning service members experience combat-related mental health problems, injuries, and disabilities. These can burden children and families. There is simply not enough research about the long-term effects on children and families of living with a parent who is experiencing such difficulties and how to help them. Longitudinal studies are needed. . . .

As already noted, most military family studies assume a traditional family and thus do not adequately sample the relevant populations. Considering the diversity of military family types, future studies should examine the impact of military life, especially deployment, on children from different types of families. Future studies should also compare the effects on children of maternal versus paternal deployment. . . .

Conclusion

Throughout history, military children and families have shown great capacity to adapt to and grow from challenges, during peace or during war. However, with U.S. involvement in current wars, military families face multiple challenges that put them at high risk of distress and mental health problems. Their needs are greater than ever. The well-being of military children and families is desirable in its own right and as a means to many other valued ends, for individuals and the larger society.

There is an urgent need for better understanding of both the challenges and the strengths and assets of military children and families to help them not only survive but also thrive. . . . Psychology as a field is in a unique position to accomplish all of these goals (Seligman & Fowler, 2011). Military children and families deserve sustained attention from psychology. One hopes that more psychologists will join and indeed help lead this worthy endeavor. About one third of the population has a direct relationship with someone in the military, and virtually everyone has an indirect relationship (Black, 1993). Military families live in our neighborhoods. Their children go to our schools. Much can be learned from them. Building and sustaining healthy, resilient, and thriving military children and families will bring benefits not just to them but ultimately to all Americans. The military family *is* the American family.

References

American Psychological Association, Presidential Task Force on Military Deployment Services for Youth, Families, and Service Members. (2007). *The psychological needs of U.S. military service members and their families: A preliminary report.* Washington, DC: American Psychological Association.

Barnes, V. A., Davis, H., & Treiber, F. A. (2007). Perceived stress, heart rate, and blood pressure among adolescents with family members deployed in Operation Iraqi Freedom. *Military Medicine, 172*, 40–43.

Black, W. G. (1993). Military-induced family separation: A stress reduction intervention. *Social Work, 38,* 273–280.

Chandra, A., Lara-Cinisomo, S., Jaycox, L. H., Tanielian, T., Burns, R. M., Ruder, T., & Han, B. (2010). Children on the homefront: The experience of children from military families. *Pediatrics, 125,* 16–25.

Department of Defense reaches out to children of soldiers. (2009, October22). U.S. Medicine. Retrieved from http://www.usmedicine.com.libproxy.lib.unc.edu/articles/Department-of-Defense-Reaches-Out-to-Children-of-Soldiers.html

Engel, R. C., Gallagher, L. B., & Lyle, D. S. (2010). Military deployments and children's academic achievement: Evidence from Department of Defense education activity schools. *Economics of Education Review, 29,* 73–82.

Flake, E. M., Davis, B. E., Johnson, P. L., & Middleton, L. S. (2009). The psychosocial effects of deployment on military children. *Journal of Developmental and Behavioral Pediatrics, 30,* 271–278. doi:10.1097/DBP.0b013e3181aac6e4

Gottman, J. M., Gottman, J. S., & Atkins, C. (2011). The Comprehensive Soldier Fitness program: Family skills component. *American Psychologist, 66,* 52–57. doi: 10.1037/a0021706.

Hammer, L. B., Cullen, J. C., Marchand, G. C., & Dezsofi, J. A. (2006). Reducing the negative impact of work-family conflict on military personnel: Individual coping strategies and multilevel interventions. In C. A. Castro, A. B. Adler, & T. W. Britt (Eds.) , *Military life: The psychology of serving in peace and combat* (Vol. 3, pp. 220– 242). Westport, CT: Praeger Security International.

Jensen, P. S., Gordon, G. A., Lewis, R. L., & Xenakis, S. N. (1986). The military family in review: Context, risk, and prevention. *Journal of the American Academy of Child Psychiatry, 25,* 225– 234. doi:10.1016/S0002-7138(09)60230-2

Jensen, P. S., & Shaw, J. A. (1996). The effects of war and parental deployment upon children and adolescents. In R. J. Ursano & A. E. Norwood (Eds.), *Emotional aftermath of the Persian Gulf War: Veterans, families, communities, and nations* (pp. 83–109). Washington, DC: American Psychiatric Press.

Jensen, P. S., Xenakis, S. N., Wolf, P., & Bain, M. W. (1991). The "military family syndrome" revisited: "By the numbers." *Journal of Nervous and Mental Disease, 179,* 102–107. doi: 10.1097/00005053-199102000-00007

Lagrone, D. M. (1978). The military family syndrome. *American Journal of Psychiatry, 135*, 1040–1043.

MacDermid, S. M. (2006). Multiple transitions of deployment and reunion for military families. Retrieved from the Military Family Research Institute, Purdue University website: http://www.cfs.purdue.edu.libproxy.lib.unc.edu/mfri/DeployReunion.ppt

Marchant, K. H., & Medway, F. J. (1987). Adjustment and achievement associated with mobility in military families. *Psychology in the Schools, 24*, 289–294. doi: 10.1002/1520-6807(198707)24:3<::AID-PITS2310240315>3.0.CO;2-A

Mental Health Advisory Team 6. (2009, November 6). Mental Health Advisory Team (MHAT) 6 Operation Enduring Freedom 2009 Afghanistan (Report chartered by the Office of the Command Surgeon US Forces Afghanistan [USFOR-A] and Office of the Surgeon General United States Army Medical Command). Retrieved from http://www.armymedicine.army.mil.libproxy.lib.unc.edu/reports/mhat/mhat_vi/MHAT_VI-OEF_Redacted.pdf

Morrison, J. (1981). Rethinking the military family syndrome. *American Journal of Psychiatry, 138*, 354–357.

Park, N. (2004). Character strengths and positive youth development. *Annals of the American Academy of Political and Social Science, 591*, 40–54. doi: 10.1177/0002716203260079

Park, N. (2009). Building strengths of character: Keys to positive youth development. *Reclaiming Children and Youth, 18*, 42–47.

Park, N., & Peterson, C. (2008). Positive psychology and character strengths: Application to strengths-based school counseling. *Professional School Counseling, 12*, 85–92.

Park, N., Peterson, C., & Brunwasser, S. M. (2009). Positive psychology and therapy. In N. Kazantzis, M. A. Reinecke, & A. Freeman (Eds.), *Cognitive and behavioral theories in clinical practice* (pp. 278–306). New York, NY: Guilford Press.

Peterson, C., & Park, N. (2003). Positive psychology as the evenhanded positive psychologist views it. *Psychological Inquiry, 14*, 141–146.

Pincus, S. H., House, R., Christensen, J., & Adler, L. E. (2001). The emotional cycle of deployment: A military family perspective. *Journal of the Army Medical Department, 4/5/6*, 615–623.

Seligman, M. E. P., & Fowler, R. D. (2011). Comprehensive Soldier Fitness and the future of psychology. *American Psychologist, 66*, 82–86. doi: 10.1037/a0021898

Shinseki, E. K. (2003). The Army family (White paper). Retrieved from http://www.whs.mil.libproxy.lib.unc.edu/library/Dig/AR-M620U_20080912.pdf

U.S. Department of Defense, Defense Manpower Data Center. (2009b). *2008 surveys of military spouses: Impact of deployments on spouses and children.* Alexandria, VA: Author.

Wiens, T. W., & Boss, P. (2006). Maintaining family resiliency before, during, and after military separation. In C. A. Castro, A. B. Adler, & T. W. Britt (Eds.), *Military life: The psychology of serving in peace and combat* (Vol. 3, pp. 13–38). Westport, CT: Praeger Security International.

Zoroya, G. (2009, June25). Troops' kids feel war toll. *USA Today*. Retrieved from http://www.usatoday.com.libproxy.lib.unc.edu/news/military/2009-06-24 -military-kids_N.htm

Think About It

(1) Does Park quote directly from her sources? If not, why not? How does she employ each source? How do the citation style, APA (Chapter 28), and discipline, psychology, for this research genre shape how Park uses sources?

(2) At the end of the introductory section, Park states, "The thesis is that greater attention to the strengths and assets of military children and families is needed in order to design and implement effective programs to support them." Were you surprised that Park stated her thesis so bluntly, introducing it with "The thesis is that . . ."? Why do you think she might have made this choice? How might it be useful for readers of this review (who are most likely psychology researchers)?

(3) What is the purpose of the "Issues and Recommendations" section of the review? What does Park want readers to do after reading this review? Is the purpose just to summarize key research, or does the review seek to do something beyond that?

Write About It

Select a set of five to six sources used in this review, and locate them from your library. Then, write a different literature review. First, read through the sources and compare them to how Park used them. Are there other interesting findings from these sources that Park does not mention? Are there other facets to the issue? Like Park, you should generate a thesis or claim that refers to what kinds of research need to be done to address this issue.

KRISTIN ANDERSON   COMING TO AMERICA

Anderson, a librarian at the Columbus Metropolitan Library, wrote this review for the School Library Journal *in 2011.*

Read About It

As you read the entries in this annotated bibliography, jot down the basic information Anderson includes for each one. Are there specific elements included in each annotation?

Give me your tired, your poor . . .

But not too tired, not too poor.

And we will give you the red tape, the long line, white bread in its wrapper, forms to fill out, and the looks, the stares that say you are not where or what you should be, not quite, not yet, you will never live up to us.

—from "Statue of Liberty Dreams of Emma Lazarus, Awakens with Tears on Her Cheeks" by Naomi Shihab Nye

To say that immigration is currently a controversial issue would be an understatement. The media is rife with misinformation and does a very poor job of making the critical distinction between legal and illegal immigration. Because of this, it is vitally important that libraries provide students with clear and unbiased material on the topic.

In addition, fiction written from a broad range of perspectives is critical to students' understanding of immigration. Stories can demonstrate that peanut butter seems as strange to some kids as hummus is to others, acknowledge the overwhelming experience of exchanging familiar faces and places with the unsettlingly unfamiliar, or underscore the challenges for children who integrate more quickly into American culture than their parents. Through reading about an immigrant's experience, nonimmigrant children and teens learn to empathize with those they might see as "different," and those who come from an immigrant background learn that they are not alone. Recent concerns about bullying in our schools make these benefits all the more important.

While this bibliography focuses on current immigration, some titles on immigration history have been included where appropriate or in cases where there are parallels between the historical experience and contemporary issues. Their inclusion serves to illustrate that the latest questions about immigration are not in any way new, even though they are often presented as such. And in a few titles, the protagonists are not immigrants themselves, but they struggle with being perceived as newcomers because of cultural practices or simply because of their appearance.

Coming to America

RECORVITS, Helen. My Name Is Yoon. illus. by Gabi Swiatkowska. Farrar/Frances Foster Bks. 2003. Tr $16. ISBN 978-0-374-35114-4.

K-Gr 2—A Korean girl comes to America and struggles with learning a new language as she tries out different names for herself in English. Imaginatively conceived, strikingly handsome paintings convey the confusion and sorrow Yoon experiences, capturing her frustration and ultimate triumph as she forges a personal path in her new home.

FLEMING, Candace. Lowji Discovers America. S&S/Atheneum/Anne Schwartz Bks. 2005. Tr $15.95. ISBN 978-0-689-86299-1.

Gr 3-5—Nine-year-old Lowji has just moved from Bombay to an apartment in Illinois with his parents. It's summer and making friends is a challenge. As he settles into his new home, his confusion about American culture leads to a string of comedic pet adoptions. Told from Lowji's perspective, this is an engaging classroom read-aloud.

APPLEGATE, Katherine. Home of the Brave. Feiwel & Friends. 2007. Tr $16.95. ISBN 978-0-312-36765-7.

Gr 4-6—In this poignant verse novel, a Sudanese refugee violently torn from a culture in which "cattle mean life" moves in with his aunt's family in Minnesota in the middle of winter and is quickly overwhelmed by the vast changes in his environment. Caring for an old cow helps Kek bridge the gap. Audiobook available from Listening Library.

GIFF, Patricia Reilly. Wild Girl. Random/Wendy Lamb Bks. 2009. Tr $15.99. ISBN 978-0-375-83890-3; PLB $18.99. ISBN 978-0-375-93890-0.

Gr 4-6—Five years after her mother's death, 12-year-old Lidie immigrates to New York from Brazil to join her brother and father, who have been training racehorses and who treat her like the little girl they remember. Strong-willed and confused, Lidie finds comfort in the relationship she builds with a horse called Wild Girl.

HOBBS, Will. Crossing the Wire. HarperCollins. 2006. Tr $15.99. ISBN 978-0-06-074138-9; PLB $16.89. ISBN 978-0-06-074139-6.

Gr 5 Up—With his family struggling to get by in Mexico, 15-year-old Victor decides that the only way he can help them is to make the dangerous trip across the American border. This is an adventure story that will also help readers understand the plight of undocumented immigrants. Audiobook available from Recorded Books.

TAN, Shaun. The Arrival. Scholastic/Arthur L. Levine Bks. 2007. Tr $19.99. ISBN 978-0-439-89529-3.

Gr 7 Up—In this wordless graphic novel, Tan captures the feelings of a man recently arrived in a new country who must make sense of his strange surroundings. Fantastical and surreal illustrations demonstrate how confusing and bizarre a new place can look to an outsider.

KAMARA, Mariatu with Susan McCleland. The Bite of the Mango. Annick. 2008. Tr $24.95. ISBN 978-1-55451-159-4; pap.$12.95. ISBN 978-1-55451-158-7.

Gr 9 Up—In this memoir, Kamara, a victim of atrocities experienced in war-torn Sierra Leone, shares her story. When she was 12, rebel soldiers chopped off her hands with a machete and left her for dead. Against all odds, she survived and immigrated to Canada. A realistic and harrowing account of the refugee experience.

The More Things Change, the More They Stay the Same (Understanding Our History)

GLASER, Linda. Emma's Poem: The Voice of the Statue of Liberty. illus. by Claire A. Nivola. Houghton Harcourt. 2010. RTE $16. ISBN 978-0-547-17184-5.

Gr 2-4—Told in spare, free verse paired with tender watercolor and gouache paintings, this biography of Emma Lazarus and the story of how she came to write "The New Colossus" illuminates the importance of immigrant advocacy and serves to remind readers that the United States has always struggled with integrating immigrants. DVD and audio version available from Spoken Arts Media.

PATERSON, Katherine. The Day of the Pelican. Clarion. 2009. Tr $16. ISBN 978-0-547-18188-2.

Gr 5-8—Eleven-year-old Meli and her family, Albanian Kosovars, must leave their home to avoid ethnic cleansing. After spending time in a refugee camp, they arrive in America and begin to integrate into the culture until the attacks of September 11th change their lives once again. Audiobook available from Brilliance Audio.

SENZAI, N. H. Shooting Kabul. S & S/Paula Wiseman Bks. 2010. Tr $16.99. ISBN 978-1-4424-0194-5.

Gr 5-8—After a traumatic escape from Afghanistan in July 2001, in which his younger sister is lost, 11-year-old Fadi and his family find a new home in San Francisco. Set against the backdrop of September 11th and the subsequent bombing of his homeland, Fadi perseveres against bullying and maintains hope in finding his sister.

BAUSUM, Ann.Denied, Detained, Deported: The Dark Side of American Immigration. National Geographic. 2009. Tr $21.95.ISBN 978-1-4263-0332-6; PLB $32.90. ISBN 978-1-4263-0333-3.

Gr 5-9—Three true stories illustrate the struggles America has faced with immigration policy over the years and how ideas of "right" and "wrong" with respect to it change over time. A concluding chapter deals with current immigration issues across our southern border. Historical photographs are included.

BURG, Ann E. All the Broken Pieces. Scholastic. 2009. Tr $16.99. ISBN 978-0-545-08092-7.

Gr 6-8—In this verse novel set in the late 1970s, 12-year-old Matt Pin, the son of an American soldier and a Vietnamese woman, tells his story of being airlifted out of Vietnam. Adopted by an American couple, he is torn between cultures, while many of his peers feel his Vietnamese heritage makes him "the enemy." Audiobook available from Scholastic Audiobooks.

MANIVONG, Laura. Escaping the Tiger. HarperCollins. 2010. Tr $15.99. ISBN 978-0-06-166177-8.

Gr 7-10—In 1982, 12-year-old Vonlai and his family escape Communist Laos by way of a dangerous trip across the Mekong River and spend four long years of deprivation in a Thai refugee camp, waiting to come to America. A gripping tale based on the author's husband's experiences.

General Nonfiction

WEISS, Gail Garfinkel. Americans from Russia and Eastern Europe. (New Americans Series). Marshall Cavendish. 2010. PLB $24.95. ISBN 978-0-7614-4310-0.

Gr 4-8—This entry in an accessible and highly visual series examines recent patterns of immigration from Eastern Europe to America, the challenges immigrants face upon arrival, their contributions to American culture, and the history of immigration. Maps, color photos, and census information are included. Other areas represented in the series are India and South Asia, the Caribbean and Central America, China, Korea, Mexico, Southeast Asia, and West Africa.

MILLER, Karen, ed. Immigration. (Social Issues Firsthand Series). Greenhaven. 2006. PLB $28.70. ISBN 978-0-7377-2893-4.

Gr 8 Up—People from all walks of life and many different countries share their stories. Sections on coming to America, adapting to this country, feeling caught between cultures, and the benefits of immigrating are included.

ANDERSON, Stuart. Immigration. (Greenwood Guide to Business and Economics Series). Greenwood. 2010. Tr $55. ISBN 978-0-313-38028-0.

Gr 9 Up—This text-dense title is ideal for students wanting more information about how immigration policy decisions can have a larger impact on the economy and the country as a whole It's a complete and unbiased discussion of current immigration from an economic and public-policy perspective.

BANKSTON, Carl L., ed. Encyclopedia of American Immigration. 3 Vols. Salem Press. 2010. PLB $395. ISBN 978-1-58765-599-9.

Gr 9 Up—Comprehensive and accessible, this alphabetically arranged, three-volume encyclopedia covers a broad range of topics, from "Au pairs" to "Green cards" to "Xenophobia" and more. Essays on immigration from various regions, historical events, various types of discrimination, and biographies of prominent immigrants are included. Photographs are incorporated with entries where appropriate.

Think About It

(1) How does the introduction to the annotated bibliography frame the sources included? In other words, how does Anderson show the importance of the topic and the usefulness of these sources?

(2) Who do you think is the audience for this annotated bibliography? How is the information Anderson provides tailored for that audience?

(3) Do the annotations simply summarize each source, or do they do more than that? How does Anderson evaluate each source?

Write About It

Write an annotated bibliography of sources on immigration (or another current issue) that would be suitable for first-year college students at your university. Your annotated bibliography could be given directly to students, or to librarians seeking to help students find relevant sources. Like Anderson, you can focus on fiction as well as non-fiction sources. Be sure to evaluate each source for its usefulness for your audience (Chapter 25).

RYAN BABICH AND SYLVIA SMITH "CRADLE TO GRAVE": AN ANALYSIS OF SUSTAINABLE FOOD SYSTEMS IN A UNIVERSITY SETTING

Ryan Babich and Sylvia Smith published this research paper in the Journal of Culinary Sciences and Technology *in 2010. At the time, Babich was an undergraduate at Southern Illinois University, where he majored in human nutrition and dietetics.*

Smith is an associate professor of hospitality and tourism administration at the same institution. Babich also presented the results from this study at the Graduate Student Research Conference in Hospitality and Tourism in 2011.

Read About It

As you read, pay attention to how this article is organized. What are the main sections, and what goes on in each section?

Abstract

The ultimate goal of this research was to understand the process of food service sustainability through a limited "cradle-to-grave" analysis of Southern Illinois University's (SIU) campus dining facilities. The process of researching the dining halls' sustainability was broken into three separate stages: food mileage analysis, food waste analysis, and vermicomposting analysis. The first stage results determined that the dining halls were 15.67% sustainable in their food purchasing process. The goal for the university was to obtain a 20% purchase rate of sustainable products. The total carbon footprint for the university was 1533.5 tons of CO_2 for 1,990 items. This carbon output is equivalent to the annual greenhouse gas emissions from 278.82 passenger vehicles. The total mileage of the food items was 775,394.50 miles.

The second stage of the research calculated the average amount of waste that was produced per student. SIU's dining halls utilize a new system of service called trayless, where trays are removed and students have to fill up a plate instead of a tray. The average food waste per student was 1.04 oz a day. Currently, the waste produced is very limited. This demonstrates that trayless dining has proven effective and needs to be continued.

The final stage was a vermicomposting analysis in which a pre-composting phase was introduced to expedite the vermicomposting process. The amount of time taken for this pre-composting phase was still longer than anticipated. The longer time frame translated into additional monies to pay for utilities for the building and payroll for the workers. Vermicomposting, although ecological[ly] friendly, does not appear cost effective in this setting.

This study demonstrates how universities can begin the process of sustainability. By using several methods that have been investigated to increase sustainability (food mileage calculations and tray-less dining), university food services should be able to implement more sustainable practices in order to encourage making our universities green.

INTRODUCTION

The ultimate goal of this research was to understand the process of foodservice sustainability through a limited "cradle-to-grave" analysis of a medium-size Midwestern university campus dining facilities. The university foodservice under study feeds 4,000 students through the dining services. On average the university prepares 7,000 meals a day (Conners, B., personal communication, May 11, 2010).

During the 2009–2010 academic calendar, the dining facilities implemented programs that would help reduce the distance that food travels, limit the amount of food waste, and recycle as much excess waste as possible. By purchasing from local food sources, implementing trayless dining, and vermicomposting excess food waste, the university was attempting to bring their dining facilities into the future of sustainability.

BACKGROUND

Sustainability has been described as development that meets the needs of the present without compromising future generations to meet their own needs. It is further defined in terms of economic and social justice by establishing a fundamental framework of ecology, economy and equity (American Dietetic Association [ADA] Sustainable Food System Task Force, 2007). With the understanding that global warming is a threat, the need for reducing our energy consumption and waste has become a goal that we all should strive to achieve. The idea of sustainability has expanded from grassroots movements to boardrooms, places of industry, and universities. Many universities are taking a lead in the movement toward environmental sustainability.

Universities play a critical role in developing environmental sustainable policies, becoming climate neutral, and educating and graduating environmentally responsible students. Universities across the nation are committed to reducing carbon emissions, employing full-time sustainability staff, incorporating "green" into the curriculum, developing eco-friendly buildings, and promoting green transportation.

University dining facilities are beginning to recognize their role in the sustainability movement. Many universities are paying attention to their campus dining facilities to reduce their ecological footprint. College dining facilities arguably have the most room for influence because they tend to take up to five times more water, five times more energy, and five times more waste than other campus buildings (Curry, 2008). In order to reduce food waste and subsequent costs, some universities are making the transition to trayless dining. Trayless dining helps to reduce the amount of food waste that is produced by limiting the amount of food that students are able to carry in a single visit through the buffet lines. A study conducted by Sarjahani, Serrano, and Johnson (2009) analyzed the food waste produced in two "all-you-can-eat" dining facilities at Virginia Polytechnic Institute to determine how much food waste was produced by the students with and without trays. The researchers found that the trayless dining systems had statistically significant lower amounts of food waste in all categories. Overall, it was concluded that a flat fee for food, in conjunction with all-you-can-eat dining is misleading to consumers and does not take into consideration the environmental and economic burdens that food production demands. . . .

Recently the university has made changes to some of their environmental food-service policies, yet very little research has been conducted to identify what is working. From the distribution of the food to the disposal of the waste, there are no concrete records to hold the university accountable to a higher standard. Through a limited "cradle-to-grave" analysis, we will be able to provide the university dining hall's data to support environmental initiatives and suggestions on how to make improvements to the sustainable dining experience.

METHODS

The university under study has three student dining halls on campus: Trueblood, Lentz, and University Hall. The process of researching the dining halls' sustainability was broken into three separate stages: food mileage analysis, food waste analysis, and vermicomposting analysis. . . . [Cut: Stage 1 and Stage 3]

Stage 2: Food Waste Analysis

The second stage of the research was the food waste analysis. From September to October 2009, time was spent in the dish room at Trueblood and Lentz dining facilities to determine the amount of food waste that the students produced. The food waste collection was based on obtaining two days' worth of student food waste from the same serving period from each dining hall (i.e., breakfast, lunch, and dinner) and then calculating a per person average food waste based on the number of students for that particular serving period. The serving periods were divided by meal time: breakfast, 7:30 a.m.–10:30 a.m., lunch, 11 a.m.–2 p.m., and dinner, 4 p.m.–7 p.m.

The dining halls use a pulping system to dispose of excess food waste. The system works as follows: students enter the dining hall and obtain their food; after they finish eating, the dishes are placed on a conveyor belt; the dishes travel on the conveyor belt to the dish room. Once in the dish room, the food is scraped into a flowing trough system as the conveyor belts moves toward the end of the belt system; once the bulk of the waste is removed, the eating utensils are collected on a tray and pushed down a series of rollers to the washer; the washer uses a series of faucet heads to rinse the excess waste into the trough system; after the residual food waste (e.g., crumbs, sauce, etc.) is removed from the plate, it is placed on another conveyor belt to be taken to the actual dishwashing machine; the food travels through the trough to the pulper and the food is cut into smaller pieces. The entire process is repeated multiple times throughout the duration of the serving period.

For our study, after the serving period had ended, the pulped waste was gathered and weighed on a scale. The scale increments were based on a rounded .25 lb differentiation (1.25–1.50–1.75–2.00). This means that when an item is weighed the item is rounded up to the next weight. Further, the scale was calibrated by weighing food products with known weights and it was determined that the scale was 3 lbs off the actual weight. This calibration was applied to the collected food waste. Food waste results were recorded in an Excel worksheet until each of the entire serving periods were collected, to calculate an average food waste per serving period.

RESULTS

Food Waste Analysis

The food waste collection was based on obtaining two days' worth of student food waste from the same serving period (i.e., breakfast, lunch, and dinner) and then calculating a per person average food waste based on the total number of students for that dining hall and the total waste produced by that dining hall.

The total waste being produced by the students was 1.04 ounces per student a day. The greatest amount of waste was being produced at Lentz Hall but only marginally more than Trueblood. University Hall was not included in this analysis because it does not work on the same pulping system as Trueblood and Lentz. . . .

DISCUSSION AND RECOMMENDATIONS

The implications of sustainability have reached into the social consciousness of the global economy. Government agencies, corporations, farming communities, and the like have all followed the same movement closely. The overall goal adopted by this Midwestern university is to reach a 20% sustainability margin for its total food budget by 2020. The purpose of this study was to examine the distance food travels to reach the university, determine the amount of waste being produced by the students, and analyze a precomposting system applied to the existing vermicomposting process. . . .

Food Waste Analysis

Trayless dining limits the amount of food students take in one sitting. Also, it reduces the amount of food required for production because students are taking less. Students were still able to obtain multiple plates; yet food servings became much more limited because they were no longer allowed to use trays. In turn, this made the dish room more ecologically friendly because of the reduction in food waste and water used to clean additional trays. One additional suggestion would be to have the students personally dispose of the food waste in designated cans to educate the students on the importance of reducing their waste.

In regards to food preparation, the kitchen is producing excessive waste during production. Much of the food is prepared ahead of time to save time and money, yet at the end of the night, the majority of the excess food is being tossed out. The food is brought to a trash compactor and then disintegrated. Over 50 lbs of food is lost per night. One recommendation would be to more closely analyze the eating patterns forecasted for a particular day and prepare and serve food based on the appropriate forecast. . . .

LIMITATIONS

. . .

Food Waste Analysis

First, one of the university dining halls did not work on the same system as the larger two. It uses a trash compactor instead of a pulping system. It was not included in this research. Second, of the two larger dining halls, some of the food waste contained a marginal amount of paper biodegradable napkins. Third, external factors may have affected total attendance for the dining halls (e.g., weather and sporting events). Lastly, menu selection would affect the waste outcome as well. For instance, on September 29, 2009, the menu provided chicken as the main dish. The bones were included in this chicken dish. The students would eat the chicken and remove the bones. The plate would be placed on the conveyor belt to the dish room and removed for proper plate cleaning. The pulper cannot break down the bones and thus the bones needed to be tossed into the garbage as general waste.

CONCLUSIONS

It is hoped that findings from this study may be used by other universities across the country in order to reduce excess resources and practice sustainability. By analyzing these cradle-to-grave steps, the university foodservice community will be able to improve sustainable practices and begin looking to other avenues as a means of continuing the sustainability movement.

REFERENCES

1. American Dietetic Association Sustainable Food System Task Force. 2007. *Healthy land, healthy people: Building a better understanding of sustainable food systems for food and nutrition professionals. A primer on sustainable food systems and emerging roles for food and nutrition professionals*, Chicago, IL: Author.

2. Carbon footprint calculator. http://www.carbonfund.org/business/calculator (http://www.carbonfund.org/business/calculator)

3. Curry, M. (2008). The war on college cafeteria trays. http://www.time.com (http://www.time.com) (Accessed: 24 January 2009).

4. Illinois General Assembly Public Act. Public Act 096–0579. http://www.ilga.gov/legislation/publicacts//fulltext.asp?Name-096—0579&GA-96 (http://www.ilga.gov/legislation/publicacts//fulltext.asp?Name-096—0579&GA-96)

5. Mileage calculator. http://www.mapquest.com/ (http://www.mapquest.com/)

6. Sarjahani, A., Serrano, E. L. and Johnson, R. 2009. Food and non-edible, compostable waste in a university dining facility. *Journal of Hunger & Environmental Nutrition*, 4(1): 95–102. [Taylor & Francis Online]

7. Vermont food audit. http://www.uvm.edu/~ecoreps/images/2009-2010/actions/2009FoodWasteWeighInResults.pdf (http://www.uvm.edu/~ecoreps/images/2009-2010/actions/2009FoodWasteWeighInResults.pdf) (Accessed: 28 January 2009).

Think About It

(1) This article describes a scientific study the authors conducted. How do the organization of the article and the contents of each section tell a story about that study? What does each section contribute to the reader's understanding of the study?

(2) Why do you think the authors include "limitations" in their study? Does this detract from their ethos, or does it increase it? Why might these be included in a scientific study?

(3) Why is this study important to researchers? Would it have an audience besides other researchers in this field?

Write About It

Conduct your own study of food waste. With your class or your group, keep a visual food diary for a week. In your food diary, write down when and where you ate each meal, and whether or not you threw away uneaten food. Use a digital camera or a cell phone to take "before and after" pictures of each meal. Before you start the study, develop a hypothesis. What factors would make individuals more likely to waste food? (Eating in the dining hall versus at home versus a restaurant, for instance; eating alone or with friends; etc.) Be sure to note this information for each meal.

Then, pool your results with your group. Using the photographs as evidence, tally how many meals were not finished overall, and then how many meals were not finished based on the factors you are tracking (for example, what percentage of meals in the dining hall were unfinished versus meals eaten at home or in a dorm room?). Using the Babich and Smith article as a model, write a research paper that explains the purpose of your study, the method you used, the results, and your conclusions. Consider how you can use a table to display your data.

ELAINE CHUN   READING RACE BEYOND BLACK AND WHITE

Elaine Chun wrote this research paper for the journal Discourse & Society *in 2011. Chun is an assistant professor of English at the University of South Carolina, where she researches language, identity, and culture in multiethnic settings.*

Read About It

Chun uses some key terms to help her analysis, such as "authenticity," "hypermasculinity," and "racialization." As you read, note these and any other terms that express concepts that seem to be key to her study. Then, see if you can generate your own definitions of these terms, based on how Chun uses them. (If you get stuck, look them up in a dictionary or online search engine).

Abstract

This article examines the practice of reading race, or the explicit labeling of people or practices with race terms. Through the close analysis of interactional moments, I examine how speakers of different ethnicities and genders across a Texas high school community strategically drew on this sociocultural practice for ideological commentary. First, I argue that readings of race often depended on an ideology of racial authenticity according to which students were expected to engage in racial performances that corresponded with their perceived racial identity. Second, I suggest that reading race was a strategy of gender and class commentary that measured speakers in relation to stereotypes of privileged white hyperfemininity and working-class black hypermasculinity. The analysis underscores the importance of attending to how racialized language is a negotiated process, how this process intersects with local ideologies of race, gender, class, and authenticity, and how reading race often achieves more than racial classification alone.

Introduction

Race remains a salient dimension of social distinction in the USA. By high school, students are typically well-practiced in placing race labels on their peers, clothing styles, and cafeteria spaces, despite the anxieties that race talk may cause in some public realms (Pollock, 2004). This article examines the sociocultural practice of reading race, or the explicit labeling of people or practices with race terms, such as black, white, ghetto, or prep, in a multiethnic high school in Texas. As a form of racialization, this practice entails the assignment of racial meanings to cultural signs that might have been read in other ways. . . .

In my analysis, I explore how reading race in fact constituted a strategic social practice for ideological commentary, not only on racial authenticity but also on gender and class performance. Reading race was a form of social action that could have important ideological consequences. Through the close analysis of various interactional moments, I examine how reading race emerged in conversations among speakers of different ethnicities and genders across the high school community and how this practice reflected and reproduced local ideologies of race. First, I argue that this practice, which was typically embedded in evaluative acts, tended to depend on an ideology of racial authenticity according to which students were expected to engage in racial performances that corresponded with their perceived racial identity. Second, I suggest that reading race was a strategy of gender and class commentary that measured speakers in relation to prep girls, viewed as embodying privileged white hyperfemininity, and ghetto boys, viewed as embodying working-class black hypermasculinity. The analysis I present underscores the importance of attending to how racialized language is a negotiated process, how this process intersects with local ideologies of race, gender, class, and authenticity, and how reading race often achieves more than racial classification alone. . . .

Reading Race at Diversity High

Diversity High, the site of my research, was located in a working-to-middle-class community in Texas that had been shaped racially and economically by families with links to a neighboring military base. The pseudonym I have chosen for the school derives from students' frequent characterizations of their own community as diverse. My analysis is based on 27 instances of reading race during 17 conversations between 10 groups of friends and classmates. These analyzed moments represent only a subset of similar moments that I observed and recorded during my time at Diversity High between August 2003 and January 2005, when I tutored nearly 200 students and joined them at lunch and afterschool activities. The students represented in the examples had all been raised in the USA, such that they oriented to mainstream US ideologies of race, class, and gender, but their own racial experiences were quite varied as they identified diversely as black, black-Filipino-Puerto Rican, black-German, black-Korean, Chinese-Hawaiian-Korean, Filipino, Filipino-Puerto Rican, Korean, Mexican, Pakistani, Puerto Rican, Vietnamese, and white. Ironically, despite the local recognition of a large variety of racial possibilities, the acts of reading race in the data I have collected largely oriented to two racial categories: blackness and whiteness. . . .

Reading Racial (In)authenticity

Reading race was not an objective description of an existing world of racial signs, but a subjective practice that not only assigned signs with racial meanings but often designated them as racially authentic or inauthentic. The local sociocultural importance of racial authenticity is clear in the next several excerpts, in which girls and boys are critiqued for engaging inauthentically in either white or black practices. In each case, race readers not only collaboratively construct other students as inauthentic but also critique their racial performance as a pathological denial of their own racial reality.

The first example takes place in a classroom where a group of classmates sometimes ate lunch, and the conversation emerges about 13 minutes after I have asked them to describe different ways of speaking at the school. The classmates, most of whom are African American, assess an African American female cheerleader named Belinda, who is read as engaging in "white" practices. Through both parodic stylization of her speech (lines 28–31) and metapragmatic evaluation of her practices with race terms (lines 19, 21, 22, 23, 24, 38), they collaboratively construct Belinda as problematically inauthentic. . . .

4 ANN: There's this girl-

5 You know Belinda.

6 DENASHA: Oh Belinda.

12 LAQUISHA: You don't like her?

13 DENASHA: I'm not fat? (Belinda stylization)

. . .

18 ANN: she's just-

19 LJ: Belinda's a oreo.

21 VIVIONI: Belinda's like a black-

22 a white girl in a black girl's body

. . .

27 LAQUISHA: She's like a-

28 VIVIONI: Miss Smith? (prep girl stylization)

29 Okay?

30 Okay we were reading

31 Romeo and Juliette?

Belinda's racial performance is constructed as problematic . . . through LJ's and Ann's uses of the term oreo (lines 19, 23, 24), a metaphor of racial incongruence that circulates in US popular culture. The negative evaluation of Belinda is additionally constructed through Vivioni's parody, which includes high-pitched falsetto and rising intonation to index her hyperfeminine whiteness (lines 28–31). . . .

Boys were also sometimes critiqued for their inauthenticity. In the next example, which takes place during another dinner interview, Grace and Heather discuss the case of a "blond and blue-eyed" (lines 23–4) European American boy named Keith who performed blackness. Grace presents Keith as an example of a wannabe, a label that students used to describe boys viewed as aspiring, but failing to achieve, masculine coolness. . . .

1 GRACE: I remember Keith.

2 Remember him?

3 HEATHER: Keith

4 GRACE: From the um

5 eight grade?

6 HEATHER: The black one?

7 GRACE: No he was white.

8 He was always trying to act black though . . .

10 I remember he said he was . . .

12 white on the outside and

13 black on the inside?

14 HEATHER: Oh yeah . . .

16 GRACE: He said h- he used to be black

17 but he fell in the washing machine . . .

20 ELAINE: Did he really seem black? . . .

23 GRACE: No he's blond and

24 blue eyed . . .

27 HEATHER: It looks like he tried

28 to be black.

29 GRACE: He does.

30 He's trying to rap

35 Oh he talked slang . . .

44 ELAINE: Um and what do you think about that . . .

46 GRACE: It's kind of annoying

47 cause he's not.

Not only do these girls explicitly read Keith's racial performance in lines 8, 13 and 28, but they provide examples of his symbolic display in response to my questions: Keith was described as "trying to rap" (line 30) and "talk[ing] slang" (line 35). As in the previous cases, his racial incongruence is constructed as a pathological inauthenticity that was . . . "annoying" (line 46).

Conclusion

Reading race may appear to parse the social world in terms of a singular social dimension, but the preceding analysis has shown this act to be linked with complex ideologies of authenticity, gender, and class. I have suggested that the embedding of these acts in negative assessments often reproduced an ideology according to which an individual's racial performance should correspond with her or his perceived racial identity. My analysis has also suggested that race readings were typically linked to meanings of gender and class; stereotypes of working-class black masculinity (ghetto boys) and middle-class white femininity (prep girls) informed the kinds of values and meanings that were implicit in race readings. In other words, the value that students assigned to racialized performance potentially were linked to two local ideologies: one that values racial authenticity and another that polices gendered performance. . . .

References

Pollack, M. (2004). Colormute: Race Talk Dilemmas in an American School. Princeton, NJ: Princeton University Press.

Think About It

(1)   The author of this article is a linguist. What forms the basis of her evidence in this article? How does she present that evidence, and how does she interpret it? How do terms like "authenticity" or "hypermasculinity" inform her analysis?

(2)   The full version of this article contained over forty references, but most of them appeared in the second section of the article, a review of recent literature on the topic. The section included here includes only one reference. Why do you think this is the case? Why does the body of the research paper focus mainly on the researcher's study results, not on prior research?

(3)   Think back to your own experiences in high school. Did students at your school "read" each other's gender and race performances? What function do you think "reading" race and gender serves in high school settings?

Write About It

Conduct your own study of student language on your campus. For your study, keep track of slang words you hear on your campus. For a week, keep a notebook in which you transcribe conversations you hear (or, record them with your cellphone—but be sure to ask for permission first). Do you find that students use different slang or speaking patterns depending on race or gender? What slang terms do you hear especially often on your campus, and what can they tell us about student culture? After collecting your data, write a research paper, using Chun's article as a model. Be sure to include concrete examples of conversations you wrote down, and to interpret what they mean.

Reading Workplace Genres

CHAPTER OUTLINE

ANONYMOUS   OPEN LETTER TO INTERIM DEAN BROWN

This business letter was published anonymously on EagleiOnline.com, *the student-run online newspaper of Boston College Law School, in October of 2010. The student published this letter anonymously, but in a public forum.*

Read About It

As you read this letter, think about the strategies that the author uses to gain the sympathy of his audience.

George D. Brown
Interim Dean
Boston College Law School
885 Centre Street
Newton Centre, MA 02459

Dear Dean Brown,

I hope this letter finds you well. I want to start by thanking you for serving as the interim Dean. I know that it is always difficult to step into a situation at the last minute, but we are all thankful for your leadership.

Unfortunately, the occasion for me writing to you is not a happy one. As a 3L, my peers and I find ourselves in the midst of one of the worst job markets in the history of our profession. A few of us have been able to find employment, but the overwhelming majority of us are desperately looking, and unable to find anything. We are discouraged, scared, and in many cases, feeling rather hopeless about our chances of ever getting to practice law.

To compound our difficulties, many of us are in an enormous amount of debt from our legal studies. Soon after our graduation, we will be asked to make very large monthly payments towards this debt, regardless of whether we've been able to find employment or not. It is a debt which, despite being the size of a mortgage, gives us no tangible asset which we could try to sell or turn in to the bank. We are not even able to seek the protection of bankruptcy from this debt.

I write to you from a more desperate place than most: my wife is pregnant with our first child. She is due in April. With fatherhood impending, I go to bed every night terrified of the thought of trying to provide for my child AND paying off my J.D, and resentful at the thought that I was convinced to go to law school by empty promises of a fulfilling and remunerative career. And although my situation puts the enormity of the problem into sharp focus, there are a lot of us facing similar financial disasters. In all of this, we have had very little help from career services, who all seem to be as confounded as we are by this job market. Kate Devlin Joyce has been an amazing and helpful ally; everyone else in that office has shrugged their shoulders at us and asked if we have tried using LinkedIn [a networking web site].

I'd like to propose a solution to this problem: I am willing to leave law school, without a degree, at the end of this semester. In return, I would like a full refund of the tuition I've paid over the last two and a half years.

This will benefit both of us: on the one hand, I will be free to return to the teaching career I left to come here. I'll be able to provide for my family without the crushing weight of my law school loans. On the other hand, this will help BC Law go up in the rankings, since you will not have to report my unemployment at graduation to *US News*. This will present no loss to me, only gain: in today's job market, a J.D. seems to be more of a liability than an asset. I will explain the gap in my resume by simply saying that I attended law school, but was unable to finish for financial reasons. In the short run, refunding my tuition might present a financial challenge to the law school, but in the long run, better *US News* rankings will help you far more than having yet another disgruntled and unemployed alumnus.

I would love to discuss this proposal with you further. I would also love to hear any other thoughts or solutions you may have. Thanks very much for your time, and I look forward to speaking with you.

Best regards,
[Name redacted]
Class of 2011

Think About It

(1)   As an "open letter," this document has multiple audiences. List as many of those audiences as you can. What does this author hope to persuade each of those audiences to believe?
(2)   Throughout the letter, the author uses the word "we" (along with "I"). Who does this "we" represent? How is using "we" a persuasive tool?
(3)   Do you think that the author is serious about his proposal to the dean? Why or why not?

Write About It

Think of an issue on your campus that you believe should be addressed by the administration. Write an open letter to the proper person in the administration, the person who would have the power to actually bring about change. Think about your multiple audiences. Using this reading and the business letters in Chapter 12 as examples.

TIGERMOM   AN OPEN LETTER TO THE CATHOLIC LEAGUE FROM AN ADOPTED CHILD

This letter was published on the progressive political website the Daily KOS. *The letter was written in response to a tweet (a note published on* Twitter.com*) by the Catholic League, a Catholic advocacy group unaffiliated with the Catholic Church. The tweet addressed adoption, as you will see. TigerMom is the anonymous pen name of a regular contributor to the* Daily KOS. *She is a married mother of two who lives in the southwestern U.S.*

Read About It

You do not have the text of the original Tweet that this letter was written in response to. As you read, see if you can imagine what the Tweet might have said.

To Whom It May Concern:

I just read your highly insulting tweet regarding Hilary Rosen, and I am livid!

In your short, snotty little tweet, you have reiterated an extremely hurtful opinion and viewpoint about adoption that I spent years having to deal with growing up.

I am 46 years old. I was adopted in 1966 through Catholic Charities in Philadelphia when I was one month old. I know very little about my biological parents: they were both teenagers; both of Irish descent; and I was born in the hospital associated with St. Vincent's Home for (Wayward) Girls. That's all I know, and that's okay with me, because I know that my parents (now deceased) who reared me were overwhelmed with joy at being able to adopt me.

My parents were always honest with me about my being adopted. They answered my questions as best they could, and made it abundantly clear that I was loved and a gift. In fact, my parents brought me home the day before my mother's birthday, so she always considered me the best birthday present she ever got! I love and miss her dearly.

But, there was always something else. It was strongly suggested that while my family knew I was adopted, I still shouldn't talk about it publicly. You see, being adopted, back then, still had a little bit of a stigma—the idea that I was an illegitimate child, although now a bit more respectable because I had parents. But they weren't "blood" relatives, and some people viewed that as being less than a true part of the family.

As an adult, I see the foolishness of this, but as a child, I felt like I had this secret, that somehow I wasn't my parents' "real" daughter. And believe me, once word got out that I was adopted, there were those in the neighborhood who told me to my face that I wasn't my parents' "real" daughter. Do you understand how hurtful that is to a child, being taunted with the notion that their family isn't "real" because they're not "blood"? All every child wants is to be loved, and an adopted child needs that just as much as any biological child, sometimes even more so. You see, we understand that, for whatever reason, we could not be with the one who bore us, yet we know that the ones who took us in chose to open their hearts and lives to us. That is a stronger bond than blood, and that is what makes a family.

And in your . . . tweet, you opened the Pandora's Box once again that adopted children are somewhat less than pure, and denigrated every adopted child and adoptive parent out there . . . .

. . . [Y]ou say . . . if the child is not born of the womb that loves and cares for her, she is less than perfect. . . .

You owe . . . me and every adopted child and parent an apology, but I won't be holding my breath.

TigerMom

Adopted Child

Think About It

(1) The preceding letter has multiple audiences. Who do you think these audiences might be? Why?

(2) The author uses narrative (Chapter 19) in an attempt to make her letter more persuasive. Which parts of the letter are narrative? Which parts are not? Do you find the use of personal narrative to be persuasive? Why or why not?

(3) The original tweet read like this: "Lesbian Dem Hilary Rosen tells Ann Romney she never worked a day in her life. Unlike Rosen, who had to adopt kids, Ann raised 5 of her own." Hilary Rosen is a political commentator for CNN who is a lesbian and an adoptive mother. Ann Romney is the wife of Mitt Romney, former governor of Massachusetts and, at the time of the tweet, the Republican nominee for the U.S. presidency. Do you think that the letter responds appropriately to this tweet? Why or why not?

Write About It

Think of a controversial current issue about which you feel strongly and have personal experience. Write a letter in which you use narrative (Chapter 19) to persuade the recipient to agree with you.

CATHOLIC BISHOPS OF WISCONSIN   TRAVELING TOGETHER IN HOPE

This letter was published online and made available to the public through Catholic websites. The authors, the five Catholic Bishops of the state of Wisconsin at the time (2011), wrote this letter collaboratively.

Read About It

As you read the following letter, notice that the authors use historical arguments throughout the letter. Mark the arguments that use history as persuasion.

December 12, 2011

A Pastoral Letter on Immigration
The Catholic Bishops of Wisconsin

Dear Brothers and Sisters in Christ,

Over the course of two thousand years, the Catholic Church has developed a special expertise in the area of immigration. Our universal Church has observed and participated in migrations all across the globe. We have helped millions of immigrants—Catholic and non-Catholic—to prosper in new lands. We have done so and will continue to do so because we see the image and likeness of God in every human being. From the Prophets to recent papal teaching, the Church has a consistent message: welcome the stranger (Mt 25:35).

We recognize that Catholics, all in good conscience, hold differing views about U.S. immigration policy. We also know that many are dissatisfied with the status quo and are looking for a workable solution. Our Catholic teaching provides important principles to guide us.

Our Catechism addresses directly the duty of wealthy nations like ours to welcome foreigners who are searching for a better life and to respect their natural right to emigrate. At the same time, it recognizes the right of governments to regulate immigration for the sake of the common good (Catechism of the Catholic Church, 2nd ed., n. 2241). This duty and this right are not incompatible; it is possible to respect both.

Most Americans recognize that we are a nation of immigrants. At the same time, many are deeply troubled that millions of immigrants reside in the U.S. without legal authorization. We too share this concern; obeying laws is essential to any stable society. As Americans, however, we have to acknowledge that some of our foreign and domestic policies and practices have contributed to the illegal entry of immigrants.

Our nation's incessant demand for inexpensive goods and services is one of the driving forces behind the export of American jobs and the hiring of immigrant workers. Our nation is a magnet for immigrants because there is work here and because of the international disparity in wages. Our aging population needs younger workers. Entire economic sectors—service, construction, agriculture—would falter without immigrant labor. Here in Wisconsin, our dairy industry relies heavily on immigrants.

The tremendous economic pull overwhelms our inadequate immigration system, and our failure to reform the system effectively ensures illegal entry. The U.S. provides only 5,000 permanent and 66,000 temporary visas annually to low-wage workers wishing to enter this country, a total far below the number of workers needed by key sectors of our economy. As a result, immigrants take the risk of working here illegally.

Large migrations are always accompanied by cultural tensions between citizens and immigrants. There is often a long period of adjustment for both groups. This is especially true in difficult economic times.

Many who fear for their jobs see immigrants as competitors. Others worry that immigrants threaten our culture. Our nation has experienced this tension before when waves of immigrants from Poland, Germany, Ireland, Italy, and China—to name just a few—were once considered undesirables and faced open discrimination.

In spite of all the challenges they faced, however, these and other immigrants helped build our nation. Again and again, America has demonstrated that its highest ideals—life, liberty, and the pursuit of happiness—can be embraced and reinvigorated by people from all around the world who come to our country searching for a better way of life. . . .

Let us then commit ourselves to helping resolve this pressing immigration crisis. We do so not just for our nation's sake, but also for the sake of millions of children and adults who live fearfully in the shadows, who are vulnerable to exploitation, whose family members are being cruelly isolated, detained, and deported.

We therefore urge all Catholics to take the following steps to help resolve the present crisis:

- Pray for immigrants, lawmakers, and for one another as we address this challenge.
- Read the accompanying Questions and Answers resource and visit the U.S. Conference of Catholic Bishops (USCCB) Justice for Immigrants website (www.justiceforimmigrants.org) for additional resources.
- Educate fellow citizens and legislators about the need for comprehensive immigration reform—a reform that is not a blanket amnesty, but rather a path to citizenship that includes restitution where it is owed.
- Reject state and federal legislation that unfairly profiles or discriminates against immigrants.
- Reach out to immigrants and begin building communities of hope. For our part, as your bishops, we commit ourselves to welcoming all—whether documented or undocumented—in our parishes and Church institutions. Our Catholic faith can and must transcend political and cultural turmoil. Let us remember that in the end we are all migrants on this earth, traveling together in hope towards our loving God. May Our Lady of Guadalupe, Mother of the Americas, protect us on our journey.

Sincerely yours in Christ,

The Most Reverend Jerome E. Listecki, Archbishop of Milwaukee

The Most Reverend Robert C. Morlino, Bishop of Madison

The Most Reverend David L. Ricken, Bishop of Green Bay

The Most Reverend William P. Callahan, Bishop of La Crosse

The Most Reverend Peter F. Christensen, Bishop of Superior

Think About It

(1)   Look over the letter. Does it resemble any other genres that you are familiar with, such as a factsheet? a political speech? an op-ed? How so? Why do you think that the authors chose the genre of a letter to present this information?

(2)   The authors quote the Declaration of Independence in their letter, when they write that "life, liberty, and the pursuit of happiness" should be open to immigrants in the U.S. As a rhetorical strategy, what does quoting the Declaration of Independence accomplish?

(3)   What strategies do the authors use to generate sympathy for immigrants?

Write About It

Read this letter carefully. Make a list of the rhetorical strategies that the authors use to persuade their audiences. Then, compose a letter in response to this one, addressed to its authors. To plan your argument, refer to the strategies described in Chapter 18.

ETHAN GENAUER   SUSTAINABLE FOOD SYSTEMS RÉSUMÉ

This résumé is published online as a way for the author to showcase his experience in a particular field: developing sustainable food systems.

Read About It

As you read, consider the amount of details the author provides for each item. For each item, note down whether you find the level of detail to be too little, too much, or just right.

Ethan Genauer
Email: ethang@email.com   Phone: (555) 222-3131

Objective

To utilize my experience and skills in farming, research and writing, community organizing, event coordination, grassroots activism and progressive policy advocacy to educate, communicate, advocate and organize for sustainable food systems.

Education

• BA Degree with Majors in History, Political Science and Middle East Studies (GPA 3.6/4) from Rutgers College, Graduated 2004, New Brunswick, NJ
• Study Abroad: Tel Aviv University Overseas School Honors Program and Arava Institute for Environmental Studies (AIES), Israel
• Coursework in Sustainable Agriculture at AIES, Spring 2000 and Volunteer, Cook Student Organic Farm, Rutgers University, Spring 2001

• Summer 2006—Certified Permaculture Design Course ("Earth Activist Training") Missouri

Sustainable Food Systems and Community Organizing Experience (selected)

• Spring–Summer 2009, Special Assistant, Abundance in Balance, Bay Area, CA
   ~ Designed and installed edible "food forest" and permaculture landscapes at homes,
   organizations and schools. Mapped designs, planted trees, shrubs, flowers, herbs and
   vegetables, placed irrigation systems, worked with volunteers, conducted outreach,
   and mobilized community participation in "Grow Food" special events and work days.

• Spring to Fall 2008, Volunteer Assistant Farmer, La Placita Gardens, Albuquerque, NM
   ~ Assisted community, interfaith and youth groups with partnership growing produce
   on 4 acres at historic County Open Space site. Helped till, plant, weed, cultivate,
   harvest and market crops, recruit and lead volunteers, and support classroom service
   learning outings. Organized events including "silent auction" benefit event at statewide
   Environmental Educators conference and "Community Gardens CYCLEbration," a
   free bike tour of numerous Albuquerque community gardens and farms.

• Summer–Fall 2008, Campaign Outreach Assistant, NM Youth Organized, Albuquerque
   ~ Conducted outreach to city residents to raise awareness and opposition regarding
   environmental impacts of oil and gas drilling inside Albuquerque, collected petition
   signatures, and encouraged democratic civil participation in local, state and national
   elections.

• Winter–Summer 2007, Farm Apprentice, Erda Gardens and Learning Center,
Albuquerque
   ~ Interned with community-supported agriculture (CSA) farm to cultivate five plots
   (8 acres) using biodynamic agriculture practices. Responsible for tilling, planting,
   transplanting, irrigation, composting, fertilizing, weeding, harvesting, supervising
   volunteers, distributing shares to CSA members, selling produce at farmers markets,
   and organizing special events.

• Winter–Spring 2006, Field Organizer, Culture Change, National "Peak Oil and Post-
Petroleum Sustainable Living" Conference, Washington, DC
   ~ Coordinated logistical planning (venue arrangements, speakers travel, audio and
   video recording), volunteer recruitment and coordination, media communications, local
   and national outreach, registration process, conference schedule, design and printing
   of conference literature. Recruited leading organic farmers and permaculture experts
   to speak about sustainable food production without dependence on fossil fuels.

• Winter–Summer 2005, Lead Field Organizer, BioDemocracy Mobilization, Institute for
Social Ecology (ISE) Biotechnology Project, Philadelphia, PA
   ~ Led development of $15,000 "BioDemocracy Conference and Mobilization"
   advocating strong environmental regulation and democratic oversight over genetically
   engineered agriculture, health care and weaponry sectors of corporate biotechnology.
   Administered website and Internet communications networks, facilitated coalition
   meetings, recruited and supervised volunteers, enlisted sponsor and participant
   organizational allies, designed and distributed outreach literature (color postcards and
   posters, dozens of flyers and e-mail alerts, 8-page newsletter, research article
   published in national environmental journal), drafted grant proposals, organized fundraising events, negotiated event venues, and compiled final weeklong schedule of over

50 BioDemocracy events, including 3-day Conference, a "Day of Action" attended by over 1,000 people, "Reclaim the Commons" festival, "Farmers Speak-Out" opposing GMOs in agriculture, and feature presentation of film "The Future of Food."

Publications, Awards, Events (selected)

2009—Wrote essay on youth leadership in sustainable food movement / Journalistic reporting on Ecological Farming Conference in Pacific Grove, "Strengthening the Roots" Student Convergence in Santa Cruz, CA, National "Slow Money" Gathering in Santa Fe, NM, and Community Food Security Coalition national conference in Des Moines, IA / Scholarship to attend national Growing Food and Justice for All Initiative gathering in Milwaukee, WI / Assisted installation of permaculture food forests at Food First! office in Oakland, CA and UCSC campus in Santa Cruz, CA / Wrote travel essay describing visit to Essene Garden of Peace in rural Oregon

2008—Attended W.K. Kellogg Foundation "Food and Society Gathering for Good Food" in Phoenix, AZ as delegate with national student group Real Food Challenge / Participated in full week of "Youth Food Movement" discussions, workshops, and advocacy at "Slow Food Nation" Gathering in San Francisco, CA / Campaigned in 3 states with White House Organic Farm Project cross-country bus tour gathering petition signatures for next President to plant organic food crops on White House lawn / Organized youth scholarships and facilitated workshop led by young farmers at NM Organic Farming Conference in Albuquerque / Presented workshop on sustainable agriculture and climate change at Sierra Student Coalition "Student Environmental Leadership Training" in Abiquiu, NM / Published "Open Letter on Food Justice" to the New Jewish Food Movement / Joined the annual Black Mesa Indigenous Support supply caravan and work party to support indigenous elders in remote, off-grid, environmentally and culturally endangered areas of Native American reservation. Organized donations of supplies and organic food in Arizona cities. Spent one month assisting elders on the land by cooking food, chopping wood, repairing buildings, herding sheep and goats

2007—Received scholarships to attend Holistic Management International and Quivira Coalition conferences in Albuquerque, and Food and Seed Sovereignty Symposium in Tesuque Pueblo / Organized and facilitated youth-led panel discussion on "Youth and the Future of Sustainable Agriculture in New Mexico" at Bioneers Conference in Santa Fe / Wrote essay on climate change, water and sustainable agriculture in New Mexico for Edible Santa Fe / Completed in-depth course of study in Fundamentals of Sustainable Herbal Medicine in the Southwest

2006—Awarded grant by Elizabeth Ann Bogert Memorial Fund to study relationship of ecological agriculture with Christian mysticism / Published "Peak Oil and Community Food Sustainability" in Journal of Cooperative Living and "Peak Opportunity! Earth Activism and the Oil Endgame" in Earth First! Journal

Think About It

(1)   This résumé is longer than most print résumés that young people submit for jobs. What does the author list that you might not list on a résumé you would write?

(2)   This résumé is published online rather than on paper. What features does it have that make it more useful to its readers than a paper version would be?

(3)   This résumé has a stated theme: sustainable food. How does the author present his experience and other qualifications in order to adhere to that theme?

Write About It

Take a draft of a résumé that you have written. Imagine that you are applying for jobs in a particular field only (such as marine biology or museum studies). Write down the name of that field. Revise your résumé with that field in mind. You will have to select certain experiences and revise all of your descriptions of your experiences so that they target only this field. When you are done, compare the targeted résumé with the original résumé. Which one would be more persuasive if you were applying for a job in the field that you selected? What have you learned?

MARTIN LUTHER KING, JR.   LETTER FROM A BIRMINGHAM JAIL (EXCERPT)

King wrote this letter while jailed in Birmingham for participating in a series of nonviolent protests against racial segregation in that city. This open letter was a response to another open letter authored by eight white clergymen from Birmingham criticizing the racial protests (titled "A Call for Unity"). The "Unity" letter argued that anti-segregation work should take place in the courts and not on the streets, and should not be led by "outsiders," namely King.

Read About It

King, a master rhetorician, used a variety of rhetorical strategies in this letter. One of these strategies was vivid imagery. As you read, mark the places where King uses vivid imagery and think about how the images help persuade a reader.

16 April 1963

My Dear Fellow Clergymen:

While confined here in the Birmingham city jail, I came across your recent statement calling my present activities "unwise and untimely." Seldom do I pause to answer criticism of my work and ideas. If I sought to answer all the criticisms that cross my desk, my secretaries would have little time for anything other than such correspondence in the course of the day, and I would have no time for constructive work. But since I feel that you are men of genuine good will and that your criticisms are sincerely set forth, I want to try to answer your statement in what I hope will be patient and reasonable terms.

I think I should indicate why I am here in Birmingham, since you have been influenced by the view which argues against "outsiders coming in." I have the honor of serving as president of the Southern Christian Leadership Conference, an organization operating in every southern state, with headquarters in Atlanta, Georgia. We have some eighty five affiliated organizations across the South, and one of them is the Alabama Christian Movement for Human Rights. Frequently we share staff, educational and financial resources with our affiliates. Several months ago the affiliate here in Birmingham asked us to be on call to engage in a nonviolent direct action program if such were deemed necessary. We readily consented, and when the hour came we lived up to our promise. So I, along with several members of my staff, am here because I was invited here. I am here because I have organizational ties here.

But more basically, I am in Birmingham because injustice is here. Just as the prophets of the eighth century B.C. left their villages and carried their "thus saith the Lord" far beyond the boundaries of their home towns, and just as the Apostle Paul left his village of Tarsus and carried the gospel of Jesus Christ to the far corners of the Greco Roman world, so am I compelled to carry the gospel of freedom beyond my own home town. Like Paul, I must constantly respond to the Macedonian call for aid.

Moreover, I am cognizant of the interrelatedness of all communities and states. I cannot sit idly by in Atlanta and not be concerned about what happens in Birmingham. Injustice anywhere is a threat to justice everywhere. We are caught in an inescapable network of mutuality, tied in a single garment of destiny. Whatever affects one directly, affects all indirectly. Never again can we afford to live with the narrow, provincial "outside agitator" idea. Anyone who lives inside the United States can never be considered an outsider anywhere within its bounds.

You deplore the demonstrations taking place in Birmingham. But your statement, I am sorry to say, fails to express a similar concern for the conditions that brought about the demonstrations. I am sure that none of you would want to rest content with the superficial kind of social analysis that deals merely with effects and does not grapple with underlying causes. It is unfortunate that demonstrations are taking place in Birmingham, but it is even more unfortunate that the city's white power structure left the Negro community with no alternative.

In any nonviolent campaign there are four basic steps: collection of the facts to determine whether injustices exist; negotiation; self purification; and direct action. We have gone through all these steps in Birmingham. There can be no gainsaying the fact that racial injustice engulfs this community. Birmingham is probably the most thoroughly segregated city in the United States. Its ugly record of brutality is widely known. Negroes have experienced grossly unjust treatment in the courts. There have been more unsolved bombings of Negro homes and churches in Birmingham than in any other city in the nation. These are the hard, brutal facts of the case. On the basis of these conditions, Negro leaders sought to negotiate with the city fathers. But the latter consistently refused to engage in good faith negotiation.

Then, last September, came the opportunity to talk with leaders of Birmingham's economic community. In the course of the negotiations, certain promises were made by the merchants—for example, to remove the stores' humiliating racial signs. On the basis of these promises, the Reverend Fred Shuttlesworth and the leaders of the Alabama Christian Movement for Human Rights agreed to a moratorium on all demonstrations. As the weeks and months went by, we realized that we were the victims of a broken promise. A few signs, briefly removed, returned; the others remained. As in so many past experiences, our hopes had been blasted, and the shadow of deep disappointment settled upon us. We had no alternative except to prepare for direct action, whereby we would present our very bodies as a means of laying our case before the conscience of the local and the national community. Mindful of the difficulties involved, we decided to undertake a process of self purification. We began a series of workshops on nonviolence, and we repeatedly asked ourselves: "Are you able to accept blows without retaliating?" "Are you able to endure the ordeal of jail?" We decided to schedule our direct action program for the Easter season, realizing that except for Christmas, this is the main shopping period of the year. Knowing that a strong economic-withdrawal program would be the by product of direct action, we felt that this would be the best time to bring pressure to bear on the merchants for the needed change.

. . .

You may well ask: "Why direct action? Why sit ins, marches and so forth? Isn't negotiation a better path?" You are quite right in calling for negotiation. Indeed, this is the very purpose of direct action. Nonviolent direct action seeks to create such a crisis and foster such a tension that a community which has constantly refused to negotiate is forced to confront the issue. It seeks so to dramatize the issue that it can no longer be ignored. My citing the creation of tension as part of the work of the nonviolent resister may sound rather shocking. But I must confess that I am not afraid of the word "tension." I have earnestly opposed violent tension, but there is a type of constructive, nonviolent tension which is necessary for growth. Just as Socrates felt that it was necessary to create a tension in the mind so that individuals could rise from the bondage of myths and half truths to the unfettered realm of creative analysis and objective appraisal, so must we see the need for nonviolent gadflies to create the kind of tension in society that will help men rise from the dark depths of prejudice and racism to the majestic heights of understanding and brotherhood. The purpose of our direct action program is to create a situation so crisis packed that it will inevitably open the door to negotiation. I therefore concur with you in your call for negotiation. Too long has our beloved Southland been bogged down in a tragic effort to live in monologue rather than dialogue.

. . .

We know through painful experience that freedom is never voluntarily given by the oppressor; it must be demanded by the oppressed. Frankly, I have yet to engage in a direct action campaign that was "well timed" in the view of those who have not suffered unduly from the disease of segregation. For years now I have heard the word "Wait!" It rings in the ear of every Negro with piercing familiarity. This "Wait" has almost always meant "Never." We must come to see, with one of our distinguished jurists, that "justice too long delayed is justice denied."

We have waited for more than 340 years for our constitutional and God given rights. The nations of Asia and Africa are moving with jetlike speed toward gaining political independence, but we still creep at horse and buggy pace toward gaining a cup of coffee at a lunch counter. Perhaps it is easy for those who have never felt the stinging darts of segregation to say, "Wait." But when you have seen vicious mobs lynch your mothers and fathers at will and drown your sisters and brothers at whim; when you have seen hate filled policemen curse, kick and even kill your black brothers and sisters; when you see the vast majority of your twenty million Negro brothers smothering in an airtight cage of poverty in the midst of an affluent society; when you suddenly find your tongue twisted and your speech stammering as you seek to explain to your six year old daughter why she can't go to the public amusement park that has just been advertised on television, and see tears welling up in her eyes when she is told that Funtown is closed to colored children, and see ominous clouds of inferiority beginning to form in her little mental sky, and see her beginning to distort her personality by developing an unconscious bitterness toward white people; when you have to concoct an answer for a five year old son who is asking: "Daddy, why do white people treat colored people so mean?"; when you take a cross county drive and find it necessary to sleep night after night in the uncomfortable corners of your automobile because no motel will accept you; when you are humiliated day in and day out by nagging signs reading "white" and "colored"; when your first name becomes "nigger," your middle name becomes "boy" (however old you are) and your last name becomes "John," and your wife and mother are never given the respected title "Mrs."; when you are harried by day and haunted by night by the fact that you are a Negro, living constantly at tiptoe stance, never quite knowing what to expect next, and are plagued with inner fears and outer resentments; when you are forever fighting a degenerating sense of "nobodiness"—then you will understand why we find it difficult to wait. There comes a time when the cup of endurance runs over, and men are no longer willing to be plunged into the abyss of despair. I hope, sirs, you can understand our legitimate and unavoidable impatience.

. . .

I wish you had commended the Negro sit inners and demonstrators of Birmingham for their sublime courage, their willingness to suffer and their amazing discipline in the midst of great provocation. One day the South will recognize its real heroes. They will be the James Merediths, with the noble sense of purpose that enables them to face jeering and hostile mobs, and with the agonizing loneliness that characterizes the life of the pioneer. They will be old, oppressed, battered Negro women, symbolized in a seventy two year old woman in Montgomery, Alabama, who rose up with a sense of dignity and with her people decided not to ride segregated buses, and who responded with ungrammatical profundity to one who inquired about her weariness: "My feets is tired, but my soul is at rest." They will be the young high school and college students, the young ministers of the gospel and a host of their elders, courageously and nonviolently sitting in at lunch counters and willingly going to jail for conscience' sake. One day the South will know that when these disinherited children of God sat down at lunch counters, they were in reality standing up for what is best in the American dream and for the most sacred values in our Judaeo Christian heritage, thereby bringing our nation back to those great wells of democracy which were dug deep by the founding fathers in their formulation of the Constitution and the Declaration of Independence.

Never before have I written so long a letter. I'm afraid it is much too long to take your precious time. I can assure you that it would have been much shorter if I had been writing from a comfortable desk, but what else can one do when he is alone in a narrow jail cell, other than write long letters, think long thoughts and pray long prayers?

If I have said anything in this letter that overstates the truth and indicates an unreasonable impatience, I beg you to forgive me. If I have said anything that understates the truth and indicates my having a patience that allows me to settle for anything less than brotherhood, I beg God to forgive me.

I hope this letter finds you strong in the faith. I also hope that circumstances will soon make it possible for me to meet each of you, not as an integrationist or a civil-rights leader but as a fellow clergyman and a Christian brother. Let us all hope that the dark clouds of racial prejudice will soon pass away and the deep fog of misunderstanding will be lifted from our fear drenched communities, and in some not too distant tomorrow the radiant stars of love and brotherhood will shine over our great nation with all their scintillating beauty.

Yours for the cause of Peace and Brotherhood,

Martin Luther King, Jr.

Think About It

(1)   The stated audience for this letter is the group of clergymen who criticized the Birmingham protests. Who were the other audiences of this letter?

(2)   How would you describe King's tone (Chapter 21) in this letter toward the clergymen who criticized him? Does he address them with respect or disrespect? Why do you think he chose the tone he did? What does his tone accomplish rhetorically?

(3)   King mentions many famous historical people in this letter. Identify a few of them, and then look up who they are using an online reference or biography database (Chapter 24). How does his mention of these people make his letter more persuasive?

Write About It

Think of a current social problem that you feel strongly about. Write an open letter in which you criticize this social problem. As evidence to support your arguments, use historical events and figures in the fashion that King did in his letter.

Reading Proposals

VINCENT CASMIRRI AND VICTOR ARCELUS   GENDER-NEUTRAL HOUSING PROPOSAL

The following student proposal was prepared in 2011 by the Office of Residence Life at Gettysburg College in Pennsylvania. It was co-authored by a student and a college administrator.

Read About It

Before you read this document, look up the term "heteronormative" in a dictionary. This complicated term is used in the following document as part of a justification for the proposal. Keep the term in mind as you read.

Introduction

During the Spring 2011 semester a group of students, faculty, and staff involved with Allies [Allies aims to promote the rights, safety, and comfort of Lesbian, Gay, Bisexual, Transgendered, Queer, and Questioning persons on the Gettysburg College campus and to spread awareness of LGBTQQ issues] shared a series of recommendations with Provost Chris Zappe and Vice President of College Life and Dean of Students Julie Ramsey. These proposals were compiled from discussions with students, faculty and staff and are intended to help support lesbian, gay, bisexual, transgender, queer, questioning and many other groups/people. One of the recommendations discussed focuses on the College shifting to gender-neutral housing.

Vincent Casmirri '13 served as the College Life Summer Intern during this past summer and he worked closely with Victor Arcelus, Assistant Dean and Director of Residence Life, to develop this gender-neutral housing proposal for Gettysburg College. Over the course of the summer, Vincent and Victor collected and reviewed many college/university gender-neutral housing proposals, policies, and practices. This information and the specific dynamics and characteristics of Gettysburg College were used to develop the proposal.

Rationale

The Office of Residence Life proposes that Gettysburg College offer gender-neutral housing, which is defined as a housing option in which two or more students mutually agree to share a multiple-occupancy bedroom, suite, or apartment regardless of students' sex or gender. Gender-neutral housing provides students increased choice in selecting roommates, regardless of gender, in order to respect and support the various needs of our students. In addition, gender-neutral housing provides more options for students who do not wish to live in more traditional room arrangements. This further demonstrates support for the college's non-discrimination policy with respect to gender, sexual orientation, gender identity, and gender expression.

Gender-neutral housing provides students maximal choice in determining and taking responsibility for their own living arrangements. This opportunity is consistent with Gettysburg's approach to education, where the College supports students' development as self-directed young adults, able to take personal responsibility over all dimensions of their lives. This learning occurs through students' active decision-making and engagement in the learning environment, both in and out of the classroom.

Gender-neutral housing intends to help create a campus climate that is welcoming, inclusive, and supportive of all students. This approach lessens the impact of heteronormative assumptions regarding housing assignments. It provides options for a variety of students: those who feel uncomfortable rooming with members of the same sex, transgender students in the process of discovering their gender identity, students who feel they would be more compatible with a roommate of a different sex or gender, and students who do not want sex or gender to be a primary factor in choosing a roommate. This policy helps create an environment that acknowledges, appreciates, and respects the diverse nature of the Gettysburg College student body, while giving students more options in finding a roommate who is truly compatible.

Policy Description

Gender-neutral housing will be available in all halls for sophomores, juniors, and seniors through the spring housing selection process. The option is available to first-year and transfer students through special requests coordinated with the Office of Residence Life. The following guiding principles apply:

- Students may choose to request a roommate of any sex or gender.
- As with all roommate requests, the Office of Residence Life will only honor those requests made by all parties living within the same living space (i.e., room, apartment, suite).
- Upperclass students must apply with their prospective roommate(s) following the same processes and deadlines of all students entering the housing selection process.
- Upperclass students will not be required to reveal their reasons for opting to live in gender-neutral housing. First-year and transfer students will have a conversation with a Residence Life professional so that the College can provide housing that best meets the needs of the student.
- Students will not be assigned to gender-neutral housing unless they have elected to do so.
- This program is intended for students who wish to share a room, suite, or apartment with friends of a different sex or gender. It is not intended for romantic couples.
- There is no specific number or limit of gender-neutral spaces on campus.
- We encourage students to maintain an open dialogue with their families. Students over 18 are legally able to make decisions about their housing placements.

Living space designation for a given academic year:

- Any space on campus can be gender-neutral. This avoids segregation and offers students gender-neutral housing within all housing styles and at the various housing price points.
- The default designation for a room, apartment, or suite will be single-sex unless the students selecting into the space opt to create a gender-neutral pair/group.
- Once a room, apartment, or suite is gender-neutral, that space will continue to be gender-neutral as long as the residents can maintain the occupancy of the living space.

When there is a vacancy:

- In a stand-alone gender-neutral double, a roommate who is left behind may elect to pull in any new roommate—including a roommate of the same sex. If the resident cannot identify a new roommate, the room will default back to single-sex status. In this case, the Office of Residence Life may place a student of the same sex in the room.

- In a gender-neutral triple, apartment, or suite, the residents may elect to pull in any roommate(s). All students in the space have to approve new resident(s) moving into the triple, apartment, or suite.
- If the residents in a triple, apartment, or suite cannot fill the vacancies, the Office of Residence Life will first attempt to place students in the apartment or suite who are interested in living in a gender-neutral space. Current residents will be asked to approve the students interested in moving into the space.

If the Office of Residence Life needs to maximize use of all available spaces on campus, and the above is not possible, then Residence Life staff will work closely with the student group to determine next steps. Two options include:

- Relocating the gender-neutral group to another location that accommodates the group's new size.
- Split the group in order to create two single-sex groups and fill vacancies with students of the same sex.

Think About It

(1) What are the reasons given in the proposal in support of gender-neutral housing? Do you find the reasons persuasive?
(2) Why do you suppose the policy states, "We encourage students to maintain an open dialogue with their families"? How did you interpret this statement?
(3) Do you find that the policy described meets the needs described in the "Rationale" section? Why or why not?

Write About It

Think of a student life policy that you would like to see changed or implemented. Search your college's website for a list of policies affecting students, such as policies pertaining to sustainability, student governance, use of campus facilities, and so on. Develop a research plan using published sources (such as newspapers or books) and/or interviews with students and administrators (Chapter 24). Then, write a short proposal directed to college administrators.

ALKA VAID MENON   PAULINE AND IRVING TANNER DEAN'S SCHOLARS GRANT PROPOSAL

Menon wrote this grant proposal in 2008, when she was an undergraduate at Cornell University in Ithaca, New York.

Read About It

The grant proposal presented here follows an organizational scheme required by the granting agency: Abstract, Biographical Sketch, Statement of Purpose, Bibliography, and Budget. As you read, think about how the writer worked within this scheme to produce a memorable grant proposal.

Abstract

The history of same-sex marriage in the United States is of great interest now that state legislatures and state supreme courts are pondering the legality of excluding same-sex couples from marriage. While many states in the last election cycle passed specific bills or state constitutional amendments banning same-sex marriage, other states (namely, Massachusetts and Connecticut) have extended civil marriage to same-sex couples. An analysis of why same-sex couples are fighting for marriage, how the fight for marriage "rights" came about, and who within the gay rights movement is in favor of and who is opposed to promoting same-sex marriage rights is instructive for legislators and policymakers who are debating same-sex marriage legislation. It is also instructive to examine the arguments for gay marriage and if and how they have changed over the past few years. Knowledge of which arguments for gay marriage were thought by gay activists to be the most persuasive to the American public and to politicians offers a sense of our national sensibility, values, and thought. I intend to investigate how same-sex marriage became central to the agenda of major gay and lesbian rights organizations in the 1990s in the United States. I seek to explore the groundwork laid during the 1970s through 1990s that later facilitated the ascendance of gay marriage to the top of the gay rights agenda in the early twenty-first century. A focus on the records of the two largest, most well-known and arguably most "mainstream" gay rights organizations, the National Gay and Lesbian Task Force and the Human Rights Campaign, will help me understand how gay marriage went from being a distant dream in the minds of a few derided as "assimilationist" to being one of the hot-button issues in the 2004 presidential election year.

Biographical Sketch

I am the child of unconventional immigrant parents; my mother, though born in India, attended high school and college in the United States, and my father was born and raised by Indian parents in Malaysia. By the time I entered the picture, my parents had settled for good in College Station, Texas, a midsize, conservative town that is dominated by a large state school, Texas A&M University. Growing up there was wonderful; the town was small, safe, and underdeveloped enough that I could play outside whenever I wanted (the nice weather helped, too). I spent my early years divided between climbing trees and playing outdoor games with my neighborhood buddies and reading anything that I could get my hands on, from fantasy and science fiction to the British classics to historical nonfiction. My childhood was punctuated by trips abroad, accompanying my academic parents to conferences and sojourns to their respective family homes in different parts of India.

As I got older though, I began to outgrow College Station, and the seasonal trips were no longer enough to keep me happy. I exhausted my local library; after attending every summer camp offered, I had run out of options there, too; and once I learned how to drive, I realized that there was nowhere within range that I wanted to drive to. After years spent successfully avoiding Texas A&M, which I associated with my parents' work, I finally turned to the university to alleviate my summer boredom.

I started out observing in science labs, which were new to me, as neither of my parents are scientists. While I turned to research to keep myself entertained, I ended up discovering that I truly enjoyed it. There is something addictive about doing experiments and getting results that kept me coming back. By my senior year, I knew that research was a career path that I wanted to pursue and took that into account when applying to colleges. Unfortunately, Texas A&M didn't make it on the list—after living in College Station for my whole life, I wanted to leave town and try my fortunes elsewhere.

Coming to Cornell was a fortuitous accident. As a high school senior, I knew only that I wanted to leave Texas and get a good liberal arts education, ideally somewhere that had good biology facilities as well. I applied to colleges somewhat haphazardly, and after being admitted to Cornell, I fell in love with the place on a gloomy April day when I came to visit. After years of adolescent restlessness, I had finally found peace.

Temporarily, that is. I spent my first year agonizing over what major to declare. Though I had made forays into science during my high school summers, I simply wasn't ready to give up on my love of literature. I have a real fondness for society novels, particularly those by Jane Austen and Edith Wharton, and this fondness was further nurtured by my first freshman writing seminar, The Politics and Poetics of American Marriage. Though I enjoyed science, particularly biology, and wanted to join the ranks of women scientists, I was unwilling to sacrifice the chance to at least try the humanities first. I resolved my dilemma by applying to the College Scholar program, an independent major program that allowed me to take classes in any department, freeing me from distribution requirements in pursuit of learning a multidisciplinary topic. I channeled my penchant for society novels into a theme of marriage and have taken courses in animal behavior, feminist studies, English, history, sociology and more, bringing me to the present.

I continue at Cornell a happy, industrious student, living out my many dreams of doing research, becoming a woman scientist, and studying the humanities.

Statement of Purpose

As it became apparent on November 5, 2008, that California had passed Proposition 8, a ballot initiative unambiguously revoking the recently won right of gay and lesbian couples to legally wed, the GLBT community and its allies were in shock; to them, the unthinkable had happened. From the comfort of their armchairs, many gay rights supporters had been so sure that California, the progressive vanguard of the states, would uphold the right of homosexuals to marry. Though the vote was close, it was clear that a blow had been struck against gay rights efforts in California. What happened? Was this outcome inevitable? What happens to same-sex marriage efforts from here? It is important to look at the bigger picture. The vote was not always this close. Less than twenty years ago, same-sex marriage was not on the agenda for any gay organization, let alone for the two leading national gay rights organizations. While some in the gay, lesbian, bisexual and transgender (GLBT) community could not imagine why anyone would ever want to marry, the consensus was universal that marriage for same-sex couples was an unattainable goal.

I would like to explore how that consensus changed in the gay rights movement by focusing on the internal and external struggles facing two movement organizations. The struggles that these organizations faced were reflective of the difficulties faced in the larger gay rights movement, so I will also trace gay movement dynamics, examining the role of specific organizations in a national movement and the coordination of diverse goals into a united movement agenda. I seek to write a tale of how far the gay rights movement has come in twenty years and to project how far it still has yet to go, a tale of friction between lesbians and gays as well as between heterosexuals and homosexuals.

How did same-sex marriage become central to the agenda of the gay rights movement in the United States? To answer this question, I will focus primarily on two prominent gay rights organizations, the National Gay and Lesbian Task Force (NGLTF), founded in 1973 as the first national gay/lesbian political organizing force, and the Human Rights Campaign (HRC), founded in 1980 as a political action committee to raise money for gay rights-friendly political candidates. I will limit the scope of my project to the late 1970s to the late 1990s in an effort to explore the groundwork laid during that time period that facilitated the ascendance of gay marriage to the top of the gay rights agenda in the early twenty-first century. This summer research project would lay the groundwork for my College Scholar senior honors thesis.

This project idea stems from research that I conducted in Fall 2008 for Professor Tamar Carroll's HIST 4141 writing seminar on Women's Activism and Social Change in the 20th Century. I wrote a twenty-five page paper chronicling the history of the NGLTF during the years 1985 through 1997. Based on my reading of the National Gay and Lesbian Task Force Records for the 1980s and 1990s and interviews with Urvashi Vaid, a former executive director and policy director of the NGLTF, I contend that the mobilization of the Religious Right around the federal Defense of Marriage Act and a host of anti-gay marriage state ballot measures catapulted advocacy of legal same-sex marriage to the top of the gay rights agenda. My focus for that project was primarily on the NGLTF, the more progressive of the two most prominent gay rights organizations. For my Tanner Dean summer project, I would like to explore the NGLTF's path to advocacy of same-sex marriage in greater detail, enriching my source base by conducting additional archival research as well as oral history interviews with gay rights leaders, and by examining coverage of same-sex marriage in the gay press, particularly *The Advocate*. This would allow me to get a sense of when same-sex marriage began to be publicly discussed within the gay rights movement and how attitudes toward same-sex marriage changed as same-sex marriage cases made their way through the courts in the early 1990s. Moreover, since other gay and lesbian organizations prioritized same-sex marriage to varying degrees before the mobilization of the Religious Right in 1995–1997, I would like to expand my focus to examine and analyze the involvement of the Human Rights Campaign, the other leading national gay and lesbian organization, in the struggle for same-sex marriage, providing a comparison to the NGLTF.

As the Carl A. Kroch Library of the Cornell University Library houses both the National Gay and Lesbian Task Force records and the Human Rights Campaign records spanning from 1973–2005, I plan to conduct the bulk of my research here at the archives in Ithaca. These collections include organization minutes, publications, press releases, budgets, plans, press clippings, and executive directors' letters, speeches, and files, providing a window into the thinking, priorities, and strategy of each organization. The Kroch Rare and Manuscript Division's Human Sexuality collection also contains a host of gay publications, including *The Advocate*. For more recent material and to interview gay rights activists, I plan to make trips to New York City and possibly Washington D.C. to the headquarters of these organizations. I will conduct oral history interviews with activists farther afield by phone. . . .

I am interested in expanding this research because there has been limited scholarship on the history of same-sex marriage to date; gay rights history is a recently emerging and greatly underserved field, and I think that we are at a pivotal cultural and political moment for capturing the early days of the push for the legalization of same-sex marriage. My research will supplement John D'Emilio's analysis of the NGLTF and its role in the gay rights movement, specifically honing in on its role in the larger same-sex marriage debate and providing detailed analysis of the NGLTF's archival records. While my original interpretation of organizational records and oral history interviews will constitute my primary contribution to research in this field, I will also situate my findings within gay and lesbian theory, including the writings of Michael Warner, Andrew Sullivan, Nancy Polikoff, and Urvashi Vaid, and within the history of family and marriage in the United States. I have attached a brief working bibliography for my research project.

I will also expand upon the ideas in Nancy Cott's history of marriage in the United States, *Public Vows: A History of Marriage and the Nation*, applying her analysis of how marriage laws have been used to restrict the rights of women, gays and lesbians, and ethnic minorities and how such laws have shaped modern gender roles. In addition, it is my goal to synthesize and present the thinking of a host of gay and lesbian theorists.

As a rough time line of my research, I plan to start work on June 1. Throughout the summer, I will meet weekly with Professor Carroll to discuss my progress and research findings. During the first two weeks of June, I will conduct four hours of archival research per day, completing my perusal of the National Gay and Lesbian Task Force records by the end of that period. During the last two weeks of June, I will conduct four hours of archival research per day focusing on newspapers and the gay press. I will also make a trip to New York to conduct oral histories during this time. During the first two weeks of July, I will travel to Washington D.C. to conduct oral history interviews of gay activists. I will also complete my perusal of the Human Rights Campaign records related to gay marriage during this time. By the last two weeks of July, I plan to have completed my secondary readings, and I will spend the first week of August outlining, organizing, and compiling my research. Hopefully by this time I will have also started the actual writing of my senior honors thesis.

Working Bibliography

Archival Collections National Gay and Lesbian Task Force Records, #7301. Division of Rare and Manuscript Collections, Cornell University Library, Ithaca, NY.

Human Rights Campaign Records, #7712. Division of Rare and Manuscript Collections, Cornell University Library.

Oral History

Vaid, Urvashi. Phone interview with author. Ithaca, NY, November 9, 2008.

Secondary Sources

Celello, Kristin. *Making marriage work: A history of marriage and divorce in the twentieth century U.S.* Chapel Hill, North Carolina: University of North Carolina Press, 2008.

Chauncey, George. *Why marriage?: The history shaping today's debate over gay equality.* New York: Basic Books, 2004.

Cott, Nancy. *Public vows: A history of marriage and the nation.* Cambridge, Massachusetts: Harvard University Press, 2000.

D'Emilio, John. "Organizational Tales: Interpreting the NGLTF Story," in *The World Turned* (Durham and London: Duke University, 2002) pp. 99–119.

Pascoe, Peggy. *What comes naturally: Miscegenation law and the making of race in America.* Oxford: Oxford University Press, 2009.

Polikoff, Nancy. *Beyond (straight and gay) marriage: Valuing all families under the law.* Boston: Beacon Press, 2008.

Stanton, Glenn, and Maier, Bill. *Marriage on trial: The case against same-sex marriage and parenting.* Downers Grove, Illinois: InterVarsity Press, 2004.

Sullivan, Andrew. *Virtually normal: An argument on homosexuality.* New York: Alfred A. Knopf, Inc, 1995.

Vaid, Urvashi. *Virtual equality: The mainstreaming of gay and lesbian liberation.* New York: Anchor Books, 1995.

Warner, Michael. *The trouble with normal: Sex, politics, and the ethics of queer life.* New York: Free Press, 1999.

Wolfson, Evan. *Why marriage matters.* New York: Simon & Schuster, 2004.

Budget

I am seeking funding to cover approximately two and a half months' living expenses in Ithaca, as I plan to be in Ithaca from June 1 until mid-August. I anticipate that my rent and utilities will be $500/month, and that I will need about $60/week for food. I will also incur transportation costs for my trips to interview activists and to visit the headquarters of the NGLTF and HRC in New York City and Washington D.C. Those trips are included below. I have also included a book allowance so that I can purchase a few of the key secondary texts so that I can mark them up.

- Rent and utilities: $500.00 × 3 = $1500
- Food: $60/week × 10 = $600
- Transportation: Round-trip busfare to New York City: $90
- Room and board for 2 days at $100/day: $200
- Books: $50
- Miscellaneous (copying, mail costs, etc.): $60
- Total = $2500

Think About It

(1)   Does Menon's biographical sketch lead you to believe that she would be a good researcher? Why or why not?

(2)   One of the purposes of a grant proposal is to show that the topic is both timely and important. Do you believe that this grant proposal accomplishes these purposes? Why or why not?

(3)   One purpose of scholarly research is to expand upon the knowledge that already exists in a research area. How does Menon convey that she will expand on existing research in her field?

Write About It

Think about an issue that you would be interested in learning more about. Following Menon's example, find an organization you could study to help you learn more about this issue and how it is being addressed. For example, if you are interested in climate change, you might research the Union of Concerned Scientists to see how they are helping to address the problem. Using Menon's proposal as an example, write a grant proposal to support your research.

JING WANG   JINGLISH DOCUMENTARY PROPOSAL

This film pitch was published by the author on her blog, Jing's Garden, *in 2010.*

Read About It

The writer of the following film pitch does not use standard English, because she is an English language learner. As you read, see if you can find ways that the language of the film pitch actually helps to enhance the proposal.

Title
JINGLISH

Film Summary
A participatory personal dairy in which a young Chinese female immigrant pursuing passion of life by adopting another culture, seeking college education and learning a new language.

Treatment
JINGLISH is a personal dairy documentary film with cute, quirky comedy style. The movie begins with a blue screen of computer based English test. A Standard English voiceover says an introduction of the exam. Learning English is a test for

immigrants who want to [pursue] American dreams in United States. The examination includes four parts: Listening, Reading, Speaking, and Writing. A shot of a Chinese girl in her late twenties, takes the test in front of the computer. Camera follows her exit the classroom, and walks in to a busy New York street.

JINGLISH is a personal diary documentary film about my four Years' journey of English study in America. JINGLISH is the symbol of confidence in my identity. JINGLISH is the sign of independent thought and action. It is a sample of a young female immigrant, pursuing her passion of life by adopting another culture, learning a new language and seeking college education. It is not only about learning new language, but also a voice to make me to be individuals.

Director's Statement

I am the best person to make this film is because this is a story I am live in, and I understand the most. I grew up in a society always looking for common. Everyone should [obey] social norms. People are looking for to become part of organization. I was a follower, who never think independently what I want to be? I choose this subject to indicate thousands of young immigrants like me. There is lots of hard working girls travel far away from home to pursue a dream. We lost our voice in the new environments, but on the same time we learn and develop our individual voice. In my Four years learning journey in America, I explore my life with thousands of possibilities. America frees me to enter one of the most creative periods of my life. As a new Chinese immigrant, I feel culture conflict, and passionate in communication in the same time. Learning to accept our accent, to identify myself is a hard but necessary lesion for all of immigrants. Research in the Asian Immigrants issues always be my favorite topics. American identity and communication between eastern-western cultures always fasnating to me. There are three research papers I have written in this kind of topic, Made in China explores issues concerning cheap labor and contemporary immigrant culture; Chinatown Voting Issues reflects Asian American's political approach in American democracy; and The Song of Chang-Gan, the critical thinking of Ezra Pound's translation about the eight century ancient Chinese poem. The Song of Chang-Gan is selected in CUNY library research paper content, and the Chinatown Voting Issues is selected as a sample essay by Urban Sociology department.

This is a hard life experience, But I will make this a comedy film full of positive actions. I prefer contemporary documentary style, Like Favelas Rising. JINGLISH will be a documentary poetry which full of young energies. I plan to Use a lot of fast pasting jumping cut images, and animation effect on the reaction frames.

Part 1—Listening

Director's voice over, "I am not a good listener. In china, we are happy to follow the social norms and are proud to belong to an organization." Footages of different groups of Chinese girls wear uniform in elementary school, middle school, High school and a group of Chinese women in business suit. An animation communism hero character Lei feng says, "We are all accessories of the big machine." My mom says in her Interview, "Jing has too much fantasy in her head. I named her 'Jing' because Its my wish for her. I wish she can be a grace lady. I dream she can be a good student in school, find a stable office job, have a simple marriage and a happy kid." Animation character Jing Doll changing in to different customs. But no matter what my parent's wishes are, I do the opposite. Images of me acts, learn arts, sing rock & Roll. One day, I decided to run across the world, so I don't need to listen to mom's old talk anymore. An animated me land by statue liberty. Voice over, "In fact, I was landed on Connecticut country side. Suddenly I was around by sounds of perfect English." Jing listens to American's conversation on street, in the store. Shots of Jing make phone calls. She listens to the machine talks for half hour to wait it breathe so she can talks to it. Footages of me stop someone on the street to ask direction, I nod and say thank you all the time. But I go to opposite direction right after. Animated Jing Doll becomes a stupid potato. Interview with my friend Yong, he says, "We all thought that Jing attending college in America, and supporting herself was a joke four years ago. She even can't speak a full sentience at that time." A voice over says, "I have to be a good listener in America." Footage of Jing watches Kids show for 3 years old children. Jing goes to language school, smiles, nods and she is excited as Elmo. I learn black street talk and Spanish accent on the subway. Shots of me use my face and body expressions to pretend that I understand American conversations.

Part 2—Reading

Shots in a literature class, Teacher asks everyone to read 100 pages for next class and writes reflection papers based on reading. Jing runs between three jobs after the class. At night, she sits down for 2 hours with help from translator machine, she reads on page 5. One of the best ways to learning reading is when I drive alone for interviewing a babysitter job. Jing is driving with a map on my hand and read signs on the high way in the same time. Doing research to find jobs and read from immigrants' website is also very helpful for improving my reading too. Reading is not only helps me understand signs, moreover reading enlighten me appreciate American culture. I am really enjoy reading and I am eager to read more, Shots of my books collection under my bed. Varieties of books open the door to understanding America.

Part 3— Speaking

On Yong's interview, he says, "Jing is always eager to talk, since she first comes to America. I remember she smiles to everyone on street. People have to stop and say hi. Then she will call her mom, "Americans are so friendly everyone talks with me." Jing barely speaks English, But She never afraid of speaking." A voice over with moving photo images. "When Jing just arrived CT, She talks to everyone who has an Asian face. After a month she knows most of the Chinese people in the little town. This is how I find my first job as a mandarin teacher. Teaching American Kids is a great way to practice speaking and self confidents. Shots I teach in my mandarin classroom, but Kids laugh at my accent in the sometime. I create a lot of chance for me to speak in public. I always sit in the front of the classroom, I ask question to my favorite film director. I stand up to be a volunteer translator in film festival.

Part 4—Writing

Some shots of my [Facebook posts]. Yong reads my [Facebook post]. He makes fun of my grammar. "One time I read Jing's face book, I can't bear her grammar mistake. I write to her, don't think your English is good. Do you know you do not use English? What you use should call JINGLISH." Shots in Jing's script writing class, classmates set part to read Jing's script. They has trouble to read through, and they don't understand what I am talking about. I try to express deep thought with an elementary level English writing skill. My formal English teacher reads her comments on my first draft, and last draft of the poetry research paper. Images of Jing standing on research competition stage and reading paper with JINGLISH Accent. Jing drive a car crossing the white stone bridge. The skyline of Manhattan slowly appear behind the huge bridge gate. Jing drives pass the gate.

Think About It

(1)   Does reading this film pitch give you a good feel for what the film will be like? Why or why not?
(2)   The title of the film is taken from an anecdote described in Part 4 of the film description. Does that anecdote help the film make sense to you?
(3)   Jing (the author and the subject of the documentary) is excited to be living in the U.S. How does she express this excitement in her pitch?

Write About It

Think of a story from your own life (or that of a friend or relative) that you would like to tell in documentary form. Using Jing's proposal and the sample film pitch in Chapter 13 as examples, write a pitch for your documentary.

THE MUSLIM STUDENTS' ASSOCIATION OF TEXAS A&M UNIVERSITY   A TASTE OF CULTURE: PROPOSAL TO ESTABLISH HALAL FOOD PROGRAM

The Muslim Students' Association of Texas A&M University (located in College Station, Texas) drafted this student proposal in 2006.

Read About It

As you read, notice when the authors make comparisons between Texas A&M University and other universities in the country that have a program similar to the one that they are proposing. Think about what effect these comparisons have on you as a reader.

A recent conversation with the mother of a prospective student from Louisiana showed that although students and their parents may prefer Texas A&M to other schools, the lack of a Halal Food program compels·them to choose otherwise. This student had also been accepted by prestigious universities such as Stanford, and he made it clear that he was choosing Stanford over A&M because of their Halal Food Program.

Over the years, universities have gradually become aware of the growing market for Halal food. Since Stanford became the pioneer for Halal food on campus in 1997, universities across the country have followed their lead.

The Muslim Students' Association requests your support in implementing a long term Halal Food Program at Texas A&M University. We would like to begin a pilot program this Fall semester, after which an assessment of the costs and benefits will be made. Since no restaurants in Brazos County serve Halal food, this program will attract a multitude of students, faculty, and families in the region. Over 300 current students, faculty, staff, and alumni have signed an appeal for Halal food to be served at SBISA Dining Hall [See Attachment A: Signed Petition].

What Is Halal Food?

Halal food refers to what is considered permissible for Muslims to eat, under the Islamic guidelines, which encompass not only the contents but also preparation. For example, Muslims may not eat food that contains or was prepared with alcohol, pork, or animals not slaughtered under Islamic guidelines.

Why Bring Halal Food to TAMU?

1. Enhance University Image

The adoption of a long term Halal Food Program will make Texas A&M the first in Texas to execute such a program, and one of the pioneer universities in the United States to offer Halal food on campus, joining the likes of Stanford, Yale, NYU, and Dartmouth. Not only will this service give TAMU an added advantage above competing universities in the nation, but it will also highlight its commitment to diversity and cultural education.

2. Improve Efforts in Recruiting Students of Diverse Backgrounds

> It is essential that the faculty, students, and larger campus community embrace this more cosmopolitan environment. The university's traditional core values will give us guidance and distinctiveness, while preparing us to interact with all people of the globe. Texas A&M University must attract and nurture a more ethnically, culturally, and geographically diverse faculty, staff, and student body.
> —Vision 2020, "Globalize and Diversify," Imperative 6

Establishing a Halal Food Program can result in recruitment of a more diverse pool of students, faculty, and staff. As illustrated in the example of the student from Louisiana, the existence of a Halal Food Program is an essential factor that many prospective students consider when selecting a university. How many more top-caliber students are we losing to other universities simply because we do not offer this service?

An essential tool in recruiting diverse groups of students is to address their needs. Meeting their dietary requirements will create an environment of respect towards other cultures, foster an atmosphere of community, and make Texas A&M a more welcoming place for all.

3. Encourage Diversity through Education

> *[Texas A&M] University must consider the world as a source and market-place for its ideas. We must bring the world to our students and faculty, and our students and faculty to the world. Our reach into the larger world and the reach of the larger world into Texas A&M University will affect both the real and perceived quality of the university. Global perspectives must be infused into all curricula.*
>
> —Vision 2020, "Globalize and Diversify," Imperative 6

Food is one of the defining aspects of a culture and has the ability to unite people of diverse backgrounds. As Halal food is an important aspect of Muslim culture, establishing this program will create awareness and understanding of a culture adhered to by one-fifth of the world's population. This will complement the other efforts being made by TAMU in this regard, such as the establishment of a branch campus of Texas A&M in Education City, Qatar as well as the initiation of an Arabic language program.

> *Texas A&M University is committed to promoting diversity in all of its dimensions as an essential enriching aspect of a quality educational experience. The real world—the world after college—is endlessly diverse; A&M students must be prepared to make their contribution in that world.*
>
> —Dr. Robert M. Gates, Texas A&M President

The promotion of "diversity in all of its dimensions" that Texas A&M aspires to will not be achieved solely within the walls of a classroom, but requires a more comprehensive approach such as the Halal Program. Exposure to the concept of Halal food would provide a unique opportunity for students to gain an understanding and appreciation for other cultures. Halal food at SBISA would provide an excellent forum for such learning and development to occur.

Feasibility

Nadeem Siddiqui, Executive Director of Food Services, and Gary Arthur, Senior Executive Chef, whom Texas A&M has recently added to their staff, have prior experience in establishing campus Halal Food programs. They have worked together to implement programs at both Stanford and Cornell University.

For the benefit of visiting Qatar students this summer, a trial run for Halal food at SBISA Dining Hall was implemented under the supervision of Mr. Siddiqui, which has proven to be both feasible and cost effective. Adopting this program long term can be a stepping-stone to implementing more services that create a welcoming environment by accommodating the religious dietary needs of its students. [. . .]

Think About It

(1)   The opening paragraph of this proposal tells a brief story about a student who chose to attend Stanford University instead of Texas A&M University ("TAMU") because of food options. Later, they mention TAMU losing "top-caliber students" because of the lack of Halal food. What effect do these arguments have on a reader? What purposes do these arguments serve?

(2)   Throughout the list of reasons provided for why TAMU should bring Halal food to campus, there are quotations from university documents and university leaders. What rhetorical purposes do these quotations serve?

(3)   What reasons do the authors provide for why this program is feasible? Why must a proposal include a statement on feasibility, do you think?

Write About It

Think about a food issue on campus that you would like to change. Write a student proposal in which you provide the reasons why this change should occur, using this reading and the student proposals found in Chapter 13 as examples.

ALFONSO JOSIA SAMM   SUMMER RESEARCH PROPOSAL: EDUCATION POLICY IMPACT: PERCEPTIONS OF HIGH SCHOOL EDUCATORS

Samm wrote this grant proposal in 2008 when he was an undergraduate student at the University of New Hampshire in Durham, New Hampshire.

Read About It

As you read the following grant proposal, note places where the author's language slips from an academic or objective tone into a more emotional or even hyperbolic tone. Ask yourself whether this strong language makes the proposal more or less persuasive.

Introduction

[. . .]

Problem Statement

Many educators and academicians raise concern that the nation is facing a crisis with regard to Black boys (Hefner, 2004; Smith, 2005). Black males have consistently struggled in the US educational system. The achievement and persistence gaps between Black and white students have been long lasting. But, increasing gaps within race groups are also causing alarm. Concluding her review of the data, Rosa Smith observed that Black siblings who were reared in the same home and communities have significantly different educational outcomes (Holzman, 2004). As a result, she raised a potent question which begs for a response: "What is it about our education environments, policies, and systems that produce this dramatic Black student gender gap (p. 3)?"

Research Question

If it can be said that schools have contributed and continue to support academic, social and economic marginalization of particular students, namely Black boys, what factors give rise to this? Lipman (2003) argued that education policy in US schools function[s] to produce inequality and marginalization, and in doing so, reinforces patterns of racial domination. Thus, in an effort to answer the question that Smith asks, this research will identify school policies that affect Black males at the secondary level. The central questions are [as follows]:

1. Do educators perceive a particular policy or practice as detrimental to Black male high school graduation?
2. Is there a relationship between educators' racial identity and educators' perception of policy effectiveness?

Significance

This research is necessary because, although there is much investigation into the negative educational outcomes of African American students and increasing attention paid to Black males, there is little inquiry into policies that produce or facilitate these outcomes. Policies are important considerations because they involve the values and processes through which a system takes action to address a situation, to include expressed intentions and consistent practices, both direct and indirect, or active and non-active (Fowler, 2000). Educational policies, while focused on schools and those within the confines of the school facility, reflect social values. Further, this research will contribute in the broader sense to the works on educational equity in the US. As some scholars warn, there are deep and widespread consequences to continued failure to educate males, Black males in particular, as effectively and efficiently as their [female] counterparts (Holzman, 2004; Mortenson, 1999). Therefore this research is important because, if society truly cares about the equality of genders and races, we must attend to the educational disparity observable between Black males and other groups, because the social cost of disenfranchised Black males is simply unbearable.

Literature Review

Race, class, and political mobilization are intertwined with school quality and the ability to resist hegemonic policies (Lipman, 2003). Teachers can help redress unequal societal relationships by creating alternative experiences in classrooms that disrupt, rather than reflect inequities (Cassidy & Bates, 2005). Unfortunately, far too many educators operate in and are rewarded by a system wherein the goal is to transform students into people much like themselves, and so they are viewed by students who hold differing worldviews as inculcators and assimilationists who de-value the students' ways of seeing and knowing the world (Trusty, 1996).

History and Background

Since the early 1500s white European traders brought millions of enslaved people from . . . Africa to the New World of the west. The Virginia Slave Code of 1705, which defined those eligible for enslavement as "black" and those who would be free as "white," used crude measures for distinguishing people. Since its beginning the United States has been a nation structured toward dominance along two lines: race and gender. And, as Patterson (1995) noted, Black males have consistently been the most demeaned by US social organization. Because of past discrimination and the way that history of discrimination has had economic impact on Blacks, Wilson (1987) argues that African Americans are the truly disadvantaged. He further as-serts that Blacks, especially young males, are dropping out of the workforce in sig-nificant numbers, and that this unfavorable trend has been happening since the end of World War II. The statistics on Black male joblessness are outrageous, and recently a report by the New England Board of Higher Education (NEBHE) stated that "nearly 53,000 Hispanic and black young adults in New England are disconnected—jobless and not in school" (Fogg & Harrington, 2004, p. 24).

Race and Gender

Sex and gender identity are likely most central to individual self-concept (White-head, 2002). Masculinity or, more specifically, white masculinity has always in-volved some sense of individual autonomy, competitiveness, and mastery or competence (Harper, 2004; Staples, 1986). Some scholars put forward that main-stream concepts of masculinity, such as the accumulation of wealth, status, and power, are often unattainable to African Americans due to the constraints of race (Franklin, 1984). Pierre, Mahalik and Woodland (2001) argue that African American males are socialized by the dominant culture in such a way that they are forced to suppress their emotions regarding social and psychological situations in which they experience a great deal of anger-hostility as a result of unfair evaluation and threat by whites. They also note that African American males are expected to operate in a nation that silences, abuses, and devalues their existence. Further, they contend that, in the US, African American males struggle to assert their masculinity amidst societal prejudice, economic hardship, educational limitations, and even unwar-ranted violence. As a coping strategy to life in a racist society, many African Ameri-can males focus on impression management, invoking the "Cool Pose" as an aggressive assertion of masculinity (Majors & Billson, 1992; Pierre, Mahalik & Woodland, 2001; Staples, 1982). According to Pierre, Mahalik, and Woodland (2001) the objectives in the use of the cool pose stance are protection, social competence and self-pride; it also moderates stressful conditions and can provide the basis for personal achievement and self-respect.

For many Black men, the adaptation of the tough guy image, the cool pose, and the hypersexual persona are central characteristics to masculine identity (Harper, 2004; Whitehead, 2002). Tough guys, according to Harper (2004), are fighters who incite fear in others and are not afraid to defend themselves. The cool pose is a combination of composure and expression oriented at appearing trendy and relaxed and is characterized by a "pimp-style" strut (Harper, 2004; Pierre, Mahalik & Woodland, 2001). Sexual activity among Black males bends toward permissiveness, begins early, occurs frequently, and involves multiple partners (Staples, 1986). These personal and political stances can be considered acts of power and resistance (Staples 1986; Whitehead, 2002).

[. . .]

Education Policy and School Marginalization

Policy, in some crude fashion, can be described as the granting of privilege to some while withholding said privilege from others. Policies then are essentially economic instruments. No matter the level or political body, policy formulation is driven by values, both personal and corporate (Fowler, 2000). Often schools are charged with supporting the public good, and to the extent that bearing up the economic system of the nation is deemed a public good, schools will replicate policies (which themselves are economic implements) to gird the economic system. Further, if as Manning Marable (1993) contends, slave owners perceived that Black males posed a potential threat to the entire system of slavery, it stands to reason that whites would have made every effort to secure their economic position. To the degree that this is true over time, public and educational policies would allow for the credentialing of some and not others, providing a gate-keeping mechanism for access to social and economic resources. [This is] only possible, as Lipman (2003) says, because policies function to control behavior and legitimate what is thought, said, and learned, framing even the social identities that are allowed to emerge, and the very meaning of the purpose of education.

Methods/Methodology

Study Design

This quantitative study will employ a cross-sectional survey design. Surveys are intended to collect information that will describe particular characteristics of a population (Fraenkel & Wallen, 2003). The purpose of this research project is to explore educators' perceptions regarding policies that inhibit Black male promotion from one grade level to the next, as well as those that prevent high school graduation and deter college enrollment. The intent of this project is to examine if there are differences in perceptions within and across certain groups of educators with regards to the impact of educational policies on African American males.

Sample and Selection

The targeted sample population is public high school teachers and administrators who work in schools with substantial portions of African American students (approximately 35% or greater). The rationale for looking at schools with large numbers of Black adolescents centers on the notion that issues which confront Black males are likely to have surfaced and generated an administrative response, whereas schools with a small African American presence are less likely to have the aforementioned and are more likely to treat a matter on an individual basis. Educators' perceptions are critical to understanding the issue of policy impact because they are the closest to the administration of practices and procedures related to them. A stratified random sample will be utilized. This will be a regional sample involving all northeastern states. Using data from the National Center for Education Statistics, schools will be selected with sufficient numbers of African Americans. Once schools within a state have been identified, schools will be randomly selected based on the alphabetized listing of all eligible schools in the northeast. Educators will be randomly selected using an alphabetical listing of educators within the school.

Instrument

The survey instrument is a self-designed questionnaire that will collect demographic information on the respondent and the school. Fraenkel and Wallen (2003) state that survey methods best provide encouragement to answer questions of a sensitive nature and allow for standardization of responses. Given that race and gender issues tend to be emotionally charged, the survey design is the ideal model for this study. Fraenkel and Wallen also say that the response rate with this type of study is poor. Because of the sensitive nature of this topic a substantial nonresponse rate is anticipated. To address this issue, 650 respondents will be targeted and a reminder follow up will be distributed. A 30 percent response rate threshold is expected, which is a projected yield of 250 responses.

To address *validity*, three or four educators or former educators who worked in settings with substantive minority populations will assess the content validity of the questionnaire. Fraenkel and Wallen call this expert judgment. To explore the issue of *reliability*, the instrument will be piloted with a group of ten to twenty educators. Fraenkel and Wallen refer to this as observer agreement.

Data Collection Procedures

The research instrument will be copied and mailed to 650 educators across all northeastern states. It is expected that 50 schools will be identified, to include ten teachers and three administrators in each school. The packet mailed to each school will include a letter explaining the study, three survey instruments, three consent forms, and three return-addressed, stamped envelopes. Respondents will be asked to complete and return the survey as soon as possible. Also, two reminder notices will be mailed. Surveys will be catalogued in the order in which they are received.

Data Analysis

Once returned surveys are received, data will be compiled into SPSS software for analysis by the researcher. Because this study will attempt to describe certain relationships and make inferences about particular perceptions of educators, both correlation and chi square analysis will be utilized.

Resources and Budget

This project will be supported in part by a $500 grant from the Education department of the University of New Hampshire. The resources necessary to carry out this project are: a copy card for the copying of materials such as the release letter and the survey instrument, envelopes, postage stamps, post cards, access to the NCES database, access to a UNH lab computer whereon the SPSS program is loaded, and room and board accommodations during the summer. It is necessary to have lodging and meals during the summer at the university because this provides the only means to complete the analysis portion of the project, as it affords access to a computer system with the applicable software and to the faculty research supervisor who will provide guidance and direction with the statistical manipulations, analysis and interpretation of the data.

[...]

Works Cited

Cassidy, W. & Bates, A. (2005, November). "Drop-outs" and "push-outs": Finding hope at a school that actualizes the ethic of care. *American Journal of Education. 112*, 66–102.

Franklin, C. W. (1984, December 2). Black male–black female conflict: Individually caused and culturally nurtured. *Journal of Black Studies, 15*, 139–154.

Fogg, N. P. & Harrington, P. E. (2004, Spring). A matter of degrees: How undergraduate college completions shape labor supply. *Connection: The Journal of the New England Board of Higher Education, 18*, 5. 21–24.

Fowler, F. C. (2000). *Policy Studies for Educational Leaders: An Introduction*. Upper Saddle River, NJ: Merrill/Prentice Hall.

Fraenkel, J. R. & Wallen, N. E. (2003). *How to Design and Evaluate Research in Education*, 5th edition. Boston, MA: McGraw-Hill.

Harper, S. (2004). The measure of a man: Conceptualizations of masculinity among high- achieving African American male college students. *Berkeley Journal of Sociology, 48*, 89–107.

Hefner, D. (2004, June 17). Where the boys aren't: The decline of black males in colleges and universities has sociologists and educators concerned about the future of the African American community. *Black Issues in Higher Education: Special Anniversary Edition*, 70–75.

Holzman, M. (2004). Public education and black male students: A state report card. *Schott Educational Equity Index*. Cambridge, MA: The Schott Foundation for Public Education.

Lipman, P. (2003, December). Chicago school policy: Regulating Black and Latino youth in the global city. *Race, Ethnicity and Education, 6*, 4. 331–335.

Majors, R. & Billson, J. M. (1992). *Cool pose: The dilemmas of Black manhood in America*. New York: Lexington.

Marable, M. (1993). The black male: Searching beyond stereotypes. In Majors, R. & Gordon, J. (Eds.), *The American Black Male*. Chicago: Nelson-Hall.

Mortenson, T. (1999, December). Where are the men: The growing gender gap in higher education. *Opportunity Outlook: Journal of the Council for Opportunity in Education*, 14–20.

Patterson, O. (1995). The crisis of gender relations among African-Americans. *Race, gender, and power in America*. Anita Faye Hill and Emma Coleman Jordan (Eds.). 56–103.

Pierre, M. R., Mahalik, J. R., & Woodland, M. H. (2001). The effects of racism, African self-consciousness and psychological functioning on black masculinity: A historical and social adaptation framework. *Journal of African American Men,* 6, 2. 19–39.

Smith, R. (2005, Spring). Saving black boys: The elusive promise of public education. NewsBrief: Publication of the National Alliance of Black School Educators.

Staples, S. (1986, Winter). Stereotypes of black male sexuality: The facts behind the myths. Changing Men.

Trusty, J. (1996). Counseling for dropout prevention: Applications from multicultural counseling. *Journal of Multicultural Counseling & Development, 24*, 2, 105–117.

Wilson, W. J. (1987). The truly disadvantaged: The inner city, the underclass, and public policy.

Whitehead, S. M. (2002). *Men and Masculinities.* Malden, MA: Blackwell Publishers.
[. . .]

Think About It

(1)   What arguments does Samm make about why his study is urgent and important? Do you find these arguments compelling? Why or why not?

(2)   Did you notice that Samm often used the passive voice? (e.g., "The research instrument will be copied and mailed to 650 educators across all northeastern states.") He also avoided use of the word "I." (He sometimes refers to himself as "the researcher.") Why do you suppose Samm uses this language style?

(3)   This is a research project that needs additional funding in order for Samm to conduct it. Looking at the grant proposal as a whole (not just at the "Resources and Budget" section, describe the strategies that Samm uses to convince his reader to provide additional funding. Do you see places where the author could be more persuasive? Consider, for instance, whether correcting minor details such as the consistency of citations or accuracy of numerical data would make this proposal more effective.

Write About It

Think of an area of research that you would like to explore. Choose a topic based on readings from one of your classes, or conduct some preliminary research to develop a topic (Chapter 23). Next, find a source of funding that is available for students at your college. Then, using this reading and the grant proposals in Chapter 13 as examples, write a grant proposal to fund your research on this topic.

Reading Reports

THE COLLEGE BOARD   "PROGRESS REPORT 2011: THE COLLEGE COMPLETION AGENDA" (EXCERPT)

The College Board's Commission on Access, Admissions and Success in Higher Education prepared this report in 2011 as part of its central mission: to identify how the United States can reach the goal of having at least 55 percent of 25- to 34-year-olds holding at least an associate's degree by 2025. In this recommendation report, the Board identifies ten factors that will help the United States to reach that goal. This section of the report includes recommendations to make college education more affordable for students.

Read About It

Before you read this recommendation report, skim the main sections and subsections. How is the report organized? What are the main sections within this section of the report, and how are they indicated by the design elements in the text?

CollegeBoard
Advocacy & Policy Center

The College Completion Agenda

2011

Progress Report

Eight

Keep college affordable

WE RECOMMEND restraining growth in college costs and prices, using available aid and resources wisely, and insisting that state governments meet their obligations for funding higher education.

In *Coming to Our Senses*, the commission called for assuring college affordability by restraining increases in college prices. In order to make this a reality, the state governments must meet their obligations for funding higher education. State appropriations are not keeping pace with the increasing enrollments at colleges and universities, contributing to rapid increases in tuition and fees.[66] The lag in appropriations by states is leaving families and students with the burden of financing an increasing portion of the cost of higher education. However, state appropriations and tuition prices cannot be viewed in a vacuum. While state appropriations and tuition are indeed important, ensuring college affordability also depends on other factors, such as living expenses, family ability to pay and the availability of financial aid. Each of these factors affects the affordability of attending a college or university. All of these areas are reflected in the measures that have been chosen for this recommendation.

Indicators of progress on this recommendation include:

- State appropriations to fund public higher education;
- Tuition, fees and other costs of attendance at colleges and universities;
- Net price students pay for college;
- Change in family income levels; and
- Earnings of college graduates.

---

66. College Board. (2011). *Trends in College Pricing*. Retrieved October 26, 2011, from http://trends.collegeboard.org/college_pricing/

completionagenda.collegeboard.org

General Findings for This Recommendation

- As of 2010-11, total state appropriations to fund public higher education are $78.9 billion.
- As of 2010-11, total state appropriations to fund public higher education per FTE are $7,171.
- From 1980-81 to 2010-11, the change in total state appropriations for public higher education has increased from $55.3 billion in 1980-81 to $78.9 billion in 2010-11, or 42.7 percent.
- From 1980-81 to 2010-11, the change in total state appropriations for public higher education per FTE decreased from $8,326 in 1980-81 to $7,171 in 2010-11, or -13.9 percent.
- As of the 2011-12 academic year, the average estimated undergraduate budget for public two-year commuter students is $15,286, including tuition and fees, room and board, books and supplies, transportation, and other expenses.
- As of the 2011-12 academic year, the average estimated undergraduate budget for public four-year in-state on-campus students is $21,447, including tuition and fees, room and board, books and supplies, transportation, and other expenses.
- As of the 2011-12 academic year, the average estimated undergraduate budget for public four-year out-of-state on-campus students is $33,973, including tuition and fees, room and board, books and supplies, transportation, and other expenses.
- As of the 2011-12 academic year, the average estimated undergraduate budget for private nonprofit four-year on-campus students is $42,224, including tuition and fees, room and board, books and supplies, transportation, and other expenses.
- As of the 2011-12 academic year, at public two-year institutions, the net price students pay for tuition and fees is -$810 (after subtracting grants and federal tax benefits).
- As of the 2011-12 academic year, at public four-year institutions, the net price students pay for tuition and fees is $2,490 (after subtracting grants and federal tax benefits).
- As of the 2011-12 academic year, at private nonprofit four-year institutions, the net price students pay for tuition and fees is $12,970 (after subtracting grants and federal tax benefits).
- From 2000 to 2010, the average family income has declined 16 percent (inflation adjusted) for low-income families.
- From 2000 to 2010, the average family income has declined 6 percent (inflation adjusted) for moderate-income families.
- As of 2009, the average amount of earnings for full-time workers ages 25 to 34 whose highest degree is a high school diploma is $34,594.
- As of 2009, the average amount of earnings for full-time workers ages 25 to 34 whose highest degree is an associate degree is $42,391.
- As of 2009, the average amount of earnings for full-time workers ages 25 to 34 whose highest degree is a bachelor's degree is $53,483.

$78.9 Billion

As of 2010-11, total public support for public higher education is $78.9 billion.

▼ **$1.6 billion**
FY2009–FY2010

$7,171

As of 2010-11, total state appropriations to fund higher education per FTE is $7,171.

▼ **$319** FY2009–FY2010

Updated data source ★

State Appropriations to Fund Higher Education

What is this measure, and why is this measure important? This indicator measures the state appropriation dollars used to support higher education in both total dollars and per full-time equivalent (FTE) student in the United States. Revenues for public colleges and universities, where about 70 percent of students are enrolled, come primarily from a combination of state appropriations and the tuition and fees students pay. This measure is important because the inability of state appropriations to keep up with enrollment growth is a primary driver of rising tuition levels.

What are the policy issues associated with this measure? State funding levels depend on the interaction of state priorities and philosophies of educational funding with fiscal constraints. With the pressures on state budgets from declining revenues and competing demands, only a strong commitment to affordable, high-quality public higher education on the part of state legislatures can assure the funding levels required to restrain tuition increases and provide adequate need-based aid.

Where are we now? In the United States, state fiscal support for education has increased 42.7 percent from 1981-82 and 2010-11 (after adjusting for inflation). Figure 8.1a shows that this increase is despite the adjustment of these numbers for inflation. Figure 8.1b shows that after increasing by 6 percent in the 1980s and by 5 percent in the 1990s, state appropriations per FTE student declined by 23% in inflation-adjusted dollars over the decade from 2000-01 to 2010-11. This decline in fiscal support per FTE can be attributed largely to the recession that has crippled state and federal budgets in the time of increasing enrollments at public institutions. The 18 percent real decline in state appropriations per FTE student from 2007-08 to 2010-11 was the largest three-year decline in the 30 years of data reported here.

When the data are disaggregated by state, fiscal support for education ranges from $66.9 million in Vermont to $11.7 billion in California. Figure 8.1c shows that when states are placed in rank order, states with the highest fiscal support for education are California, Texas, New York, North Carolina and Florida. The states with the lowest fiscal support for education are Vermont, New Hampshire, South Dakota, Rhode Island and Montana.

201

completionagenda.collegeboard.org

42.7%

From 1980-81 to 2010-11 total public support for public higher education increased from $55.3 billion (in 2010 constant dollars) in 1980-81 to $78.9 billion in 2010-11, or 42.7 percent.

-13.9%

From 1980-81 to 2010-11 total public support for public higher education per FTE decreased from $8,326 (in 2010 constant dollars) in 1980-81 to $7,171 in 2010-11, or -13.9 percent.

When the data are disaggregated by state, state fiscal support for education per FTE ranges from $2,754 in Vermont to $13,090 in Wyoming. Figure 8.1d shows that when states are placed in rank order, states with the highest fiscal support for education per FTE are Wyoming, Alaska, North Carolina, Texas and Connecticut. The states with the lowest fiscal support for education per FTE are Vermont, New Hampshire, Colorado, Ohio and Montana.

When interpreting this measure, what should be kept in mind? State appropriation levels and patterns differ considerably across states. Both enrollment levels and economic circumstances must be understood to put appropriations into context. However, national appropriations do provide an important snapshot. It is much more important to understand the support in education per FTE because this value takes into account the enrollment of the state in addition to the allocation of education dollars. Further, this mitigates the advantage that larger states have in allocating more money to higher education.

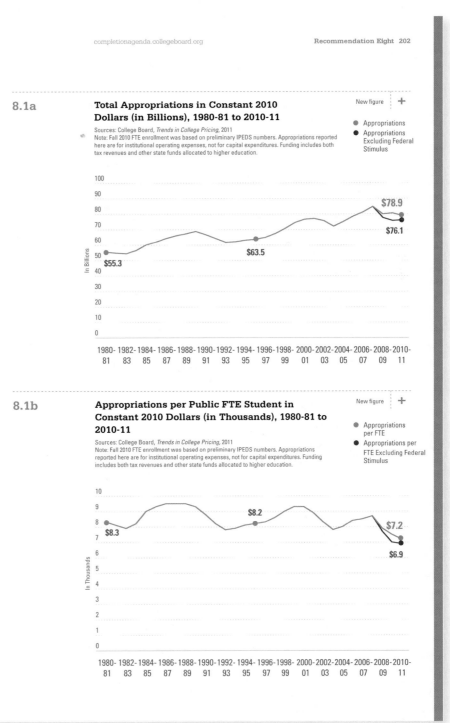

8.1a

Total Appropriations in Constant 2010 Dollars (in Billions), 1980-81 to 2010-11

New figure +

● Appropriations
● Appropriations Excluding Federal Stimulus

Sources: College Board, *Trends in College Pricing*, 2011
Note: Fall 2010 FTE enrollment was based on preliminary IPEDS numbers. Appropriations reported here are for institutional operating expenses, not for capital expenditures. Funding includes both tax revenues and other state funds allocated to higher education.

$78.9
$76.1
$63.5
$55.3

In Billions

1980-81 1982-83 1984-85 1986-87 1988-89 1990-91 1992-93 1994-95 1996-97 1998-99 2000-01 2002-03 2004-05 2006-07 2008-09 2010-11

8.1b

Appropriations per Public FTE Student in Constant 2010 Dollars (in Thousands), 1980-81 to 2010-11

New figure +

● Appropriations per FTE
● Appropriations per FTE Excluding Federal Stimulus

Sources: College Board, *Trends in College Pricing*, 2011
Note: Fall 2010 FTE enrollment was based on preliminary IPEDS numbers. Appropriations reported here are for institutional operating expenses, not for capital expenditures. Funding includes both tax revenues and other state funds allocated to higher education.

$8.2
$8.3
$7.2
$6.9

In Thousands

1980-81 1982-83 1984-85 1986-87 1988-89 1990-91 1992-93 1994-95 1996-97 1998-99 2000-01 2002-03 2004-05 2006-07 2008-09 2010-11

203   completionagenda.collegeboard.org

8.1c   **Educational Fiscal Support by State Rank, FY 2010–2011**   New figure   +
            Source: State Higher Education Finance, State Higher Education, Executive Officers, 2011

In Billions

		0	1	2	3	4	5	6	7	8	9	10	11	12	13	14	15

California	$11,683,824,350
Texas	$6,581,785,758
New York	$4,817,473,365
North Carolina	$3,541,451,114
Florida	$3,408,549,094
Illinois	$3,325,837,582
Georgia	$2,558,404,198
Michigan	$2,291,948,391
Ohio	$2,041,142,065
Pennsylvania	$1,977,641,215
New Jersey	$1,929,769,000
Arizona	$1,673,804,800
Maryland	$1,658,253,134
Wisconsin	$1,607,966,188
Virginia	$1,583,189,711
Washington	$1,555,846,701
Tennessee	$1,317,599,357
Indiana	$1,313,270,756
Minnesota	$1,280,857,000
Massachusetts	$1,196,403,246
Louisiana	$1,174,964,909
Missouri	$1,174,959,206
Alabama	$1,137,010,562
Kentucky	$1,040,087,184
Oklahoma	$981,978,880
Connecticut	$889,346,452
South Carolina	$834,817,353
Colorado	$825,096,369
Mississippi	$796,728,225
Kansas	$785,116,448
Oregon	$750,948,945
New Mexico	$747,161,865
Iowa	$741,743,209
Arkansas	$705,599,663
Utah	$672,510,100
Nebraska	$607,145,616
Nevada	$516,471,637
Hawaii	$461,116,903
West Virginia	$386,020,036
Idaho	$354,996,631
Alaska	$302,853,868
Wyoming	$298,261,301
North Dakota	$246,221,389
Maine	$237,532,814
Delaware	$228,167,650
Montana	$190,346,889
Rhode Island	$168,351,962
South Dakota	$155,341,395
New Hampshire	$127,897,496
Vermont	$66,931,354
District of Columbia	N/A

completionagenda.collegeboard.org   Recommendation Eight 204

- -

8.1d   **Educational Fiscal Support per FTE by State Rank, FY 2010–2011**   New figure +

Source: State Higher Education Finance, State Higher Education, Executive Officers, 2011

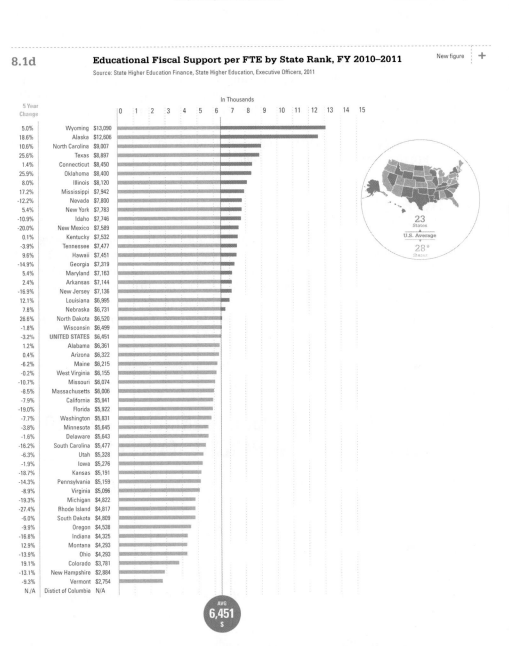

5 Year Change	State	Value
5.0%	Wyoming	$13,090
18.6%	Alaska	$12,606
10.6%	North Carolina	$9,007
25.6%	Texas	$8,897
1.4%	Connecticut	$8,450
25.9%	Oklahoma	$8,400
8.0%	Illinois	$8,120
17.2%	Mississippi	$7,942
-12.2%	Nevada	$7,800
5.4%	New York	$7,783
-10.9%	Idaho	$7,746
-20.0%	New Mexico	$7,589
0.1%	Kentucky	$7,532
-3.9%	Tennessee	$7,477
9.6%	Hawaii	$7,451
-14.9%	Georgia	$7,319
5.4%	Maryland	$7,163
2.4%	Arkansas	$7,144
-16.9%	New Jersey	$7,136
12.1%	Louisiana	$6,995
7.8%	Nebraska	$6,731
26.6%	North Dakota	$6,520
-1.8%	Wisconsin	$6,499
-3.2%	UNITED STATES	$6,451
1.2%	Alabama	$6,361
0.4%	Arizona	$6,322
-6.2%	Maine	$6,215
-0.2%	West Virginia	$6,155
-10.7%	Missouri	$6,074
-8.5%	Massachusetts	$6,006
-7.9%	California	$5,941
-19.0%	Florida	$5,922
-7.7%	Washington	$5,831
-3.8%	Minnesota	$5,645
-1.6%	Delaware	$5,643
-16.2%	South Carolina	$5,477
-6.3%	Utah	$5,328
-1.9%	Iowa	$5,276
-18.7%	Kansas	$5,191
-14.3%	Pennsylvania	$5,159
-8.9%	Virginia	$5,096
-19.3%	Michigan	$4,822
-27.4%	Rhode Island	$4,817
-6.0%	South Dakota	$4,809
-9.9%	Oregon	$4,538
-16.8%	Indiana	$4,325
12.9%	Montana	$4,293
-13.9%	Ohio	$4,293
19.1%	Colorado	$3,781
-13.1%	New Hampshire	$2,884
-9.3%	Vermont	$2,754
N./A	District of Columbia	N/A

In Thousands
0 1 2 3 4 5 6 7 8 9 10 11 12 13 14 15

23 States
U.S. Average
28* States

AVG
6,451
$

Think About It

(1)   This report incorporates a variety of design elements (Chapter 29). How do these design elements contribute to the overall message or claims in the report, and how do they appeal to the audience? Why do you think the report was designed in this way?

(2)   We might assume that reports simply provide information from a study or inquiry. But recommendation reports, especially, also make an argument. What are the main claims made in this report section, and how are they supported?

(3)   Compare the factors identified in this report section to your own experiences with college so far. Do you agree with the recommendations in the report, or are their other factors to consider?

Write About It

Find your state in the graphs 8.1c-d. Where does your state rank in college funding? How does the level of fiscal support in your state affect students? Research and write a news report about state support for education and how it affects students in your state. First, research the problem: you might start by looking up other news accounts, reports, and articles, but you might also wish to interview students, professors, or administrators to learn their perspectives on education funding (Chapter 24). Next, draft a news report that might appear in a local magazine, website or newspaper.

SCOTT D. RYAN, SUE PEARLMUTTER, AND VICTOR GROZA
COMING OUT OF THE CLOSET: OPENING AGENCIES TO GAY AND LESBIAN ADOPTIVE PARENTS (EXCERPT)

The authors of this recommendation report are professors of social work. They published this report in the journal Social Work *in 2004.*

Read About It

One purpose for a recommendation report is to offer solutions to problems. As you read, write down the main problems the authors identify, and then list the solutions they propose.

Empirical and clinical knowledge of adoption policy and practice has increased greatly in recent years. However, a crisis remains in this arena, as many more children are available for adoption than there are families to adopt them. As a result of the 1997 enactment of the Adoption and Safe Families Act (P.L. 105-89), which requires more expedient termination of birth parent rights than had previously existed, the number of children available for adoption continues to grow. The Adoption and Foster Care Analysis and Reporting System (AFCARS), established as part of the act, estimated that as of September 30, 2001, 126,000 children were waiting to be adopted. These were children for whom the public child welfare agency had a goal of adoption, for whom parental rights had been terminated, or both. During the fiscal year ending September 30, 2001, AFCARS reported that an estimated 46,668 children were adopted through the public child welfare system (AFCARS, 2002).

Defining Suitable Adoptive Families

Child welfare agencies most often seek adoptive families from among traditional heterosexual two-parent or single-parent families. In doing this, they follow state adoption statutes, many dating to the mid-1900s that favor those families (Appell, 2001; Hollinger, 1999), even though a great deal of evidence exists that family constellations have changed significantly in the past three decades. Fields and Casper (cited in the U.S. Census Bureau, 2001) reported that the traditional two-parent nuclear family (that is, married households with one or more children under the age of 18) constituted 24 percent of all U.S. households in 2000—down from 40 percent in 1970. Although the total number of households in the United States is estimated to increase 15.5 percent from 1995 to 2010, the number of traditional families is projected to decline 6.4 percent from 24.6 million to 23.1 million. Such families would then constitute only 20.1 percent of total households (U.S. Census Bureau, 1996).

Greater flexibility in the conceptualization and interpretation of the word "family" (Ricketts & Achtenberg, 1989) would benefit children awaiting adoptive families. The effect of excluding nontraditional placement resources through an overly narrow definition of family is that some children will languish longer in foster care without permanence. Brooks and colleagues (1999) have discussed recent federal legislation intended to increase the pool of multiethnic foster and adoptive families. Their principles for recruitment and adoption placement practice show that commitment to considering gay and lesbian singles and couples as potential adoptive families would expand the possibilities for permanent child placement.

Gay men and lesbians have adopted children for many years, despite fear and discrimination. They have adopted as single parents through public child welfare agencies, private sources, and international organizations. They have sought older children from various racial and ethnic groups, as well as sibling groups and children with disabilities. And, although international adoptions have permitted more flexibility, they too have become more restrictive, as countries such as China, Thailand, and Guatemala have prohibited gay and lesbian adoption applications (Brodzinsky, 2002; Chibbaro, 2002). . . .

Laws and regulations, narrow definitions of family, homophobia, and heterosexism limit the possibility that lesbians and gay men will be considered as adoptive parents. The cumulative effect of actions by states, local jurisdictions, agencies, and individual staff members is to prevent or discourage consideration of their availability and interest. Even if child welfare staff members overcome these initial barriers, the decision-making tool most often available to them may further limit the inclusion of gay and lesbian families as placement candidates. This standard, the "best interest of the child," is used as a measure to guide placement of children in the custody of the child welfare system.

The Best Interest Decision-Making Standard

All states allow social workers, judges, and professionals involved in the placement of children with prospective adoptive families to apply the best interest of the child standard for decision making (Ricketts, 1991). This standard requires that child welfare workers base their recommendations and decisions on what is best for the child, not what is best for the potential adoptive parents or the agency and not the worker's personal opinion. Workers must assess the match between short- and long-term needs of the child or children awaiting placement and the resources, strengths, and vulnerabilities of a particular family.

However, the capacity of social workers to fully and objectively assess parenting ability among a range of family types may be limited. Berkman and Zinberg (1997) found that heterosexism is prevalent among social workers. . . .

Literature suggests that considerations surrounding gay men and lesbians' suitability as adoptive parents focus first on the applicants themselves. These concerns include the mental health of the applicant (Falk, 1989; Green, Mandel, Hotvedt, Gray, & Smith, 1986), parenting skills (Cramer, 1986; Patterson, 2000a), and his or her relationship quality and stability (Flaks, Ficher, Masterpasqua, & Joseph, 1995; Koepke, Hare, & Moran, 1992). Next, consideration focuses on the effect of gay or lesbian adoption on the child's psychological and psychosexual development (Allen & Burrell, 1996; Falk, 1989; Gibbs, 1988; Green et al.; Knight & Garcia, 1994; Patterson, 1992, 2000a), sexual safety (Cramer, 1986; Falk, 1989; Knight & Garcia), and social stigmatization (Donaldson, 2000). In addition, studies have examined permutations of these subthemes among gay and lesbian biological and adoptive families (Sullivan, 1995). Currently, no empirical evidence demonstrates that living with a gay or lesbian parent has any significant negative effects on children (for an overview of the available research, see Patterson, 2000b).

In using the best interest standard, social workers may be influenced by peers, supervisors, their organizational context, and the larger sociocultural arena, and this may restrict their decision making.

Practice Implications

The characteristics and definitions of family change with the realities of demographic shifts in this country. However, application of the best interest standard can become more inclusive only if workers, their supervisors, and child welfare organizations begin to consciously accept gay and lesbian people as potential adoptive parents.

Aligning Personal Attitudes, Beliefs, and Behaviors with Professional Guidelines

A primary intervention tool for changing behavior is the use of training. Ryan (2000) found that training focused specifically on adoptions by gay men and lesbians was the most significant predictor of social worker placement recommendation. Others have also noted the positive effects of general training on attitudes held toward gay men and lesbians (Ben-Ari, 1998; Christensen & Sorensen, 1994; Serdahely & Ziemba, 1984; Wells, 1991). Trainers should begin this work by helping social workers define their beliefs and attitudes about gay men and lesbians, including attitudes about them as parents. Identifying individual values and beliefs regarding this issue is essential to the growth process (Taylor, 1998). . . .

Research suggests that interventions directly addressing stereotypes and unfounded beliefs may be most effective in countering negative attitudes toward gay men and lesbians as parents (Crawford & Solliday, 1996). Adoption workers could meet with gay and lesbian applicants, birth families, and adoptive families (Berkman & Zinberg, 1997; Herek, 1988; Herek & Glunt, 1993), thereby enlisting collective support. Other strategies for changing attitudes have been suggested. For instance, special committees focused on gay and lesbian issues within an agency "increased the visibility of gay/lesbian employees and have led to a more tolerant attitude [among staff]" (Brooks et al., 1996, p. 26). Providing social workers with information from relevant research may further help to illuminate and broaden their perceptions of family. For example, the majority of students in one study attributed their attitude changes to meeting with a gay man and his mother and obtaining additional theoretical and empirical information about gay men and lesbians (Ben-Ari, 1998).

Child welfare workers also need to understand how to apply the best interest standard in ways that are inclusive. In training, they should be encouraged to examine applicant information and materials with an awareness of the child's needs and interests, recognizing that their own values may impede that process. Definitions of family could be discussed and broadened in a training or educational setting so that workers begin their consideration of applicants from a larger pool of adoptive candidates. . . .

Moderating Supervisor and Peer Influences

As noted earlier, homophobic peers or supervisors might negatively influence an accepting social worker. Most training focuses on the individual social worker. In this instance, training could address the effects of agency policy and other employees, providing workers with tools and strategies to implement new policies and deal with other system constraints. To counter any negative effects of supervisors, peers, or other groups, Brooks and colleagues (1996) described one agency's practice of having representatives of the gay and lesbian community present at the meeting at which placements are considered. This practice humanizes the victims of prejudicial behavior (Bandura, 1990) and reminds decision makers of their responsibility to consider the best interest of the child rather than the sexual orientation of the applicants.

The inclusion of a gay or lesbian community representative, the hiring of gay and lesbian social workers, or both, could shift the power balance within the group, providing more support for consideration of placements with gay and lesbian applicants. Bandura (1977) indicated that because behavior is learned, it can be unlearned as well. Thus, interacting with gay and lesbian coworkers and community members can help social workers become comfortable working with gay and lesbian applicants. . . .

Organizational Changes

Only a few laws or policies explicitly require child welfare organizations to consider gay and lesbian applicants equally with heterosexual individuals in child placement decisions. This double standard for placement decisions seems antithetical to a mission of social justice and runs counter to the ethical guidelines of NASW and recommendations from the Child Welfare League of America, the American Psychiatric Association, the American Psychological Association, and other organizations. The clear positions these professional organizations have taken can provide an agency with support to implement inclusive policies, procedures, and practices.

Although decision makers' lack of guidance may encourage ambiguity and homophobia, these position statements can provide legitimacy for an organization's positive actions in the larger professional community. In addition, agencies can engage community activists knowledgeable on adoption by gay and lesbian individuals to assist in developing clear policies that help remove this veil of ambiguity. . . .

Conclusion

Social work professionals have a responsibility to challenge problems that have been socially sanctioned and created. Leadership requires doing what is right, not necessarily what is popular or consistent with expressed community standards and values. Working to ensure the best interests of children may require joining the fight against gay and lesbian prejudice. A recognition of struggles in the civil rights movement and the women's movement can help us understand how such normative prejudice has denied large segments of the population full participation in society. These struggles also help identify the significance of any change in values, attitudes, and behaviors that were once perceived as acceptable.

No one has the right to adopt; children do have a right to loving, permanent homes. This article has proposed that one step toward that goal is a critical re-evaluation at the intrapersonal, interpersonal, and organizational levels of the ways in which the best interest of the child standard is defined and applied.

References

Adoption and Safe Families Act of 1997, P.L. 105-89, 111 Stat. 2115. See also http://www.abanet.org/ftp/ pub/child/pl105-89.txt

AFCARS. (2002). *Adoption and foster care analysis and reporting system.* Retrieved November 4, 2003, from http://www.acf.dhhs.gov/programs/cb/publications/afcars/report8.pdf

Allen, M., & Burrell, N. (1996). Comparing the impact of homosexual and heterosexual parents on children: Meta-analysis of existing research. *Journal of Homosexuality, 32*(2), 19–35.

American Psychiatric Association. (1986). Position statement on discrimination in selection of foster parents. *American Journal of Psychiatry, 143*, 1506.

American Psychological Association. (1975). *Policy statements on lesbian, gay, and bisexual concerns: Discrimination against homosexuals*. Retrieved June 2000, from http://www.apa.org/pi/lgbpolicy/child.html

American Psychological Association. (1976). *Policy statements on lesbian, gay, and bisexual concerns: Child custody or placement*. Retrieved June 2000, from http://www.apa.org/pi/lgbpolicy/against.html

Appell, A. R. (2001). Lesbian and gay adoption. *Adoption Quarterly, 4*, 75–86.

Bandura, A. (1977). *Social learning theory*. Englewood Cliffs, NJ: Prentice Hall.

Bandura, A. (1990). Selective activation and disengagement of moral control. *Journal of Social Issues, 46*, 27–46.

Ben-Ari, A. (1998). An experiential attitude change: Social work students and homosexuality. *Journal of Homosexuality, 36*(2), 59–71.

Berkman, C., & Zinberg, G. (1997). Homophobia and heterosexism in social workers. *Social Work, 42*, 319–332.

Brodzinsky, D. (2002). Adoption agency perspectives on lesbian and gay prospective parents: A national study. *Adoption Quarterly, 5*(3), 5–23.

Brooks, D., Barth, R., Bussiere, A., & Patterson, G. (1999). Adoption and race: Implementing the Multiethnic Placement Act (MEPA) and the Interethnic Adoption Provisions. *Social Work, 44*, 167–178.

Brooks, D., Goldberg, S., Berrick, J., & Austin, M. (1996). *Considerations relating to the placement of children in gay/lesbian foster and adoptive homes*. Berkeley, CA: Bay Area Social Services Consortium.

Chibbaro, L., Jr. (2002). *Most agencies OK gay adoptions*. Retrieved February 27, 2003, from http://www.hrc.org/familynet/newsstand.asp?ID=1866

Child Welfare League of America. (2000). *Standards for adoption service* (rev. ed.). Washington, DC: Author.

Christensen, S., & Sorensen, L. (1994). Effects of a multi-factor education program on the attitude of child and youth worker students towards gays and lesbians. *Child and Youth Care Forum, 23*, 119–133.

Cramer, D. (1986). Gay parents and their children: A review of research and practical implications. *Journal of Counseling and Development, 64*, 504–507.

Crawford, I., & Solliday, E. (1996). The attitudes of undergraduate college students toward gay parenting. *Journal of Homosexuality, 30*(4), 63–77.

Donaldson, C. (2000). Midlife lesbian parenting. *Journal of Gay & Lesbian Social Services: Issues in Practice, Policy, &Research, 11*, 119–138.

Falk, P. (1989). Lesbian mothers: Psychological assumptions in family law. *American Psychologist, 44*, 941–947.

Flaks, D. K., Ficher, I., Masterpasqua, F., & Joseph, G. (1995). Lesbians choosing motherhood: A comparative study of lesbian and heterosexual parents and their children. *Developmental Psychology, 31*, 105–114.

Gibbs, E. D. (1988). Psychosocial development of children raised by lesbian mothers: A review of research. *Women and Therapy, 8*, 65–75.

Green, R., Mandel, J., Hotvedt, M., Gray, J., & Smith, L. (1986). Lesbian mothers and their children: A comparison with solo parent heterosexual mothers and their children. *Archives of Sexual Behavior, 15*, 167–184.

Herek, G. (1988). Heterosexuals' attitudes toward lesbians and gay men: Correlates and gender differences. *Journal of Sex Research, 25*, 451–477.

Herek, G., & Glunt, E. (1993). Interpersonal contact and heterosexuals' attitudes toward gay men: Results from a national survey. *Journal of Sex Research, 30*, 239–244.

Knight, R., & Garcia, D. (1994). *Homosexual parenting: Bad for children, bad for society*. Washington, DC: Family Research Council.

Koepke, L., Hare, J., & Moran, P. B. (1992). Relationship quality in a sample of lesbian couples with children and child-free lesbian couples. *Family Relations, 41*, 224–229.

Patterson, C. (1992). Children of lesbian and gay parents. *Child Development, 63*, 1025–1042.

Patterson, C. (2000a). Family relationships of lesbians and gay men. *Journal of Marriage and the Family, 62*, 1052–1069.

Patterson, C. (2000b, February 23). *Lesbian and gay parenting: A resource for psychologists*. Retrieved October 2002, from http://www.apa.org/pi/parent.html

Ricketts, W. (1991). *Lesbians and gay men as foster parents*. Portland, ME: National Child Welfare Resource Center for Child and Family Policy.

Ricketts, W., & Achtenberg, R. (1989). Adoption and foster parenting for lesbians and gay men: Creating new traditions in family. *Marriage and Family Review*, i4, 83–n6.

Ryan, S. (2000). Examining social workers' placement recommendations of children with gay and lesbian adoptive parents. *Families in Society, 81*, 517–528.

Serdahely, W., & Ziemba, G. (1984). Changing homophobic attitudes through college sexuality education. *Journal of Homosexuality, 10*, 109–116.

Sullivan, A. (1995). Policy issues. In A. Sullivan (Ed.), *Issues of gay and lesbian adoption: Proceedings of the Fourth Annual Pierce-Warwick Adoption Symposium* (pp. 1–9). Washington, DC: Child Welfare League of America.

Taylor, M. (1998, October). *Attitudes of social workers toward gay and lesbian adoption*. Unpublished master's thesis, California State University, Long Beach. (UMI No. 1390139, MAI 36/05, p. 1276)

U.S. Census Bureau. (1996, May). *National households and families projections*. Retrieved June 2000, from http://www.census.gov/population/www/projections/nathh.ktml

Weinberg, G. (1972). *Society and the healthy homosexual*. New York: St. Martin's Press.

Wells, J. (1991). What makes a difference? Various teaching strategies to reduce homophobia in university students. *Annals of Sex Research, 3*, 229–238.

Think About It

(1)   Who do you think is the audience for this recommendation report? Are there multiple types of readers for this report? If so, how do the authors address these different readers?

(2)   How do the authors dramatize the problems they identify in the report? Do

you think readers of this report would be convinced that these problems should be addressed? If not, what objections do you think readers might have?

(3) How do the authors use official statements, policies, and laws in their report? Did you find them effective sources of evidence? Why or why not?

Write About It

Research an issue affecting families in your community, such as affordable housing for families, access to child care, divorce rates, or teen pregnancy. How well does your community provide resources that address the issue? Conduct research on your issue, using published sources (such as newspapers and reports) and/or interviews and surveys (Chapter 24). Then, write a recommendation report. Choose an audience that is in a position to act on your issue. Drawing on your research, develop a set of recommendations that will help to address the issue.

WENDY CERVANTES AND YALI LINCROFT   THE IMPACT OF IMMIGRATION ENFORCEMENT ON CHILD WELFARE

Wendy Cervantes and Yali Lincroft wrote this recommendation report for First Focus, a bipartisan advocacy organization that seeks to make children and families a priority in federal decision-making. This report appeared in 2010, when new immigration enforcement policies were being debated in many states.

Read About It

This recommendation report centers on the effects of immigration on children. While the report is often considered an objective, informational genre, it may also evoke appeals to emotions or values—especially when a report deals with a topic such as children. As you read, mark down places where you think the authors may be appealing to the reader's emotions or values.

While children of immigrants have a lot at stake in the discussions surrounding U.S. immigration policy, their interests remain largely ignored in the debate. For instance, little consideration is given to the impact of immigration enforcement on the 5.5 million children, the vast majority of whom are native-born U.S. citizens, living with at least one undocumented parent.[1] Similarly overlooked are the significant challenges experienced by public child welfare agencies that encounter children separated from their parents due to immigration enforcement measures.

The U.S. child welfare system is based on the notion of ensuring the safety and best interest of the child; however, this principle is often compromised in the face of conflicting federal immigration policies and practices. This policy brief examines the intersection of immigration enforcement and child welfare and the difficulties facing immigrant families caught between the two systems. Recommendations are provided to prioritize keeping children with their families and out of the public child welfare system whenever possible and to ensure that separated children who do encounter the child welfare system receive appropriate care and parents receive due process.

An Overview of Immigration Enforcement

Immigration enforcement activities conducted by Immigration and Customs Enforcement (ICE), the interior enforcement arm of the Department of Homeland Security (DHS), have increased significantly over the past decade. The number of immigrants in ICE detention has risen 45% from about 21,000 in FY 2005 to about 31,000 in FY 2008.[2] Under the Bush administration, there was a particularly dramatic increase in enforcement activities with several large, highly publicized worksite raids. The practice of large-scale worksite raids generally ended under the Obama administration in early 2009. However, the historically high level of arrests, detentions and deportations has remained consistent since 2006.[3]

Beginning in late 2007, a new enforcement strategy was adopted to prioritize the apprehension of serious criminals, resulting in the merging of several programs under the ICE ACCESS Initiative (Agreements of Cooperation in Communities to Enhance Safety and Security). One of the most well-known programs within ICE ACCESS are 287(g) agreements, formal collaborations between ICE and local officials which allow local police to be deputized to enforce immigration laws. Other related programs within the criminal justice system include the Secure Communities and the Criminal Alien programs, which use fingerprint and database checks and detainers or holds to ensure transfer to immigration officials once a person's criminal case is concluded. The National Fugitive Operations Program (NFOP) is another widely used initiative which utilizes Fugitive Operation Teams (FOTs) to arrest immigrants with outstanding deportation orders or other immigration-related violations, often through targeted home raids.[4]

While the ultimate goal of ICE ACCESS programs is to target the most serious criminals, recent studies demonstrate that many of these programs have resulted in the apprehension of thousands of immigrants for minor non-criminal offenses as well as the deportation of thousands of lawful permanent residents (LPRs).[5] Nonetheless, these programs have grown exponentially over recent years, with 287(g) agreements up from just 8 agreements in 2006 to 66 agreements in 2009 and plans to implement the Secure Communities program nationwide by 2013.[6,7] The rapid growth of these new enforcement activities raises serious concerns for child and family well-being.

Unintended Consequences for Children and Families

The exact overall number of children impacted by immigration enforcement, including those that end up in the care and custody of state or local child welfare agencies, is unknown since this information is currently not collected in a consistent way by DHS, the Department of Health and Human Services, or by state and local child welfare agencies themselves. However, a 2007 study of worksite raids by the Urban Institute found that on average for every two adults apprehended in a raid, at least one child is impacted.[8] Furthermore, according to a January 2009 report for the DHS Security Inspector General's Office, over 108,000 undocumented parents of U.S. citizen children were removed from the U.S. between 1997 and 2007.[9] Another recent study focusing on the deportation of LPRs during the same ten-year period reveals that nearly 88,000 U.S. citizen children were impacted by the deportation of an LPR parent, and over a third of the impacted children were under the age of five at the time of the parent's deportation.[10] . . .

Separation from a parent poses a variety of serious risks for a child, and in the context of immigration enforcement, a child can sometimes face sudden separation from both parents. A recent report by the Urban Institute demonstrates that in addition to emotional trauma, separated children face other short-term and long-term threats to their safety, economic security, and overall well-being.[11] For example, housing insecurity and food shortages were common hardships experienced by children in the study due to the loss of one or more parental income.[12] Adverse behavior changes such as more frequent crying and increased fear and anxiety were also noted in two-thirds of children in the six months following a parental arrest, and these changes were most significant in children who witnessed a parental arrest in the home.[13] Nearly a quarter of families included in the study ultimately had to make the difficult decision whether children—many of whom are U.S. citizens— would accompany a deported parent or remain behind in the United States.[14] . . .

Challenges for the Public Child Welfare System

There are multiple ways in which a child may enter the child welfare system due to immigration enforcement. In some cases, arrested parents may simply not be provided with the opportunity to make child care and temporary custody arrangements at the time of apprehension. Or, a child may enter the child welfare system as a result of a parent's criminal arrest or conviction, which can then precipitate the parent's deportation. As mentioned, ICE has prioritized immigration enforcement against such parents and other persons deemed to be "criminal aliens." These persons can be mandatorily detained and deported even if they have some form of protected legal status, are responsible for the care of dependent U.S. citizen children, and/or are now rehabilitated.

Once an immigrant family is involved in the child welfare system, there are several challenges immigrant parents face in reunifying with their child. In some cases, biased family court judges may inappropriately base their decision on a parent's immigration status rather than their demonstrated parenting capacity.[15] Language and cultural barriers, limited access to services, and the difficulty of navigating both the immigration and child welfare systems also threaten an immigrant parent's ability to meet case plan requirements and timelines. . . .

Conclusion: Protecting Child Well-being and Family Unity

As policymakers consider the future of U.S. immigration policy, the interests of children and families must be made a priority. The enforcement of our immigration laws should not conflict with our American values of protecting all children and keeping families together. Policies and practices should be developed to preserve family unity and prevent the unnecessary involvement of children in the child welfare system during all immigration enforcement activities.

Policy Recommendations for Child Welfare:

- Protocols should be created and implemented to guide federal, state, and local child welfare staff, and their contractors, in handling cases involving children separated from their parents due to immigration enforcement. For example, Memorandums of Understanding should be developed between child welfare agencies and DHS, other federal, state and local agencies, the judiciary, dependency and immigration attorneys, and consulates/embassies. These MOUs should ensure coordination among all the entities involved so that parents are able to participate in all state court proceedings that affect their child and that parents facing deportation are provided with adequate time and assistance to make arrangement for their children to either accompany them or remain in the U.S. after their parents' departure.
- Guidelines for privacy and confidentiality should be established for separated children and their families. These guidelines should prevent the disclosure by child welfare agency personnel or their contracting agencies of sensitive information, including the immigration status of children or potential substitute caretakers, to other government agencies or individuals.
- Exceptions to ASFA timelines should be allowed in the event of complicated immigration cases when such an exception is in the best interest of the child. Immigrant families face many challenges which justify a longer time period than allowed under ASFA's timeframe. These extensions should consider delays in the immigration court process, parent language barriers, lack of accessible services, required international relative searches and home studies, and working with foreign consulates and embassies.
- Undocumented children who are separated from their parents due to immigration enforcement should be provided with child welfare services, including foster care placement, when needed. Sometimes, a child left behind after a parent is apprehended in an immigration enforcement action will not be a U.S. citizen but rather an undocumented immigrant. Immigration status should not be a barrier to the provision of all appropriate child protective services, including foster care placement and services, by a state/local child welfare agency.

Endnotes

[1] Terrazas, A., Batalova, J. (2009). *Frequently Requested Statistics on Immigrants and Immigration in the United States*. Washington, DC: Migration Policy Institute.

[2] Ibid.

[3] Ibid.

[4] Mendelson, M., Strom, S. Wishnie, M. (2009). *Collateral Damage: An Examination of ICE's Fugitive Operations Program*. Washington, DC: Migration Policy Institute.

[5] Mendelson, M., Strom, S. (2009). *Collateral Damage: An Examination of ICE's Fugitive Operations Program*. Washington, DC: Migration Policy Institute.

[6] ICE Fact Sheet (January 2010). "Delegation of Immigration Authority Section 287(g) Immigration and Naturalization Act."

[7] ICE Fact Sheet (2009). "Secure Communities Fact Sheet." www.ICE.gov .Secure_Communities.

[8] Capps, R., Castaneda, R. (2007). *Paying the Price: The Impact of Immigration Raids on America's Children*. Washington, DC: Urban Institute for the National Council of La Raza.

[9] Office of the Inspector General, Department of Homeland Security (2009). *Removals Involving Illegal Alien Parents of United States Citizen Children*.

[10] *In the Child's Best Interest? The Consequences of Losing a Lawful Immigrant Parent to Deportation*. (March 2010). University of California, Berkeley School of Law and University of California, Davis, School of Law.

[11] Chaudry, A., Capps, R. (2010). *Facing Our Future: Children in the Aftermath of Immigration Enforcement*. Washington, DC: Urban Institute.

[12] Ibid.

[13] Ibid.

[14] Ibid.

[15] Thronson, D. (Fall 2005). "Of borders and best interests: Examining the experiences of undocumented immigrants in U.S. family courts." *Texas Hispanic Journal of Law & Policy*, 11: 47–72.

Think About It

(1)   Immigration is a contentious political issue in the United States, but this report was written by a bipartisan organization (that is, one that includes members from both political parties). How well do the authors frame this issue and their recommendations to appeal to readers from different political orientations? Are there places where they seemed biased toward one political stance or another?

(2)   This report is organized according to a problem-solution framework: the authors first outline the nature of the problem, and then provide recommendations. Where do the authors use most of their sources—in the problem sections, or in the recommendation sections? Why do you think that is the case?

(3)   Examine places where the authors use statistics to support their points. How are these statistics framed by the authors? Do the authors simply present the statistics, or do they use words to dramatize the numbers? What effect do you think their framing of the data might have on readers?

Write About It

How could your state or community better support the children of immigrants? For example, could your community provide better resources for parents? Could they provide better resources to help children of immigrants learn English, integrate into the larger community, or learn more about their culture? Research and write a recommendation report, drawing on database sources and/or empirical research, such as surveys or interviews (Chapter 24).

● ●

SCOTT M. STRINGER   FOOD NYC: A BLUEPRINT FOR A SUSTAINABLE FOOD SYSTEM

Scott M. Stringer wrote this report in February, 2010, when he was borough chief of Manhattan. The report was prompted by a 2009 summit held in New York City to discuss food and climate change.

Read About It

What kinds of research go into a recommendation report like this one? As you read, pay attention to the footnotes the authors use to cite information. Tally up the type of information cited in each case. How often does the author quote, summarize or paraphrase other sources (Chapter 26)? Consider how each type of reference is used, and how it contributes to the report's credibility and persuasiveness.

In December 2009, world leaders convened in Copenhagen for the United Nations Climate Change Conference, the final meeting of the international community before the Kyoto Protocol expires in 2011. As the conference drew to a close, the participating nations disappointed millions when they emerged without any consensus or comprehensive plan. Even if the two weeklong meetings in Copenhagen had produced such a plan, advocates and scientists knew that an essential piece of the climate change puzzle had been left out: the potential for sustainable food systems to combat the climate crisis.

Across the Atlantic on December 12, several hundred New Yorkers took their seats in an auditorium at New York University to address that issue and to discuss the role that urban communities must play in the fight to halt and reverse climate change. The New York City Food & Climate Summit, hosted by Borough President Scott Stringer in partnership with Just Food and New York University, was a daylong feast of public policy sessions and skill-building workshops designed to bring this international challenge home. . . .

Until recently, it would have been unheard of to host a conversation about farming and agriculture in a city that paved the pastures of Harlem more than a century ago. But with the world's population expected to reach 9.1 billion by 2050, and the majority of people living in cities for the first time in history,[1] it has become clear that cities will play a pivotal role in both feeding the world and meeting the climate change challenge. . . .

Here in New York City, the rate of asthma in some neighborhoods is five times the national average. Unbalanced development has left entire communities in "food deserts" without access to fresh food and saddled with the deadly pairing of obesity and hunger. As the unemployment rate rises, fewer families are able to afford a healthy diet. Last year, 1.6 million New Yorkers received food stamps and 3.3 million had trouble paying for food.[2] The rise of cities, the encroaching impact of climate change on the health of humanity, and the paralysis of the international community has created a situation where urban, industrialized localities must step up and launch the movement to prevent climate change at home.

Given this challenge, what city is better equipped to lead the way than New York? . . . The recommendations featured in this report identify specific opportunities for city government to design a food policy that integrates energy and climate objectives with environmental, social, and economic goals. In doing so, we can shape the kind of future that will make New Yorkers not just survive, but thrive, and create a blueprint for progress that can position the City as a leader in both environmental and health policy innovation around the world.

II. REPORT RECOMMENDATIONS

1. URBAN AGRICULTURE

GOAL: Establish urban food production as a priority in New York City for personal, community, or commercial use by the year 2030.

Recommendations

1. Assess Land Availability and Suitability for Urban Agriculture: The New York City Council should pass legislation mandating that City agencies conduct an annual assessment of City-owned property and nominate suitable sites for urban agriculture. This effort is similar to the "Diggable City" project in Portland, Oregon that integrated urban agriculture into planning and policymaking.[3] Based on a preliminary analysis of data provided by the Department of Housing Preservation and Development in 2008, there are 454 total vacant lots above 110th Street in Manhattan. Of those, over 100 are owned by the City and many have no development plans. In 2008, the Manhattan Borough President's office also identified significant amounts of open land on New York City Housing Authority properties which should be evaluated as possible garden sites. Where appropriate and following a public review process, City and State parkland should also be considered for urban agriculture.

2. Create a Citywide Urban Agriculture Program: The Mayor should establish a citywide Urban Agriculture Program to support the creation of food growing spaces. The program should be similar to Capital Growth, London's campaign to plant 2,012 growing spaces by the 2012 Olympics by connecting people to land, providing funding, and offering practical guidance on how to grow food.[4] New York City's Urban Agriculture Program should be modeled on and keep pace with "Million Trees NYC," an initiative announced by Mayor Bloomberg on Earth Day in 2007 to plant one million trees throughout the city by 2030.[5] It would thus be operated through a public-private partnership and draw a large volunteer base. The Urban Agriculture Program, which would also reduce the City's GHG emissions, should offer technical assistance to facilitate the creation of new gardens, enhance existing gardens, and attract new gardeners.[6] The first new growing space, a vegetable garden, should be planted in City Hall Park to mark the program's launch.

3. Ensure the Permanence of Community Gardens: The Mayor should preserve community gardens as parks, as proposed in a resolution introduced in the City Council by Council Member Helen Foster,[7] to help establish the permanence of existing gardens in perpetuity.[1] Cleveland, Boston, and Seattle are among other cities that have all established similar initiatives.[8]

4. Facilitate the Development of Rooftop Agricultural Greenhouses: A number of property owners who are interested in building rooftop agricultural greenhouses have faced zoning barriers, including those pertaining to permitted uses, maximum allowable floor area, and light and air regulations. The City should consider addressing these barriers by creating an authorization process for certain use and bulk waivers to facilitate the development of rooftop agricultural greenhouses. Such an authorization process would provide for the case-by-case consideration of requested waivers. In addition to building plans, applications would include performance standards (e.g., amount of food produced, water use, energy conservation, programming, jobs, etc.); findings to determine public benefits (e.g., environment, economic, health, education); the identification of significant adverse impacts (e.g., shadows, traffic, character, etc.); and protocols for compliance reporting. Priority should be given to projects that create green collar jobs by training and employing New York City residents, especially those who are unemployed or underemployed.

Context

Urban agriculture refers to the production of food within or on the fringe of cities. People have grown food in cities for centuries and the practice endures across the globe. In Vancouver, for example, 44 percent of residents produce their own food.[9]

The defining characteristic of urban agriculture may not be its location as much as its role in the economic, environmental, and social fabric of an urban community.[10] Urban agriculture can help meet nutritional needs and provide jobs for those who grow, harvest, and sell food.[11] It creates opportunities for the young and old, as well as people from all walks of life to strengthen communities and reshape their relationship with food in the process. Urban agriculture can filter and reduce the volume of rainwater run-off, which decreases combined sewage overflow in our city waterways, can reduce the heat-island effect, absorb carbon through photosynthesis, and sequester CO_2 in the soil. It can also help businesses offset food overhead costs. For example, the Fairmount Waterfront Hotel in Vancouver, Canada grows herbs, vegetables, fruits and edible flowers for its restaurant, saving between $25,000 and $30,000 annually and more than offsetting the $16,000 annual maintenance cost.[17]

Because of these benefits, a number of large cities have developed concrete policies to promote urban agriculture, including London, Brisbane, and San Francisco.[12] Although there has been a resurgence of interest in urban agriculture in New York City,[13] a long list of impediments prevent it from growing beyond a small number of community gardens.

In addition to sun, seeds, soil, and water, urban agriculture requires land. However, the scarcity of land in the five boroughs is a major obstacle to gardening and farming. In 1998, the Giuliani administration auctioned off City land that had been used for community gardens. City policy still reflects the longstanding view that urban agriculture is a transitional use of land, available until the land is ready for urban development. The city's Community Gardens Coalition is currently campaigning for future access to property once the Memorandum of Understanding, signed by the State Attorney General and the Mayor in 2002 to protect many existing gardens, expires in September 2010.[14] Although the Bloomberg administration is generally supportive of community gardens, food infrastructure is not officially part of City land use and planning decisions, nor is it considered when communities, elected officials, and developers think about how land could and should be used.

The scarcity of traditional spaces for gardens and farms has prompted the exploration of underutilized areas, such as rooftops, basements, or warehouses, as well as innovative technologies to serve the unique needs of an urban environment. For example, a company called Gotham Greens is constructing the city's first hydroponic rooftop farm on a church in Queens. The 12,000 square foot farm will produce[14] tons of fruits and vegetables annually, be powered by 2,000 square feet of solar panels, and collect rainwater through a large sistern.[15] At the Food and Climate Summit, New School professor Nevin Cohen estimated that New York City has 52,000 acres of backyard space that collectively could provide vegetables for 700,000 people. Opportunities to use traditionally under-utilized space for growing food, training workers, and implementing new technology may have substantial health, economic and environmental benefits.

[1] Worldwatch Institute, "State of the World 2007: Our Urban Future." November 21, 2006. <http://www.worldwatch.org/taxonomy/term/467>

[2] *The Economist*. "Food and Poverty: The Big Apple Is Hungry," January 14, 2010. <http://www.economist.com/research/articlesBySubject/displaystory.cfm?subjectid=348876&story_id=1 5271055>

[3] Mendes, W., Balmer, K., Kaethler, T., Rhoades, A. "Using Land Inventories to Plan for Urban Agriculture: Experiences From Portland and Vancouver." *Journal of the American Planning Association*, September, 2008. <http://www.informaworld.com/smpp/content~content=a902335069~db=all>

[4] Capital Growth Campaign homepage: <http://www.capitalgrowth.org/>

[5] Million Trees NYC homepage: <http://www.milliontreesnyc.org/html/about/about.shtml:

[6] McLaughlin, L. "Inner City Farms." Time v. 172 no. 5 (August 4 2008) p. 67–8.

[7] New York City Council: Resolution 1980-2009, sponsored by Councilwoman Helen Foster. Text can be found here: <http://legistar.council.nyc.gov/LegislationDetail.aspx?ID=452496&GUID=FA0344AA-52E5-42DE-AE7A-EB53E89D3386&Options=ID%7cText%7c&Search=community+gardens>

[8] Cleveland, OH: The nation's first zoning code for "Urban Garden Districts" was created in March 2008 to ensure that urban gardens are appropriately located and protected to meet the city's needs: <http://caselaw.lp.findlaw.com/clevelandcodes/cco_part3_336.html> Boston, MA: An Open Space zoning designation with a

community garden sub-district within that district. Greenhouses explicitly mentioned as accessory structures: <www.cityofboston.gov/parks/pdfs/os4b.pdf> Seattle, WA: Twenty year Comprehensive Plan includes community gardens and sets specific goals for a community garden for every 2,500 households: <http://www.communitygarden.org/docs/cg_policies.pdf>

[9] City Farmer, Canada's Office of Urban Agriculture. "44% of Vancouver Households Grow Food says City Farmer." Urban Agriculture Notes. September 22, 2002. <http://www.cityfarmer.org/44percent.html>

[10] Cities Farming for the Future: Urban Agriculture for Green and Productive Cities. Edited by René van Veenhuizen, RUAF Foundation, International Institute of Rural Reconstruction, International Development Research Center. 2006.

[11] Alberto Zezzo and Luca Tasciotti. "Does Urban Agriculture Enhance Dietary Diversity? Empirical Evidence from a Sample of Developing Countries." Food and Agriculture Organization (FAO), Agriculture and Development Economic Division. October 23, 2007. <ftp://ftp.fao.org/docrep/fao/011/aj306e/aj306e.pdf>

[12] "Design Considerations for the Implementation of Green Roofs." Metro Vancouver. April, 2009. <http://www.metrovancouver.org/about/publications/Publications/greenroofreporttext.pdf>

[13] "World First Brisbane Addresses Climate Change with Urban Agriculture and Green Roofs." Urban Agriculture Network Australia. May 1, 2007. <http://urbanagriculture.wordpress.com/2007/05/01/world-first-brisbane-addresses-climate-change-with-urban-agriculture-and-green-roofs/>

[14] Miller, T. "New York City Farms and Community Gardens Gear Up for Spring with Increased Interest." New York Daily News, April 8, 2009. <http://www.nydailynews.com/lifestyle/food/2009/04/09/2009-04-09_new_york_city_farms_and_community_gardens_gear_up_for_spring_with_increased_inte.html>

[15] Schwartz, A. "Gotham Greens Building First Hydroponic Rooftop Farm in NYC." Fast Company. June 15, 2009. <http://www.fastcompany.com/blog/ariel-schwartz/sustainability/gotham-greens-building-first-hydroponic-rooftop-farm-nyc>

Think About It

(1)   How does the author make this issue seem timely and important?

(2)   In each section of this report, the author provides recommendations first, and then fills out the context for those recommendations. Why do you think the author chose to organize the report that way? Did you find this organization effective?

(3)   The author often relies on comparisons to initiatives undertaken in other major cities. Do you find these comparisons effective? How do they support the recommendations in this report?

Write About It

How can your college or community develop new ways to promote sustainable food? Choose one of the ideas in this report (you can find more in the complete report, here: http://www.mbpo.org/uploads/policy_reports/mbp/FoodNYC.pdf). Then, research which of those ideas might work in your own locale. Write a recommendation report to your town council or college administrators providing your recommendations and a context that supports each recommendation.

. . . .

MICHAELA KRAUSER   SEGREGATION CONTINUES IN URBAN SCHOOLS

Michaela Krauser wrote this news report for the website Next American City in 2012. Krauser is a writer for Next American City, a non-profit organization that seeks to connect cities and inform readers about the work being done to improve them.

Read About It

This news report was posted on the website Salon.com *and on the website for the* Next American City. *How does the report take advantage of Internet capabilities, such as linking (represented by underlined text)? As you read, note how each link functions in the article. Which links would you feel compelled to click on if you were reading this online?*

Nearly 60 years have passed since the Supreme Court made its landmark *Brown v. Board of Education* decision, legally ending school segregation across the U.S. Today, the legacy of school segregation persists, as racial isolation remains the reality of many students nationwide.

Though it is expected that the U.S. population will shift from a white-majority to a minority-majority by 2046, currently most students do not see that diversity reflected in their school experience. Nationally, according to the National Center for Education Statistics, 52 percent of black students and 58 percent of Latino students attend school where minority students make up 75 percent or more of the entire student body.

In Chicago, America's most segregated city, it's typical for students to go through their entire K-12 education without ever having met a classmate of another race, as GOOD reported this week. In a recent radio interview on a local station, a Chicago student described having thought that schools were still legally segregated, based solely on her surroundings.

Advocates for reform argue that the incentives to foster greater diversity in schools are clear: Exposing students to racially and culturally diverse environments prepares them for the world outside school doors. Recent studies have also shown that students fare better academically in schools with greater levels of socioeconomic diversity.

Throughout the past decade, public school reformers have focused largely on building schools in the 90/90/90 model—schools with populations made up of more than 90 percent low-income students, more than 90 percent ethnic minorities and more than 90 percent students who meet set academic standards—as a way to provide high-performing schools to students in their own neighborhoods.

Some argue that the model fails to address issues of segregation, as discriminatory housing practices continue to create segregated communities—a fact that is especially problematic given that housing prices have been linked to school quality.

A recent study by the Brookings Institution reports that homes located in neighborhoods with high-performing schools cost, on average, about 2.4 times as much as those located in neighborhoods with low-performing schools. Since students of color are more likely to live in low-income neighborhoods than their white peers, students of color thereby have less access to high-performing schools.

Though redlining has long been part of the desegregation conversation, reformers are increasingly focusing their attention on charter schools—a model that has radically changed the landscape of the U.S. public school system in the last 30 years.

The popularity of charter schools has continued to escalate in recent years, despite the fact that charter schools have been found to be, on average, more segregated than traditional schools.

KIPP (the Knowledge Is Power Program) is one of the most prominent examples of high-performing charter school networks, and includes more than 100 schools nationwide. KIPP's program is designed to cater to low-income students, and features a longer school day, a tough disciplinary structure and a curriculum aimed at catching students up to grade level. With an enrollment made up of 95 percent Latino or black students, KIPP's focus is clearly to serve minority students.

What would the model for an urban charter school look like that would meet the needs of its students, while fostering a diverse student population?

This, among others, is a question reformers are tackling from coast to coast.

Think About It

(1)   How does this report draw on research? Skim some of the other reports in this section. Does this online news report use research differently? Or does it simply cite its research differently from a print report?

(2)   Do you think the author of this report has a particular claim to make about segregation in schools? If so, how explicit is the claim in the report?

(3)   How does your experience in elementary and high school education match up with the article? Would you describe your previous schools as diverse? How does that experience affect your experiences in college thus far?

Write About It

How do students at your college view diversity initiatives on your campus? Interview at least ten students about their views on a particular policy or program. For example, if your college has diversity requirements for course selections, interview students about that. Or, you might interview students about their perceptions of diversity (gender, racial, economic, etc.) at your school. Then, write a news report for your college newspaper that details the findings of your investigation.

Illustration Credits

Chapter Five

p. 74 Reprinted courtesy of Sarah Davignon and The Most Loyals.

p. 74 Reproduced in accordance with Facebook Brand Assets requirements.

p. 75 Images courtesy of Nintendo.

p. 75 Reproduced in accordance with Facebook Brand Assets requirements.

p. 75 Reprinted by permission of Habitat for Humanity International, Inc./Jason Asteros.

p. 78 Copyright © 2013 by MINOR STARS. http://www.minorstars.com. Reprinted by permission.

p. 78 Reprinted by permission of Matthew Scott Myers, FatHeart-Galleries (http://www.fatheart-galleries.com).

p. 79 Reprinted by permission of Andrea Selch (http://www.andreaselch.com).

p. 82 Reprinted by permission of the World Bank Publications.

p. 83 http://durhamtech.edu/health/medicalassisting.htm. Reprinted by permission of Durham Technical Community College.

Chapter Six

p. 99 Reprinted by permission of Gawker Media, http://www.gawkermedia.com.

p. 100 "3 Ways to Kill Ants without Pesticides," wikiHow, http://www.wikihow.com/Kill-Ants-Without-Pesticides. Reprinted by permission of wikiHow.

p. 100 "Work at Home—Stay Focused," LifeTips (2013), http://relationship.lifetips.com/tip/125712/work-and-office/working-at-home/work-at-home-ndash-stay-focused.html. Reprinted by permission of IdeaLaunch.com.

p. 102 "How to Roll Out Pizza Dough," *Bon Appetit* on-line—tips and tools, 11/2008. Copyright © 2013 by Conde Nast. All rights reserved. Originally published in *Bon Appetit*. Reprinted by permission.

p. 103 The content from ProQuest products is published with permission of ProQuest LLC. Further reproduction is prohibited without permission. www.proquest.com.

p. 107 "Genetic Engineering," Greenpeace. http://www.greenpeace.org/new-zealand/Global/new-zealand/P3/publications/ge/2010/GPN_Factsheet-GE.web.pdf.

p. 108 "Shingles Fact Sheet," CDC. http://www.cdc.gov/vaccines/vpd-vac/shingles/downloads/factsheet_pss.pdf.

p. 109 http://www.eeoc.gov/youth/downloads/harassment_en.pdf.

p. 112 http://wwwnc.cdc.gov/eid/article/19/5/ad-1905_article.htm.

Chapter Eight

p. 150 Courtesy of Wordle.net.

p. 150 Courtesy of Wordle.net.

p. 151 Courtesy of Wordle.net.

Chapter Ten

p. 219 Courtesy of U.S. Army Recruiting Command Public Affairs.

p. 220 Courtesy of U.S. Army Recruiting Command Public Affairs.

p. 221 Courtesy of U.S. Army Recruiting Command Public Affairs.

Chapter Twelve

p. 315 Reprinted by permission of California State University, Fresno.

p. 316 Reprinted by permission of KCRW 89.9.

p. 316 http://www.fns.usda.gov/snap/outreach/pdfs/340.pdf.

Chapter Twenty-Four

p. 506 Reprinted by permission of University of Mississippi.

p. 508 http://digilib.usm.edu/cdm/search/searchterm/This%20item%20is%20part%20of%20the%20Civil%20Rights%20in%20Mississippi%20Digital%20Archive. Courtesy of McCain

Library and Archives, University of Southern Mississippi.

p. 510 http://www.lib.ncsu .edu/databases/. Images courtesy of North Carolina State University Libraries.

p. 511 http://www.lib.ncsu .edu/databases/. Images courtesy of North Carolina State University Libraries.

p. 513 http://www.lib.ncsu .edu/databases/. Images courtesy of North Carolina State University Libraries.

p. 519 Reprinted from Vani R. Henderson & Bridget Kelly, "Food Advertising in the Age of Obesity: Content Analysis of Food Advertising on General Market and African American Television," *Journal of Nutrition Education and Behavior*, 37(4), 191–196 (2005). Copyright © 2005 by Elsevier. Reprinted by permission of Elsevier.

p. 520 Reprinted with permission of EBSCO Information Services.

p. 521 Reprinted from Dunn, Richard A. "The Effect of Fast-Food Availability on Obesity: An Analysis by Gender, Race, and Residential Location." *American Journal of Agricultural Economics* 92.4 (2010): 1149–64. Copyright © 2010 by Oxford University Press. Reprinted by permission of Oxford University Press.

p. 523 The content from ProQuest products is published with permission of ProQuest LLC. Further reproduction is prohibited without permission. http://www.proquest .com.

Chapter Twenty-Five

p. 526 Stephen Pinker, *Language, Cognition, and Human Nature: Selected Articles*. New York: Oxford University Press (2013).

p. 527 Stephen Pinker, *Language, Cognition, and Human Nature: Selected Articles*. New York: Oxford University Press (2013).

p. 529 Richard A. Dunn, "The Effect of Fast-Food Availability on Obesity: An Analysis by Gender, Race, and Residential Location." *American Journal of Agricultural Economics* (2010), 92, (4). Reprinted by permission of Oxford University Press.

p. 532 Jason Kuznicki, "Marriage against the State: Toward a New View of Civil Marriage," *Cato Institute* (Jan 12, 2011), http://www.cato .org/publications/policy-analysis/marriage-against -state-toward-new -view-civil-marriage. Reprinted by permission of Cato Institute.

p. 537 http://en.wikipedia.org/ wiki/Fast_food. In-N-Out cheeseburgers.JPG by Jef Poskanzer, Berkeley, CA, USA (http://www.flickr.com/ photos/jef/). Licensed under the Creative Commons Attribution 2.0 Generic License. Fast Food language.JPG by Bryan Allison, Las Vegas, NV, USA (http://www.flickr.com/ people/37996647372@N01). Licensed under the Creative Commons Attribution-Share Alike 2.0 Generic License. Chinese noodles.JPG by Kenneth Chan, youngjediboy@ hotmail.com. CC-BY-3.0; Released under the GNU Free Documentation License.

p. 538 Reprinted from Dunn, Richard A. "The Effect of Fast-Food Availability on Obesity: An Analysis by Gender, Race, and Residential Location." *American Journal of Agricultural Economics* 92.4 (2010): 1149–64. Copyright © 2010 by Oxford University Press. Reprinted by permission of Oxford University Press.

Chapter Twenty-Nine

p. 626 Tornado Factsheet: Get Ready PDF (http://www .getreadyforflu.org/facts/ TornadoesFacts.pdf). American Public Health Association, 2013. First page. Reprinted by permission by American Public Health Association.

p. 628 http://carolinawomen .web.unc.edu/. Created and reprinted here by permission of Holly M. Holbrook, Emi Bunner, Latoya Holland, Caitlin Hooks, Averi Harper, Amber Emerson, and Taylor Fulton.

p. 629 http://www.ers.usda .gov/publications/eib58/ eib58.pdf.

p. 631 Photos from http//www .act.hhs.gov/programs/css/

quick-fact and http://www2 .archivists.org/sties/all/files/ KCFinal.pdf.

p. 635 "Median Age at First Marriage," http://www .whitehouse.gov/sites/ default/files/rss_viewer/ Women_in_America.pdf.

p. 636 "Earnings by Educational Attainment," http://www .whitehouse.gov/sites/ default/files/rss_viewer/ Women_in_America.pdf.

p. 637 NCES Common Core Standards, Department of Education, http://nces .ed.gov/nceskids/help/user _guide/graph/pie.asp.

p. 637 Federal Trade Commission, "Ten Years of Do Not Call," http://www.consumer .ftc.gov/articles/0108 -national-do-not-call-registry.

p. 638 Bureau of Labor Statistics, http://bls.gov/news .release/pdf/atus.pdf.

p. 640 National Oceanic and Air Administration, http://www .esrl.noaa.gov/about/ directorsoffice.html.

p. 641 National Institutes of Health, http://www.nhlbi .nih.gov/health/health -topics/topics/brnchi/.

p. 642 Library of Congress, http://www.loc.gov/exhibits/ us.capitol/svntfive.jpg.

p. 642 National Gallery of Art, http://www.nga.gov/ exhibitions/2008/pompeii/ images/us_cap.jpg.

p. 643 Architect of the Capitol, http://www.aoc.gov/cc/cc _map.cfm.

p. 644 Food & Drug Administration, http:///www.fda.gov.

p. 648 Department of Health & Human Services, Administration for Children and Families, http://www.acf .hhs.gov/programs/css/ quick-fact?page=1.

Chapter Thirty

p. 659 LaGuardia Community College—Registered Nursing Program Capstone Course. https://lagcc-cuny.digication .com/de_gracias_shane_ep/ Introduction/published. Reprinted by permission of LaGuardia Community College Nursing Program, Shane de Garcia, Deborah Mcmillan-Coddington, and Philip Gimber.

p. 660 Bajomo, Darryle. "Palm Peach Place." http://bajomo

.web.unc.edu/. Reprinted by permission of Darryle Bajomo.

p. 661 http://business.fullerton .edu/marketing/program Require/MP%20-%20Sample %20Portfolio%20(Sotelo% 2008-11-2010).pdf. Reprinted by permission of Mihaylo College.

p. 661 http://www.kon.org/ CFP/cfp_urjhs.html. Copyright © 2013 by Kappa Omicron Nu, The Human Sciences Honor Society. All rights reserved. Reprinted by permission.

READINGS: Chapter Seven

p. 786 Kelly Huston, "Did I Vote on Your Marriage?" flickr (Nov. 9, 2008), http://www .flickr.com/photos/ doxiehaus/3018087812/.

READINGS: Chapter Eleven

p. 858 College Board Advocacy & Policy Center. The College Completion Agenda - 2011 Progress Report. Copyright © 2011. The College Board. www .collegeboard.org. Reproduced with permission.

Text Credits

Preface

p. xxvi http://wpacouncil.org/positions/outcomes.html.

p. xxviii http://wpacouncil.org/framework.

Chapter One

p. 2 "My Bondage and My Freedom." Frederick Douglass (1855).

p. 6 Excerpt from pp. 16–18, "My Bismillah and Nasra" from MEMOIRS OF A REBEL PRINCESS by Abida Sultaan. Copyright © 2004. Reprinted by permission of Oxford University Press, Karachi, PAKISTAN.

p. 8 Copyright © 1989 by Amy Tan. First appeared in *The Threepenny Review*. Reprinted by permission of the author and Sandra Djikstra Literary Agency.

Chapter Two

p. 25 Meriwether Lewis, "The Journals of the Lewis and Clark Expedition: September 17, 1804".

Chapter Three

p. 36 Claire Zhang, "Amy Tan Phase," *Modality* (July 9, 2012), http://modalityblog.wordpress.com/2012/07/09/amy-tan-phase/. Reprinted by permission of Claire Zhang.

p. 49 "The Way of a Cherokee," by Foxxy, http://www.teenink.com/nonfiction/all/article/64974/The-Way-of-a-Cherokee/. Reprinted with permission by Teen Ink Magazine and TeenInk.com.

Chapter Four

p. 57 "Two Worlds, One Great Nation". Copyright © 2012 by Maisha S., part of the *This I Believe* Essay Collection found at http://www.thisibelieve.org. Copyright © 2005–2014 by This I Believe, Inc. Reprinted with permission.

p. 58 "I Believe in the Senses." Copyright © 2010 by Mark Carlson, part of the *This I Believe* Essay Collection found at http://www.thisibelieve.org. Copyright © 2005–2014 by This I Believe, Inc. Reprinted with permission.

Chapter Five

p. 85 "Oregon Ballet Theatre's Lucas Threefoot," *1859 Oregon's Magazine* (Oct. 1, 2011), http://1859oregonmagazine.com/obts-lucas-threefoot. Reprinted by permission of the publisher.

p. 87 Jaime Schroeder, "Goals for Life," *Idaho State University Magazine*, vol. 43, no. 1 (Fall 2012), http://www.isu.edu/magazine/fall12/goals-for-life.shtml. Reprinted by permission of Idaho State University, Department of Intercollegiate Athletics.

p. 88 Stephanie Gottschlich, "The New Recruits," *Wright State University Magazine* (Fall 2012), http://webapp2.wright.edu/web1/community/2012/the-new-recruits/. Reprinted by permission of Wright State University.

Chapter Six

p. 120 Asawin Suebsaeng, Deanna Pan, and Gavin Aronsen, "What Happened in the Newtown School Shooting," *Mother Jones* (Dec. 14, 2012 1:52 PM), http://www.motherjones.com/print/211036. Reprinted by permission of Mother Jones, The Foundation for National Progress.

Chapter Seven

p. 130 Reprinted by permission of Patrick Lam, University of Waterloo.

p. 131 Reprinted by permission of Jenna Shrewsbury, ROADCS.com.

p. 133 L'eau de vie, "Disappointment: *Rizzoli & Isles*," Sur le Seuil (Dec. 22, 2011), http://surleseuil.com/2011/12/22/on-disappointment/. Reprinted by permission of Brandy Grabow writing as L'eau-de-vie.

p. 142 Courtesy of Belinda Walzer, Northeastern University.

p. 144 Courtesy of Peggy Kline, Santa Monica College.

Chapter Eight

p. 165 Reprinted by permission of Kerri Zuiker. http://www .squareways.com/ brokeback.html.

p. 174 Reprinted by permission of Cody Poplin.

p. 185 "An Open Statement to Fans of 'The Help'," Association of Black Women Historians, Ida E. Jones, Daina Ramey Berry, Tiffany M. Gill, Kali Nicole Gross & Janice Sumler-Edmond (Sept. 20, 2011), http://www.abwh.org/ index.php?option=com _content&view=article &id=2%3Aopen-statement -the-help. Reprinted by permission of the Association of Black Women Historians.

Chapter Nine

p. 195 Reprinted by permission of Jacob Clayton.

p. 196 "Of Montreal's New Album a Mix of Weird Sounds and Intrigue" by Katie Fennelly, *Daily Nebraskan* (Feb. 7, 2012). http://www .dailynebraskan.com/arts _and_entertainment/ article_9299ad1e-c722-5f92 -9bf9-de23ba384a01.html. Reprinted by permission of the *Daily Nebraskan*.

p. 197 Nathan Cook, "Film Review: 'Epic'," *The UCSD Guardian* (May 23, 2013), http://www.ucsdguardian .org/arts-entertainment/ film-a-tv/item/26808-film -review-epic#.UkMDsT_he6l. Reprinted by permission of *The UCSD Guardian*.

p. 200 "Top Pick! Brian's 99 Cents: Review of *The Quill Pen* by Michelle Isenhoff," by Brian L. Braden, *Underground Book Reviews* (Feb. 3, 2012), http://www.under groundbookreviews.com/3/ post/2012/02/top-pick -brians-99-cents-review-of -the-quill-pen-by-michelle -isenhoff.html. Reprinted by permission of Brian L. Braden.

p. 201 "Review of *The Change-over* by Margaret Mahy" by Risa Applegarth. http://www .goodreads.com/book/show/ 351461.The_Changeover. Reprinted by permission of Risa Applegarth.

p. 201 Reprinted by permission of Adriana Lorenzini (2010).

p. 208 Reprinted by permission of Megan McDermott.

Chapter Ten

p. 223 Nate Rushing, "UF's Meatless Mondays Are Ridiculous", *Alligator: The Independent Florida* (Nov. 18, 2010 12:15 AM), http://www .alligator.org/opinion/ columns/article_8707ff31 -1984-5389-b3e4-ed2af9 c1a034.html. Reprinted by permission of The Independent Florida Alligator. Campus Communications, Inc. makes no representation or warranty that it has any interest in the work other than a license to reproduce the work in its own publication.

p. 224 Amelia Jensen, "Meatless Mondays," *The Index*: Letters to the Editors (Apr. 27, 2011),

http://kzindex.wordpress .com/2011/04/27/meatless -mondays/. Reprinted by permission of The Index at Kalamazoo College.

p. 225 "Insults against Disabled People Must Be Eradicated" by Rini Sampath, *The Daily Trojan* Op-Ed (April 30, 2013). http://wwww.daily trojan.com/2013/04/30/ insults-against-disabled -people-must-be-eradicated/. Reprinted by permission of *The Daily Trojan*.

p. 229 As reported by The Associated Press, "Illinois Sen. Barack Obama's Announcement Speech." *The Washington Post:* Politics (Feb. 10, 2007 3:28 PM), http://www .washingtonpost.com/ wp-dyn/content/article/ 2007/02/10/AR200702 1000879.html.

p. 233 http://madisonpeace forstudentbodypresident .blogspot.com. Reprinted by permission of John Hundscheid and Madison Peace.

p. 236 http://cityroom.blogs .nytimes.com/2009/11/04/ text-of-bloombergs-victory -speech/?pagewanted=print

p. 249 Reprinted with the permission of *The Onion*. Copyright © 2013 by Onion, Inc. http://www.theonion.com.

Chapter Eleven

p. 259 Reprinted by permission of PLOS. http://www .plosbiology.org.

p. 260 Mike Duncan, "Polemical Ambiguity and the Composite Audience: Bush's 20

September 2001 Speech to Congress and the Epistle of 1 John." *Rhetoric Society Quarterly*, Fall 2011, 41:5, pp. 455–471. http://www.tandfonline.com/doi/abs/10.1080/02773945.2011.596178#preview.

p. 260 Jessica Ross, "Closing Guantanamo Bay: The Future of Detainees," *NeoAmericanist*. Vol. 5, no. 1 (Spring/Summer 2010), http://neoamericanist.org/issues/issue/vol-5-no-1-spring summer-2010?page=1.

p. 263 Reprinted by permission of Chris Clayman.

p. 264 Lisa Garmire, "Comprehensive Annotated Bibliography of American AIDS Novels: 1982–1992," (excerpted). http://www.oocities.org/lisagarmire/AnnotatedBiblio.htm. Reprinted by permission of Lisa Frieden.

p. 265 Sandra Kerka and Susan Imel, excerpt from "Annotated Bibliography: Women and Literacy" from *Women's Study Quarterly* 32, nos. 1 & 2 (Spring–Summer 2004). Copyright © 2004 by The Feminist Press at the City University of New York. Used by permission of the publishers. http://www.feministpress.org. All rights reserved.

p. 268 Reprinted by permission of Kirby Diamaduros.

p. 275 *J Med Internet Res.* 2007 Jul-Sep; 9(3): e26. http://www.ncbi.nlm.nih.gov/pmc/articles/PMC2047289/?report=printable.

p. 281 Property of Agustin Fuentes.

p. 285 Reprinted by permission of Kristine Thompson.

p. 295 Reprinted by permission of Rick Ingram.

p. 312 Reprinted by permission of Rick Ingram.

Chapter Thirteen

p. 344 Reprinted by permission of Vincent Abiona.

p. 350 Reprinted by permission of Grace McDermott.

Chapter Fourteen

p. 360 "Men's Basketball's Stoglin Named Second-Team All-ACC" by Chris Eckard, *DiamondbackOnline*, March 5, 2012. http://www.diamondbackonline.com/article_b1c3903c-aba8-5d25-8bb5-8d3c6bff609c.html. Reprinted by permission of *The Diamondback,* University of Maryland.

p. 361 "UNL Psychology Study Finds College-Aged Men Struggle with Image, Objectification" by Daniel Wheaton, *Daily Nebraskan*, June 10, 2013, http://www.dailynebraskan.com/news/article_c85a5474-d17c-11e2-933b-0019bb30f31a.html. Reprinted by permission of the *Daily Nebraskan.*

p. 362 Reprinted by permission of *The Collegian*/Fresno State.

p. 375 Reprinted by permission of Mr. Bradley J. Kinnison, RN BSN.

p. 393 Reprinted by permission of Mr. Bradley J. Kinnison, RN BSN.

Chapters Fifteen/Sixteen

p. 399 Courtesy of Terrence Bogans.

p. 404 Courtesy of Terrence Bogans.

Chapter Seventeen

p. 410 Courtesy of Terrence Bogans.

p. 411 Courtesy of Terrence Bogans.

p. 412 Courtesy of Terrence Bogans.

p. 413 Courtesy of Terrence Bogans.

p. 415 Courtesy of Terrence Bogans.

p. 417 Courtesy of Terrence Bogans.

p. 418 Courtesy of Terrence Bogans.

p. 419 Courtesy of Terrence Bogans.

Chapter Eighteen

p. 423 Courtesy of Terrence Bogans.

p. 428 Courtesy of Terrence Bogans.

p. 430 Courtesy of Terrence Bogans.

Chapter Nineteen

p. 441 Courtesy of Terrence Bogans.

Chapter Twenty

p. 449 Courtesy of Terrence Bogans.

p. 454 Courtesy of Terrence Bogans.

p. 457 Courtesy of Terrence Bogans.

p. 460 Courtesy of Terrence Bogans.

p. 462 Courtesy of Terrence Bogans.

Chapter Twenty-One

p. 464 Schenwar, Maya. "The Prison System Welcomes My Newborn Niece to this World" (September 12, 2013), http://www.truth-out.org/news/item/18776-the-prison-system-welcomes-my-newborn-niece-to-this-world. Reprinted by permission of Truthout.org.

p. 465 Loper, Ann Booker, and Elena Hontoria Tuerk. "Improving the Emotional Adjustment and Communication Patterns of Incarcerated Mothers: Effectiveness of a Prison Parenting Intervention," *Journal of Child and Family Studies* 20.1 (2011): 89–101. Copyright © 2011 by Springer. Reprinted by permission of the publisher.

p. 466 Reprinted by permission of Ashley McAlarney.

p. 466 This article was originally published in *The Dialectics: Journal of Leadership, Politics, and Society* housed at the Pennsylvania State University, Abington. Reprinted by permission.

p. 473 "I Have a Dream" by Dr. Martin Luther King, Jr. Copyright © 1963 by Dr. Martin Luther King, Jr. Copyright renewed 1991 by Coretta Scott King. Reprinted by arrangement with The Heirs to the Estate of Martin Luther King Jr., c/o Writers House as agent for the proprietor New York, NY.

Chapter Twenty-Two

p. 480 Courtesy of Terrence Bogans.

p. 484 Courtesy of Terrence Bogans.

Chapter Twenty-Three

p. 489 *Young Scholars in Writing: Undergraduate Research in Writing and Rhetoric.*

p. 492 Courtesy of Jay C. Zhang.

p. 493 Courtesy of Jay C. Zhang.

Chapter Twenty-Four

p. 504 Reprinted by permission of Kristine Thompson.

p. 521 Courtesy of Jay C. Zhang.

Chapter Twenty-Five

p. 533 "Reading and Communicating with Your Child Builds Reading and Language Skills," *Pocket Literacy Coach* (Sept. 20, 2011), http://pocketliteracy.com/blog/post/reading-and-communicating-your-child-builds-reading-and-language-skills/. Reprinted by permission of Chris Drew, Parent University.

Chapter Twenty-Six

p. 539 Reprinted by permission of Jay C. Zhang.

p. 541 Ray M. Marín & Jiří Vaníček, "Optimal Use of Conservation and Accessibility Filters in MicroRNA Target Prediction," *PLoS ONE* 7(2) (Feb. 27, 2012), http://www.plosone.org/article/info%3Adoi%2F10.1371%2Fjournal.pone.0032208#pone.0032208-Filipowicz1.

p. 542 Shulman, J. L., Gotta, G., & Green, R. (2012). "Will Marriage Matter? Effects of Marriage Anticipated by Same-Sex Couples", *Journal of Family Issues*, 33(2), 158–181. Reprinted by permission of SAGE Publications.

p. 546 Courtesy of Terrence Bogans.

p. 546 http://www.mcdonalds.com/us/en/food/food_quality/see_what_we_are_made_of/moms_quality_correspondents.html.

Chapter Twenty-Seven

p. 552 Reprinted by permission of Jay C. Zhang.

p. 555 Reprinted by permission of Jay C. Zhang.

Chapter Twenty-Eight

p. 559 Editorial Board, "A Campus Climate Change," *The New University* (Jan. 15, 2013), http://www.newuniversity.org/2013/01/opinion/a-campus-climate-change/.

p. 559 Reprinted by permission of Jay C. Zhang.

p. 604 Courtesy of Terrence Bogans.

Chapter Twenty-Nine

p. 646 Courtesy of Terrence Bogans.

READINGS: Chapter One

p. 696 Juan Garcia, "Spring Broken," *The Daily Californian* (Apr. 9, 2012), http://www.thedailycal.org/2012/04/09/spring-broken/. Reprinted by permission of *The Daily Californian*.

p. 698 Jacque Weber, "Love and Loss." *University Daily Kansan* (Oct. 7, 2010, 6 AM), http://www.kansan.com/news/2010/oct/07/love-and-loss/. Reprinted by permission of *The University Daily Kansan*.

p. 700 Andrea Viejo, "Mexican in New York," *The Columbia Daily Spectator* (Jan. 30, 2012, 1:13 AM), http://www.columbiaspectator.com/printer/view?nid=34740. Copyright © 2012 by *The Columbia Daily Spectator*. All rights reserved. Printed with permission.

p. 703 Jane Kramer, "The Food at Our Feet: Why Is Foraging All the Rage?" *The New Yorker* (Nov. 21, 2011), http://www.newyorker.com/reporting/2011/11/21/111121fa_fact_kramer?currentPage=all. This essay was first published in *The New Yorker*. Copyright © 2011 by Jane Kramer. Reprinted by permission of Jane Kramer.

p. 706 Tamara Winfrey Harris, "Nappy Love: Or How I Learned to Stop Worrying and Embrace the Kinks" (September 15, 2007), http://www.whattamisaid.com/2007/09/nappy-love-or-how-i-learned-to-stop.html.

Reprinted by permission of Tamara Winfrey Harris. Originally published at What Tami Said.

READINGS: Chapter Two

p. 709 Audrey Watters, "A College Student and a CEO: A Profile of 21 Year Old Entrepreneur Jay Rodrigues." *ReadWrite*, (June 9, 2010 1:00 PM), http://readwrite.com/2010/06/09/a-college-student-and-a-ceo-a. Reprinted by permission of ReadWrite.

p. 712 Linda Wasmer Andrews, "Adoptive Mothers Share Stories," *American Profile* (Apr. 28, 2011), http://americanprofile.com/articles/adoption-mothers-share-stories-help-struggle/. Reprinted by permission of American Profile, Athlon Media Group.

p. 714 "Illegal Immigrant Becomes World-Renowned Brain Surgeon," WBAL-TV11 (Mar. 5, 2007 7:38 AM), http://wbaltv.com/Illegal-Immigrant-Becomes-World-Renowned-Brain-Surgeon/-/9380084/.../index.html. Reprinted by permission of WBAL-TV. All rights reserved.

p. 716 Yale Sustainable Food Project: About Us, http://www.yale.edu/sustainablefood/about_history.html. Reprinted by permission of Yale Sustainable Food Project.

p. 720 Julie Slaymaker, "Door Opener." *Indiana State*

University Magazine (Apr. 19, 2010 1:29 PM), http://www.isumagazine.com/2010/04/door-opener/. Reprinted by permission of *Indiana State University Magazine*.

READINGS: Chapter Three

p. 724 National Institute of Health, National Inst. on Alcohol Abuse & Alcoholism, NIH publication no. 10-5640, "Fall Semester: A Time for Parents to Revisit Discussions about College Drinking" (2010). http://www.collegedrinkingprevention.gov/niaaacollegematerials/collegefactsheetforparents.aspx.

p. 726 National Conference of State Legislatures, "How the Child Support System Affects Low-Income Fathers" from *Connecting Low-Income Families and Fathers: A Guide to Practical Policies*, 2000. http://www.ncsl.org/issues-research/human-services/how-child-support-affects-low-income-fathers.aspx. Reprinted by permission of The National Conference of State Legislatures.

p. 729 Futures Without Violence, "The Facts on Immigrant Women and Domestic Violence," available at http://www.endabuse.org. Reprinted courtesy of Futures Without Violence.

p. 731 Sarah Starkey, "How to Make Your Own Indoor Compost Bin," *Apartment Therapy* (Feb. 7, 2011 1:30

PM), http://www.apartment therapy.com/howtomake yourownindoorco138645. Reprinted by permission of Apartment Therapy Media LLC.

p. 733 "How to Fight Racism in Your School." wikiHow, http://www.wikihow.com/Fight -Racism-in-Your-School.

READINGS: Chapter Four

p. 736 "Visiting College Campuses: Observations by a Professional Tour Taker" by Mark Montgomery, April 22, 2008 from http://greatcollege advice.com/visiting-college -campuses-observations -by-a-professional-tour-taker/. Copyright © 2008 by Montgomery Educational Consulting, Inc. Reprinted by permission.

p. 739 "Dealing with Deployment" by Victoria Simmons from http://www.lovemilitary .blogspot.com/2012/10/ dealing-with-deployment .html. Reprinted by permission of Victoria Simmons.

p. 741 Ruth Brown, "Diary of an Immigrant: 'Welcome to America. Are You Finding Everything OK?'" *Willamette Week* (June 15, 2010) http://www.wweek.com/portland/ blog-1196-diary_of_an _immigrant_welcome_to _america_are_you_f.html. Reprinted by permission of *Willamette Week*.

p. 742 Stefanie Hollmichel, "Eating Animals," *So Many Books* (Nov. 18, 2010), http://somanybooksblog.com/

2010/11/18/eating-animals/. Reprinted by permission of the author.

p. 745 "Boys Rules, Girls Lose— Women at Work" by Steve Blank, August 30, 2010. http://www.steveblank .com/2010/08/30/boys -rules-girls-lose-%E2%80 %93-women-at-work/. Reprinted by permission of Steve Blank.

READINGS: Chapter Five

p. 748 Abrams, Max, "Immigrants and Galactus: Junot Diaz's World in *The Brief Wondrous Life of Oscar Wao,*" *English and Comparative Literary Studies Comps* (Spring 2009), http://scholar .oxy.edu/ecls_student/1. Part of the Literature in English, North American Commons. "

p. 751 Christina LaVecchia, "Of Peerenting, Trophy Wives, and Effeminate Men: *Modern Family*'s Surprisingly Conservative Remediation of the Family Sitcom Genre." *Harlot* (2011), http://harlotofthearts .org/index.php/harlot/article/ view/85/65. Reprinted by permission of Christina M. LaVecchia, some rights reserved. (Creative Commons License, Attribution- NonCommerical-ShareAlike 3.0 United States).

p. 757 Debarati Bandyopadhyay, "Negotiating Borders of Culture: Jhumpa Lahiri's Fiction," 7(1) *Journal of Literature, Culture, and Media Studies* 97, 97–108 (2009). Reprinted here in

accordance with use as an open-access journal.

p. 761 Greg Boone, "Globalizing Korea: A Rhetoric of Food." HarmsBoone.org (Apr. 25, 2010), http://www .harmsboone.org/globalizing -korea-rhetoric-of-food. Originally published in Schoolhouse: ROK. Reprinted here by permission of Greg Boone, Harmsboone.org.

p. 765 Roy Peter Clark, "Why It Worked: A Rhetorical Analysis of Obama's Speech on Race," Poynter (Apr. 1, 2008, 6:30 PM), http://www .poynter.org/how-tos/.../ why-it-worked-a-rhetorical -analysis-of-obamas -speech-on-race/. Reprinted by permission of The Poynter Institute.

READINGS: Chapter Six

p. 771 Lauren Honeycutt, "*A Midsummer Night's Dream* at Howard Community College's Theatre Program and Student Arts Collective," *Maryland Theatre Guide* (Aug. 9, 2011), http://www .mdtheatreguide.com/2011/ 08/a-midsummer-nights -dream-at-howard -community-colleges -theatre-program-and -student-arts-collective/. Reprinted by permission of MD Theatre Guide.

p. 774 Copyright © 2012 by National Public Radio, Inc. NPR news report titled "In Childhood, When 'I Wish' Equals an Action Plan" by NPR's

READINGS: Chapter Seven

READINGS: Chapter Eight

READINGS: Chapter Nine

READINGS: Chapter Ten

READINGS: Chapter Eleven

Index